CHEVROLET

CAPRICE 1990-93
REPAIR MANUAL

President, Chilton Enterprises	David S. Loewith
Senior Vice President	Ronald A. Hoxter
Publisher & Editor-In-Chief	Kerry A. Freeman, S.A.E.
Managing Editors	Peter M. Conti, Jr., W. Calvin Settle, Jr., S.A.E.
Assistant Managing Editor	Nick D'Andrea
Senior Editors	Debra Gaffney, Ken Grabowski, A.S.E., S.A.E.
	Michael L. Grady, Richard J. Rivele, S.A.E.
	Richard T. Smith, Jim Taylor, Ron Webb
Project Managers	Martin J. Gunther, Jeffrey M. Hoffman
Director of Manufacturing	Mike D'Imperio
Editor	Don Schnell, A.S.E

ONE OF THE **DIVERSIFIED PUBLISHING COMPANIES,** A PART OF **CAPITAL CITIES/ABC,INC.**

Manufactured in USA
© 1993 Chilton Book Company
Chilton Way, Radnor, PA 19089
ISBN 0-8019-8421-1
Library of Congress Catalog Card No. 92-054896
2345678901   3210987654

Contents

Contents

	7
DRIVE TRAIN	

	8
SUSPENSION AND STEERING	

	9
BRAKES	

	10
BODY	

GLOSSARY

MASTER INDEX

SAFETY NOTICE

Proper service and repair procedures are vital to the safe, reliable operation of all motor vehicles, as well as the personal safety of those performing repairs. This manual outlines procedures for servicing and repairing vehicles using safe, effective methods. The procedures contain many NOTES, CAUTIONS, and WARNINGS which should be followed along with standard procedures to eliminate the possibility of personal injury or improper service which could damage the vehicle or compromise its safety.

It is important to note that the repair procedures and techniques, tools and parts for servicing motor vehicles, as well as the skill and experience of the individual performing the work vary widely. It is not possible to anticipate all of the conceivable ways or conditions under which vehicles may be serviced, or to provide cautions as to all of the possible hazards that may result. Standard and accepted safety precautions and equipment should be used when handling toxic or flammable fluids, and safety goggles or other protection should be used during cutting, grinding, chiseling, prying,or any other process that can cause material removal or projectiles.

Some procedures require the use of tools specially designed for a specific purpose. Before substituting another tool or procedure, you must be completely satisfied that neither your personal safety, nor the performance of the vehicle will be endangered.

Although information in this manual is based on industry sources and is complete as possible at the time of publication, the possibility exists that some car manufacturers made later changes which could not be included here. While striving for total accuracy, Chilton Book Company cannot assume responsibility for any errors, changes or omissions that may occur in the compilation of this data.

PART NUMBERS

Part numbers listed in this reference are not recommendation by Chilton for any product by brand name. They are references that can be used with interchange manuals and aftermarket supplier catalogs to locate each brand supplier's discrete part number.

SPECIAL TOOLS

Special tools are recommended by the vehicle manufacturer to perform their specific job. Use has been kept to a minimum, but where absolutely necessary, they are referred to in the text by the part number of the tool manufacturer. These tools can be purchased, under the appropriate part number, from your Honda dealer or regional distributor, or an equivalent tool can be purchased locally from a tool supplier or parts outlet. Before substituting any tool for the one recommended, read the SAFETY NOTICE at the top of this page.

ACKNOWLEDGMENTS

The Chilton Book Company expresses appreciation to General Motors Corporation for their generous assistance.

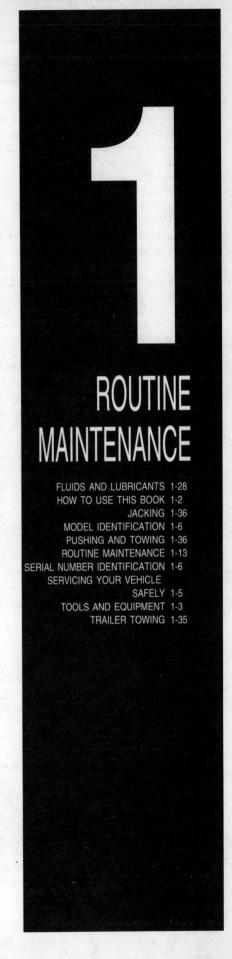

1
ROUTINE MAINTENANCE

HOW TO USE THIS BOOK

Chilton's Total Car Care Manual for the 1990-93 Caprice is intended to help you learn more about the inner workings of your car and save you money on its upkeep and operation.

The first two sections will be the most used, since they contain maintenance and tune-up information and procedures. Studies have shown that a properly tuned and maintained car can get at least 10% better gas mileage than an out-of-tune car. The other sections deal with the more complex systems of your car. Operating systems from engine through brakes are covered to the extent that the average do-it-yourselfer becomes mechanically involved. This book will not explain such things as rebuilding the automatic transmission for the simple reason that the expertise required and the investment in special tools make this task uneconomical. It will give you detailed instructions to help you change your own brake pads and shoes, replace spark plugs, and do many more jobs that will save you money, give you personal satisfaction, and help you avoid expensive problems.

A secondary purpose of this book is a reference for owners who want to understand their car and/or their mechanics better. In this case, no tools at all are required.

Before removing any bolts, read through the entire procedure. This will give you the overall view of what tools and supplies will be required. There is nothing more frustrating than having to walk to the bus stop on Monday morning because you were short one bolt on Sunday afternoon. So read ahead and plan ahead. Each operation should be approached logically and all procedures thoroughly understood before attempting any work.

All sections contain adjustments, maintenance, removal and installation procedures, and repair or overhaul procedures. When repair is not considered practical, we tell you how to remove the part and then how to install the new or rebuilt replacement. In this way, you at least save the labor costs. Backyard repair of such components as the alternator is just not practical.

Two basic mechanic's rules should be mentioned here. One, whenever the left side of the car or engine is referred to, it is meant to specify the driver's side of the car. Conversely, the right side of the car means the passenger's side. Secondly, most screws and bolts are removed by turning counterclockwise, and tightened by turning clockwise.

Safety is always the most important rule. Constantly be aware of the dangers involved in working on an automobile and take the proper precautions. See the reference in this Section, Servicing Your Vehicle Safely and the SAFETY NOTICE on the acknowledgment page. Pay attention to the instructions provided. There are 3 common mistakes in mechanical work:

1. Incorrect order of assembly, disassembly or adjustment. When taking something apart or putting it together, doing things in the wrong order usually costs you extra time; however, it CAN break something. Read the entire procedure before beginning disassembly. Do everything in the order in which the instructions say you should do it, even if you can't

immediately see a reason for it. When you're taking apart something that is very intricate (for example, a carburetor), you might want to draw a picture of how it looks when assembled at one point in order to make sure you get everything back in its proper position. (We will supply exploded view whenever possible). When making adjustments, especially tune-up adjustments, do them in order; often, one adjustment affects another, and you cannot expect even satisfactory results unless each adjustment is made only when it cannot be changed by any other.

2. Overtorquing (or undertorquing). While it is more common for overtorquing to cause damage, undertorquing can cause a fastener to vibrate loose causing serious damage. Especially when dealing with aluminum parts, pay attention to torque specifications and utilize a torque wrench in assembly. If a torque figure is not available, remember that if you are using the right tool to do the job, you will probably not have to strain yourself to get a fastener tight enough. The pitch of most threads is so slight that the tension you put on the wrench will be multiplied many, many times in actual force on what you are tightening. A good example of how critical torque is can be seen in the case of spark plug installation, especially where you are putting the plug into an aluminum cylinder head. Too little torque can fail to crush the gasket, causing leakage of combustion gases and consequent overheating of the plug and engine parts. Too much torque can damage the threads, or distort the plug which changes the spark gap.

There are many commercial products available for ensuring that fasteners won't come loose, even if they are not torqued just right (a very common brand is Loctite®). If you're worried about getting something together tight enough to hold, but loose enough to avoid mechanical damage during assembly, one of these products might offer substantial insurance. Read the label on the package and make sure the products is compatible with the materials, fluids, etc. involved before choosing one.

3. Crossthreading. This occurs when a part such as a bolt is screwed into a nut or casting at the wrong angle and forced. Cross threading is more likely to occur if access is difficult. It helps to clean and lubricate fasteners, and to start threading with the part to be installed going straight in. Then, start the bolt, spark plug, etc. with your fingers. If you encounter resistance, unscrew the part and start over again at a different angle until it can be inserted and turned several turns without much effort. Keep in mind that many parts, especially spark plugs, used tapered threads so that gentle turning will automatically bring the part you're treading to the proper angle if you don't force it or resist a change in angle. Don't put a wrench on the part until it's been turned a couple of turns by hand. If you suddenly encounter resistance, and the part has not seated fully, don't force it. Pull it back out and make sure it's clean and threading properly.

Always take your time and be patient; once you have some experience, working on your car will become an enjoyable hobby.

TOOLS AND EQUIPMENT

▶ **See Figure 1**

Naturally, without the proper tools and equipment it is impossible to properly service your car. It would be impossible to catalog each tool that you would need to perform each or any operation in this book. It would also be unwise for the amateur to rush out and buy an expensive set of tools on the theory that he may need on or more of them at sometime.

The best approach is to proceed slowly, gathering together a good quality set of those tools that are used most frequently. Don't be misled by the low cost of bargain tools. It is far better to spend a little more for better quality. Forged wrenches, 10 or 12 point sockets and fine tooth ratchets are by far preferable to their less expensive counterparts. As any good mechanic can tell you, there are few worse experiences than trying to work on a vehicle with bad tools. Your monetary savings will be far outweighed by frustration and mangled knuckles.

Begin accumulating those tools that are used most frequently; those associated with routine maintenance and tune-up.

In addition to the normal assortment of screwdrivers and pliers you should have the following tools for routine maintenance jobs:

1. Metric and SAE wrenches, sockets and combination open end/box end wrenches in sizes from 1/8 in. (3mm) to 3/4 in. (19mm) and a spark plug socket 13/16 in. or 5/8 in. depending on plug type).

If possible, buy various length socket drive extensions. One break in this department is that the metric sockets available in the U.S. will all fit the ratchet handles and extensions you may already have (1/4 in., 3/8 in., and 1/2 in. drive).

2. A hydraulic floor jack of at least 1½ ton capacity. If you are serious about maintaining your own car, then a floor jack is as necessary as a spark plug socket. The greatly increased utility, strength, and safety of a hydraulic floor jack makes it pay for itself many times over through the years.

3. Jackstands for support.
4. A drop light, to light up the work area (make sure yours is Underwriter's approved, and has a shielded bulb).
5. Oil filter wrench.
6. Oil filler spout for pouring oil.
7. Grease gun for chassis lubrication.
8. Hydrometer for checking the battery.
9. A container for draining oil.
10. Many rags for wiping up the inevitable mess.

In addition to the above items there are several others that are not absolutely necessary, but handy to have around. These include oil dry, a transmission funnel and the usual supply of lubricants, antifreeze and fluids, although these can be purchased as needed. This is a basic list for routine maintenance, but only your personal needs and desire can accurately determine you list of tools.

The second list of tools is for tune-ups. While the tools involved here are slightly more sophisticated, they need not be outrageously expensive. There are several inexpensive tach/dwell meters on the market that are every bit as good for the average mechanic as a $100.00 professional model. Just be sure that it goes to a least 1200-1500 rpm on the tach scale and that it works on 4, 6, or 8 cylinder engines. A basic list of tune-up equipment could include:

11. Tach/dwell meter.
12. Spark plug wrench.
13. Timing light (a DC light that works from the vehicle's battery is best, although an AC light that plugs into 110V house current will suffice at some sacrifice in brightness).
14. Wire spark plug gauge/adjusting tools.
15. Set of feeler blades.

In addition to these basic tools, there are several other tools and gauges you may find useful. These include:

16. A compression gauge. The screw-in type is slower to use, but eliminates the possibility of a faulty reading due to escaping pressure.
17. A manifold vacuum gauge.
18. A test light.
19. An induction meter. This is used for determining whether or not there is current in a wire. These are handy for use if a wire is broken somewhere in a wiring harness.

As a final note, you will probably find a torque wrench necessary for all but the most basic work. The beam type models are perfectly adequate, although the newer click type are more precise.

Special Tools

Normally, the use of special factory tools are avoided for repair procedures, since these are not readily available for the do-it-yourself mechanic. When it is possible to perform the job with more commonly available tools, it will be pointed out, but occasionally, a special tool was designed to perform a specific function and should be used. Before substituting another tool, you should be convinced that neither your safety nor the performance of the car will be compromised.

When a special tool is indicated, it will be referred to by a manufacturer's part number. Where possible, an illustration of the tool will be provided so that an equivalent tool may be used. Some special tools are available commercially from major tool manufacturers. Others can be purchased from: General Motors Service Tool Division, Kent-Moore, 29784 Little Mack, Roseville, MI 48066-2298.

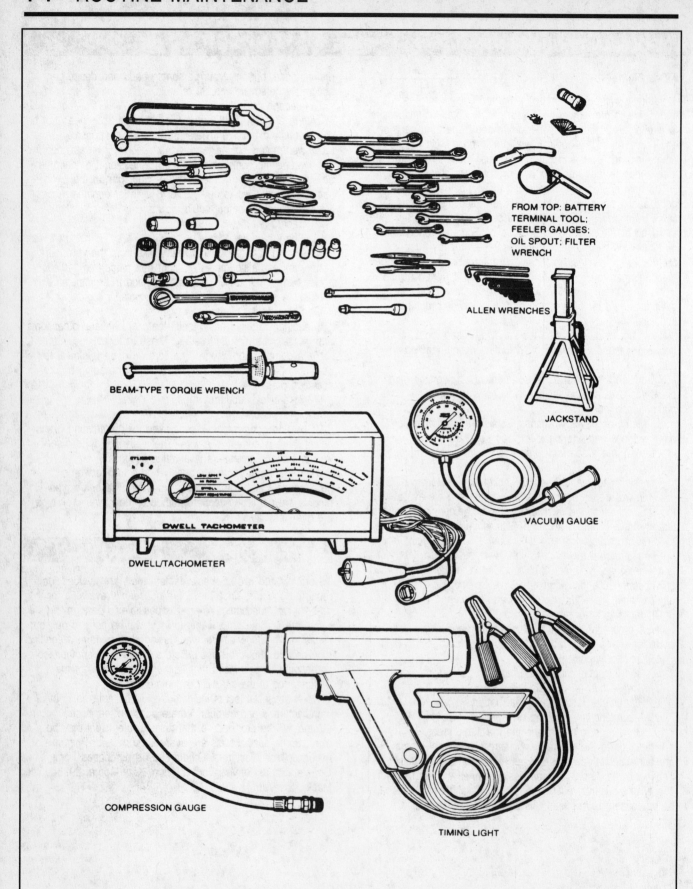

FROM TOP: BATTERY TERMINAL TOOL; FEELER GAUGES; OIL SPOUT; FILTER WRENCH

ALLEN WRENCHES

BEAM-TYPE TORQUE WRENCH

JACKSTAND

DWELL/TACHOMETER

VACUUM GAUGE

COMPRESSION GAUGE

TIMING LIGHT

Fig. 1 You need only a basic assortment of hand tools and test instruments for most maintenance and repair jobs

SERVICING YOUR VEHICLE SAFELY

It is virtually impossible to anticipate all of the hazards involved with automotive maintenance and service, but care and common sense will prevent most accidents.

The rules of safety for mechanics range from 'don't smoke around gasoline,' to 'use the proper tool for the job.' The trick to avoiding injuries is to develop safe work habits and take every possible precaution.

Do's

▶ See Figures 2 and 3

• Do keep a fire extinguisher and first aid kit within easy reach.

• Do wear safety glasses or goggles when cutting, drilling, grinding or prying, even if you have 20/20 vision. If you wear glasses for the sake of vision, they should be made of hardened glass that can serve also as safety glasses, or wear safety goggles over your regular glasses.

• Do shield your eyes whenever you work around the battery. Batteries contain sulfuric acid. In case of contact with the eyes or skin, flush the area with water or a mixture of water and baking soda and get medical attention immediately.

• Do use safety stands for any under car service. Jacks are for raising cars; safety stands are for making sure the car stays raised until you want it to come down. Whenever the car

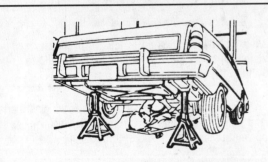

Fig. 2 Always use jackstands when supporting the car, never use cylinder blocks or tire changing jacks

Fig. 3 Ensure floor jack is positioned properly. Correct placement of both front and/or rear jackstands

is raised, block the wheels remaining on the ground and set the parking brake.

• Do use adequate ventilation when working with any chemicals or hazardous materials. Like carbon monoxide, the asbestos dust resulting from brake lining wear can be poisonous in sufficient quantities.

• Do disconnect the negative battery cable when working on the electrical system. The secondary ignition system can contain up to 40,000 volts.

• Do follow manufacturer's directions whenever working with potentially hazardous materials. Both brake fluid and antifreeze are poisonous if taken internally.

• Do properly maintain your tools. Loose hammerheads, mushroomed punches and chisels, frayed or poorly grounded electrical cords, excessively worn screwdrivers, spread wrenches (open end), cracked sockets, slipping ratchets, or faulty droplight sockets can cause accidents.

• Likewise, keep your tools clean; a greasy wrench can slip off a bolt head, ruining the bolt and often ruining your knuckles in the process.

• Do use the proper size and type of tool for the job being done.

• Do when possible, pull on a wrench handle rather than push on it, and adjust your stance to prevent a fall.

• Do be sure that adjustable wrenches are tightly closed on the nut or bolt and pulled so that the face is on the side of the fixed jaw.

• Do select a wrench or socket that fits the nut or bolt. The wrench or socket should sit straight, not cocked.

• Do strike squarely with a hammer; avoid glancing blows.

• Do set the parking brake and block the drive wheels if the work requires the engine running.

Don'ts

• Don't run the engine in a garage or anywhere else without proper ventilation — EVER! Carbon monoxide is poisonous; it takes a long time to leave the human body and you can build up a deadly supply of it in your system by simply breathing in a little every day. You may not realize you are slowly poisoning yourself. Always use power vents, windows, fans or open the garage doors.

• Don't work around moving parts while wearing a necktie or other loose clothing. Short sleeves are much safer than long, loose sleeves; hard — toed shoes with neoprene soles protect your toes and give a better grip on slippery surfaces. Jewelry such as watches, fancy belt buckles, beads or body adornment of any kind is not safe working around a car. Long hair should be tied back under a hat or cap.

• Don't use pockets for toolboxes. A fall or bump can drive a screwdriver deep into your body. Even a wiping cloth hanging from the back pocket can wrap around a spinning shaft or fan.

• Don't smoke when working around gasoline, cleaning solvent or other flammable material.

• Don't smoke when working around the battery. When the battery is being charged, it gives off explosive hydrogen gas.

• Don't use gasoline to wash your hands; there are excellent soaps available. Gasoline may contain lead, and lead can enter the body through a cut, accumulating in the body until you are very ill. Gasoline also removes all the natural oils from the skin so that bone dry hands will soak up oil and grease.

• Don't service the air conditioning system unless you are equipped with the necessary tools and training. The refrigerant, R-12, is extremely cold when compressed, and when released into the air will instantly freeze any surface it contacts, including your eyes. Although the refrigerant is normally non-toxic, R-12 becomes a deadly poisonous gas in the presence of an open flame. One good whiff of the vapors from burning refrigerant can be fatal.

• Don't use screwdrivers for anything other than driving screws! A screwdriver used as an prying tool can snap when you least expect it, causing injuries. At the very least, you'll ruin a good screwdriver.

• Don't use a bumper jack (that little ratchet, scissors, or pantograph jack supplied with the car) for anything other than changing a flat! These jacks are only intended for emergency use out on the road; they are NOT designed as a maintenance tool. If you are serious about maintaining your car yourself, invest in a hydraulic floor jack of a least 1½ ton capacity, and at least two sturdy jackstands.

MODEL IDENTIFICATION

The Caprice, the 'B-body' car line of General Motors, carries only two series, the Sedan and the Station Wagon. Within the series, the Caprice branches out into the Classic and Brougham, the more sophisticated interior, with more electronic instrumentation and controls.

SERIAL NUMBER IDENTIFICATION

Vehicle

Vehicle Identification Number (VIN) Plate

▶ See Figures 4, 5, 6 and 7

The Vehicle Identification Number (VIN) is stamped on a plate located on the top left hand side of the instrument panel, so it can be seen by looking through the windshield. The VIN is a seventeen digit sequence of numbers and letters important for ordering parts and for servicing.

➡The tenth digit of the (VIN) represents the model and is designated as a letter. Starting with 1990 (L), 1991 (M), 1992 (N) and 1993 (P).

Body Identification Label

▶ See Figure 8

The body number plate was last used on some of the 1990 vehicles. The ID plate is located on the upper surface of the

Fig. 5 View of VIN tag located in left front corner of dash; visible through the windshield. Use the VIN to correctly identify body and engine

firewall. The plate supplies various information for original parts ordering and body, engine and transmission identification. As of 1991 all vehicles use the Service Parts identification Label.

Service Parts Identification Label

▶ See Figures 9, 10 and 11

The service parts identification label has been developed and placed on the vehicle to aid in identifying parts and options originally installed on the vehicle. This is extremely helpful when purchasing a used vehicle, or restoring a used vehicle to its original state. The label is located on the underside of the luggage compartment lid on sedans, and on the inner right rear quarter panel of wagons.

Engine

▶ See Figure 12

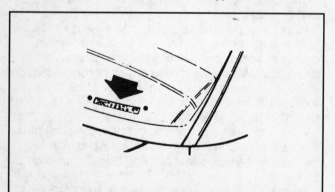

Fig. 4 Vehicle Identification Number (VIN) location

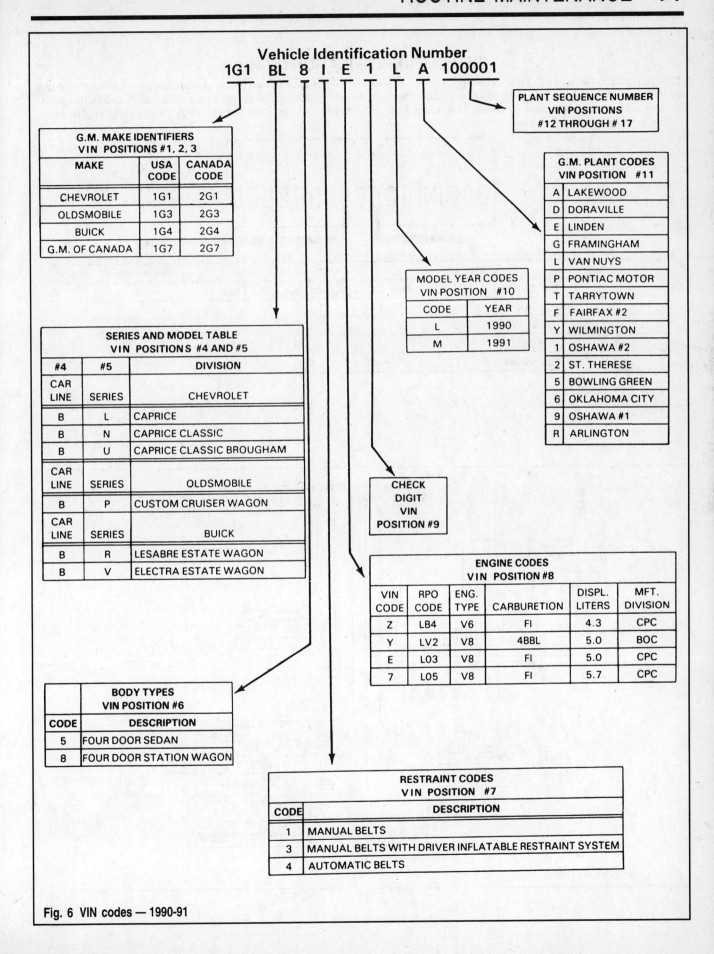

Vehicle Identification Number

1G1 BL 8 I E 1 L A 100001

PLANT SEQUENCE NUMBER
VIN POSITIONS
#12 THROUGH #17

G.M. MAKE IDENTIFIERS
VIN POSITIONS #1, 2, 3

MAKE	USA CODE	CANADA CODE
CHEVROLET	1G1	2G1
OLDSMOBILE	1G3	2G3
BUICK	1G4	2G4
G.M. OF CANADA	1G7	2G7

G.M. PLANT CODES
VIN POSITION #11

A	LAKEWOOD
D	DORAVILLE
E	LINDEN
G	FRAMINGHAM
L	VAN NUYS
P	PONTIAC MOTOR
T	TARRYTOWN
F	FAIRFAX #2
Y	WILMINGTON
1	OSHAWA #2
2	ST. THERESE
5	BOWLING GREEN
6	OKLAHOMA CITY
9	OSHAWA #1
R	ARLINGTON

MODEL YEAR CODES
VIN POSITION #10

CODE	YEAR
L	1990
M	1991

SERIES AND MODEL TABLE
VIN POSITIONS #4 AND #5

#4	#5	DIVISION
CAR LINE	SERIES	CHEVROLET
B	L	CAPRICE
B	N	CAPRICE CLASSIC
B	U	CAPRICE CLASSIC BROUGHAM
CAR LINE	SERIES	OLDSMOBILE
B	P	CUSTOM CRUISER WAGON
CAR LINE	SERIES	BUICK
B	R	LESABRE ESTATE WAGON
B	V	ELECTRA ESTATE WAGON

CHECK DIGIT VIN POSITION #9

ENGINE CODES
VIN POSITION #8

VIN CODE	RPO CODE	ENG. TYPE	CARBURETION	DISPL. LITERS	MFT. DIVISION
Z	LB4	V6	FI	4.3	CPC
Y	LV2	V8	4BBL	5.0	BOC
E	LO3	V8	FI	5.0	CPC
7	LO5	V8	FI	5.7	CPC

BODY TYPES
VIN POSITION #6

CODE	DESCRIPTION
5	FOUR DOOR SEDAN
8	FOUR DOOR STATION WAGON

RESTRAINT CODES
VIN POSITION #7

CODE	DESCRIPTION
1	MANUAL BELTS
3	MANUAL BELTS WITH DRIVER INFLATABLE RESTRAINT SYSTEM
4	AUTOMATIC BELTS

Fig. 6 VIN codes — 1990-91

VEHICLE IDENTIFICATION CHART

It is important for servicing and ordering parts to be certain of the vehicle and engine identification. The VIN (vehicle identification number) is a 17 digit number visible through the windshield on the driver's side of the dash and contains the vehicle and engine identification codes. The tenth digit indicates model year and the eighth digit indicates engine code. It can be interpreted as follows:

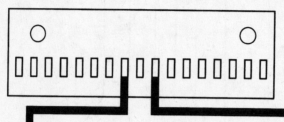

Engine Code

Code	Liters	Cu. In. (cc)	Cyl.	Fuel Sys.	Eng. Mfg.
Z	4.3	262 (4300)	6	TBI	CPC
Y	5.0	305 (5000)	8	Carb	BOC
E	5.0	305 (5000)	8	TBI	CPC
7	5.7	350 (5700)	8	TBI	CPC

BOC—Buick, Oldsmobile, Cadillac
CPC—Chevrolet, Pontiac, Canada
Carb—Carbureted
TBI—Throttle Body Injection

Model Year

Code	Year
L	1990
M	1991
N	1992
P	1993

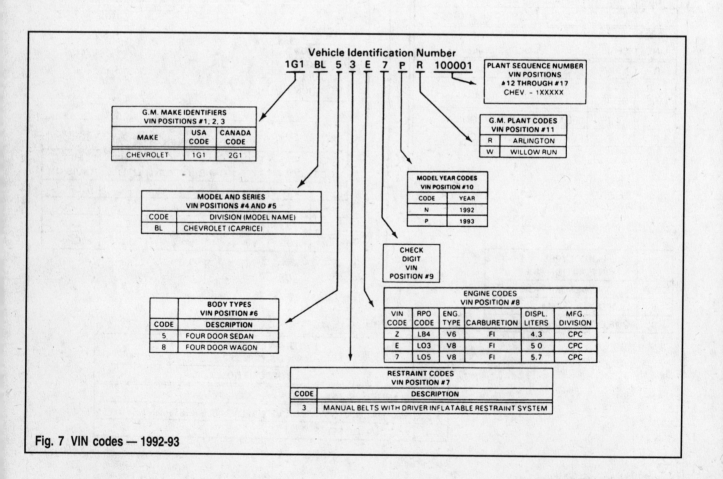

Fig. 7 VIN codes — 1992-93

ENGINE IDENTIFICATION

Year	Model	Engine Displacement Liters (cc)	Engine Series (ID/VIN) ③	Fuel System	No. of Cylinders	Engine Type
1990	Caprice ①	4.3 (4300)	Z	TBI	6	OHV
	Caprice	5.0 (5000)	Y	Carb	8	OHV
	Caprice	5.0 (5000)	E	TBI	8	OHV
	Caprice	5.7 (5700)	7	TBI	8	OHV
1991	Caprice ①	4.3 (4300)	Z	TBI	6	OHV
	Caprice	5.0 (5000)	E	TBI	8	OHV
	Caprice ②	5.7 (5700)	7	TBI	8	OHV
1992	Caprice ①	4.3 (4300)	Z	TBI	6	OHV
	Caprice	5.0 (5000)	E	TBI	8	OHV
	Caprice ②	5.7 (5700)	7	TBI	8	OHV
1993	Caprice ①	4.3 (4300)	Z	TBI	6	OHV
	Caprice	5.0 (5000)	E	TBI	8	OHV
	Caprice ②	5.7 (5700)	7	TBI	8	OHV

Carb—Carbureted
OHV—Overhead Valves
TBI—Throttle Body Injection
VIN—Vehicle Identification Number
① Fleet Sales
② Station Wagon and Police only
③ 8th digit of Vehicle Identification Number

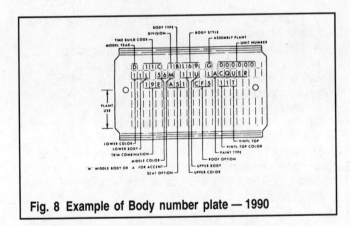

Fig. 8 Example of Body number plate — 1990

There are several ways to identify the engine size, manufacturer and year. The first is by comparing digits 3 and 10 through 17 of the VIN plate with the VIN derivative which is stamped on the engine block.

If the 2 sets of numbers correspond, then it is safe to say that this is the original installed engine. The next thing to do is correctly identify the size of the engine by checking the 8th digit of the VIN plate and comparing the digit to the VIN chart.

On the V6 and all V8 engines, except the 307 c.i. (VIN Y) Oldsmobile carbureted engine, the serial number is found on a pad at the front right hand side of the cylinder block, just below the cylinder head. On the 231 c.i. V6, the number can be found on a pad on the left side of the cylinder block, where it meets the transmission. On the 307 c.i. (VIN Y) Oldsmobile carbureted engine, the number can be found below the front of the left exhaust manifold assembly.

The engines are also stamped with a number which identifies the assembly plant, the day and month produced and the engine type code.

Stick on labels are also used to identify engine unit number and code. The sticker also contains bar coding for in-plant identification.

Transmission

♦ **See Figures 13 and 14**

Each transmission has a VIN derivative and an identification label located on the housing. The identification label gives the model of transmission and the build date. The location of the numbers on each transmission are shown in the illustration.

Drive Axle

♦ **See Figure 15**

The axle identification number is located either on a metal tag (attached to the rear axle cover) or stamped onto the right front side of the axle tube.

To service the rear axle, the 4th digit must be known, which is the manufacturers identity. The codes are: K for GM of Canada or G for Saginaw. The rear axle identification number must be known to order the Original Equipment Manufacturer (OEM) parts.

If the identification tag is missing, or it does not have the gear ratio stamped on it, a quick way to determine the axle ratio is as follows:

1. Raise and safely support the rear of the vehicle on jack stands.

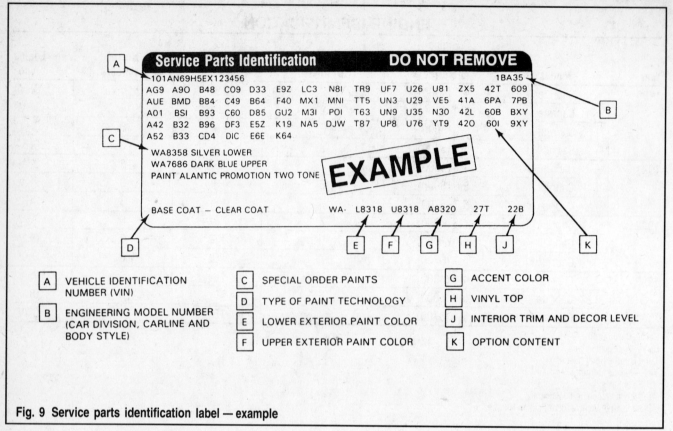

Fig. 9 Service parts identification label — example

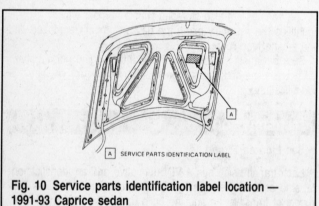

Fig. 10 Service parts identification label location — 1991-93 Caprice sedan

Fig. 11 Service parts identification label location — 1991-93 Caprice station wagon

2. Matchmark the inside of one rear wheel and the ground with chalk or other suitable marker.

3. Matchmark the pinion yoke and the axle housing.

4. With transmission in neutral, turn the driveshaft (or pinion) and count the number of turns it takes to turn the wheel one complete revolution.

5. Lower vehicle.

You now have an estimated axle ratio, examples being: 2½ turns of the pinion to 1 turn of the wheel equals a 2.50 ratio. A 3¼ turn of the pinion to 1 turn of the wheel equals a 3.25 ratio. Remember this is just an estimated ratio and the actual ratio may be slightly different upon ordering replacement parts.

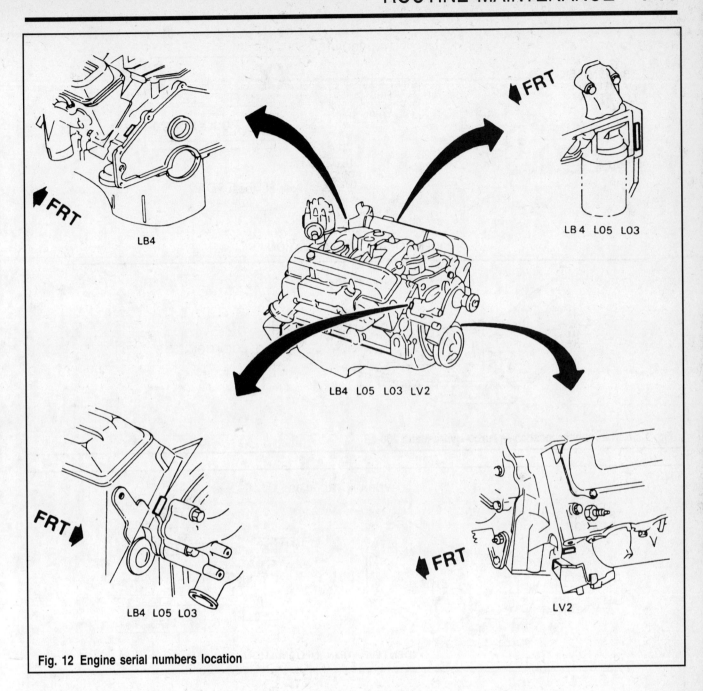

Fig. 12 Engine serial numbers location

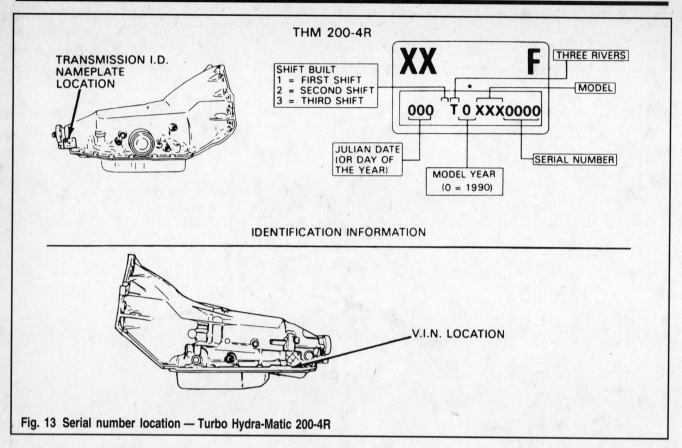

Fig. 13 Serial number location — Turbo Hydra-Matic 200-4R

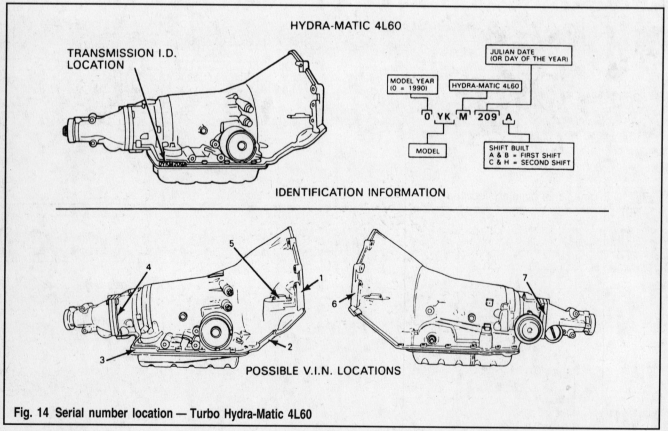

Fig. 14 Serial number location — Turbo Hydra-Matic 4L60

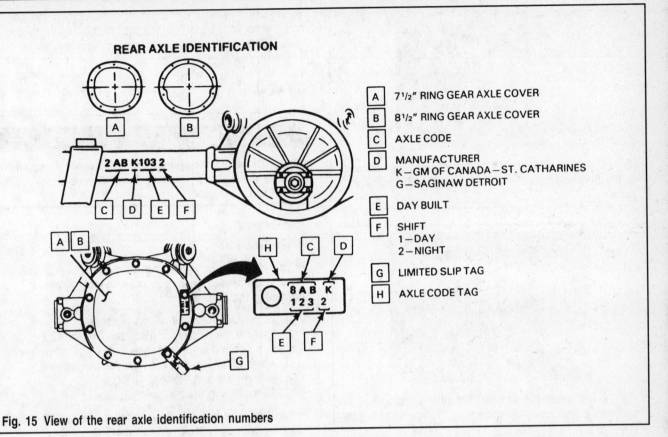

REAR AXLE IDENTIFICATION

2 AB K103 2

A	7½" RING GEAR AXLE COVER
B	8½" RING GEAR AXLE COVER
C	AXLE CODE
D	MANUFACTURER K — GM OF CANADA — ST. CATHARINES G — SAGINAW DETROIT
E	DAY BUILT
F	SHIFT 1 — DAY 2 — NIGHT
G	LIMITED SLIP TAG
H	AXLE CODE TAG

8 AB K
1 2 3 2

Fig. 15 View of the rear axle identification numbers

ROUTINE MAINTENANCE

▶ See Figure 16

Vehicle Emission Control Information Label

▶ See Figure 17

The Vehicle Emission Control Information Label is located in the engine compartment (fan shroud, radiator support, hood underside, etc.) of every car produced by General Motors. The label contains important emission specifications and setting procedures, as well as a vacuum hose schematic with various emissions components identified.

Fig. 16 Underhood of engine compartment general component locations — 1992 5.0L (VIN E) engine shown

Fig. 17 Emission decal containing pertinent engine specifications — 1992 5.0L (VIN E) — example only

When servicing your Chevrolet, this label should always be checked for up-to-date information pertaining specifically to your car.

➡ Always follow the timing procedures on this label when adjusting ignition timing.

Air Cleaner

▶ See Figures 18 and 19

The air cleaner has a dual purpose. It not only filters the air going to the carburetor, but also acts as a flame arrester if the engine should backfire through the carburetor. If an engine

Fig. 18 Unsnap the air cleaner box clips to gain access to the filter assembly — 1992-93 5.0L (VIN E) engine shown

Fig. 19 Removing the air filter. The filter should be replaced if noticeably dirty, such as the one shown here.

maintenance procedure requires the temporary removal of the air cleaner, remove it; otherwise, never run the engine without it. Unfiltered air to the carburetor will eventually result in a dirty, inefficient carburetor and possible engine damage.

To replace the filter, simply remove the wingnut located on the top of the air cleaner assembly and remove the air cleaner lid. Replace the filter assembly and reinstall the lid. Inspect the air filter and housing assembly for excessive contaminants, such as leaves and oil. If an excessive amount of oil is present in or on the filter assembly, inspect the PCV system for proper operation or the engine for mechanical damage such as bad piston rings.

Fuel Filter

There are three different types of fuel filters that may be used on the Caprice: internal filter, in-line filter and an in-tank filter.

The internal filter is used on all carburetors and is located in the inlet fitting. A spring is installed behind the filter to hold the filter outward, sealing it against the inlet fitting. A check valve is also built into the fuel filter element to prevent fuel from draining back out of the carburetor when the engine is not running.

The in-line fuel filter is just that, installed in the fuel tank-to-engine fuel line, usually mounted near the rear crossmember of the Caprice. The lines are made of nylon and care must be taken not to kink the lines.

The in-tank fuel filter is located on the lower end of the fuel pick-up tube in the fuel tank. The filter is made of woven

plastic and prevents dirt from entering the fuel line and also stops water unless the filter becomes completely submerged in water. This filter is self-cleaning and normally requires no maintenance.

REMOVAL & INSTALLATION

✳✳CAUTION

Never smoke when working around gasoline! Avoid all sources of sparks or ignition. Gasoline vapors are EXTREMELY volatile!

Carbureted Engine
▶ See Figure 20

➡To avoid twisting or kinking a brake, oil or fuel line, always use a backup wrench when loosening and/or tightening the line.

1. Disconnect the negative battery cable.
2. Remove the air cleaner assembly. Disconnect the fuel line connection at the fuel inlet filter nut using 2 wrenches.
3. Remove the fuel inlet nut from the carburetor.
4. Remove the fuel filter and spring.
5. To install, replace the fuel filter.

➡The fuel filter has a built in check valve and must be installed with the check valve to meet with safety standards. Ensure the check valve is not sticking closed by lightly pushing the valve open.

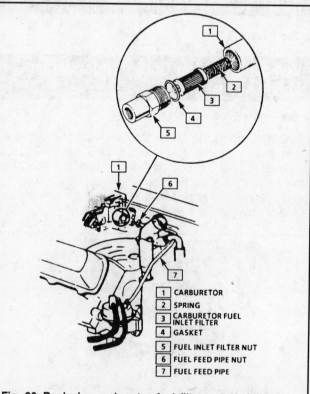

1	CARBURETOR
2	SPRING
3	CARBURETOR FUEL INLET FILTER
4	GASKET
5	FUEL INLET FILTER NUT
6	FUEL FEED PIPE NUT
7	FUEL FEED PIPE

Fig. 20 Replacing carburetor fuel filter — 5.0L (VIN Y) engine

6. Install the filter spring, filter and check valve assembly in carburetor. The check valve end of filter should face toward the fuel line. The ribs on the closed end of the filter element will prevent the filter from being installed incorrectly unless it is forced.

7. Install the nut in the carburetor and tighten nut to 46 ft. lbs. (62 Nm).

8. Install the fuel line and tighten connection. Reconnect the negative battery cable.

9. Start the engine and check for leaks. Install the air cleaner.

In-Line Filter

▶ See Figures 21 and 22

✳✳CAUTION

Before removing any component of the fuel system, make sure the fuel system pressure is properly relieved as described in this section.

1. Disconnect the negative battery cable. Disconnect the nylon fuel line fittings by squeezing the plastic tabs of the male connector together, twisting the lines a ¼ turn and pulling the connection apart. Repeat the procedure for the remaining line.

2. Remove the fuel filter from the retainer or mounting bolt.

3. To install, reverse the removal procedures. Start the engine and check for leaks.

➡The filter has an arrow (fuel flow direction) on the side of the case, be sure to install it correctly in the system, with the arrow facing in the direction of flow toward the front of the vehicle.

In-Tank Filter

To service the in-tank fuel filter, refer to the Electric Fuel Pump Removal and Installation procedure in Section 5.

FUEL PRESSURE RELEASE

Carbureted Engine

To release the fuel pressure on the carbureted system, remove and replace the fuel tank cap.

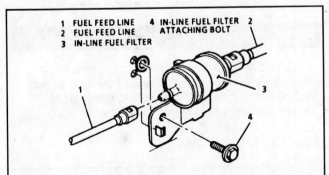

Fig. 21 In-line fuel filter replacement — fuel injected engines

1	FUEL FEED LINE	4	IN-LINE FUEL FILTER
2	FUEL FEED LINE		ATTACHING BOLT
3	IN-LINE FUEL FILTER		

Fuel Injected Engine

The TBI unit used on the fuel injected engines contains a constant bleed feature in the pressure regulator that relieves pressure any time the engine is turned off. Therefore, no special relief procedure is required, however, a small amount of fuel may be released when the fuel line is disconnected.

✳✳CAUTION

To reduce the chance of personal injury, cover the fuel line with cloth to collect the fuel and then place the cloth in an approved container.

Positive Crankcase Ventilation (PCV) Valve

▶ See Figures 23 and 24

The crankcase ventilation system (PCV) must be operating correctly to provide complete removal of the crankcase vapors. Fresh air is supplied to the crankcase from the air filter, mixed with the internal exhaust gases, passed through the PCV valve and into the intake manifold.

The PCV valve meters the flow at a rate depending upon the manifold vacuum. If the manifold vacuum is high, the PCV restricts the flow to the intake manifold. If abnormal operating conditions occur, excessive amounts of internal exhaust gases back flow through the crankcase vent tube into the air filter to be burned by normal combustion.

If the engine is idling roughly, a quick check of the PCV valve can be made. While the engine is idling, pull the PCV valve from the valve cover, place your thumb over the end of the PCV valve and check for vacuum. If no vacuum exists, check for a plugged PCV valve, manifold port, hoses or deteriorated hoses. Turn the engine **OFF**, remove the PCV valve and shake it. Listen for the rattle of the check needle inside the valve. If it does not rattle, replace the valve.

The PCV system should be checked at every oil change and serviced every 30,000 miles.

✳✳WARNING

Never operate an engine without a PCV valve or a ventilation system, otherwise oil leaks from excessive crankcase pressure and/or engine damage may result.

Fuel Vapor Canister

▶ See Figure 25

To limit gasoline vapor discharge into the air this system is designed to trap fuel vapors, which normally escape from the fuel system. Vapor arrest is accomplished through the use of the charcoal canister. This canister absorbs fuel vapors and stores them until they can be removed to be burned in the engine. Removal of the vapors from the canister is accomplished by a solenoid operated bowl vent or vacuum operated purge valve mounted on the canister. In addition to the fuel system modifications and the canister, the fuel tank requires a non-vented gas cap. The domed fuel tank positions a vent high enough above the fuel to keep the vent pipe in

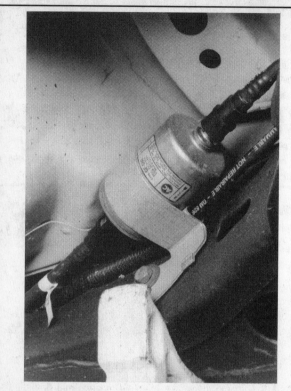

Fig. 22 Fuel filter location, right side forward of rear axle — fuel injected engines

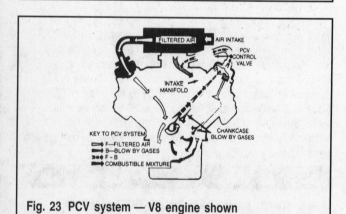

Fig. 23 PCV system — V8 engine shown

Fig. 24 PCV valve located on the left side valve cover — except 5.0L (VIN Y) engine

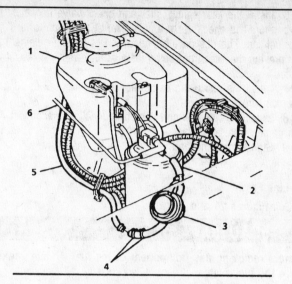

1	**WINDSHIELD WIPER WASHER FLUID TANK**
2	**FUEL VAPOR CANISTER**
3	**FUEL VAPOR PRESSURE CONTROL VALVE**
4	**CLAMPS**
5	**FUEL VAPOR PIPE FROM TANK**
6	**FUEL VAPOR HOSE TO TBI**

Fig. 25 Vapor canister location — 1991-93 Caprice

the vapor at all times. The single vent pipe is routed directly to the canister. From the canister, the vapors are routed to the PCV system, where they will be burned during normal combustion.

REPLACEMENT

1. Tag and disconnect all hoses connected to the charcoal canister.
2. Loosen the retaining clamps and then lift out the canister.
3. Grasp the filter in the bottom of the canister with your fingers and pull it out. Replace it with a new one.
4. Install canister and tighten retaining clamps.
5. Install all hoses to canister.

➡**Some vehicles do not have replaceable filters.**

Battery

All General Motors vehicles have a 'maintenance free' battery as standard equipment, eliminating the need for fluid level checks and the possibility of specific gravity tests. However, the battery does require some attention.

GENERAL MAINTENANCE

Once a year, the battery terminals and the cable clamps should be cleaned. Remove the side terminal bolts and the cables, negative cable first. Clean the cable clamps and the battery terminals with a wire brush until all corrosion, grease, etc. is removed and the metal is shiny. It is especially important to clean the inside of the clamp thoroughly, since a small deposit of foreign material or oxidation there will prevent a sound electrical connection and inhibit either starting or charging. Special tools are available for cleaning the side terminal clamps and terminals.

Before installing the cables, loosen the battery hold-down clamp, remove the battery, and check the battery tray. Clear it of any debris and check it for corrosion. Rust should be wire-brushed away, and the metal given a coat of anti-rust paint. Install the battery and tighten the hold-down clamp securely, but be careful not to over tighten, which will crack the battery case.

After the clamps and terminals are clean, reinstall the cables, negative cable last. Give the clamps and terminals a thin external coat of grease after installation, to retard corrosion.

Check the cables at the same time that the terminals are cleaned. If the cable insulation is cracked or broken, or if the ends are frayed, the cable should be replaced with a new cable of the same length and gauge.

✳✳CAUTION

Keep flames or sparks away from the battery; it gives off explosive hydrogen gas! Battery electrolyte contains sulfuric acid. If you should get any on your skin or in your eyes, flush the affected areas with plenty of clear water; if it lands in your eyes, get medical help immediately!

TESTING

▶ **See Figures 26 and 27**

The sealed top battery cannot be checked for charge in the normal manner, since there is no provision for access to the electrolyte. The battery has a label containing the model, cold cranking amps, load test amps and replacement number affixed to it. To check the condition of the battery proceed as follows:

1. Check the built in hydrometer on top of the battery:
a. If a green dot appears in the middle of the indicator eye on top of the battery , the battery is sufficiently charged.

b. If the indicator eye is clear or light yellow, the electrolyte fluid is too low and the battery must be replaced.
c. If the indicator eye is dark, the battery has a low charge and should be charged.
2. Load test the battery:
a. Connect a battery load tester and a voltmeter across the battery terminals (the battery cables should be disconnected from the battery).
b. Apply a 300 ampere load to the battery for 15 seconds to remove the surface charge. Remove the load.
c. Wait 15 seconds to allow the battery to recover. Apply the appropriate test load, as specified:
- 730 Battery (std. V8) — Test load: 260 amperes
- 731 Battery (opt. V8) — Test load: 280 amperes
- 601 Battery (std. V6) — Test load: 310 amperes
- 735 Battery (fleet and police) — Test load: 260 amperes

Take a voltage reading at the end of 15 seconds of load. Disconnect the load.
3. Check the results against the following chart. If the battery voltage is at or above the specified voltage for the temperature listed, the battery is good. If the voltage falls below what's listed, the battery should be replaced.

CHARGING THE BATTERY

➡**Do not charge a battery if the indicator eye is clear or light yellow. The battery should be replaced. If the battery feels hot (125°F) or if violent gassing or spewing of the electrolyte through the vent hole(s) occurs, discontinue charging or reduce the charging rate. Always follow the battery charger manufacturer's information for charging the battery.**

1. To charge a sealed terminal battery out of the car, install adapter kit ST-1201 or 1846855 or equivalent.
2. Make sure that all charger connections are clean and tight.

➡**For best results, the battery should be charged while the battery electrolyte and plates are at room temperature. A battery that is extremely cold may not accept the charging current for several hours after starting the charger.**

3. Charge the battery until the indicator eye shows a green dot. (It may be necessary to tip the battery from side to side

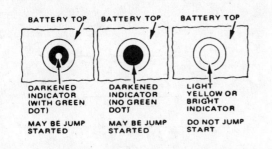

Fig. 26 Maintenance free batteries contain their own built-in hydrometer

Temperature (°F)	Minimum Voltage
70 or above	9.6
60	9.5
50	9.4
40	9.3
30	9.1
20	8.9
10	8.7
0	8.5

Fig. 27 Battery temperature versus voltage drop

to get the green dot to appear after charging.) The battery should be checked every half hour while charging.

REPLACEMENT

When it becomes necessary to replace the battery, select a battery with a rating equal to or greater than the battery originally installed. Details on battery removal and installation are covered in Section 3.

Early Fuel Evaporation System (EFE)Heat Riser Valve

▶ See Figure 28

The EFE system is used on the 5.0L (VIN Y) engine to provide a source of quick heat to the engine induction system during cold drive away. The EFE system consists of a vacuum servo (located in the exhaust manifold) and Thermo Vacuum Switch (TVS).

Every 30,000 miles, check the EFE valve (make sure it is free, not sticking), the TVS for proper function and the hoses for cracking or deterioration. If necessary, replace or lubricate.

To check the valve, ensure the engine is cool and move the valve through its full stroke by hand, making sure that the linkage does not bind and is properly connected. Using a hand held vacuum pump, apply 10 in. Hg. of vacuum to valve and verify the vacuum holds and the valve opens. If the valve sticks, free it with a solvent. If the vacuum falls, replace the valve. Also check that all vacuum hoses are properly

connected and free of cracks or breaks. Replace hoses or broken or bent linkage parts as necessary.

Belts

INSPECTION

The belts which drive the engine accessories such as the alternator or generator, the air pump, power steering pump, air conditioning compressor and water pump are of either the V-belt design or flat, serpentine design. Older belts show wear and damage readily, since their basic design was a belt with a rubber casing. As the casing wore, cracks and fibers were readily apparent. Newer design, caseless belts do not show wear as readily, and an untrained eye cannot distinguish between a good serviceable belt and one that is worn to the point of failure.

It is a good idea, therefore, to visually inspect the belts regularly and replace them, routinely, every two to three years.

ADJUSTING

V-Belts
▶ See Figures 29, 30, 31, 32 and 33

Belts are normally adjusted by loosening the bolts of the accessory being driven and moving that accessory on its pivot points until the proper tension is applied to the belt. The accessory is held in this position while the bolts are tightened. To determine proper belt tension, you can purchase a belt tension gauge or simply use the deflection method. To determine deflection, press inward on the belt at the mid-point of its longest straight run. The belt should deflect (move inward) 3/8-1/2 in. A general rule for alternator belt tension is the pulley should not be capable of being turned with hand pressure.

➡The bolts securing the power steering pivot bolts are accessible thru the holes in the power steering pulley.

It is important to note, however, that on engines with many driven accessories, several or all of the belts may have to be removed to get at the one to be replaced.

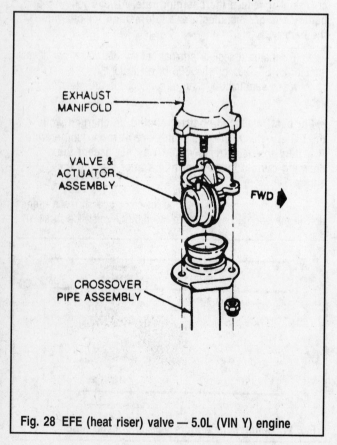

Fig. 28 EFE (heat riser) valve — 5.0L (VIN Y) engine

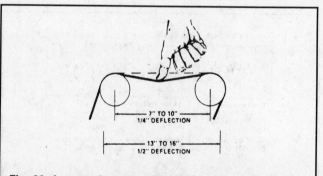

Fig. 29 A gauge is recommended, but you can check the belt tension with moderate thumb pressure

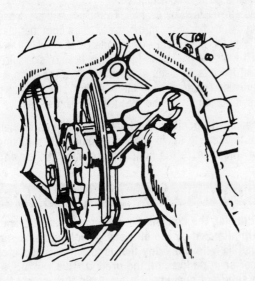

Fig. 30 To adjust belt tension, or to replace belts, first loosen the component's mounting and adjusting bolts slightly

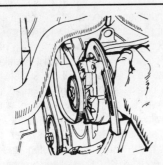

Fig. 31 Push the component toward the engine and slip off the belt

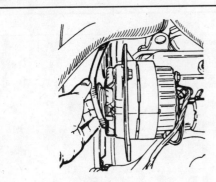

Fig. 32 Slip the new belt over the pulley

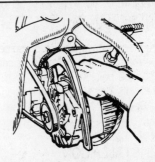

Fig. 33 Pull outward on the component and tighten the mounting bolts

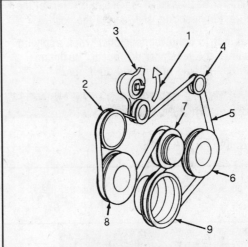

1. Rotate tensioner in direction shown to install or remove belt
2. A/C Compressor
3. Belt tensioner
4. Generator assembly pulley
5. Serpentine belt
6. P/S Pump pulley
7. Water pump pulley
8. Air pump pulley
9. Crankshaft pulley

Fig. 34 Serpentine belt routing and components

Fig. 35 Serpentine belt routing label located on the radiator shroud

Serpentine Belt

▶ See Figures 34, 35, 36 and 37

A single belt is used to drive all of the engine accessories formerly driven by multiple drive belts. The single belt is referred to a serpentine belt. All the belt driven accessories are rigidly mounted with belt tension maintained by a spring loaded tensioner. Because of the belt tensioner, no adjustment is necessary.

REMOVAL & INSTALLATION

To remove a drive belt, simply loosen the accessory being driven and move it on its pivot point to free the belt. Then, remove the belt. If a belt tensioner is used, push (rotate) the tensioner using a 15mm socket, and remove the belt.

➡ Take care as not to bend the tensioner when applying torque. Damage to the tensioner will occur. Maximum torque to load belt should not exceed 30 ft. lbs.

Hoses

REMOVAL & INSTALLATION

Radiator hoses are generally of two constructions, the preformed (molded) type, which is custom made for a

Fig. 37 Use a rachet or breaker bar to loosen serpentine belt tensioner when removing or installing the belt

particular application, and the spring-loaded type, which is made to fit several different applications. Heater hoses are all of the same general construction.

Hoses are retained by clamps. To replace a hose, loosen the clamp and slide it down the hose, away from the attaching point. Twist the hose from side to side carefully until it is free, then pull it off. Before installing the new hose, make sure that the outlet fitting is as clean as possible. Coat the fitting with non-hardening sealer and slip the hose into place. Install the clamp and tighten it. Fill and bleed the cooling system.

➡ Remember to position the hoses and clamps in their original location to avoid rubbing against other moving components; ensure the hoses and clamps are beyond the pipe lip.

✳✳CAUTION

When draining the coolant, keep in mind that cats and dogs are attracted by the ethylene glycol antifreeze, and are quite likely to drink any that is left in an uncovered container or in puddles on the ground. This will prove fatal in sufficient quantity. Always drain the coolant into a sealable container. Coolant should be reused unless it is contaminated or several years old.

Air Conditioning System

▶ See Figure 38

The Cycling Clutch Orifice Tube (CCOT) system includes the compressor, condenser, evaporator, an accumulator/drier with fixed orifice tube, a clutch cycling switch with or without a temperature probing capillary tube to maintain a selected comfortable temperature within the vehicle, while preventing evaporator freeze-up. Full control of the system is maintained through the use of a selector control, mounted in the dash assembly. The selector control makes use of a vacuum supply and electrical switches to operate mode doors and the blower motor. A sight glass is not used in this system and one should not be installed. When charging the system, the correct quantity of refrigerant must be installed to obtain maximum system performance.

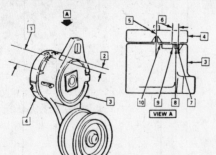

1. Used belt acceptable wear range
2. New belt range
3. Arm
4. Spindle
5. Fixed belt length indicator
6. With new belt installed, fixed pointer must fall within this range
7. Minimum length—new belt
8. Nominal length—new belt
9. Maximum length—new belt
10. Replace belt position

Fig. 36 Serpentine belt tensioner

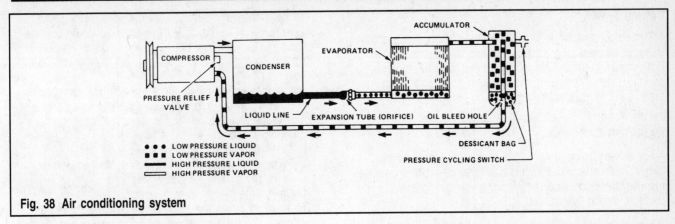

Fig. 38 Air conditioning system

GENERAL SERVICING PROCEDURES

The most important aspect of air conditioning service is the maintenance of pure and adequate charge of refrigerant in the system; likewise, the systems greatest enemy is moisture and therefore a system cannot function properly and will be damaged if leaks are not repaired in a timely manner. A refrigeration system cannot function properly if a significant percentage of the charge is lost. Refrigerant leaks can occur because of oil contamination on the hoses and lines or vibration can cause a cracking or loosening of the air conditioning fittings. As a result, the extreme operating pressures of the system force refrigerant out.

SAFETY WARNINGS

The following is a list of general precautions that should be observed while servicing the air conditioning system:

1. Always wear safety goggles when performing any work on or around the refrigerant system.

2. If refrigerant should contact the eyes or skin, flush the exposed area with cold water and seek medical assistance immediately.

3. Wrap a towel around the fitting valves when connecting or disconnecting the lines.

4. Thoroughly purge the service gauges and hoses of air and moisture before connecting them to the system. Keep them capped when not in use.

5. Thoroughly clean any refrigerant fitting before disconnecting it, in order to minimize the entrance of dirt into the system.

6. Plan any operation that requires opening the system beforehand in order to minimize the length of time it will be exposed to open air. Cap or seal the open ends to minimize the entrance of foreign material.

7. Never disconnect the air conditioning gauge service line at the gauges, always disconnect the line at the service fitting, otherwise the Schrader valve in the fitting will remain open and completely discharge the system, causing possible injury or system damage.

8. When adding oil, ensure the system has been properly discharged and pour the oil through an extremely clean and dry tube or funnel. Keep the oil capped whenever possible. Do not use oil that has not been kept tightly sealed.

9. Use only Refrigerant 12. Purchase refrigerant intended for use only in automotive air conditioning systems. Avoid the use of Refrigerant 12 that may be packaged for another use, such as cleaning, or powering a horn, as it is impure.

10. Using an approved recovery/recycling machine, completely evacuate a system that has been opened to replace a component, other than when isolating the compressor, or that has leaked sufficiently to draw in moisture and air. This requires evacuating air and moisture with a good vacuum pump for at least one hour.

11. Use a wrench on both halves of a fitting that is to be disconnected, so as to avoid placing torque on any of the refrigerant lines.

SYSTEM INSPECTION

❄❄CAUTION

Refrigerant will freeze any surface, including your eyes, that it contacts. In addition, the refrigerant changes into a poisonous gas in the presence of a flame.

1. Operation of the air conditioning blower at all four speeds with the mode button in any position except OFF, and engagement of the compressor clutch would indicate that the electrical circuits are functioning properly. (The blower will not operate in any speed with the mode button in the OFF position.)

2. Operation of the air conditioning control selector (mode) button to distribute air from designated outlets would indicate proper functioning.

Oil Leaks

System leaks can usually be identified as oily areas around the hoses or components. If a hose is thought to be leaking, simply grasp the hose with one hand and the line with the other and attempt to turn the line, if the line turns it is defective and must be replaced.

➡**If it is determined that the system has a leak, it should be corrected as soon as possible. Leaks may allow moisture to enter and cause expensive repairs.**

Cooling System

The air conditioning system depends on the cooling system to lower the condenser temperature and change the vapors into a liquid; therefore the cooling system must be in proper working order. The cooling system quantity and protection factor must be satisfactory. The cooling fan must also be operating properly.

RADIATOR CAP

For efficient operation of an air conditioned car's cooling system, the radiator cap should hold pressure which meets the manufacturer's specifications. A cap which fails to hold pressure should be replaced.

Condenser

Any obstruction of or damage to the condenser fin configuration will restrict the air flow which is essential to its efficient operation. It is therefore a good rule to keep this unit clean and in proper physical shape.

➡**Bug screens are regarded as obstructions.**

Condensation Drain Tube

A molded drain tube allows the condensation which accumulates in the bottom of the evaporator housing to drain outside of the vehicle. Occasionally over time, this tube, which is generally located on the engine firewall below the evaporator housing will become obstructed and allow the evaporator housing to fill up with water (condensation). Simply unclog any obstruction in the drain tube and allow the water to drain. Be careful not to damage the evaporator core.

➡**If this tube is obstructed, the air conditioning performance can be restricted and condensation buildup can spill over onto the vehicle's floor.**

REFRIGERANT LEVEL CHECKS

The same hand-felt temperature of the evaporator inlet pipe and the accumulator surface of an operating system would indicate a properly charged system. The system contains NO sightglass.

GAUGE SETS

Most of the service work performed in air conditioning requires the use of a set of two gauges, one for the high (head) pressure side of the system, the other for the low (suction) pressure side.

The low side gauge records both pressure and vacuum. Vacuum readings are calibrated from 0 to 30 inches and the pressure graduations read from 0 to no less than 60 psi.

The high side gauge measures pressure from 0 to at last 600 psi.

Both gauges are threaded into a manifold that contains two hand shut-off valves. Proper manipulation of these valves and the use of the attached test hoses allow the user to perform the following services:

1. Test high and low side pressures.
2. Remove air, moisture, and contaminated refrigerant.
3. Purge the system (of refrigerant).
4. Charge the system (with refrigerant).

The manifold valves are designed so that they have no direct effect on gauge readings, but serve only to provide for, or cut off, flow of refrigerant through the manifold. During all testing and hook-up operations, the valves are kept in a closed position to avoid disturbing the refrigeration system. The valves are opened only to purge the system of air or refrigerant and/or to charge it.

TESTING THE SYSTEM

▶ **See Figures 39, 40 and 41**

1. Close (clockwise) the gauge set valves.
2. Connect the gauge set as follows:

➡**It is recommended that the use of an approved recovery/recycling machine only be used to perform all discharging, evacuating and recharging of the system.**

   a. Locate the 2 service fittings in the air conditioning system.

   b. The low pressure fitting is located on the accumulator, connect the blue gauge hose to the fitting.

   c. The high pressure (smaller) fitting is located on the thinner line going from the accumulator to the condenser, connect the red gauge hose with special adapter to the fitting.

3. Set the parking brake, place the transmission in **N** and establish an idle of 2,000 rpm.

4. Place a high volume fan in front of the radiator grille to ensure proper airflow across the condenser.

5. Run the air conditioning system in the **MAX** and **COOL** mode with the blower on **HI**. Ensure the windows and doors are closed.

6. Insert a thermometer into the center air outlet. The thermometer should drop to approximately 45° (7°C) within a short period of time.

7. Use the accompanying performance chart for specifications.

RELATIVE HUMIDITY (%)	AMBIENT AIR TEMP		LOW SIDE		ENGINE SPEED (rpm)	CENTER DUCT AIR TEMPERATURE		HIGH SIDE	
	°F	°C	kPa	PSIG		°F	°C	kPa	PSIG
20	70	21	200	29	2000	40	4	1034	150
	80	27	200	29		44	7	1310	190
	90	32	207	30		48	9	1689	245
	100	38	214	31		57	14	2103	305
30	70	21	200	29	2000	42	6	1034	150
	80	27	207	30		47	8	1413	205
	90	32	214	31		51	11	1827	265
	100	38	221	32		61	16	2241	325
40	70	21	200	29	2000	45	7	1138	165
	80	27	207	30		49	9	1482	215
	90	32	221	32		55	13	1931	280
	100	38	269	39		65	18	2379	345
50	70	21	207	30	2000	47	8	1241	180
	80	27	221	32		53	12	1620	235
	90	32	234	34		59	15	2034	295
	100	38	276	40		69	21	2413	350
60	70	21	207	30	2000	48	9	1241	180
	80	27	228	33		56	13	1655	240
	90	32	249	36		63	17	2069	300
	100	38	296	43		73	23	2482	360
70	70	21	207	30	2000	50	10	1276	185
	80	27	234	34		58	14	1689	245
	90	32	262	38		65	18	2103	305
	100	38	303	44		75	24	2517	365
80	70	21	207	30	2000	50	10	1310	190
	80	27	234	34		59	15	1724	250
	90	32	269	39		67	19	2137	310
90	70	21	207	30	2000	50	10	1379	200
	80	27	249	36		62	17	1827	265
	90	32	290	42		71	22	2275	330

Fig. 39 Air conditioning performance test

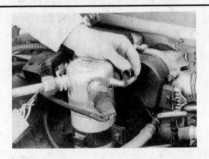

Fig. 40 A/C low pressure side service fitting with low pressure switch next to the fitting, located on the accumulator in right rear of engine compartment

Fig. 41 A/C high pressure side service fitting, located on the back of the compressor. Note that the high pressure service fitting will always be found in the thinner line; Do not charge the system through this fitting!

DISCHARGING THE SYSTEM

When replacing any of the air conditioning refrigeration components, the system must be completely discharged of refrigerant.

➡R-12 refrigerant is a chlorofluorocarbon which, when released into the atmosphere, can contribute to the depletion of the ozone layer in the upper atmosphere. The Ozone filters out harmful radiation from the sun. Consult the laws in your area before servicing the air conditioning system. In some states it is illegal to perform repairs involving refrigerant unless the work is done by a certified professional. If possible, an approved R-12 Recovery/Recycling machine that meets SAE standards should be employed when discharging the system. Follow the operating instructions provided with the approved equipment exactly to properly discharge the system.

✳✳WARNING

Always discharge the system at the low side service fitting.

1. With ignition turned OFF, remove protection cap from the low side service fitting on the accumulator and connect an approved Recycling/Recovery station, charging station J-23500-01.

2. With the low side of the system fully discharged, check the high side system fitting (on the liquid line or muffler) for the remaining pressure.

3. If some pressure is found, attempt to discharge the high side using the same procedure as was used for the low side. (This condition indicates a restriction on the high side and the cause must be diagnosed and corrected before evacuating and charging the system.

4. When the system is completely discharged (no vapor escaping with hose fully tightened down), measure, record amount, and discard the collected refrigerant oil. If the measured quantity is ½ fl. oz. (15ml) or more, this amount of new 525 viscosity refrigerant oil must be added to the system, plus any quantity in removed parts before system evacuation and charging with R-12.

ADDING OIL TO THE AIR CONDITIONING SYSTEM

Adding oil to the air conditioning system should take place after discharging and before evacuation procedures by removing the refrigeration suction hose at the accumulator outlet pipe connection, pouring the correct quantity of new refrigerant oil into the hose or pipe and then properly reconnecting the hose to the pipe. The R-4 compressor system requires 6 fl. oz. (180ml) of 525 viscosity refrigerant oil.

1. Remove only the accumulator.

2. Drain, measure and record quantity of oil in the accumulator.

➡It is not necessary to remove and drain the compressor because the compressor only retains a minimum quantity of oil.

3. If less than 3 fl. oz. (90ml) of oil was drained, add 3 fl. oz. (90ml) of new oil to the system.

4. If more than 3 fl. oz. (90ml) of oil was drained, add the same amount of new oil drained.

5. If a new accumulator must be added to the system, add 2 fl. oz. (60ml) additional oil to compensate for that retained by the original accumulator desiccant.

EVACUATING THE SYSTEM

1. Connect a gauge and vacuum pump assembly as follows:
   a. Connect low pressure gauge to the accumulator fitting.
   b. Connect the gauge set center hose to R-12 source.
   c. Connect the high pressure gauge to vacuum pump.

2. To begin evacuation of the air conditioning system with the manifold gauge set and vacuum pump, slowly open the high and low side gauge valves and begin vacuum pump operation. Pump the system until the low side gauge reaches 26 in. Hg of vacuum.

➡The vacuum specified can only be reached at or near sea level. For every 1000 ft. above sea level, the vacuum should be decreased by one inch. If the prescribed vacuum cannot be reached, close the vacuum control valve, shut off the vacuum pump and look for a leak at the components, connections or pump.

3. When the gauge reaches the prescribed vacuum, the system is fully evacuated. Close the high side gauge set valve and turn off the vacuum pump.

4. Watch the low side gauge to be sure that vacuum holds for five minutes. If the vacuum does hold, disconnect the vacuum hose at the gauge set and then proceed to charge the system.

5. If the system loses more than 2 in. Hg. of vacuum in five minutes, charge the system with ½ lb. (420ml) of R-12 and leak check. Discharge the system again and repair the leak as necessary. Then repeat evacuation procedure.

CHARGING THE SYSTEM

✱✱CAUTION

Never attempt to open the high pressure side gauge control when the compressor is operating. The compressor high pressure can burst the refrigerant container, causing severe personal injuries.

1. Start and run the engine until it reaches operating temperature. Then set the air conditioning mode control button on **OFF**.

2. Open the R-12 source valve and allow 14 oz. of liquid R-12 to flow into the system through the low side service fitting into the accumulator.

3. As soon as the R-12 has been added to the system, immediately engage the compressor by setting the air conditioning control button to **NORM** and the blower speed on **HI**, to draw in the remainder of the R-12 charge.

➡Total system capacity is 3.5 lbs. of R-12. The charging operation can be speeded up by using a large volume fan to pass air over the condenser. If the condenser temperature is maintained below the charging cylinder temperature, R-12 will enter the system more rapidly.

4. Turn OFF the R-12 source valve and run engine for 30 seconds to clear the lines and gauges.

5. With the engine running, remove the charging low side hose adapter from the accumulator service fitting. Unscrew rapidly to avoid excess R-12 escaping from the system.

✱✱CAUTION

Never remove a gauge line from its adapter when the line is connected to the air conditioning system. Always remove the line adapter from the service fitting to disconnect a line. Do not remove charging hose at the gauge set while attached to the accumulator. This will result in complete discharge of the system due to the depressed Schrader valve in service low side fitting, and may cause personal injury due to escaping R-12.

6. Replace protective cap on accumulator fitting.

7. Turn engine off.

8. Leak check system with electronic leak detector J-29547 or equivalent.

9. Start engine.

10. With the system fully charged and leak checked, continue to check the system performance.

Windshield Wipers

▶ **See Figure 42**

For maximum effectiveness and longest element life, the windshield and wiper blades should be kept clean. Dirt, tree sap, road tar and so on will cause streaking, smearing and blade deterioration if left on the windshield. It is advisable to wash the windshield carefully with a commercial glass cleaner at least once a month. Wipe off the rubber blades with a wet rag afterwards. Do not attempt to move the wipers back and forth by hand; damage to the motor and drive mechanism will result.

If the blades are found to be cracked, broken or torn, they should be replaced immediately. Replacement intervals will vary with usage, although ozone deterioration usually limits blade lift to about one year. If the wiper pattern is smeared or streaked, or if the blade chatters across the glass, the blades should be replaced. It is easiest and most sensible to replace them in pairs.

There are basically three different types of wiper blade refills, which differ in their method of replacement. One type has two release buttons, approximately ⅓ of the way up from the ends of the blade frame. Pushing the buttons down releases a lock and allows the rubber blade to be removed from the frame. The new blade slides back into the frame and locks in place.

The second type of refill has two metal tabs which are unlocked by squeezing them together. The rubber blade can then be withdrawn from the frame jaws. A new one is installed by inserting it into the front frame jaws and sliding it rearward to engage the remaining frame jaws. There are usually four jaws; be certain when installing that the refill is engaged in all

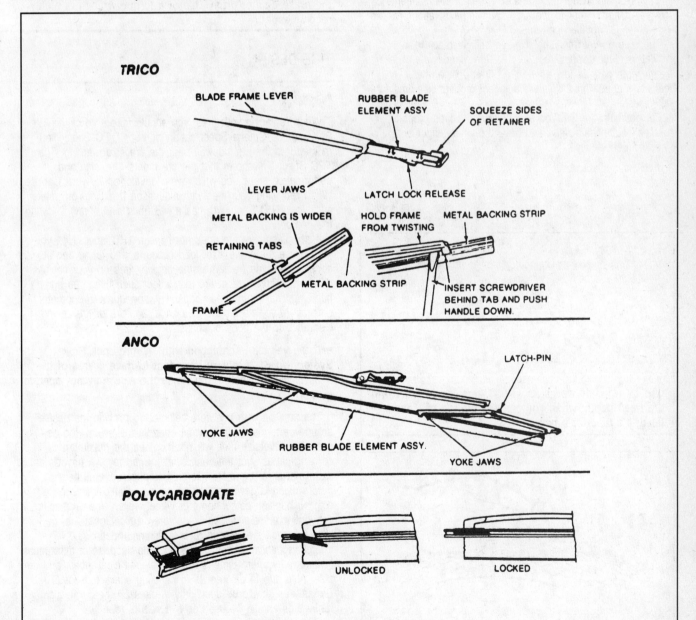

Fig. 42 The three types of wiper blade retention

of them. At the end of its travel, the tabs will lock into place on the front jaws of the wiper blade frame.

The third type is a refill made from polycarbonate. The refill has a simple locking device at one end which flexes downward out of the groove into which the jaws of the holder fit, allowing easy release. By sliding the new refill through all the jaws and pushing through the slight resistance when it reaches the end of its travel, the refill will lock into position.

Regardless of the type of refill used, make sure that all of the frame jaws are engaged as the refill is pushed into place and locked. The metal blade holder and frame will scratch the glass if allowed to touch it.

Tires and Wheels

▶ **See Figures 43, 44 and 45**

The tires should be rotated as specified in the Maintenance Intervals Chart. Refer to the accompanying illustrations for the recommended rotation patterns.

The tires on your car should have built-in tread wear indicators, which appear as ½″ (12.7mm) bands when the tread depth gets as low as 1/16″ (1.6mm). When the indicators appear in 2 or more adjacent grooves, it's time for new tires.

For optimum tire life, you should keep the tires properly inflated, rotate them often and have the wheel alignment checked periodically.

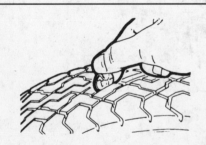

Fig. 43 A penny works as well as anything for checking tire tread depth; when you can see the top of Lincoln's head, it's time for a new tire

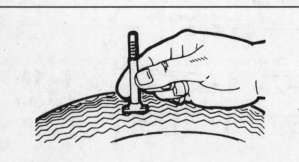

Fig. 44 Tread depth can be checked with an inexpensive gauge

TIRE ROTATION

▶ **See Figure 46**

Tire rotation is recommended at 7,500 miles and 15,000 miles thereafter, to obtain maximum tire wear. For all tire sizes, rotate the rear tires straight up to the front without crisscross and the front tires crisscross to the rear without dismounting the tires from the wheels. Torque wheel nuts as follows:

1990 Sedan — 81 ft. lbs. (110 Nm).
1990 Wagon and Police — 100 ft. lbs. (140 Nm).
1991 — 93 All Vehicles — 100 ft. lbs. (140 Nm).

❋❋WARNING

Avoid overtightening the lug nuts to prevent damage to the brake disc or drum. Use of a torque wrench is highly recommended.

TIRE DESIGN

▶ **See Figure 47**

When replacing your tires, you should take note of the Tire Performance Criteria Specification Number (TPC Spec. No.) molded into the tire sidewall near the tire size marking. The TPC Spec. No. shows that the tire meets rigid size and performance standards which were developed for your Caprice. When replacing your tires with all-season tread design, make sure your TPC Spec. No. has a MS (mud and snow) following the number.

If a replacement tire does not have a TPC Spec. No., you should use the same size, load range, speed rating and construction type (radial) as the original tires on your car. A different size or type of tire may affect such things as ride, handling, maximum speed capability, speedometer/odometer calibration, vehicle ground clearance, and tire or tire chain clearance to the body or chassis.

➡**If the vehicle is equipped with an Anti-Lock Brake System (ABS), it is very important to have 4 tires of the same size and design, otherwise the ABS may not operate properly.**

The tires on your car were selected to provide the best all around performance for normal operation when inflated as specified. Oversize tires will not increase the maximum carrying capacity of the vehicle, although they will provide an extra margin of tread life. Be sure to check overall height before using larger size tires which may cause interference with suspension components or wheel wells. When replacing conventional tire sizes with other tire size designations, be sure to check the manufacturer's recommendations. Interchangeability is not always possible because of differences in load ratings, tire dimensions, wheel well clearances, and rim size. Also due to differences in handling characteristics, 70 Series tires should be used only in pairs on the same axle; radial tires should be used only in sets of four.

The wheels must be the correct width for the tire. Tire dealers have charts of tire and rim compatibility. A mismatch can cause sloppy handling and rapid tread wear. The old rule

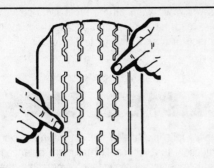

Fig. 45 Tread wear indicators will appear when the tire is worn out

of thumb is that the tread width should match the rim width (inside bead to inside bead) within an inch. For radial tires, the rim width should be 80% or less of the tire (not tread) width.

The height (mounted diameter) of the new tires can greatly change speedometer accuracy, engine speed at a given road speed, fuel mileage, acceleration, and ground clearance. Tire manufacturers furnish full measurement specifications.

➡**Dimensions of tires marked the same size may vary significantly, even among tires from the same manufacturer.**

The spare tire should be usable, at least for low speed operation, with the new tires.

For maximum satisfaction, tires should be used in sets of five. Mixing of different types (radial, bias-belted, fiberglass belted) should be avoided. Conventional bias tires are constructed so that the cords run bead-to-bead at an angle. Alternate plies run at an opposite angle. This type of construction gives rigidity to both tread and sidewall. Bias-belted tires are similar in construction to conventional bias ply tires. Belts run at an angle and also at a 90° angle to the bead, as in the radial tire. Tread life is improved considerably over the conventional bias tire. The radial tire differs in construction, but instead of the carcass plies running at an angle of 90° to each other, they run at an angle of 90° to the bead. This gives the tread a great deal of rigidity and the sidewall a great deal of flexibility and accounts for the characteristic bulge associated with radial tires.

Radial tire are recommended for use on all models. If they are used, tire sizes and wheel diameters should be selected to maintain ground clearance and tire load capacity equivalent to the minimum specified tire. Radial tires should always be used in sets of five, but in an emergency radial tires can be used with caution on the rear axle only. If this is done, both tires on the rear should be of radial design.

➡**Radial tires should never be used on only the front axle.**

TIRE STORAGE

Store the tires at the proper inflation pressure if they are mounted on wheels. Keep them in a cool dry place, laid on their sides. If the tires are stored in the garage or basement, do not let them stand on a concrete floor; set them on strips of wood.

TIRE INFLATION

The tire pressure is the most often ignored item of automotive maintenance. Gasoline mileage can drop as much as 0.8 percent for every 1 pound/square inch (psi) of under inflation.

Pressures should be checked before driving, since pressure can increase as much as 6 psi due to heat. It is a good idea to have an accurate gauge and to check pressures weekly. Not all gauges on service station air pumps are accurate.

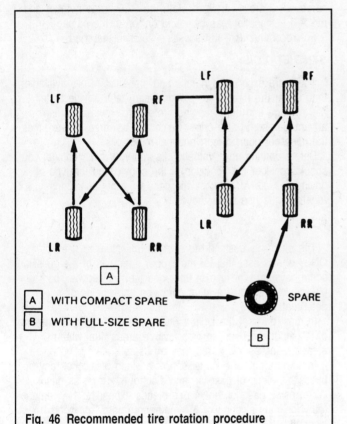

Fig. 46 Recommended tire rotation procedure

A   WITH COMPACT SPARE

B   WITH FULL-SIZE SPARE

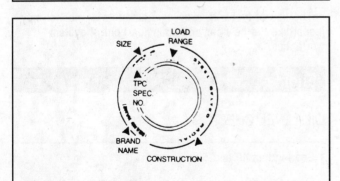

Fig. 47 Tire Performance Criteria (TPC) information location

CARE OF SPECIAL WHEELS

A protective coating is applied to all aluminum wheels to prevent degradation. Avoid prolonged use of automatic car washes which will wear off the protective coating. When using cleaners, read the label on the package and make sure it will not damage or remove the protective coating.

FLUIDS AND LUBRICANTS

Fluid Disposal

Used fluid such as engine oil, transmission fluid, antifreeze and brake fluid are considered hazardous wastes and must be disposed of properly. Before draining any fluids consult with the local authorities; in many areas, waste oil, etc. is being accepted as a part of recycling programs. A number of service stations and auto parts stores are accepting waste fluids for recycling.

Be sure of the recycling center's policies before draining any fluids, as many will not accept different fluids which have been mixed together.

Fuel and Engine Oil Recommendations

Engine Oil
▶ See Figure 48

The SAE (Society of Automotive Engineers) grade number indicates the viscosity of the engine oil and thus its ability to lubricate at a given temperature. The lower the SAE grade number, the lighter the oil; the lower the viscosity, the easier it is to crank the engine in cold weather.

Oil viscosities should be chosen from those oils recommended for the lowest anticipated temperatures during the oil change interval.

Multi-viscosity oils (10W-30, 20W-50 etc.) offer the important advantage of being adaptable to temperature extremes. They allow easy starting at low temperatures, yet they give good protection at high speeds and engine temperatures. This is a decided advantage in changeable climates or in long distance touring.

The API (American Petroleum Institute) designation indicates the classification of engine oil used under certain given operating conditions. Only oils designated for use Service SG, SG/CC or SG/CD should be used. Oils of the SG type perform a variety of functions inside the engine in addition to their basic function as a lubricant. Through a balanced system of metallic detergents and polymeric dispersants, the oil prevents the formation of high and low temperature deposits and also keeps sludge and particles of dirt in suspension. Acids, particularly sulfuric acid, as well as other by-products of combustion, are neutralized. Both the SAE grade number and the API designation can be found on top of the oil can.

For recommended oil viscosities, refer to the chart.

SYNTHETIC OIL

There are excellent synthetic and fuel-efficient oils available that, under the right circumstances, can help provide better fuel mileage and better engine protection. However, these advantages come at a price, which can be three or four times the price per quart of conventional motor oils.

Before pouring any synthetic oils into your car's engine, you should consider the condition of the engine and the type of driving you do. Also, check the car's warranty conditions regarding the use of synthetics.

Fuel

The engine is designed to operate on unleaded gasoline ONLY and is essential for the proper operation of the emission control system. The use of unleaded fuel will reduce spark plug fouling, exhaust system corrosion and engine oil deterioration.

In most parts of the United States, fuel with an octane rating of 87 should be used; in high altitude areas, fuel with an octane rating as low as 85 may be used.

In some areas, fuel consisting of a blend of alcohol may be used; this blend of gasoline and alcohol is known as gasohol. When using gasohol, never use blends exceeding 10% ethanol (ethyl or grain alcohol) or 5% methanol (methyl or wood alcohol).

➡The use of fuel with excessive amounts of alcohol may jeopardize the new car and emission control system warranties.

Engine

OIL LEVEL CHECK

▶ See Figures 49 and 50

Every time you stop for fuel, check the engine oil as follows:
1. Make sure the car is parked on level ground.
2. When checking the oil level it is best for the engine to be at normal operating temperature, although checking the oil immediately after stopping will lead to a false reading. Wait a

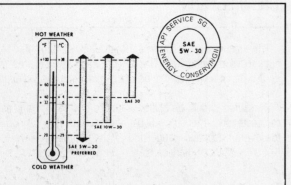

Fig. 48 Engine oil viscosity recommendation

Fig. 49 The oil level is checked with the dipstick — 5.0L (VIN E) engine shown

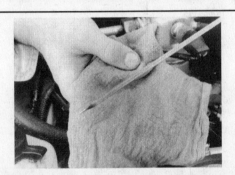

Fig. 50 The oil level should be between the ADD and FULL marks on the dipstick — 5.0L (VIN E) engine shown

few minutes after turning off the engine to allow the oil to drain back into the crankcase.

3. Open the hood and locate the dipstick which will be on either the right or left side depending upon your particular engine. Pull the dipstick from its tube, wipe it clean and then reinsert it.

4. Pull the dipstick out again and, holding it horizontally, read the oil level. The oil should be between the FULL and ADD marks on the dipstick. If the oil is below the ADD mark, add oil of the proper viscosity through the capped opening in the top of the cylinder head cover. See the Oil and Fuel Recommendations chart in this Section for the proper viscosity and rating of oil to use.

5. Replace the dipstick and check the oil level again after adding any oil. Be careful not to overfill the crankcase. Approximately one quart of oil will raise the level from the

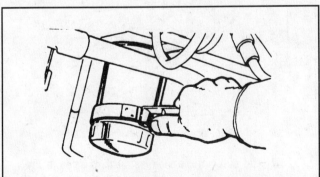

Fig. 51 Remove the oil filter with a strap wrench

ADD mark to the FULL mark. Excess oil will generally be consumed at an accelerated rate.

OIL AND FILTER CHANGE

▶ See Figures 51, 52, 53 and 54

Under normal operating conditions, the oil is to be changed every 7,500 miles or 12 months, whichever occurs first. Change the filter at first oil change and then at every other oil change, unless 12 months pass between changes. However, for best protection against premature engine wear, a new filter should be installed with every oil change.

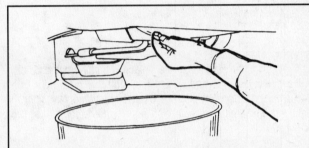

Fig. 52 By keeping an inward pressure on the plug as you unscrew it, oil won't escape past the threads

Fig. 53 Coat the new oil filter gasket with clean oil

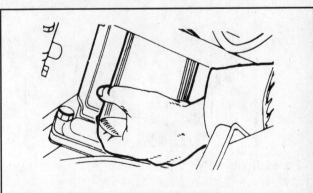

Fig. 54 Install the new oil filter by hand

If driving under conditions such as: dusty areas, trailer towing, idling for long periods of time, low speed operation, or when operating with temperatures below freezing and driving short distances (under 4 miles), change the oil and filter every 3,000 miles or 3 months.

The oil should be disposed of properly after it is drained from the vehicle. Store the oil in a suitable container and take the container to an official oil recycling station. Most gas or oil and lube facilities will take the used oil at little or no expense to you.

1. Raise the car and safely support on jackstands. Remove the oil pan drain plug and drain oil into a suitable pan.

✳✳CAUTION

The engine oil will be hot. Keep your arms, face and hands away from the oil as it drains out.

2. Using an oil filter wrench, remove the oil filter and place it in the oil catch pan. Using a clean rag, wipe oil filter mounting surface.

3. When installing the oil filter, place a small amount of oil on the sealing gasket and tighten the filter only hand tight or ¾ of a turn past gasket contact. Do not overtighten the filter.

4. Install the oil pan drain plug and torque to 18 ft. lbs. (25 Nm).

5. Using a funnel, add oil through the oil fill cap. Lower car, start the engine and inspect for oil leaks.

✳✳CAUTION

The EPA warns that prolonged contact with used engine oil may cause a number of skin disorders, including cancer! You should make every effort to minimize your exposure to used engine oil. Protective gloves should be worn when changing the oil. Wash your hands and any other exposed skin areas as soon as possible after exposure to used engine oil. Soap and water, or waterless hand cleaner should be used.

Automatic Transmission

FLUID RECOMMENDATIONS AND LEVEL CHECK

▶ **See Figures 55, 56 and 57**

Check the automatic transmission fluid level at least every 6000 miles. The dipstick can be found in the rear of the engine compartment. The fluid level should be checked only when the transmission is hot (normal operating temperature). Use only Dexron®II automatic transmission fluid..

1. Park the car on a level surface with the engine idling. Shift the transmission into Park and set the parking brake.

2. Remove the dipstick, wipe it clean and then reinsert it firmly. Be sure that it has been pushed all the way in. Remove the dipstick again and check the fluid level while holding it horizontally. With the engine running, the fluid level should be between the second notch and the FULL HOT line. If the fluid must be checked when it is cool, the level should be between the first and second notches.

3. If the fluid level is below the second notch (engine hot) or the first notch (engine cold), add DEXRON®II automatic transmission fluid through the dipstick tube. This is easily done with the aid of a funnel. Check the level often as you are filling the transmission, be extremely careful not to overfill it. Overfilling will cause slippage, seal damage and overheating. Approximately one pint of ATF will raise the fluid level from one notch/line to the other.

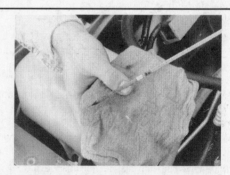

Fig. 56 Automatic transmission dipstick marks; the proper level is within the shaded area

Fig. 55 Remove the transmission dipstick to check the fluid level with the engine idling in Park

Fig. 57 Add automatic transmission fluid through the dipstick tube

The fluid on the dipstick should always be a bright red color. If it is discolored (brown or black), or smells burnt, serious transmission troubles, probably due to overheating, should be suspected. The transmission should be inspected by a qualified technician to locate the cause of the burnt fluid.

DRAIN AND REFILL

Refer to the PAN AND FILTER SERVICE procedure.

PAN AND FILTER SERVICE

The automatic transmission fluid and filter should be changed every 15,000 miles if your Caprice is driven in heavy city traffic in hot weather, in hilly or mountainous terrain, frequent trailer pulling, or uses such as found in taxi, police car or delivery service. If your Caprice is driven other than the conditions listed above, change the fluid and filter every 30,000 miles.

1. Raise and safely support the car on jackstands. Place an oil catch pan under the transmission.
2. Remove the oil pan bolts from the front and sides only.
3. Loosen rear oil pan bolts approximately 4 turns.

❋❋WARNING

Do not damage the transmission case or oil pan sealing surfaces.

4. Lightly tap the oil pan with a rubber mallet or a pry it to allow fluid to drain.
5. Remove the remaining oil pan bolts, then remove the oil pan and pan gasket.
6. Remove the filter and O-ring.
7. Clean the transmission case and oil pan gasket surfaces with suitable solvent and air dry. Make sure to remove all traces of the old gasket.
8. To install, coat the O-ring seal with a small amount of oil.
9. Install the new O-ring onto the filter.
10. Install the new filter into the case.
11. Install the oil pan and new gasket.
12. Install the oil pan bolts and tighten them to 15 ft. lbs. (20 Nm).
13. Lower the car.
14. Fill the transmission to proper level with Dexron®II fluid.
15. Check cold fluid level reading for initial fill. Do not overfill the transmission.
16. Follow the fluid level check procedure described before.
17. Check the oil pan gasket for leaks.

Drive Axle

FLUID RECOMMENDATIONS

SAE 80W or SAE 80W-90 GL-5 (SAE 80W GL-5 in Canada) gear lubricant is recommended.

LEVEL CHECK

▶ **See Figure 58**

The gear lubricant in the drive axle should be checked every 12 months or 15,000 miles.

1. Raise the car and support on jackstands as close to level as possible.
2. Remove the filler plug from the side of the drive axle housing.
3. If lubricant begins to trickle out of the hole, there is enough and you need not go any further. Otherwise, carefully insert your finger (watch out for sharp threads) and check to see if the lubricant is up to the edge of the hole.
4. If not, add oil through the hole until the level is at the edge of the hole. Most gear lubricants come in a plastic squeeze bottle with a nozzle; making additions simple.
5. Install and tighten the filler plug.

DRAIN AND REFILL

If equipped with limited slip differential, the rear axle should have the gear lubricant changed at the first 7500 miles; be sure to add 4 oz. of GM limited slip additive part No. 1052358.

If the vehicle is used for trailer towing, the gear lubricant should be changed every 7500 miles.

1. Raise the car and support on Jackstands. Place a container under the differential to catch the fluid.
2. Remove the bolts retaining the cover to the housing. Pry the cover from the differential housing and allow the fluid to drain into the catch pan.
3. Clean and inspect the differential. With the cover and housing washed free of oil, apply sealer to the mating surfaces.
4. Using a new gasket, install the cover and torque the bolts to 20 ft. lbs. (27 Nm) in a clockwise pattern to insure uniform draw on the gasket. Fill the differential with fluid through the fill plug and add limited slip additive, as required.
5. The fluid level should reach a level within ³⁄₈ in. of the filler plug hole. Replace the filler plug. Lower the car and inspect for leaks.

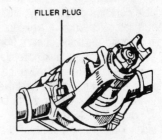

FILLER PLUG

Fig. 58 Remove the plug to check the lubricant level in the rear axle; fluid may also be added through the inspection hole

Cooling System

➡The 1992-93 Caprices are experiencing considerable radiator clogging problems, therefore it is highly recommended that the cooling system be flushed at least once a year.

FLUID RECOMMENDATION

When adding or changing the fluid in the system, create a 50/50 mixture of high quality ethylene glycol antifreeze and water.

LEVEL CHECK

The fluid level may be checked by observing the fluid level marks of the recovery tank. The level should be below the ADD mark when the system is cold. At normal operating temperatures, the level should be between the ADD and the FULL marks. Only add coolant to bring the level to the FULL mark.

❄❄CAUTION

Should it be necessary to remove the radiator cap, make sure that the system has had time to cool, reducing the internal pressure.

DRAINING AND REFILLING

❄❄CAUTION

Do not remove a radiator cap while the engine and radiator are still hot. Danger of burns by scalding fluid and steam under pressure may result!

1. With a cool engine, slowly rotate the radiator cap counterclockwise to the detent without pressing down on the cap.
2. Wait until any remaining pressure is relieved by listening for a hissing sound.
3. After all the pressure is relieved, press down on the cap and continue to rotate the radiator cap counterclockwise.
4. With a suitable container to catch the fluid under the radiator, open the radiator draincock. If equipped, remove the engine block drain plugs to drain the coolant from the block.
5. Loosen or slide the recovery tank hose clamp at the radiator filler neck overflow tube and remove the hose. Holding the hose down to the drain pan, drain the recovery tank. Attach the hose to the filler neck overflow and tighten the clamp.
6. Close the radiator draincock and install the engine block drain plug.
7. With the engine idling, add coolant until the level reaches the bottom of the filler neck. Install the radiator cap,

making sure that the arrows on the cap line up with the overflow tube.

➡Never add cold water to an overheated engine while the engine is not running.

8. Add coolant to the recovery tank.
9. After filling the radiator and recovery tank, run the engine until it reaches normal operating temperature, to make sure that the thermostat has opened and all the air is bled from the system.

FLUSHING AND CLEANING THE SYSTEM

▸ See Figure 59

The cooling system should be drained, thoroughly flushed and refilled at least every 30,000 miles or 24 months according to manufacturer recommendations, although it is recommended that the system be flushed once a year. These operations should be done with the engine cold.

❄❄CAUTION

To drain the cooling system, allow the engine to cool down BEFORE ATTEMPTING TO REMOVE THE RADIATOR CAP. Then turn the cap until it hisses. Wait until all pressure is off the cap before removing it completely. To avoid burns and scalding, always handle a warm radiator cap with a heavy rag.

1. Remove the radiator and recovery tank caps. Run the engine until the upper radiator hose gets hot. This means that the thermostat is open and the coolant is flowing through the system.
2. Turn the engine OFF and place a large container under the radiator. Open the draincock at the bottom of the radiator. Remove the block drain plugs to speed up the draining process.
3. At the dash, set the heater TEMP control lever to the fully HOT position. Close the drain valve, install the block drain plug and add water until the system is full. Repeat the draining and filling process several times, until the liquid is nearly colorless.
4. Remove the recovery tank and rinse it out with clean water. Install the recovery tank.
5. After the last draining, fill the system with a 50/50 mixture of ethylene glycol and water. Run the engine until the

Fig. 59 Drain plug for the cooling system is located on the bottom of the radiator

system is hot and add coolant, if necessary. Replace the caps and check for any leaks.

Master Cylinder

FLUID RECOMMENDATIONS

When adding or replacing the brake fluid, always use a top quality fluid, such as Delco Supreme II or DOT-3. DO NOT allow the brake fluid container or master cylinder reservoir to remain open for long periods of time; brake fluid absorbs moisture from the air, reducing its effectiveness and causing corrosion in the lines.

LEVEL CHECK

▶ **See Figure 60**

The master cylinder is located in the left rear section of the engine compartment. The brake master cylinder consists of an aluminum body and a translucent nylon reservoir with minimum fill indicators. The fluid level of the reservoirs should be kept near the top of the observation windows.

✳✳WARNING

Any sudden decrease in the fluid level indicates a possible leak in the system and should be checked out immediately. Do not allow brake fluid to spill on the vehicle's finish; it will remove the paint. In case of a spill, flush the area with water and mild soap.

Although it is not mandatory, it is recommend that you periodically flush the brake lines with new brake fluid, this will help stop the corrosion buildup in the brake system. However, if the vehicle is equipped with an Anti-Lock Brake System (ABS), it is essential that the system be flushed once a year. Use the brake bleeding method, described in Section 9, to accomplish this procedure.

Power Steering Pump

FLUID RECOMMENDATIONS

When filling or replacing the fluid of the power steering pump reservoir, use GM power steering fluid, part #1050017 or equivalent.

LEVEL CHECK

▶ **See Figures 61, 62 and 64**

Power steering fluid level should be checked at least twice a year. To prevent possible overfilling, check the fluid level only when the fluid has warmed to operating temperatures and the wheels are turned straight ahead. If the level is low, fill the pump reservoir until the fluid level measures between the COLD and HOT marks on the reservoir dipstick. Low fluid level usually produces a moaning sound as the wheels are turned (especially when standing still or parking) and increases steering wheel effort.

Chassis Greasing

▶ **See Figures 64, 65 and 66**

Chassis greasing can be performed with a pressurized grease gun or it can be performed at home by using a hand-

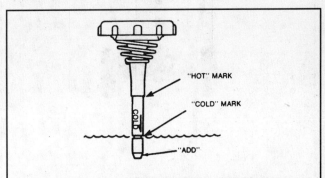

Fig. 61 Use the dipstick to check the power steering fluid

Fig. 60 Checking master cylinder fluid level

Fig. 62 With the engine OFF, remove the power steering pump cap to fill or check the fluid level

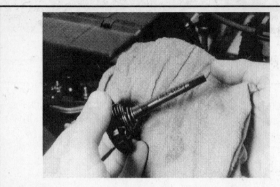

Fig. 63 Verify the fluid is at the correct level

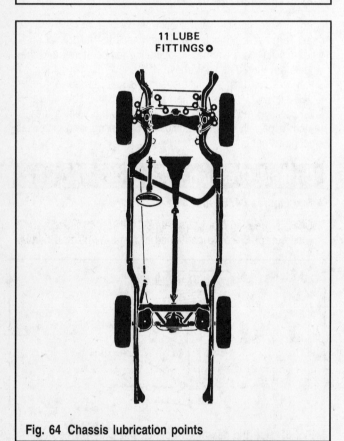

11 LUBE FITTINGS ⊙

Fig. 64 Chassis lubrication points

Fig. 65 Be sure to lube all 4 tie rod ends and the 2 upper and lower ball joints

Fig. 66 Also lube the idler and centerlink joints

operated grease gun. Wipe the grease fittings clean before greasing in order to prevent the possibility of forcing any dirt into the component.

Body Lubrication

Transmission Shift Linkage

Lubricate the manual transmission shift linkage contact points with the EP grease used for chassis greasing, which should meet GM specification 6031M. The automatic transmission linkage should be lubricated with clean engine oil.

Hood Latch and Hinges

Clean the latch surfaces and apply clean engine oil to the latch pilot bolts and the spring anchor. Use the engine oil to lubricate the hood hinges as well. Use a chassis grease to lubricate all the pivot points in the latch release mechanism.

Door Hinges

The gas tank filler door, car door, and rear hatch or trunk lid hinges should be wiped clean and lubricated with clean engine oil. Silicone spray also works well on these parts, but must be applied more often. Use engine oil to lubricate the trunk or hatch lock mechanism and the lock bolt and striker. The door lock cylinders can be lubricated easily with a shot of silicone spray or one of the many dry penetrating lubricants commercially available.

Parking Brake Linkage

Use chassis grease on the parking brake cable where it contacts the guides, links, levers, and pulleys. The grease should be a water resistant one for durability under the car.

Accelerator Linkage

Lubricate the throttle cable stud, throttle lever, and the accelerator pedal lever at the support inside the car with clean engine oil.

Wheel Bearings

Once every 12 months or 12,000 miles, clean and repack wheel bearings with a wheel bearing grease. Use only enough grease to completely coat the rollers. Remove any excess grease from the exposed surface of the hub and seal.

It is important that wheel bearings be properly adjusted after installation. Improperly adjusted wheel bearings can cause steering instability, front-end shimmy and wander, and increased tire wear.

REMOVAL, REPACKING, INSTALLATION AND ADJUSTMENT

1. Raise the car and support it at the lower arm. Remove the wheel. Remove the brake caliper and support it on a wire.
2. Remove the dust cap, cotter pin, castle nut, thrust washer and outside wheel bearing. Pull the disc/hub assembly from the steering knuckle.
3. Pry out the inner seal and remove the inner bearing.
4. Wipe out the grease from inside the hub.
5. Clean the wheel bearings thoroughly with solvent and check their condition before installation. After cleaning, check parts for excessive wear and replace damaged parts.

✳✳WARNING

Do not allow the bearing to spin when blowing dry with compressed air, as this would allow the bearing to turn without lubrication.

6. Apply a sizable amount of lubricant to the palm of one hand. Using your other hand, work the bearing into the lubricant so that the grease is pushed through the rollers and out the other side. Keep rotating the bearing while continuing to push the lubricant through it.
7. Apply grease to the inside of the hub and install the inner bearing in the hub. Install a new grease seal, being careful not to damage the seal.
8. Install the disc/hub assembly onto the steering knuckle. Install the outer bearing, thrust washer and castle nut. Torque the nut to 16 ft. lbs. while turning the wheel.
9. Back the nut off and retighten until nearest slot aligns with the cotter pin hole.
10. Insert a new cotter pin. End-play should be between 0.001-0.005″ (0.025-0.127mm). If play exceeds this tolerance, the wheel bearings should be replaced.

TRAILER TOWING

General Recommendations

Your car was primarily designed to carry passengers and cargo. It is important to remember that towing a trailer will place additional loads on your car's engine, drive train, steering, braking and other systems. However, if you find it necessary to tow a trailer, using the proper equipment is a must. Local laws may require specific equipment such as trailer brakes or fender mounted mirrors. Check your local laws.

Trailer Weight

The weight of the trailer is the most important factor. A good weight-to-horsepower ratio is about 35:1, 35 lbs. of GCW (Gross Combined Weight) for every horsepower your engine develops. Multiply the engine's rated horsepower by 35 and subtract the weight of the car passengers and luggage. The result is the approximate ideal maximum weight you should tow, although a numerically higher axle ratio can help compensate for heavier weight.

Hitch Weight

Figure the hitch weight to select a proper hitch. Hitch weight is usually 9-11% of the trailer gross weight and should be measured with the trailer loaded. Hitches fall into three types: those that mount on the frame and rear bumper or the bolt-on or weld-on distribution type used for larger trailers. Axle mounted or clamp-on bumper hitches should never be used.

Check the gross weight rating of your trailer. Tongue weight is usually figured as 10% of gross trailer weight. Therefore, a trailer with a maximum gross weight of 2000 lb. will have a maximum tongue weight of 200 lb. Class I trailers fall into this category. Class II trailers are those with a gross weight rating of 2000-3500 lb., while Class III trailers fall into the 3500-6000 lb. category. Class IV trailers are those over 6000 lb. and are for use with fifth wheel trucks, only.

When you've determined the hitch that you'll need, follow the manufacturer's installation instructions, exactly, especially when it comes to fastener torques. The hitch will be subjected to a lot of stress and good hitches come with hardened bolts. Never substitute an inferior bolt for a hardened bolt.

Cooling

ENGINE

One of the most common, if not THE most common, problems associated with trailer towing is engine overheating.

If you have a standard cooling system, without an expansion tank, you'll definitely need to get an aftermarket expansion tank kit, preferably one with at least a 2 quart capacity. These kits are easily installed on the radiator's overflow hose, and come with a pressure cap designed for expansion tanks.

Another helpful accessory is a Flex Fan. These fans are large diameter units and are designed to provide more airflow at low speeds, with blades that have deeply cupped surfaces. The blades then flex, or flatten out, at high speed, when less cooling air is needed. These fans are far lighter in weight than stock fans, requiring less horsepower to drive them. Also, they are far quieter than stock fans.

If you do decide to replace your stock fan with a flex fan, note that if your car has a fan clutch, a spacer between the flex fan and water pump hub will be needed.

Aftermarket engine oil coolers are helpful for prolonging engine oil life and reducing overall engine temperatures. Both of these factors increase engine life. While not absolutely necessary in towing Class I and some Class II trailers, they are recommended for heavier Class II and all Class III towing. Engine oil cooler systems consist of an adapter, screwed on in place of the oil filter, a remote filter mounting and a multi-tube, finned heat exchanger, which is mounted in front of the radiator or air conditioning condenser.

TRANSMISSION

An automatic transmission is usually recommended for trailer towing. Modern automatics have proven reliable and, of course, easy to operate, in trailer towing.

The increased load of a trailer, however, causes an increase in the temperature of the automatic transmission fluid. Heat is the worst enemy of an automatic transmission. As the temperature of the fluid increases, the life of the fluid decreases.

PUSHING AND TOWING

Push Starting

Your Chevrolet has an automatic transmission and should not be pushed nor should push starting be attempted.

Towing

The car can be towed safely (with the transmission in Neutral) from the front at speeds of 35 mph or less. The car

JACKING

▶ See Figure 67

The standard jack utilizes slots in the bumper to raise the car. The jack supplied with the car should never be used for any service operation other than tire changing. Never get under the car while it is supported by only a jack. Always block the wheels when changing tires.

The service operations in this book often require that one end of the car, or the entire car, be raised and safely supported. The ideal method, of course, would be a hydraulic hoist. Since this is beyond both the resource and requirement of the do-it-yourselfer, a small hydraulic, screw or scissors jack will suffice for the procedures in this guide. Two sturdy jackstands should be acquired if you intend to work under the

It is essential, therefore, that you install an automatic transmission cooler. The cooler, which consists of a multi-tube, finned heat exchanger, is usually installed in front of the radiator or air conditioning compressor, and hooked in-line with the transmission cooler tank inlet line. Follow the cooler manufacturer's installation instructions.

Select a cooler of at least adequate capacity, based upon the combined gross weights of the car and trailer.

Cooler manufacturers recommend that you use an aftermarket cooler in addition to, and not instead of, the present cooling tank in your radiator. If you do want to use it in place of the radiator cooling tank, get a cooler at least two sizes larger than normally necessary.

➡A transmission cooler can, sometimes, cause slow or harsh shifting in the transmission during cold weather, until the fluid has a chance to come up to normal operating temperature. Some coolers can be purchased with or retrofitted with a temperature bypass valve which will allow fluid flow through the cooler only when the fluid has reached operating temperature, or above.

Handling A Trailer

Towing a trailer with ease and safety requires a certain amount of experience. It's a good idea to learn the feel of a trailer by practicing turning, stopping and backing in an open area such as an empty parking lot.

must either be towed with the rear wheels off the ground or the driveshaft disconnected if: towing speeds are to be over 35 mph, or towing distance is over 50 miles, or transmission or rear axle problems exist.

When towing the car on its front wheels, the steering wheel must be secured in a straight-ahead position and the steering column locked. Tire-to-ground clearance should not exceed 6 in. during towing.

car at any time. An alternate method of raising the car would be drive-on ramps. These are available commercially. Be sure to block the wheels when using ramps. Never use concrete blocks to support the car. They may break if the load is not evenly distributed.

Regardless of the method of jacking or hoisting the car, there are only certain areas of the undercarriage and suspension you can safely use to support it. See the illustration, and make sure that only the shaded areas are used. In addition, be especially careful not to damage the catalytic converter. Remember that various cross braces and supports on a lift can sometimes contact low hanging parts of the car.

SCHEDULED MAINTENANCE SERVICES
SCHEDULE I

Follow Schedule I if your vehicle is MAINLY driven under one or more of the following conditions:
- When most trips are less than 6 kilometers (4 miles).
- When most trips are less than 16 kilometers (10 miles) and outside temperatures remain below freezing.
- When most trips include extended idling and/or frequent low-speed operation as in stop-and-go traffic.†
- Towing a trailer.**
- Operating in dusty areas.

ITEM NO.	TO BE SERVICED	WHEN TO PERFORM Kilometers (Miles) or Months, Whichever Occurs First	The services shown in this schedule up to 80 000 km (48,000 miles) are to be performed after 80 000 km (48,000 miles) at the same intervals.															
		KILOMETERS (000)	5	10	15	20	25	30	35	40	45	50	55	60	65	70	75	80
		MILES (000)	3	6	9	12	15	18	21	24	27	30	33	36	39	42	45	48
1.	Engine Oil & Oil Filter Change*	Every 5 000 km (3,000 mi.) or 3 mos.	●	●	●	●	●	●	●	●	●	●	●	●	●	●	●	●
2.	Chassis Lubrication	Every other oil change		●		●		●		●		●		●		●		●
3.	Carburetor Choke & Hose Inspection (if equipped)*‡	At 10 000 km (6,000 mi.) and then at each 50 000 km (30,000 mi.) interval		●								●						
4.	Carburetor or Throttle Body Mounting Bolt Torque (some models)*	At 10 000 km (6,000 mi.) only		●														
5.	Engine Idle Speed Adjustments (some models)*			●														
6.	Tire & Wheel Inspection & Rotation	At 10 000 km (6,000 mi.) and then every 25 000 km (15,000 mi.)		●						●				●				
7.	Vacuum or AIR Pump Drive Belt Inspection*	Every 50 000 km (30,000 mi.) or 24 mos.										●						
8.	Cooling System Service*											●						
9.	Front Wheel Bearing Repack (Rear-Wheel-Drive Cars Only)	See explanation for service interval.																
10.	Transmission/Transaxle Service																	
11.	Spark Plug Replacement*											●						
12.	Spark Plug Wire Inspection (some models)*‡	Every 50 000 km (30,000 mi.)										●						
13.	PCV Valve Inspection (some models)*‡											●						
14.	EGR System Inspection (some models)*‡	Every 50 000 km (30,000 mi.) or 36 mos.										●						
15.	Air Cleaner & PCV Filter Replacement*											●						
16.	Engine Timing Check (some models)*											●						
17.	Fuel Tank, Cap & Lines Inspection*‡	Every 50 000 km (30,000 mi.)										●						
18.	Thermostatically Controlled Air Cleaner Inspection (some models)*											●						

† Note: Schedule I should also be followed if the vehicle is used for delivery service, police, taxi or other commercial applications.
‡ The U.S. Environmental Protection Agency has determined that the failure to perform this maintenance item will not nullify the emission warranty or limit recall liability prior to the completion of vehicle useful life. General Motors, however, urges that all recommended maintenance services be performed at the indicated intervals and the maintenance be recorded in section C of the owner's maintenance schedule.
* An Emission Control Service
** Trailering is not recommended for some models. See your Owner's Manual for details.

SCHEDULED MAINTENANCE SERVICES
SCHEDULE II

Follow Schedule II ONLY if none of the driving conditions specified in Schedule I apply.

ITEM NO.	TO BE SERVICED	WHEN TO PERFORM Kilometers (Miles) or Months, Whichever Occurs First	The services shown in this schedule up to 75 000 km (45,000 miles) are to be performed after 75 000 km (45,000 miles) at the same intervals.					
		KILOMETERS (000)	12.5	25	37.5	50	62.5	75
		MILES (000)	7.5	15	22.5	30	37.5	45
1.	Engine Oil Change (Turbocharged, see †)*	Every 12 500 km (7,500 mi.) or 12 mos.	●	●	●	●	●	●
	Oil Filter Change†*	At first and then every other oil change or 12 mos.	●		●		●	
2.	Chassis Lubrication	Every 12 500 km (7,500 mi.) or 12 mos.	●	●	●	●	●	●
3.	Carburetor Choke & Hose Inspection (if equipped)*‡	At 12 500 km (7,500 mi.) and then each 50 000 km (30,000 mi.) interval	●			●		
4.	Carburetor or Throttle Body Mounting Bolt Torque (some models)*	At 12 500 km (7,500 mi.) only	●					
5.	Engine Idle Speed Adjustments (some models)*		●					
6.	Tire & Wheel Inspection & Rotation	At 10 000 km (6,000 mi.) and then every 25 000 km (15,000 mi.)	●		●		●	
7.	Vacuum or AIR Pump Drive Belt Inspection*	Every 50 000 km (30,000 mi.) or 24 mos.				●		
8.	Cooling System Service*					●		
9.	Front Wheel Bearing Repack (Rear-Wheel-Drive Cars Only)	Every 50 000 km (30,000 mi.)				●		
10.	Transmission/Transaxle Service	See explanation for service interval.						
11.	Spark Plug Replacement*					●		
12.	Spark Plug Wire Inspection (some models)*‡	Every 50 000 km (30,000 mi.)				●		
13.	PCV Valve Inspection (some models)*‡					●		
14.	EGR System Inspection (some models)*‡	Every 50 000 km (30,000 mi.) or 36 mos.				●		
15.	Air Cleaner & PCV Filter Replacement*					●		
16.	Engine Timing Check (some models)*					●		
17.	Fuel Tank, Cap & Lines Inspection*‡	Every 50 000 km (30,000 mi.)				●		
18.	Thermostatically Controlled Air Cleaner Inspection (some models)*					●		

† Turbocharged Engines (VIN engine codes M and V): Change oil every 5 000 km (3,000 miles) or 3 months, whichever comes first. Change engine oil filter at first oil change, then every other oil change.
‡ The U.S. Environmental Protection Agency has determined that the failure to perform this maintenance item will not nullify the emission warranty or limit recall liability prior to the completion of vehicle useful life. General Motors, however, urges that all recommended maintenance services be performed at the indicated intervals and the maintenance be recorded in section C of the owner's maintenance schedule.
* An Emission Control Service

SCHEDULED MAINTENANCE SERVICES
SCHEDULE I

Follow Schedule I if your vehicle is MAINLY driven under one or more of the following conditions:
- When most trips are less than 6 kilometers (4 miles).
- When most trips are less than 16 kilometers (10 miles) and outside temperatures remain below freezing.
- When most trips include extended idling and/or frequent low-speed operation as in stop-and-go traffic.†
- Towing a trailer.**
- Operating in dusty areas.

ITEM NO.	TO BE SERVICED	WHEN TO PERFORM Kilometers (Miles) or Months, Whichever Occurs First	The services shown in this schedule up to 80 000 km (48,000 miles) are to be performed after 80 000 km (48,000 miles) at the same intervals.															
		KILOMETERS (000)	5	10	15	20	25	30	35	40	45	50	55	60	65	70	75	80
		MILES (000)	3	6	9	12	15	18	21	24	27	30	33	36	39	42	45	48
1.	Engine Oil & Oil Filter Change*	Every 5 000 km (3,000 Miles) or 3 mos.	•	•	•	•	•	•	•	•	•	•	•	•	•	•	•	•
2.	Chassis Lubrication	Every other oil change.		•		•		•		•		•		•		•		•
3.	Throttle Body Mounting Bolt Torque*	At 10 000 km (6,000 mi.) only.		•														
4.	Tire and Wheel Assembly Inspection & Rotation	At 10 000 km (6,000 mi.) and then every 25 000 km (15,000 mi.).		•					•					•				
5.	Serpentine Drive Belt Inspection*	Every 50 000 km (30,000 mi.) or 24 mos.										•						
6.	Cooling System Service*											•						
7.	Front Wheel Bearing Assembly Repack	See explanation for service interval.																
8.	Transmission Service																	
9.	Spark Plug Assembly Replacement*	Every 50 000 km (30,000 mi.).										•						
10.	Spark Plug Wire Assembly Inspection*‡											•						
11.	Positive Crankcase Ventilation (PCV) Valve Inspection*‡											•						
12.	Thermostatically Controlled Air Cleaner Inspection*											•						
13.	EGR System Inspection*‡											•						
14.	Air Cleaner Filter Replacement*											•						
15.	Engine Timing Check*											•						
16.	Fuel Tank, Cap & Lines Inspection*‡											•						

† Note: Schedule I should also be followed if the vehicle is used for delivery service, police, taxi or other commercial applications.
‡ The U.S. Environmental Protection Agency has determined that the failure to perform this maintenance item will not nullify the emission warranty or limit recall liability prior to the completion of vehicle useful life. General Motors, however, urges that all recommended maintenance services be performed at the indicated intervals and the maintenance be recorded in section E of the owner's maintenance schedule.
* An Emission Control Service
** Do not exceed trailering limits. See your Owner's Manual for details.

SCHEDULED MAINTENANCE SERVICES
SCHEDULE II

Follow Schedule II ONLY if none of the driving conditions specified in Schedule I apply.

ITEM NO.	TO BE SERVICED	WHEN TO PERFORM Kilometers (Miles) or Months, Whichever Occurs First	The services shown in this schedule up to 75 000 km (45,000 miles) are to be performed after 75 000 km (45,000 miles) at the same intervals.					
		KILOMETERS (000)	12.5	25	37.5	50	62.5	75
		MILES (000)	7.5	15	22.5	30	37.5	45
1.	Engine Oil Change*	Every 12 500 km (7,500 mi.) or 12 mos.	•	•	•	•	•	•
	Oil Filter Change*	At first and then every other oil change or 12 mos.	•		•		•	
2.	Chassis Lubrication	Every 12 500 km (7,500 mi.) or 12 mos.	•	•	•	•	•	•
3.	Throttle Body Mounting Bolt Torque*	At 12 500 km (7,500 mi.) only.	•					
4.	Tire and Wheel Assembly Inspection & Rotation	At 12 500 km (7,500 mi.) and then every 25 000 km (15,000 mi.).	•		•			
5.	Serpentine Drive Belt Inspection*	Every 50 000 km (30,000 mi.) or 24 mos.				•		
6.	Cooling System Service*					•		
7.	Front Wheel Bearing Assembly Repack	Every 50 000 km (30,000 mi.).				•		
8.	Transmission Service	See explanation for service interval.						
9.	Spark Plug Assembly Replacement*	Every 50 000 km (30,000 mi.).				•		
10.	Spark Plug Wire Assembly Inspection*‡					•		
11.	Positive Crankcase Ventilation (PCV) Valve Inspection*‡					•		
12.	Thermostatically Controlled Air Cleaner Inspection*					•		
13.	EGR System Inspection*‡					•		
14.	Air Cleaner Filter Replacement*					•		
15.	Engine Timing Check*					•		
16.	Fuel Tank, Cap & Lines Inspection*‡					•		

‡ The U.S. Environmental Protection Agency has determined that the failure to perform this maintenance item will not nullify the emission warranty or limit recall liability prior to the completion of vehicle useful life. General Motors, however, urges that all recommended maintenance services be performed at the indicated intervals and the maintenance be recorded in section E of the owner's maintenance schedule.
* An Emission Control Service

CAPACITIES

Year	Model	Engine ID/VIN	Engine Displacement Liters (cc)	Engine Crankcase with Filter	Transmission (pts.) Auto.	Drive Axle Rear (pts.)	Fuel Tank (gal.)	Cooling System (qts.)
1990	Caprice Sedan ①	Z	4.3 (4300)	5	7 ③	④	24.5	12.0–12.6
	Caprice Wagon	Y	5.0 (5000)	5	7 ③	④	22.0	16.1–16.7
	Caprice Sedan	E	5.0 (5000)	5	7 ③	④	24.5	16.3–17.3
	Caprice Sedan ②	7	5.7 (5700)	5	7 ③	④	24.5	14.8
1991	Caprice Sedan ①	Z	4.3 (4300)	5	10	④	24.5	12.0–12.6
	Caprice Sedan	E	5.0 (5000)	5	10	④	24.5	16.3–17.3
	Caprice Wagon	E	5.0 (5000)	5	10	④	24.5	16.3–17.3
	Caprice Sedan ②	7	5.7 (5700)	5	10	④	24.5	14.8
1992	Caprice Sedan ①	Z	4.3 (4300)	5	10	⑤	23	12.6–13.2
	Caprice Sedan	E	5.0 (5000)	5	10	⑤	23	16.7–17.3
	Caprice Sedan ②	7	5.7 (5700)	5	10	⑤	23	15.1
	Caprice Wagon	E	5.0 (5000)	5	10	⑤	22	16.7–17.3
	Caprice Wagon	7	5.7 (5700)	5	10	⑤	22	14.6
1993	Caprice Sedan ①	Z	4.3 (4300)	5	10	⑤	23	12.6–13.2
	Caprice Sedan	E	5.0 (5000)	5	10	⑤	23	16.7–17.3
	Caprice Sedan ②	7	5.7 (5700)	5	10	⑤	23	15.1
	Caprice Wagon	E	5.0 (5000)	5	10	⑤	22	16.7–17.3
	Caprice Wagon	7	5.7 (5700)	5	10	⑤	22	14.6

① Fleet Sales
② Police only
③ Turbo-hydramatic 4L60—10 pints
④ 7½ in. ring gear—3.50 pints
   8½ in. ring gear—4.25 pints
⑤ 7½ in. ring gear—2.90 pints
   8½ in. ring gear—3.50 pints

TORQUE SPECIFICATIONS

Component	U.S.	Metric
Carburetor fuel inlet nut	46 ft. lbs.	62 Nm
Oil drain plug	18 ft. lbs.	25 Nm
Rear axle cover	20 ft. lbs.	27 Nm
Transmission pan	15 ft. lbs.	20 Nm
Wheels 1990 Sedan 1990 Wagon and Police 1991–93 All	81 ft. lbs. 100 ft. lbs. 100 ft. lbs.	110 Nm 140 Nm 140 Nm

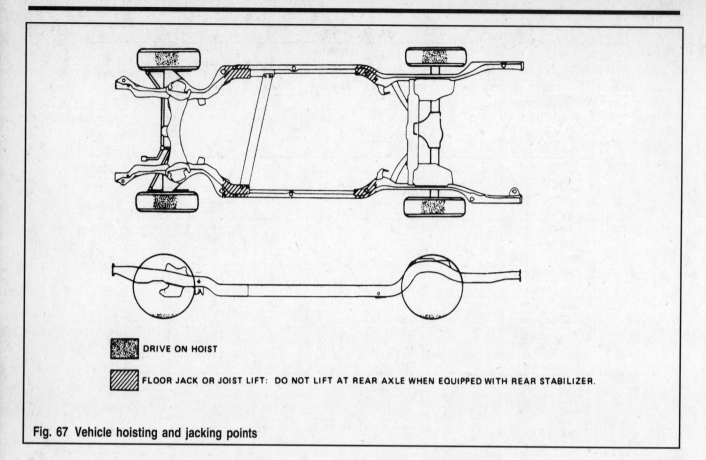

DRIVE ON HOIST

FLOOR JACK OR JOIST LIFT: DO NOT LIFT AT REAR AXLE WHEN EQUIPPED WITH REAR STABILIZER.

Fig. 67 Vehicle hoisting and jacking points

2

ENGINE PERFORMANCE AND TUNE-UP

TUNE-UP PROCEDURES

▶ See Figure 1

GASOLINE ENGINE TUNE-UP SPECIFICATIONS

Year	Engine VIN	Engine Displacement Liters (cc)	Spark Plugs Gap (in.)	Ignition Timing ③ (deg.) MT	AT	Fuel Pump (psi)	Idle Speed (rpm) MT	AT	Valve Clearance In.	Ex.
1990	Z	4.3 (4300)	0.035	—	①	9–13	—	②	Hyd.	Hyd.
	E	5.0 (5000)	0.035	—	0	9–13	—	②	Hyd.	Hyd.
	Y	5.0 (5011)	0.060	—	20	9–13	—	②	Hyd.	Hyd.
	7	5.7 (5733)	0.035	—	0	5.5–6.5	—	②	Hyd.	Hyd.
1991	Z	4.3 (4300)	0.035	—	①	9–13	—	②	Hyd.	Hyd.
	E	5.0 (5011)	0.035	—	0	9–13	—	②	Hyd.	Hyd.
	7	5.7 (5733)	0.035	—	0	9–13	—	②	Hyd.	Hyd.
1992	Z	4.3 (4300)	0.035	—	①	9–13	—	②	Hyd.	Hyd.
	E	5.0 (5011)	0.035	—	0	9–13	—	②	Hyd.	Hyd.
	7	5.7 (5733)	0.035	—	0	9–13	—	②	Hyd.	Hyd.
1993	Z	4.3 (4300)	0.035	—	①	9–13	—	②	Hyd.	Hyd.
	E	5.0 (5011)	0.035	—	0	9–13	—	②	Hyd.	Hyd.
	7	5.7 (5733)	0.035	—	0	9–13	—	②	Hyd.	Hyd.

NOTE: The lowest cylinder pressure should be within 75% of the highest cylinder pressure reading. For example, if the highest cylinder is 134 psi, the lowest should be 101. Engine should be at normal operating temperature with throttle valve in the wide open position.
The underhood specifications sticker often reflects tune-up specification changes in production. Sticker figures must be used if they disagree with those in this chart.
Hyd.—Hydraulic
① See the Underhood Emission Decal for specification
② Idle speed is controlled by the ECM and is non-adjustable
③ Before Top Dead Center

In order to extract the full measure of performance and economy from your engine, it is essential that it is properly tuned at regular intervals. A regular tune-up will keep your vehicles engine running smoothly and will prevent the annoying breakdowns and poor performance associated with an untuned engine.

A complete tune-up should be performed every 30,000 miles. This interval should be halved if the car is operated under severe conditions such as trailer towing, prolonged idling, start-and-stop driving, or if starting or running problems are noticed. It is assumed that the routine maintenance described in Section 1 has been kept up, as this will have a decided effect on the results of a tune-up. All of the applicable steps of a tune-up should be followed in order, as the result is a cumulative one.

If the specifications on the underhood tune-up sticker in the engine compartment of your car disagree with the Tune-Up Specifications chart in this section, the figures on the sticker must be used. The sticker often reflects changes made during the production run.

➡ **All 1990-93 Caprices use electronic ignition.**

Spark Plugs

A typical spark plug consists of a metal shell surrounding a ceramic insulator. A metal electrode extends downward through the center of the insulator and protrudes a small distance. Located at the end of the plug and attached to the side of the outer metal shell is the side electrode. The side electrode bends in at a 90° angle so that its tip is even with, and parallel to, the tip of the center electrode. The distance between these two electrodes (measured in thousandths of an inch) is called the spark plug gap. The spark plug in no way produces a spark but merely provides a gap across which the current can arc. The coil produces anywhere from 20,000 to 40,000 volts or more, which travels to the distributor where it is distributed through the spark plug wires to the spark plugs. The current passes along the center electrode and jumps the

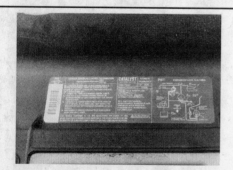

Fig. 1 Example of emission decal located in engine compartment

gap to the side electrode, and, in so doing, ignites the air/fuel mixture in the combustion chamber.

SPARK PLUG HEAT RANGE

▶ See Figure 2

Spark plug heat range is the ability of the plug to dissipate heat. The longer the insulator (or the farther it extends into the engine), the hotter the plug will operate; the shorter the insulator the cooler it will operate. A plug that absorbs little heat and remains too cool will quickly accumulate deposits of oil and carbon since it is not hot enough to burn them off. This leads to plug fouling and consequently to misfiring. A plug that absorbs too much heat will have deposits to, but due to the excessive heat the electrodes will burn them away quickly and in some instances, pre-ignition may result. Pre-ignition takes place when the combustion chamber temperature is to high and the air/fuel mixture explodes before the actual spark occurs. This early ignition will usually cause a pinging during low speeds and heavy loads.

The general rule of thumb for choosing the correct heat range when picking a spark plug is: if most of your driving is long distance, high speed travel, use a colder plug; if most of your driving is stop and go, use a hotter plug. Original equipment plugs are your best choice, but most people never have occasion to change their plugs from the factory recommended heat range. It is first recommended that the cause of the fouled plug be diagnosed instead of temporarily fixing the problem by increasing or decreasing the spark plug heat range.

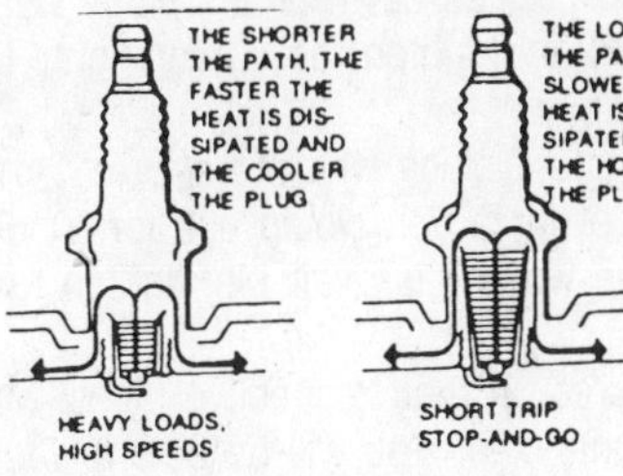

REMOVAL

▶ See Figures 3 and 4

Spark plug replacement is recommended every 30,000 miles. When you're removing spark plugs, you should work on one at a time. Don't start by removing the plug wires all at once, because, unless you number them, they're going to get mixed up. On some models though, it will be more convenient for you to remove all the wires before you start to work on the plugs. If this is necessary, take a minute before you begin and number the wires with tape before you take them off. The time you spend here will pay off later.

1. Twist the spark plug boot and remove the boot from the plug. You may also use a plug wire removal tool designed especially for this purpose. Do not pull on the wire itself. When the wire has been removed, take a wire brush and clean the area around the plug. Make sure that all the grime is removed so that none will enter the cylinder after the plug has been removed.

2. Remove the plug using the proper size socket, extensions, and universals as necessary.

3. If removing the plug is difficult, apply some penetrating oil near the plug threads, allow it to work in, then remove the plug. Also, be sure that the socket is straight on the plug, especially on those hard to reach plugs.

INSPECTION

▶ See Figures 5, 6, 7 and 8

Check the plugs for deposits and wear. If they are not going to be replaced, clean the plugs thoroughly. Remember that any kind of deposit will decrease the efficiency of the plug. Plugs can be cleaned in a spark plug cleaning machine, which can sometimes be found in service stations, or you can do an acceptable job of cleaning with a stiff brush. If the plugs are cleaned, the electrodes must be filed flat. Use an ignition points file, not an emery board or the like, which will leave deposits. The electrodes must be filed perfectly flat with sharp edges; rounded edges reduce the spark plug voltage by as much as 50%.

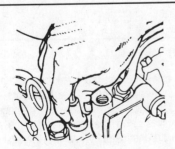

Fig. 2 Spark plug heat range

Fig. 3 Twist the boot and pull the wire off the spark plug; never pull on the wire itself

Fig. 4 Spark plug removal

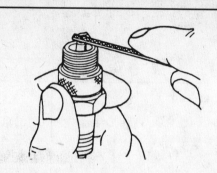

Fig. 5 Used spark plugs in good condition may be filed and re-used

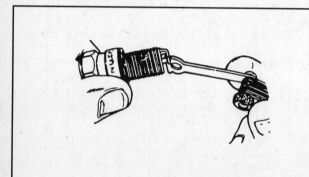

Fig. 6 Adjust the plug gap by bending the side electrode

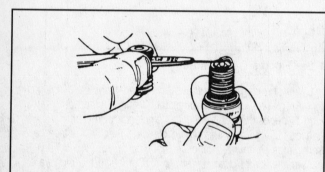

Fig. 7 Spark plug gap may also be set using a wire gauge

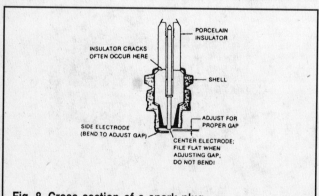

Fig. 8 Cross section of a spark plug

HEI Plug Wire Resistance Chart

Wire Length	Minimum	Maximum
0–15 inches	3000 ohms	10,000 ohms
15–25 inches	4000 ohms	15,000 ohms
25–35 inches	6000 ohms	20,000 ohms
Over 35 inches		25,000 ohms

Fig. 9 HEI Plug Wire Resistance Chart

Check spark plug gap before installation. The ground electrode (the L-shaped one connected to the body of the plug) must be parallel to the center electrode and the specified size wire/blade gauge (see Tune-Up Specifications) should pass through the gap with a slight drag. Always check the gap on new plugs, they are not always set correctly at the factory. Do not use a flat feeler gauge when measuring the gap, because the reading will be inaccurate.

Wire gapping tools usually have a bending tool attached. Use that to adjust the side electrode until the proper distance is obtained. Absolutely never bend the center electrode. Also, be careful not to bend the side electrode too far or too often; it may weaken and break off within the engine, requiring removal of the cylinder head to retrieve it.

INSTALLATION

1. Lubricate the threads of the spark plugs with a drop of oil. Install the plugs and tighten them hand-tight. Take care not to cross-thread them.

2. Tighten the spark plugs with the socket. Do not apply the same amount of force you would use for a bolt; just snug them in. If a torque wrench is available, tighten to 11 ft. lbs. (15 Nm).

3. Install the wires on their respective plugs. Make sure the wires are firmly connected. You will be able to feel them click into place.

Spark Plug Wires

CHECKING AND REPLACING

▶ **See Figure 9**

Every 15,000 miles, inspect the spark plug wires for burns, cuts, or breaks in the insulation. Check the boots and the nipples on the distributor cap. Replace any damaged wiring.

Every 30,000 miles or so, the resistance of the wires should be checked with an ohmmeter. Wires with excessive resistance will cause misfiring, and may make the engine difficult to start in damp weather. Generally, the useful life of the cables is 40,000-60,000 miles.

To check resistance, remove the distributor cap, leaving the wires in place. Connect one lead of an ohmmeter to an electrode within the cap; connect the other lead to the corresponding spark plug terminal (remove it from the spark plug for this test). Replace any wire which shows a resistance over 30,000 ohms. Generally speaking, however, resistance should not be over 25,000 ohms, and 30,000 ohms must be considered the outer limit of acceptability.

It should be remembered that resistance is also a function of length; the longer the wire, the greater the resistance. Thus, if the wires on your car are longer than the factory originals, resistance will be higher, quite possibly outside these limits.

When installing new wires, replace them one at a time to avoid mix-ups. Start by replacing the longest one first. Install the boot firmly over the spark plug. Route the wire over the same path as the original. Insert the nipple firmly onto the tower on the distributor cap, then install the cap cover and latches to secure the wires.

FIRING ORDER

▶ See Figures 10, 11 and 12

➡To avoid confusion always remove and tag the spark plug wires one at a time, for replacement.

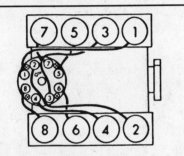

Fig. 10 5.0L (VIN Y) Engine
Engine Firing Order: 1-8-4-3-6-5-7-
Distributor Rotation: Counterclockwise

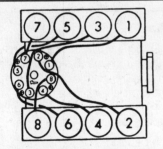

Fig. 11 5.0L (VIN E) and 5.7L (VIN 7) Engines
Engine Firing Order: 1-8-4-3-6-5-7-2
Distributor Rotation: Clockwise

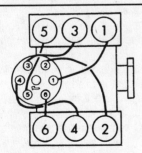

Fig. 12 4.3L Engines
Engine Firing Order: 1-6-5-4-3-2
Distributor Rotation: Clockwise

ELECTRONIC IGNITION

Description and Operation

▶ **See Figures 13 and 14**

The Caprice uses a High Energy Ignition (HEI) system with Electronic Spark Timing (EST) and is completely self-contained unit — all parts are contained within the distributor except the ignition coil which is externally mounted on all engines except the 5.0L (VIN Y) engine.

The distributor contains the electronic module, and the magnetic triggering device. The magnetic pick-up assembly contains a permanent magnet, a pole piece with internal teeth, and a pickup coil (not to be confused with the ignition coil).

All spark timing changes are done electronically by the Electronic Control Module (ECM) which monitors information from various engine sensors, computes the desired spark timing and then signals the distributor to change the timing accordingly. No vacuum or mechanical advance systems are used.

In the HEI system, as in other electronic ignition systems, the breaker points have been replaced with an electronic switch (a transistor) which is located within the control module. This switching transistor performs the same function the points had in a conventional ignition system; it simply turns the coil's primary current on and off at the correct time. Essentially, electronic and conventional ignition systems operate on the same principle.

The module which houses the switching transistor is controlled (turned on and off) by a magnetically generated

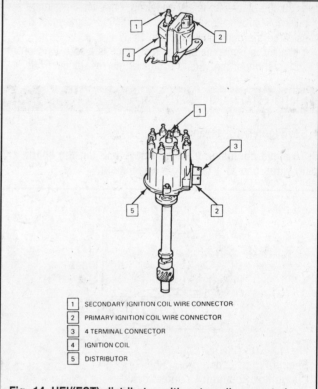

1	SECONDARY IGNITION COIL WIRE CONNECTOR
2	PRIMARY IGNITION COIL WIRE CONNECTOR
3	4 TERMINAL CONNECTOR
4	IGNITION COIL
5	DISTRIBUTOR

Fig. 14 HEI/(EST) distributor with externally mounted ignition coil

impulse induced in the pick-up coil. When the teeth of the rotating timer align with the teeth of the pole piece, the induced voltage in the pick-up coil signals the electronic module to open the coil primary circuit. The primary current then decreases, and a high voltage is induced in the ignition coil secondary windings which is then directed through the rotor and high voltage leads (spark plug wires) to fire the spark plugs.

In essence, the pick-up coil/module system simply replaces the conventional breaker points and condenser. The condenser found within the distributor is for radio suppression purposes only and has nothing to do with the ignition process. The module automatically controls the dwell period, increasing it with increasing engine speed. Since dwell is automatically controlled, it cannot be adjusted. The module itself is non-adjustable and non-repairable and must be replaced if found defective.

All engines are also equipped with Electronic Spark Control (ESC). The ESC system is used in conjunction with the EST system to reduce spark knock by retarding the ignition timing. A knock sensor, which is installed in the cylinder block, sends a signal to the ESC control module and then in turn to the ECM, which then adjusts the timing accordingly.

HEI SYSTEM PRECAUTIONS

Before going on to troubleshooting, it might be a good idea to take note of the following precautions:

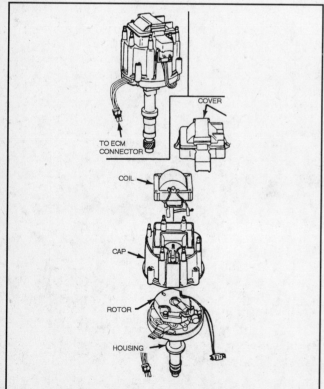

Fig. 13 HEI/(EST) distributor with internally mounted ignition coil

Timing Light Use

Inductive pick-up timing lights are the best kind to use with HEI. Timing lights which connect between the spark plug and the spark plug wire occasionally (not always) give false readings.

Spark Plug Wires

The plug wires used with HEI systems are of a different construction than conventional wires. When replacing them, make sure you get the correct wires, since conventional wires won't correctly handle the high secondary voltage. Also, handle the wires carefully to avoid cracking or splitting. Never pierce the HEI ignition wires.

Tachometer Use

Not all tachometers will operate or indicate correctly when used on a HEI system. While some tachometers may give a reading, this does not necessarily mean the reading is correct. In addition, some tachometers hook up differently from others. If you can't figure out whether or not your tachometer will work on your car, check with the tachometer manufacturer. Dwell readings, of course, have no significance at all with the HEI system.

HEI System Testers

Instruments designed specifically for testing HEI systems are available from several tool manufacturers. Some of these will even test the module itself. However, the tests given in the following section will require only an ohmmeter and a voltmeter.

Diagnosis and Testing

The symptoms of a defective component within the HEI system are exactly the same as those you would encounter in a conventional system. Some of these symptoms are:
- Hard or no Starting
- Rough Idle or Backfiring
- Poor Fuel Economy
- Engine misses under load or while accelerating.

If you suspect a problem in your ignition system, there are certain preliminary checks which you should carry out before you begin to check the electronic portions of the system. First, it is extremely important to make sure the vehicle battery is in good state of charge. A defective or poorly charged battery will cause the various components of the ignition system to read incorrectly when they are being tested. Second, make sure all wiring connections are clean and tight, not only at the battery, but also at the distributor cap, ignition coil, and at the electronic control module.

Since the only change between electronic and conventional ignition systems is in the distributor component area, it is imperative to check the secondary ignition circuit first (plugs, wires, rotor and cap). If the secondary circuit checks out properly, then the engine condition is probably not the fault of the ignition system. To check the secondary ignition system, perform a simple spark test. Remove one of the plug wires and insert some sort of extension in the plug socket. An old spark plug with the ground electrode removed makes a good extension. Hold the wire and extension about 1/4 inch away

from the block and crank the engine. If a normal bright blue spark occurs, then the problem is most likely not in the ignition system. Check for fuel system problems, or fouled spark plugs.

➡ **It is also possible for there to be some type of internal engine damage (timing chain) and still have good spark.**

If, however, there is no spark or a weak spark, then further ignition system testing will have to be done. Troubleshooting techniques fall into two categories, depending on the nature of the problem. The categories are (1) Engine cranks, but won't start or (2) Engine runs, but runs rough or cuts out. To begin with, let's consider the first case.

Engine Fails to Start

If the engine won't start, perform a spark test as described earlier. This will narrow the problem area down considerably. If no spark occurs, check for the presence of normal battery voltage at the battery (BAT) terminal on the ignition coil. The ignition switch must be in the **ON** position for this test. Either a voltmeter or a test light may be used for this test. Connect the test light wire to ground and the probe end to the BAT terminal at the coil. If the light comes on, you have voltage to the distributor. If the light fails to come on, this indicates an open circuit in the ignition primary wiring leading to the distributor. In this case, you will have to check wiring continuity back to the ignition switch. If there is battery voltage at the BAT terminal, but no spark at the plugs, then the problem lies within the distributor assembly. Go on to the distributor components test section.

Engine Runs, But Runs Rough or Cuts Out

1. Make sure the plug wires are in good shape first. There should be no obvious cracks or breaks. You can check the plug wires with an ohmmeter, but do not pierce the wires with a probe. Check the chart for the correct plug wire resistance.

2. If the plug wires are good, remove the cap assembly and check for moisture, cracks, chips, or carbon tracks, or any other high voltage leaks or failures. Perform a 'wiggle test' (feeling the wire for bad or broken connections) on all wires leading to and in the distributor. Replace any defective parts. Make sure the distributor rotates (checking timing chain and gears) when the engine is cranked. If everything is all right so far, go on to the distributor components test section following.

DISTRIBUTOR COMPONENTS TESTING

▶ **See Figures 19, 20, 21, 22, 23, 24, 25, 26, 27 and 28**

If the trouble has been narrowed down to the components within the distributor, the following tests can help pinpoint the defect. An ohmmeter with both high and low ranges should be used. These tests are made with the distributor wires disconnected and the cap removed from the distributor.

✳✳WARNING

The tachometer terminals must never be allowed to touch ground, otherwise damage to the module or coil is possible.

Ignition Coil

MOUNTED IN CAP

▶ See Figure 15

1. Connect an ohmmeter between the TACH and BAT terminals on the ignition coil. The primary coil resistance should be less than one ohm.

2. To check the coil secondary resistance, connect an ohmmeter between the high tension terminal and the BAT terminal. Note the reading. Connect the ohmmeter between the high tension terminal and the TACH terminal. Note the reading. The resistance in both cases should be 6,000-30,000 ohms. Be sure to test between the high tension terminal and both the BAT and TACH terminals.

3. Replace the coil only if the readings in Step 1 and Step 2 are infinite.

➡These resistance checks will not disclose shorted coil windings. This condition can only be detected with scope analysis or a suitably designed coil tester. If these instruments are unavailable, replace the coil with a known good coil as a final coil test.

EXTERNALLY MOUNTED

▶ See Figure 16

1. Disconnect the coil wires and set the ohmmeter on the high scale.
2. Connect the ohmmeter as illustrated in test No. 1.
3. The ohmmeter should read near infinite or very high.
4. Next, set the ohmmeter to the low scale.
5. Connect the ohmmeter as illustrated in test No. 2.
6. The ohmmeter should read zero or very low.

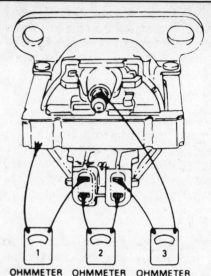

CHECK IGNITION COIL WITH OHMMETER FOR OPENS AND GROUNDS:
STEP 1. — USE HIGH SCALE. SHOULD READ VERY HIGH (INFINITE). IF NOT, REPLACE COIL.
STEP 2. — USE LOW SCALE. SHOULD READ VERY LOW OR ZERO. IF NOT, REPLACE COIL.
STEP 3. — USE HIGH SCALE. SHOULD NOT READ INFINITE. IF IT DOES, REPLACE COIL.

Fig. 16 Testing externally mounted ignition coil — Except 5.0L (VIN Y) Engine

7. Next, set the ohmmeter on the high scale again.
8. Connect the ohmmeter as illustrated in test No. 3.
9. The ohmmeter should NOT read infinite.
10. If the reading are not as specified, replace the coil.

Pickup Coil

▶ See Figures 17 and 18

1. Remove the distributor cap and rotor.
2. Disconnect the pick-up coil lead.
3. Set the ohmmeter on the high scale and connect it as illustrated in test No. 1.
4. The ohmmeter should read infinity at all times.
5. Next, set the ohmmeter on the low scale and connect it as illustrated in test No. 2.
6. The ohmmeter should read a steady value between 500-1500 ohms.

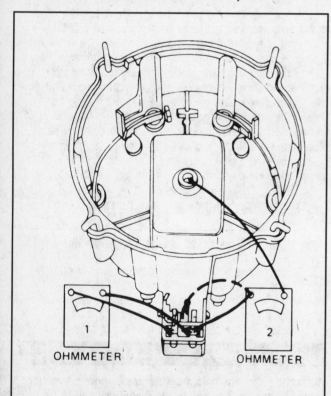

Fig. 15 Testing Internally mounted ignition coil — 5.0L (VIN Y) Engine

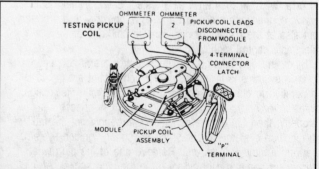

Fig. 17 Testing the pick-up coil — with ignition coil mounted in cap

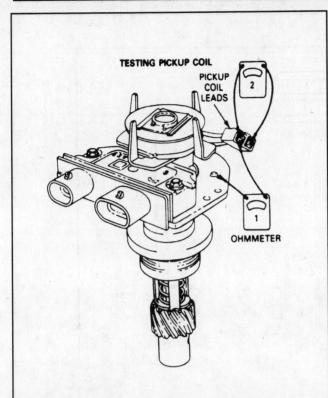

Fig. 18 Testing the pick-up coil — with ignition coil externally mounted

7. If the readings are not as specified, replace the pick-up coil.

8. If no defects have been found at this time, and you still have a problem, then the module will have to be checked. If you do not have access to a module tester, the only possible alternative is a substitution test.

HEI System Maintenance

Except for periodic checks on the spark plug wires, and an occasional check ot the distributor cap for cracks (see Steps 1 and 2 under Engine Runs, But Runs Rough or Cuts Out for details), no maintenance is required on the HEI system. No periodic lubrication is necessary; engine oil lubricates the lower bushing, and an oil-filled reservoir lubricates the upper bushing.

Component Replacement

CAPACITOR

Removal and Installation

The capacitor, if equipped, is part of the coil wire harness assembly. The capacitor is used only for radio noise suppression, it will seldom need replacement.

ESC KNOCK SENSOR

▶ **See Figures 29, 30 and 31**

Removal and Installation

The knock sensor is located on the passenger side of the block above the oil pan, on the 5.0L (VIN E) and 5.7L (VIN 7) engine. On the 5.0L (VIN Y) it is located on the drivers side of the engine, near the front corner of the block. On the 4.3L (VIN Z) engine the knock sensor is located on the top left rear of the block behind the cylinder head.

ESC MODULE

▶ **See Figure 32**

Removal and Installation

The module is located on a bracket in the right inner fender well, in the engine compartment.

HEI DISTRIBUTOR

▶ **See Figure 33**

Removal and Installation

➡**The distributor will have to be removed from the engine and disassembled if the pick-up coil or distributor shaft need to be replaced.**

1. Disconnect the negative battery cable.
2. Remove the air cleaner assembly.
3. Disconnect the electrical connectors from the side of the distributor.
4. Remove the distributor cover and wire retainer, if equipped. Turn the retaining screws counterclockwise and remove the cap.
5. Mark the relationship of the rotor to the distributor housing and the housing relationship to the engine.
6. Remove the distributor retaining bolt and hold-down clamp.
7. Pull the distributor up until the rotor just stops turning counterclockwise and again note the position of the rotor.
8. Remove the distributor from the engine.
   To install:
9. Insert the distributor into the engine, with the rotor aligned to the last mark made, then slowly install the distributor the rest of the way until all marks previously made are aligned.
10. Install the distributor hold-down clamp and retaining bolt. Torque the hold-down bolt to 27 ft. lbs. (36 Nm).
11. If removed, install the wiring harness retainer and secondary wires.
12. Install the distributor cap.
13. Reconnect the wire connectors to the side of the distributor. Make certain the connectors are fully seated and latched.

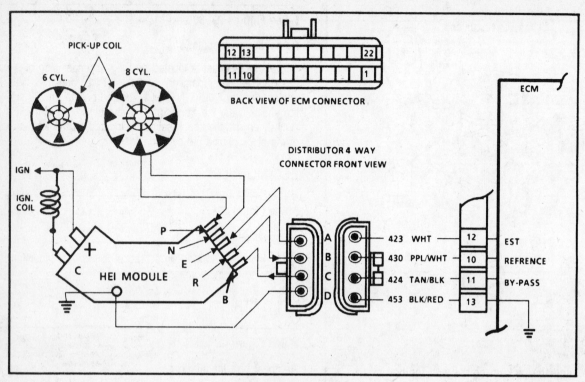

BACK VIEW OF ECM CONNECTOR

DISTRIBUTOR 4 WAY
CONNECTOR FRONT VIEW

CHART C-4A

IGNITION SYSTEM CHECK

5.0L
CARBURETED

1. Checks for proper output from the ignition system. The spark tester requires a minimum of 25, 000 volts to fire. This check can be used in case of an ignition miss because the system may provide enough voltage to run the engine but not enough to fire a spark plug under heavy load.

1A. If spark occurs with EST connector disconnected, pick-up coil output is too low for EST operation.

2. Normal reading during cranking is about 8-10 volts.

3. Checks for a shorted module or grounded circuit from the ignition coil to the module. The distributor module should be turned off so normal voltage should be about 12 volts. If the module is turned "ON", the voltage would be low but above 1 volt. This could cause the ignition coil to fail from excessive heat. With an open ignition coil primary winding, a small mount of voltage will leak through the module from the "Bat." to the tach. terminal.

4. Checks the voltage output with the pick-up coil triggering the module. A spark indicates that the ignition system has sufficient output, however intermittent no-starts or poor performance could be the result of incorrect polarity between the ignition coil and the pick-up coil.
The color of the pick-up coil connector has to be yellow if one of the ignition coil leads is yellow. If the ignition coil has a white lead, any pick-up coil connector color except yellow is OK.

5. Checks for an open module or circuit to it. 12 volts applied to the module "P" terminal should turn the module "ON" and the voltage should drop to about 7-9 volts.

6. This should turn off the module and cause a spark. If no spark occurs, the fault is most likely in the ignition coil because most module problems would have been found before this point in the procedure. A module tester could determine which is at fault.

Fig. 19 Ignition system diagnostic procedure with integral coil — 5.0L (VIN Y) Engine

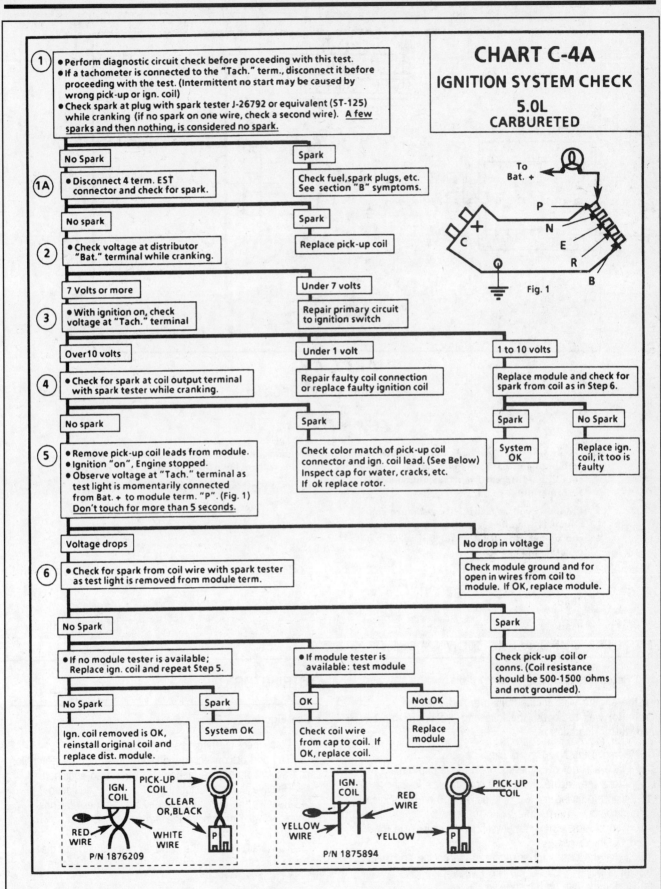

① • Perform diagnostic circuit check before proceeding with this test.
   • If a tachometer is connected to the "Tach." term., disconnect it before proceeding with the test. (Intermittent no start may be caused by wrong pick-up or ign. coil)
   • Check spark at plug with spark tester J-26792 or equivalent (ST-125) while cranking (if no spark on one wire, check a second wire). A few sparks and then nothing, is considered no spark.

CHART C-4A
IGNITION SYSTEM CHECK
5.0L
CARBURETED

No Spark | Spark

1A • Disconnect 4 term. EST connector and check for spark.

Check fuel, spark plugs, etc. See section "B" symptoms.

No spark | Spark

② • Check voltage at distributor "Bat." terminal while cranking.

Replace pick-up coil

7 Volts or more | Under 7 volts

③ • With ignition on, check voltage at "Tach." terminal

Repair primary circuit to ignition switch

Over 10 volts | Under 1 volt | 1 to 10 volts

④ • Check for spark at coil output terminal with spark tester while cranking.

Repair faulty coil connection or replace faulty ignition coil

Replace module and check for spark from coil as in Step 6.

No spark | Spark | Spark | No Spark

⑤ • Remove pick-up coil leads from module.
   • Ignition "on", Engine stopped.
   • Observe voltage at "Tach." terminal as test light is momentarily connected from Bat. + to module term. "P". (Fig. 1) Don't touch for more than 5 seconds.

Check color match of pick-up coil connector and ign. coil lead. (See Below) Inspect cap for water, cracks, etc. If ok replace rotor.

System OK

Replace ign. coil, it too is faulty

Voltage drops | No drop in voltage

⑥ • Check for spark from coil wire with spark tester as test light is removed from module term.

Check module ground and for open in wires from coil to module. If OK, replace module.

No Spark | Spark

• If no module tester is available; Replace ign. coil and repeat Step 5.

• If module tester is available: test module

Check pick-up coil or conns. (Coil resistance should be 500-1500 ohms and not grounded).

No Spark | Spark | OK | Not OK

Ign. coil removed is OK, reinstall original coil and replace dist. module.

System OK

Check coil wire from cap to coil. If OK, replace coil.

Replace module

Fig. 20 Ignition system diagnostic procedure with integral coil — 5.0L (VIN Y) Engine

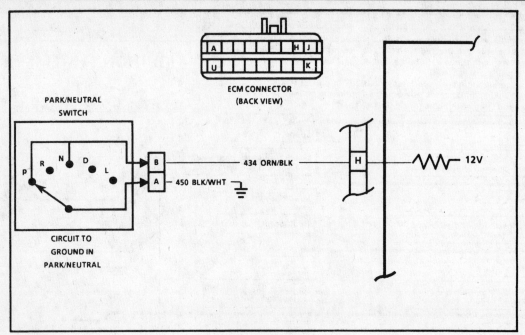

CHART C-4 K

EST PERFORMANCE CHECK
5.0L
CARBURETED

1. Grounding the "test" terminal causes the system to go to a fixed spark advance which should be different from that obtained with EST operating.

   Engine is run at fast idle to get more spark advance. Usually the change is enough so it can be heard in RPM change. If so, it is not necessary to check timing.

2. The check in drive is made because some engines will not have EST operating in P/N.

3. Checks to see if fault is in MAP/VAC system.

Fig. 21 EST performance test — 5.0L (VIN Y) Engine

14. Reconnect the negative battery cable.

➡ If the engine was accidentally cranked after the distributor was removed, the following procedure can be used during installation.

15. Remove the No. 1 spark plug.
16. Place a finger over the spark plug hole and have a helper crank the engine slowly until compression is felt.
17. Align the timing mark on the pulley to **0** on the engine timing indicator.
18. Turn the rotor to point between No. 1 spark plug tower on the distributor cap.
19. Install the distributor assembly in the engine and ensure the rotor is pointing toward the No. 1 spark plug tower.
20. Install the cap and spark plug wires.
21. Check and adjust engine timing.

DISTRIBUTOR CAP

▶ See Figure 34

1. Disconnect the negative battery cable.
2. Tag and disconnect the ignition wires from the distributor cap. Also disconnect the tachometer wire, if so equipped.
3. Release the connectors from the cap, if equipped.
4. Remove the distributor cap by turning the 4 latches counterclockwise or remove the 2 mounting screws.
5. Remove the cap.
6. To install, position the cap into place, matching the notch in the cap with the distributor housing and secure it by turning the latches or screws.
7. Connect the wire to the cap.

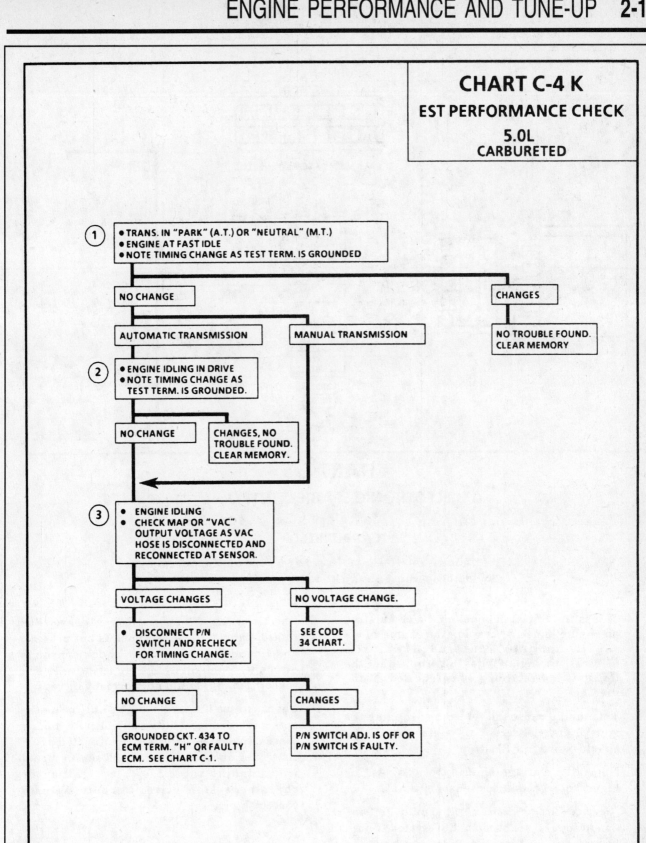

CHART C-4 K
EST PERFORMANCE CHECK
5.0L
CARBURETED

① • TRANS. IN "PARK" (A.T.) OR "NEUTRAL" (M.T.)
   • ENGINE AT FAST IDLE
   • NOTE TIMING CHANGE AS TEST TERM. IS GROUNDED

NO CHANGE

CHANGES

AUTOMATIC TRANSMISSION

MANUAL TRANSMISSION

NO TROUBLE FOUND. CLEAR MEMORY

② • ENGINE IDLING IN DRIVE
   • NOTE TIMING CHANGE AS TEST TERM. IS GROUNDED.

NO CHANGE

CHANGES, NO TROUBLE FOUND. CLEAR MEMORY.

③ • ENGINE IDLING
   • CHECK MAP OR "VAC" OUTPUT VOLTAGE AS VAC HOSE IS DISCONNECTED AND RECONNECTED AT SENSOR.

VOLTAGE CHANGES

NO VOLTAGE CHANGE.

• DISCONNECT P/N SWITCH AND RECHECK FOR TIMING CHANGE.

SEE CODE 34 CHART.

NO CHANGE

CHANGES

GROUNDED CKT. 434 TO ECM TERM. "H" OR FAULTY ECM. SEE CHART C-1.

P/N SWITCH ADJ. IS OFF OR P/N SWITCH IS FAULTY.

Fig. 22 EST performance test — 5.0L (VIN Y) Engine

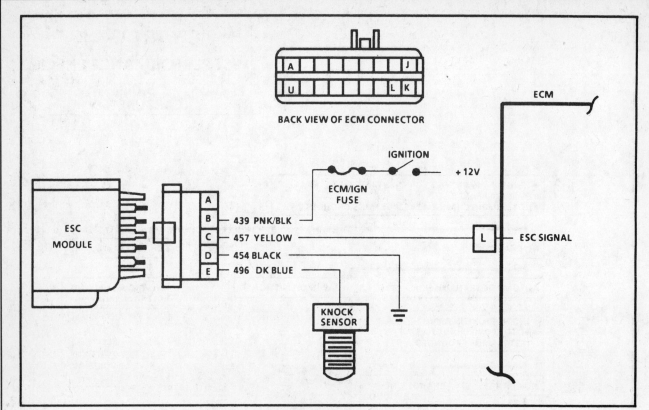

CHART C-5

ELECTRONIC SPARK CONTROL

5.0L
CARBURETED

If the timing is retarded at idle, it may be due to ESC operating.
ESC should not operate unless a knock is present.

1. This is the ESC functional check. Simulating an engine knock by tapping the engine block should normally cause an RPM drop (decrease timing). If it doesn't drop, either the timing is not retarding or is retarded all the time.

2. This should cause full retard by dropping the voltage at ECM term. "L." Retarded timing should cause an RPM drop.

3. Normally, voltage should be .08V AC or higher for a good knock sensor circuit.

4. "Service Engine Soon" light should be "on" and a Code 43 set because ESC system would be retarded too long. If no light comes on, the ECM is not retarding the spark because of a voltage on CKT. 457 to terminal "L" or the ECM is faulty.

5. Checks to see if knock sensor is reason for retard signal. If engine knock is not present, and timing increases when knock sensor is disconnected, fault is an over sensitive knock sensor. Timing should not normally increase.

6. Checks to see if retard signal is due to "noise" on signal wire or faulty controller. If timing increases when wire is disconnected from controller, fault is due to knock sensor signal wire running too close to an ignition or charging system wire. Reroute wire to correct.

Fig. 23 ESC system diagnostic procedure — 5.0L (VIN Y) Engine

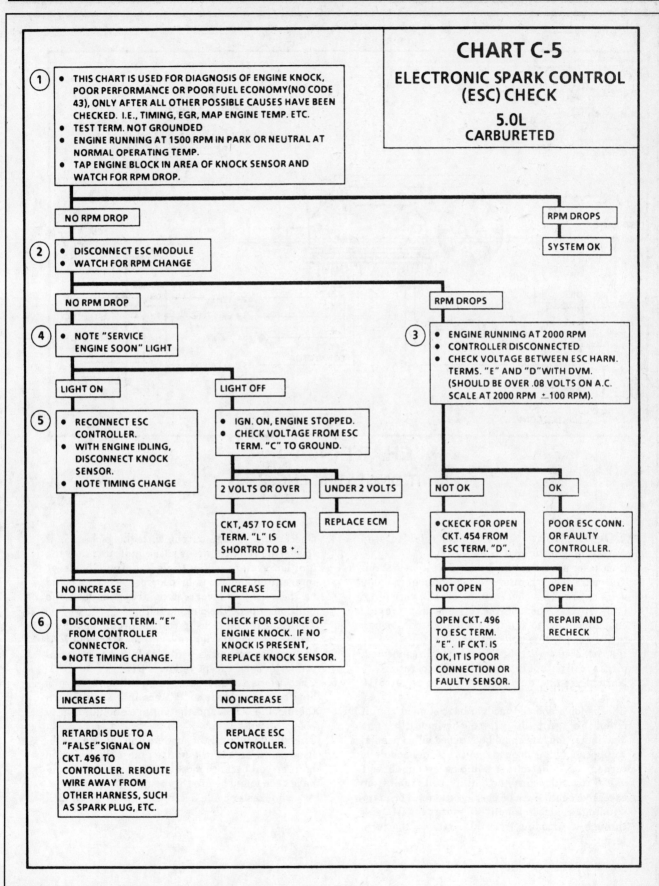

CHART C-5

ELECTRONIC SPARK CONTROL (ESC) CHECK

5.0L
CARBURETED

① • THIS CHART IS USED FOR DIAGNOSIS OF ENGINE KNOCK, POOR PERFORMANCE OR POOR FUEL ECONOMY(NO CODE 43), ONLY AFTER ALL OTHER POSSIBLE CAUSES HAVE BEEN CHECKED. I.E., TIMING, EGR, MAP ENGINE TEMP. ETC.
• TEST TERM. NOT GROUNDED
• ENGINE RUNNING AT 1500 RPM IN PARK OR NEUTRAL AT NORMAL OPERATING TEMP.
• TAP ENGINE BLOCK IN AREA OF KNOCK SENSOR AND WATCH FOR RPM DROP.

NO RPM DROP

RPM DROPS

② • DISCONNECT ESC MODULE
• WATCH FOR RPM CHANGE

SYSTEM OK

NO RPM DROP

RPM DROPS

④ • NOTE "SERVICE ENGINE SOON" LIGHT

③ • ENGINE RUNNING AT 2000 RPM
• CONTROLLER DISCONNECTED
• CHECK VOLTAGE BETWEEN ESC HARN. TERMS. "E" AND "D" WITH DVM. (SHOULD BE OVER .08 VOLTS ON A.C. SCALE AT 2000 RPM ± 100 RPM).

LIGHT ON

LIGHT OFF

⑤ • RECONNECT ESC CONTROLLER.
• WITH ENGINE IDLING, DISCONNECT KNOCK SENSOR.
• NOTE TIMING CHANGE

• IGN. ON, ENGINE STOPPED.
• CHECK VOLTAGE FROM ESC TERM. "C" TO GROUND.

NOT OK

OK

2 VOLTS OR OVER

UNDER 2 VOLTS

• CKECK FOR OPEN CKT. 454 FROM ESC TERM. "D".

POOR ESC CONN. OR FAULTY CONTROLLER.

CKT, 457 TO ECM TERM. "L" IS SHORTRD TO B +.

REPLACE ECM

NOT OPEN

OPEN

NO INCREASE

INCREASE

OPEN CKT. 496 TO ESC TERM. "E". IF CKT. IS OK, IT IS POOR CONNECTION OR FAULTY SENSOR.

REPAIR AND RECHECK

⑥ • DISCONNECT TERM. "E" FROM CONTROLLER CONNECTOR.
• NOTE TIMING CHANGE.

CHECK FOR SOURCE OF ENGINE KNOCK. IF NO KNOCK IS PRESENT, REPLACE KNOCK SENSOR.

INCREASE

NO INCREASE

RETARD IS DUE TO A "FALSE"SIGNAL ON CKT. 496 TO CONTROLLER. REROUTE WIRE AWAY FROM OTHER HARNESS, SUCH AS SPARK PLUG, ETC.

REPLACE ESC CONTROLLER.

Fig. 24 ESC system diagnostic procedure — 5.0L (VIN Y) Engine

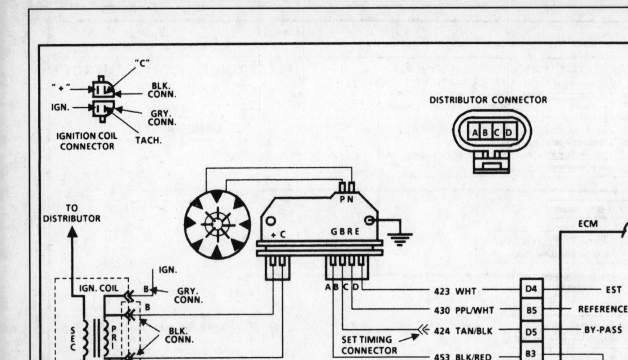

CHART C-4A

IGNITION SYSTEM CHECK

Test Description: Step numbers refer to step numbers on diagnostic chart.

1. Checks for proper output from the ignition system. The spark tester requires a minimum of 25,000 volts to fire. This check can be used in case of an ignition miss because the system may provide enough voltage to run the engine but not enough to fire a spark plug under heavy load.

1A. If spark occurs with EST connector disconnected, pick-up coil output is too low for EST operation.

2. Normal reading during cranking is about 8-10 volts.

3. Checks for a shorted module or grounded circuit from the ignition coil to the module. The distributor module should be turned off so normal voltage should be about 12 volts. If the module is turned "ON", the voltage would be low but above 1 volt. This could cause the ignition coil to fail from excessive heat. With an open ignition coil primary winding, a small mount of voltage will leak through the module from the "Bat." to the tach. terminal.

4. Checks the voltage output with the pick-up coil triggering the module. A spark indicates that the ignition system has sufficient output, however intermittent no-starts or poor performance could be the result of incorrect polarity between the ignition coil and the pick-up coil.
The color of the pick-up coil connector has to be yellow if one of the ignition coil leads is yellow. If the ignition coil has a white lead, any pick-up coil connector color except yellow is OK.

5. Checks for an open module or circuit to it. 12 volts applied to the module "P" terminal should turn the module "ON" and the voltage should drop to about 7-9 volts.

6. This should turn off the module and cause a spark. If no spark occurs, the fault is most likely in the ignition coil because most module problems would have been found before this point in the procedure. A module tester could determine which is at fault.

Fig. 25 Ignition system diagnostic procedure with remote coil — Except 5.0L (VIN Y) Engine

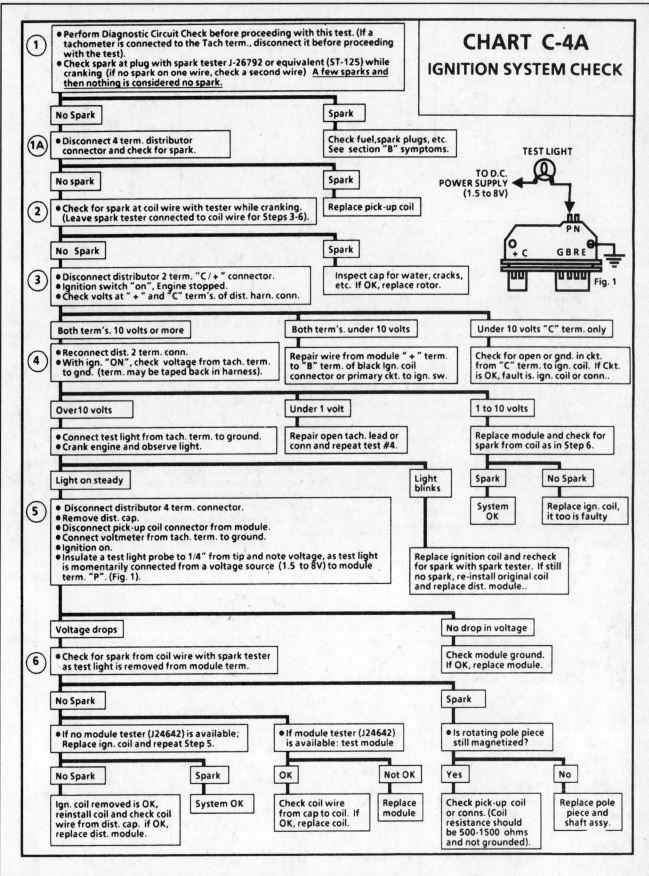

CHART C-4A
IGNITION SYSTEM CHECK

1 • Perform Diagnostic Circuit Check before proceeding with this test. (If a tachometer is connected to the Tach term., disconnect it before proceeding with the test).
• Check spark at plug with spark tester J-26792 or equivalent (ST-125) while cranking (if no spark on one wire, check a second wire) A few sparks and then nothing is considered no spark.

No Spark | Spark

1A • Disconnect 4 term. distributor connector and check for spark.

Check fuel, spark plugs, etc. See section "B" symptoms.

TEST LIGHT
TO D.C. POWER SUPPLY (1.5 to 8V)

No spark | Spark

2 • Check for spark at coil wire with tester while cranking. (Leave spark tester connected to coil wire for Steps 3-6).

Replace pick-up coil

P N
+ C G B R E
Fig. 1

No Spark | Spark

3 • Disconnect distributor 2 term. "C/+" connector.
• Ignition switch "on", Engine stopped.
• Check volts at " + " and "C" term's. of dist. harn. conn.

Inspect cap for water, cracks, etc. If OK, replace rotor.

Both term's. 10 volts or more | Both term's. under 10 volts | Under 10 volts "C" term. only

4 • Reconnect dist. 2 term. conn.
• With ign. "ON", check voltage from tach. term. to gnd. (term. may be taped back in harness).

Repair wire from module " + " term. to "B" term. of black Ign. coil connector or primary ckt. to ign. sw.

Check for open or gnd. in ckt. from "C" term. to ign. coil. If Ckt. is OK, fault is. ign. coil or conn..

Over 10 volts | Under 1 volt | 1 to 10 volts

• Connect test light from tach. term. to ground.
• Crank engine and observe light.

Repair open tach. lead or conn and repeat test #4.

Replace module and check for spark from coil as in Step 6.

Light on steady | Light blinks | Spark | No Spark

System OK | Replace ign. coil, it too is faulty

5 • Disconnect distributor 4 term. connector.
• Remove dist. cap.
• Disconnect pick-up coil connector from module.
• Connect voltmeter from tach. term. to ground.
• Ignition on.
• Insulate a test light probe to 1/4" from tip and note voltage, as test light is momentarily connected from a voltage source (1.5 to 8V) to module term. "P". (Fig. 1).

Replace ignition coil and recheck for spark with spark tester. If still no spark, re-install original coil and replace dist. module..

Voltage drops | No drop in voltage

6 • Check for spark from coil wire with spark tester as test light is removed from module term.

Check module ground. If OK, replace module.

No Spark | Spark

• If no module tester (J24642) is available; Replace ign. coil and repeat Step 5.

• If module tester (J24642) is available: test module

• Is rotating pole piece still magnetized?

No Spark | Spark | OK | Not OK | Yes | No

Ign. coil removed is OK, reinstall coil and check coil wire from dist. cap. if OK, replace dist. module.

System OK

Check coil wire from cap to coil. If OK, replace coil.

Replace module

Check pick-up coil or conns. (Coil resistance should be 500-1500 ohms and not grounded).

Replace pole piece and shaft assy.

Fig. 26 Ignition system diagnostic procedure with remote coil — Except 5.0L (VIN Y) Engine

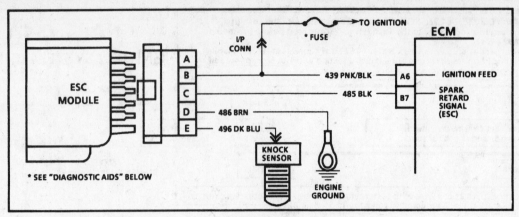

CHART C-5

ELECTRONIC SPARK CONTROL (ESC) SYSTEM CHECK
(ENGINE KNOCK, POOR PERFORMANCE, OR POOR ECONOMY)
(TBI)

Circuit Description:

Electronic Spark Control (ESC) is accomplished with a module that sends a voltage signal to the ECM. When the knock sensor detects engine knock, the voltage from the ESC module to the ECM is shut "OFF" and this signals the ECM to retard timing, if engine rpm is over about 900.

Test Description: Numbers below refer to circled numbers on the diagnostic chart.

1. If a Code 43 is not set, but a knock signal is indicated while running at 1500 rpm, listen for an internal engine noise. Under a no load condition, there should not be any detonation, and if knock is indicated, an internal engine problem may exist.
2. Usually a knock signal can be generated by tapping on the exhaust manifold. This test can also be performed at idle. Test number 1 was run at 1500 rpm, to determine if a constant knock signal was present, which would affect engine performance.
3. This tests whether the knock signal is due to the knock sensor, a basic engine problem, or the ESC module.
4. If the ESC module ground circuit is faulty, the ESC module will not function correctly. The test light should light indicating the ground circuit is OK.

5. Contacting CKT 496, with a test light to 12 volts, should generate a knock signal to determine whether the knock sensor is faulty, or the ESC module can't recognize a knock signal.

Diagnostic Aids:

* ECM Fuse

"Scan" tools have two positions to diagnose the ESC system. The knock signal can be monitored to see if the knock sensor is detecting a knock condition and if the ESC module is functioning, knock signal should display "YES", whenever detonation is present. The knock retard position on the "Scan" displays the amount of spark retard the ECM is commanding. The ECM can retard the timing up to 20 degrees.

If the ESC system checks OK, but detonation is the complaint, refer to "Detonation/Spark Knock" in Section "B".

Fig. 27 ESC system diagnostic procedure — Except 5.0L (VIN Y) Engine

8. Connect the tachometer wire, if so equipped, and connect the ignition wires to the distributor cap, in there original location.

Rotor

1. Disconnect the negative battery cable.
2. Remove the distributor cap.
3. Unscrew the two rotor attaching screws (integral coil only) and then lift off the rotor.
4. To install, position the rotor into place and secure the rotor with the 2 rotor attaching screws (integral coil only).
5. Install the distributor cap.
6. Connect the negative battery cable.

HEI MODULE

◆ See Figure 35

Removal and Installation

1. Disconnect the negative battery cable.
2. Remove the air cleaner assembly, as required.
3. Remove the distributor cap and rotor.
4. Remove the module retaining screws, then lift the module upwards.
5. Disconnect the module leads. Note the color code on the leads, as these cannot be interchanged.

➡Do not wipe the grease from the module or distributor base, if the same module is to be replaced.

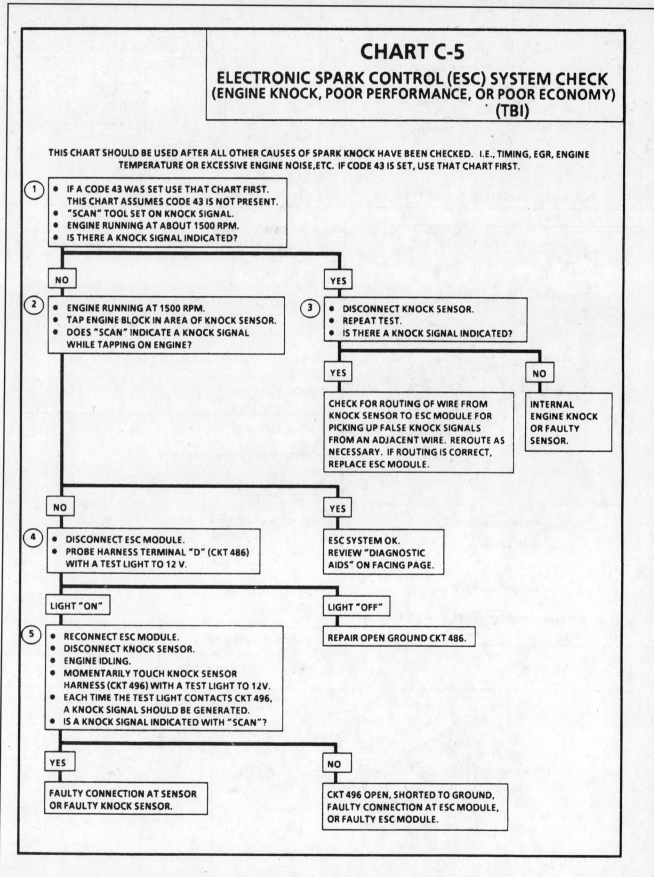

CHART C-5

ELECTRONIC SPARK CONTROL (ESC) SYSTEM CHECK
(ENGINE KNOCK, POOR PERFORMANCE, OR POOR ECONOMY)
(TBI)

THIS CHART SHOULD BE USED AFTER ALL OTHER CAUSES OF SPARK KNOCK HAVE BEEN CHECKED. I.E., TIMING, EGR, ENGINE TEMPERATURE OR EXCESSIVE ENGINE NOISE, ETC. IF CODE 43 IS SET, USE THAT CHART FIRST.

1
- IF A CODE 43 WAS SET USE THAT CHART FIRST. THIS CHART ASSUMES CODE 43 IS NOT PRESENT.
- "SCAN" TOOL SET ON KNOCK SIGNAL.
- ENGINE RUNNING AT ABOUT 1500 RPM.
- IS THERE A KNOCK SIGNAL INDICATED?

NO

YES

2
- ENGINE RUNNING AT 1500 RPM.
- TAP ENGINE BLOCK IN AREA OF KNOCK SENSOR.
- DOES "SCAN" INDICATE A KNOCK SIGNAL WHILE TAPPING ON ENGINE?

3
- DISCONNECT KNOCK SENSOR.
- REPEAT TEST.
- IS THERE A KNOCK SIGNAL INDICATED?

YES

NO

CHECK FOR ROUTING OF WIRE FROM KNOCK SENSOR TO ESC MODULE FOR PICKING UP FALSE KNOCK SIGNALS FROM AN ADJACENT WIRE. REROUTE AS NECESSARY. IF ROUTING IS CORRECT, REPLACE ESC MODULE.

INTERNAL ENGINE KNOCK OR FAULTY SENSOR.

NO

YES

4
- DISCONNECT ESC MODULE.
- PROBE HARNESS TERMINAL "D" (CKT 486) WITH A TEST LIGHT TO 12 V.

ESC SYSTEM OK. REVIEW "DIAGNOSTIC AIDS" ON FACING PAGE.

LIGHT "ON"

LIGHT "OFF"

5
- RECONNECT ESC MODULE.
- DISCONNECT KNOCK SENSOR.
- ENGINE IDLING.
- MOMENTARILY TOUCH KNOCK SENSOR HARNESS (CKT 496) WITH A TEST LIGHT TO 12V.
- EACH TIME THE TEST LIGHT CONTACTS CKT 496, A KNOCK SIGNAL SHOULD BE GENERATED.
- IS A KNOCK SIGNAL INDICATED WITH "SCAN"?

REPAIR OPEN GROUND CKT 486.

YES

NO

FAULTY CONNECTION AT SENSOR OR FAULTY KNOCK SENSOR.

CKT 496 OPEN, SHORTED TO GROUND, FAULTY CONNECTION AT ESC MODULE, OR FAULTY ESC MODULE.

Fig. 28 ESC system diagnostic procedure — Except 5.0L (VIN Y) Engine

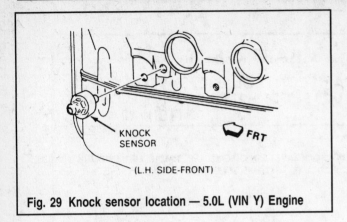

Fig. 29 Knock sensor location — 5.0L (VIN Y) Engine

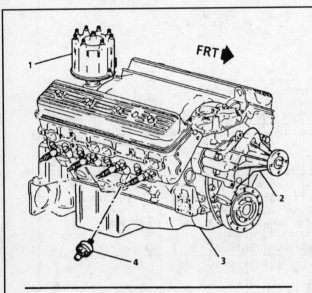

1	DISTRIBUTOR
2	WATER PUMP
3	OIL PAN
4	ESC KNOCK SENSOR

Fig. 31 Knock sensor location — 5.0L (VIN E) and 5.7L (VIN 7) Engines

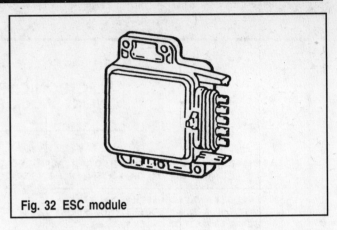

Fig. 32 ESC module

To install:

6. Spread the silicone grease, included in package, on the metal face of the module and on the distributor base where the module seats.

7. Fit the module leads to the module. Make certain the leads are fully seated and latched. Seat the module and metal shield into the distributor and install the retaining screws.

8. Install the rotor and cap.

9. Install the air cleaner assembly.

10. Reconnect the negative battery cable.

PICK-UP COIL

▶ See Figure 36

Removal and Installation

1. Disconnect the negative battery cable.

2. Remove the distributor assembly.

3. Support the distributor assembly in a vice and drive the roll pin from the gear. Remove the shaft assembly.

4. To remove the pick-up coil, remove the retainer and shield, on external coil distributors. Remove the 3 pick-up coil retaining screws and remove the magnetic shield and C-clip.

5. Lift the pick-up coil assembly straight up to remove it from the distributor.

To install:

6. Assembly the pick-up coil, shield, screws and retainer.

7. Install the shaft.

8. Install the gear and roll pin to the shaft. Make certain the matchmarks are aligned.

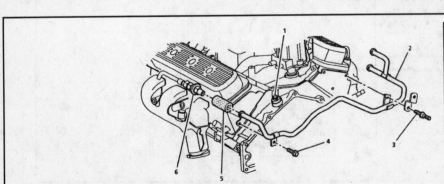

1	KNOCK SENSOR
2	AIR INJECTION CROSSOVER PIPE
3	35 N·m (26 lb. ft.)
4	35 N·m (26 lb. ft.)
5	HOSE
6	AIR INJECTION CHECK VALVE

Fig. 30 Knock sensor location — 4.3L (VIN Z) Engine

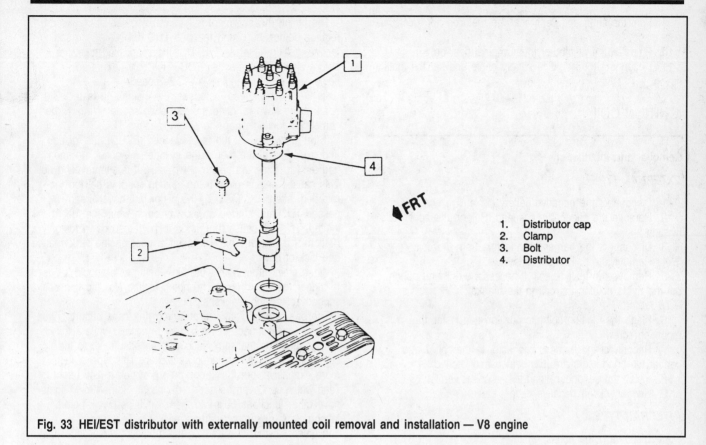

1. Distributor cap
2. Clamp
3. Bolt
4. Distributor

Fig. 33 HEI/EST distributor with externally mounted coil removal and installation — V8 engine

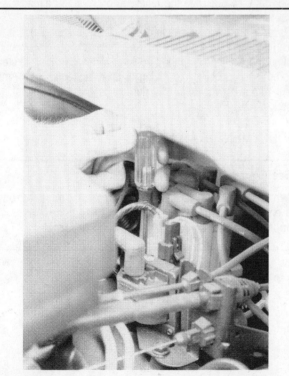

Fig. 34 HEI distributor cap removal — 5.0L (VIN E) Engine; Note that the original equipment ignition wires are numbered.

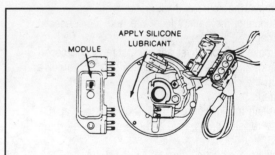

Fig. 35 Module replacement; ensure the mating surfaces are coated with silicone lubricant — 5.0L (VIN Y) Engine

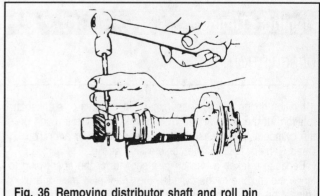

Fig. 36 Removing distributor shaft and roll pin

9. Spin the shaft and verify that the teeth do not touch the pole piece.

10. Reinstall the distributor in its original position.

11. Reconnect the negative battery cable and set the ignition timing.

IGNITION COIL

Removal and Installation

EXTERNAL TYPE

1. Disconnect the negative battery cable.

2. Remove the secondary coil lead. Pull on the boot while twisting it.

3. Disconnect the harness connectors from the coil.

4. Remove the coil mounting screws.

5. Remove the ignition coil. If necessary, drill and punch out the rivets holding the coil to the bracket.

To install:

6. Place the ignition coil into position and install the mounting screws.

7. Reconnect the harness connector to the coil. Make certain the connectors are fully seated and latched.

8. Install the secondary lead to the coil tower.

9. Reconnect the negative battery cable.

INTEGRAL TYPE

1. Disconnect the negative battery cable.

2. Remove the cover and wire retainer.

3. Disconnect the battery feed wire and coil connections from the cap.

4. Remove the coil cover attaching screws and cover.

5. Remove the coil attaching screws and lift the coil and leads from the cap.

To install:

6. Position the ignition coil and leads into the cap. Be certain the resistor brush, seal and coil grounds are properly positioned.

7. Install the mounting screws.

8. Install the coil cover and retaining screws.

9. Reconnect the feed wire and coil connection to the cap.

10. Install the cover and wire retainer.

11. Reconnect the negative battery cable.

Ignition Timing

DESCRIPTION

Ignition timing is the measurement, in degrees of crankshaft rotation, of the point at which the spark plugs fire in each of the cylinders. It is measured in degrees before or after Top Dead Center (TDC) of the compression stroke.

Because it takes a fraction of a second for the spark plug to ignite the mixture in the cylinder, the spark plug must fire a little before the piston reaches TDC. Otherwise, the mixture will not be completely ignited as the piston passes TDC and the full power of the explosion will not be used by the engine.

The timing measurement is given in degrees of crankshaft rotation before the piston reaches TDC (BTDC). If the setting for the ignition timing is 5°BTDC, the spark plug must fire 5° before each piston reaches TDC. This only holds true, however, when the engine is at idle speed.

As the engine speed increases, the pistons go faster. The spark plugs have to ignite the fuel even sooner if it is to be completely ignited when the piston reaches TDC.

If the ignition is set too far advanced (BTDC), the ignition and explosion of the fuel in the cylinder will occur too soon and tend to force the piston down while it is still traveling up. This causes engine ping. If the ignition spark is set too far retarded, after TDC (ATDC), the piston will have already passed TDC and started on its way down when the fuel is ignited. This will cause the piston to be forced down for only a portion of its travel. This will result in poor engine performance and lack of power.

When timing the engine, the No. 1 plug wire should be used to trigger the timing light. The notch for the No. 1 cylinder is scribed across the crankshaft pulley.

The basic timing light operates from the car's battery. Two alligator clips connect to the battery terminals, while a third wire connects to the spark plug with an adapter or to the spark plug wire with an inductive pickup. This type of light is more expensive, but the xenon bulb provides a nice bright flash which can even be seen in sunlight. Some timing lights have other functions built into them, such as dwell meters, tachometers, or remote starting switches. These are convenient, in that they reduce the tangle of wires under the hood, but may duplicate the functions of tools you already have.

Because the car has electronic ignition, you should use a timing light with an inductive pickup. This pickup simply clamps around the Number 1 spark plug wire, eliminating the adapter. It is not susceptible to crossfiring or false triggering, which may occur with a conventional light due to the greater voltages produced by HEI.

ADJUSTMENT

◗ See Figures 37, 38 and 39

➡ **When adjusting the timing, refer to the instructions on the emission control label located in the engine compartment. Follow all instructions on the label.**

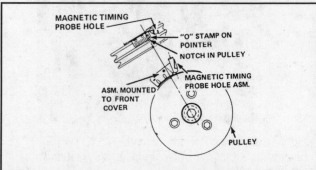

Fig. 37 View of the timing marks on the front crankshaft pulley

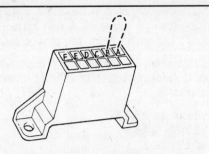

Fig. 38 Jumper the A and B terminals of the ALDL connector located under the driver's side instrument panel prior to setting the timing — 1990-91 vehicles

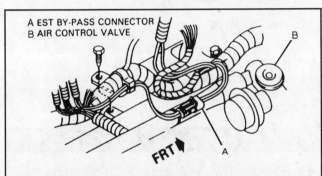

A EST BY-PASS CONNECTOR
B AIR CONTROL VALVE

Fig. 39 Disconnect the EST by-pass connector prior to setting the ignition timing — 1992-93 vehicles

1. Locate the timing marks on the crankshaft pulley and the front of the engine. They may be viewed easier by looking down between the timing cover and the back of the water pump.

2. Clean off the marks and coat them with white paint or chalk, so that they may be easily identified.

3. Warm the engine to normal operating temperatures and stop the engine. Connect a tachometer to the distributor.

4. Install a timing light with an inductive pick-lead to the No. 1 spark plug wire. Front left (driver's side cylinder).

5. To set the base timing the ECM EST must be bypassed. To do this, do the following:
   • For all 1990-91 vehicles — ground diagnostic terminal (terminals A and B) in the ALDL diagnostic connector
   • For all 1992-93 vehicles — disconnect the single connector tan/black wire at the right rear valve cover

6. Turn off all accessories, place the transmission in **N** for manual and **PARK** for auto. Set the parking brake.

7. Loosen the distributor bolt so that the distributor may be turned.

8. Start the engine and aim the timing light at the timing marks. With the engine idling, adjust the timing marks.

9. Turn the engine off and tighten the distributor bolt. Turn the engine on and recheck the timing marks.

10. Turn the engine off and disconnect the timing light and tachometer. Reconnect the distributor connectors.

Valve Lash

All models utilize a hydraulic valve lifter system to obtain zero lash. No adjustment is necessary. An initial adjustment is required anytime that the lifters are removed or the valve train is disturbed.

ADJUSTMENT

EXCEPT 5.0L (VIN Y) ENGINE
▶ See Figure 40

The valves may be adjusted with the engine idling or shut off. If you choose to adjust the valves with the engine idling, the use of oil stopper clips, which prevent oil splatter is recommended and the valves may be adjusted in any sequence.

If you adjust the valves with the engine shut off it will be a much cleaner process, but you will need to follow a cylinder and valve adjustment procedure.

To adjust the valves with the engine running proceed as follows:

Establish normal operating temperature by running the engine for several minutes. Shut the engine off and remove the valve cover(s). After valve cover removal, torque the cylinder heads to specification. Plug all open vacuum lines.

Restart the engine. Valve lash is set with the engine warm and idling. Turn the rocker arm nut counterclockwise until the rocker arm begins to clatter. Reverse the direction and turn the rocker arm down slowly until the clatter just stops. This is the zero lash position. Turn the nut down an additional ¼ turn and wait ten seconds until the engine runs smoothly. Continue with additional ¼ turns, waiting ten seconds each time, until the nut has been turned down one full turn from the zero lash position. This one turn, pre-load adjustment must be performed to allow the lifter to adjust itself and prevents possible interference between the valves and pistons. Noisy lifters should be cleaned or replaced.

To adjust the valves with the engine **OFF** proceed as follows:
   1. Adjust the valves as follows:
   a. Crank the engine until the mark on the damper aligns with the TDC or 0° mark on the timing tab and the engine is in No. 1 firing position. This can be determined by placing the fingers on the No. 1 cylinder valves as the marks align.

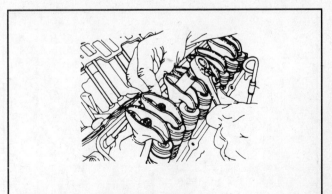

Fig. 40 Valve adjustment — V8 engine

If the valves do not move, it is in No. 1 firing position. If the valves move, it is in No. 4 (V6) or No. 6 (V8) firing position and the crankshaft should be rotated one more revolution to the No. 1 firing position.

b. The adjustment is made in the same manner on both engines.

c. With the engine in No. 1 firing position, the following valves can be adjusted:

➡**Distinguishing the exhaust from intake valves is easy, simply look for the intake or exhaust runner directly in-line with the valve.**

- V8-Exhaust-1,3,4,8
- V8-Intake-1,2,5,7
- V6-Exhaust-1,5,6
- V6-Intake-1,2,3

2. Back the adjusting nut out until lash can be felt at the push rod, then turn the nut until all lash is removed (this can be determined by rotating the push rod while turning the adjusting nut). When all lash has been removed, turn the nut in 1 additional turn, this will center the lifter plunger.

3. Crank the engine 1 full revolution until the marks are again in alignment. This is No. 4 (V6) or No. 6 (V8) firing position. The following valves can now be adjusted:

➡**Distinguishing the exhaust from intake valves is easy, simply look for the intake or exhaust runner directly in-line with the valve.**

- V8-Exhaust-2,5,6,7
- V8-Intake-3,4,6,8
- V6-Exhaust-2,3,4
- V6-Intake-4,5,6

4. Reinstall the rocker arm covers using new gaskets or sealer.

5. Install the distributor cap and wire assembly.

6. Adjust the carburetor idle speed.

5.0L (VIN Y) ENGINE

The 5.0L (VIN Y) engine uses a positive stop type rocker bolt; the lifters are automatically adjusted and centered when the rocker bolts are properly torqued down to 22 ft. lbs. (28 Nm). If a lifter is still noisy; refer to Section 3 — Camshaft Inspection.

IDLE SPEED AND MIXTURE ADJUSTMENTS

Carbureted Engines

➡**Idle speed and mixture settings are factory set and sealed; adjustment of the idle mixture requires special tools including an exhaust gas analyzer and should not be attempted by the do-it-yourselfer, but only by an authorized GM dealer.**

A cover is in place over the idle air bleed valve, and the access holes to the idle mixture needles are sealed with hardened plugs to prevent the factory settings from being tampered with. These items are NOT to be removed unless required for cleaning, part replacement, improper dwell readings or if the System Performance Check indicates the carburetor is the cause of the trouble.

5.0L Engine

MIXTURE PLUG REMOVAL
▶ **See Figure 41**

1. Remove the carburetor from the engine, following normal service procedures to gain access to the plugs covering the idle mixture needles.

2. Invert carburetor and drain fuel into a suitable container.

❋❋CAUTION

Take precautions to avoid the risk of fire.

3. Place the carburetor on a suitable holding fixture, with the intake manifold side up. Use care to avoid damaging linkage, tubes and parts protruding from air horn.

4. Make 2 parallel cuts in the throttle body, 1 on each side of the locator points beneath the idle mixture needle plug (manifold side), with a hacksaw.

➡**The cuts should reach down to the steel plug, but should not extend more than 1/8 inch beyond the locator points. The distance between the saw cuts depends on the size of the punch to be used.**

5. Place a flat punch near the ends of the saw marks in the throttle body. Hold the punch at a 45 degree angle and drive it into the throttle body until the casting breaks away, exposing the steel plug. The hardened plug will break, rather than remaining intact. It is not necessary to remove the plug in a whole piece, but do remove the loose pieces.

6. If equipped with a 4 barrel carburetor, repeat the procedure for the remaining mixture needle plug.

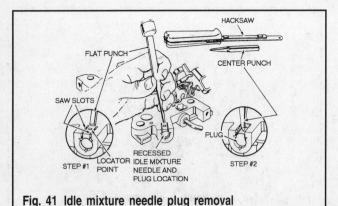

Fig. 41 Idle mixture needle plug removal

7. Reinstall the carburetor using a new gasket.

PRE-ADJUSTMENT PROCEDURE

▶ See Figure 42

1. Block the drive wheels, set the parking brake and place the transmission in **P** for vehicles equipped with an automatic transmission or neutral for manual transmissions.

2. Remove the idle mixture needle plugs and turn the idle mixture screw in until lightly seated, then back out approximately 3 3/8 turns using tool J-29030 or equivalent.

3. Reinstall the carburetor, if previously removed.

4. Do not install the air cleaner.

5. Disconnect and plug the hoses as directed on the Emission Control Information Label under the hood.

6. Check the ignition timing as shown on the Emission Control Information Label.

7. Connect the positive lead of a dwell meter to the mixture control solenoid test lead (green connector generally located on right fenderwell) and connect the other lead to ground. Set the dwell meter to the 6-cylinder position.

MIXTURE ADJUSTMENT PROCEDURE

▶ See Figures 43 and 44

1. Start the engine and allow it run until thoroughly warm and dwell begins to vary.

2. Check idle speed and compare to the specifications on the underhood Emission Control Information Label. If necessary adjust the curb idle speed.

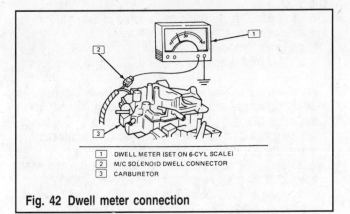

1	DWELL METER (SET ON 6-CYL SCALE)
2	M/C SOLENOID DWELL CONNECTOR
3	CARBURETOR

Fig. 42 Dwell meter connection

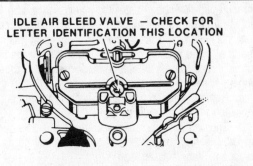

IDLE AIR BLEED VALVE – CHECK FOR
LETTER IDENTIFICATION THIS LOCATION

Fig. 43 Idle air bleed valve identification letter location — 5.0L (VIN Y) Engine

3. With the engine idling in **D** for automatic transmissions or neutral for manual transmissions, observe the dwell reading on the 6 cylinder scale.

4. If the reading is varying within the 10-50 degree range, the adjustment is correct.

5. If the reading is not as specified remove the idle air bleed valve cover. Refer to Fuel System, Section 5. With cover removed, look for presence (or absence) of a letter identification on top of idle air bleed valve.

➡**A missing cover indicates that the idle air bleed valve setting has been changed from its original factory setting.**

6. If no identifying letter appears on top of the valve, begin with Procedure A, below. If the valve is identified with a letter, begin Procedure B.

Procedure A (No Letter On Idle Air Bleed Valve)

➡**Presetting the idle air bleed valve to a gauge dimension is necessary only if the valve was serviced prior to on-vehicle adjustment.**

1. Install idle air bleed valve gauging Tool J-33815-2, BT-8253-B, or equivalent, in throttle side D-shaped vent hole in the air horn casting. The upper end of the tool should be positioned over the open cavity next to the idle air bleed valve.

2. While holding the gauging tool down lightly, so that the solenoid plunger is against the solenoid stop, adjust the idle air bleed valve so that the gauging tool will pivot over and just contact the top of the valve. The valve is now preset for on-vehicle adjustment. Remove the gauging tool and proceed as follows:

   a. Disconnect the vacuum hose from the canister purge valve and plug it.

   b. Start engine and allow it to reach normal operating temperature.

   c. While idling in **D** for automatic transmission or neutral for manual transmission, use a screwdriver to slowly turn the valve counterclockwise or clockwise, until the dwell reading varies within the 25-35° range, attempting to be as close to 30° as possible.

➡**Perform this step carefully. The air bleed valve is very sensitive and should be turned in ⅛ turn increments only.**

   d. If the reading is not as specified, the idle mixture needles will have to be adjusted.

   e. If the reading is within specifications, reconnect all hoses previously removed and install air cleaner.

3. If unable to set dwell to 25-35°, and the dwell is below 25°, turn both mixture needles counterclockwise an additional turn. If dwell is above 35°, turn both mixture needles clockwise an additional turn. Readjust idle air bleed valve to obtain dwell limits.

4. After adjustments are complete, seal the idle mixture needle openings in the throttle body, using silicone sealant, RTV rubber, or equivalent. The sealer is required to discourage unnecessary adjustment of the setting, and to prevent fuel vapor loss in that area.

5. On vehicles without a carburetor-mounted Idle Speed Control or Idle Load Compensator, adjust curb idle speed if necessary.

6. Check, and only if necessary adjust, fast idle speed as described on Vehicle Emission Control Information label.

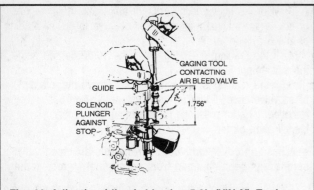

Fig. 44 Adjusting idle air bleed — 5.0L (VIN Y) Engine

Procedure B (Letter Appears On Idle Air Bleed Valve)

1. Install idle air bleed valve gauging Tool J-33815-2, BT-8253-B, or equivalent, in throttle side D-shaped vent hole in the air horn casting. The upper end of the tool should be positioned over the open cavity next to the idle air bleed valve.

2. While holding the gauging tool down lightly, so that the solenoid plunger is against the solenoid stop, adjust the idle air bleed valve so that the gauging tool will pivot over and just contact the top of the valve.

3. The valve is now set properly. No further adjustment of the valve is necessary. Remove gauging tool.

4. Disconnect vacuum hose to canister purge valve and plug it.

5. Start engine and allow it to reach normal operating temperature.

6. While idling in **D** for automatic transmissions or neutral for manual transmission, adjust both mixture needles equally, ⅛ turn increments, until dwell reading varies within the 25-35 degree range, attempting to be as close to 30 degrees as possible.

7. If reading is too low, turn mixture needles counterclockwise. If reading is too high, turn mixture needles clockwise. Allow time for dwell reading to stabilize after each adjustment.

➡️**After adjustments are complete, seal the idle mixture needle openings in the throttle body, using silicone sealant, RTV rubber, or equivalent. The sealer is required to discourage unnecessary readjustment of the setting, and to prevent fuel vapor loss in that area.**

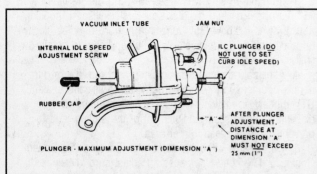

Fig. 45 Idle Load Compensator (ILC) adjustment — 5.0L (VIN Y) Engine

8. On vehicles without a carburetor-mounted Idle Speed Control or Idle Load Compensator, adjust curb idle speed if necessary.

9. Check, and if necessary, adjust fast idle speed, as described on the Vehicle Emission Control Information label.

IDLE LOAD COMPENSATOR (ILC) ADJUSTMENT
▶ See Figure 45

1. Prepare the vehicle for adjustments-see emission label.
2. Connect a tachometer (distributor side of TACH filter, if used).
3. Remove the air cleaner and plug vacuum hose to thermal vacuum valve (TVV).
4. Disconnect and plug the vacuum hose to EGR.
5. Disconnect and plug the vacuum hose to canister purge port.
6. Disconnect and plug the vacuum hose to ILC.
7. Back out the idle stop screw on the carburetor 3 turns.
8. Turn the air conditioning **OFF**.

✳✳CAUTION

Before starting engine, place the transmission in the Park position, set parking brake and block drive wheels.

9. With the engine running (engine warm, choke off), transmission in **D** position and ILC plunger fully extended (no vacuum applied), using tool J-29607, BT-8022, or equivalent, adjust plunger to obtain 650-750 rpm. Locknut on plunger must be held with wrench to prevent damage to guide tabs.

10. Remove plug from vacuum hose, reconnect hose to ILC and observe idle speed. Idle speed should be 425-475 rpm in **D** position.

11. If rpm in Step 10 is correct, proceed to Step 13. No further adjustment of the ILC is necessary.

12. If rpm in Step 10 is not correct:
   a. Stop engine and remove the ILC. Plug vacuum hose to ILC.
   b. With the ILC removed, remove the rubber cap from the center outlet tube and remove the metal plug (if used) from this same tube.
   c. Install ILC on carburetor and re-attach throttle return spring and any other related parts removed during disassembly. Remove plug from vacuum hose and reconnect hose to ILC.
   d. Using a spare rubber cap with hole punched to accept a 0.090 in. (3/32 ″) hex key wrench, install cap on center outlet tube (to seal against vacuum loss) and insert wrench through cap to engage adjusting screw inside tube. Start engine and turn adjusting screw with wrench to obtain 550 rpm in **D** position. Turning the adjusting screw will change the idle speed approximately 75-100 rpm for each complete turn. Turning the screw counterclockwise will increase the engine speed.
   e. Remove wrench and cap (with hole) from center outlet tube and install new rubber cap.
   f. Engine running, transmission in **D** position, observe idle speed. If a final adjustment is required, it will be necessary to repeat Steps 12a through 12e.

13. After adjustment of the ILC plunger, measure distance from the lock nut to tip of the plunger, dimension must not exceed 1 in. (25mm).

14. Disconnect and plug vacuum hose to ILC. Apply vacuum source such as hand vacuum pump J-23768, BT-7517 or equivalent to ILC vacuum inlet tube to fully retract the plunger.

15. Adjust the idle stop on the carburetor float bowl to obtain 500 rpm in **D** position.

16. Place transmission in **P** position and stop engine.

17. Remove plug from vacuum hose and install hose on ILC vacuum inlet tube.

18. Remove plugs and reconnect all vacuum hoses.

19. Install air cleaner and gasket.

20. Remove block from drive wheels.

Differential Vacuum Delay Valve (DVDV) Adjustment

▶ **See Figure 46**

The DVDV is located in the vacuum line between the Idle Load Compensator (ILC) and the vacuum source. It is used on all 5.0L engines (engine code Y).

The DVDV acts as cushioning device by slightly delaying the operation of the ILC until a constant vacuum change has occurred. Without the DVDV the ILC would react too quickly to changes in engine vacuum, causing a stalling or run-on condition.

To check the operation of the DVDV, install a vacuum gauge with a tee between the hose from the DVDV to the ILC. Install a vacuum pump to port 1 of the DVDV and apply 17.8 in. Hg while watching the other vacuum gauge, it should take 6-9 seconds for the vacuum to rise to 16.9 in. Hg Remove the vacuum gauge with tee, install the vacuum pump to port 2 and leave port 1 open. Air should flow through the valve after 0.5 in. Hg is applied.

Fuel Injected Engines

➡ The fuel/air mixture is controlled by the ECM and is non-adjustable.

MINIMUM IDLE SPEED ADJUSTMENT

➡ **This adjustment should be performed only when throttle body parts have been replaced. Engine must be at normal operating temperature before making an adjustment.**

Throttle Body Injection

▶ **See Figure 47**

1. Using a suitable tool, pierce the idle stop screw plug and remove it. Plug any necessary vacuum ports and connect a tachometer to the engine.

2. With the IAC valve connected, ground the diagnostic terminal (ALDL connector).

3. Turn ignition switch to the **ON** position, but do not start the engine. Wait for at least 45 seconds, allowing the IAC valve pintle to fully extend and seat.

4. With the ignition switch still **ON** and test terminal grounded, disconnect Idle Air Control (IAC) electrical connector.

5. Remove the ground from diagnostic lead and start the engine.

6. Adjust the idle speed screw to obtain 400-450 rpm with the transmission in **N**.

7. Turn the ignition OFF and reconnect connector at IAC motor.

8. Adjust the Throttle Position Sensor (TPS) to specifications.

9. Recheck the setting, start the engine and check for proper idle operation.

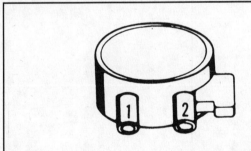

Fig. 46 Differential Vacuum Delay Valve (DVDV) port identification-5.0L engine

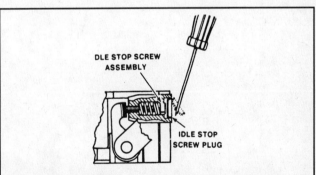

Fig. 47 Throttle stop screw plug removal procedure — TBI Engine

TORQUE SPECIFICATIONS

Component	U.S.	Metric
Spark plugs:	11 ft. lbs.	15 Nm
Distributor hold-down bolt:	27 ft. lbs.	36 Nm

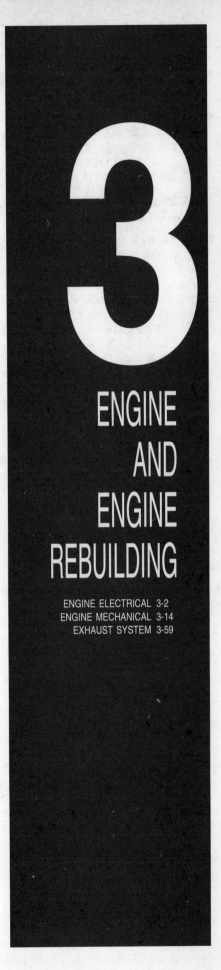

3

ENGINE AND ENGINE REBUILDING

ENGINE ELECTRICAL

The engine electrical system can be broken down into three separate and distinct systems:
1. The starting system.
2. The charging system.
3. The ignition system.

Battery and Starting System

The battery is the first link in the chain of mechanisms which work together to provide cranking of the automobile engine. In most modern cars, the battery is a lead-acid electrochemical device consisting of six two-volt (2 V) subsections connected in series so the unit is capable of producing approximately 12 V of electrical pressure. Each subsection, or cell, consists of a series of positive and negative plates held a short distance apart in a solution of sulfuric acid and water. The two types of plates are of dissimilar metals. This causes a chemical reaction to be set up, and it is this reaction which produces current flow from the battery when its positive and negative terminals are connected to an electrical appliance such as a lamp or motor.

The continued transfer of electrons would eventually convert the sulfuric acid in the electrolyte to water and make the two plates identical in chemical composition. As electrical energy is removed from the battery, its voltage output tends to drop. Thus, measuring battery voltage and battery electrolyte composition are two ways of checking the ability of the unit to supply power. During the starting of the engine, electrical energy is removed from the battery. However, if the charging circuit is in good condition and the operating conditions are normal, the power removed from the battery will be replaced by the generator (or alternator) which will force electrons back through the battery, reversing the normal flow, and restoring the battery to its original chemical state.

The battery and starting motor are linked by very heavy electrical cables designed to minimize resistance to the flow of current. Generally, the major power supply cable that leaves the battery goes directly to the starter, while other electrical system needs are supplied by a smaller cable. During the starter operation, power flows from the battery to the starter and is grounded through the car's frame and the battery's negative ground strap.

The starting motor is a specially designed, direct current electric motor capable of producing a very great amount of power for its size. One thing that allows the motor to produce a great deal of power is its tremendous rotating speed. It drives the engine through a tiny pinion gear (attached to the starter's armature), which drives the very large flywheel ring gear at a greatly reduced speed. Another factor allowing it to produce so much power is that only intermittent operation is required of it. Thus, little allowance for air circulation is required, and the windings can be built into a very small space.

The starter solenoid is a magnetic device which employs the small current supplied by the starting switch circuit of the ignition switch. This magnetic action moves a plunger which mechanically engages the starter and electrically closes the heavy switch which connects it to the battery. The starting switch circuit consists of the starting switch contained within the ignition switch, a transmission neutral safety switch or clutch pedal switch, and the wiring necessary to connect these with the starter solenoid or relay.

A pinion, which is a small gear, is mounted to a one-way drive clutch. This clutch is splinted to the starter armature shaft. When the ignition switch is moved to the **start** position, the solenoid plunger slides the pinion toward the flywheel ring gear via a collar and spring. If the teeth on the pinion and flywheel match properly, the pinion will engage the flywheel immediately. If the gear teeth butt one another, the spring will be compressed and will force the gears to mesh as soon as the starter turns far enough to allow them to do so. As the solenoid plunger reaches the end of its travel, it closes the contacts that connect the battery and starter and then the engine is cranked.

As soon as the engine starts, the flywheel ring gear begins turning fast enough to drive the pinion at an extremely high rate of speed. At this point, the one-way clutch begins allowing the pinion to spin faster than the starter shaft so that the starter will not operate at excessive speed. When the ignition switch is released from the starter position, the solenoid is de-energized, and a spring contained within the solenoid assembly pulls the gear out of mesh and interrupts the current flow to the starter.

Some starters employ a separate relay, mounted away from the starter, to switch the motor and solenoid current on and off. The relay thus replaces the solenoid electrical switch, but does not eliminate the need for a solenoid mounted on the starter used to mechanically engage the starter drive gears. The relay is used to reduce the amount of current the starting switch must carry.

The Charging System

The automobile charging system provides electrical power for operation of the vehicle's ignition and starting systems and all the electrical accessories. The battery serves as an electrical surge or storage tank, storing (in chemical form) the energy originally produced by the engine driven generator. The system also provides a means of regulating alternator output to protect the battery from being overcharged and to avoid excessive voltage to the accessories.

The storage battery is a chemical device incorporating parallel lead plates in a tank containing a sulfuric acid-water solution. Adjacent plates are slightly dissimilar, and the chemical reaction of the two dissimilar plates produces electrical energy when the battery is connected to a load such as the starter motor. The chemical reaction is reversible, so that when the generator is producing a voltage (electrical pressure) greater than that produced by the battery, electricity is forced into the battery, and the battery is returned to its fully charged state.

Alternators are used on the modern automobiles because they are lighter, more efficient, rotate at higher speeds and have fewer brush problems. In an alternator, the field rotates while all the current produced passes only through the stators windings. The brushes bear against continuous slip rings rather than a commutator. This causes the current produced to periodically reverse the direction of its flow. Diodes (electrical one-way switches) block the flow of current from traveling in the wrong direction. A series of diodes is wired together to permit the alternating flow of the stator to be converted to a pulsating, but unidirectional flow at the alternator output. The alternator's field is wired in series with the voltage regulator.

Ignition System

➡**Please refer to Section 2 for all ignition system testing procedures.**

Ignition Coil

REMOVAL AND INSTALLATION

Coil In Cap

1. Disconnect wires from cap.
2. Remove distributor cap from distributor.
3. On the distributor cap, remove coil cover attaching screws and remove cover.
4. Remove ignition coil attaching screws and lift coil with leads from the cap.
5. To install, position the coil into position and secure with attaching screws.
6. Install coil cover and attaching screws.
7. Install distributor cap.
8. Connect the wires to the cap.

Fig. 1 HEI distributor with external coil mounted in front of assembly

Externally Mounted Coil

▶ **See Figure 1**

1. Disconnect wires from coil.
2. Remove ignition coil mounting bolts and remove coil.
3. To install, position coil into place and secure with the mounting bolts.
4. Connect the wires to the coil.

Ignition Module

REMOVAL AND INSTALLATION

1. Disconnect wires from cap.
2. Remove distributor cap from distributor.
3. Remove the two module attaching screws and capacitor attaching screw. Lift module, capacitor and harness assembly from base.
4. Disconnect wiring harness and capacitor assembly.
5. To install, apply silicone lubricant on housing under module.
6. Connect wiring harness and capacitor assembly.
7. Install module and attaching screws.
8. Install the distributor cap and wires.

HEI Distributor

REMOVAL AND INSTALLATION

➡**The distributor will have to be removed from the engine and disassembled if the pick-up coil or distributor shaft need to be replaced.**

1. Disconnect the negative battery cable.
2. Remove the air cleaner assembly.
3. Disconnect the electrical connectors from the side of the distributor.
4. Remove the distributor cover and wire retainer, if equipped. Turn the retaining screws counterclockwise and remove the cap.
5. Mark the relationship of the rotor to the distributor housing and the housing relationship to the engine.
6. Remove the distributor retaining bolt and hold-down clamp.
7. Pull the distributor up until the rotor just stops turning counterclockwise and again note the position of the rotor.
8. Remove the distributor from the engine.
   To install:
9. Insert the distributor into the engine, with the rotor aligned to the last mark made, then slowly install the distributor the rest of the way until all marks previously made are aligned.
10. Install the distributor hold-down clamp and retaining bolt.
11. If removed, install the wiring harness retainer and secondary wires.
12. Install the distributor cap.
13. Reconnect the wire connectors to the side of the distributor. Make certain the connectors are fully seated and latched.

14. Reconnect the negative battery cable.

➡**If the engine was accidentally cranked after the distributor was removed, the following procedure can be used during installation.**

15. Remove the No. 1 spark plug.

16. Place a finger over the spark plug hole and have a helper crank the engine slowly until compression is felt.

17. Align the timing mark on the pulley to **0** on the engine timing indicator.

18. Turn the distributor rotor to point between No. 1 spark plug tower on the distributor cap.

19. Install the distributor assembly in the engine and ensure the rotor is pointing toward the No. 1 spark plug tower.

20. Install the cap and spark plug wires.

21. Check and adjust engine timing.

Alternator

DESCRIPTION

An alternator differs from a DC shunt generator in that the armature is stationary, and is called the stator, while the field rotates and is called the rotor. The higher current values in the alternator's stator are conducted to the external circuit through fixed leads and connections, rather than through a rotating commutator and brushes as in a DC generator. This eliminates a major point of maintenance.

The rotor assembly is supported in the drive end frame by a ball bearing and at the other end by a roller bearing. These bearings are lubricated during assembly and require no maintenance. There are six diodes in the end frame assembly. These diodes are electrical check valves that also change the alternating current developed within the stator windings to a direct (DC) current at the output (BAT) terminal. Three of these diodes are negative and are mounted flush with the end frame while the other three are positive and are mounted into a strip called a heat sink. The positive diodes are easily identified as the ones within small cavities or depressions.

The alternator charging system is a negative (-) ground system which consists of an alternator, a regulator, a charge indicator, a storage battery and wiring connecting the components, and fuse link wire.

The alternator is belt-driven from the engine. Energy is supplied from the alternator/regulator system to the rotating field through two brushes to two slip-rings. The slip-rings are mounted on the rotor shaft and are connected to the field coil. This energy supplied to the rotating field from the battery is called excitation current and is used to initially energize the field to begin the generation of electricity. Once the alternator starts to generate electricity, the excitation current comes from its own output rather than the battery.

The alternator produces power in the form of alternating current. The alternating current is rectified by 6 diodes into direct current. The direct current is used to charge the battery and power the rest of the electrical system.

When the ignition key is turned on, current flows from the battery, through the charging system indicator light on the instrument panel, to the voltage regulator, and to the alternator. Since the alternator is not producing any current,

the alternator warning light comes on. When the engine is started, the alternator begins to produce current and turns the alternator light off. As the alternator turns and produces current, the current is divided in two ways: part to the battery to charge the battery and power the electrical components of the vehicle, and part is returned to the alternator to enable it to increase its output. In this situation, the alternator is receiving current from the battery and from itself. A voltage regulator is wired into the current supply to the alternator to prevent it from receiving too much current which would cause it to put out too much current. Conversely, if the voltage regulator does not allow the alternator to receive enough current, the battery will not be fully charged and will eventually go dead.

The battery is connected to the alternator at all times, whether the ignition key is turned on or not. If the battery were shorted to ground, the alternator would also be shorted. This would damage the alternator. To prevent this, a fuse link is installed in the wiring between the battery and the alternator. If the battery is shorted, the fuse link is melted, protecting the alternator.

An alternator is better than a conventional, DC shunt generator because it is lighter and more compact, because it is designed to supply the battery and accessory circuits through a wide range of engine speeds, and because it eliminates the necessary maintenance of replacing brushes and servicing commutators.

PRECAUTIONS

To prevent serious damage to the alternator and the rest of the charging system, the following precautions must be observed:

• Never reverse the battery connections.

• Booster batteries for starting must be connected properly: positive-to-positive and negative-to-groups.

• Disconnect the battery cables before using a fast charger; the charger has a tendency to force current through the diodes in the opposite direction for which they were designed. This burns out the diodes.

• Never use a fast charger as a booster for starting the vehicle.

• Never disconnect the voltage regulator while the engine is running.

• Avoid long soldering times when replacing diodes or transistors. Prolonged heat is damaging to AC generator.

• Do not use test lamps of more than 12 volts (V) for checking diode continuing.

• Do not short across or ground any of the terminals on the AC generator.

• The polarity of the battery, generator, and regulator must be matched and considered before making any electrical connections within the system.

• Never operate the alternator on an open circuit. make sure that all connections within the circuit are clean and tight.

• Disconnect the battery terminals when performing any service on the electrical system. This will eliminate the possibility of accidental reversal of polarities.

• Disconnect the battery ground cable if arc welding is to be done on any part of the car.

CHARGING SYSTEM TROUBLESHOOTING

There are many possible ways in which the charging system can malfunction. Often the source of a problem is difficult to diagnose, requiring special equipment and a good deal of experience. However, when the charging system fails completely and causes the dash board warning light to come on or the battery to become dead the following items may be checked:

1. The battery is known to be good and fully charged.
2. The alternator belt is in good condition and adjusted to the proper tension.
3. All connections in the system are clean and tight.

REMOVAL AND INSTALLATION

▶ **See Figures 2, 3, 4, 5, 6, 7, 8 and 9**

➡**The model CS-130 alternator may not be disassembled for testing or repairs, otherwise damage to the unit may occur. While internal CS-144 alternator repairs are possible, they require specialized tools and training. Therefore, it is advisable to replace a defective alternator as an assembly, or have it repaired by a qualified shop.**

1. Disconnect the battery ground cable.
2. Tag and disconnect the alternator wiring.
3. Remove the alternator brace bolt. Detach the drive belt(s).
4. Support the alternator and remove the mount bolt(s). Remove the unit from the vehicle.

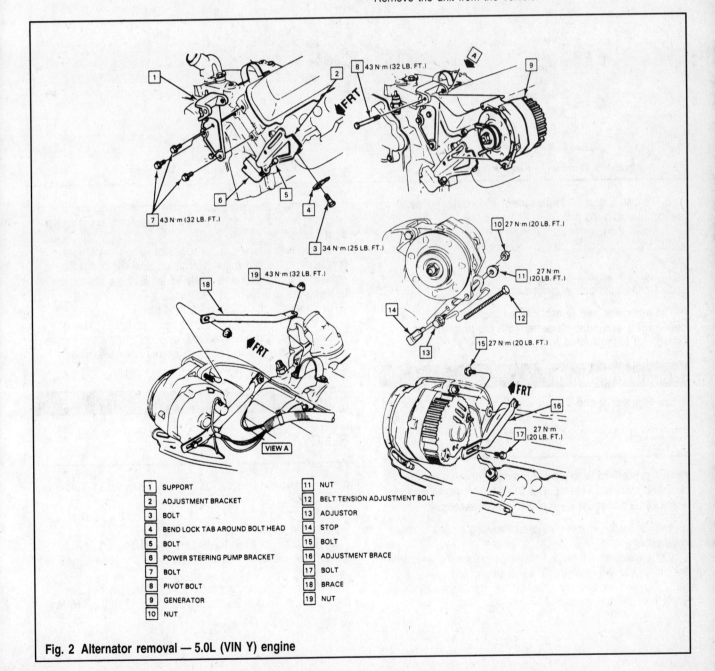

1	SUPPORT	11	NUT	
2	ADJUSTMENT BRACKET	12	BELT TENSION ADJUSTMENT BOLT	
3	BOLT	13	ADJUSTOR	
4	BEND LOCK TAB AROUND BOLT HEAD	14	STOP	
5	BOLT	15	BOLT	
6	POWER STEERING PUMP BRACKET	16	ADJUSTMENT BRACE	
7	BOLT	17	BOLT	
8	PIVOT BOLT	18	BRACE	
9	GENERATOR	19	NUT	
10	NUT			

Fig. 2 Alternator removal — 5.0L (VIN Y) engine

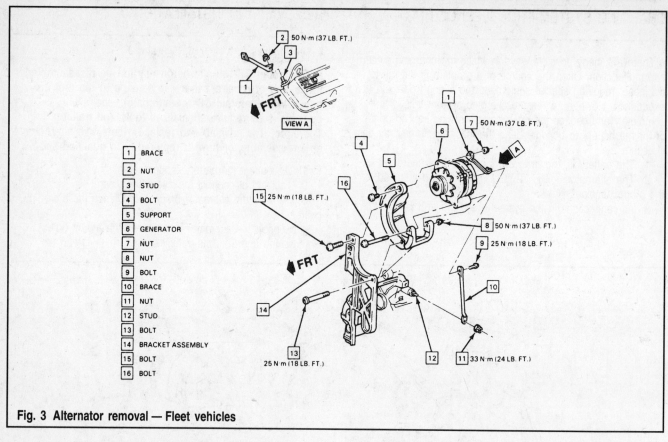

Fig. 3 Alternator removal — Fleet vehicles

1	BRACE
2	NUT
3	STUD
4	BOLT
5	SUPPORT
6	GENERATOR
7	NUT
8	NUT
9	BOLT
10	BRACE
11	NUT
12	STUD
13	BOLT
14	BRACKET ASSEMBLY
15	BOLT
16	BOLT

5. To install, position the alternator into place and install the mount bolt(s) loosely.

6. Install the drive belt(s). Tighten belt enough to allow approximately ½ inch of play on the longest run between pulleys.

7. Connect the alternator wiring.

8. Connect the battery ground cable.

➡ **The alternator belt is properly adjusted when the cooling fins and pulley assembly on the unit are not capable of being turned by hand.**

Voltage Regulator

◗ **See Figures 10 and 11**

REMOVAL AND INSTALLATION

➡ **This procedure is to be performed with the alternator removed from the vehicle. The CS-130 alternators are non-serviceable and must be replaced as an assembly.**

1. Make scribe marks on the end housing frames to make reassembly easier.

2. Remove the 4 through-bolts and separate the end frame assembly from the rectifier end frame assembly.

3. Remove the 3 stator attaching nuts and remove the stator from the end frame.

4. Unsolder the connections, remove the 2 regulator attaching screws and separate the regulator and brush holder from the vehicle.

5. To install, assemble the regulator, brush holder and connector to the end frame. Securely solder the connection between the regulator and brush holder, and the connection between the regulator and brush strap.

6. Assemble the stator to the end frame.

7. Install the halves of the alternator, ensuring the end frames are aligned as previously removed. Secure the halves with the 4 through-bolts. After the alternator is assembled, remove the brush retainer.

Battery

REMOVAL AND INSTALLATION

1. Remove the negative battery cable and then the positive battery cable.

2. Remove the battery retainer screw and the retainer. Remove the battery.

3. To install, position the battery into place.

4. Install the battery retainer and secure it with the retaining screw.

5. Connect the positive battery cable then the negative battery cable. Torque the battery cables to 11 ft. lbs. (15 Nm).

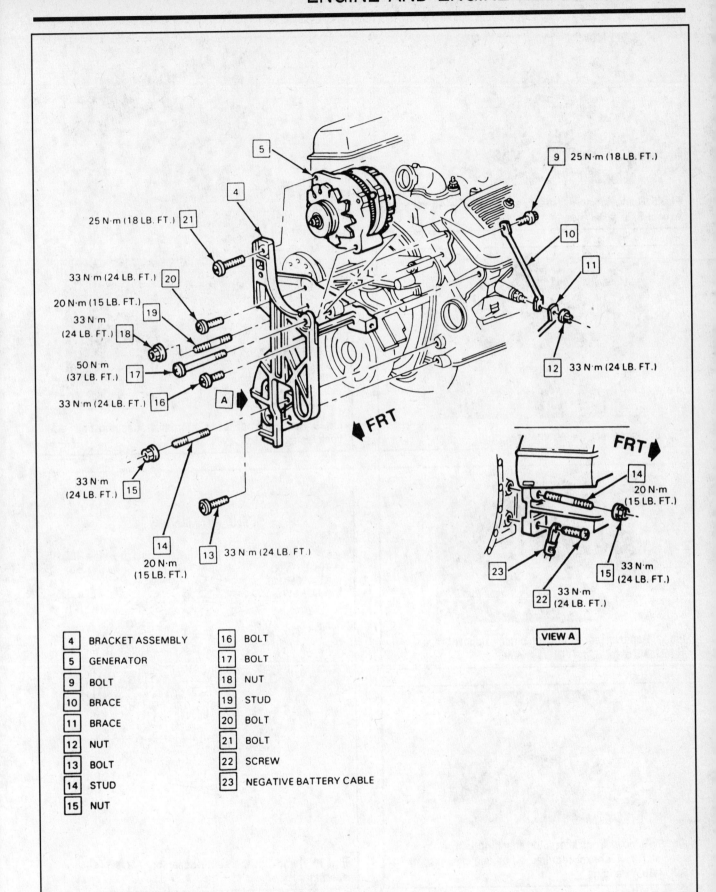

25 N·m (18 LB. FT.) 21

33 N·m (24 LB. FT.) 20

20 N·m (15 LB. FT.) 19

33 N·m (24 LB. FT.) 18

50 N·m (37 LB. FT.) 17

33 N·m (24 LB. FT.) 16

33 N·m (24 LB. FT.) 15

5

4

9 25 N·m (18 LB. FT.)

10

11

12 33 N·m (24 LB. FT.)

A

FRT

14

13 33 N·m (24 LB. FT.)

20 N·m (15 LB. FT.)

FRT

14

20 N·m (15 LB. FT.)

23

22 33 N·m (24 LB. FT.)

15 33 N·m (24 LB. FT.)

VIEW A

4	BRACKET ASSEMBLY	16	BOLT
5	GENERATOR	17	BOLT
9	BOLT	18	NUT
10	BRACE	19	STUD
11	BRACE	20	BOLT
12	NUT	21	BOLT
13	BOLT	22	SCREW
14	STUD	23	NEGATIVE BATTERY CABLE
15	NUT		

Fig. 4 Alternator removal — 4.3L, 5.0L (VIN E) and 5.7L engines

Fig. 5 Removing the serpentine drive belt — All vehicles except 5.0L (VIN Y) engine

Fig. 6 Disconnect the alternator wiring

Fig. 9 Remove front lower alternator attaching bolt — All vehicles except 5.0L (VIN Y) engine

Fig. 7 Remove rear alternator brace support brace — All vehicles except 5.0L (VIN Y) engine

Fig. 8 Remove front alternator attaching bolt; Note special Torx® socket required on all vehicles except 5.0L (VIN Y) engine

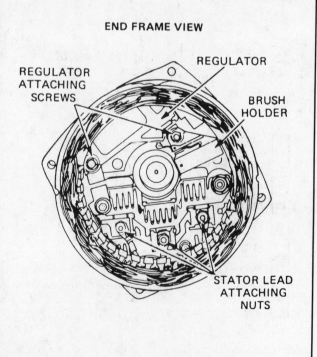

Fig. 10 Removing the stator assembly — CS-144 alternator

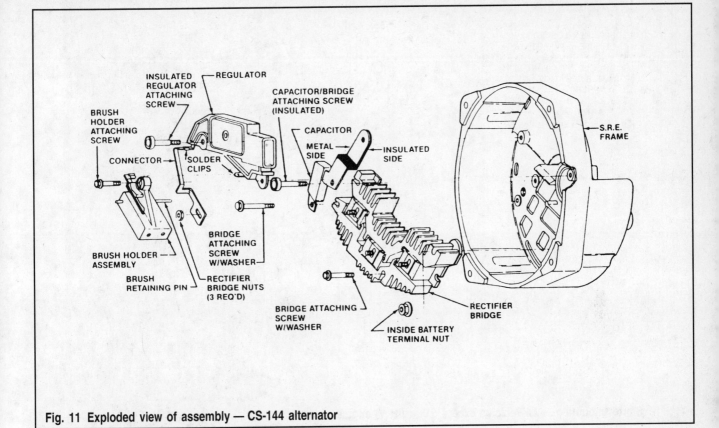

Fig. 11 Exploded view of assembly — CS-144 alternator

Starter

▶ See Figure 12

REMOVAL AND INSTALLATION

1. Disconnect the negative battery cable.
2. Raise and safely support the vehicle.
3. Disconnect all wiring from the starter solenoid. Replace each nut as the connector is removed, as thread sizes differ from connector to connector. Note or tag the wiring positions for installation.
4. Remove the bracket from the starter and the two mounting bolts. On engines with a solenoid heat shield, remove the front bracket upper bolt and detach the bracket from the starter.
5. Remove the front bracket bolt or nut. Lower the starter front end first, and then remove the unit from the car.
6. To install, position the starter into place and secure it with the front bracket bolt and nut. Torque the two mounting bolts to 25-35 ft. lbs. (32-42 Nm).

✳✳CAUTION

If shims were removed, they must be replaced to ensure proper pinion-to-flywheel engagement.

7. On engines with a solenoid heat shield, attach the bracket to the starter. Install the bracket to the starter and the two mounting bolts. Install the front bracket upper bolt.
8. Connect all wiring to the starter solenoid and tighten wire lug nuts.
9. Lower the vehicle.
10. Connect the negative battery cable.

SOLENOID REPLACEMENT

1. Remove the screw and washer from the motor connector strap terminal.
2. Remove the two solenoid retaining screws.
3. Twist the solenoid housing clockwise to remove the flange key from the keyway in the housing. Then remove the housing.
4. To re-install the unit, place the return spring on the plunger and place the solenoid body on the drive housing. Turn counterclockwise to engage the flange key. Place the two retaining screws in position and install the screw and washer which secures the strap terminal. Install the unit on the starter.

Sending Units and Sensors

Refer to Section 4 for all sending unit and sensor testing.

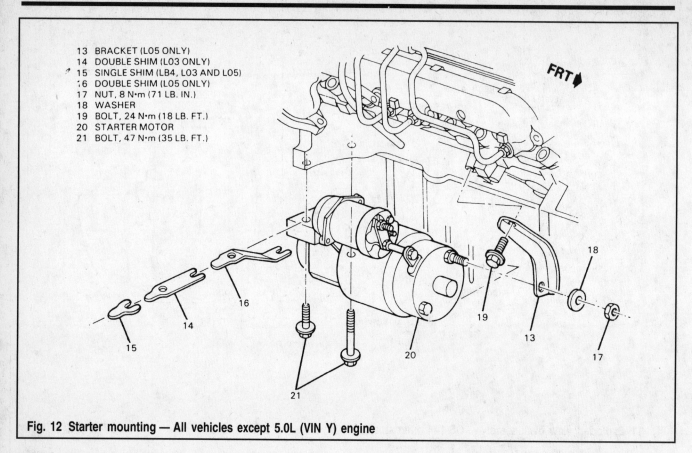

13 BRACKET (L05 ONLY)
14 DOUBLE SHIM (L03 ONLY)
15 SINGLE SHIM (LB4, L03 AND L05)
16 DOUBLE SHIM (L05 ONLY)
17 NUT, 8 N·m (71 LB. IN.)
18 WASHER
19 BOLT, 24 N·m (18 LB. FT.)
20 STARTER MOTOR
21 BOLT, 47 N·m (35 LB. FT.)

FRT

Fig. 12 Starter mounting — All vehicles except 5.0L (VIN Y) engine

REMOVAL AND INSTALLATION

▶ See Figures 13, 14, 15 and 16

Coolant Temperature

Replace the sensor by disconnecting the electrical connector, draining the coolant and then remove the sensor using the appropriate wrench or socket.

Oil Pressure

Replace the sensor by disconnecting the electrical connector and using a special socket, remove the sensor.

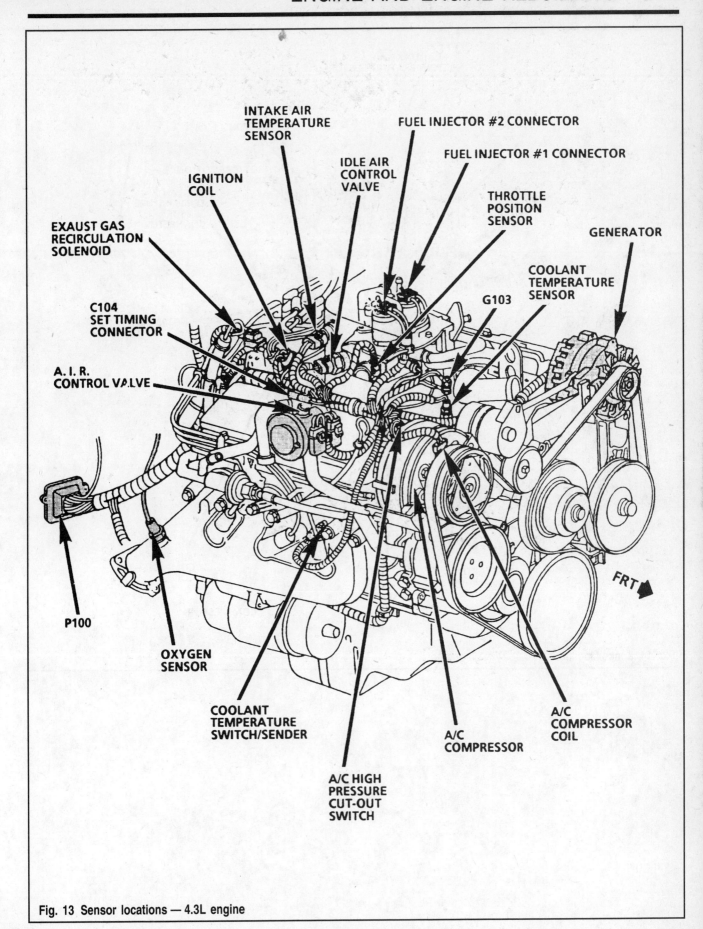

Fig. 13 Sensor locations — 4.3L engine

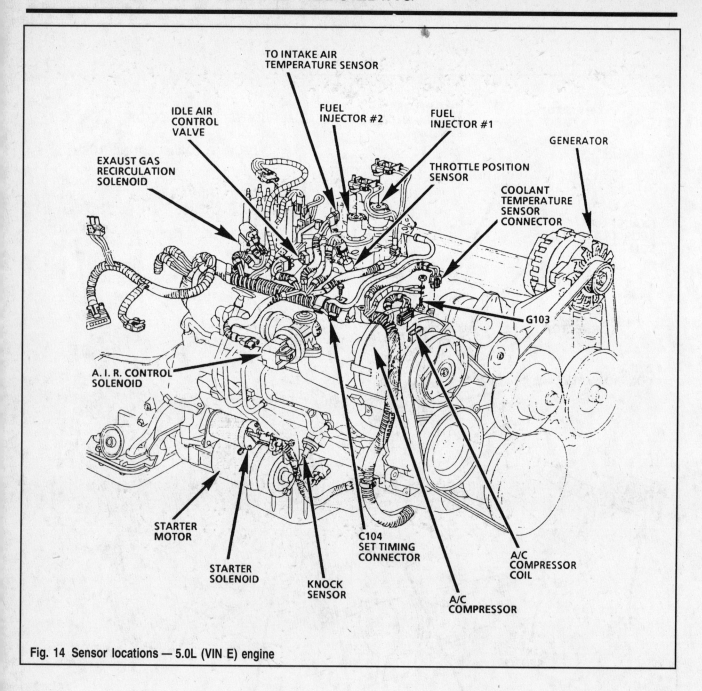

TO INTAKE AIR
TEMPERATURE SENSOR

IDLE AIR
CONTROL
VALVE

FUEL
INJECTOR #2

FUEL
INJECTOR #1

GENERATOR

EXAUST GAS
RECIRCULATION
SOLENOID

THROTTLE POSITION
SENSOR

COOLANT
TEMPERATURE
SENSOR
CONNECTOR

G103

A. I. R. CONTROL
SOLENOID

STARTER
MOTOR

STARTER
SOLENOID

KNOCK
SENSOR

C104
SET TIMING
CONNECTOR

A/C
COMPRESSOR

A/C
COMPRESSOR
COIL

Fig. 14 Sensor locations — 5.0L (VIN E) engine

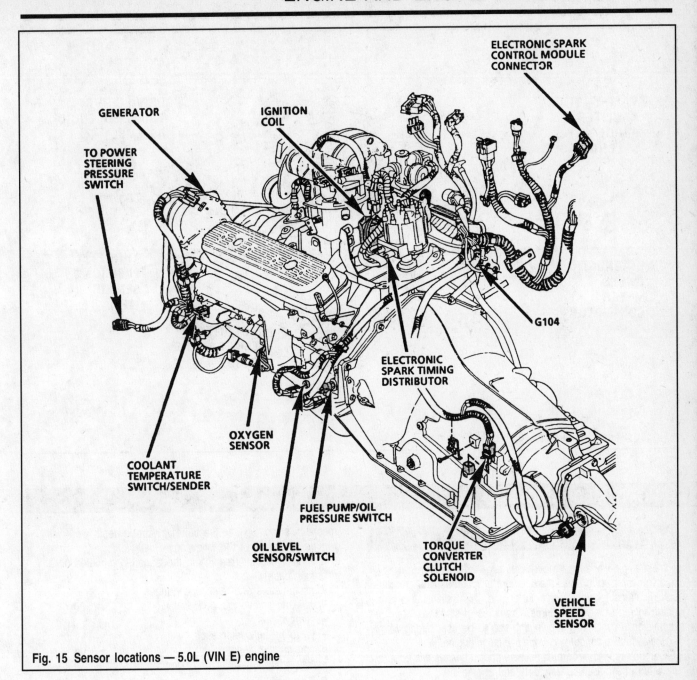

ELECTRONIC SPARK
CONTROL MODULE
CONNECTOR

GENERATOR

IGNITION
COIL

TO POWER
STEERING
PRESSURE
SWITCH

G104

ELECTRONIC
SPARK TIMING
DISTRIBUTOR

OXYGEN
SENSOR

COOLANT
TEMPERATURE
SWITCH/SENDER

FUEL PUMP/OIL
PRESSURE SWITCH

OIL LEVEL
SENSOR/SWITCH

TORQUE
CONVERTER
CLUTCH
SOLENOID

VEHICLE
SPEED
SENSOR

Fig. 15 Sensor locations — 5.0L (VIN E) engine

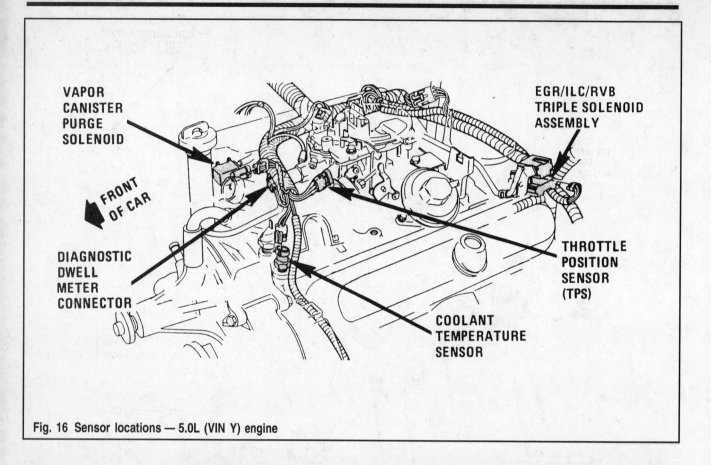

VAPOR CANISTER PURGE SOLENOID

FRONT OF CAR

DIAGNOSTIC DWELL METER CONNECTOR

EGR/ILC/RVB TRIPLE SOLENOID ASSEMBLY

THROTTLE POSITION SENSOR (TPS)

COOLANT TEMPERATURE SENSOR

Fig. 16 Sensor locations — 5.0L (VIN Y) engine

ENGINE MECHANICAL

Engine Overhaul Tips

Most engine overhaul procedures are fairly standard. In addition to specific parts replacement procedures and complete specifications for your individual engine, this Section also is a guide to rebuilding procedures. Examples of standard rebuilding practice are shown and should be used along with specific details concerning your particular engine.

Competent and accurate machine shop services will ensure maximum performance, reliability and engine life.

In most instances it is more profitable for the do-it-yourself mechanic to remove, clean and inspect the component, buy the necessary parts and deliver these to a shop for actual machine work.

On the other hand, much of the rebuilding work (crankshaft, block, bearings, piston rods, and other components) are well within the scope of the do-it-yourself mechanic.

TOOLS

The tools required for an engine overhaul or parts replacement will depend on the depth of your involvement. With a few exceptions, they will be the tools found in a mechanic's tool kit (see Section 1). More in-depth work will require any or all of the following:

- a dial indicator (reading in thousandths) mounted on a universal base
- micrometers and telescope gauges
- jaw and screw-type pullers
- scraper
- valve spring compressor
- ring groove cleaner
- piston ring expander and compressor
- ridge reamer
- cylinder hone or glaze breaker
- Plastigage®
- engine stand

The use of most of these tools is illustrated in this section. Many can be rented for a one-time use from a local parts jobber or tool supply house specializing in automotive work.

Occasionally, the use of special tools is called for. See the information on Special Tools and Safety Notice in the front of this book before substituting another tool.

INSPECTION TECHNIQUES

Procedures and specifications are given in this section for inspecting, cleaning and assessing the wear limits of most major components. Other procedures such as Magnaflux® and Zyglo® can be used to locate material flaws and stress cracks. Magnaflux® is a magnetic process applicable only to ferrous materials. The Zyglo® process coats the material with a fluorescent dye penetrant and can be used on any material to check for suspected surface cracks. Other spray-type dyes are available through parts retailers and can also be used to check for cracks.

OVERHAUL TIPS

Aluminum has become extremely popular for use in engines, due to its low weight. Observe the following precautions when handling aluminum parts:
- Never hot tank aluminum parts (the caustic hot tank solution will eat the aluminum.
- Remove all aluminum parts (identification tag, etc.) from engine parts prior to the tanking.
- Always coat threads lightly with engine oil or anti-seize compounds before re-installation, to prevent seizure.
- Never overtorque bolts or spark plugs especially in aluminum threads.

Stripped threads in any component can be repaired using any of several commercial repair kits (Heli-Coil®, Microdot®, Keenserts®, etc.).

When assembling the engine, any parts that will be experiencing frictional contact must be prelubed to provide lubrication at initial start-up. Any product specifically formulated for this purpose can be used, but engine oil is not recommended as a prelube.

When semi-permanent (locked, but removable) installation of bolts or nuts is desired, threads should be cleaned and coated with Loctite® or other similar, commercial non-hardening sealant.

REPAIRING DAMAGED THREADS

▶ **See Figures 17, 18, 19 and 20**

Several methods of repairing damaged threads are available. Heli-Coil® (shown here), Keenserts® and Microdot® are among the most widely used. All involve basically the same principle, drilling out stripped threads, tapping the hole and installing a prewound insert, making welding, plugging and oversize fasteners unnecessary.

Two types of thread repair inserts are usually supplied: a standard type for most Inch Coarse, Inch Fine, Metric Course and Metric Fine thread sizes and a spark lug type to fit most spark plug port sizes. Consult the individual manufacturer's catalog to determine exact applications. Typical thread repair kits will contain a selection of pre-wound threaded inserts, a tap (corresponding to the outside diameter threads of the insert) and an installation tool. Spark plug inserts usually differ because they require a tap equipped with pilot threads and a combined reamer/tap section. Most manufacturers also supply blister-packed thread repair inserts separately in addition to a master kit containing a variety of taps and inserts plus installation tools.

Prior to proceeding with a repair to a threaded hole, remove any snapped, broken or damaged bolts or studs. Penetrating oil can be used to free frozen threads. The offending item can be removed with locking pliers or with a screw or stud extractor. Often when a bolt is overtightened and snaps it may be removed easily by the drilling 2 small holes right next to each other on the top of the bolt; then use a small screwdriver to remove the broken bolt or stud. After the hole is clear, the threads can be repaired if damaged, as shown in the series of accompanying illustrations.

Checking Engine Compression

▶ **See Figure 21**

A noticeable lack of engine power, excessive oil consumption and/or poor fuel mileage measured over an extended period are all indicators of internal engine war. Worn piston rings, scored or worn cylinder bores, blown head gaskets, sticking or burnt valves and worn valve seats are all possible culprits here. A check of each cylinder's compression will help you locate the problems.

As mentioned in the Tools and Equipment section of Section 1, a screw-in type compression gauge is more accurate then the type you simply hold against the spark plug hole, although it takes slightly longer to use. It's worth it to obtain a more accurate reading. Follow the procedures below.

1. Warm up the engine to normal operating temperature.
2. Remove all the spark plugs.
3. Disconnect the high tension lead from the ignition coil.
4. Fully open the throttle, either by operating the carburetor throttle linkage by hand or by having an assistant hold the accelerator pedal to the floor.
5. Screw the compression gauge into the No. 1 spark plug hole until the fitting is snug.

✳✳WARNING

Be careful not to crossthread the plug hole.

6. Ask an assistant to depress the accelerator pedal fully on both carbureted and fuel injected vehicles. Then, while you read the compression gauge, ask the assistant to crank the engine 4 to 6 revolutions using the ignition switch. Repeat the test two or three times until a consistent reading is obtained.

7. Read the compression gauge at the end of each series of cranks, and record the highest of these readings. Repeat this procedure for each of the engine's cylinders. The lowest reading recorded should not be less than 70% of the highest reading and no cylinder should be less than 100 psi.

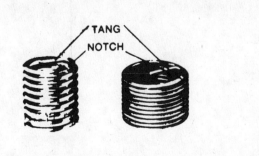

Fig. 17 Using the thread repair kit to fix a damaged hole

Fig. 18 Using the specified drill to remove the damaged threads and prepare the hole for the specified tap. Drill completely through the hole or the bottom of a blind hole

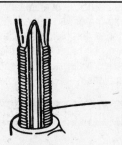

Fig. 19 Using the tap supplied with the kit, tap the hole to receive the new thread insert. Keep the tap sufficiently oiled and back it out frequently to avoid clogging it

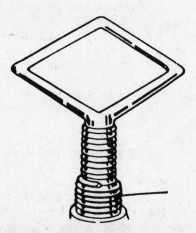

FIG. 12 Screw the threaded insert onto the tool until the tang engages the slot. Screw the insert into the hole until it is $\frac{1}{4}$ to a $\frac{1}{2}$ turn below the top of the hole. After installation break off the tang with a hammer and punch

Fig. 20 Screw the threaded insert onto the tool until the tang engages the slot. Screw the insert into the hole until it is $\frac{1}{4}$ to a $\frac{1}{2}$ turn below the top of the hole. After installation break off the tang with a hammer and punch

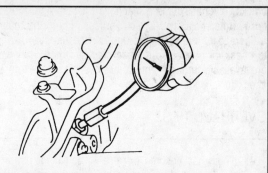

Fig. 21 Screw-in type compression gauge is more accurate

For example, if the highest reading obtained was 150 psi. then the lowest acceptable cylinder reading would be 105 psi. (150 x .70 = 105). The difference between any two cylinders should be no more than 12-14 pounds.

8. If a cylinder is unusually low, pour a tablespoon of clean engine oil into the cylinder through the spark plug hole and repeat the compression test. If the compression comes up after adding the oil, it appears that the cylinder's piston rings or bore are damaged or worn. If the pressure remains low, the valves may not be seating properly (a valve job is needed), or the head gasket may be blown near that cylinder. If compression in any two adjacent cylinders is low, and if the addition of oil doesn't help the compression, there is leakage past the head gasket. Oil and coolant water in the combustion chamber can result from this problem. There may be evidence of water droplets on the engine dipstick when a head gasket has blown.

GENERAL ENGINE SPECIFICATIONS

Year	Engine ID/VIN	Engine Displacement Liters (cc)	Fuel System Type	Net Horsepower @ rpm	Net Torque @ rpm (ft. lbs.)	Bore × Stroke (in.)	Compression Ratio	Oil Pressure @ rpm
1990	Z	4.3 (4300)	TBI	140 @ 4000	225 @ 2000	4.000 × 3.480	9.3:1	18 @ 2000
	E	5.0 (5011)	TBI	170 @ 4400	255 @ 2400	3.740 × 3.480	9.3:1	18 @ 2000
	Y	5.0 (5011)	Carb	140 @ 3200	255 @ 2000	3.800 × 3.385	8.0:1	18 @ 2000
	7	5.7 (5733)	TBI	195 @ 4200	295 @ 2400	4.000 × 3.480	9.8:1	18 @ 2000
1991	Z	4.3 (4300)	TBI	140 @ 4000	225 @ 2000	4.000 × 3.480	9.3:1	18 @ 2000
	E	5.0 (5011)	TBI	170 @ 4200	255 @ 2400	3.740 × 3.480	9.3:1	18 @ 2000
	7	5.7 (5733)	TBI	195 @ 4200	295 @ 2400	4.000 × 3.480	9.8:1	18 @ 2000
1992	Z	4.3 (4300)	TBI	140 @ 4000	225 @ 2000	4.000 × 3.480	9.3:1	18 @ 2000
	E	5.0 (5011)	TBI	170 @ 4200	255 @ 2400	3.740 × 3.480	9.3:1	18 @ 2000
	7	5.7 (5733)	TBI	195 @ 4200	295 @ 2400	4.000 × 3.480	9.8:1	18 @ 2000
1993	Z	4.3 (4300)	TBI	140 @ 4000	225 @ 2000	4.000 × 3.480	9.3:1	18 @ 2000
	E	5.0 (5011)	TBI	170 @ 4200	255 @ 2400	3.740 × 3.480	9.3:1	18 @ 2000
	7	5.7 (5733)	TBI	195 @ 4200	295 @ 2400	4.000 × 3.480	9.8:1	18 @ 2000

NOTE: Horsepower and torque are SAE net figures. They are measured at the rear of the transmission with all accessories installed and operating. Since the figures vary when a given engine is installed in different models, some are representative rather than exact.
Carb—Carbureted
TBI—Throttle Body Injection
① Minimum

VALVE SPECIFICATIONS

Year	Engine ID/VIN	Engine Displacement Liters (cc)	Seat Angle (deg.)	Face Angle (deg.)	Spring Test Pressure (lbs. @ in.)	Spring Installed Height (in.)	Stem-to-Guide Clearance (in.)		Stem Diameter (in.)	
							Intake	Exhaust	Intake	Exhaust
1990	Z	4.3 (4300)	46	45	194–206 @ 1.25	1.70	0.0011–0.0027	0.0011–0.0027	NA	NA
	E	5.0 (5011)	①	②	180–194 @ 1.27	③	0.0010–0.0027	0.0015–0.0032	0.3425–0.3432	0.3420–0.3427
	Y	5.0 (5011)	46	45	194–206 @ 1.25	1.70	0.0011–0.0027	0.0011–0.0027	NA	NA
	7	5.7 (5733)	46	45	194–206 @ 1.25	1.70	0.0011–0.0027	0.0011–0.0027	NA	NA
1991	Z	4.3 (4300)	46	45	194–206 @ 1.25	1.70	0.0011–0.0027	0.0011–0.0027	NA	NA
	E	5.0 (5011)	46	45	194–206 @ 1.25	1.70	0.0011–0.0027	0.0011–0.0027	NA	NA
	7	5.7 (5733)	46	45	194–206 @ 1.25	1.70	0.0011–0.0027	0.0011–0.0027	NA	NA
1992	Z	4.3 (4300)	46	45	194–206 @ 1.25	1.70	0.0011–0.0027	0.0011–0.0027	NA	NA
	E	5.0 (5011)	46	45	194–206 @ 1.25	1.70	0.0011–0.0027	0.0011–0.0027	NA	NA
	7	5.7 (5733)	46	45	194–206 @ 1.25	1.70	0.0011–0.0027	0.0011–0.0027	NA	NA
1993	Z	4.3 (4300)	46	45	194–206 @ 1.25	1.70	0.0011–0.0027	0.0011–0.0027	NA	NA
	E	5.0 (5011)	46	45	194–206 @ 1.25	1.70	0.0011–0.0027	0.0011–0.0027	NA	NA
	7	5.7 (5733)	46	45	194–206 @ 1.25	1.70	0.0011–0.0027	0.0011–0.0027	NA	NA

① Intake: 45
  Exhaust: 31
② Intake: 44
  Exhaust: 30
③ Use valve stem height gauge tool BT-6428 or
  J-25289

CAMSHAFT SPECIFICATIONS

All measurements given in inches.

Year	Engine ID/VIN	Engine Displacement Liters (cc)	Journal Diameter					Lobe Lift		Bearing Clearance (in.)	Camshaft Endplay (in.)
			1	2	3	4	5	Intake	Exhaust		
1990	Z	4.3 (4300)	1.8682–1.8692	1.8682–1.8692	1.8682–1.8692	1.8682–1.8692	1.8682–1.8692	0.234	0.257	NA	0.0040–0.0120
	E	5.0 (5011)	1.8682–1.8692	1.8682–1.8692	1.8682–1.8692	1.8682–1.8692	1.8682–1.8692	0.234	0.257	NA	0.0040–0.0120
	Y	5.0 (5011)	2.0362	2.0360	1.9959	1.9759	1.9559	0.247	0.251	0.0038	0.0050–0.0220
	7	5.7 (5733)	1.8682–1.8692	1.8682–1.8692	1.8682–1.8692	1.8682–1.8692	1.8682–1.8692	0.257	0.269	NA	0.0040–0.0120
1991	Z	4.3 (4300)	1.8682–1.8692	1.8682–1.8692	1.8682–1.8692	1.8682–1.8692	1.8682–1.8692	0.234	0.257	NA	0.0040–0.0120
	E	5.0 (5011)	1.8682–1.8692	1.8682–1.8692	1.8682–1.8692	1.8682–1.8692	1.8682–1.8692	0.234	0.257	NA	0.0040–0.0120
	7	5.7 (5733)	1.8682–1.8692	1.8682–1.8692	1.8682–1.8692	1.8682–1.8692	1.8682–1.8692	0.257	0.269	NA	0.0040–0.0120
1992	Z	4.3 (4300)	1.8682–1.8692	1.8682–1.8692	1.8682–1.8692	1.8682–1.8692	1.8682–1.8692	0.234	0.257	NA	0.0040–0.0120
	E	5.0 (5011)	1.8682–1.8692	1.8682–1.8692	1.8682–1.8692	1.8682–1.8692	1.8682–1.8692	0.234	0.257	NA	0.0040–0.0120
	7	5.7 (5733)	1.8682–1.8692	1.8682–1.8692	1.8682–1.8692	1.8682–1.8692	1.8682–1.8692	0.257	0.269	NA	0.0040–0.0120
1993	Z	4.3 (4300)	1.8682–1.8692	1.8682–1.8692	1.8682–1.8692	1.8682–1.8692	1.8682–1.8692	0.234	0.257	NA	0.0040–0.0120
	E	5.0 (5011)	1.8682–1.8692	1.8682–1.8692	1.8682–1.8692	1.8682–1.8692	1.8682–1.8692	0.234	0.257	NA	0.0040–0.0120
	7	5.7 (5733)	1.8682–1.8692	1.8682–1.8692	1.8682–1.8692	1.8682–1.8692	1.8682–1.8692	①	②	NA	0.0040–0.0120

NA—Not available

① Police: 0.257 in.
  Non-Police: 0.233 in.
② Police: 0.269 in.
  Non-Police: 0.256 in.

CRANKSHAFT AND CONNECTING ROD SPECIFICATIONS

All measurements are given in inches.

Year	Engine ID/VIN	Engine Displacement Liters (cc)	Crankshaft Main Brg. Journal Dia.	Crankshaft Main Brg. Oil Clearance	Crankshaft Shaft End-play	Crankshaft Thrust on No.	Connecting Rod Journal Diameter	Connecting Rod Oil Clearance	Connecting Rod Side Clearance
1990	Z	4.3 (4300)	2.4481–2.4490 ①	0.0011–0.0020 ②	0.001–0.007	4	2.2487–2.2498	0.0013–0.0035	0.006–0.014
	E	5.0 (5011)	2.4481–2.4490 ①	0.0011–0.0020 ②	0.001–0.007	5	2.0893–2.0998	0.0013–0.0035	0.006–0.014
	Y	5.0 (5011)	2.4481–2.4490 ①	0.0011–0.0020 ②	0.001–0.007	5	2.0893–2.0998	0.0013–0.0035	0.006–0.014
	7	5.7 (5733)	2.4481–2.4490 ①	0.0011–0.0020 ②	0.001–0.007	5	2.0893–2.0998	0.0013–0.0035	0.006–0.014
1991	Z	4.3 (4300)	2.4481–2.4490 ①	0.0011–0.0020 ②	0.001–0.007	4	2.2487–2.2498	0.0013–0.0035	0.006–0.014
	E	5.0 (5011)	2.4481–2.4490 ①	0.0011–0.0020 ②	0.001–0.007	5	2.0893–2.0998	0.0013–0.0035	0.006–0.014
	7	5.7 (5733)	2.4481–2.4490 ①	0.0011–0.0020 ②	0.001–0.007	5	2.0893–2.0998	0.0013–0.0035	0.006–0.014
1992	Z	4.3 (4300)	2.4485–2.4494 ①	0.0011–0.0023 ②	0.002–0.007	4	2.2487–2.2498	0.0013–0.0035	0.006–0.014
	E	5.0 (5011)	2.4481–2.4490 ①	0.0011–0.0020 ②	0.001–0.007	5	2.0893–2.0998	0.0013–0.0035	0.006–0.014
	7	5.7 (5733)	2.4481–2.4490 ①	0.0011–0.0020 ②	0.001–0.007	5	2.0893–2.0998	0.0013–0.0035	0.006–0.014
1993	Z	4.3 (4300)	2.4485–2.4494 ①	0.0011–0.0023 ②	0.002–0.007	4	2.2487–2.2498	0.0013–0.0035	0.006–0.014
	E	5.0 (5011)	2.4481–2.4490 ①	0.0011–0.0020 ②	0.001–0.007	5	2.0893–2.0998	0.0013–0.0035	0.006–0.014
	7	5.7 (5733)	2.4481–2.4490 ①	0.0011–0.0020 ②	0.001–0.007	5	2.0893–2.0998	0.0013–0.0035	0.006–0.014

① Journal No. 1: 2.4488–2.4493
Journal No. 5: 2.4480–2.4489
② Journal No. 1: 0.0008–0.0020
Journal No. 5: 0.0017–0.0032

PISTON AND RING SPECIFICATIONS
All measurements are given in inches.

Year	Engine ID/VIN	Engine Displacement Liters (cc)	Piston Clearance	Ring Gap			Ring Side Clearance		
				Top Compression	Bottom Compression	Oil Control	Top Compression	Bottom Compression	Oil Control
1990	Z	4.3 (4300)	0.0007–0.0021	0.010–0.020	0.010–0.025	0.015–0.055	0.0012–0.0032	0.0012–0.0032	0.0020–0.0070
	E	5.0 (5011)	0.0007–0.0021	0.010–0.020	0.010–0.025	0.015–0.055	0.0012–0.0032	0.0012–0.0032	0.0020–0.0070
	Y	5.0 (5011)	0.0008–0.0018	0.009–0.019	0.009–0.019	0.015–0.055	0.0018–0.0038	0.0018–0.0038	0.0010–0.0050
	7	5.7 (5733)	0.0007–0.0021	0.010–0.020	0.010–0.025	0.015–0.055	0.0012–0.0032	0.0012–0.0032	0.0020–0.0070
1991	Z	4.3 (4300)	0.0007–0.0021	0.010–0.020	0.010–0.025	0.015–0.055	0.0012–0.0032	0.0012–0.0032	0.0020–0.0070
	E	5.0 (5011)	0.0007–0.0021	0.010–0.020	0.010–0.025	0.015–0.055	0.0012–0.0032	0.0012–0.0032	0.0020–0.0070
	7	5.7 (5733)	0.0007–0.0021	0.010–0.020	0.010–0.025	0.015–0.055	0.0012–0.0032	0.0012–0.0032	0.0020–0.0070
1992	Z	4.3 (4300)	0.0007–0.0017	0.010–0.020	0.017–0.025	0.015–0.055	0.0014–0.0032	0.0014–0.0032	0.0014–0.0032
	E	5.0 (5011)	0.0007–0.0021	0.010–0.020	0.018–0.026	0.015–0.055	0.0012–0.0032	0.0012–0.0032	0.0020–0.0070
	7	5.7 (5733)	0.0005–0.0022	0.010–0.020	0.018–0.026	0.015–0.055	0.0012–0.0032	0.0012–0.0032	0.0020–0.0070
1993	Z	4.3 (4300)	0.0005–0.0022	0.010–0.020	0.018–0.026	0.015–0.055	0.0012–0.0032	0.0012–0.0032	0.0020–0.0070
	E	5.0 (5011)	0.0005–0.0022	0.010–0.020	0.018–0.026	0.015–0.055	0.0012–0.0032	0.0012–0.0032	0.0020–0.0070
	7	5.7 (5733)	0.0005–0.0022	0.010–0.020	0.018–0.026	0.015–0.055	0.0012–0.0032	0.0012–0.0032	0.0020–0.0070

TORQUE SPECIFICATIONS
All readings in ft. lbs.

Year	Engine ID/VIN	Engine Displacement Liters (cc)	Cylinder Head Bolts	Main Bearing Bolts	Rod Bearing Bolts	Crankshaft Damper Bolts	Flywheel Bolts	Manifold		Spark Plugs	Lug Nut
								Intake	Exhaust		
1990	Z	4.3 (4300)	65	65	44	70	74	35	②	22	①
	E	5.0 (5011)	68	77	44	70	74	35	②	22	①
	Y	5.0 (5011)	③	④	⑤	200–310	60	40	25	25	①
	7	5.7 (5733)	68	77	44	70	74	35	②	22	①
1991	Z	4.3 (4300)	65	65	44	70	74	35	②	22	①
	E	5.0 (5011)	68	77	44	70	74	35	②	22	①
	7	5.7 (5733)	68	77	44	70	74	35	②	22	①
1992	Z	4.3 (4300)	65	65	44	70	74	35	②	11	100
	E	5.0 (5011)	68	77	44	70	74	35	②	11	100
	7	5.7 (5733)	68	77	44	70	74	35	②	11	100
1993	Z	4.3 (4300)	65	65	44	70	74	35	②	11	100
	E	5.0 (5011)	68	77	44	70	74	35	②	11	100
	7	5.7 (5733)	68	77	44	70	74	35	②	11	100

① Sedan: 81
Wagon and Police: 103
② Nuts: 26
Studs: 20
③ 1st step: 40 ft. lbs.
2nd step: (positions 1 thru 7 & 9) rotate
120 degree turn
3rd step: (positions 8 & 10) rotate
95 degree turn
④ Except No. 5: 80 ft. lbs.
No. 5: 210 ft. lbs.
⑤ 1st step: 18 ft. lbs.
2nd step: rotate 70 degree turn

Engine

REMOVAL AND INSTALLATION

▶ **See Figure 22**

In the process of removing the engine you will come across a number of steps which call for the removal of a separate component or system, i.e. Disconnect the exhaust system or Remove the radiator. In all of these instances, a detailed removal procedure can be found elsewhere in this section.

It is virtually impossible to list each individual wire and hose which must be disconnected, simply because so many different model and engine combinations have been manufactured. Careful observation and common sense are the best possible additions to any repair procedure. Be absolutely sure to tag any wire or hose before disconnecting it, so that it may be reconnected properly during installation. If at all possible, remove the component, leaving the wires or hoses connected and place the component on top of the engine assembly. This will help make reassembly easier and less confusing.

✳✳CAUTION

The EPA warns that prolonged contact with used engine oil may cause a number of skin disorders, including cancer! You should make every effort to minimize your exposure to used engine oil. Protective gloves should be worn when changing the oil. Wash your hands and any other exposed skin areas as soon as possible after exposure to used engine oil. Soap and water, or waterless hand cleaner should be used.

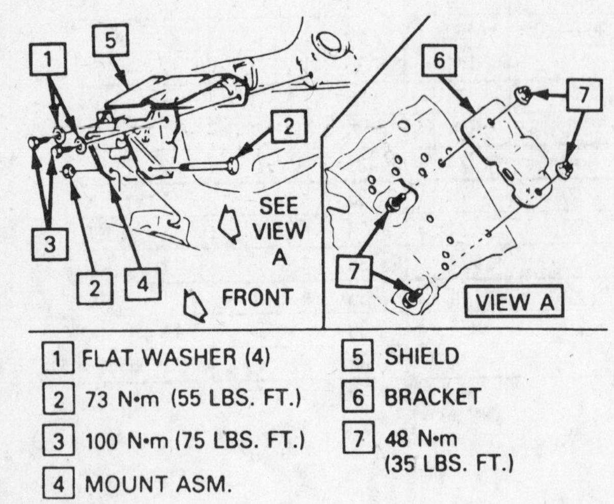

4.3L ENGINE

1. Relieve the fuel system pressure and disconnect the negative battery cable.
2. Remove the hood from hinges and mark for reassembly.
3. Drain coolant into a suitable container.
4. Raise and safely support vehicle.
5. Disconnect the exhaust crossover pipe at the exhaust manifolds.
6. Remove the flywheel housing cover.
7. Remove the flexplate to torque converter attaching bolts. Scribe chalk mark on the flywheel and converter for reassembly alignment.
8. Disconnect transmission oil cooler lines at the oil pan.
9. Remove right side motor mount through-bolt and loosen left side motor mount through-bolt.
10. Remove transmission to engine attaching bolts.
11. Disconnect wires at the knock sensor.
12. Disconnect the front fuel hoses from front fuel pipes.
13. Remove the lower fan shroud bolts
14. Lower the vehicle.
15. Disconnect the ECM wiring harness at the engine, and other wiring harnesses as necessary.
16. Remove the air cleaner assembly.
17. Remove the upper fan shroud.
18. Disconnect the vacuum supply hoses which supply all non-engine mounted components with engine vacuum. If equipped, the vacuum modulator, load leveler and power brake vacuum hoses should all be disconnected at the engine.
19. Disconnect accelerator and TV cables.
20. Disconnect radiator and heater hoses from engine.
21. Remove the radiator.
22. If equipped with air conditioning, disconnect compressor ground wire from the mounting bracket. Remove the electrical connector from the compressor clutch, remove the compressor to mounting bracket attaching bolts and position the compressor aside.
23. Remove power steering pump to mounting bracket bolts and position pump assembly aside.
24. Disconnect the positive battery cable and wires from the starter motor.
25. Disconnect engine to body ground strap(s) at engine.
26. Remove the AIR hose at the Catalytic converter AIR pipe and the pipe from the exhaust manifold.
27. Remove fan blade, pulleys and, if not removed already, belt(s).
28. Support the transmission.
29. Attach a safe lifting device to the engine and raise the engine enough so the remaining mounting through-bolt can be removed. Ensure the wiring harness, vacuum hoses and other parts are free and clear before lifting engine out of the vehicle.
30. Raise engine far enough to clear engine mounts, raise transmission support accordingly and alternately until engine can be disengaged from the transmission and removed.

To install:
31. With the engine and transmission safely supported, lower engine into position and align with the transmission.
32. Install the motor mount through-bolts.

1. FLAT WASHER (4)
2. 73 N•m (55 LBS. FT.)
3. 100 N•m (75 LBS. FT.)
4. MOUNT ASM.
5. SHIELD
6. BRACKET
7. 48 N•m (35 LBS. FT.)

Fig. 22 Engine mounts — 5.0L (VIN Y) engine. Only engine-to-mount through bolt removal is necessary for engine removal

33. Install the fan blade and pulley assembly.

34. Connect the AIR hose to the catalytic converter AIR pipe and the pipe to the exhaust manifold.

35. Connect the engine ground strap(s) to the engine.

36. Connect the positive battery cable and wires to the starter motor.

37. Attach the power steering pump to mounting bracket bolts.

38. If equipped with air conditioning, connect the compressor and mounting bracket. Connect the compressor ground wire to the mounting bracket and the electrical connector to the compressor clutch.

39. Reconnect belts or serpentine belt.

40. Install radiator and connect radiator and heater hoses.

41. Connect accelerator and TV cables.

42. Reconnect vacuum hoses.

43. Install upper fan shroud.

44. Connect the air cleaner assembly.

45. Reconnect the ECM wiring harness and other engine electrical connectors.

46. Safely raise and support the vehicle.

47. Install the lower fan shroud and bolts.

48. Connect front fuel hoses to fuel pipes.

49. Connect wires to knock sensors.

50. Install the transmission to engine attaching bolts and tighten to 35 ft. lbs. (47 Nm).

51. Connect the transmission oil cooler lines to the pan.

52. Align the flexplate to torque converter chalk marks and install the attaching bolts. Install the flywheel cover.

53. Connect the exhaust crossover pipe to the exhaust manifolds.

54. Lower vehicle. Fill cooling system and check all engine fluids

55. Align hood hinges to marks and install hood.

56. Tighten fuel filler cap and connect the negative battery cable.

57. Check the fluid levels, engine specifications and inspect for leaks and proper operation.

5.0L (VIN Y) ENGINE

1. Disconnect the negative battery cable.

2. Remove the hood from hinges and mark for reassembly.

3. Drain coolant into a suitable container.

4. Remove the air cleaner assembly and hot air pipe.

5. Remove the radiator hoses and upper fan shroud.

6. Remove the radiator.

7. Remove the engine cooling fan.

8. Disconnect the heater hoses at the engine.

9. Disconnect the power steering pump, air conditioning compressor and brackets, and position out of the way leaving the hoses attached.

10. Disconnect the accelerator, TV, and cruise control cables.

11. Disconnect all necessary vacuum hoses and the fuel hose from the fuel line.

12. Disconnect the ECM wiring harness, the engine wiring harness at the engine bulkhead, engine to bulkhead ground straps and all other wires between body and engine.

13. Set the engine on TDC and remove the distributor.

14. Remove the battery ground-to-cylinder head cable.

15. Raise and support the vehicle safely.

16. Disconnect the battery positive cable and wires at the starter motor.

17. Disconnect the crossover pipe at the manifolds.

18. Remove the flywheel cover and mark the relationship of the torque converter to the flywheel, remove the torque converter bolts.

19. Remove the engine mount through-bolts.

20. Disconnect the front fuel hoses from the front fuel pipes.

21. Disconnect the transmission converter clutch wiring at the transmission and the transmission oil cooler lines at the clip on the oil pan.

22. Disconnect the catalytic converter AIR pipe at the exhaust manifold.

23. Remove the transmission to engine bolts.

24. Lower the vehicle.

25. Support the transmission and connect a suitable lifting device to the engine.

26. Remove the engine.

To install:

27. With the engine safely supported, lower into position with the lifting device and align with the motor mounts and transmission.

28. Install motor mount through-bolts and the transmission to engine bolts. Tighten the transmission to engine bolts to 35 ft. lbs. (47 Nm).

29. Raise and support the vehicle safely.

30. Connect the catalytic converter AIR pipe to the exhaust manifold.

31. Connect the transmission converter clutch wiring to the transmission and the transmission oil cooler lines to the clip on the oil pan.

32. Connect the front fuel hoses to the front fuel pipes.

33. Install the torque converter to flywheel bolts and the flywheel housing cover.

34. Connect the crossover pipe to the exhaust manifolds.

35. Connect the battery positive cable and wires to the starter motor.

36. Lower vehicle.

37. Connect the battery ground to cylinder head cable.

38. Set the engine on TDC and install the distributor.

39. Connect the ECM wiring harness, the engine wiring harness at the engine bulkhead, engine to bulkhead ground straps and all other wires between body and engine.

40. Connect all necessary vacuum hoses.

41. Connect the accelerator, TV and cruise control cables.

42. Connect the power steering pump and air conditioning compressor brackets, if equipped.

43. Connect the heater hoses to the engine.

44. Install the engine cooling fan.

45. Install the radiator, hoses and fan shroud.

46. Install the air cleaner assembly.

47. Install the hood, aligning the marks made during removal.

48. Connect the negative battery cable.

49. Fill the cooling system to the proper level.

50. Inspect vehicle fluid levels, specifications and verify there are no fluid leaks.

5.0L (VIN E) AND 5.7L ENGINES

1. Relieve the fuel system pressure and disconnect the negative battery cable.

2. Remove the hood from hinges and mark for reassembly.

3. Drain coolant into a suitable container.

4. Remove the air cleaner assembly.

5. Remove the radiator hoses and upper fan shroud.

6. Remove the radiator.

7. Remove the engine cooling fan.

8. Disconnect the heater hoses at the engine

9. Disconnect the power steering pump and air conditioning compressor brackets, if equipped, and position out of the way.

10. Disconnect the accelerator, TV, and cruise control cables.

11. Disconnect all necessary vacuum hoses.

12. Disconnect the ECM wiring harness, the engine wiring harness at the engine bulkhead, engine to bulkhead ground straps and all other wires between body and engine.

13. Set the engine on TDC and remove the distributor.

14. Remove the wiper motor, MAP sensor and battery negative to cylinder head cable.

15. Raise and support the vehicle safely.

16. Disconnect the battery positive cable and wires at the starter motor.

17. Disconnect the crossover pipe and catalytic converter as an assembly.

18. Remove the flywheel cover and torque converter to flywheel bolts.

19. Remove the engine mount through-bolts.

20. Disconnect the front fuel hoses from the front fuel pipes.

21. Disconnect the transmission converter clutch wiring at the transmission and the transmission oil cooler lines at the clip on the oil pan.

22. Disconnect the catalytic converter AIR pipe at the exhaust manifold.

23. Remove the transmission to engine bolts.

24. Lower the vehicle.

25. Support the transmission and connect a suitable lifting device to the engine.

26. Remove the engine.

To install:

27. With the engine safely supported, lower into position with the lifting device and align with the motor mounts and transmission.

28. Install motor mount through-bolts and the transmission to engine bolts. Tighten the transmission to engine bolts to 35 ft. lbs. (47 Nm).

29. Raise and support the vehicle safely.

30. Connect the catalytic converter AIR pipe to the exhaust manifold.

31. Connect the transmission converter clutch wiring to the transmission and the transmission oil cooler lines to the clip on the oil pan.

32. Connect the front fuel hoses to the front fuel pipes.

33. Install the torque converter to flywheel bolts and the flywheel housing cover.

34. Connect the crossover pipe and catalytic converter assembly.

35. Connect the battery positive cable and wires to the starter motor.

36. Lower vehicle.

37. Install the wiper motor, MAP sensor and the negative battery to cylinder head cable.

38. Set the engine on TDC and install the distributor.

39. Connect the ECM wiring harness, the engine wiring harness at the engine bulkhead, engine to bulkhead ground straps and all other wires between body and engine.

40. Connect all necessary vacuum hoses.

41. Connect the accelerator, TV and cruise control cables.

42. Connect the power steering pump and air conditioning compressor brackets, if equipped.

43. Connect the heater hoses to the engine.

44. Install the engine cooling fan.

45. Install the radiator, hoses and fan shroud.

46. Install the air cleaner assembly.

47. Install the hood, aligning the marks made during removal.

48. Connect the negative battery cable.

49. Fill the cooling system to the proper level.

50. Inspect vehicle fluid levels, specifications and verify there are no fluid leaks.

Rocker Arm (Valve) Cover

▶ See Figures 23 and 24

REMOVAL AND INSTALLATION

4.3L ENGINE

Right Side

1. Disconnect the negative battery cable. Remove the air cleaner.

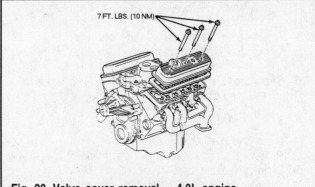

Fig. 23 Valve cover removal — 4.3L engine

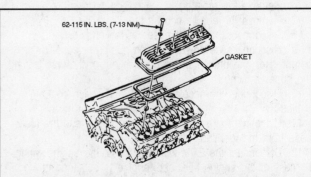

Fig. 24 Valve cover removal — 5.0L (VIN E) and 5.7L engines

2. At the engine, disconnect the heater hoses from the evaporator case and bracket.

3. At the intake manifold, disconnect the heater hose and the wiring harness bracket. Remove the rocker arm cover bolts and the breather pipe.

4. Disconnect and plug the fuel lines. Disconnect the clips and the spark plug wires at the distributor.

5. Remove the rocker arm cover retaining bolts. Remove the rocker arm cover.

To install:

6. Thoroughly clean old gasket from valve cover and cylinder head.

7. Install a new gasket onto the valve cover.

8. Install the rocker arm cover. Install the rocker arm cover retaining bolts. Torque the bolts to 97 inch lbs. (11 Nm).

9. Connect the fuel lines. Connect the clips and the spark plug wires at the distributor.

10. Connect the heater hose and the wiring harness bracket at the manifold. Install the breather pipe.

11. At the engine, connect the heater hoses to the evaporator case and bracket.

12. Connect the negative battery cable. Install the air cleaner.

13. Inspect for leaks.

Left Side

1. Disconnect the negative battery cable and remove the air cleaner.

2. At the rocker arm cover, disconnect the PCV valve.

3. Remove the AIR hose at the manifold and spark plug wire clips.

4. Disconnect the alternator wire harness.

5. Remove the rocker arm cover bolts and the cover.

To install:

6. Thoroughly clean old gasket from valve cover and cylinder head.

7. Install a new gasket onto the valve cover.

8. Install the rocker arm cover. Install the rocker arm cover retaining bolts. Torque the bolts to 97 inch lbs. (11 Nm).

9. Connect the alternator wire harness.

10. At the rocker arm cover, connect the PCV valve.

11. Install the AIR hose at the manifold and spark plug wire clips.

12. Connect the negative battery cable and Install the air cleaner.

5.0L (VIN E) AND 5.7L ENGINES

Right Side

1. Disconnect the negative battery cable. Remove the air cleaner.

2. Disconnect the ECM wire harness from the intake manifold and the oxygen sensor, as necessary.

3. At the exhaust manifold, disconnect the AIR valve and hose.

4. Disconnect the wires from the alternator and the spark plugs, then the harness from the rocker cover, position it to the side.

5. Remove the EGR valve. Remove the rocker arm cover bolts and the cover.

To install:

6. Thoroughly clean old gasket from valve cover and cylinder head.

7. Install a new gasket onto the valve cover.

8. Install the rocker arm cover. Install the rocker arm cover retaining bolts. Torque the bolts to 97 inch lbs. (11 Nm).

9. Install the EGR valve and spark plug wires.

10. Connect the wires to the alternator, then the position the harness onto the rocker cover.

11. At the exhaust manifold, connect the AIR valve and hose.

12. Connect the ECM wire harness to the intake manifold and the oxygen sensor.

13. Connect the negative battery cable. Install the air cleaner.

Left Side

1. Disconnect the negative battery cable. Remove the air cleaner.

2. Disconnect the power brake pipe from the manifold and the booster.

3. Disconnect the AIR hose from the exhaust manifold. Remove the PCV valve.

4. Disconnect the wire from the oxygen sensor. Disconnect the fuel lines from the TBI unit.

5. Remove the A/C evaporator hose, as required.

6. Remove the rocker arm cover bolts and the cover.

To install:

7. Thoroughly clean old gasket from valve cover and cylinder head.

8. Install a new gasket onto the valve cover.

9. Install the rocker arm cover. Install the rocker arm cover retaining bolts. Torque the bolts to 97 inch lbs. (11 Nm).

10. Install the A/C evaporator hose, if removed.

11. Connect the wire to the oxygen sensor. Connect the fuel lines from the TBI unit.

12. Connect the AIR hose to the exhaust manifold. Install the PCV valve.

13. Connect the power brake pipe to the intake manifold and the brake booster.

14. Connect the negative battery cable. Install the air cleaner.

5.0L (VIN Y) ENGINE

RIGHT SIDE

1. Disconnect the negative battery cable. Remove the air cleaner.

2. Disconnect the spark plug wires. Remove the air conditioning compressor bracket, as required.

3. Disconnect the required electrical wires and vacuum hoses. Remove the PCV valve and hose.

4. Remove the canister purge hose.

5. Remove the AIR pump pulley, belt, hoses and valve.

6. Remove the valve cover retaining bolts. Remove the valve cover.

To install:

7. Thoroughly clean old gasket from valve cover and cylinder head.

8. Install a new gasket onto the valve cover.

9. Install the rocker arm cover. Install the rocker arm cover retaining bolts. Torque the bolts to 97 inch lbs. (11 Nm).

10. Install the AIR pump pulley, belt, hoses and valve.

11. Install the canister purge hose.

12. Disconnect the required electrical wires and vacuum hoses. Install the PCV valve and hose.

13. Connect the spark plug wires. Install the air conditioning compressor bracket, if removed.

14. Connect the negative battery cable. Install the air cleaner.

LEFT SIDE

1. Disconnect the negative battery cable. Remove the air cleaner.

2. Disconnect the spark plug wires. Remove the EGR valve assembly to gain clearance.

3. Disconnect the required electrical wires. Loosen the exhaust manifold upper shroud assembly.

4. Remove the ILC anti-dieseling solenoid.

5. Remove the alternator drive belt and rear bracket.

6. Remove the oil level indicator.

7. Remove the valve cover retaining bolts. Remove the valve cover.

To install:

8. Thoroughly clean old gasket from valve cover and cylinder head.

9. Install a new gasket onto the valve cover.

10. Install the rocker arm cover. Install the rocker arm cover retaining bolts. Torque the bolts to 97 inch lbs. (11 Nm).

11. Install the oil level indicator.

12. Install the alternator drive belt and rear bracket.

13. Install the ILC anti-dieseling solenoid.

14. Connect all previously disconnected electrical wires. Tighten the exhaust manifold upper shroud assembly.

15. Connect the spark plug wires. Install the EGR valve assembly.

16. Connect the negative battery cable. Install the air cleaner.

Rocker Arms

REMOVAL AND INSTALLATION

EXCEPT 5.0L (VIN Y) ENGINE
▶ See Figures 25 and 26

Rocker arms are removed by removing the adjusting nut. Be sure to keep all the components in the exact order of removal so they may be installed in there original location; adjust the valve lash after replacing the rocker arms. Coat the replacement rocker arm and ball with engine oil before installation.

Rocker arms studs that have damaged threads or are loose in the cylinder heads may be replaced by reaming the bore and installing oversize studs. Oversized available are 0.003″ and 0.013″. The bore may also be tapped and screw-in studs installed. Several aftermarket companies produce complete rocker arm stud kits with installation tools.

5.0L (VIN Y) ENGINE
▶ See Figure 27

1. Disconnect the negative battery cable. Remove the valve cover.

2. Remove the retaining bolts from a set of rocker arm assemblies.

3. Remove the rocker arms, bolts and the rocker arm pivots from their mounting.

4. Installation is the reverse of the removal procedure.

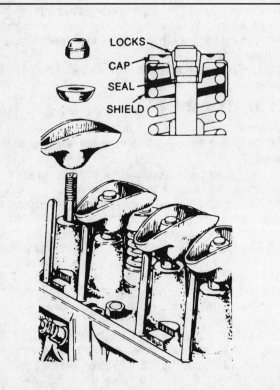

Fig. 25 Rocker arm components — except 5.0L (VIN Y) engine

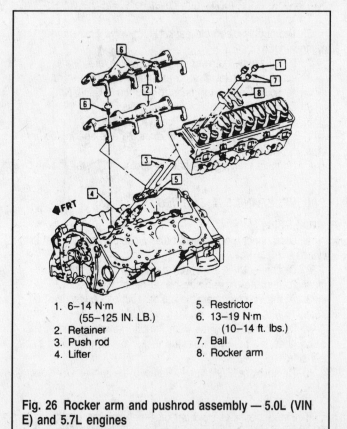

1. 6–14 N·m (55–125 IN. LB.)
2. Retainer
3. Push rod
4. Lifter
5. Restrictor
6. 13–19 N·m (10–14 ft. lbs.)
7. Ball
8. Rocker arm

Fig. 26 Rocker arm and pushrod assembly — 5.0L (VIN E) and 5.7L engines

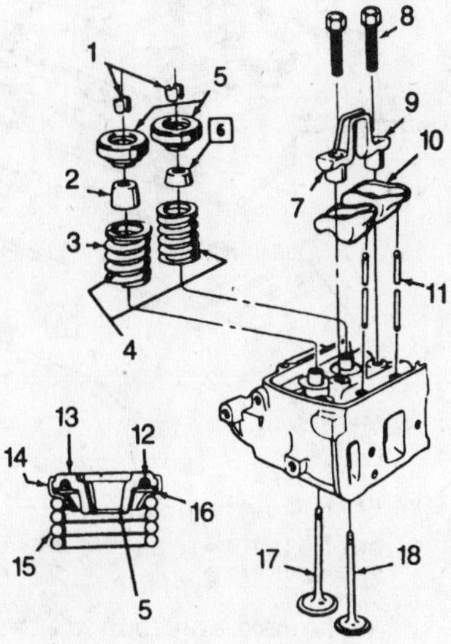

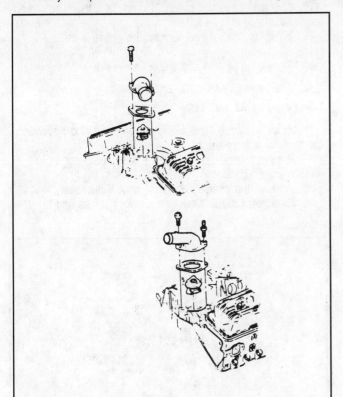

1. Valve keys
2. Intake valve seal
3. Spring
4. Dampener rotator
5. Valve rotator
6. Exhaust valve seal
7. Identification pad
8. 22 ft. lbs.
9. Rocker arm pivot
10. Rocker arms
11. Pushrods
12. Coil spring
13. Body
14. Collar
15. Valve spring
16. Flat washer
17. Intake valve
18. Exhaust valve

Fig. 27 Rocker arm assembly — 5.0L (VIN Y) engine

5. Inspect the rocker pivots for wear and replace as necessary. Torque the rocker arm bolts to 22 ft. lbs. (30 Nm).

Fig. 28 Thermostat servicing — 5.0L (VIN E) and 5.7L engines

Thermostat

▶ See Figures 28 and 29

REMOVAL AND INSTALLATION

1. Drain the cooling system to below the thermostat level.

✳✳CAUTION

When draining the coolant, keep in mind that cats and dogs are attracted by the ethylene glycol antifreeze, and are quite likely to drink any that is left in an uncovered container or in puddles on the ground. This will prove fatal in sufficient quantity. Always drain the coolant into a sealable container. Coolant should be reused unless it is contaminated or several years old.

2. Disconnect the upper radiator hose from the thermostat housing. Loosen the clamp on the coolant by-pass hose, on the 5.0L (VIN Y) engine only.
3. Remove the two retaining bolts or studs from the thermostat housing and remove the thermostat.
4. Use a new gasket when replacing the thermostat.
5. Fill and bleed the cooling system.

Intake Manifold

REMOVAL AND INSTALLATION

➡When servicing all vehicles, be absolutely sure to mark vacuum hoses and wiring so that these items may be properly reconnected during installation. Also, when disconnecting fitting lines (fuel lines, power brake vacuum lines, transmission and engine cooler lines, etc.), always use two flare nut (or line) wrenches. Hold the wrench on the large fitting with pressure on the wrench as if you were tightening the fitting (clockwise), THEN loosen and disconnect the smaller fitting from the larger fitting. If this is not done, damage to the line will result.

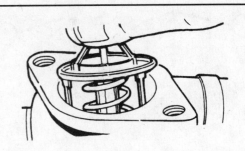

Fig. 29 Removing the thermostat from the intake manifold

5.0L (VIN Y) ENGINE

▶ See Figures 30 and 31

1. Disconnect the negative battery cable and drain the radiator.
2. Remove the air cleaner.
3. Disconnect hoses and pipes; upper radiator, thermostat by-pass at water pump, heater at rear of manifold, fuel, vacuum (label each hose) and AIR.
4. Disconnect the throttle and TV cables.
5. Remove generator rear brace and air conditioning rear brace.
6. Disconnect all necessary electrical leads.
7. Disconnect rear vacuum brake/idle load compensator/exhaust gas recirculation solenoid assembly and idle load compensator and bracket assembly.
8. Disconnect EGR valve.
9. Remove intake manifold bolts and manifold.

To install:

10. Clean mating surfaces and discard old gaskets.
11. Apply 1050026 sealer or equivalent, to both sides of the manifold gasket. Then apply 1052915 or equivalent RTV sealer, to the front and rear seals.
12. Place gaskets on cylinder heads and seals to block.
13. Position intake manifold, taking care not to dislodge gaskets.
14. Lubricate bolts with engine oil, and torque in proper sequence. First tighten all bolts to 15 ft. lbs. (20 Nm), then tighten to 40 ft. lbs. (54 Nm).
15. Connect EGR valve and tighten bolts to 20 ft. lbs. (27 Nm).
16. Connect electrical leads.

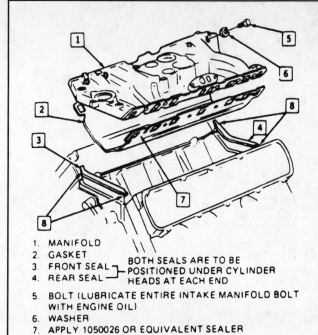

1. MANIFOLD
2. GASKET
3. FRONT SEAL ⎤ BOTH SEALS ARE TO BE
4. REAR SEAL ⎦ POSITIONED UNDER CYLINDER HEADS AT EACH END
5. BOLT (LUBRICATE ENTIRE INTAKE MANIFOLD BOLT WITH ENGINE OIL)
6. WASHER
7. APPLY 1050026 OR EQUIVALENT SEALER TO BOTH SIDES OF THE INTAKE MANIFOLD GASKET AT ALL THE PORT AREAS.
8. APPLY 1052915, GE 1673 OR EQUIVALENT SEALER TO BOTH ENDS OF INTAKE MANIFOLD SEALS.

Fig. 31 Intake manifold installation — 5.0L (VIN Y) engine

17. Connect air conditioning and generator braces.
18. Connect throttle and TV cables.
19. Connect hoses and pipes; AIR, vacuum, fuel, heater and upper radiator.
20. Install air cleaner and connect the negative battery cable.
21. Fill cooling system and inspect for leaks.

4.3L, 5.0L (VIN E) AND 5.7L ENGINES

▶ See Figures 32 and 33

1. Properly relieve the fuel system pressure and disconnect the negative battery cable.
2. Drain the engine coolant into a suitable container and remove the air cleaner.
3. Remove the throttle body assembly, if necessary.
4. Disconnect the ECM engine control harness and lay it aside.

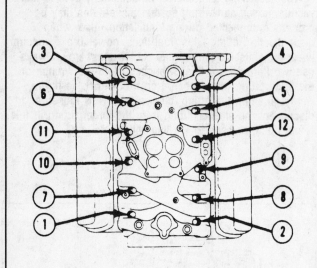

1. LUBRICATE ENTIRE BOLT IN ENGINE OIL
2. TIGHTEN ALL BOLTS IN SEQUENCE SHOWN TO 20 N·m (15 LBS. FT.)
3. RETIGHTEN IN SEQUENCE SHOWN TO 54 N·m (40 LBS. FT.)

Fig. 30 Intake manifold bolt torque sequence — 5.0L (VIN Y) engine

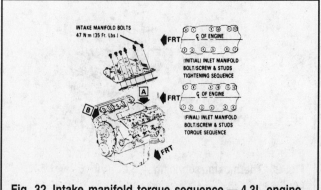

INTAKE MANIFOLD BOLTS 47 N·m (35 Ft. Lbs.)

(INITIAL) INLET MANIFOLD BOLT/SCREW & STUDS TIGHTENING SEQUENCE

(FINAL) INLET MANIFOLD BOLT/SCREW & STUDS TORQUE SEQUENCE

Fig. 32 Intake manifold torque sequence — 4.3L engine

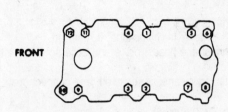

Fig. 33 Intake manifold torque sequence — 5.0L (VIN E) and 5.7L engine

5. Disconnect the upper radiator hose at thermostat housing and heater hose at the manifold.

6. Remove thermostat housing and gasket, if necessary.

7. Disconnect all necessary electrical connections.

8. Disconnect fuel pipe clips at AIR pump bracket and intake manifold.

9. Disconnect accelerator and TV cables.

10. Remove the spark plug wires at the distributor cap. Mark 1 wire and location to assist in reinstallation.

11. Remove the EGR valve and EGR solenoid valve, as applicable.

12. Remove the distributor cap and mark the position of the rotor, then remove the distributor. Remove the coil and bracket as required.

13. Remove the accessory mounting brackets, as required.

14. Remove the coolant temperature sensor.

15. Remove the manifold bolts, studs and remove the intake manifold. Remove and discard the intake manifold gaskets.

To install:

16. Thoroughly clean the intake manifold and cylinder block surfaces to remove any trace of gasket material or sealant.

17. Place gasket and seals on cylinder heads and block, apply a thin bead of RTV sealer 1052289 or equivalent, to the front and rear of cylinder block. Extend the RTV bead ½ inch up each cylinder head to seal and retain gasket.

18. Install the intake manifold, manifold retaining bolts and studs taking care not to dislodge the gaskets and seals. Tighten bolts and studs in proper sequence, first to 10 ft. lbs. (14 Nm) and then to 35 ft. lbs. (47 Nm).

19. Install coolant temperature sensor.

20. Attach accessory mounting brackets, if removed. Tighten compressor brace to manifold nut to 18 ft. lbs. (24 Nm), compressor brace to compressor nut to 24 ft. lbs. (32 Nm) and/or generator to brace nut to 37 ft. lbs. (50 Nm)

21. Install distributor, align rotor with mark and attach cap. Attach coil and bracket if removed.

22. Install the EGR valve and EGR solenoid valve, as applicable.

23. Attach the spark plug wires to the distributor cap in proper firing order.

24. Connect the accelerator and TV cables.

25. Connect fuel pipe clips to AIR pump bracket and intake manifold.

26. Connect all necessary electrical connections.

27. Install the thermostat housing and gasket, if removed. Connect the upper radiator hose to the thermostat housing and heater hose at the manifold.

28. Connect the ECM engine control harness.

29. Install the throttle body assembly, if removed.

30. Install the air cleaner and connect the negative battery cable.

31. Replace fuel filler cap and add engine coolant.

32. Start the engine and inspect for leaks. Adjust timing if necessary.

Exhaust Manifold

▶ See Figures 34, 35 and 36

REMOVAL & INSTALLATION

1. Disconnect the negative battery cable.

2. Raise and support vehicle safely.

3. Disconnect crossover pipe at the exhaust manifold.

4. Lower the vehicle.

5. Tag and remove spark plug wires and, if necessary, remove air cleaner.

6. Disconnect hoses, pipes, and accessory brackets, as required.

7. Remove oil level indicator and tube, if necessary and/or oxygen sensor electrical connection, if equipped.

8. Remove exhaust manifold bolts, studs, locks and washers.

9. Remove the exhaust manifold and gasket.

To install:

10. Clean mating surfaces on manifold and cylinder head.

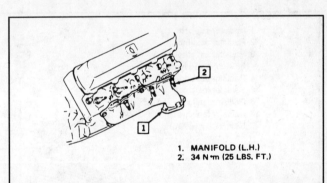

1. MANIFOLD (L.H.)
2. 34 N·m (25 LBS. FT.)

Fig. 34 Left side exhaust manifold removal — 5.0L (VIN Y) engine

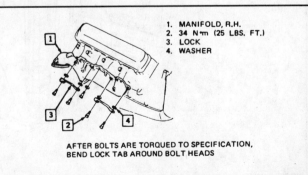

1. MANIFOLD, R.H.
2. 34 N·m (25 LBS. FT.)
3. LOCK
4. WASHER

AFTER BOLTS ARE TORQUED TO SPECIFICATION, BEND LOCK TAB AROUND BOLT HEADS

Fig. 35 Right side exhaust manifold removal — 5.0L (VIN Y) engine

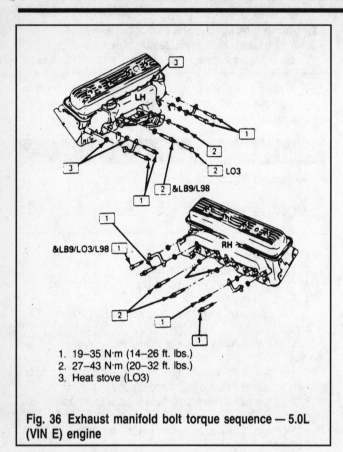

1. 19–35 N·m (14–26 ft. lbs.)
2. 27–43 N·m (20–32 ft. lbs.)
3. Heat stove (LO3)

Fig. 36 Exhaust manifold bolt torque sequence — 5.0L (VIN E) engine

11. Place exhaust manifold and gasket into position on cylinder head.

12. Install shields, washers, locks, studs and bolts. Tighten bolts to 25-26 ft. lbs. (34-35 Nm) and studs to 20 ft. lbs. (27 Nm).

13. Connect oxygen sensor electrical connector, if equipped and install oil level indicator tube, if removed.

14. Connect any hoses, pipes and accessory brackets which were removed.

15. Install air cleaner, if removed, and connect spark plug wires.

16. Raise and support vehicle safely.

17. Connect crossover pipe to the exhaust manifold and tighten nuts to 15 ft. lbs. (20 Nm).

18. Lower vehicle and connect the negative battery cable.

19. Start engine and check for leaks.

Radiator

▶ See Figure 37

REMOVAL AND INSTALLATION

✳✳CAUTION

When draining the coolant, keep in mind that cats and dogs are attracted by the ethylene glycol antifreeze, and are quite likely to drink any that is left in an uncovered container or in puddles on the ground. This will prove fatal in sufficient quantity. Always drain the coolant into a sealable container. Coolant should be reused unless it is contaminated or several years old.

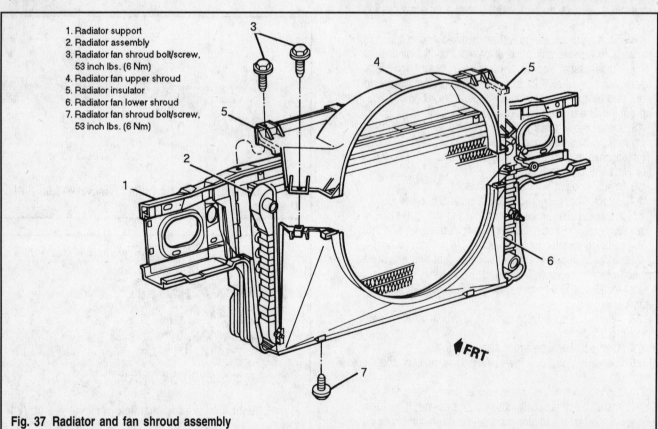

1. Radiator support
2. Radiator assembly
3. Radiator fan shroud bolt/screw, 53 inch lbs. (6 Nm)
4. Radiator fan upper shroud
5. Radiator insulator
6. Radiator fan lower shroud
7. Radiator fan shroud bolt/screw, 53 inch lbs. (6 Nm)

Fig. 37 Radiator and fan shroud assembly

1. Disconnect the negative battery cable.
2. Drain the radiator and remove the fan shrouds.
3. Disconnect the radiator inlet and outlet hoses.
4. Disconnect and plug the transmission fluid and/or oil cooler lines from the radiator.
5. Disconnect the low fluid sensor connector, if equipped.
6. Disconnect the coolant reservoir hose from the radiator.
7. Disconnect the heater hose, if applicable, and remove the radiator from the vehicle.

To install:

8. Position radiator in place making sure the radiator is seated on the insulators.
9. Connect the coolant recovery hose to the filler neck.
10. Connect the transmission fluid lines to the radiator and tighten to 18 ft. lbs. (24 Nm).
11. Connect the engine oil cooler lines to the radiator, if equipped, and tighten to 18 ft. lbs. (24 Nm).
12. Connect the radiator inlet and outlet hoses and clamps to the radiator.
13. Connect the heater hose and clamp to the radiator.
14. If equipped, connect the low coolant sensor.
15. Connect the upper and lower fan shrouds.
16. Connect the negative battery cable, add coolant and check system for leaks.

Engine Oil Cooler

The engine oil cooler consists of an adapter bolted to the engine block which the oil filter is screwed onto. The adapter has 2 hoses which attach to the oil cooler mounted in front of the radiator support on police and taxi use or connected internally to the left radiator tank, these hoses are the inlet and return lines.

REMOVAL AND INSTALLATION

1. Disconnect the negative battery cable. Drain the cooling system into a suitable container.

✳✳CAUTION

When draining the coolant, keep in mind that cats and dogs are attracted by the ethylene glycol antifreeze, and are quite likely to drink any that is left in an uncovered container or in puddles on the ground. This will prove fatal in sufficient quantity. Always drain the coolant into a sealable container. Coolant should be reused unless it is contaminated or several years old.

2. On all vehicles except police and taxi, Remove the radiator, if the oil cooler is to be repaired or replaced, otherwise remove the engine oil cooler from the front of the radiator as necessary.
3. Remove the oil filter.
4. Remove the hoses from the oil cooler adapter.
5. Unscrew the oil cooler adapter retainer and remove the assembly. Discard the gasket.

6. Installation is the reverse of the removal procedure. Use new gaskets.

Clutch Fan

▶ See Figure 38

REMOVAL AND INSTALLATION

1. Disconnect the negative battery cable.
2. Remove the upper fan shroud.
3. Remove nuts and fan clutch with cooling fan.
4. Remove spacer if equipped, and if necessary remove bolts connecting cooling fan and clutch.

➡Keep the fan in an upright position during repairs to prevent the silicone fluid from leaking out.

To install:

✳✳WARNING

Inspect fan blade for bends or damage. Do not use or attempt to repair a fan blade which has been bent or damaged. It is essential that a fan blade remains in balance to prevent failure and possible injury.

5. Attach cooling fan to the fan clutch, if removed, with bolts. Tighten bolts to 18 ft. lbs. (24 Nm).
6. Place spacer, if equipped, and attach fan assembly to the cooling pump. Be sure to align reference marks on the fan clutch and coolant pump hub.
7. Tighten nuts to 18 ft. lbs. (24 Nm).
8. Attach upper fan shroud and tighten screws to 53 inch lbs. (5.8 Nm).
9. Connect the negative battery cable.

Water Pump

REMOVAL & INSTALLATION

EXCEPT 5.0L (VIN Y) ENGINE

▶ See Figure 39

1. Disconnect the negative battery cable.
2. Remove cooling fan as follows:
   a. Remove upper and lower fan shrouds.
   b. Remove nuts and fan clutch with cooling fan.
   c. Remove spacer if equipped, and if necessary remove bolts connecting cooling fan and clutch.

➡If equipped with a clutch fan, keep the fan in an upright position during repairs to prevent the silicone fluid from leaking out.

3. Loosen and remove the serpentine belt from the coolant pump pulley and remove the pulley.

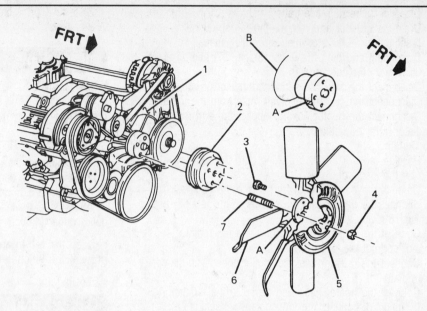

A   ALIGNMENT REFERENCE MARK
B   HUB, WATER PUMP
1   PUMP ASSEMBLY, WATER
2   PULLEY ASSEMBLY, WATER PUMP
3   BOLT/SCREW, FAN BLADE, 24 N·m (18 LB. FT.)
4   NUT, FAN BLADE CLUTCH, 24 N·m (18 LB. FT.)
5   CLUTCH ASSEMBLY, FAN BLADE
6   BLADE ASSEMBLY, FAN
7   STUD, FAN BLADE CLUTCH

Fig. 38 Fan and clutch assembly

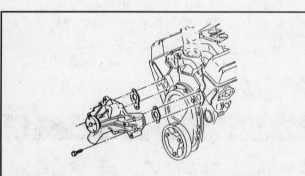

Fig. 39 Water pump assembly — Except 5.0L (VIN Y) engine

4. Drain the cooling system.

✳✳CAUTION

When draining the coolant, keep in mind that cats and dogs are attracted by the ethylene glycol antifreeze, and are quite likely to drink any that is left in an uncovered container or in puddles on the ground. This will prove fatal in sufficient quantity. Always drain the coolant into a sealable container. Coolant should be reused unless it is contaminated or several years old.

5. Unfasten the heater bypass and radiator hose from the pump, as equipped.

6. If required, remove the alternator, air conditioning compressor and/or power steering brackets.

7. Remove the bolts securing the water pump and remove the pump.
    To install:
8. Clean cylinder block and coolant pump gasket surfaces and discard old gaskets.
9. Place new gaskets on coolant pump and mounting bolts and attach coolant pump making sure gaskets remain in proper position. Tighten mounting bolts to 30 ft. lbs. (41 Nm).
10. If removed, connect the alternator, air conditioning compressor and/or power steering brackets.
11. Fasten heater bypass and radiator hose, as equipped, to the pump.
12. Attach coolant pump pulley and serpentine belt to the coolant pump.

✳✳WARNING

Inspect fan blade for bends or damage. Do not use or attempt to repair a fan blade which has been bent or damaged. It is essential that a fan blade remains in balance to prevent failure and possible injury.

13. Attach cooling fan as follows:
    a. Attach cooling fan to the fan clutch, if removed, with bolts. Tighten bolts to 18 ft. lbs. (24 Nm).
    b. Place spacer, if equipped, and attach fan assembly to the cooling pump. Be sure to align reference marks on the fan clutch and coolant pump hub.
    c. Tighten nuts to 18 ft. lbs. (24 Nm).
    d. Attach upper and lower fan shrouds and tighten screws to 53 inch lbs. (5.8 Nm).

14. Connect the negative battery cable and add coolant to engine.

15. Start engine and check for leaks.

5.0L (VIN Y) ENGINE

1. Disconnect the negative battery cable. Drain the cooling system.

✳✳CAUTION

When draining the coolant, keep in mind that cats and dogs are attracted by the ethylene glycol antifreeze, and are quite likely to drink any that is left in an uncovered container or in puddles on the ground. This will prove fatal in sufficient quantity. Always drain the coolant into a sealable container. Coolant should be reused unless it is contaminated or several years old.

2. Disconnect the lower radiator hose, the heater hose and the by-pass hose from the water pump.

3. Remove the fan assembly, the drive belts and the water pump pulley.

4. Remove the alternator, the power steering pump and the air conditioning compressor brackets, then move the units aside.

5. Remove the water pump mounting bolts, noting where each bolt came from since several different bolt sizes are used and then remove the pump assembly.

To install:

6. Clean the gasket mounting surfaces. Use new gaskets apply sealant to the gasket mating surface on the pump.

7. Install the water pump and bolts. Torque the mounting bolts to 22 ft. lbs. (30 Nm).

8. Install the alternator, the power steering pump and the air conditioning compressor brackets.

9. Install the pulley and fan assembly, then the drive belts.

10. Reconnect the lower radiator hose, the heater hose and the by-pass hose to the water pump.

11. Connect the negative battery cable. Fill the cooling system, start the engine and inspect for leaks.

Cylinder Head

▶ See Figures 40, 41 and 42

REMOVAL AND INSTALLATION

➡When servicing the engine, be absolutely sure to mark vacuum hoses and wiring so that these items may be properly reconnected during installation. Also, when disconnecting fittings of metal lines (fuel, power brake vacuum), always use two flare nut (or line) wrenches. Hold the wrench on the large fitting with pressure on the wrench as if you were tightening the fitting (clockwise), THEN loosen and disconnect the smaller fitting from the larger fitting. If this is not done, damage (twisting) to the line will result.

✳✳CAUTION

Properly relieve the fuel system pressure before disconnecting any lines.

1. Relieve the fuel system pressure and disconnect negative battery cable.

2. Drain cooling system into a suitable container, loosen and remove belt(s).

3. Remove the intake manifold.

4. Remove the exhaust manifold.

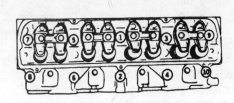

Fig. 41 Cylinder head tightening sequence — 5.0L (VIN Y) engine

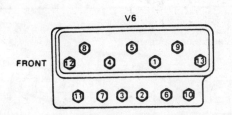

Fig. 40 Cylinder head tightening sequence — 4.3L engine

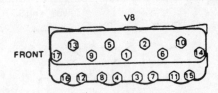

Fig. 42 Cylinder head tightening sequence — 5.0L (VIN E) and 5.7L engines

5. Remove the diverter valve, if equipped. If removing the left cylinder head on the 4.3L engine, remove the oil level indicator and guide tube.

6. Disconnect the power steering pump, generator, and/or air conditioning brackets, as necessary, and position aside.

7. Remove the rocker arm cover or valve cover.

8. Tag and disconnect spark plug wires from the spark plugs. Disconnect ground strap and/or negative battery cable from cylinder head as applicable.

9. Loosen cylinder head bolts gradually and in 3 passes.

10. Clean dirt from cylinder head and adjacent area to avoid getting dirt into engine.

11. If necessary, remove rocker arm assemblies and lift out pushrods.

12. Remove cylinder head.

To install:

13. Cylinder heads using a steel gasket should have both sides of the new gasket coated with a good sealer. The coating should be thin and even. Do not use sealer on composite type gaskets.

14. Place gasket over dowel pins.

15. Place cylinder head over dowel pins and gasket.

16. Coat the threads of the cylinder head bolts with sealing compound, part 1052080 or equivalent for all engines except 5.0L (VIN Y) engine. For the 5.0L (VIN Y) engine, dip the bolts in clean engine oil. Insert bolts finger-tight.

17. Following the proper torque sequence, tighten the cylinder head bolts, in 3 passes, to 68 ft. lbs. (92 Nm) for the 5.0L (VIN E) and 5.7L engines or to 65 ft. lbs. (88 Nm) for the 4.3L engine. For the 5.0L (VIN Y) engine tighten bolts to 40 ft. lbs. (54 Nm) on the first pass, then in the 2nd pass, tighten bolts 1-7 and 9 and additional 120 degrees. Finally, in a third pass, tighten bolts 8 and 10 an additional 95 degrees.

18. If removed, position pushrods and attach rocker arm assemblies. Adjust the valves.

19. Connect spark plug wires, and the body ground strap.

20. Attach rocker arm cover or valve cover.

21. Attach power steering pump, generator and/or air conditioning brackets if removed. Install the diverter valve, the oil level indicator and tube, if removed.

22. Attach the intake and exhaust manifolds.

23. Attach both ends of the negative battery to cylinder head cable.

24. Attach fuel filler cap, add coolant and inspect the engine for fluid leakage.

25. Change the engine oil and filter.

26. Start the engine and set the idle and timing to specification.

CLEANING AND INSPECTION

▶ **See Figure 43**

Chip carbon away from the valve heads, combustion chambers, and ports, using a chisel made of hardwood. Remove the remaining deposits with a stiff wire brush.

➡**Be sure that the deposits are actually removed, rather than burnished.**

Have the cast iron cylinder heads hot-tanked to remove grease, corrosion, and scale from the water passages. Clean the remaining cylinder head parts in an engine cleaning solvent. Do not remove the protective coating from the springs.

Place a straightedge across the gasket surface of the cylinder head. Using feeler gauges, determine the clearance at the center of the straightedge. If warpage exceeds 0.003″ in a 6″ span, or 0.006″ over the total length, the cylinder head must be resurfaced.

➡**If warpage exceeds the manufacturer's maximum tolerance for material removal, the cylinder head must be replaced.   When milling the cylinder heads, the intake manifold mounting position is altered, and must be corrected by milling the manifold flange a proportionate amount.**

RESURFACING

▶ **See Figure 44**

➡**This procedure should only be performed by a machine shop.**

When the cylinder head is removed, check the flatness of the cylinder head gasket surfaces.

1. Place a straightedge across the gasket surface of the cylinder head. Using feeler gauges, determine the clearance at the center of the straightedge.

2. If warpage exceeds 0.003″ (0.076mm) in a 6″ (152mm) span, or 0.006″ (0.152mm) over the total length, the cylinder head must be resurfaced.

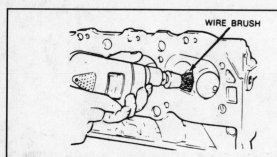

Fig. 43 Removing carbon from the cylinder head chamber

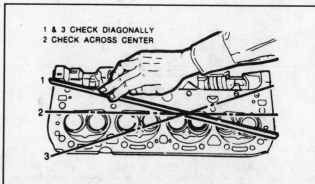

Fig. 44 Checking the cylinder head for warpage

3. If it is necessary to refinish the cylinder head gasket surface, do not plane or grind off more than 0.254mm (0.010") from the original gasket surface.

➡When milling the cylinder heads, the intake manifold mounting position is altered, and must be corrected by milling the manifold flange a proportionate amount. Consult an experienced machinist about this.

Valves and Springs

▶ See Figures 45, 46 and 47

REMOVAL AND INSTALLATION

1. Block the head on its side, or install a pair of head-holding brackets made especially for valve removal.
2. Use a socket slightly larger than the valve stem and keepers, place the socket over the valve stem and gently hit the socket with a plastic hammer to break loose any varnish buildup.
3. Remove the valve keepers, retainer, spring shield and valve spring using a valve spring compressor (the locking C-clamp type is the easiest kind to use).
4. Keep all parts organized in a separate container numbered for the cylinder being worked on; do not mix them with other parts removed.
5. Remove and discard the valve stem oil seals. A new seal will be used at assembly time.

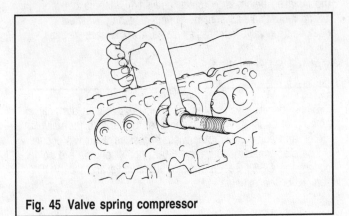

Fig. 45 Valve spring compressor

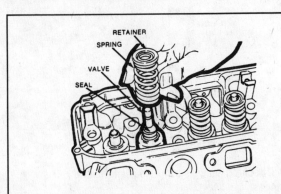

Fig. 46 Valve spring and seal removal and installation

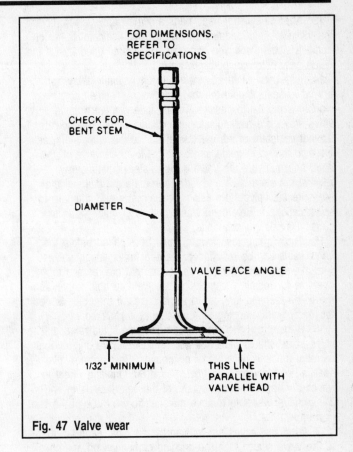

FOR DIMENSIONS, REFER TO SPECIFICATIONS

CHECK FOR BENT STEM

DIAMETER

VALVE FACE ANGLE

1/32" MINIMUM

THIS LINE PARALLEL WITH VALVE HEAD

Fig. 47 Valve wear

6. Remove the valves from the cylinder head and place them, in order, through numbered holes punched in a stiff piece of cardboard or wood valve holding stick.

➡The exhaust valve stems, on some engines, are equipped with small metal caps. Take care not to lose the caps. Make sure to reinstall them at assembly time. Replace any caps that are worn.

7. Use an electric drill and rotary wire brush to clean the intake and exhaust valve ports, combustion chamber and valve seats. In some cases, the carbon will need to be chipped away. Use a blunt pointed drift for carbon chipping. Be careful around the valve seat areas.
8. Use a wire valve guide cleaning brush and safe solvent to clean the valve guides.
9. Clean the valves with a revolving wires brush. Heavy carbon deposits may be removed with the blunt drift.

➡When using a wire brush to clean carbon on the valve ports, valves etc., be sure that the deposits are actually removed, rather than burnished.

10. Wash and clean all valve springs, keepers, retaining caps etc., in safe solvent.
11. Clean the head with a brush and some safe solvent and wipe dry.
12. Check the head for cracks. Cracks in the cylinder head usually start around an exhaust valve seat because it is the hottest part of the combustion chamber. If a crack is suspected but cannot be detected visually have the area checked with dye penetrant or other method by the machine shop.

13. After all cylinder head parts are reasonably clean, check the valve stem-to-guide clearance. If a dial indicator is not on hand, a visual inspection can give you a fairly good idea if the guide, valve stem or both are worn.

14. Insert the valve into the guide until slightly away from the valve seat. Wiggle the valve sideways. A small amount of wobble is normal, excessive wobble means a worn guide or valve stem. If a dial indicator is on hand, mount the indicator so that the stem of the valve is at 90° to the valve stem, as close to the valve guide as possible. Move the valve off the seat, and measure the valve guide-to-stem clearance by rocking the stem back and forth to actuate the dial indicator. Measure the valve stem using a micrometer and compare to specifications to determine whether stem or guide wear is causing excessive clearance.

15. The valve guide, if worn, must be repaired before the valve seats can be resurfaced. Manufacturers supply valves with oversize stems to fit valve guides that are reamed to oversize for repair. The machine shop will be able to handle the guide reaming for you. In some cases, if the guide is not too badly worn, knurling may be all that is required.

16. Reface, or have the valves and valve seats refaced. The valve seats should be a true 45° angle. Remove only enough material to clean up any pits or grooves. Be sure the valve seat is not too wide or narrow. Use a 60° grinding wheel to remove material from the bottom of the seat for raising and a 30° grinding wheel to remove material from the top of the seat to narrow.

17. After the valves are refaced by machine, hand lap them to the valve seat. Clean the grinding compound off and check the position of face-to-seat contact. Contact should be close to the center of the valve face. If contact is close to the top edge of the valve, narrow the seat; if too close to the bottom edge, raise the seat.

18. Valves should be refaced to a true angle of 44°. Remove only enough metal to clean up the valve face or to correct runout. If the edge of a valve head, after machining, is 1/32" (0.8mm) or less replace the valve. The tip of the valve stem should also be dressed on the valve grinding machine, however, do not remove more than 0.010" (0.254mm).

19. After all valve and valve seats have been machined, check the remaining valve train parts (springs, retainers, keepers, etc.) for wear. Check the valve springs for straightness and tension.

20. Install the valves in the cylinder head and metal caps.

21. Install new valve stem oil seals.

22. Install the valve keepers, retainer, spring shield and valve spring using a valve spring compressor (the locking C-clamp type is the easiest kind to use).

23. Check the valve spring installed height, shim or replace as necessary.

CHECKING SPRINGS

▶ See Figures 48 and 49

Place the spring on a flat surface next to a square. Measure the height of the spring, and rotate it against the edge of the square to measure distortion. If spring height varies (by comparison) by more than $1/16$ inch or if distortion exceeds $1/16$ inch, replace the spring.

In addition to evaluating the spring as above, test the spring pressure at the installed and compressed (installed height minus valve lift) height using a valve spring tester. Springs used on small displacement engines (up to 3 liters) should be ±1 lb. of all other springs in either position. A tolerance of ±5 lbs is permissible on larger engines.

VALVE SPRING INSTALLED HEIGHT

▶ See Figure 50

After installing the valve spring, measure the distance between the spring mounting pad and the lower edge of the spring retainer. Compare the measurement to specifications. If the installed height is incorrect, add shim washers between the spring mounting pad and the spring. Use only washers designed for valve springs, available at most parts houses.

VALVE STEM OIL SEALS

When installing valve stem oil seals, ensure that a small amount of oil is able to pass the seal to lubricate the valve stems and guide walls, otherwise, excessive wear will occur.

The stem seals used on the 5.0L (VIN Y) engine are color coded; the GREY seal is for the intake valve and the IVORY seal is for the exhaust valve.

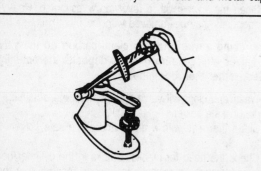

Fig. 48 Testing valve spring tension using tool J-8056 and torque wrench

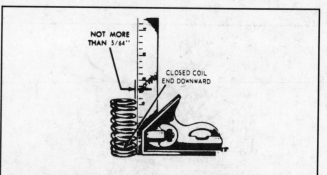

Fig. 49 Checking valve spring free length and straightness

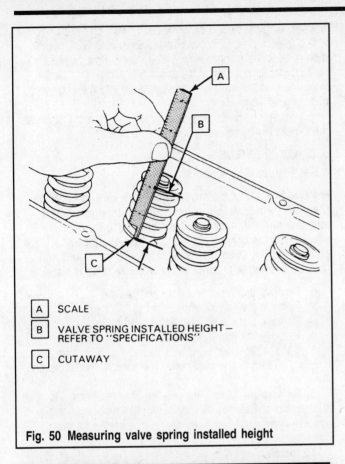

A   SCALE

B   VALVE SPRING INSTALLED HEIGHT — REFER TO "SPECIFICATIONS"

C   CUTAWAY

Fig. 50 Measuring valve spring installed height

Valve Seats

➡The valve seats are not removable, they are an integral part of the cylinder head. Any cutting or grinding operation performed on the valve guides, should be done by a qualified machine shop.

LAPPING THE VALVES

▶ See Figure 51

When valve faces and seats have been refaced and recut, or if they are determined to be in good condition, the valves

Fig. 51 Lapping the valves using a hand valve lapping stick

must be lapped-in to ensure efficient sealing when the valve closes against the seat.

1. Invert the cylinder head so that the combustion chambers are facing up.

2. Lightly lubricate the valve stems with clean oil, and coat the valve seats with valve grinding compound. Install the valves in the head as numbered.

3. Attach the suction cup of a valve lapping tool to a valve head. You'll probably have to moisten the cup to securely attach the tool to the valve.

4. Rotate the tool between the palms, changing position and lifting the tool often to prevent grooving. Lap the valve until a smooth, polished seat is evident (you may have to add a bit more compound after some lapping is done).

5. Remove the valve and tool, and remove ALL traces of grinding compound with solvent-soaked rag, or rinse the head with solvent.

➡Valve lapping can also be done by fastening a suction cup to a piece of drill rod in a hand eggbeater type drill. Proceed as above, using the drill as a lapping tool. Due to the higher speeds involved when using the hand drill, care must be exercised to avoid grooving the seat. Lift the tool and change direction of rotation often.

Valve Guides

➡The valve guides are not removable, they are an integral part of the cylinder head. Any cutting or grinding operation performed on the valve guides, should be done by a qualified machine shop.

REAMING VALVE GUIDES

If it becomes necessary to ream a valve guide to install with an oversize stem, a reaming kit is available which contains a oversize reamers and pilot tools.

When replacing a standard size valve with an oversize valve always use the reamer in sequence (smallest oversize first, then next smallest, etc.) so as not to overload the reamers. Always reface the valve seat after the valve guide has been reamed, and use a suitable scraper to brake the sharp corner at the top of the valve guide.

KNURLING

Valve guides which are not excessively worn or distorted may, in some cases, be knurled. Knurling is a process in which metal is displaced and raised, thereby reducing clearance. Knurling also provides excellent oil control.

➡This procedure should only be performed by a qualified machine shop.

STEM-TO-GUIDE CLEARANCE

Valve stem-to-guide clearance should be checked upon assembling the cylinder head, and is especially necessary if the valve guides have been reamed or knurled, or if oversize valve have been installed. Excessive oil consumption often is a result of too much clearance between the valve guide and valve stem.

1. Clean the valve stem with lacquer thinner or a similar solvent to remove all gum and varnish. Clean the valve guides using solvent and an expanding wire-type valve guide cleaner (a rifle cleaning brush works well here).

2. Mount a dial indicator so that the stem is 90° to the valve stem and as close to the valve guide as possible.

3. Move the valve off its seat, and measure the valve guide-to-stem clearance by rocking the stem back and forth to actuate the dial indicator. Measure the valve stems using a micrometer and compare to specifications, to determine whether stem or guide wear is responsible for excessive clearance.

Valve Lifters

REMOVAL AND INSTALLATION

EXCEPT 5.0L (VIN Y) ENGINE

▶ See Figure 52

1. Remove the intake manifold, valve cover and push rod cover (4-cylinder). Disassemble the rocker arms and remove the push rods.

2. Remove the lifters. If they are coated with varnish, clean with carburetor cleaning solvent.

3. If installing new lifters or you have disassembled the lifters, they must be primed before installation. Submerge the lifters in SAE 10 oil and carefully push down on the plunger with a ⅛ inch drift. Hold the plunger down (DO NOT pump), then release the plunger slowly. The lifter is now primed.

4. Coat the bottoms of the lifters with Molykote® before installation. Install the lifters and pushrods into the engine in their original position.

5. Install the rocker arms and adjust the valves. Complete the installation by reversing the removal procedure.

5.0L (VIN Y) ENGINE

▶ See Figures 53, 54 and 55

➡ Valve lifters and pushrods should be kept in order so they can be reinstalled in their original position. Some engines will have both standard and 0.010 in. oversize valve lifters as original equipment. The oversize lifters are etched with an O on their sides; the cylinder block will also be marked with an O if the oversize lifter is used.

1. Remove the intake manifold and gasket.
2. Remove the valve covers.
3. Remove the valve lifter retainer and guide.
4. Remove the rocker arm assemblies and pushrods.
5. If the lifters are coated with varnish, apply carburetor cleaning solvent to the lifter body. The solvent should dissolve the varnish.
6. Remove the lifters. Remove the lifter retainer guide bolts, and remove the guides. A special tool for removing lifters is available from local part suppliers, and is helpful for this procedure.

To install:

7. New lifters must be primed before installation. Submerge the lifters in SAE 10 oil, which is very thin. Carefully insert the

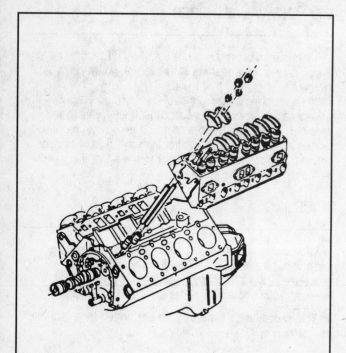

Fig. 52 Exploded view of lifters, rockers and pushrods-V8 engine; Note that cylinder head removal is not necessary.

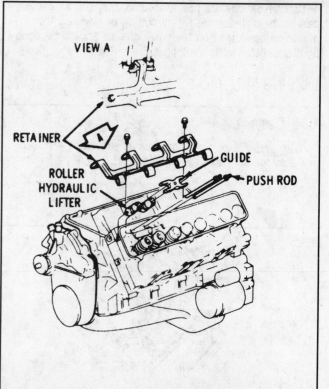

Fig. 53 Valve lifter guides and retainer — 5.0L (VIN Y) engine

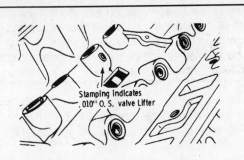

Fig. 54 Oversize valve lifter bore identification — 5.0L (VIN Y) engine

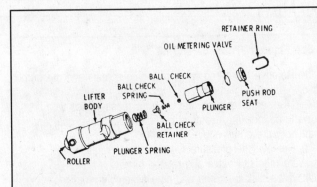

Fig. 55 Roller tip valve lifter — 5.0L (VIN Y) engine

end of a ⅛ inch (3mm) drift into the lifter and pump up and down on the plunger. The lifter is now primed.

8. Coat the bottoms of the lifters and the rollers with Molykote® or an equivalent molybdenum-disulfide lubricant before installation. Install the lifters and pushrods into the engine in their original order. Install the lifter retainer guide.

9. Install the rocker arm assemblies and pushrods. Torque the rocker arm to 22 ft. lbs. (28 Nm).

10. Install the valve lifter retainer and guide.

11. Install the intake manifold gaskets and manifold.

12. Install the valve covers.

13. Change the engine oil and filter, connect the negative battery cable, check and fill the coolant to the proper level.

14. Start the engine and check for leaks.

Oil Pan

REMOVAL AND INSTALLATION

EXCEPT 5.0L (VIN Y) ENGINE

1. Disconnect the negative battery cable and remove the air cleaner assembly.

2. Disconnect the wire connectors at the wiper motor and remove the fuse cover on V8 engines only. Remove the distributor cap and wires.

3. Remove the transmission and oil dipsticks.

4. Remove the upper fan shroud.

5. Raise and safely support the vehicle.

6. Drain the engine oil.

7. Disconnect the exhaust pipe at the manifolds. Remove the flywheel cover. On the 4.3L engine, disconnect the AIR pipe to converter at the exhaust manifold.

8. Disconnect the transmission fluid cooler lines at the clips on the oil pan.

9. Remove the transmission dipstick tube and linkage as required.

10. Remove the starter motor assembly.

11. If equipped with an oil level sensor, it must be disconnected and removed to prevent possible damage to the oil level sensor, oil pump pickup screen and pipe.

12. Disconnect the engine mount through-bolts and safely raise and support the front of the engine only as far as necessary to remove the oil pan.

13. Remove the oil pan attaching nuts, bolts and reinforcement.

14. Place the crankshaft timing mark to the 6 o'clock position in order to move the crankshaft out of the way, then remove the pan and discard the old gasket.

To install:

15. Clean the gasket mating surfaces. Apply a small amount of 1052914 or equivalent sealer to the front and rear cover to cylinder block junctions and continue bead 1 inch in either direction from the radius of the cavity.

16. Install the new gasket on the oil pan, and position the oil pan in place with loosely installed nuts, bolts and reinforcement.

17. Lower the engine.

18. Tighten the oil pan nuts to 17 ft. lbs. (23 Nm) and bolts to 97 inch lbs. (11 Nm).

19. Connect the engine mount through-bolts.

20. If equipped, install the oil level sensor and electrical connection.

21. Install the starter motor assembly.

22. Connect the transmission fluid cooler lines to the clips on the oil pan and install the transmission dipstick tube and linkage.

23. Install the flywheel cover. Connect the exhaust pipe to the manifolds. On the 4.3L engine, connect the AIR pipe to converter at the exhaust manifold.

24. Lower the vehicle.

25. Install the upper fan shroud.

26. Install the transmission and oil dipsticks.

27. Install the distributor cap and wires. Install the fuse cover and connect the wiper motor wiring connector.

28. Install the air cleaner assembly.

29. Reconnect the battery cable, refill crankcase with proper engine oil and check engine for leaks.

5.0L (VIN Y) ENGINE

▶ See Figure 56

1. Disconnect negative battery cable.

2. Remove oil level indicator.

3. Remove upper fan shroud and attaching screws.

4. Raise and safely support vehicle.

5. Drain oil pan.

6. Remove flywheel cover, crossover pipe and starter.

7. Install engine support and adapter tools BT-7109, BT-7203 and BT-6501 or equivalent.

8. Disconnect engine mounts at cylinder block.

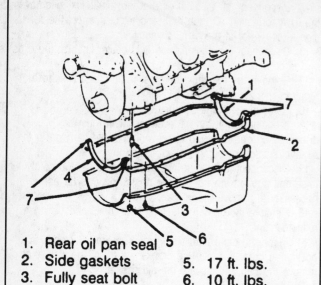

1. Rear oil pan seal
2. Side gaskets
3. Fully seat bolt
4. Front oil pan seal
5. 17 ft. lbs.
6. 10 ft. lbs.
7. Apply sealer

Fig. 56 Oil pan and gasket assembly — 5.0L (VIN Y) engine

9. Carefully raise front of engine high enough and remove oil pan.

To install:

10. Clean the gasket mating surfaces and apply 1050026 or equivalent sealer to both sides of the new gasket.

11. Position gasket in place on the oil pan. Wipe front and rear seals with engine oil and position in place.

12. Apply 1052915 or equivalent RTV sealer to oil pan seals and install oil pan.

13. Install oil pan bolts, tighten to 97 inch lbs. (11 Nm), and nuts, tighten to 17 ft. lbs. (23 Nm).

14. Lower engine sufficiently to install mounts, then lower engine fully and remove bar.

15. Install the crossover pipe, starter and flywheel cover.

16. Lower vehicle and install oil level indicator.

17. Install upper fan shroud and attaching screws.

18. Fill crankcase with engine oil, connect the negative battery cable and check for leaks.

Oil Pump

REMOVAL

1. Drain and remove the oil pan.

✳✳CAUTION

The EPA warns that prolonged contact with used engine oil may cause a number of skin disorders, including cancer! You should make every effort to minimize your exposure to used engine oil. Protective gloves should be worn when changing the oil. Wash your hands and any other exposed skin areas as soon as possible after exposure to used engine oil. Soap and water, or waterless hand cleaner should be used.

2. Remove the oil pump-to-rear main bearing cap bolt. Remove the pump and the extension shaft.

3. Remove the cotter pin, spring and pressure regulator valve.

➡Place your thumb over the pressure regulators bore before removing the cotter pin, as the spring is under pressure.

OVERHAUL

▶ See Figures 57, 58, 59 and 60

1. Remove the pump cover attaching screws and the pump cover.

2. Mark gear teeth so they may be reassembled with the same teeth indexing. Remove the idler gear, drive gear and shaft from the pump body.

3. Remove the pressure regulator valve retaining pin, pressure regulator valve and related parts.

4. If the pickup screen and pipe assembly need replacing, mount the pump in a soft-jawed vise and extract the pipe from pump by twisting the assembly as if you are unscrewing the pickup tube from the pump assembly. Do not disturb the pickup screen on the pipe. This is serviced as an assembly.

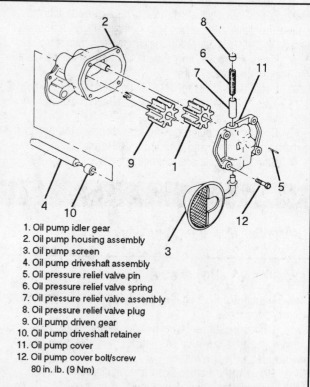

1. Oil pump idler gear
2. Oil pump housing assembly
3. Oil pump screen
4. Oil pump driveshaft assembly
5. Oil pressure relief valve pin
6. Oil pressure relief valve spring
7. Oil pressure relief valve assembly
8. Oil pressure relief valve plug
9. Oil pump driven gear
10. Oil pump driveshaft retainer
11. Oil pump cover
12. Oil pump cover bolt/screw
    80 in. lb. (9 Nm)

Fig. 57 Exploded view of oil pump — Except 5.0L (VIN Y) engine

Fig. 58 Measuring gear side clearance

5. Wash all parts in cleaning solvent and dry with compressed air.

6. Inspect the pump body and cover for cracks or excessive wear. Inspect pump gears for damage or excessive wear.

➡ **The pump gears and body are not serviced separately. If the pump gears or body are damaged or worn, replacement of the entire oil pump assembly is necessary.**

7. Check the drive gear shaft for looseness in the pump body. Inspect inside of pump cover for wear that would permit oil to leak past the ends of the gears.

8. Inspect the pickup screen and pipe assembly for damage to screen, pipe or relief grommet.

9. Check the pressure regulator valve for fit.

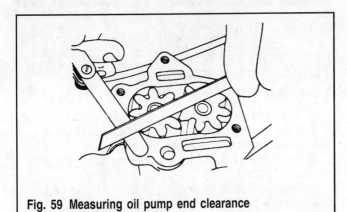

Fig. 59 Measuring oil pump end clearance

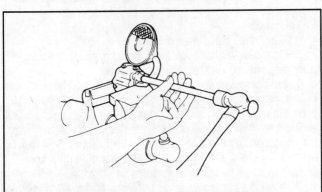

Fig. 60 Installing the oil pump pickup and screen

10. If the pickup screen and pipe assembly was removed, it should be replaced with a new part. Loss of press fit condition could result in an air leak and loss of oil pressure. Mount the pump in a soft-jawed vise, apply sealer to end of pipe, and use a suitable tool to tap the pipe in place.

➡ **Be careful of twisting, shearing or collapsing pipe while installing in pump. Do not use excessive force.**

11. Install the pressure regulator valve and related parts.

12. Install the drive gear and shaft in the pump body.

13. Install the idler gear in the pump body with the smooth side of gear towards pump cover opening.

➡ **Pack the inside of the pump completely with petroleum jelly. DO NOT use engine oil. The pump MUST be primed this way or it won't produce any oil pressure when the engine is started.**

14. Install the pump cover and torque attaching screws to specifications.

15. Turn drive shaft by hand to check for smooth operation.

16. Install a new shaft extension clip onto the pump drive shaft and snap the extension shaft into the clip, on all except 5.0L (VIN Y) engine.

INSTALLATION

1. Assemble pump and extension shaft to rear main bearing cap. On the 5.0L (VIN Y) engine, ensure the shaft extension washer be $1/32$ from the tip of the shaft and then insert the washer end of the shaft into the pump and install the pump assembly. On all except the 5.0L (VIN Y) engine, install a new shaft extension with clip onto the pump drive shaft and snap the extension shaft into the clip, then align the slot on top end of extension shaft with drive tang on lower end of distributor drive shaft and install the pump.

➡ **When assembling the drive shaft extension to the drive shaft, the end of the extension nearest the washers must be inserted into the drive shaft.**

2. Insert the drive shaft extension through the opening in the main bearing cap and block until the shaft mates into the distributor drive gear.

3. Install the pump onto the rear main bearing cap and install the attaching bolts. Torque the bolts to specifications:
   - 4.3L engine: 65 ft. lbs. (88 Nm)
   - 5.0L (VIN E) and 5.7L engines: 77 ft. lbs. (105 Nm)
   - 5.0L (VIN Y) engine: 35 ft. lbs. (47 Nm)
4. Install the oil pan and fill the crankcase with engine oil.
5. Start the engine and check the oil pressure.

Crankshaft Damper

▸ **See Figures 61 and 62**

The damper may be replaced by removing the fan shroud, belts, crankshaft pulley bolts and then remove the damper center bolts. Install a suitable damper removing tool (J-23523 or equivalent), remove the damper from the crankshaft. Use the appropriate end of the removal tool for reinstalling the damper. Do not hammer the pulley ON.

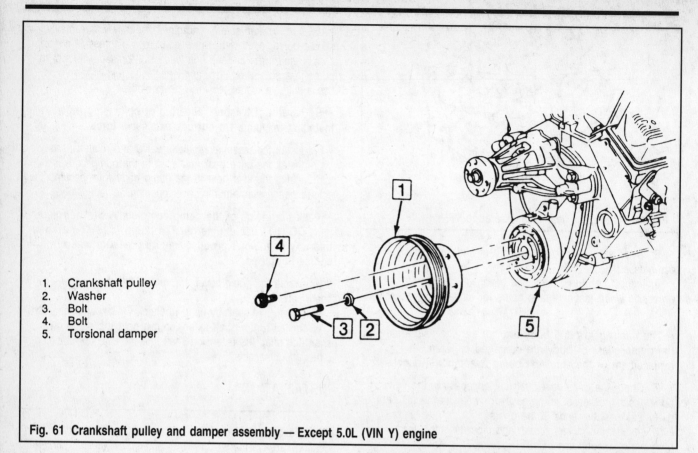

1. Crankshaft pulley
2. Washer
3. Bolt
4. Bolt
5. Torsional damper

Fig. 61 Crankshaft pulley and damper assembly — Except 5.0L (VIN Y) engine

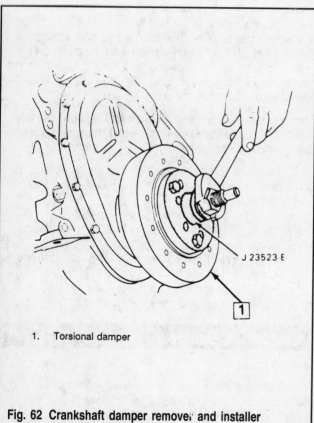

J 23523-E

1. Torsional damper

Fig. 62 Crankshaft damper remover and installer

Timing Chain Cover and Seal

REMOVAL AND INSTALLATION

EXCEPT 5.0L (VIN Y) ENGINE

▶ See Figures 63 and 64

1. Disconnect the negative battery cable.
2. Drain the cooling system into a suitable container and remove the water pump assembly.
3. Using tool J-23523-E or equivalent, remove the torsional damper assembly.
4. Raise and safely support the vehicle. Remove the oil pan assembly.
5. Remove the engine front cover retaining bolts. Remove the front cover and discard the gasket.

To install:

6. Clean the gasket mating surfaces.
7. Coat new engine front cover gasket with sealant and place into position on the engine front cover.
8. Position cover and gasket in place and loosely install the engine front cover to block upper attaching bolts. Tighten bolts alternately while carefully pressing downward on the engine front cover so the dowels in the block are aligned with the corresponding holes in the engine front cover. Be careful not to force the the front cover over the dowels to the point where the cover flange or dowels become distorted.
9. Install the remaining cover bolts and tighten all cover bolts alternately and evenly to 97 inch lbs. (11 Nm).
10. Install the oil pan.

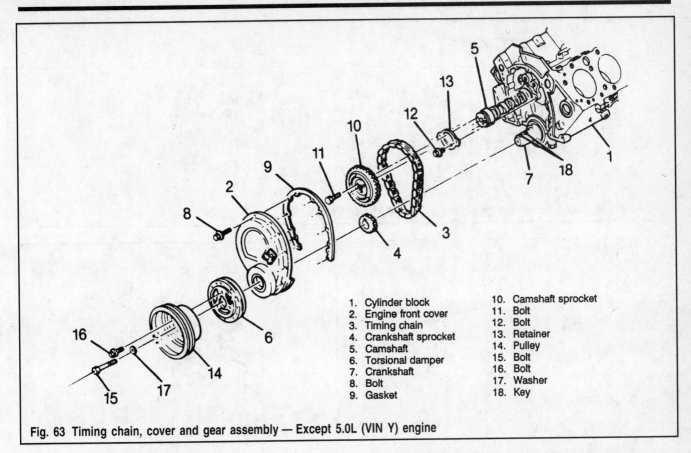

1. Cylinder block	10. Camshaft sprocket
2. Engine front cover	11. Bolt
3. Timing chain	12. Bolt
4. Crankshaft sprocket	13. Retainer
5. Camshaft	14. Pulley
6. Torsional damper	15. Bolt
7. Crankshaft	16. Bolt
8. Bolt	17. Washer
9. Gasket	18. Key

Fig. 63 Timing chain, cover and gear assembly — Except 5.0L (VIN Y) engine

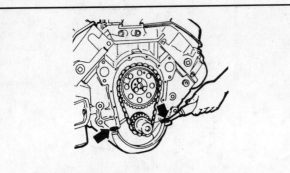

Fig. 64 Apply sealer to these joints prior to assembly — Except 5.0L (VIN Y) engine

11. Install the torsional damper.

12. Install the coolant pump, hoses and belts.

13. Connect the negative battery cable and add engine coolant.

5.0L (VIN Y) ENGINE

▶ **See Figures 65, 66 and 67**

1. Disconnect the negative battery cable and drain the coolant.

2. Disconnect the radiator hose, heater hose and the bypass hose. Remove the fan, belts and pulley.

3. Disconnect the power steering pump bracket and, if equipped, the air conditioner compressor bracket. Position accessories and brackets aside.

4. Remove the torsional damper and crankshaft pulley.

5. Remove the front cover attaching bolts/studs and remove the cover and water pump assembly from the front of the engine.

6. Remove the dowel pins. If necessary grind a flat surface on the dowel pins to aid in removal.

To install:

7. Clean gasket mating surfaces.

8. Apply 1050026 or equivalent sealer around the coolant holes of the new cover gasket. Trim about 1/8 inch from each end of the new front pan seal and trim any excess material from the front edge of the oil pan gasket.

9. Position gasket on block and seal on front cover. Apply 1052915 or equivalent RTV sealer on the oil pan, on the seal mating surface.

10. Position front cover in place on the block, pressing to compress the oil pan seal. Guide the seal into place between the oil pan and cylinder block with a suitable small tool.

11. Apply engine oil to bolts/studs and insert 2 bolts, finger tight.

12. Install the dowel pins, chamfer ends first, through the holes in the cover.

13. Install the remaining front cover attaching bolts/studs, tighten alternately and evenly to 22 ft. lbs. (28 Nm).

14. Install the torsional damper and pulley

15. Connect the power steering pump bracket and, if equipped, the air conditioner compressor bracket.

16. Install the fan, belts and pulley. Connect the radiator hose, heater hose and the bypass hose.

17. Connect the negative battery cable and add engine coolant.

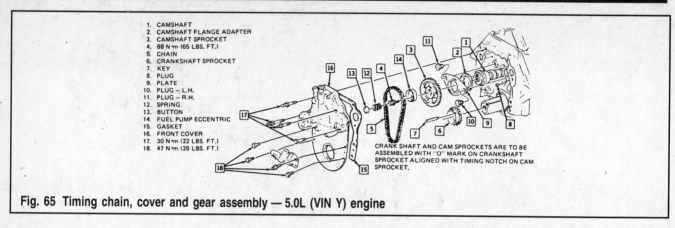

1. CAMSHAFT
2. CAMSHAFT FLANGE ADAPTER
3. CAMSHAFT SPROCKET
4. 88 N·m (65 LBS. FT.)
5. CHAIN
6. CRANKSHAFT SPROCKET
7. KEY
8. PLUG
9. PLATE
10. PLUG — L.H.
11. PLUG — R.H.
12. SPRING
13. BUTTON
14. FUEL PUMP ECCENTRIC
15. GASKET
16. FRONT COVER
17. 30 N·m (22 LBS. FT.)
18. 47 N·m (35 LBS. FT.)

CRANK SHAFT AND CAM SPROCKETS ARE TO BE ASSEMBLED WITH "O" MARK ON CRANKSHAFT SPROCKET ALIGNED WITH TIMING NOTCH ON CAM SPROCKET.

Fig. 65 Timing chain, cover and gear assembly — 5.0L (VIN Y) engine

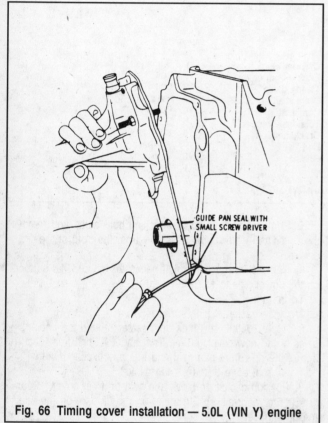

GUIDE PAN SEAL WITH SMALL SCREW DRIVER

Fig. 66 Timing cover installation — 5.0L (VIN Y) engine

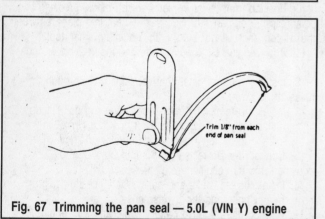

Trim 1/8" from each end of pan seal

Fig. 67 Trimming the pan seal — 5.0L (VIN Y) engine

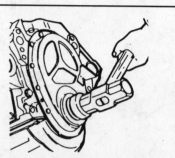

Fig. 68 Installing oil seal with front cover on engine — Except 5.0L (VIN Y) engine

Fig. 69 Installing oil seal with front cover removed from engine — Except 5.0L (VIN Y) engine

TIMING CHAIN COVER OIL SEAL REPLACEMENT

EXCEPT 5.0L (VIN Y) ENGINE

▶ See Figures 68 and 69

1. Disconnect the negative battery cable.
2. With the torsional damper removed, remove the old seal using a suitable prying tool. Take care not to damage the front cover when removing seal.

To install:

3. Position new seal with the open end toward the inside of the engine front cover and carefully drive in the new seal with tool J-35468 or equivalent.

4. Reinstall torsional damper, connect the negative battery cable and check cover for oil leaks.

5.0L (VIN Y) ENGINE

◗ See Figure 70

1. Disconnect the negative battery cable.
2. Remove the crankshaft pulley and torsional balancer.
3. Remove the oil seal using tool BT-6406 or J-23129 and J-1859-03 or their equivalents.

To install:

4. Coat the outside diameter of the new seal with sealer.
5. Install seal with lip facing the engine, using tool BT-6405, J-25264-A or equivalent and tighten until 0.005 inch gauge fits between front cover and tool.
6. Install crankshaft pulley and balancer.
7. Install the belts and adjust tension.

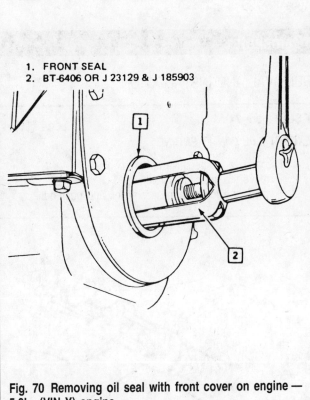

1. FRONT SEAL
2. BT-6406 OR J 23129 & J 185903

Fig. 70 Removing oil seal with front cover on engine — 5.0L (VIN Y) engine

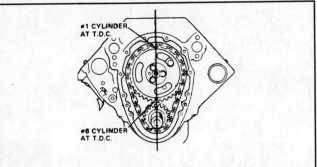

Fig. 71 Timing gear alignment — Except 5.0L (VIN Y) engine

8. Reconnect the negative battery cable. Inspect cover for oil leaks.

Timing Chain or Gear

REMOVAL AND INSTALLATION

EXCEPT 5.0L (VIN Y) ENGINE

◗ See Figure 71

➡ **To remove the timing gear cover, refer to the Timing Gear Cover Removal and Installation in this Section.**

1. With the timing gear cover removed, rotate the engine so that the No. 6 cylinder T.D.C. mark (V8 engine) or the No. 4 cylinder T.D.C. mark (V6 engine) on the camshaft sprocket, aligns with the mark on the crankshaft sprocket.
2. Remove the 3 bolts holding the camshaft sprocket to the camshaft. Pull the camshaft sprocket forward.
3. If the camshaft sprocket will not move, give the sprocket a light blow with a plastic mallet, on the lower edge. Remove the sprocket and timing chain.
4. To install, position the sprocket into place and secure with the 3 camshaft sprocket bolts without changing the engines position. Torque the bolts to 15-25 ft. lbs. (20-35 Nm).
5. Install the timing gear cover.

5.0L (VIN Y) Engine

◗ See Figure 72

1. Disconnect the negative battery cable.
2. Remove the front cover and gasket.
3. Rotate the engine until the marks on the camshaft sprocket and crankshaft sprocket are aligned with the shaft centers.
4. Remove the crankshaft oil slinger.
5. Remove the camshaft thrust button and spring.
6. Remove the fuel pump, fuel pump gasket and fuel pump eccentric.
7. Remove the camshaft sprocket and timing chain.

To install:

8. Install the camshaft timing sprocket and the timing chain with the timing marks aligned.
9. After the timing gear alignment is verified, torque the camshaft sprocket (fuel pump eccentric) bolt to 65 ft. lbs. (88 Nm).

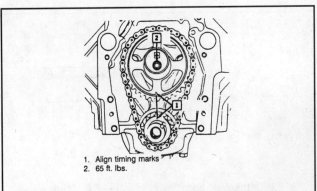

1. Align timing marks
2. 65 ft. lbs.

Fig. 72 Timing gear alignment — 5.0L (VIN Y) engine

10. Install the camshaft thrust button and spring. Install the crankshaft oil slinger.
11. Install front cover using new gasket.
12. Install fuel pump using new gasket.
13. Connect the negative battery cable.

Crankshaft Sprocket

REMOVAL & INSTALLATION

EXCEPT 5.0L (VIN Y) ENGINE

1. Disconnect the negative battery terminal.
2. Remove the timing chain and camshaft sprocket.
3. Remove the crankshaft sprocket using tool J-5825-A or equivalent.
4. Remove crankshaft key, if required.
To install:
5. Install crankshaft key, if removed.
6. Install the crankshaft sprocket using tool J-5590 or equivalent.
7. Install timing chain and camshaft.
8. Connect the negative battery.

5.0L (VIN Y) ENGINE
▶ See Figure 73

1. Disconnect negative battery cable.
2. Remove the timing chain and camshaft sprocket.
3. Remove the spark plugs.

➡The crankshaft key has a blind keyway. The key must be removed before removing the crankshaft sprocket.

4. Remove the crankshaft key.
5. Remove the crankshaft sprocket, using removal tool BT-6812, J-25287, J-21052 or equivalent.
To install:
6. Place the timing chain on a flat surface.
7. Insert the camshaft and crankshaft timing sprockets into the timing chain with the timing marks aligned. Ensure this alignment is maintained through out the remaining procedure.
8. Place the sprockets with the timing chain into position.
9. Rotate the camshaft sprocket as required until it engages with the camshaft. With the camshaft sprocket engaged, install the fuel pump eccentric with the flat side toward the engine.

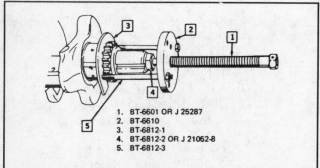

1. BT-6601 OR J 25287
2. BT-6610
3. BT-6812-1
4. BT-6812-2 OR J 21052-8
5. BT-6812-3

Fig. 73 Crankshaft sprocket removal — 5.0L (VIN Y) engine

10. Install the camshaft sprocket bolt until finger-tight.
11. Rotate the crankshaft until the crankshaft sprocket and keyway are in alignment. When the keyway is aligned, tap the crankshaft key into place with a brass hammer until the key bottoms.
12. Check the timing marks are still in alignment.

➡When the timing marks are aligned, the No. 6 piston is at TDC. When both timing marks are on top, the No. 1 piston is in the firing position.

13. After the timing gear alignment is verified, torque the camshaft sprocket (fuel pump eccentric) bolt to 65 ft. lbs. (88 Nm).
14. Install the camshaft thrust button and spring. Install the crankshaft oil slinger.
15. Install front cover using new gasket.
16. Install fuel pump using new gasket.
17. Install the spark plugs and connect the negative battery cable.

Camshaft

REMOVAL AND INSTALLATION

▶ See Figure 74
EXCEPT 5.0L (VIN Y) ENGINE

1. Disconnect the negative battery cable.
2. Remove the intake manifold
3. Remove the rocker arm assemblies and pushrods.

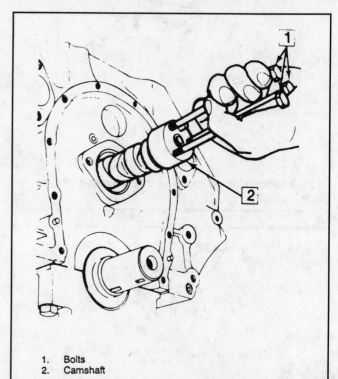

1. Bolts
2. Camshaft

Fig. 74 Install 3 long bolts in camshaft to aid in removal and installation of camshaft

4. Loosen the belt tensioner and remove the serpentine belt.

5. Remove the upper fan shroud, radiator hoses, oil cooler lines and the radiator.

6. Remove the timing chain.

7. Properly discharge the air conditioning, disconnect and remove the condenser.

8. Remove the valve lifters.

9. Remove the camshaft retainer bolts and the camshaft retainer.

10. Install three 4 inch long bolts in the camshaft bolt holes and carefully pull camshaft from bearings.

To install:

11. Coat camshaft lobes and journals with prelube 1052365 or equivalent.

12. Carefully slide camshaft into the block.

13. Install the camshaft retainer and retainer bolts. Tighten bolts to 106 inch lbs. (12 Nm).

14. Install the timing chain.

15. Install new valve lifters to assure durability of the camshaft lobes and lifter rollers.

16. Install the air conditioning condenser.

17. Install the radiator, oil cooler lines and radiator hoses.

18. Install the serpentine drive belt.

19. Install the upper fan shroud.

20. Install the pushrods and rocker arm assemblies

21. Install the intake manifold.

22. Connect the negative battery, change the oil and filter, add coolant, and adjust valves.

5.0L (VIN Y) ENGINE

1. Properly discharge the air conditioning system. Disconnect the negative battery cable.

2. Drain the cooling system into a suitable container.

3. Remove the upper radiator baffle.

4. Disconnect the upper radiator hose.

5. Remove the radiator assembly.

6. Remove the air cleaner assembly.

7. Disconnect the throttle cable.

8. Remove accessory brackets and drive belts. Position accessories aside with lines and connectors attached.

9. Remove AIR pump pulley.

10. Remove the fan, fan clutch and water pump pulley.

11. Disconnect the thermostat bypass.

12. Disconnect the electrical and vacuum connections.

13. Remove the AIR pump.

14. Remove distributor with cap and wiring intact.

15. Remove crankshaft pulley and hub.

16. Remove the fuel pump.

17. Remove engine front cover.

18. Remove both valve covers.

19. Remove intake manifold, gaskets and seals.

20. Remove rocker arms assemblies, pushrods and valve lifters.

➡**All parts for each assembly must be kept together and reinstalled in the same location.**

21. Disconnect and plug the air conditioner condenser lines.

22. Remove the condenser assembly.

23. Remove bolt securing fuel pump eccentric, remove eccentric, camshaft gear, oil slinger and timing chain.

24. Remove camshaft retaining plate and flange adapter.

25. Remove camshaft by carefully sliding it out the front of the engine.

To install:

26. Lubricate the camshaft with 1051396 or equivalent, and carefully insert into journals.

27. Install camshaft flange adapter and retaining plate.

28. Timing chain and sprockets.

29. Install fuel pump eccentric.

30. Install camshaft thrust spring and button.

31. Install the front cover and fuel pump with new gaskets.

32. Install condenser assembly and lines.

33. Install valve lifters, pushrods and rocker arm assemblies.

34. Install valve covers.

35. Install intake manifold, with new gaskets. Connect fuel lines.

36. Install crankshaft pulley and hub.

37. Install AIR pump.

38. Connect all electrical connections and vacuum hoses.

39. Connect thermostat bypass hose.

40. Install water pump pulley, fan clutch and fan.

41. Connect AIR pump pulley.

42. Install remaining accessory brackets and drive belts.

43. Connect the throttle cable.

44. Install the air cleaner assembly.

45. Install the radiator, hoses and baffle.

46. Connect the negative battery cable and add engine coolant.

47. Check for leaks and recharge air conditioning.

Camshaft Bearing Removal and Installation

▶ **See Figure 75**

➡**It is recommended that the engine be removed from the vehicle before attempting this procedure.**

ALL ENGINES

To remove the camshaft bearings, the camshaft lifters, flywheel, rear camshaft expansion plug, and crankshaft must be removed.

Camshaft bearings can be replaced with engine completely or partially disassembled. To replace bearings without complete disassembly remove the camshaft and crankshaft leaving cylinder heads attached and pistons in place. Before removing crankshaft, tape threads of connecting rod bolts to prevent damage to crankshaft. Fasten connecting rods against sides of engine so they will not be in the way while replacing camshaft bearings.

If excessive wear is indicated, or if the engine is being completely rebuilt, camshaft bearings should be replaced as follows: Drive the camshaft rear plug from the block. Assembly the removal puller with its shoulder on the bearing to be removed. Gradually tighten the puller nut until bearing is removed. Remove remaining bearings, leaving the front and rear for last. To remove front and rear bearings, reverse position of the tool, so as to pull the bearings in toward the center of the block. Leave the tool in this position, pilot the new front and rear bearings on the installer, and pull them into position as follows:

• Except 5.0L (VIN Y) engine: Ensure the No. 1 (front) camshaft bearing holes are an equal distance from the 6 o'clock position on 1990-91 engines or positioned at the 1 o'clock and 5 o'clock positions on 1992-93 engines. The No. 2

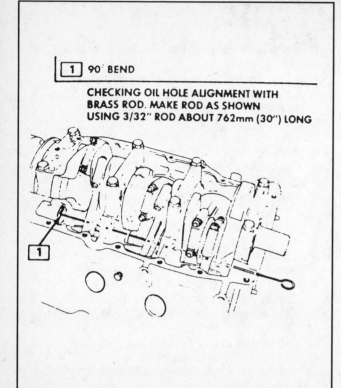

Fig. 75 Checking camshaft bearing oil hole alignment — 5.0L (VIN Y) engine

thru 4 (3 on V6 engine) inner bearing holes must be positioned at the 5 o'clock position towards the left side (drivers) of the engine, even with the bottom of the cylinder bore. The No. 5 (4 on V6 engine) rear bearing oil holes must be positioned at 12 o'clock.

• 5.0L (VIN Y) engine: Ensure the bearing oil holes and engine block oil passages are aligned. Use a piece of 3/32 in. brass rod as illustrated to check for proper alignment.

Return the tool to its original position and pull remaining bearings into position.

➡Ensure that oil holes are properly aligned. Replace camshaft rear plug, and stake it into position to aid retention.

CAMSHAFT INSPECTION

The lobe lift may be checked without removing the camshaft, simply remove the valve cover and rotate the engine while observing each rocker assembly. There should be a substantial and consistent amount of lift between all rockers. If a camshaft lobe is excessively worn there is usually some rocker arm play and valve noise during engine operation.

➡The 5.0L (VIN Y) is prone to excessive rocker arm and bridge wear, these parts should be thoroughly cleaned and inspected.

If the camshaft is suspected of excessive wear, removal will be necessary for a more thorough examination. Once removed,

the camshaft lobes should be examined for wear or pitting. The camshaft journals and bearings should also be inspected for wear and pitting. The journals can be measured using a micrometer and then compared to factory specifications.

Pistons and Connecting Rods

▶ **See Figures 76 and 77**

REMOVAL

Before removal of piston(s), connecting rod(s) and cap(s), mark them with their respective cylinder numbers. Place the mark on the side of the connecting rod as in the figure and also on the top of the piston, nearest to the front of the engine. This will ensure a proper match during reinstallation.

➡**This procedure is easily completed if the engine has been removed from the car.**

1. Remove the cylinder head(s), intake manifold, exhaust manifold, oil pan, and oil pump as outlined in this Section.
2. Mount the engine on a stand. In order to facilitate removal of the piston and connecting rod, the ridge at the top of the cylinder (unworn area; see illustration) must be removed. Place the piston at the bottom of the bore, and cover it with a rag. Cut the ridge away using a ridge reamer,

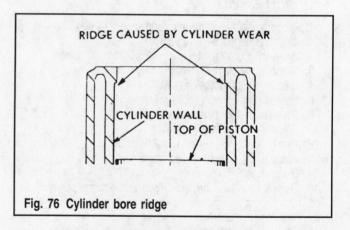

Fig. 76 Cylinder bore ridge

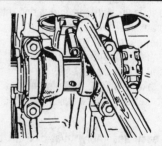

Fig. 77 Pushing the piston assembly from the engine using a hammer handle

exercising extreme care to avoid cutting too deeply. Remove the rag, and remove cuttings that remain on the piston.

❋❋CAUTION

If the ridge is not removed, and new rings are installed, damage to rings will result.

3. Remove the connecting rod bearing caps and bearings.
4. Install a section of rubber hose over the connecting rod bolts to prevent damage to the crankshaft.
5. Slide the piston/connecting rod assembly through the top of the cylinder block.

❋❋CAUTION

To avoid damaging the rings, do not attempt to force the piston past the cylinder ridge (see above).

POSITIONING

▶ See Figure 78

➡ Most pistons are notched or marked to indicate which way they should be installed. If your pistons are not marked, mark the top front of the piston and the connecting rods with there respective cylinder number before removal. Then reinstall them in the proper position.

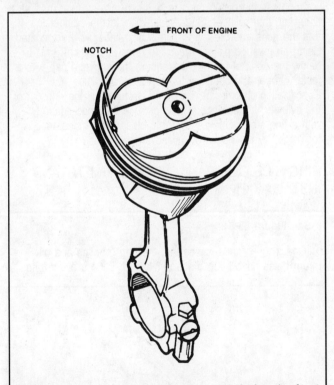

Fig. 78 Install the pistons with the notch facing the front of the engine and the oil bearing tang slots facing the opposite side of the camshaft

CLEANING AND INSPECTING

▶ See Figures 79, 80, 81, 82 and 83

A piston ring expander is necessary for removing piston rings without damaging them; any other method (screwdriver blades, pliers, etc.) usually results in the rings being broken or distorted, or the piston itself being damaged. When the rings are removed, clean the ring grooves using a ring groove

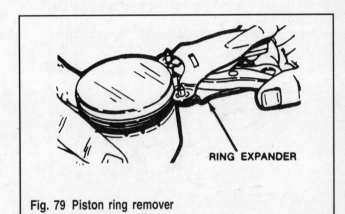

Fig. 79 Piston ring remover

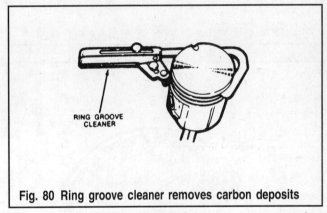

Fig. 80 Ring groove cleaner removes carbon deposits

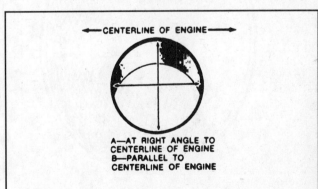

Fig. 81 Cylinder bore measuring points

cleaning tool, using care not to cut too deeply. Thoroughly clean all carbon and varnish from the piston with solvent.

✳✳CAUTION

Do not use a wire brush or caustic solvent (acids, etc.) on piston.

Inspect the pistons for scuffing, scoring, cracks, pitting, or excessive ring groove wear. If these are evident, the piston must be replaced.

The piston should also be checked in relation to the cylinder diameter. Using a telescoping gauge and micrometer, or a dial gauge, measure the cylinder bore diameter perpendicular to the piston pin, 2 ½ inch below the cylinder block deck (surface where the block mates with the heads). Then, with the

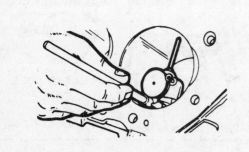

Fig. 82 Measuring the cylinder bore with a dial gauge

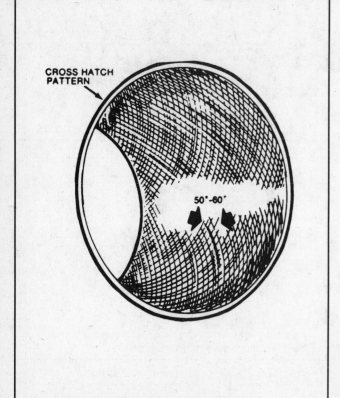

Fig. 83 Correct cylinder bore honing pattern

micrometer, measure the piston perpendicular and a ½ inch below the wrist pin on the skirt. The difference between the two measurements is the piston clearance.

If the clearance is within specifications or slightly below (after the cylinders have been bored or honed), finish honing is all that is necessary. If the clearance is excessive, try to obtain a slightly larger piston to bring clearance to within specifications. If this is not possible obtain the first oversize piston and hone (or if necessary, bore) the cylinder to size. Generally, if the cylinder bore is tapered 0.005″ or more, or is out-of-round 0.003″ or more, it is advisable to re-bore for the smallest possible oversize piston and rings. After measuring, mark pistons with a felt-tip pen for reference and for assembly.

➡**Cylinder block boring should be performed by a reputable machine shop with the proper equipment. In some cases, cleanup honing can be done with the cylinder block in the car, but most excessive honing and all cylinder boring must be done with the block stripped and removed from the car.**

CHECKING RING END GAP

▶ **See Figure 84**

Piston ring end gap should be checked while the rings are removed from the pistons. Incorrect end gap indicates that the wrong size rings are being used; ring breakage could occur.

Compress the piston rings to be used in a cylinder, one at a time, into that cylinder. Squirt clean oil into the cylinder, so that the rings and the top 2 inches of cylinder wall are coated. Using an inverted piston, press the rings approximately 1″ below the deck of the block. Measure the ring end gap with a feeler gauge, and compare to the Piston and Ring Specification chart in this Section. Carefully pull the ring out of the cylinder. If clearance is too tight, file the ends squarely with a fine file to obtain the proper clearance. If clearance is too large, try too obtain oversized rings.

RING SIDE CLEARANCE MEASUREMENT AND INSTALLATION

▶ **See Figure 85**

Check the pistons to see that the ring grooves and oil return holes have been properly cleaned. Slide a piston ring

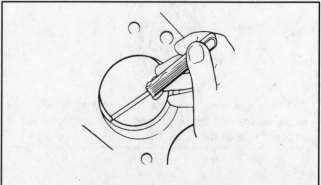

Fig. 84 Checking the piston ring end gap

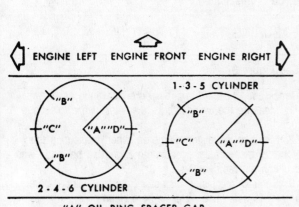

Fig. 85 Piston ring end gaps in correct locations — V6 engine illustrated; V8 engine the same

into its groove, and check the side clearance with a feeler gauge. Make sure the feeler gauge is inserted between the ring and its lower land (lower edge of the groove), because any wear that occurs forms a step at the inner portion of the lower land. If the piston grooves have worn to the extent that relatively high steps exist on the lower land, the piston should be replaced, because these will interfere with the operation of the new rings and ring clearances will be excessive. Piston rings are not furnished in oversize widths to compensate for ring groove wear.

Install the rings on the piston, lowest ring first, using a piston ring expander. There is a high risk of breaking or distorting the rings, or scratching the piston, if the rings are installed by hand or other means.

Position the rings on the piston as illustrated; spacing of the various piston ring gaps is crucial to proper oil retention and even cylinder wear. When installing new rings, refer to the installation diagram furnished with the new parts.

PISTON PIN REPLACEMENT

The piston pins are made of chromium steel. The fit within the piston is floating and the connecting rod is pressed on all except the 5.0L (VIN Y) engine. The fit within the piston and rod is floating on the 5.0L (VIN Y) engine.

➡ **Pin replacement should only be attempted by a qualified machine shop.**

Connecting Rod Bearings

Connecting rod bearings for the engines covered in this guide consist of two halves or shells which are interchangeable in the rod and cap. When the shells are placed in position, the ends extend slightly beyond the rod and cap surfaces so that when the rod bolts are torqued the shells will be clamped tightly in place to ensure positive seating and to prevent turning. A tang holds the shells in place.

➡ **The ends of the bearing shells must never be filed flush with the mating surface of the rod and cap.**

If a rod bearing becomes noisy or is worn so that its clearance on the crank journal is excessive, a new bearing of the correct undersize must be selected and installed since there is no provision for adjustment.

✳✳CAUTION

Under no circumstances should the rod end or cap be filed to adjust the bearing clearance, nor should shims of any kind be used.

Inspect the rod bearings while the rod assemblies are out of the engine. If the shells are scored or show flaking, they should be replaced. If they are in good shape check for proper clearance on the crank journal (see below). Any scoring or ridges on the crank journal means the crankshaft must be replaced, or re-ground and fitted with undersized bearings.

➡ **If journals are deeply scored or ridged the crankshaft must be replaced, as regrinding will reduce the durability of the crankshaft.**

ROD BEARING INSPECTION AND REPLACEMENT

▶ **See Figure 86**

➡ **Make sure connecting rods and their caps are kept together, and that the caps are installed in the proper direction.**

Replacement bearings are available in standard size, and in undersizes for reground crankshafts. Connecting rod-to-crankshaft bearing clearance is checked using Plastigage® at

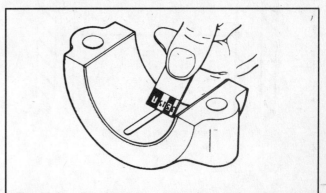

Fig. 86 Use Plastigage® to determine bearing clearances

either the top or bottom of each crank journal. The Plastigage® has a range of 0.001-0.003″.

1. Remove the rod cap with the bearing shell, Completely clean the bearing shell and the crank journal, and blow any oil from the oil hole in the crankshaft; Plastigage® lengthwise along the bottom center of the lower bearing shell, then install the cap with shell and torque the bolt or nuts to specification. DO NOT turn the crankshaft with Plastigage® in the bearing.

2. Remove the bearing cap with the shell. The flattened Plastigage® will be found sticking to either the bearing shell or crank journal. Do not remove it yet.

3. Use the scale printed on the Plastigage® envelope to measure the flattened material at its widest point. The number within the scale which most closely corresponds to the width of the Plastigage® indicates bearing clearance in thousandths of an inch.

4. Check the specifications chart in this section for the desired clearance. It is advisable to install a new bearing if clearance exceeds 0.003″; however, if the bearing is in good condition and is not being checked because of bearing noise, bearing replacement is not necessary.

5. If you are installing new bearings, try a standard size, then each undersize in order until one is found that is within the specified limits when checked for clearance with Plastigage. Each undersize shell has its size stamped on it.

6. When the proper size shell is found, clean off the Plastigage, oil the bearing thoroughly, reinstall the cap with its shell and torque the rod bolt nuts to specification.

→ With the proper bearing selected and the nuts torqued, it should be possible to move the connecting rod back and forth freely on the crank journal as allowed by the specified connecting rod end clearance. If the rod cannot be moved, either the rod bearing is too far undersize or the rod is misaligned.

MEASURING THE OLD PISTONS

▶ See Figure 87

Check used piston-to-cylinder bore clearance as follows:
1. Measure the cylinder bore diameter with a telescope gauge.
2. Measure the piston diameter. When measuring the pistons for size or taper, measurements must be made with the piston pin removed.
3. Subtract the piston diameter from the cylinder bore diameter to determine piston-to-bore clearance.
4. Compare the piston-to-bore clearances obtained with those clearances recommended. Determine if the piston-to-bore clearance is in the acceptable range.
5. When measuring taper, the largest reading must be at the bottom of the skirt.

SELECTING NEW PISTONS

1. If the used piston is not acceptable, check the service piston size and determine if a new piston can be selected. (Service pistons are available in standard, high limit and standard oversize.

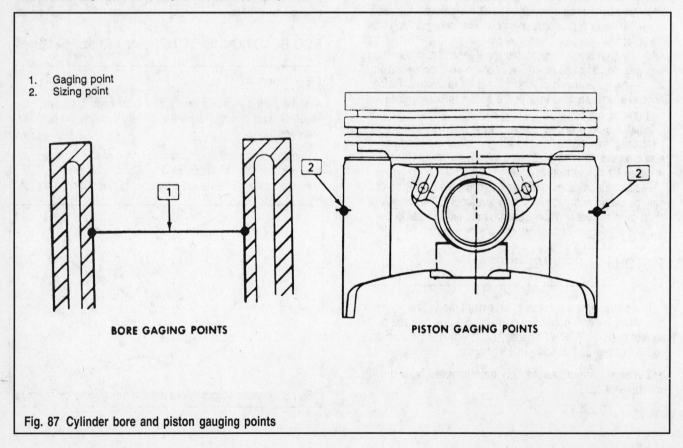

1. Gaging point
2. Sizing point

BORE GAGING POINTS

PISTON GAGING POINTS

Fig. 87 Cylinder bore and piston gauging points

2. If the cylinder bore must be reconditioned, measure the new piston diameter, then hone the cylinder bore to obtain the preferred clearance.

3. Select a new piston and mark the piston to identify the cylinder for which it was fitted. (On some vehicles, oversize pistons may be found. These pistons will be 0.254mm (0.010 inch) oversize).

CYLINDER HONING

▶ **See Figure 83**

1. When cylinders are being honed, follow the manufacturer's recommendations for the use of the hone.

2. Occasionally, during the honing operation, the cylinder bore should be thoroughly cleaned and the selected piston checked for correct fit.

3. When finish-honing a cylinder bore, the hone should be moved up and down at a sufficient speed to obtain a very fine uniform surface finish in a cross-hatch pattern of approximately 45-65° included angle. The finish marks should be clean but not sharp, free from embedded particles and torn or folded metal.

4. Permanently mark the piston for the cylinder to which it has been fitted and proceed to hone the remaining cylinders.

❈❈WARNING

Handle the pistons with care. Do not attempt to force the pistons through the cylinders until the cylinders have been honed to the correct size. Pistons can be distorted through careless handling.

5. Thoroughly clean the bores with hot water and detergent. Scrub well with a stiff bristle brush and rinse thoroughly with hot water. It is extremely essential that a good cleaning operation be performed. If any of the abrasive material is allowed to remain in the cylinder bores, it will rapidly wear the new rings and cylinder bores. The bores should be swabbed several times with light engine oil and a clean cloth and then wiped with a clean dry cloth. CYLINDERS SHOULD NOT BE CLEANED WITH KEROSENE OR GASOLINE! Clean the remainder of the cylinder block to remove the excess material spread during the honing operation.

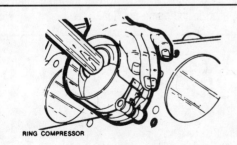

Fig. 88 Install the piston ring compressor, then tap the piston into the cylinder bore. Make sure that the piston marks are correctly positioned

PISTON AND CONNECTING ROD ASSEMBLY AND INSTALLATION

▶ **See Figures 88 and 89**

Install the connecting rod to the piston, making sure piston installation notches and marks on the rod are in proper relation to one another. Lubricate the wrist pin with clean engine oil, and install the pin into the rod and piston assembly, by using a press, as required. Install snaprings if equipped, and rotate them in their grooves to make sure they are seated. To install the piston and connecting rod assembly into the engine, proceed as follows:

1. Make sure connecting rod bearings are of the correct size and properly installed.

2. Fit rubber hoses over the connecting rod bolts to protect the crankshaft journals, as in the Piston Removal procedure. Coat the rod bearings with clean oil.

3. Using the proper ring compressor, insert the piston assembly into the cylinder so that the notch in the top of the piston faces the front of the engine and the connecting rod bearing tang slots on the side opposite the camshaft (this assumes that the dimple(s) or other markings on the connecting rods are in correct relation to the piston notch).

4. From beneath the engine, coat each crank journal with clean oil. Pull the connecting rod, with the bearing shell in place, into position against the crank journal.

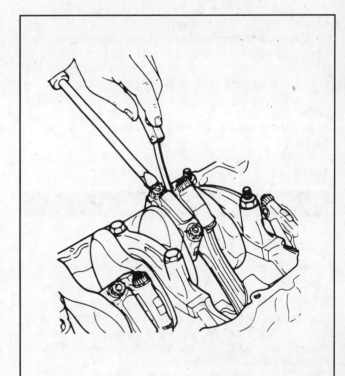

Fig. 89 Check the connecting rod side clearance with a feeler gauge. Use a small pry bar to carefully spread the rods to specified clearance

5. Remove the rubber hoses. Install the bearing cap and cap nuts and torque to specification.

➡When more than one rod and piston assembly is being installed, the connecting rod cap attaching nuts should only be tightened enough to keep each rod in position until all have been installed. This will ease the installation of the remaining piston assembles.

6. Check the clearance between the sides of the connecting rods and the crankshaft using a feeler gauge. Spread the rods slightly with a small prybar to insert the gauge. If clearance is below the minimum tolerance, the rod may be machined to provide adequate clearance. If clearance is excessive, substitute an unworn rod, and recheck. If clearance is still outside specifications, the crankshaft must be welded and reground, or replaced.

7. Replace the oil pump, if removed, and the oil pan.

8. Install the cylinder head(s) and intake manifold, as previously described.

Freeze Plugs

REMOVAL AND INSTALLATION

1. Disconnect the negative battery cable.
2. Drain the cooling system.
3. Raise and support the vehicle safely.
4. Remove the coolant drain plug on the side of the block, if equipped. Or you can use a punch to put a small hole in the center of the freeze plug being replaced.
5. Remove all components in order to gain access to the freeze plug(s).
6. Using a punch, tap the bottom corner of the freeze plug to cock it in the bore. Remove the plug using pliers.
7. Clean the freeze plug hole and coat the new plug with sealer.
8. Using a suitable tool, install the freeze plug into the block.
9. Connect the negative battery cable, fill the cooling system, start the engine and check for leaks.

Crankshaft and Main Bearings

CLEANING AND INSPECTION

Crankshaft servicing literally makes or breaks any engine; especially a high performance one. The most critical maintenance operation is the replacement of the crankshaft main bearings. These bearings are of the precision insert design and do not require adjustment through shims. They are offered in several undersizes.

Despite the advent of these inserts and accompanying precision machine work, it does happen that sizing mistakes are made and no crankshaft should be installed in a block without checking clearances. One of the simplest means of doing so is to use Plastigage®. This is a wax-like plastic material that is formed into precision threads. It will compress

evenly between two surfaces, without damage, and when measured, will indicate the actual clearance.

It is easiest to check bearing clearance with the engine removed from the car and the block inverted. This ensures that the crank is resting against the upper bearing shells. If Plastigage® is to be used on an engine still in the vehicle, it will be necessary to support the crankshaft at both ends so that clearance between the crankshaft and the upper bearing shells is eliminated.

REMOVAL

▶ See Figure 90

1. Drain the engine oil and remove the engine from the car. Mount the engine on a work stand in a suitable working area. Invert the engine, so the oil pan is facing up.

✳✳CAUTION

The EPA warns that prolonged contact with used engine oil may cause a number of skin disorders, including cancer! You should make every effort to minimize your exposure to used engine oil. Protective gloves should be worn when changing the oil. Wash your hands and any other exposed skin areas as soon as possible after exposure to used engine oil. Soap and water, or waterless hand cleaner should be used.

2. Remove the engine water pump and front (timing) cover.
3. Remove the timing chain (if equipped) and gears.
4. Remove the oil pan.
5. Remove the oil pump.
6. Stamp or mark the cylinder number on the machined surfaces of the bolt bosses of the connecting rods and caps for identification when reinstalling. If the pistons are to be removed from the connecting rod, mark the cylinder number on the pistons with silver paint or felt-tip pen for proper cylinder identification and cap-to-rod location.
7. Remove the connecting rod caps. Install lengths of rubber hose on each of the connecting rod bolts, to protect the crank journals when the crank is removed.
8. Mark the main bearing caps with a number punch or punch so that they can be reinstalled in their original positions.
9. Remove all main bearing caps.
10. Note the position of the keyway in the crankshaft so it can be installed in the same position.

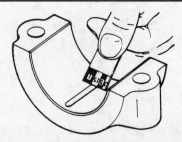

Fig. 90 Support the connecting rods with rubber bands and install rubber hose over the cap bolts during crankshaft removal and installation

11. Install rubber bands between a bolt on each connecting rod and oil pan bolts that have been reinstalled in the block (see illustration). This will keep the rods from banging on the block when the crank is removed.

12. Carefully lift the crankshaft out of the block. The rods will pivot to the center of the engine when the crank is removed.

MAIN BEARING INSPECTION

◗ **See Figure 91**

Like connecting rod big-end bearings, the crankshaft main bearings are shell-type inserts that do not utilize shims and cannot be adjusted. The bearings are available in various standard and undersizes; if main bearing clearance is found to be excessive, a new bearing (both upper and lower halves) is required.

➡**It is not uncommon for the factory to use undersize bearings and sometimes mix some standard and undersize bearings to achieve a perfect fit.**

Generally, the lower half of the bearing shell (except No. 1 bearing) shows greater wear and fatigue. If the lower half only shows the effects of normal wear (no heavy scoring or discoloration), it can usually be assumed that the upper half is also in good shape; conversely, if the lower half is heavily worn or damaged, both halves should be replaced. Never replace one bearing half without replacing the other.

MEASURING MAIN BEARING CLEARANCE

Main bearing clearance can be checked both with the crankshaft in the car and with the engine out of the car. If the engine block is still in the car, the crankshaft should be supported both front and rear (by the damper and the transmission) to remove clearance from the upper bearing. Total clearance can then be measured between the lower bearing and journal. If the block has been removed from the car, and is inverted, the crank will rest on the upper bearings and the total clearance can be measured between the lower

bearing and journal. Clearance is checked in the same manner as the connecting rod bearings, with Plastigage®.

➡**Crankshaft bearing caps and bearing shells should NEVER be filed flush with the cap-to-block mating surface to adjust for wear in the old bearings. Always install new bearings.**

1. If the crankshaft has been removed, install it (block removed from car). If the block is still in the car, remove the oil pan and oil pump. Starting with the rear bearing cap, remove the cap and wipe all oil from the crank journal and bearing cap.

2. Place a strip of Plastigage® the full width of the bearing, (parallel to the crankshaft), on the journal.

➡**Plastigage® is soluble in oil; therefore, oil on the journal or bearing could result in erroneous readings.**

✳✳CAUTION

Do not rotate the crankshaft while the gaging material is between the bearing and the journal.

3. Install the bearing cap and evenly torque the cap bolts to specification.

4. Remove the bearing cap. The flattened Plastigage® will be sticking to either the bearing shell or the crank journal.

5. Use the graduated scale on the Plastigage® envelope to measure the material at its widest point. If the flattened Plastigage® tapers toward the middle or ends, there is a difference in clearance indicating the bearing or journal has a taper, low spot or other irregularity. If this is indicated, measure the crank journal with a micrometer.

6. If bearing clearance is within specifications, the bearing insert is in good shape. Replace the insert if the clearance is not within specifications. Always replace both upper and lower inserts as a unit.

7. Standard, 0.001″ or 0.002″ undersize bearings should produce the proper clearance. If these sizes still produce too sloppy a fit, the crankshaft must be reground for use with the next undersize bearing. Recheck all clearances after installing new bearings.

8. Replace the rest of the bearings in the same manner. After all bearings have been checked, rotate the crankshaft to make sure there is no excessive drag. When checking the No. 1 main bearing, loosen the accessory drive belts (engine in car) to prevent a tapered reading with the Plastigage®.

MAIN BEARING REPLACEMENT

◗ **See Figure 92**

Engine Out of Car

1. Remove and inspect the crankshaft.

2. Remove the main bearings from the bearing saddles in the cylinder block and main bearing caps.

3. Coat the bearing surfaces of the new, correct size main bearings with clean engine oil and install them in the bearing saddles in the block and in the main bearing caps.

4. Install the crankshaft. See Crankshaft Installation.

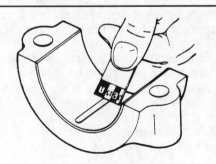

Fig. 91 Measure the main bearing clearance by comparing the flattened strip of Plastigage with the scale

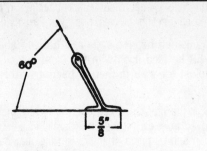

Fig. 92 Fabricated cotter pin for removal of main bearings with the engine in the vehicle

Engine in Car

1. With the oil pan, oil pump and spark plugs removed, remove the cap from the main bearing needing replacement and remove the bearing from the cap.

2. Make a bearing roll-out pin, using a bent cotter pin as shown in the illustration. Install the end of the pin in the oil hole in the crankshaft journal.

3. Rotate the crankshaft clockwise as viewed from the front of the engine. This will roll the upper bearing out of the block.

4. Lube the new upper bearing with clean engine oil and insert the plain (un-notched) end between the crankshaft and the indented or notched side of the block. Roll the bearing into place, making sure that the oil holes are aligned. Remove the roll pin from the oil hole.

5. Lube the new lower bearing and install the main bearing cap. Install the main bearing cap, making sure it is positioned in proper direction with the matchmarks in alignment.

6. Torque the main bearing cap bolts to specification.

➡The thrust bearing must be aligned before torquing cap bolts.

REGRINDING JOURNALS

➡Regrinding rod and/or main bearing journals should be performed by a qualified machine shop.

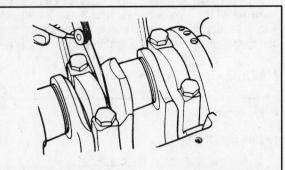

Fig. 93 Use a feeler gauge to check the crankshaft end play during assembly

CRANKSHAFT INSTALLATION

▶ **See Figures 93 and 94**

When main bearing clearance has been checked, bearings examined and/or replaced, the crankshaft can be installed. Thoroughly clean the upper and lower bearing surfaces, and lube them with clean engine oil. Install the crankshaft and main bearing caps.

Dip all main bearing cap bolts in clean oil, and torque all main bearing caps, excluding the thrust bearing cap, to specifications (see the Crankshaft and Connecting Rod chart in this section to determine which bearing is the thrust bearing). Tighten the thrust bearing bolts finger tight. To align the thrust bearing, pry the crankshaft the extent of its axial travel several times, holding the last movement toward the front of the engine. Add thrust washers if required for proper alignment. Torque the thrust bearing cap to specifications.

To check crankshaft end-play, pry the crankshaft to the extreme rear of its axial travel, then to the extreme front of its travel. Using a feeler gauge, measure the end-play at the front of the rear main bearing. End play may also be measured at the thrust bearing. Install a new rear main bearing oil seal in the cylinder block and main bearing cap. Continue to reassemble the engine in reverse of disassembly procedures.

Rear Main Oil Seal

REMOVAL AND INSTALLATION

The Oldsmobile produced 5.0L (VIN Y) engine came equipped with either a 2-piece neoprene seal or a rope seal. All other Chevrolet produced engines come equipped with a new 1-piece neoprene seal.

1-Piece Neoprene Seal

▶ **See Figures 95 and 96**

➡The rear main seal is a one piece unit. It can be removed or installed without removing the oil pan or crankshaft.

1. Jack up your vehicle and support it with jackstands.
2. Remove the transmission assembly.
3. Remove the flywheel and block plate assembly.
4. Using a suitable tool, pry the old seal out.
5. Inspect the crankshaft for nicks or burrs, correct as required.
6. To install, clean the area and coat the seal with engine oil. Install the seal onto tool J-34686 or equivalent. Install the seal into the engine.
7. Install the flywheel and block plate. Torque to specification.
8. Install the transmission.
9. Check the fluid levels, start the engine and check for leaks.

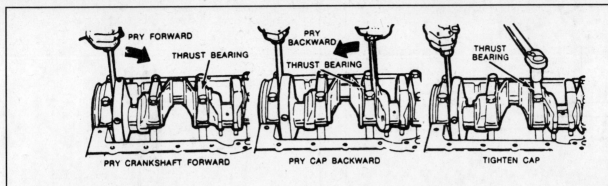

Fig. 94 Align the thrust bearing as illustrated. Torque the main caps to specification

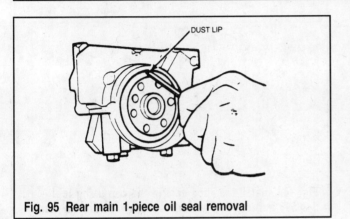

Fig. 95 Rear main 1-piece oil seal removal

Fig. 97 Rear main 2-piece oil seal lower half removal

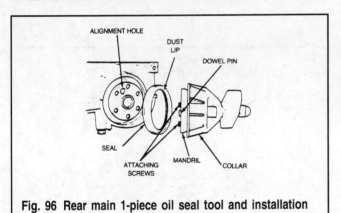

Fig. 96 Rear main 1-piece oil seal tool and installation

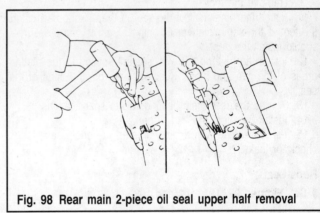

Fig. 98 Rear main 2-piece oil seal upper half removal

2-piece Neoprene Seal

▶ See Figures 97, 98, 99 and 100

Both halves of the rear main oil seal can be replaced without removing the crankshaft. Always replace the upper and lower seal together. The lip should face the front of the engine. Be very careful that you do not break the sealing bead in the channel on the outside portion of the seal while installing it. An installation tool can be fabricated to protect the seal bead.

1. Remove the oil pan, oil pump and rear main bearing cap.

2. Remove the oil seal from the bearing cap by prying it out.

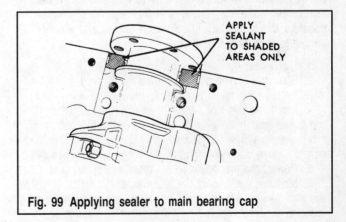

Fig. 99 Applying sealer to main bearing cap

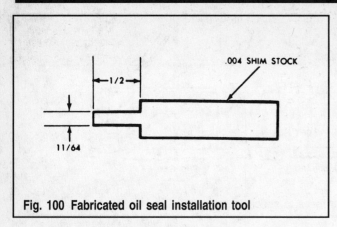

Fig. 100 Fabricated oil seal installation tool

3. Remove the upper half of the seal with a small punch. Drive it around far enough to be gripped with pliers.

4. Clean the crankshaft and bearing cap.

5. Coat the lips and bead of the seal with light engine oil, keeping oil from the ends of the seal.

6. Position the fabricated tool between the crankshaft and seal seat.

7. Position the seal between the crankshaft and tip of the tool so that the seal bead contacts the tip of the tool. The oil seal lip should face THE front of the engine.

8. Roll the seal around the crankshaft using the tool to protect the seal bead from the sharp corners of the crankcase.

9. The installation tool should be left installed until the seal is properly positioned with both ends flush with the block.

10. Remove the tool.

11. Install the other half of the seal in the bearing cap using the tool in the same manner as before. Light thumb pressure should install the seal.

12. Install the bearing cap with sealant applied to the mating areas of the cap and block. Keep sealant from the ends of the seal.

13. Torque the rear main bearing cap to specifications.

14. Install the oil pump and oil pan.

15. Fill the engine with engine oil, start the engine and check for leaks.

Rope Seal

▶ **See Figures 99, 101, 102 and 103**

➡️**The following procedure is only to be used as an oil seal repair while the engine is in the vehicle. Whenever possible the crankshaft should be removed and a new complete rope seal installed.**

1. Disconnect the negative battery cable.

2. Drain the engine oil and remove the oil pan.

3. Remove the rear main bearing cap.

4. Insert packing tool J-29114-2 or equivalent, against 1 end of the seal in the cylinder block. Drive the old seal gently into the groove until it is packed tight. This will vary from 1/4 inch to 3/4 inch depending on the amount of pack required.

5. Repeat the procedure on the other end of the seal.

6. Measure the amount the seal was driven up on one side and add 1/16 inch. Using a suitable cutting tool, cut that length from the old seal removed from the rear main bearing cap. Repeat the procedure for the other side. Use the rear main bearing cap as a holding fixture when cutting the seal.

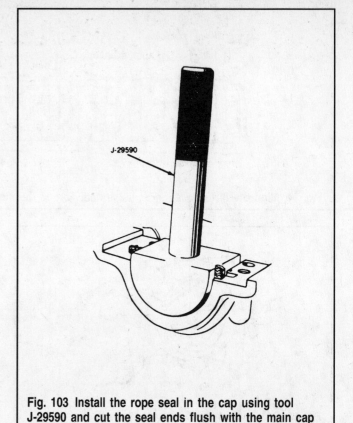

Fig. 103 Install the rope seal in the cap using tool J-29590 and cut the seal ends flush with the main cap

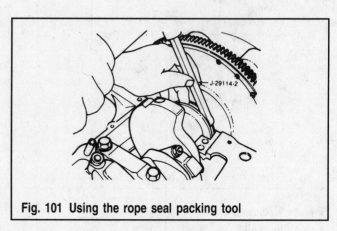

Fig. 101 Using the rope seal packing tool

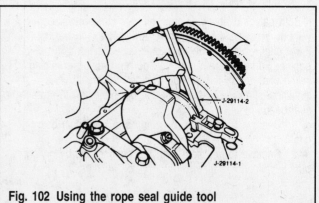

Fig. 102 Using the rope seal guide tool

7. Install guide tool J-29114-1 or equivalent, onto the cylinder block.

8. Using the packing tool, work the short pieces cut in Step 6 into the guide tool and then pack into the cylinder block. The guide tool and packing tool are machined to provide a built in stop. Use this procedure for both sides. It may help to use oil on the short pieces of the rope seal when packing them into the cylinder block.

9. Remove the guide tool.

10. Apply Loctite 414 or equivalent, to the seal groove in the rear main bearing cap. Within 1 minute, insert a new seal into the groove and push into place with tool J-29590 until the seal is flush with the block. Cut the excess seal material with a sharp cutting tool at the bearing cap parting line.

11. Apply a thin film of chassis grease to the rope seal. Apply a thin film of RTV sealant on the bearing cap mating surface around the seal groove. Use the sealer sparingly.

12. Plastigage the rear main bearing cap as outlined in MEASURING REAR MAIN CLEARANCE in this Section and check with specification. If out of specification, check for fraying of the rope seal which may be causing the cap to not seat properly.

13. Install all remaining components and inspect for leaks.

Flywheel and Ring Gear

REMOVAL AND INSTALLATION

The ring gear is an integral part of the flywheel and is not replaceable.

1. Remove the transmission.

2. Remove the six bolts attaching the flywheel to the crankshaft flange. Remove the flywheel.

3. Inspect the flywheel for cracks, and inspect the ring gear for burrs or worn teeth. Replace the flywheel if any damage is apparent. Remove burrs with a mill file.

4. Install the flywheel. The flywheel will only attach to the crankshaft in one position, as the bolt holes are unevenly spaced. Install the bolts and torque to specification. Tighten bolts in crisscross pattern.

EXHAUST SYSTEM

▶ **See Figures 104, 105 and 106**

Safety Precautions

For a number of reasons, exhaust system work can be the most dangerous type of work you can do on your car. Always observe the following precautions:

• Support the car safely. Not only will you often be working directly under it, but you'll frequently be using a lot of force, say, heavy hammer blows, to dislodge rusted parts. This can cause a car that's improperly supported to shift and possibly fall.

• Wear goggles. Exhaust system parts are always rusty. Metal chips can be dislodged, even when you're only turning rusted bolts. Attempting to pry pipes apart with a chisel makes the chips fly even more frequently.

• If you're using a cutting torch, keep it a safe distance from either the fuel tank or lines. Stop what you're doing and feel the temperature of the fuel bearing pipes on the tank frequently. Even slight heat can expand and/or vaporize fuel, resulting in accumulated vapor, or even a liquid leak, near your torch.

• Watch where your hammering and make sure you hit squarely. You could easily tap a brake or fuel line when you hit an exhaust system part with a glancing blow. Inspect all lines and hoses in the area where you've been working.

Special Tools

A number of special exhaust system tools can be rented from auto supply houses or local stores that rent special equipment. A common one is a tail pipe expander, designed to enable you to join pipes of identical diameter.

It may also be quite helpful to use solvents designed to loosen rusted bolts or flanges. Soaking rusted parts the night before you do the job can speed the work of freeing rusted parts considerably. Remember that these solvents are often flammable. Apply only to parts after they are cool!

Checking

Check complete exhaust system and nearby body areas and trunk lid for broken, damaged, missing or mispositioned parts, open seams, holes, loose connections or other deterioration which could permit exhaust fumes to seep into the trunk or passenger compartment. Dust or water in the trunk may be an indication of a problem in one of these areas. Any defects should be corrected immediately. To help ensure continued integrity, the exhaust system pipe rearward of the muffler must be replaced whenever a new muffler is installed. Also perform the following checks:

• After completing any repairs to the exhaust system check for possible leaks by performing the following: start the vehicle, ensure the emergency brake is on and the transmission is in **P** for automatic transmission, then have an assistant hold a rag up the tailpipe(s), listen for exhaust leaks, if possible carefully listen under the vehicle and if the exhaust system is still cool place hands around the pipes and feel for leaks. The engine may begin to stall because of excessive backpressure, which is normal and so the test should be performed quickly.

• After completing any repairs to the exhaust system, lower the vehicle so the suspension is fully compressed and with the aid of an assistant rock the back end of the vehicle up and down while you listen and carefully look for any system components which might be rubbing on fuel, brake or other items such as: shock absorbers, the rear axle, driveshaft and the body or floor of the vehicle.

A. LV2 (Right)
B. LB4
C. LV2 (Left)
D. LO3/LO5 (Right)
E. LO3/LO5 (Left)
1. Crossover pipe bolt
2. Seal
3. Manifold
4. Crossover pipe
5. Exhaust pipe bolt
6. Exhaust pipe
7. Spring
8. Exhaust pipe flange
9. EFE Valve gasket
10. Engine
11. Manifold stud
12. Crossover pipe
13. Crossover pipe nut
14. Crossover pipe spacer
15. Spacer gasket
16. EFE valve

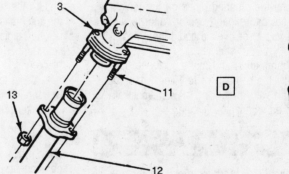

Fig. 104 Exhaust manifold attachments

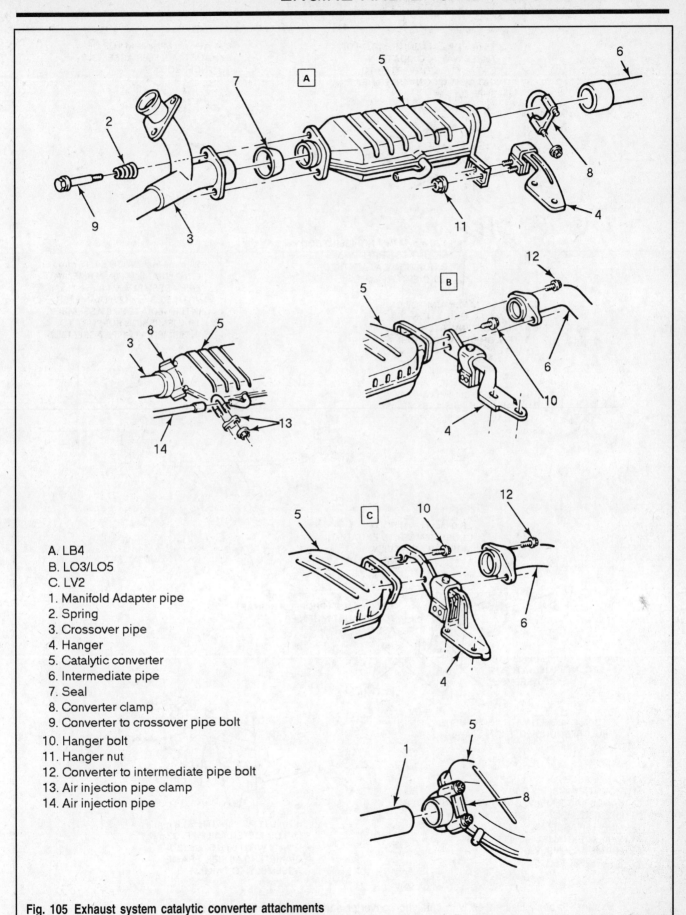

A. LB4
B. LO3/LO5
C. LV2
1. Manifold Adapter pipe
2. Spring
3. Crossover pipe
4. Hanger
5. Catalytic converter
6. Intermediate pipe
7. Seal
8. Converter clamp
9. Converter to crossover pipe bolt
10. Hanger bolt
11. Hanger nut
12. Converter to intermediate pipe bolt
13. Air injection pipe clamp
14. Air injection pipe

Fig. 105 Exhaust system catalytic converter attachments

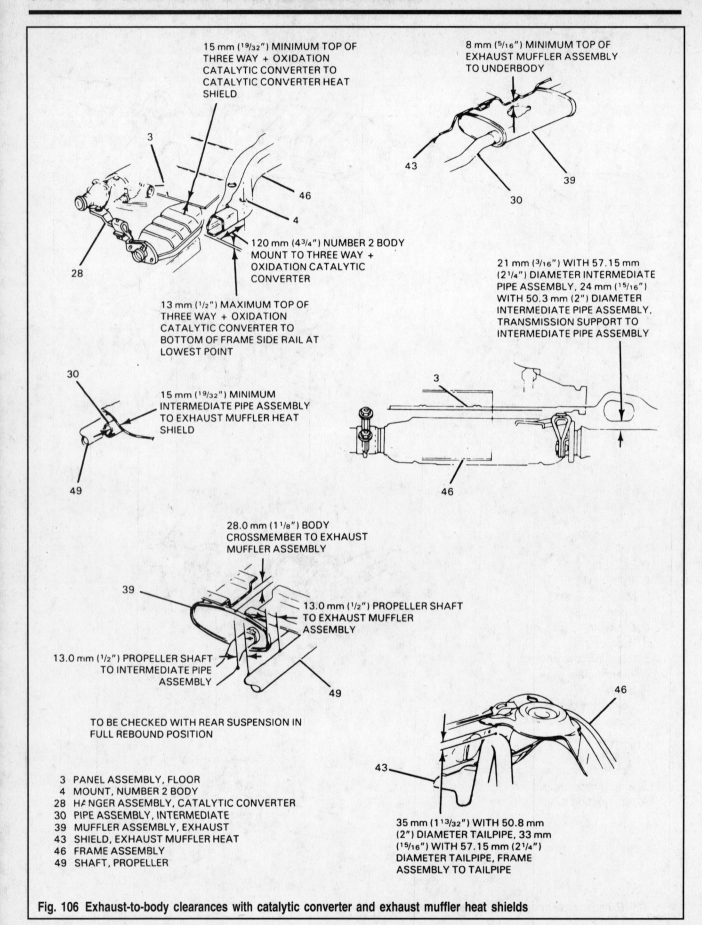

15 mm ($^{19}/_{32}$") MINIMUM TOP OF
THREE WAY + OXIDATION
CATALYTIC CONVERTER TO
CATALYTIC CONVERTER HEAT
SHIELD

8 mm ($^{5}/_{16}$") MINIMUM TOP OF
EXHAUST MUFFLER ASSEMBLY
TO UNDERBODY

120 mm (4$^{3}/_{4}$") NUMBER 2 BODY
MOUNT TO THREE WAY +
OXIDATION CATALYTIC
CONVERTER

13 mm ($^{1}/_{2}$") MAXIMUM TOP OF
THREE WAY + OXIDATION
CATALYTIC CONVERTER TO
BOTTOM OF FRAME SIDE RAIL AT
LOWEST POINT

21 mm ($^{3}/_{16}$") WITH 57.15 mm
(2$^{1}/_{4}$") DIAMETER INTERMEDIATE
PIPE ASSEMBLY, 24 mm ($^{15}/_{16}$")
WITH 50.3 mm (2") DIAMETER
INTERMEDIATE PIPE ASSEMBLY,
TRANSMISSION SUPPORT TO
INTERMEDIATE PIPE ASSEMBLY

15 mm ($^{19}/_{32}$") MINIMUM
INTERMEDIATE PIPE ASSEMBLY
TO EXHAUST MUFFLER HEAT
SHIELD

28.0 mm (1$^{1}/_{8}$") BODY
CROSSMEMBER TO EXHAUST
MUFFLER ASSEMBLY

13.0 mm ($^{1}/_{2}$") PROPELLER SHAFT
TO EXHAUST MUFFLER
ASSEMBLY

13.0 mm ($^{1}/_{2}$") PROPELLER SHAFT
TO INTERMEDIATE PIPE
ASSEMBLY

TO BE CHECKED WITH REAR SUSPENSION IN
FULL REBOUND POSITION

3 PANEL ASSEMBLY, FLOOR
4 MOUNT, NUMBER 2 BODY
28 HANGER ASSEMBLY, CATALYTIC CONVERTER
30 PIPE ASSEMBLY, INTERMEDIATE
39 MUFFLER ASSEMBLY, EXHAUST
43 SHIELD, EXHAUST MUFFLER HEAT
46 FRAME ASSEMBLY
49 SHAFT, PROPELLER

35 mm (1$^{13}/_{32}$") WITH 50.8 mm
(2") DIAMETER TAILPIPE, 33 mm
($^{15}/_{16}$") WITH 57.15 mm (2$^{1}/_{4}$")
DIAMETER TAILPIPE, FRAME
ASSEMBLY TO TAILPIPE

Fig. 106 Exhaust-to-body clearances with catalytic converter and exhaust muffler heat shields

Crossover Pipe

REMOVAL AND INSTALLATION

The exhaust manifold-to-crossover pipe connections are either of the ball type, donut type or flange type with gaskets. Remove the front pipe retaining nuts, space and heat riser, if equipped. Separate the front pipe from the converter using a torch (to heat the pipe to aid in removal), or if the pipe is be replaced you can cut the outside pipe carefully and remove it. Remove the air injection pipes, as required. Installation is the reverse of the removal, pay special attention to the fit and alignment of the system. Secure with new clamps.

Catalytic Converter

REMOVAL AND INSTALLATION

The catalytic converter is an emission control device added to the exhaust system to reduce pollutants from the exhaust gas stream. Remove the front crossover pipe assembly and front pipe to converter. Remove any AIR injection tubes, as necessary. Remove the converter hanger and intermediate pipe-to-flange retaining bolts. Installation is the reverse of the removal procedure, pay special attention to the fit and alignment of the system. Secure with new clamps.

Periodic maintenance of the exhaust system is not required, however, if the car is raised for other service, it is advisable to check the general condition of the catalytic converter, pipes and mufflers.

Intermediate Pipe, Muffler and Tail Pipe

REMOVAL AND INSTALLATION

This vehicle uses a 1 piece system from the converter back from the factory. Unless this system has been replaced with an aftermarket assembly, you will have to replace the entire factory system with separate components. Remove any necessary clamps and carefully separate the pipe from the converter using a suitable tool. Install the replacement components paying special attention to the fit and alignment of the system, using the factory mounting positions and brackets. Secure with new clamps.

ENGINE MECHANICAL SPECIFICATIONS

Component	U.S.	Metric
CAMSHAFT		
Maximum end play		
Except 5.0L (VIN Y)	0.004-0.012 in.	0.1016-0.3048 mm
5.0L (VIN Y)	0.006-0.022 in.	0.1524-0.5590 mm
Bearing diameter		
Except 5.0L (VIN Y)	NA	NA
5.0L (VIN Y)	NA	NA
Journal diameter		
Except 5.0L (VIN Y)	1.8682-1.8692 in.	47.452-47.477 mm
5.0L (VIN Y)		
No. #1	2.0365-2.0352 in.	51.7271-51.7067 mm
No. #2	2.0166-2.0152 in.	51.2166-51.1988 mm
No. #3	1.9965-1.9952 in.	50.7111-50.6780 mm
No. #4	1.9765-1.9752 in.	50.2031-50.1700 mm
No. #5	1.9565-1.9552 in.	49.6951-49.6200 mm
Bearing clearance		
Except 5.0L (VIN Y)	NA	NA
5.0L (VIN Y)	0.0020-0.0058 in.	0.0508-0.0147 mm
Lobe lift		
4.3L & 5.0L (VIN E)		
Intake:	0.234 in.	5.940 mm
Exhaust:	0.257 in.	6.530 mm
5.0L (VIN Y)		
Intake:	0.247 in.	6.2738 mm
Exhaust:	0.251 in.	6.3754 mm
5.7L (VIN 7)		
Intake:	0.257 in.	6.530 mm
Exhaust:	0.269 in.	6.830 mm
Connecting rod		
Piston pin bore diameter		
Except 5.0L (VIN Y)	0.9270-0.9273 in.	23.546-23.553 mm
5.0L (VIN Y)	0.9804-0.9806 in.	24.900-24.906 mm
Bearing oil clearance		
Except 5.0L (VIN Y)	0.0013-0.0035 in.	0.033-0.088 mm
5.0L (VIN Y)	0.0004-0.0033 in.	0.010-0.080 mm
Side clearance		
Except 5.0L (VIN Y)	0.006-0.014 in.	0.16-0.35 mm
5.0L (VIN Y)	0.006-0.020 in.	0.15-0.50 mm
Crankshaft		
Connecting rod journal		
Diameter		
4.3L	2.2487-2.2498 in.	57.120-57.140 mm
5.0L (VIN E) & 5.7L	2.0893-2.0998 in.	53.068-53.334 mm
5.0L (VIN Y)	2.1238-2.1248 in.	53.945-53.970 mm
Out-of-round (max.)		
Except 5.0L (VIN Y)	0.0005 in.	0.013 mm
5.0L (VIN Y)	0.0002 in.	0.005 mm
Taper (max.)		
All	0.0005 in.	0.013 mm
Main bearing journal		
Diameter		
Except 5.0L (VIN Y)		
No. 1	2.4488-2.4493 in.	62.189-62.212 mm
No. 2, 3 & 4	2.4481-2.4490 in.	62.182-62.205 mm
No. 5	2.4481-2.4488 in.	62.177-62.120 mm
5.0L (VIN Y)		
No. 1	2.4988-2.4998 in.	63.470-63.495 mm
No. 2, 3, 4 & 5	2.4985-2.4995 in.	63.462-63.487 mm
Out-of-round (max.)		
Except 5.0L (VIN Y)	0.0002 in.	0.005 mm
5.0L (VIN Y)	0.0002 in.	0.005 mm
Taper (max.)		
Except 5.0L (VIN Y)	0.0002 in.	0.005 mm
5.0L (VIN Y)	0.0002 in.	0.005 mm

ENGINE MECHANICAL SPECIFICATIONS

Component	U.S.	Metric
Main bearing oil clearance		
Except 5.0L (VIN Y)		
No. 1	0.0008-0.0020 in.	0.020-0.051 mm
No. 2, 3 & 4	0.0011-0.0020 in.	0.028-0.051 mm
No. 5	0.0017-0.0032 in.	0.043-0.081 mm
5.0L (VIN Y)		
No. 1, 2, 3 & 4	0.0005-0.0021 in.	0.013-0.053 mm
No. 5	0.0015-0.0031 in.	0.040-0.081 mm
Crankshaft endplay		
Except 5.0L (VIN Y)	0.0010-0.0070 in.	0.030-0.170 mm
5.0L (VIN Y)	0.0035-0.0135 in.	0.090-0.343 mm
Cylinder block		
Cylinder bore out-of-round limit		
Except 5.0L (VIN Y)	0.0010 in.	0.020 mm
5.0L (VIN Y)	0.0015 in.	0.038 mm
Cylinder bore maximum taper		
Except 5.0L (VIN Y)	0.0010 in.	0.025 mm
5.0L (VIN Y)	0.0015 in.	0.038 mm
Cylinder bore diameter		
4.3L	4.000 in.	101.60 mm
5.0L (VIN E)	3.740 in.	94.99 mm
5.0L (VIN Y)	3.800 in.	96.50 mm
5.7L	4.000 in.	101.60 mm
Cylinder bore maximum oversize		
All	NA	NA
Cylinder head		
Maximum surface warpage		
4 cyl.	NA	NA
6 cyl.	NA	NA
8 cyl.	NA	NA
Maximum refinish		
Except 5.0L (VIN Y)	NA	NA
5.0L (VIN Y)	0.006 in.	0.152 mm
Valve seat angle		
Except 5.0L (VIN Y)		
Intake	46°	46°
Exhaust	46°	46°
5.0L (VIN Y)		
Intake	45°	45°
Exhaust	45°	45°
Valve stem-to-guide clearance		
Except 5.0L (VIN Y)	0.0011-0.0027 in.	0.027-0.069 mm
5.0L (VIN Y)		
Intake	0.0010-0.0027 in.	0.026-0.068 mm
Exhaust	0.0015-0.0032 in.	0.038-0.081 mm
Hydraulic lifters		
Body diameter		
Except 5.0L (VIN Y)	NA	NA
5.0L (VIN Y)	0.920-0.922 in.	23.390-23.410 mm
Bore diameter	NA	NA
OIL PUMP		
Gear lash		
Except 5.0L (VIN Y)	NA	NA
5.0L (VIN Y)	0.0004-0.0065 in.	0.01-0.19 mm
Gear pocket depth		
Except 5.0L (VIN Y)	NA	NA
5.0L (VIN Y)	1.500-1.509 in.	38.100-38.125 mm
Gear pocket diameter		
Except 5.0L (VIN Y)	NA	NA
5.0L (VIN Y)	1.534-1.539 in.	38.960-39.090 mm
Gear length		
Except 5.0L (VIN Y)	NA	NA
5.0L (VIN Y)	1.5075-1.5095 in.	38.290-38.341 mm
Gear diameter		
Except 5.0L (VIN Y)	NA	NA
5.0L (VIN Y)	1.529-1.531 in.	38.836-38.887 mm

ENGINE MECHANICAL SPECIFICATIONS

Component	U.S.	Metric
Gear side clearance (max.)		
Except 5.0L (VIN Y)	NA	NA
5.0L (VIN Y)	0.04 in.	0.12 mm
End clearance		
Except 5.0L (VIN Y)	NA	NA
5.0L (VIN Y)	0.0025-0.0065 in.	0.0635-0.165 mm
Valve-to-bore clearance		
Except 5.0L (VIN Y)	NA	NA
5.0L (VIN Y)	0.0025-0.0050 in.	0.063-0.127 mm
Pistons		
Ring end gap		
Except 5.0L (VIN Y)		
No. 1	0.010-0.020 in.	0.250-0.500 mm
No. 2	0.010-0.025 in.	0.250-0.630 mm
Oil	0.015-0.055 in.	0.380-1.400 mm
5.0L (VIN Y)		
No. 1	0.009-0.019 in.	0.229-0.483 mm
No. 2	0.009-0.019 in.	0.229-0.483 mm
Oil	0.015-0.055 in.	0.381-1.397 mm
Ring side clearance		
Except 5.0L (VIN Y)		
No. 1	0.0012-0.0032 in.	0.030-0.081 mm
No. 2	0.0012-0.0032 in.	0.030-0.081 mm
Oil	0.0020-0.0070 in.	0.051-0.170 mm
5.0L (VIN Y)		
No. 1	0.0018-0.0038 in.	0.0457-0.0965 mm
No. 2	0.0018-0.0038 in.	0.0457-0.0965 mm
Oil	0.0010-0.0050 in.	0.0300-0.1300 mm
Piston-to-bore clearance		
Except 5.0L (VIN Y)	0.0007-0.0021 in.	0.0180-0.0530 mm
5.0L (VIN Y)	0.0008-0.0018 in.	0.0190-0.0440 mm
Pin-to-piston clearance		
Except 5.0L (VIN Y)	0.0003-0.0004 in.	0.0064-0.0088 mm
5.0L (VIN Y)	0.0003-0.0005 in.	0.0076-0.0127 mm
Pin-to-rod clearance		
Except 5.0L (VIN Y)	0.0008-0.0016 in.	0.0210-0.0400 mm
5.0L (VIN Y)	0.0002-0.0010 in.	0.0038-0.0240 mm
Pin diameter		
Except 5.0L (VIN Y)	0.9270-0.9273 in.	23.5460-23.5530 mm
5.0L (VIN Y)	0.9804-0.9806 in.	24.9000-24.9060 mm
VALVES		
Face angle		
Except 5.0L (VIN Y)	45°	45°
5.0L (VIN Y)	44°	44°
Head diameter		
Except 5.0L (VIN Y)	NA	NA
5.0L (VIN Y)		
Intake	1.745-1.755 in.	44.323-44.570 mm
Exhaust	1.497-1.507 in.	38.024-38.278 mm
Spring test pressure		
Except 5.0L (VIN Y)		
Closed	76-84 lbs. @ 1.700 in.	338-373 N @ 43.00 mm
Open	194-206 lbs. @ 1.270 in.	863-916 N @ 32.00 mm
5.0L (VIN Y)		
Closed	76-84 lbs. @ 1.670 in.	338-374 N @ 42.42 mm
Open	180-194 lbs. @ 1.270 in.	800-863 N @ 32.26 mm
Spring Installed height		
Except 5.0L (VIN Y)	1.724 in.	43.700 mm
5.0L (VIN Y)	NA	NA
Spring free length		
Except 5.0L (VIN Y)	2.030 in.	51.500 mm
5.0L (VIN Y)	1.960 in.	49.780 mm
Stem diameter		
Except 5.0L (VIN Y)	NA	NA
5.0L (VIN Y)		
Intake	0.3425-0.3432 in.	8.6995-8.7170 mm
Exhaust	0.3420-0.3427 in.	8.6868-8.7045 mm

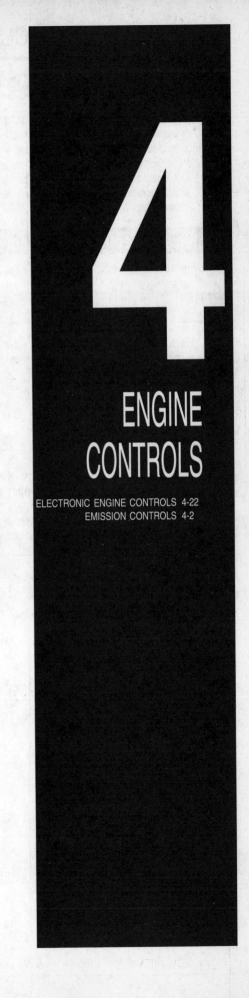

4

ENGINE
CONTROLS

EMISSION CONTROLS

There are three sources of automotive pollutants: crankcase fumes, exhaust gases, and gasoline evaporation. The pollutants formed from these substances fall into three categories: unburned hydrocarbons (HC), carbon monoxide (CO), and oxides of nitrogen (NOx). The equipment that is used to limit these pollutants is commonly called emission control equipment.

Crankcase Ventilation System

▶ See Figures 1, 2, 3 and 4

OPERATION

The positive crankcase ventilation (PCV) system is used to control crankcase blow-by vapors. The system functions as follows:

The crankcase (blow-by) gases are recycled in the following way:

As the engine is running, clean, filtered air is drawn through the air filter and into the crankcase. As the air passes through the crankcase, it picks up the combustion gases and carries them out of the crankcase, through the PCV valve, and into the induction system. As they enter the intake manifold, they are drawn into the combustion chamber where they are reburned.

The most critical component in the system is the PCV valve. This valve controls the amount of gases which are recycled

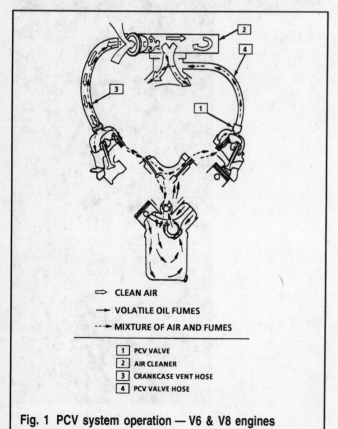

CLEAN AIR
VOLATILE OIL FUMES
MIXTURE OF AIR AND FUMES

1 PCV VALVE
2 AIR CLEANER
3 CRANKCASE VENT HOSE
4 PCV VALVE HOSE

Fig. 1 PCV system operation — V6 & V8 engines

into the combustion chamber. At low engine speeds, the valve is partially closed, limiting the flow of gases into the intake manifold. As engine speed increases, the valve opens to admit greater quantities of gases into the intake manifold. If the PCV valve becomes clogged, the system is designed to allow excessive amounts of blow-by gases to flow back through the crankcase tube and into the air cleaner where they become consumed by normal combustion.

SERVICE

Inspect the PCV system hose and connections at each tune-up and replace any deteriorated hoses. Check the PCV valve at every tune-up and replace it at 30,000 mile intervals.

TESTING

A good indication of a faulty or clogged PCV system is generally represented by external oil leaks or oil being pushed back up through the crankcase ventilation tube into the air cleaner. Remember that the purpose of the PCV system is two-fold, one is to relieve the crankcase of excessive vapors and the other is to relieve excessive pressure caused by normal amounts of piston ring blow-by.

1. Remove the PCV valve from the intake manifold or valve cover.
2. Run the engine at idle.
3. Place your thumb over the end of the valve. Check for vacuum. If there is no vacuum at the valve, check for plugged valve or vacuum lines.
4. Shut off the engine. Shake the valve and listen for the rattle. If valve doesn't rattle, replace it.
5. Reinstall the valve and start the engine.
6. Remove the oil dipstick. Connect a vacuum gauge to the dipstick tube.
7. Remove the PCV fresh vent hose at the air cleaner and plug the opening in the hose.
8. Run the engine at 1500 rpm for approximately 30 seconds. Verify there is vacuum present.
9. If there is no vacuum, inspect the valve cover, oil pan and intake manifold gaskets for leaks. If the gauge is showing pressure or pushes the gauge out of the dipstick tube, inspect the PCV valve or hoses for restriction; also inspect the engine for excessive blow-by.

Evaporative Emission Controls

▶ See Figures 5, 6, 7 and 8

OPERATION

This system reduces the amount of gasoline vapors escaping into the atmosphere. Some models employ a purge control solenoid which is controlled by the ECM, to open and close the EEC system. Other models use a vacuum purge

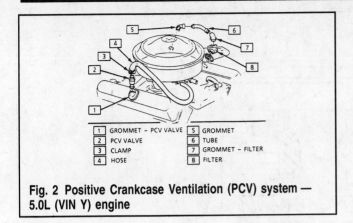

1	GROMMET – PCV VALVE	5	GROMMET
2	PCV VALVE	6	TUBE
3	CLAMP	7	GROMMET – FILTER
4	HOSE	8	FILTER

Fig. 2 Positive Crankcase Ventilation (PCV) system — 5.0L (VIN Y) engine

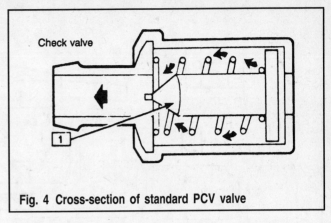

Fig. 4 Cross-section of standard PCV valve

valve; when the engine vacuum reaches a certain pressure, the valve opens allowing the gas vapors to be drawn off to the carburetor for burning.

Carburetor models use an exhaust tube from the float bowl to the charcoal canister; fuel injected models eliminate the fuel bowl tube. Fuel vapors from the gas tank travel from the tank to the vapor canister, where they are collected. Although the system varies from vehicle to vehicle, the operations are basically the same.

Canister

REMOVAL & INSTALLATION

1. Loosen the screw holding the canister retaining bracket.

2. Rotate the canister retaining bracket and remove the canister.
3. Tag and disconnect the hoses leading from the canister.
4. To install, connect the hoses to the canister according to the tags.
5. Install the canister into the retaining bracket.
6. Tighten the screw holding the canister retaining bracket.

FILTER REPLACEMENT

1. Remove the vapor canister.
2. Pull the filter out from the bottom of the canister.
3. Install a new filter and then replace the canister.

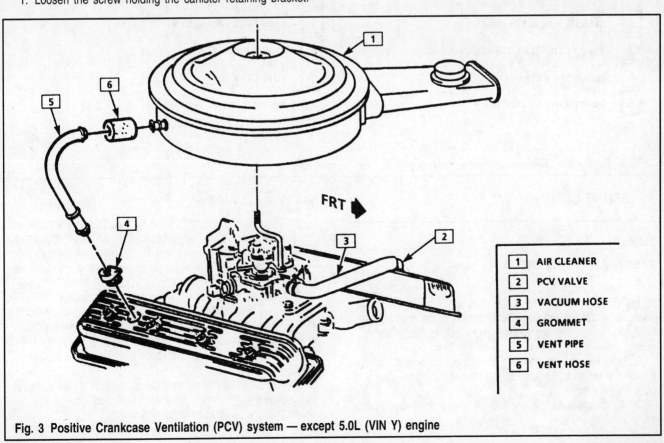

1	AIR CLEANER
2	PCV VALVE
3	VACUUM HOSE
4	GROMMET
5	VENT PIPE
6	VENT HOSE

Fig. 3 Positive Crankcase Ventilation (PCV) system — except 5.0L (VIN Y) engine

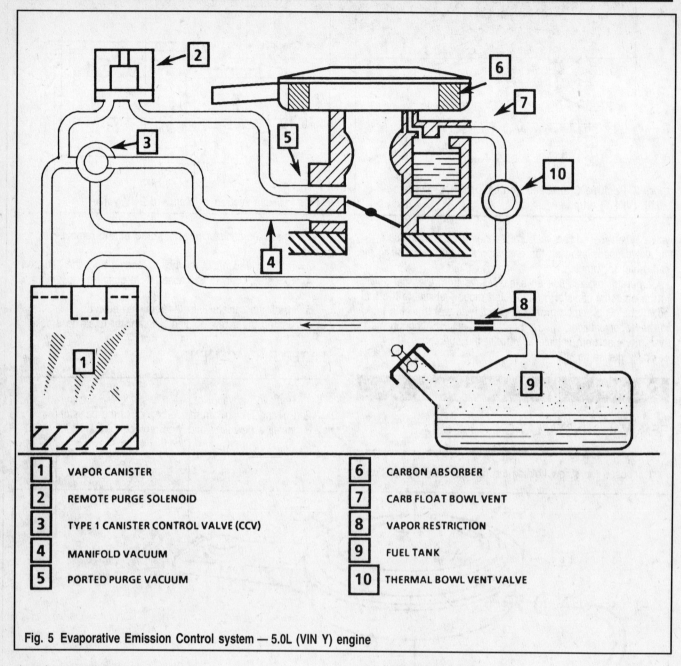

Fig. 5 Evaporative Emission Control system — 5.0L (VIN Y) engine

1	VAPOR CANISTER	
2	REMOTE PURGE SOLENOID	
3	TYPE 1 CANISTER CONTROL VALVE (CCV)	
4	MANIFOLD VACUUM	
5	PORTED PURGE VACUUM	
6	CARBON ABSORBER	
7	CARB FLOAT BOWL VENT	
8	VAPOR RESTRICTION	
9	FUEL TANK	
10	THERMAL BOWL VENT VALVE	

PRESSURE CONTROL VALVE

Testing

EXCEPT 5.0L (VIN Y) ENGINE

1. Using a hand-held vacuum pump, apply a vacuum of 15 in. Hg. (51kPa) through the control vacuum tube to the purge valve diaphragm. If the diaphragm does not hold 5 in Hg. at least for 10 seconds, the diaphragm is leaking. Replace the control valve.

2. With the vacuum still applied to the control vacuum tube, attach a short piece of hose to the valve's tank tube side and blow into the hose.

3. Air should pass through the valve. If it does not, replace the control valve.

5.0L (VIN Y) ENGINE

1. Disconnect the control valve hoses. Connect a piece of hose to the carburetor bowl tube opening at the control valve.

2. Blow air into the hose and air should pass through the valve and out of the ported purge vacuum fitting and canister purge fitting of the control valve.

3. If not as specified the valve must be replaced.

4. Using a hand-held vacuum pump, apply a vacuum of 15 in. Hg. (51kPa) to the manifold vacuum tube on the control valve. If the diaphragm does not hold vacuum for at least for 20 seconds, the diaphragm is leaking. Replace the control valve.

5. With the vacuum still applied to the control valve, again try to blow into the hose. Air should not pass through the valve. If it does, replace the control valve.

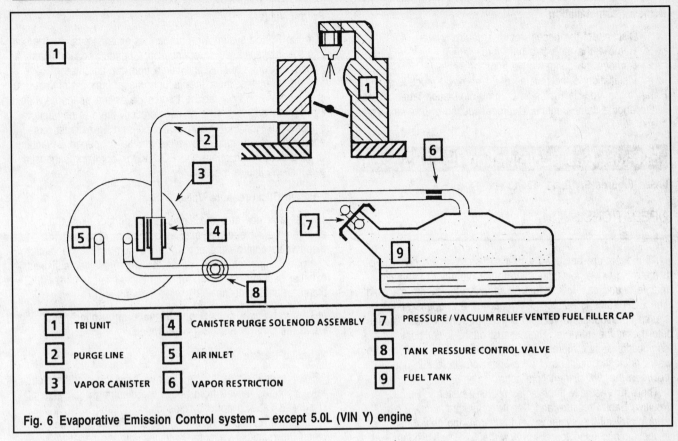

1	TBI UNIT	**4**	CANISTER PURGE SOLENOID ASSEMBLY	**7**	PRESSURE / VACUUM RELIEF VENTED FUEL FILLER CAP
2	PURGE LINE	**5**	AIR INLET	**8**	TANK PRESSURE CONTROL VALVE
3	VAPOR CANISTER	**6**	VAPOR RESTRICTION	**9**	FUEL TANK

Fig. 6 Evaporative Emission Control system — except 5.0L (VIN Y) engine

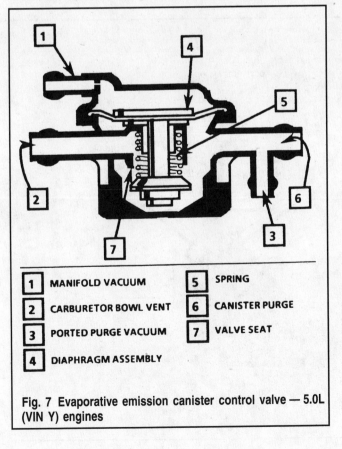

1	MANIFOLD VACUUM	**5**	SPRING
2	CARBURETOR BOWL VENT	**6**	CANISTER PURGE
3	PORTED PURGE VACUUM	**7**	VALVE SEAT
4	DIAPHRAGM ASSEMBLY		

Fig. 7 Evaporative emission canister control valve — 5.0L (VIN Y) engines

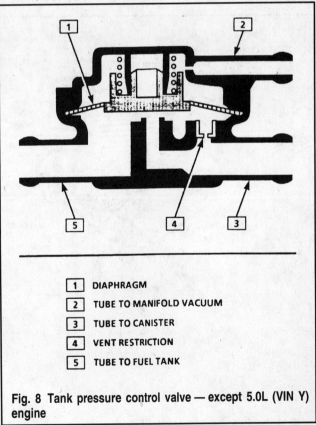

1	DIAPHRAGM
2	TUBE TO MANIFOLD VACUUM
3	TUBE TO CANISTER
4	VENT RESTRICTION
5	TUBE TO FUEL TANK

Fig. 8 Tank pressure control valve — except 5.0L (VIN Y) engine

Removal & Installation

1. Disconnect the hoses from the control valve.
2. Remove the mounting hardware.
3. Remove the control valve from the vehicle.
4. Installation is the reverse of the removal procedure.

Refer to the Vehicle Emission Control Information label, located in the engine compartment, for proper routing of the vacuum hoses.

Exhaust Gas Recirculation (EGR) System

▶ See Figures 9, 10, 11, 12, 13 and 14

OPERATIONS

All models are equipped with this system, which consists of a metering valve, a vacuum line to the carburetor or intake manifold, and cast-in exhaust passages in the intake manifold. The EGR valve is controlled by vacuum, and opens and closes in response to vacuum signals to admit exhaust gases into the air/fuel mixture. The exhaust gases lower peak combustion temperatures, reducing the formation of NOx. The valve is closed at idle and wide open throttle, but is open between the two extreme positions.

There are actually three types of EGR systems: Ported, Positive Back-Pressure and Negative Backpressure. The principle of all the systems are the same; the only difference is in the method used to control how the EGR valve opens.

Ported Valve

In the Ported system, the amount of exhaust gas admitted into the intake manifold depends on a ported vacuum signal. A ported vacuum signal is one taken from the carburetor above the throttle plates; thus, the vacuum signal (amount of vacuum) is dependent on how far the throttle plates are opened. When the throttle is closed (idle or deceleration) there is no vacuum signal. Thus, the EGR valve is closed, and no exhaust gas enters the intake manifold. As the throttle is opened, a vacuum is produced, which opens the EGR valve, admitting exhaust gas into the intake manifold.

Positive Backpressure Valve

This valve operates the same as the ported, except, it has an internal air bleed that acts as a vacuum regulator. The bleed valve controls the amount of vacuum inside the vacuum chamber during operation. When the valve receives sufficient exhaust back-pressure through the hollow shaft, it closes the bleed; at this point the EGR valve opens.

➡**This valve will not open, with vacuum applied to it, while the engine is idling or stopped.**

Negative Backpressure Valve

This valve is similar to the Positive Type, except, the bleed valve spring is moved from above the diaphragm to below it. The bleed valve is normally closed.

At certain manifold pressures, the EGR valve will open. When the manifold vacuum combines with the negative

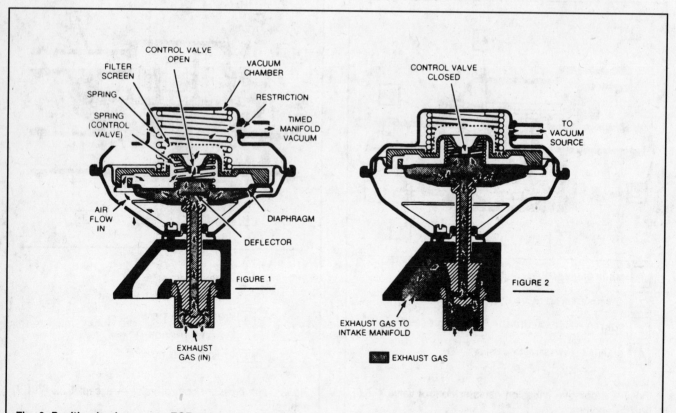

Fig. 9 Positive backpressure EGR valve

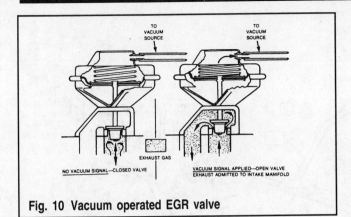

Fig. 10 Vacuum operated EGR valve

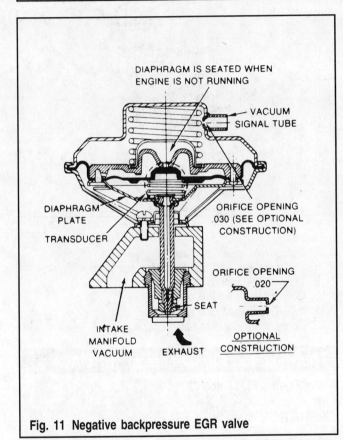

Fig. 11 Negative backpressure EGR valve

exhaust backpressure, the bleed hole opens and the EGR valve closes.

➡**This valve will open when vacuum is applied and the engine is not running.**

INCORRECT EGR OPERATION

Too much EGR flow at idle, cruise or during cold operation may result in the engine stalling after cold start, the engine stalling at idle after deceleration, vehicle surge during cruise and rough idle. If the EGR valve is always open, the vehicle may not idle. Too little or no EGR flow allows combustion temperatures to get too high which could result in spark knock (detonation), engine overheating and/or emission test failure.

EGR VALVE IDENTIFICATION

- Positive backpressure EGR valves will have a 'P" stamped on the top side of the valve below the date built.
- Negative backpressure EGR valves will have a 'N' stamped on the top side of the valve below the date built.
- Port EGR valves have no identification stamped below the date built.

Additional Controls

EGR VACUUM/SOLENOID CONTROL

Some systems use the coolant temperature sensor, throttle position sensor and manifold air temperature sensor with the EGR valve. The EGR control solenoid uses a Pulse Width Modulation system which turns the solenoid **ON** and **OFF** numerous times a second and varies the amount of **ON** time (pulse width) to vary the amount of ported vacuum supplied the EGR valve.

TESTING

EGR Valve

▶ See Figures 15, 16, 17, 18, 19, 20, 21 and 22

The following charts may be used to diagnose EGR system malfunctions.

REMOVAL & INSTALLATION

EGR Valve

1. Disconnect the negative battery cable.
2. Remove the air cleaner assembly.
3. Tag and disconnect the necessary hoses and wiring to gain access to the EGR valve.
4. Remove the EGR valve retaining bolts.
5. Remove the EGR valve. Discard the gasket.
6. Buff the exhaust deposits from the mounting surface and around the valve using a wire wheel.
7. Remove deposits from the valve outlet.
8. Clean the mounting surfaces of the intake manifold and valve assembly.

To install:
9. Install a new EGR gasket.
10. Install the EGR valve to the manifold.
11. Install the retaining bolts.
12. Connect the wiring and hoses.
13. Install the air cleaner assembly.
14. Connect the negative battery cable.

EGR Solenoid

1. Disconnect the negative battery cable.
2. Remove the air cleaner, as required.
3. Disconnect the electrical connector at the solenoid.
4. Disconnect the spark plug wires and vacuum hoses, as required.
5. Remove the retaining bolts and the solenoid.
6. Remove the filter, as required.

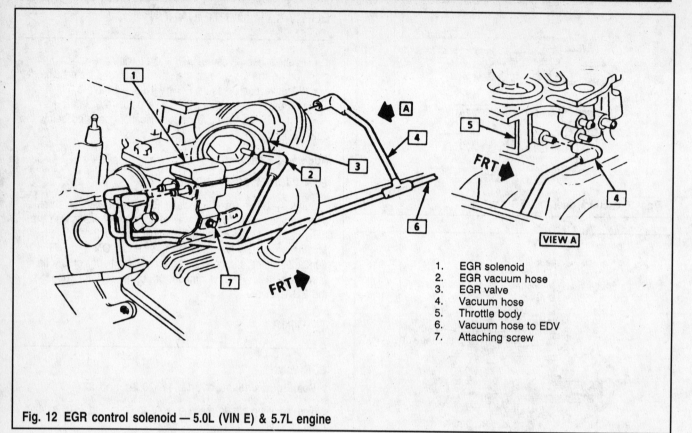

Fig. 12 EGR control solenoid — 5.0L (VIN E) & 5.7L engine

1. EGR solenoid
2. EGR vacuum hose
3. EGR valve
4. Vacuum hose
5. Throttle body
6. Vacuum hose to EDV
7. Attaching screw

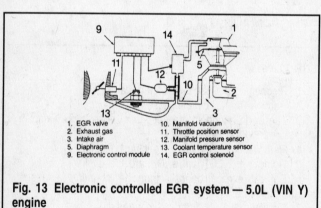

1. EGR valve
2. Exhaust gas
3. Intake air
5. Diaphragm
9. Electronic control module
10. Manifold vacuum
11. Throttle position sensor
12. Manifold pressure sensor
13. Coolant temperature sensor
14. EGR control solenoid

Fig. 13 Electronic controlled EGR system — 5.0L (VIN Y) engine

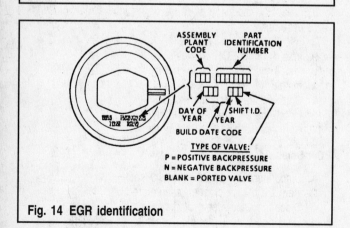

Fig. 14 EGR identification

To install:

7. If removed, install the filter.
8. Install the solenoid and retaining bolts.
9. Connect the vacuum hoses.
10. Connect the electrical connector.
11. If removed, install the air cleaner.
12. Connect the negative battery cable.

Thermostatic Air Cleaner (THERMAC)

▶ See Figures 23, 24 and 25

OPERATION

All engines use the THERMAC system. This system is designed to warm the air entering the manifold when underhood temperatures are low, and to maintain a controlled air temperature into the manifold at all times. By allowing preheated air to enter the carburetor or throttle body, the amount of time needed to bring the engine up to normal operating temperature is reduced, resulting in better fuel economy and lower emissions.

1990-91

The THERMAC system is composed of the air cleaner body, a filter, sensor unit, vacuum diaphragm, damper door, and associated hoses and connections. Heat radiating from the exhaust manifold is trapped by a heat stove and is ducted to the air cleaner to supply heated air to the carburetor or throttle body. A movable door in the air cleaner case snorkel allows

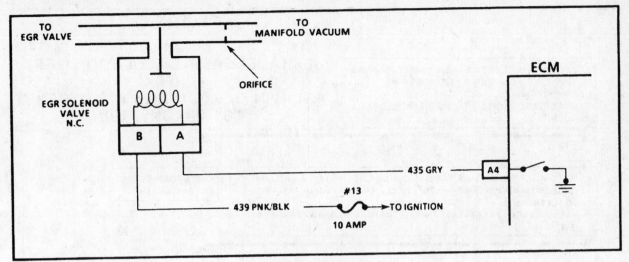

CHART C-7

(Page 1 of 3)
EXHAUST GAS RECIRCULATION (EGR) CHECK
4.3L (VIN Z), 5.0L (VIN E) & 5.7L (VIN 7) "B" CARLINE (TBI)

Circuit Description:

The ECM operates a solenoid valve to control the Exhaust Gas Recirculation (EGR) valve. This solenoid valve is normally closed. By providing a ground path, the ECM energizes the solenoid valve which then allows vacuum to pass to the EGR valve. The ECM control of the EGR is based on the following inputs:

- Engine Coolant Temperature (ECT) above 25°C (77°F).
- Throttle Position (TP) sensor off idle.
- Manifold Absolute Pressure (MAP).

If DTC 24 is stored, use that chart first.

Test Description: Number(s) below refer to circled number(s) on the diagnostic chart.

1. **Intake Passage:** Shut "OFF" engine and remove the EGR valve from the manifold. Plug the exhaust side hole with a shop rag or suitable stopper. Leaving the intake side hole open, attempt to start the engine. If the engine runs at a very high idle (up to 3000 RPM is possible) or starts and stalls, the EGR passages are not restricted. If the engine starts and idles normally, the EGR intake side passage in the intake manifold is restricted.

   Exhaust Passage: With EGR valve still removed, plug the intake side hole with a suitable stopper. With the exhaust side hole open, check for the presence of exhaust gas. If no exhaust gas is present, the EGR exhaust side passage in the intake manifold is restricted.

2. By grounding the diagnostic "test" terminal, the EGR solenoid valve should be energized and allow vacuum to be applied to the gage. The vacuum at the gage may or may not <u>slowly</u> bleed off. It is important that the gage is able to read the amount of vacuum being applied.

3. When the diagnostic "test" terminal is ungrounded, the vacuum gage should bleed off through a vent in the solenoid. The pump gage may or may not bleed off but this does not indicate a problem.

4. This test will determine if the electrical control part of the system is at fault or if the connector or solenoid valve is at fault.

5. EGR valves used with this engine are stamped on the top side of the valve with: (P) for Positive backpressure valves or (N) for Negative backpressure valves. Refer to "EGR Valve Identification," in this section for more information.

Diagnostic Aids:

Vacuum lines should be thoroughly checked for proper routing. Vacuum source goes to the orifice side of the EGR valve. Refer to "Vehicle Emission Control Information" label.

Suction from shop exhaust hoses can alter exhaust backpressure and may affect the functional check of the EGR system.

Fig. 15 EGR system testing — except 5.0L (VIN Y) engine

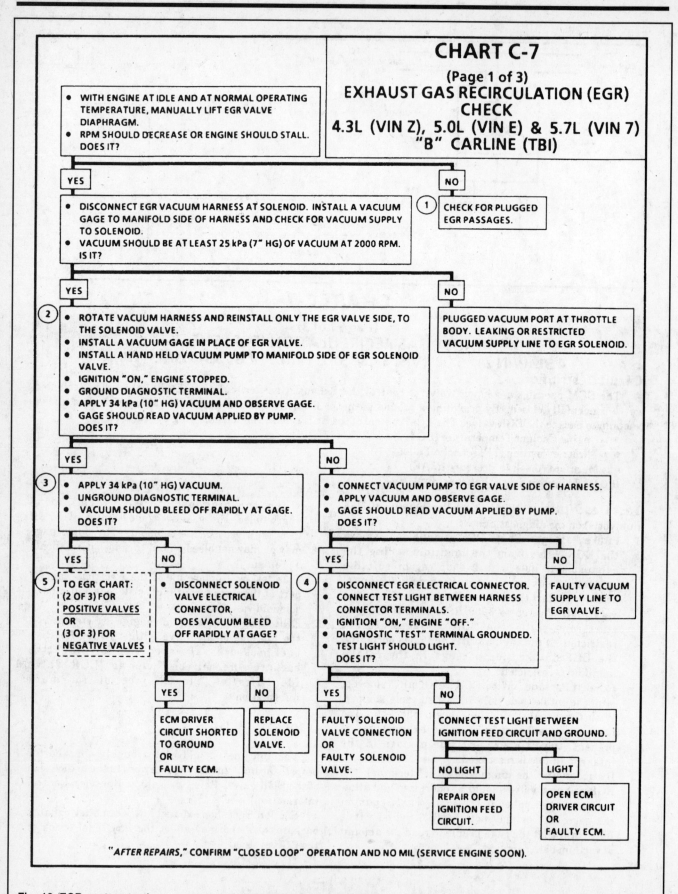

CHART C-7

(Page 1 of 3)
EXHAUST GAS RECIRCULATION (EGR) CHECK
4.3L (VIN Z), 5.0L (VIN E) & 5.7L (VIN 7) "B" CARLINE (TBI)

- WITH ENGINE AT IDLE AND AT NORMAL OPERATING TEMPERATURE, MANUALLY LIFT EGR VALVE DIAPHRAGM.
- RPM SHOULD DECREASE OR ENGINE SHOULD STALL. DOES IT?

YES

- DISCONNECT EGR VACUUM HARNESS AT SOLENOID. INSTALL A VACUUM GAGE TO MANIFOLD SIDE OF HARNESS AND CHECK FOR VACUUM SUPPLY TO SOLENOID.
- VACUUM SHOULD BE AT LEAST 25 kPa (7" HG) OF VACUUM AT 2000 RPM. IS IT?

NO

① CHECK FOR PLUGGED EGR PASSAGES.

YES

②
- ROTATE VACUUM HARNESS AND REINSTALL ONLY THE EGR VALVE SIDE, TO THE SOLENOID VALVE.
- INSTALL A VACUUM GAGE IN PLACE OF EGR VALVE.
- INSTALL A HAND HELD VACUUM PUMP TO MANIFOLD SIDE OF EGR SOLENOID VALVE.
- IGNITION "ON," ENGINE STOPPED.
- GROUND DIAGNOSTIC TERMINAL.
- APPLY 34 kPa (10" HG) VACUUM AND OBSERVE GAGE.
- GAGE SHOULD READ VACUUM APPLIED BY PUMP. DOES IT?

NO

PLUGGED VACUUM PORT AT THROTTLE BODY. LEAKING OR RESTRICTED VACUUM SUPPLY LINE TO EGR SOLENOID.

YES

③
- APPLY 34 kPa (10" HG) VACUUM.
- UNGROUND DIAGNOSTIC TERMINAL.
- VACUUM SHOULD BLEED OFF RAPIDLY AT GAGE. DOES IT?

NO

- CONNECT VACUUM PUMP TO EGR VALVE SIDE OF HARNESS.
- APPLY VACUUM AND OBSERVE GAGE.
- GAGE SHOULD READ VACUUM APPLIED BY PUMP. DOES IT?

YES

⑤ TO EGR CHART:
(2 OF 3) FOR <u>POSITIVE VALVES</u> OR
(3 OF 3) FOR <u>NEGATIVE VALVES</u>

NO

- DISCONNECT SOLENOID VALVE ELECTRICAL CONNECTOR. DOES VACUUM BLEED OFF RAPIDLY AT GAGE?

YES

④
- DISCONNECT EGR ELECTRICAL CONNECTOR.
- CONNECT TEST LIGHT BETWEEN HARNESS CONNECTOR TERMINALS.
- IGNITION "ON," ENGINE "OFF."
- DIAGNOSTIC "TEST" TERMINAL GROUNDED.
- TEST LIGHT SHOULD LIGHT. DOES IT?

NO

FAULTY VACUUM SUPPLY LINE TO EGR VALVE.

YES

ECM DRIVER CIRCUIT SHORTED TO GROUND OR FAULTY ECM.

NO

REPLACE SOLENOID VALVE.

YES

FAULTY SOLENOID VALVE CONNECTION OR FAULTY SOLENOID VALVE.

NO

CONNECT TEST LIGHT BETWEEN IGNITION FEED CIRCUIT AND GROUND.

NO LIGHT

REPAIR OPEN IGNITION FEED CIRCUIT.

LIGHT

OPEN ECM DRIVER CIRCUIT OR FAULTY ECM.

"AFTER REPAIRS," CONFIRM "CLOSED LOOP" OPERATION AND NO MIL (SERVICE ENGINE SOON).

Fig. 16 EGR system testing — except 5.0L (VIN Y) engine, continued

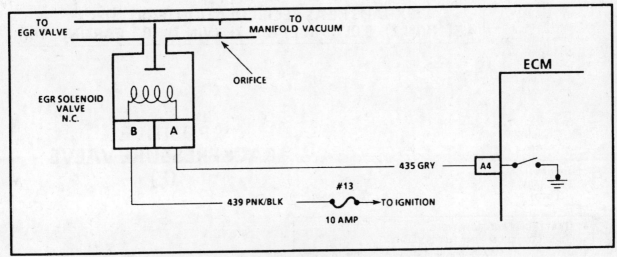

CHART C-7
(Page 2 of 3)
EXHAUST GAS RECIRCULATION (EGR) CHECK
4.3L (VIN Z), 5.0L (VIN E) & 5.7L (VIN 7) "B" CARLINE (TBI)

Circuit Description:

The ECM operates a solenoid valve to control the Exhaust Gas Recirculation (EGR) valve. This solenoid valve is normally closed. By providing a ground path, the ECM energizes the solenoid valve which then allows vacuum to pass to the EGR valve. The ECM control of the EGR is based on the following inputs:

- Engine Coolant Temperature (ECT) above 25°C (77°F).
- Throttle Position (TP) sensor off idle.
- Manifold Absolute Pressure (MAP).

If DTC 24 is stored, use that chart first.

Test Description (continued): Number(s) below refer to circled number(s) on the diagnostic chart.

6. The remaining tests check the ability of the EGR valve to interact with the exhaust system. This system uses a positive backpressure EGR valve which will not hold vacuum until sufficient exhaust backpressure is at the base of the valve.

7. The EGR valve diaphragm should move when sufficient exhaust backpressure is present at the base of the valve and when vacuum is being supplied to the valve. Rapidly "snapping" the throttle from idle should provide sufficient exhaust backpressure to the base of the valve which will close an internal vacuum bleed. With the EGR valve's internal vacuum bleed closed, the "jumpered" vacuum supply can now lift the valve off its seat.

8. Excessive exhaust backpressure from bent or restricted exhaust system components could provide enough backpressure at the base of the EGR valve to close the valve's internal bleed and allow undesired EGR valve operation at idle.

9. Plugged EGR exhaust passages can block exhaust backpressure from reaching the EGR valve. With no EGR exhaust backpressure at the base of the valve, the valve's internal bleed will remain open and prevent vacuum from operating the valve.

Fig. 17 EGR system testing — except 5.0L (VIN Y) engine, continued

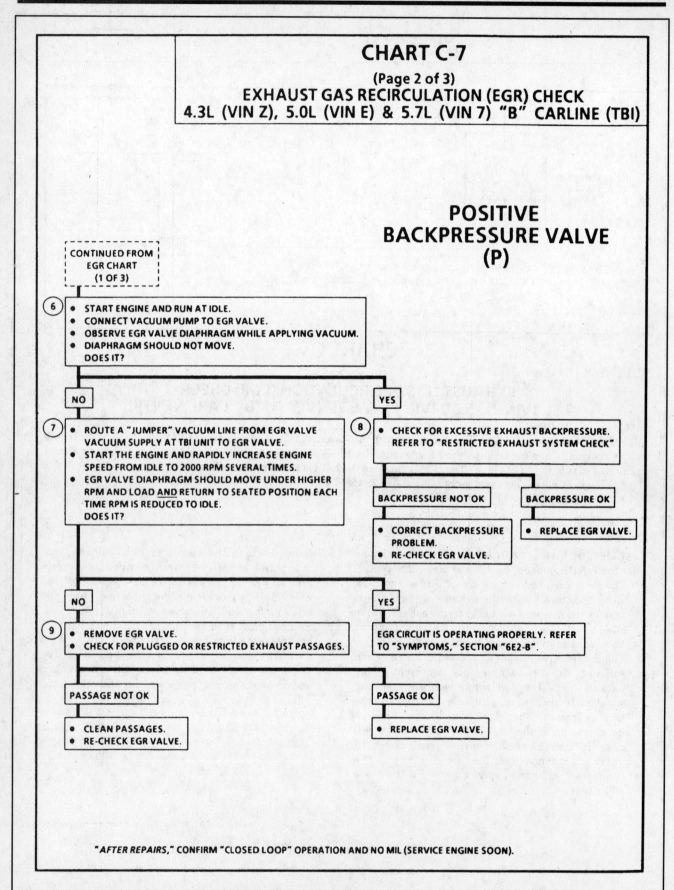

CHART C-7
(Page 2 of 3)
EXHAUST GAS RECIRCULATION (EGR) CHECK
4.3L (VIN Z), 5.0L (VIN E) & 5.7L (VIN 7) "B" CARLINE (TBI)

POSITIVE BACKPRESSURE VALVE (P)

CONTINUED FROM EGR CHART (1 OF 3)

6
- START ENGINE AND RUN AT IDLE.
- CONNECT VACUUM PUMP TO EGR VALVE.
- OBSERVE EGR VALVE DIAPHRAGM WHILE APPLYING VACUUM.
- DIAPHRAGM SHOULD NOT MOVE. DOES IT?

NO

YES

7
- ROUTE A "JUMPER" VACUUM LINE FROM EGR VALVE VACUUM SUPPLY AT TBI UNIT TO EGR VALVE.
- START THE ENGINE AND RAPIDLY INCREASE ENGINE SPEED FROM IDLE TO 2000 RPM SEVERAL TIMES.
- EGR VALVE DIAPHRAGM SHOULD MOVE UNDER HIGHER RPM AND LOAD <u>AND</u> RETURN TO SEATED POSITION EACH TIME RPM IS REDUCED TO IDLE. DOES IT?

8
- CHECK FOR EXCESSIVE EXHAUST BACKPRESSURE. REFER TO "RESTRICTED EXHAUST SYSTEM CHECK"

BACKPRESSURE NOT OK

BACKPRESSURE OK

- CORRECT BACKPRESSURE PROBLEM.
- RE-CHECK EGR VALVE.

- REPLACE EGR VALVE.

NO

YES

9
- REMOVE EGR VALVE.
- CHECK FOR PLUGGED OR RESTRICTED EXHAUST PASSAGES.

EGR CIRCUIT IS OPERATING PROPERLY. REFER TO "SYMPTOMS," SECTION "6E2-B".

PASSAGE NOT OK

PASSAGE OK

- CLEAN PASSAGES.
- RE-CHECK EGR VALVE.

- REPLACE EGR VALVE.

"AFTER REPAIRS," CONFIRM "CLOSED LOOP" OPERATION AND NO MIL (SERVICE ENGINE SOON).

Fig. 18 EGR system testing — except 5.0L (VIN Y) engine, continued

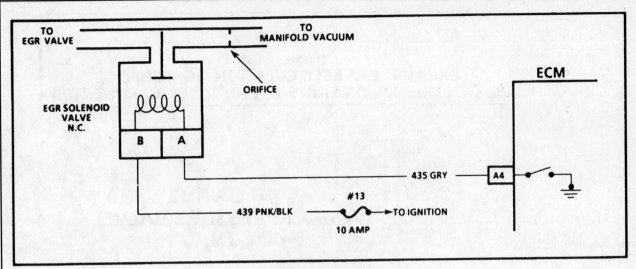

CHART C-7

(Page 3 of 3)
EXHAUST GAS RECIRCULATION (EGR) CHECK
4.3L (VIN Z), 5.0L (VIN E) & 5.7L (VIN 7) "B" CARLINE (TBI)

Circuit Description:

The ECM operates a solenoid valve to control the Exhaust Gas Recirculation (EGR) valve. This solenoid valve is normally closed. By providing a ground path, the ECM energizes the solenoid valve which then allows vacuum to pass to the EGR valve. The ECM control of the EGR is based on the following inputs:

- Engine Coolant Temperature (ECT) above 25°C (77°F).
- Throttle Position (TP) sensor off idle.
- Manifold Absolute Pressure (MAP).

If DTC 24 is stored, use that chart first.

Test Description (continued): Number(s) below refer to circled number(s) on the diagnostic chart.

6. The remaining tests check the ability of the EGR valve to interact with the exhaust system. This system uses a negative backpressure EGR valve which should hold vacuum with engine "OFF."

7. When engine is started, exhaust backpressure at the base of the EGR valve should open the valve's internal bleed and vent the applied vacuum allowing the valve to seat.

Fig. 19 EGR system testing — except 5.0L (VIN Y) engine, continued

air to be drawn in from the heat stove (cold operation). The door position is controlled by the vacuum motor, which receives intake manifold vacuum as modulated by the temperature sensor.

1992-93

This system regulates incoming air temperature without the use of vacuum; instead it uses a wax pellet actuator contained within the air cleaner assembly. Depending upon temperature, the wax pellet actuator changes its state from a solid to liquid state, which forces the actuator piston out and closes off the hot manifold air.

➡A vacuum door which remains open will cause throttle plate icing and poor cold driveability; a door which remains closed during normal engine operating temperatures can cause sluggishness, engine knocking and overheating.

SYSTEM CHECK

1990-91

➡Verify there is approximately 16 in Hg. at the air cleaner temperature sensor at all times.

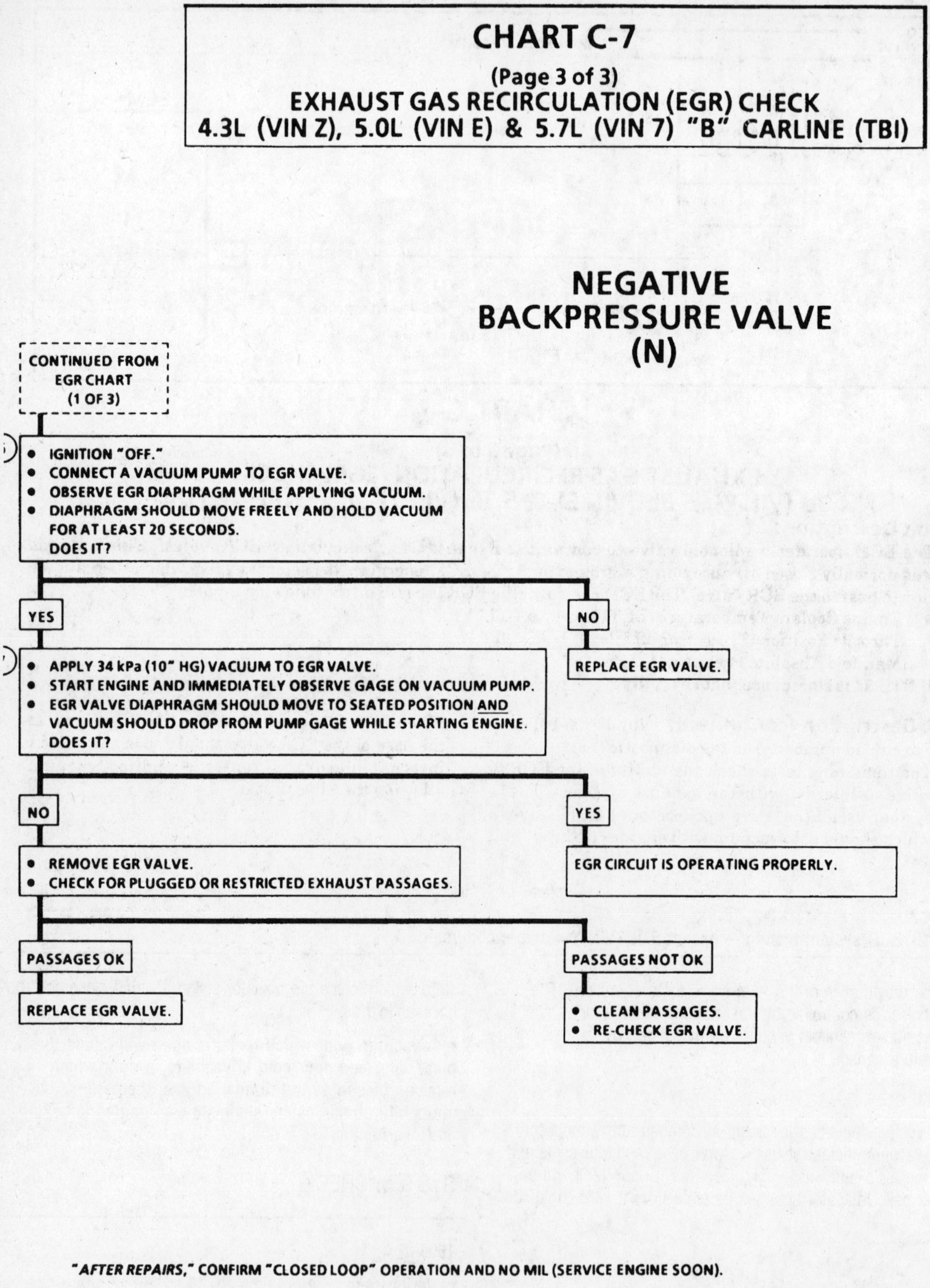

CHART C-7

(Page 3 of 3)
EXHAUST GAS RECIRCULATION (EGR) CHECK
4.3L (VIN Z), 5.0L (VIN E) & 5.7L (VIN 7) "B" CARLINE (TBI)

NEGATIVE BACKPRESSURE VALVE (N)

CONTINUED FROM
EGR CHART
(1 OF 3)

- IGNITION "OFF."
- CONNECT A VACUUM PUMP TO EGR VALVE.
- OBSERVE EGR DIAPHRAGM WHILE APPLYING VACUUM.
- DIAPHRAGM SHOULD MOVE FREELY AND HOLD VACUUM FOR AT LEAST 20 SECONDS.
  DOES IT?

YES

NO

- APPLY 34 kPa (10" HG) VACUUM TO EGR VALVE.
- START ENGINE AND IMMEDIATELY OBSERVE GAGE ON VACUUM PUMP.
- EGR VALVE DIAPHRAGM SHOULD MOVE TO SEATED POSITION AND VACUUM SHOULD DROP FROM PUMP GAGE WHILE STARTING ENGINE.
  DOES IT?

REPLACE EGR VALVE.

NO

YES

- REMOVE EGR VALVE.
- CHECK FOR PLUGGED OR RESTRICTED EXHAUST PASSAGES.

EGR CIRCUIT IS OPERATING PROPERLY.

PASSAGES OK

PASSAGES NOT OK

REPLACE EGR VALVE.

- CLEAN PASSAGES.
- RE-CHECK EGR VALVE.

"AFTER REPAIRS," CONFIRM "CLOSED LOOP" OPERATION AND NO MIL (SERVICE ENGINE SOON).

Fig. 20 EGR system testing — except 5.0L (VIN Y) engine, continued

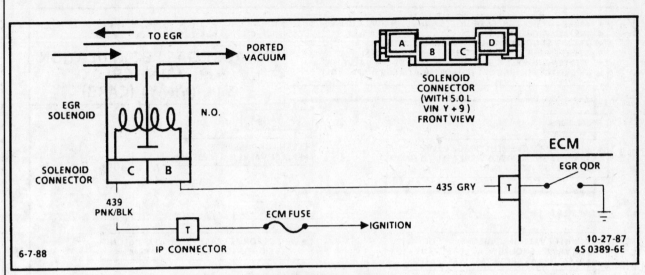

CHART C-7C
EXHAUST GAS RECIRCULATION (EGR) VALVE CHECK
5.0L (VIN Y) (CARB)

Circuit Description:

The Exhaust Gas Recirculation (EGR) valve is controlled by a normally open solenoid (allows vacuum to pass when de-energized).

When the ECM energizes the solenoid by completing a ground circuit, the EGR is turned "OFF." The ECM controls EGR based on the following inputs:

- Coolant temperature
- Throttle position
- Engine rpm
- TCC state
- Barometric pressure

Test Description: Numbers below refer to circled numbers on the diagnostic chart.

1. This tests for restricted valve or passage in manifold. Engine should run roughly or stall as valve is opened manually.
2. EGR valve diaphragm should begin to move as the engine speed approaches 2000 rpm.
3. This test should result in the EGR solenoid being energized, shutting off vacuum to the EGR valve diaphragm. This indicates EGR system is functioning properly.
4. Vacuum below 23.6 kPa (7" Hg) at 2000 rpm is insufficient for proper EGR operation. Lower vacuum readings require repair.

STEPS 1, 2 AND 3 represent an EGR system operation check.
---

5. With the ignition "ON" and engine stopped, the ECM normally grounds terminal "T" to energize the EGR solenoid. This step checks for a defective (always open) solenoid or an electrical circuit problem.
6. The EGR solenoid is normally de-energized with the engine idling at normal operating temperature. This step checks for a defective (always closed) solenoid or an electrical circuit problem.
7. This step determines whether ECM is providing ground to terminal "T" or CKT 435 is shorted to ground.

Diagnostic Aids:

Vacuum lines should be <u>thoroughly</u> checked for internal restrictions.

Fig. 21 EGR system testing — 5.0L (VIN Y) engine

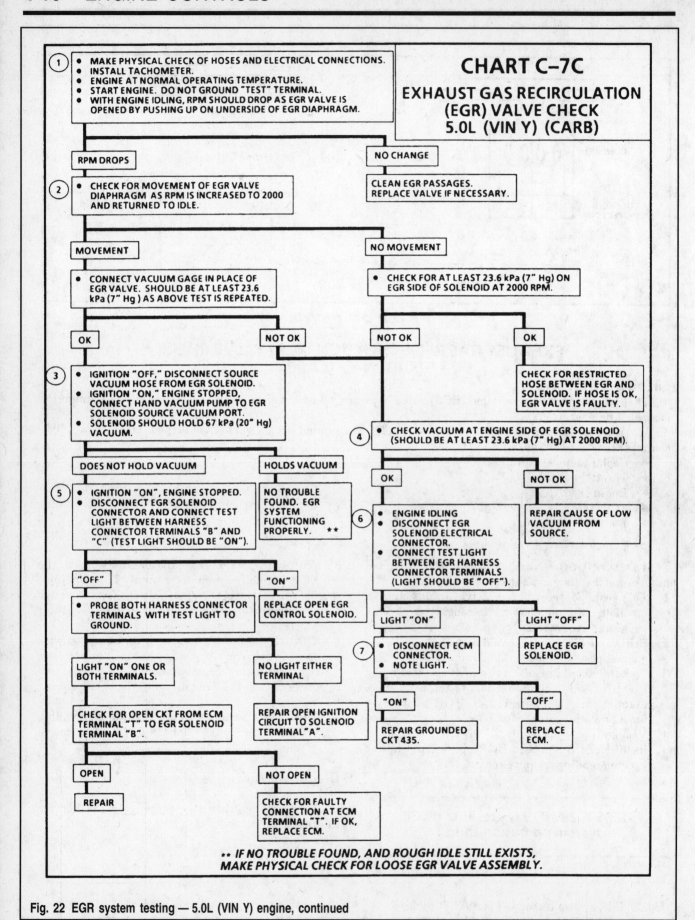

CHART C–7C

EXHAUST GAS RECIRCULATION (EGR) VALVE CHECK 5.0L (VIN Y) (CARB)

① • MAKE PHYSICAL CHECK OF HOSES AND ELECTRICAL CONNECTIONS.
• INSTALL TACHOMETER.
• ENGINE AT NORMAL OPERATING TEMPERATURE.
• START ENGINE. DO NOT GROUND "TEST" TERMINAL.
• WITH ENGINE IDLING, RPM SHOULD DROP AS EGR VALVE IS OPENED BY PUSHING UP ON UNDERSIDE OF EGR DIAPHRAGM.

RPM DROPS

② • CHECK FOR MOVEMENT OF EGR VALVE DIAPHRAGM AS RPM IS INCREASED TO 2000 AND RETURNED TO IDLE.

NO CHANGE

CLEAN EGR PASSAGES. REPLACE VALVE IF NECESSARY.

MOVEMENT

• CONNECT VACUUM GAGE IN PLACE OF EGR VALVE. SHOULD BE AT LEAST 23.6 kPa (7" Hg) AS ABOVE TEST IS REPEATED.

NO MOVEMENT

• CHECK FOR AT LEAST 23.6 kPa (7" Hg) ON EGR SIDE OF SOLENOID AT 2000 RPM.

OK

③ • IGNITION "OFF," DISCONNECT SOURCE VACUUM HOSE FROM EGR SOLENOID.
• IGNITION "ON," ENGINE STOPPED, CONNECT HAND VACUUM PUMP TO EGR SOLENOID SOURCE VACUUM PORT.
• SOLENOID SHOULD HOLD 67 kPa (20" Hg) VACUUM.

NOT OK

NOT OK

OK

CHECK FOR RESTRICTED HOSE BETWEEN EGR AND SOLENOID. IF HOSE IS OK, EGR VALVE IS FAULTY.

④ • CHECK VACUUM AT ENGINE SIDE OF EGR SOLENOID (SHOULD BE AT LEAST 23.6 kPa (7" Hg) AT 2000 RPM).

DOES NOT HOLD VACUUM

HOLDS VACUUM

NO TROUBLE FOUND. EGR SYSTEM FUNCTIONING PROPERLY. **

OK

NOT OK

⑤ • IGNITION "ON", ENGINE STOPPED.
• DISCONNECT EGR SOLENOID CONNECTOR AND CONNECT TEST LIGHT BETWEEN HARNESS CONNECTOR TERMINALS "B" AND "C" (TEST LIGHT SHOULD BE "ON").

⑥ • ENGINE IDLING
• DISCONNECT EGR SOLENOID ELECTRICAL CONNECTOR.
• CONNECT TEST LIGHT BETWEEN EGR HARNESS CONNECTOR TERMINALS (LIGHT SHOULD BE "OFF").

REPAIR CAUSE OF LOW VACUUM FROM SOURCE.

"OFF"

"ON"

• PROBE BOTH HARNESS CONNECTOR TERMINALS WITH TEST LIGHT TO GROUND.

REPLACE OPEN EGR CONTROL SOLENOID.

LIGHT "ON"

LIGHT "OFF"

⑦ • DISCONNECT ECM CONNECTOR.
• NOTE LIGHT.

REPLACE EGR SOLENOID.

LIGHT "ON" ONE OR BOTH TERMINALS.

NO LIGHT EITHER TERMINAL

"ON"

"OFF"

CHECK FOR OPEN CKT FROM ECM TERMINAL "T" TO EGR SOLENOID TERMINAL "B".

REPAIR OPEN IGNITION CIRCUIT TO SOLENOID TERMINAL "A".

REPAIR GROUNDED CKT 435.

REPLACE ECM.

OPEN

REPAIR

NOT OPEN

CHECK FOR FAULTY CONNECTION AT ECM TERMINAL "T". IF OK, REPLACE ECM.

⋆⋆ IF NO TROUBLE FOUND, AND ROUGH IDLE STILL EXISTS, MAKE PHYSICAL CHECK FOR LOOSE EGR VALVE ASSEMBLY.

Fig. 22 EGR system testing — 5.0L (VIN Y) engine, continued

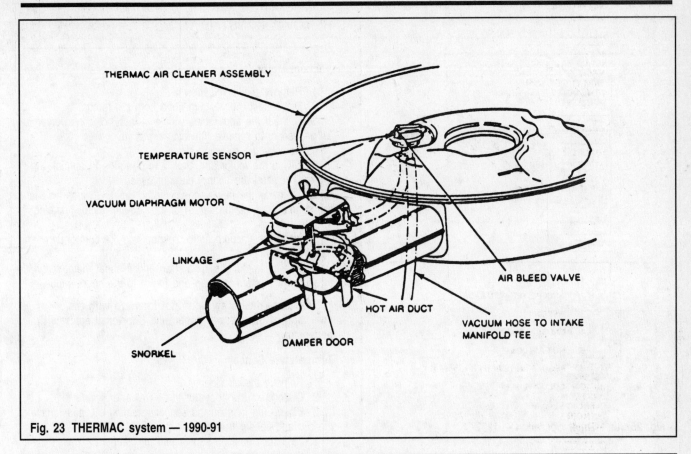

THERMAC AIR CLEANER ASSEMBLY

TEMPERATURE SENSOR

VACUUM DIAPHRAGM MOTOR

LINKAGE

AIR BLEED VALVE

SNORKEL

DAMPER DOOR

HOT AIR DUCT

VACUUM HOSE TO INTAKE MANIFOLD TEE

Fig. 23 THERMAC system — 1990-91

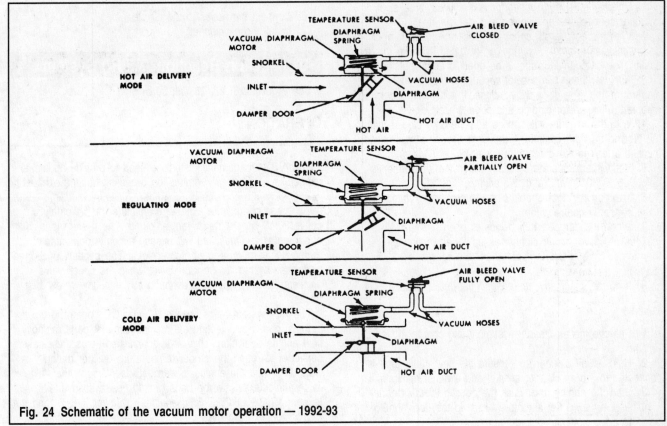

TEMPERATURE SENSOR
DIAPHRAGM SPRING
VACUUM DIAPHRAGM MOTOR
AIR BLEED VALVE CLOSED
SNORKEL
VACUUM HOSES
HOT AIR DELIVERY MODE
INLET
DIAPHRAGM
DAMPER DOOR
HOT AIR DUCT
HOT AIR

VACUUM DIAPHRAGM MOTOR
TEMPERATURE SENSOR
DIAPHRAGM SPRING
AIR BLEED VALVE PARTIALLY OPEN
SNORKEL
VACUUM HOSES
REGULATING MODE
INLET
DIAPHRAGM
DAMPER DOOR
HOT AIR DUCT

TEMPERATURE SENSOR
VACUUM DIAPHRAGM MOTOR
AIR BLEED VALVE FULLY OPEN
DIAPHRAGM SPRING
SNORKEL
VACUUM HOSES
COLD AIR DELIVERY MODE
INLET
DIAPHRAGM
DAMPER DOOR
HOT AIR DUCT

Fig. 24 Schematic of the vacuum motor operation — 1992-93

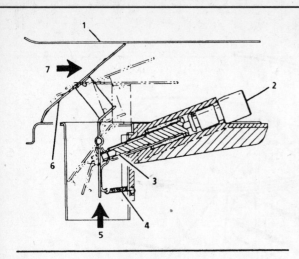

1	SNORKEL
2	WAX PELLET ACTUATOR
3	PISTON
4	CALIBRATED SPRING
5	HOT AIR INLET
6	REGULATING DAMPER ASSEMBLY
7	COLD AIR INLET

Fig. 25 Air cleaner operation — 1992-93

1. Check the vacuum hoses for leaks, kinks, breaks, or improper connections and correct any defects.

2. With the engine off, check the position of the damper door within the snorkel. A mirror can be used to make this job easier. The damper door should be open to admit outside air.

3. Apply at least 7 in. Hg. of vacuum to the damper diaphragm unit. The door should close. If it doesn't, check the diaphragm linkage for binding and correct hookup.

4. With the vacuum still applied and the door closed, clamp the tube to trap the vacuum. If the door doesn't remain closed, there is a leak in the diaphragm assembly.

5. Verify the temperature sensor within the air cleaner is below 86°F (30°C) and start the engine.

6. The damper door should close to outside air immediately if the sensor is cool enough.

7. When the damper door begins to open (within a few minutes), remove the air cleaner assembly and using a thermometer, verify the temperature of the sensor is 131°F (55°C).

8. If not as specified, the sensor must be replaced.

1992-93

1. Remove the air cleaner assembly and cool to 40°F (4°C).

2. Reinstall air cleaner and ensure the heat stove tube is connected to the air cleaner snorkel and exhaust manifold.

3. Start the engine and watch the door in the air cleaner.

4. As the wax pellet actuator warms up the door should begin to open slowly to outside air.

5. if not as specified, replace the assembly.

REMOVAL & INSTALLATION

Vacuum Motor

1. Remove the air cleaner.

2. Disconnect the vacuum hose from the motor.

3. Drill out the spot welds with a ⅛ inch hole, then enlarge as necessary to remove the retaining strap.

4. Remove the retaining strap.

5. Lift up the motor and cock it to one side to unhook the motor linkage at the control damper assembly.

6. To install the new vacuum motor, drill a ¹⁄₁₆ inch hole in the snorkel tube as the center of the vacuum motor retaining strap.

7. Insert the vacuum motor linkage into the control damper assembly.

8. Use the motor retaining strap and a sheet metal screw to secure the retaining strap and motor to the snorkel tube.

➡**Make sure the screw does not interfere with the operation of the damper assembly. Shorten the screw if necessary.**

Temperature Sensor

1. Remove the air cleaner.

2. Disconnect the hoses at the air cleaner.

3. Pry up the tabs on the sensor retaining clip and remove the clip and sensor from the air cleaner.

4. To install, position sensor into air cleaner.

5. Install retaining clip.

6. Connect the hoses to the air cleaner.

7. Install the air cleaner.

Air Injection Reaction (A.I.R.) System

▶ **See Figures 26, 27, 28, 29, 30 and 31**

OPERATION

The AIR management system, is used to provide additional oxygen to continue the combustion process after the exhaust gases leave the combustion chamber. Air is injected into either the exhaust port(s), the exhaust manifold(s) or the catalytic converter by an engine driven air pump. The system is in operation at all times and will bypass air only momentarily during deceleration and at high speeds. The bypass function is performed by the Air Control Valve, while the check valve protects the air pump by preventing any backflow of exhaust gases.

The AIR system helps reduce HC and CO content in the exhaust gases by injecting air into the exhaust ports during cold engine operation. This air injection also helps the catalytic converter to reach the proper temperature quicker during warmup. When the engine is warm (Closed Loop), the AIR system injects air into the beds of a three-way converter (except 1992-93 5.0L & 5.7L engines) to lower the HC and the CO content in the exhaust.

The Air Injection Reduction system utilizes the following components:

1. An engine driven AIR pump.

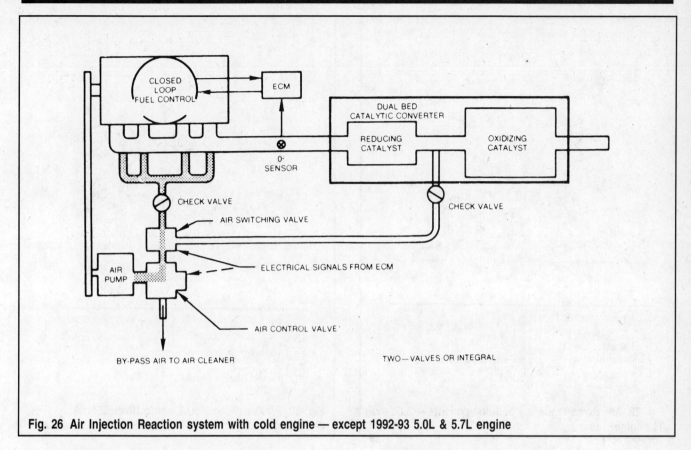

Fig. 26 Air Injection Reaction system with cold engine — except 1992-93 5.0L & 5.7L engine

2. AIR Control valves (Air Control, Air Switching).
3. Air flow and control hoses.

4. Check valves.
5. A dual-bed, three-way catalytic converter.

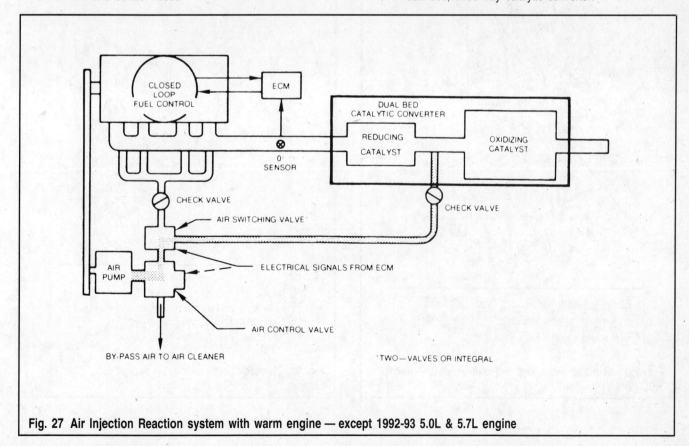

Fig. 27 Air Injection Reaction system with warm engine — except 1992-93 5.0L & 5.7L engine

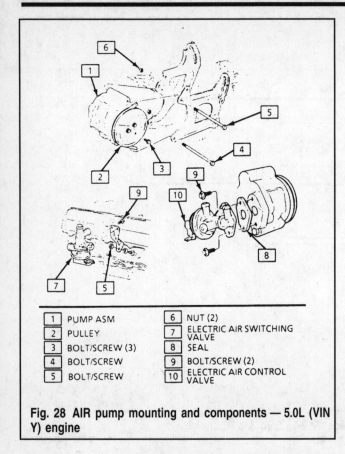

1	PUMP ASM	6	NUT (2)
2	PULLEY	7	ELECTRIC AIR SWITCHING VALVE
3	BOLT/SCREW (3)	8	SEAL
4	BOLT/SCREW	9	BOLT/SCREW (2)
5	BOLT/SCREW	10	ELECTRIC AIR CONTROL VALVE

Fig. 28 AIR pump mounting and components — 5.0L (VIN Y) engine

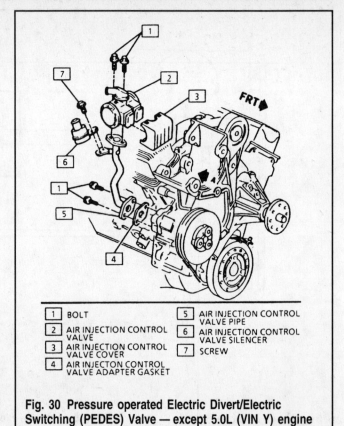

1	BOLT	5	AIR INJECTION CONTROL VALVE PIPE
2	AIR INJECTION CONTROL VALVE	6	AIR INJECTION CONTROL VALVE SILENCER
3	AIR INJECTION CONTROL VALVE COVER	7	SCREW
4	AIR INJECTON CONTROL VALVE ADAPTER GASKET		

Fig. 30 Pressure operated Electric Divert/Electric Switching (PEDES) Valve — except 5.0L (VIN Y) engine

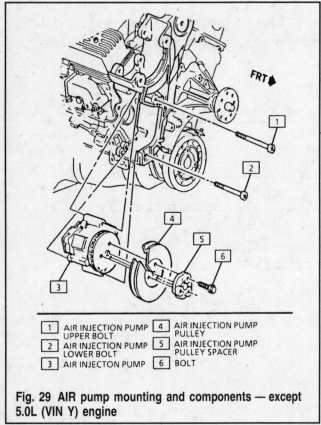

1	AIR INJECTION PUMP UPPER BOLT	4	AIR INJECTION PUMP PULLEY
2	AIR INJECTION PUMP LOWER BOLT	5	AIR INJECTION PUMP PULLEY SPACER
3	AIR INJECTON PUMP	6	BOLT

Fig. 29 AIR pump mounting and components — except 5.0L (VIN Y) engine

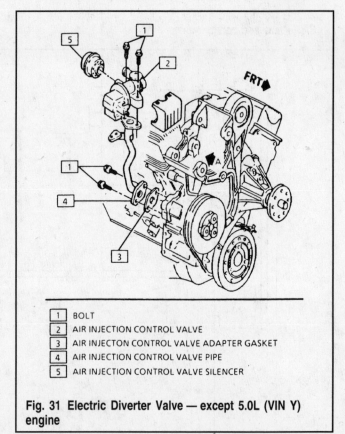

1	BOLT
2	AIR INJECTION CONTROL VALVE
3	AIR INJECTON CONTROL VALVE ADAPTER GASKET
4	AIR INJECTION CONTROL VALVE PIPE
5	AIR INJECTION CONTROL VALVE SILENCER

Fig. 31 Electric Diverter Valve — except 5.0L (VIN Y) engine

The belt driven, vane-type air pump is located at the front of the engine and supplies clean air to the AIR system for purposes already stated. When the engine is cold, the Electronic Control Module (ECM) energizes an AIR control solenoid. This allows air to flow to the AIR switching valve. The AIR switching valve is then energized to direct air to the exhaust ports.

When the engine is warm, the ECM de-energizes the AIR switching valve, thus directing the air between the beds of the catalytic converter (except 1992-93 5.0L & 5.7L engines). This provides additional oxygen for the oxidizing catalyst in the second bed to decrease HC and CO, while at the same time keeping oxygen levels low in the first bed, enabling the reducing catalyst to effectively decrease the levels of NOx.

If the AIR control valve detects a rapid increase in manifold vacuum (deceleration), certain operating modes (wide open throttle, etc.) or if the ECM self-diagnostic system detects any problem in the system, air is diverted to the air cleaner or directly into the atmosphere.

The primary purpose of the ECM's divert mode is to prevent backfiring. Throttle closure at the beginning of deceleration will temporarily create air/fuel mixtures which are too rich to burn completely. These mixtures become burnable when they reach the exhaust if combined with the injection air. The next firing of the engine will ignite this mixture causing an exhaust backfire. Momentary diverting of the injection air from the exhaust prevents this.

The AIR system check valves and hoses should be checked periodically for any leaks, cracks or deterioration.

TESTING

Air Pump

1. Check the drive belt tension.
2. Increase the engine speed and observe an increase in air flow. If air flow does not increase, replace the air pump.

Control Valve

1. Remove the hoses. Blow through the valve (toward the cylinder head).
2. Then, blow air through the other side of the valve in the direction of the pump. Air should only flow in one direction, toward the cylinder head. If not, replace the control valve.

REMOVAL & INSTALLATION

Air Pump

1. Remove the AIR control valves and/or adapter at the pump.
2. On 1990-91 Caprice, loosen the air pump adjustment bolt and remove the drive belt. On 1992-93 Caprice, hold the pump pulley from turning and loosen the pulley bolts. Lift the belt drive tensioner to the raised position remove the pump and pulley assembly.
3. Unscrew the pump mounting bolts and then remove the pump pulley.
4. Unscrew the pump mounting bolts and then remove the pump.

5. To install, position the pump into place and secure it with the mounting bolts.
6. Install the pump pulley.
7. Install the air pump drive belt and adjust pump belt with the pump adjustment bolt, as required.
8. Install the AIR control valves and/or adapter.

Check Valve

1. Release the clamp and disconnect the air hoses from the valve.
2. Unscrew the check valve from the air injection pipe using a back-up wrench.
3. Installation is in the reverse order of removal.

Air Control Valve

1. Disconnect the negative battery cable.
2. Remove the air cleaner.
3. Tag and disconnect the vacuum hose from the valve.
4. Tag and disconnect the air outlet hoses from the valve.
5. Bend back the lock tabs and then remove the bolts holding the elbow to the valve.
6. Tag and disconnect any electrical connections at the valve and then remove the valve from the elbow.
7. To install, position the valve into the elbow.
8. Connect any electrical connections at the valve.
9. Install the bolts holding the elbow to the valve and bend the lock tabs.
10. Connect the air outlet hoses to the valve.
11. Connect the vacuum hose to the valve.
12. Install the air cleaner.
13. Connect the negative battery cable.

Early Fuel Evaporation (EFE)

▶ See Figure 32

OPERATION

The EFE system is used on the 5.0L (VIN Y) engine to provide a source of rapid engine heat up during cold operations. It helps reduce the time that carburetor choking is required and helps reduce exhaust emissions.

The Vacuum Servo type consists of a valve, an actuator and a Thermal Vacuum Switch (TVS)-the valve is located in the exhaust manifold and the TVS switch is on the engine coolant housing.

A check of the operation should be made at regular maintenance intervals.

SYSTEM CHECK

1. With the engine cold, observe the position of the actuator arm. Start the engine. The arm should move toward the diaphragm (closing the valve).
2. If the arm does not move, remove the hose and check for vacuum. If still no vacuum, remove the top hose from the TVS switch and check for vacuum.
3. If vacuum is present in the top hose, replace the TVS switch.

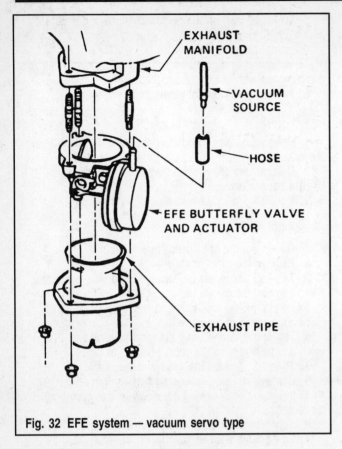

EXHAUST MANIFOLD

VACUUM SOURCE

HOSE

EFE BUTTERFLY VALVE AND ACTUATOR

EXHAUST PIPE

Fig. 32 EFE system — vacuum servo type

REMOVAL & INSTALLATION

1. Disconnect the vacuum hose at the EFE.
2. Remove exhaust pipe to manifold nuts.
3. Remove the crossover pipe. Complete removal is not always necessary.
4. Remove the EFE valve.
5. To install, position the EFE valve into place.
6. Install the crossover pipe.
7. Install the exhaust pipe to manifold nuts.
8. Connect the vacuum hose at the EFE.

4. If vacuum is present at the actuator and it does not move, try to free the valve or replace the valve.

ELECTRONIC ENGINE CONTROLS

▶ See Figures 33, 34, 35, 36 and 37

COMPUTER COMMAND CONTROL (CCC) SYSTEM

▶ See Figures 38, 39 and 40

The Computer Command Control System (CCC) is an electronically controlled exhaust emission system that can monitor and control a large number of interrelated emission control systems. It can monitor up to 15 various engine/vehicle operating conditions and then use this information to control as many as 9 engine related systems. The system is thereby making constant adjustments to maintain good vehicle performance under all normal driving conditions while at the same time allowing the catalytic converter to effectively control the emissions of HC, CO and NOx.

Electronic Control Module

The Electronic Control Module (ECM) is required to maintain the exhaust emissions at acceptable levels. The module is a small, solid state computer which receives signals from many sources and sensors; it uses these data to make judgements about operating conditions and then control output signals to the fuel and emission systems to match the current requirements.

Inputs are received from many sources to form a complete picture of engine operating conditions. Some inputs are simply Yes or No messages, such as that from the Park/Neutral switch; the vehicle is either in gear or in Park/Neutral; there are no other choices. Other data is sent in quantitative input, such as engine RPM or coolant temperature. The ECM is pre-programmed to recognize acceptable ranges or combinations of signals and control the outputs to control emissions while providing good driveability and economy. The ECM also monitors some output circuits, making sure that the components function as commanded. For proper engine operation, it is essential that all input and output components function properly and communicate properly with the ECM.

Since the control module is programmed to recognize the presence and value of electrical inputs, it will also note the lack of a signal or a radical change in values. It will, for example, react to the loss of signal from the vehicle speed sensor or note that engine coolant temperature has risen beyond acceptable (programmed) limits. Once a fault is recognized, a numeric code is assigned and held in memory. The dashboard warning lamp — CHECK ENGINE or SERVICE ENGINE SOON — will illuminate to advise the operator that the system has detected a fault.

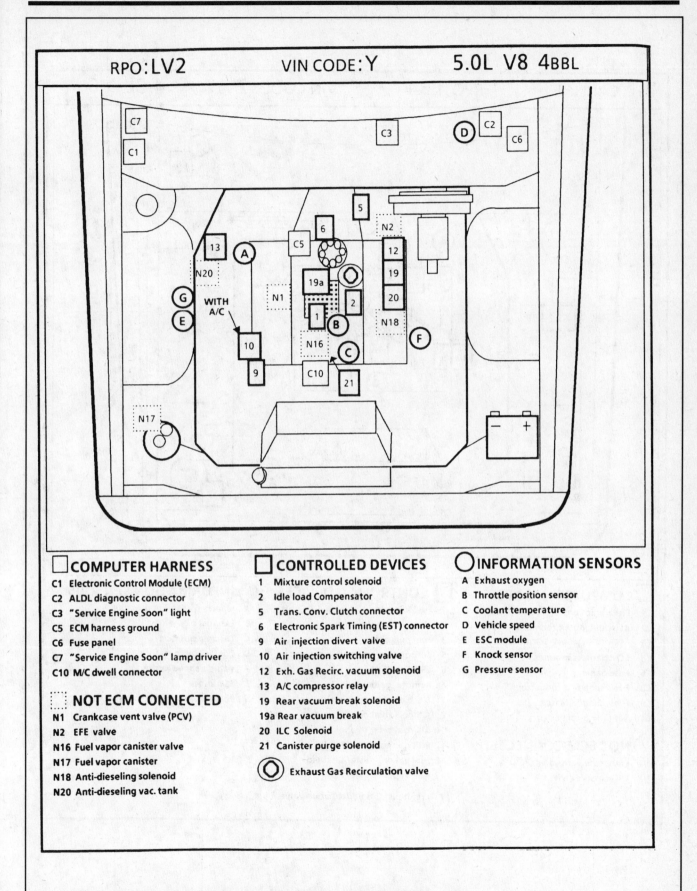

RPO: LV2   VIN CODE: Y   5.0L V8 4BBL

COMPUTER HARNESS

C1 Electronic Control Module (ECM)
C2 ALDL diagnostic connector
C3 "Service Engine Soon" light
C5 ECM harness ground
C6 Fuse panel
C7 "Service Engine Soon" lamp driver
C10 M/C dwell connector

NOT ECM CONNECTED

N1 Crankcase vent valve (PCV)
N2 EFE valve
N16 Fuel vapor canister valve
N17 Fuel vapor canister
N18 Anti-dieseling solenoid
N20 Anti-dieseling vac. tank

CONTROLLED DEVICES

1 Mixture control solenoid
2 Idle load Compensator
5 Trans. Conv. Clutch connector
6 Electronic Spark Timing (EST) connector
9 Air injection divert valve
10 Air injection switching valve
12 Exh. Gas Recirc. vacuum solenoid
13 A/C compressor relay
19 Rear vacuum break solenoid
19a Rear vacuum break
20 ILC Solenoid
21 Canister purge solenoid

Exhaust Gas Recirculation valve

INFORMATION SENSORS

A Exhaust oxygen
B Throttle position sensor
C Coolant temperature
D Vehicle speed
E ESC module
F Knock sensor
G Pressure sensor

Fig. 33 Electronic Engine Control component locations — 1990 5.0L (VIN Y) engine

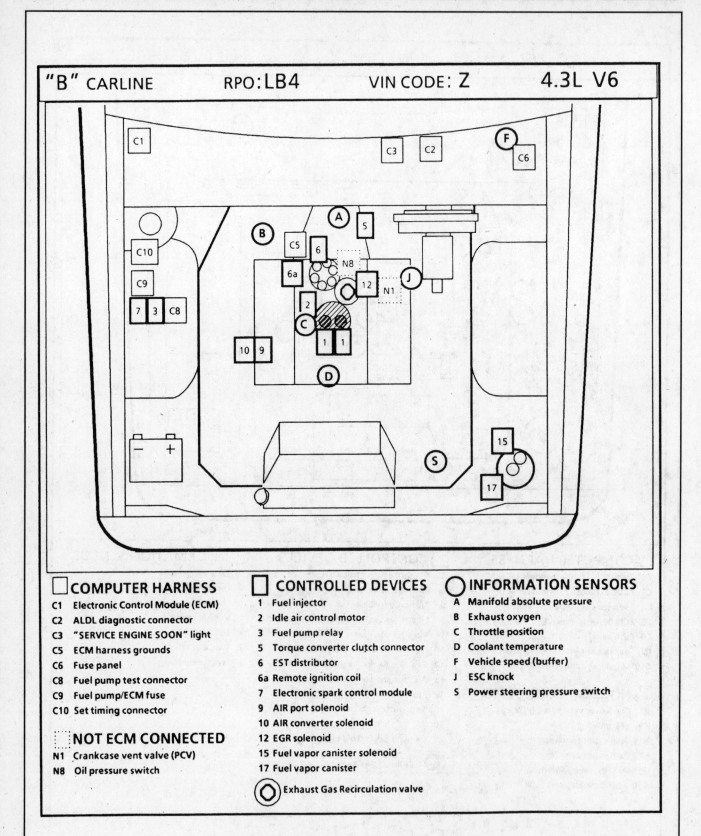

"B" CARLINE   RPO: **LB4**   VIN CODE: **Z**   **4.3L V6**

☐ **COMPUTER HARNESS**

C1   Electronic Control Module (ECM)
C2   ALDL diagnostic connector
C3   "SERVICE ENGINE SOON" light
C5   ECM harness grounds
C6   Fuse panel
C8   Fuel pump test connector
C9   Fuel pump/ECM fuse
C10 Set timing connector

☐ **NOT ECM CONNECTED**

N1   Crankcase vent valve (PCV)
N8   Oil pressure switch

☐ **CONTROLLED DEVICES**

1   Fuel injector
2   Idle air control motor
3   Fuel pump relay
5   Torque converter clutch connector
6   EST distributor
6a   Remote ignition coil
7   Electronic spark control module
9   AIR port solenoid
10   AIR converter solenoid
12   EGR solenoid
15   Fuel vapor canister solenoid
17   Fuel vapor canister

⬡ Exhaust Gas Recirculation valve

◯ **INFORMATION SENSORS**

A   Manifold absolute pressure
B   Exhaust oxygen
C   Throttle position
D   Coolant temperature
F   Vehicle speed (buffer)
J   ESC knock
S   Power steering pressure switch

Fig. 34 Electronic Engine Control component locations — 1990-91 4.3L engine

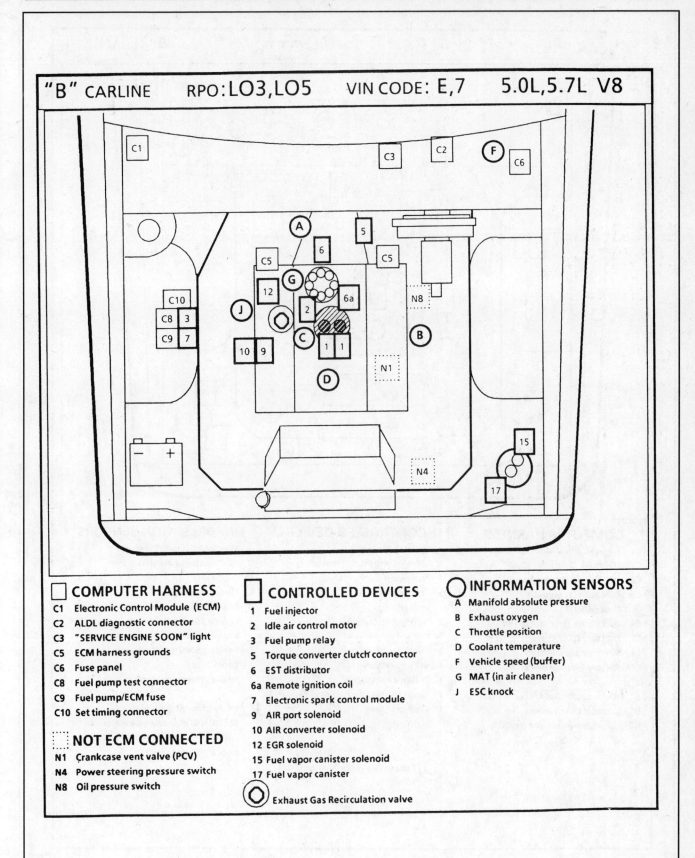

"B" CARLINE   RPO: LO3, LO5   VIN CODE: E, 7   5.0L, 5.7L V8

COMPUTER HARNESS
- C1 Electronic Control Module (ECM)
- C2 ALDL diagnostic connector
- C3 "SERVICE ENGINE SOON" light
- C5 ECM harness grounds
- C6 Fuse panel
- C8 Fuel pump test connector
- C9 Fuel pump/ECM fuse
- C10 Set timing connector

NOT ECM CONNECTED
- N1 Crankcase vent valve (PCV)
- N4 Power steering pressure switch
- N8 Oil pressure switch

CONTROLLED DEVICES
- 1   Fuel injector
- 2   Idle air control motor
- 3   Fuel pump relay
- 5   Torque converter clutch connector
- 6   EST distributor
- 6a Remote ignition coil
- 7   Electronic spark control module
- 9   AIR port solenoid
- 10 AIR converter solenoid
- 12 EGR solenoid
- 15 Fuel vapor canister solenoid
- 17 Fuel vapor canister
-     Exhaust Gas Recirculation valve

INFORMATION SENSORS
- A   Manifold absolute pressure
- B   Exhaust oxygen
- C   Throttle position
- D   Coolant temperature
- F   Vehicle speed (buffer)
- G   MAT (in air cleaner)
- J   ESC knock

Fig. 35 Electronic Engine Control component locations — 1990-91 5.0L (VIN E) & 5.7L engines

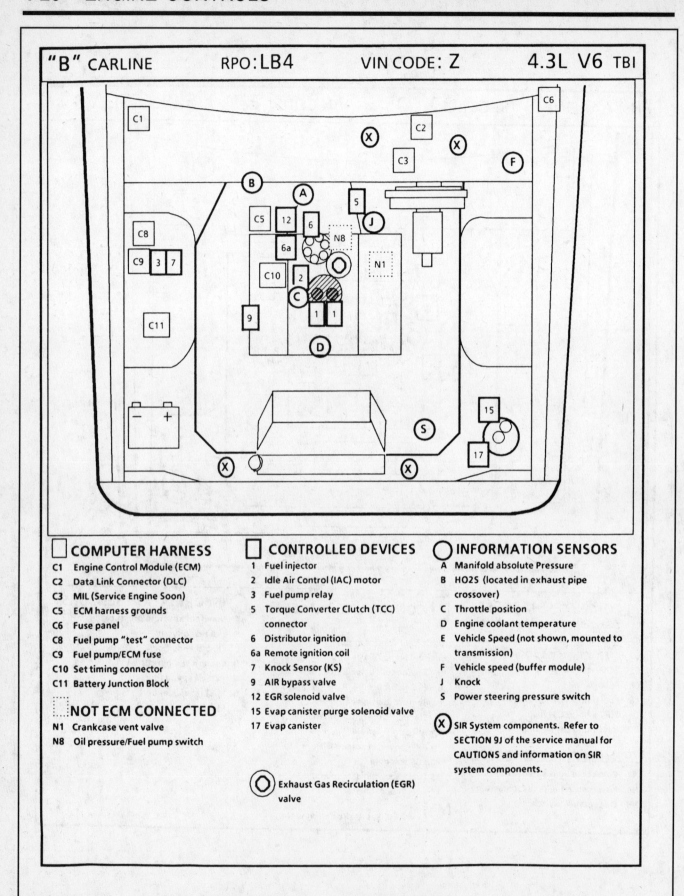

"B" CARLINE   RPO: LB4   VIN CODE: Z   4.3L V6 TBI

COMPUTER HARNESS
- C1 Engine Control Module (ECM)
- C2 Data Link Connector (DLC)
- C3 MIL (Service Engine Soon)
- C5 ECM harness grounds
- C6 Fuse panel
- C8 Fuel pump "test" connector
- C9 Fuel pump/ECM fuse
- C10 Set timing connector
- C11 Battery Junction Block

NOT ECM CONNECTED
- N1 Crankcase vent valve
- N8 Oil pressure/Fuel pump switch

CONTROLLED DEVICES
- 1   Fuel injector
- 2   Idle Air Control (IAC) motor
- 3   Fuel pump relay
- 5   Torque Converter Clutch (TCC) connector
- 6   Distributor ignition
- 6a Remote ignition coil
- 7   Knock Sensor (KS)
- 9   AIR bypass valve
- 12 EGR solenoid valve
- 15 Evap canister purge solenoid valve
- 17 Evap canister

Exhaust Gas Recirculation (EGR) valve

INFORMATION SENSORS
- A   Manifold absolute Pressure
- B   HO2S (located in exhaust pipe crossover)
- C   Throttle position
- D   Engine coolant temperature
- E   Vehicle Speed (not shown, mounted to transmission)
- F   Vehicle speed (buffer module)
- J   Knock
- S   Power steering pressure switch

(X) SIR System components. Refer to SECTION 9J of the service manual for CAUTIONS and information on SIR system components.

Fig. 36 Electronic Engine Control component locations — 1992-93 4.3L engine

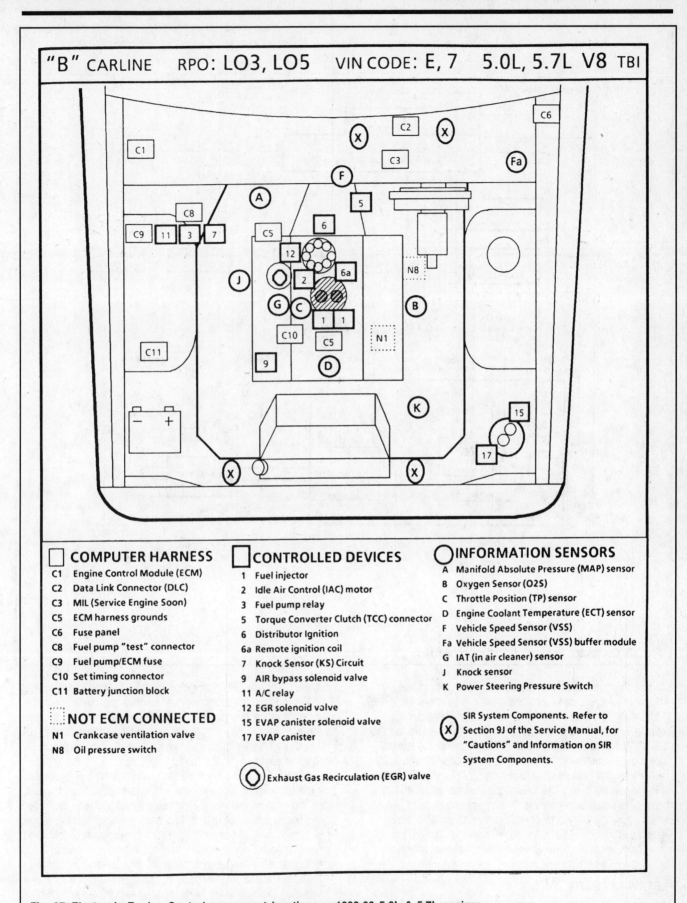

"B" CARLINE   RPO: LO3, LO5   VIN CODE: E, 7   5.0L, 5.7L V8 TBI

☐ **COMPUTER HARNESS**
C1   Engine Control Module (ECM)
C2   Data Link Connector (DLC)
C3   MIL (Service Engine Soon)
C5   ECM harness grounds
C6   Fuse panel
C8   Fuel pump "test" connector
C9   Fuel pump/ECM fuse
C10 Set timing connector
C11 Battery junction block

⠿ **NOT ECM CONNECTED**
N1   Crankcase ventilation valve
N8   Oil pressure switch

☐ **CONTROLLED DEVICES**
1   Fuel injector
2   Idle Air Control (IAC) motor
3   Fuel pump relay
5   Torque Converter Clutch (TCC) connector
6   Distributor Ignition
6a   Remote ignition coil
7   Knock Sensor (KS) Circuit
9   AIR bypass solenoid valve
11   A/C relay
12   EGR solenoid valve
15   EVAP canister solenoid valve
17   EVAP canister

⬡ Exhaust Gas Recirculation (EGR) valve

○ **INFORMATION SENSORS**
A   Manifold Absolute Pressure (MAP) sensor
B   Oxygen Sensor (O2S)
C   Throttle Position (TP) sensor
D   Engine Coolant Temperature (ECT) sensor
F   Vehicle Speed Sensor (VSS)
Fa   Vehicle Speed Sensor (VSS) buffer module
G   IAT (in air cleaner) sensor
J   Knock sensor
K   Power Steering Pressure Switch

Ⓧ SIR System Components. Refer to Section 9J of the Service Manual, for "Cautions" and Information on SIR System Components.

Fig. 37 Electronic Engine Control component locations — 1992-93 5.0L & 5.7L engines

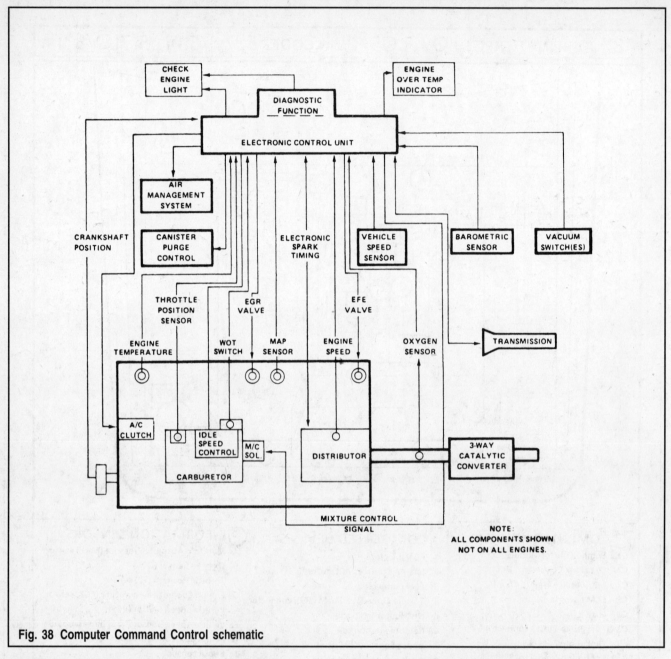

Fig. 38 Computer Command Control schematic

More than one code may be stored. Although not every engine uses every code, possible codes range from 12 to 999. Additionally, the same code may carry different meanings relative to each engine or engine family. For example, on the 3.3L (VIN N), code 46 indicates a fault found in the power steering pressure switch circuit. The same code on the 5.7L (VIN F) engine indicates a fault in the VATS anti-theft system.

In the event of an ECM failure, the system will default to a pre-programmed set of values. These are compromise values which allow the engine to operate, although possibly at reduced efficiency. This is variously known as the default, limp-in or back-up mode. Driveability is almost always affected when the ECM enters this mode.

LEARNING ABILITY

The ECM can compensate for minor variations within the fuel system through the block learn and fuel integrator

systems. The fuel integrator monitors the oxygen sensor output voltage, adding or subtracting fuel to drive the mixture rich or lean as needed to reach the ideal air fuel ratio of 14.7:1. The integrator values may be read with a scan tool; the display will range from 0-255 and should center on 128 if the oxygen sensor is seeing a 14.7:1 mixture.

The temporary nature of the integrator's control is expanded by the block learn function. The name is derived from the fact that the entire engine operating range (load vs. rpm) is divided into 16 sections or blocks. Within each memory block is stored the correct fuel delivery value for that combination of load and engine speed. Once the operating range enters a certain block, that stored value controls the fuel delivery unless the integrator steps in to change it. If changes are made by the integrator, the new value is memorized and stored within the block. As the block learn makes the correction, the integrator correction will be reduced until the integrator returns to 128;

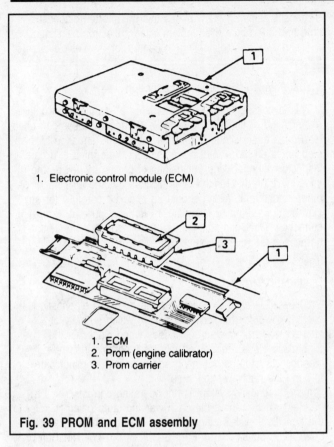

1. Electronic control module (ECM)

1. ECM
2. Prom (engine calibrator)
3. Prom carrier

Fig. 39 PROM and ECM assembly

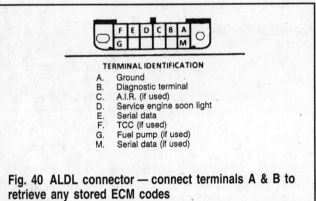

TERMINAL IDENTIFICATION
A. Ground
B. Diagnostic terminal
C. A.I.R. (if used)
D. Service engine soon light
E. Serial data
F. TCC (if used)
G. Fuel pump (if used)
M. Serial data (if used)

Fig. 40 ALDL connector — connect terminals A & B to retrieve any stored ECM codes

the block learn then controls the fuel delivery with the new value.

The next time the engine operates within the block's range, the new value will be used. The block learn data can also be read by a scan tool; the range is the same as the integrator and should also center on 128. In this way, the systems can compensate for engine wear, small air or vacuum leaks or reduced combustion.

Any time the battery is disconnected, the block learn values are lost and must be relearned by the ECM. This loss of corrected values may be noticed as a significant change in driveability. To reteach the system, make certain the engine is fully warmed up. Drive the vehicle at part throttle using moderate acceleration and idle until normal performance is felt.

DASHBOARD WARNING LAMP

The primary function of the dash warning lamp is to advise the operator and the technician that a fault has been detected, and, in most cases, a code stored. Under normal conditions, the dash warning lamp will illuminate when the ignition is turned **ON**. Once the engine is started and running, the ECM will perform a system check and extinguish the warning lamp if no fault is found.

Additionally, the dash warning lamp can be used to retrieve stored codes after the system is placed in the Diagnostic Mode. Codes are transmitted as a series of flashes with short or long pauses. When the system is placed in the Field Service Mode, the dash lamp will indicate open loop or closed loop function to the technician.

Intermittent

If a fault occurs intermittently, such as a loose connector pin breaking contact as the vehicle hits a bump, the ECM will note the fault as it occurs and energize the dash warning lamp. If the problem self-corrects, as with the terminal pin again making contact, the dash lamp will extinguish after 10 seconds but a code will remain stored in the ECM memory.

When an unexpected code appears during diagnostics, it may have been set during an intermittent failure that self-corrected; the codes are still useful in diagnosis and should not be discounted.

TOOLS AND EQUIPMENT
Scan Tools

Although stored codes may be read with only the use of a small jumper wire, the use of a hand-held scan tool such as GM's TECH 1 or equivalent is recommended. There are many manufacturers of these tools; a purchaser must be certain that the tool is proper for the intended use.

The scan tool allows any stored codes to be read from the ECM memory. The tool also allows the operator to view the data being sent to the ECM while the engine is running. This ability has obvious diagnostic advantages; the use of the scan tool is frequently required by the diagnostic charts. Use of the scan tool provides additional data but does not eliminate the need for use of the charts. The scan tool makes collecting information easier; the data must be correctly interpreted by an operator familiar with the system.

An example of the usefulness of the scan tool may be seen in the case of a temperature sensor which has changed its electrical characteristics. The ECM is reacting to an apparently warmer engine (causing a driveability problem), but the sensor's voltage has not changed enough to set a fault code. Connecting the scan tool, the voltage signal being sent to the ECM may be viewed; comparison to either a chart of normal values or a known good vehicle reveals the problem quickly.

The ECM is capable of communicating with a scan tool in 3 modes:

NORMAL OR OPEN MODE

This mode is not applicable to all engines. When engaged, certain engine data can be observed on the scanner without affecting engine operating characteristics. The number of items readable in this mode varies with engine family. Most scan tools are designed to change automatically to the ALDL mode if this mode is not available.

ALDL MODE

Also referred to as the 10K or SPECIAL mode, the scanner will present all readable data as available. Certain operating characteristics of the engine are changed or controlled when this mode is engaged. The closed loop timers are bypassed, the spark (EST) is advanced and the PARK/NEUTRAL restriction is bypassed. If applicable, the IAC controls the engine speed to 1000 rpm ± 50, and, on some engines, the canister purge solenoid is energized.

FACTORY TEST

Sometimes referred to as BACK-UP mode, this level of communication is primarily used during vehicle assembly and testing. This mode will confirm that the default or limp-in system is working properly within the ECM. Other data obtainable in this mode has little use in diagnosis.

➡ **A scan tool that is known to display faulty data should not be used for diagnosis. Although the fault may be believed to be in only one area, it can possibly affect many other areas during diagnosis, leading to errors and incorrect repair.**

To properly read system values with a scan tool, the following conditions must be met. All normal values given in the charts will be based on these conditions:

- Engine running at idle, throttle closed
- Engine warm, upper radiator hose hot
- Vehicle in park or neutral
- System operating in closed loop
- All accessories **OFF**

Electrical Tools

The most commonly required electrical diagnostic tool is the Digital Multimeter, allowing voltage, ohmage (resistance) and amperage to be read by one instrument. The multimeter must be a high-impedance unit, with 10 megohms of impedance in the voltmeter. This type of meter will not place an additional load on the circuit it is testing; this is extremely important in low voltage circuits. The multimeter must be of high quality in all respects. Replace batteries frequently in the unit.

Other necessary tools include an unpowered test light, a quality tachometer with inductive (clip-on) pick up and the proper tools for releasing GM's Metri-Pack, Weather Pack and Micro-Pack electrical terminals as necessary. The Micro-Pack connectors are used at the ECM connector. A vacuum pump/gauge may also be required for checking sensors, solenoids and valves.

Diagnosis and Testing

TROUBLESHOOTING

Diagnosis of a driveablility and/or emissions problems requires attention to detail and following the diagnostic procedures in the correct order. Resist the temptation to perform any repairs before performing the preliminary diagnostic steps. In many cases this will shorten diagnostic time and often cure the problem without electronic testing.

The proper troubleshooting procedure for the vehicle is as follows:

Visual/Physical Underhood Inspection

This is possibly the most critical step of diagnosis. A detailed examination of connectors, wiring and vacuum hoses can often lead to a repair without further diagnosis. Performance of this step relies on the skill of the technician performing it; a careful inspector will check the undersides of hoses as well as the integrity of hard-to-reach hoses blocked by the air cleaner or other component. Wiring should be checked carefully for any sign of strain, burning, crimping, or terminal pull-out from a connector. Checking connectors at components or in harnesses is required; usually, pushing them together will reveal a loose fit.

Diagnostic Circuit Check

This step is used to check that the on-board diagnostic system is working correctly. A system which is faulty or shorted may not yield correct codes when placed in the Diagnostic Mode. Performing this test confirms that the diagnostic system is not failed and is able to communicate through the dash warning lamp.

If the diagnostic system is not operating correctly, or if a problem exists without the dash warning lamp being lit, refer to the specific vehicle's diagnostic 'A-" Charts. These charts cover such conditions as Engine Cranks but Will Not Run or No Service Engine Soon Light.

Reading Codes and Use of Scan Tool

Once the integrity of the system is confirmed, enter the Diagnostic Mode and read any stored codes. To enter the diagnostic mode:

1. Turn the ignition switch **OFF**. Locate the Assembly Line Diagnostic Link (ALDL), usually under the instrument panel. It may be within a plastic cover or housing labeled DIAGNOSTIC CONNECTOR. This link is used to communicate with the ECM.

2. The code(s) stored in memory may be read either through the flashing of the dashboard warning lamp or through the use of a hand-held scan tool. If using the scan tool, connect it correctly to the ALDL.

3. If reading codes via the dash warning lamp, use a small jumper wire to connect Terminal B of the ALDL to Terminal A. As the ALDL connector is viewed from the front, Terminal A is on the extreme right of the upper row; Terminal B is second from the right on the upper row.

4. After the terminals are connected, turn the ignition switch to the **ON** position but do not start the engine. The dash warning lamp should begin to flash Code 12. The code will display as one flash, a pause and two flashes. Code 12 is not a fault code. It is used as a system acknowledgment or handshake code; its presence indicates that the ECM can communicate as requested. Code 12 is used to begin every diagnostic sequence. Some vehicles also use Code 12 after all diagnostic codes have been sent.

5. After Code 12 has been transmitted 3 times, the fault codes, if any, will each be transmitted 3 times. The codes are stored and transmitted in numeric order from lowest to highest.

➤**The order of codes in the memory does not indicate the order of occurrence.**

6. If there are no codes stored, but a driveability or emissions problem is evident, refer to the Symptoms and Intermittents Chart for the specific fuel system.

7. If one or more codes are stored, record them. At the end of the procedure, refer to the applicable Diagnostic Code chart.

8. If no fault codes are transmitted, connect the scan tool (if not already connected). Use the scan functions to view the values being sent to the ECM. Compare the actual values to the typical or normal values for the engine.

9. Switch the ignition **OFF** when finished with code retrieval or scan tool readings.

Circuit/Component Diagnosis and Repair

Using the appropriate chart(s) based on the Diagnostic Circuit Check, the fault codes and the scan tool data will lead to diagnosis and checking of a particular circuit or component. It is important to note that the fault code indicates a fault or loss of signal in an ECM-controlled system, not necessarily in the specific component. Detailed procedures to isolate the problem are included in each code chart; these procedures must be followed accurately to insure timely and correct repair. Following the procedure will also insure that only truly faulty components are replaced.

DIAGNOSTIC MODE

The ECM may be placed into the diagnostic mode by turning the ignition switch from **OFF** to **ON**, then grounding ALDL Terminal B to Terminal A. When in the Diagnostic Mode, the ECM will:

• Display Code 12, indicating the system is operating correctly.

• Display any stored fault codes 3 times in succession.

• Energize all the relays controlled by the ECM except the fuel pump relay. This will allow the relays and circuits to be checked in the shop without recreating certain driving conditions.

• Move the IAC valve to its fully extended position, closing the idle air passage.

➤**Due to increased battery draw, do not allow the vehicle to remain in the Diagnostic Mode for more than 30 minutes. If longer periods are necessary, connect a battery charger.**

FIELD SERVICE MODE

If ALDL terminal B is grounded to terminal A with the engine running, the system enters the Field Service Mode. In this mode, the dash warning lamp will indicate whether the system is operating in open loop or closed loop.

If working in open loop, the dash warning lamp will flash rapidly 2½ times per second. In closed loop, the flash rate slows to once per second. Additionally, if the system is running lean in closed loop, the lamp will be off most of the cycle. A rich condition in closed loop will cause the lamp to remain lit for most of the 1 second cycle.

When operating in the Field Service Mode, additional codes cannot be stored by the ECM. The closed loop timer is bypassed in this mode.

CLEARING THE TROUBLE CODES

Stored fault codes may be erased from memory at any time by removing power from the ECM for at least 30 seconds. It may be necessary to clear stored codes during diagnosis to check for any recurrence during a test drive, but the stored codes must be written down when retrieved. The codes may still be required for subsequent troubleshooting. Whenever a repair is complete, the stored codes must be erased and the vehicle test driven to confirm correct operation and repair.

➤**The ignition switch must be OFF any time power is disconnected or restored to the ECM. Severe damage may result if this precaution is not observed.**

Depending on the electric distribution of the particular vehicle, power to the ECM may be disconnected by removing the ECM fuse in the fusebox, disconnecting the in-line fuse holder near the positive battery terminal or disconnecting the ECM power lead at the battery terminal. Disconnecting the negative battery cable to clear codes is not recommended as this will also clear other memory data in the vehicle such as radio presets or seat memory.

➤**Refer to the appropriate Diagnostic Code Charts at the end of this Section for all testing and diagnosis of computer controlled components and sensors.**

Oxygen Sensor

▶ **See Figure 41**

OPERATION

An oxygen sensor is used on all models. The sensor protrudes into the exhaust stream and monitors the oxygen

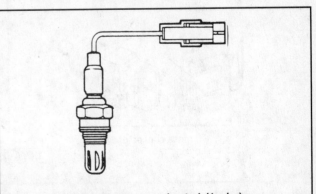

Fig. 41 Oxygen sensor — non-heated (1-wire)

content of the exhaust gases. The difference between the oxygen content of the exhaust gases and that of the outside air generates a voltage signal to the ECM. The ECM monitors this voltage and, depending upon the value of the signal received, issues a command to adjust for a rich or a lean condition.

There are 2 different oxygen sensors used: a heated oxygen (HO2S) and non heated oxygen sensor (O2S). The 1992-93 4.3L engine uses the heated sensor to achieve and maintain closed loop status. The sensor needs to operate at 600°F. (315°C) in order to become a semiconductor and produce a voltage output between 0.01-1 volt. A lower voltage output would indicate the leaner (higher oxygen content) exhaust emissions. A higher voltage reading would indicate a richer (lower oxygen content) exhaust emission.

REMOVAL & INSTALLATION

The sensor may be difficult to remove when the engine temperature is below 120° F (48 ° C). Excessive removal force may damage the threads in the exhaust manifold or pipe; follow the removal procedure carefully.

1. Locate the oxygen sensor. It protrudes from the center of the exhaust manifold at the front of the engine compartment (it looks somewhat like a spark plug).
2. Disconnect the electrical connector from the oxygen sensor.
3. Spray a commercial solvent onto the sensor threads and allow it to soak in for at least five minutes.
4. Carefully unscrew and remove the sensor.
5. To install, first coat the new sensor's threads with GM anti-seize compound No. 5613695 or the equivalent. This is not a conventional anti-seize paste. The use of a regular compound may electrically insulate the sensor, rendering it inoperative. You must coat the threads with an electrically conductive anti-seize compound.
6. Installation torque is 30 ft. lbs. (42 Nm). Do not overtighten.
7. Reconnect the electrical connector. Be careful not to damage the electrical pigtail. Check the sensor boot for proper fit and installation.

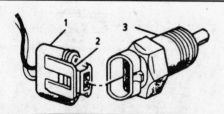

1. Harness connector to ECM
2. Locking tab
3. Temperature sensor

Fig. 42 Coolant temperature sensor (CTS)

Coolant Temperature Sensor (CTS)

♦ See Figure 42

OPERATION

Most engine functions are effected by the coolant temperature. Determining whether the engine is hot or cold is largely dependent on the temperature of the coolant. An accurate temperature signal to the ECM is supplied by the coolant temperature sensor. The coolant temperature sensor is a thermistor mounted in the engine coolant stream. A thermistor is an electrical device that varies its resistance in relation to changes in temperature. Low coolant temperature produces a high resistance (100,000 ohms at -40°F/-40°C) and high coolant temperature produces low resistance (70 ohms at 266°F/130°C). The ECM supplies a signal of 5 volts to the coolant temperature sensor through a resistor in the ECM and measures the voltage. The voltage will be high when the engine is cold and low when the engine is hot.

TESTING

1. Disconnect the negative battery cable.
2. Disconnect the coolant temperature sensor wire connector.
3. Connect a volt/ohmmeter to the terminals of the coolant temperature sensor and verify the reading is within range on the appropriate diagnostic CODE chart.

REMOVAL & INSTALLATION

1. Disconnect the negative battery cable.
2. Drain the cooling system into a clean container for reuse.
3. Disconnect the electrical connector from the coolant temperature sensor.
4. Remove the coolant temperature sensor.
To install:
5. Install the coolant temperature sensor.
6. Connect the electrical connector.
7. Fill the cooling system.
8. Connect the negative battery cable.
9. Start the engine and check for leaks.

Idle Air Control (IAC) Valve

♦ See Figure 43

OPERATION

Engine idle speeds are controlled by the ECM through the IAC valve mounted on the throttle body. The ECM sends voltage pulses to the IAC motor windings causing the IAC motor shaft and pintle to move **IN** or **OUT** a given distance (number of steps) for each pulse (called counts). The movement of the pintle controls the airflow around the throttle

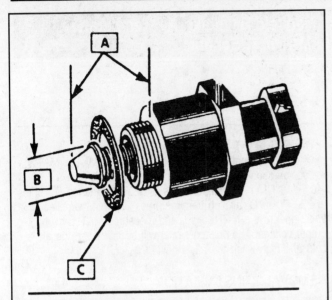

A. Distance of pintle extension
B. Diameter and shape of pintle
C. IAC valve gasket

Fig. 43 Idle Air Control (IAC) valve — Throttle Body Injection (TBI)

plate, which in turn, controls engine idle speed. IAC valve pintle position counts can be observed using a Scan tool. Zero counts correspond to a fully closed passage, while 140 counts or more corresponds to full flow.

Idle speed can be categorized in 2 ways: actual (controlled) idle speed and minimum idle speed. Controlled idle speed is obtained by the ECM positioning the IAC valve pintle. Resulting idle speed is determined by total air flow (IAC/passage + PCV + throttle valve + calibrated vacuum leaks). Controlled idle speed is specified at normal operating conditions, which consists of engine coolant at normal operating temperature, air conditioning compressor **OFF**, manual transmission in neutral or automatic transmission in **D**.

Minimum idle air speed is set at the factory with a stop screw. This setting allows enough air flow by the throttle valves to cause the IAC valve pintle to be positioned a calibrated number of steps (counts) from the seat during normal controlled idle operation.

The idle speed is controlled by the ECM through the IAC valve. No adjustment is required during routine maintenance. Tampering with the minimum idle speed adjustment may result in premature failure of the IAC valve.

REMOVAL & INSTALLATION

1. Disconnect the negative battery cable. Disconnect the IAC valve electrical connector.
2. Remove the IAC valve by performing the following:
    a. On thread-mounted units, use a 1¼ in. (32mm) wrench.

    b. On flange-mounted units, remove the mounting screw assemblies.
3. Remove the IAC valve gasket or O-ring and discard.
To install:
4. Clean the mounting surfaces by performing the following:
    a. If servicing a thread-mounted valve, remove the old gasket material from the surface of the throttle body to ensure proper sealing of the new gasket.
    b. If servicing a flange-mounted valve, clean the IAC valve surfaces on the throttle body to assure proper seal of the new O-ring and contact of the IAC valve flange.
5. If installing a new IAC valve, measure the distance between the tip of the IAC valve pintle and the mounting flange. If the distance is greater than 1.102 in. (28mm), use finger pressure to slowly retract the pintle. The force required to retract the pintle of a new valve will not cause damage to the valve. If reinstalling the original IAC valve, do not attempt to adjust the pintle in this manner.
6. Install the IAC valve into the throttle body by performing the following:
    a. If installing a thread-mounted valve, install with a new gasket. Using a 1¼ in. (32mm) wrench, tighten to 13 ft. lbs. (18 Nm).
    b. If installing a flange-mounted valve, lubricate a new O-ring with transmission fluid and install on the IAC valve. Install the IAC valve to the throttle body. Install the mounting screws using a suitable thread locking compound. Tighten to 28 inch lbs. (3.2 Nm).
7. Connect the IAC valve electrical connector.
8. Connect the negative battery cable.
9. No physical adjustment of the IAC valve assembly is required after installation. Reset the IAC valve pintle position by performing the following:
    a. Depress the accelerator pedal slightly.
    b. Start the engine and run for 5 seconds.
    c. Turn the ignition switch to the **OFF** position for 10 seconds.
    d. Restart the engine and check for proper idle operation.

Manifold Absolute Pressure (MAP) Sensor

▶ See Figure 44

OPERATION

The MAP sensor measures the changes in intake manifold pressure, which result from engine load and speed changes and converts this information to a voltage output. The MAP sensor reading is the opposite of a vacuum gauge reading: when manifold pressure is high, MAP sensor value is high and vacuum is low. A MAP sensor will produce a low output on engine coastdown with a closed throttle while a wide open throttle will produce a high output. The high output is produced because the pressure inside the manifold is the same as outside the manifold, so 100 percent of the outside air pressure is measured.

The MAP sensor is also used to measure barometric pressure under certain conditions, which allows the ECM to automatically adjust for different altitudes.

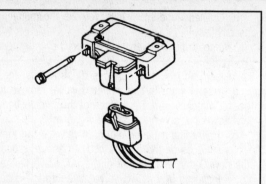

Fig. 44 Manifold Absolute Pressure (MAP) sensor

The MAP sensor changes the 5 volt signal supplied by the ECM, which reads the change and uses the information to control fuel delivery and ignition timing.

REMOVAL & INSTALLATION

1. Disconnect the negative battery cable.
2. Disconnect the vacuum harness assembly.
3. Release the electrical connector locking tab.
4. Remove the bolts or release the MAP sensor locking tabs and remove the sensor.
To install:
5. Install the bolts or snap sensor onto the bracket.
6. Connect the MAP sensor electrical connector.
7. Connect the MAP sensor vacuum harness connector.
8. Connect the negative battery cable.

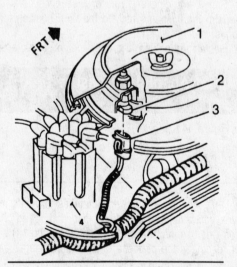

1. Air cleaner
2. Intake Air TGemperature (IAT) sensor
3. Harness connector to ECM
4. Distributor

Fig. 45 Manifold Air Temperature (MAT) sensor — 1990-91 vehicles except 5.0L (VIN Y) engine

Manifold or Intake Air Temperature (MAT/IAT) Sensor

▶ See Figure 45

OPERATION

The MAT or IAT sensor is a thermistor which supplies manifold air temperature information to the ECM. The MAT sensor produces high resistance (100,000 ohms at -40°F/-40°C) at low temperatures and low resistance (70 ohms at 226°F/130°C) at high temperatures. The ECM supplies a 5 volt signal to the MAT sensor and measures MAT sensor output voltage. The voltage signal will be low when the air is cold and high when the air is hot.

REMOVAL & INSTALLATION

1. Disconnect the negative battery cable.
2. Disconnect the sensor electrical connector locking tab.
3. Remove the sensor.
To install:
4. Install the sensor.
5. Connect the electrical connector.
6. Connect the negative battery cable.

Throttle Position Sensor (TPS)

▶ See Figure 46

OPERATION

The TPS is mounted in the carburetor bowl below the accelerator pump plunger on the 5.0L (VIN Y) engine or on the throttle body, opposite the throttle lever shaft on all other TBI engines. Its function is to sense the current throttle valve position and relay that information to the ECM. Throttle position information allows the ECM to generate the required injector or mixture control signals. The TPS consists of a potentiometer which alters the flow of voltage according to the position of the throttle shaft.

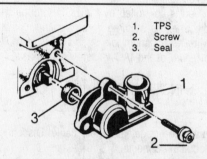

1. TPS
2. Screw
3. Seal

Fig. 46 Throttle Position Sensor (TPS) — 5.0L (VIN E) engine

REMOVAL & Installation

EXCEPT 5.0L (VIN Y) ENGINE

1. Disconnect the negative battery cable.
2. Disconnect the TPS electrical connector.
3. Remove the 2 mounting screws.
4. Remove the TPS and, if equipped, TPS seal from the throttle body.

To install:

5. Place the TPS in position. Align the TPS lever with the TPS drive lever on the throttle body.
6. Install the 2 TPS mounting screws.
7. Connect the electrical connector.
8. Connect the negative battery cable.

5.0L (VIN Y) ENGINE

Refer to Section 5 for all carburetor service and adjustments.

Vehicle Speed Sensor

▶ **See Figure 47**

OPERATION

The VSS is located on the transmission and sends a pulsing voltage signal to the ECM which is converted to miles per hour. This sensor mainly controls the operation of the Torque Converter Clutch (TCC) system.

REMOVAL & INSTALLATION

1. Disconnect the negative battery cable.
2. Raise and safely support the vehicle.
3. Disconnect the VSS electrical connector.

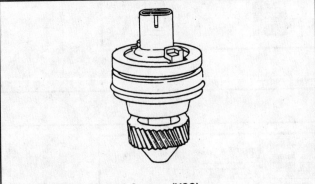

Fig. 47 Vehicle Speed Sensor (VSS)

4. Remove the retaining bolt.
5. Have a clean container to catch the transmission fluid and remove the VSS.
6. Remove and discard the O-ring.

To install:

7. Lubricate a new O-ring with a thin film of transmission fluid. Install the O-ring and VSS.
8. Install the retaining bolt.
9. Connect the electrical connector.
10. Lower the vehicle.
11. Connect the negative battery cable.
12. Refill transmission to proper level.

➡**Due to the intricacy of the system and the special testing equipment required, it is recommended that a qualified technician perform any testing, adjusting, or replacement of the system components.**

Diagnostic Trouble Codes

CODE	COMPONENT NO.
12=	No engine speed signal
13=	Open O2 sensor circuit
14=	CTS circuit (high temperature)
15=	CTS circuit (low temperature)
21=	TPS circuit (signal voltage high)
22=	TPS circuit (signal voltage low)
23=	M/C solenoid circuit (signal voltage low) — CARB
23=	IAT sensor circuit (low temp indicated) — TBI
24=	VSS circuit
25=	IAT sensor circuit (high temp indicated) — TBI
31=	Canister purge solenoid circuit — CARB
32=	EGR circuit — TBI
33=	MAP sensor circuit (signal voltage high-low vacuum) — TBI
34=	MAP sensor circuit (signal voltage low-high vacuum) — TBI
34=	Pressure sensor circuit (signal voltage out of range) — CARB
41=	No distributor reference pulse
42=	Ignition control or EST circuit
43=	ESC circuit — CARB
43=	Knock sensor circuit — TBI
44=	O2 sensor circuit (lean exhaust indicated)
45=	O2 sensor circuit (rich exhaust indicated)
51=	PROM error (faulty or incorrect PROM)
53=	EGR system malfunction (California only) — CARB
54=	M/C solenoid circuit (signal voltage high) — CARB
54=	Fuel pump circuit (low voltage) — TBI
55=	ECM error — TBI

Fig. 48 Vehicle emission decal and vacuum schematic — 1992 4.3L (Federal) engine

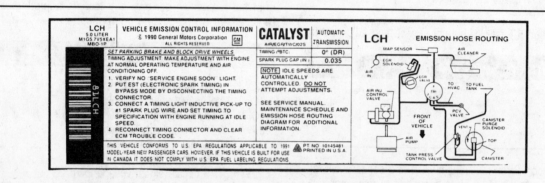

Fig. 49 Vehicle emission decal and vacuum schematic — 1991 5.0L (Federal) engine

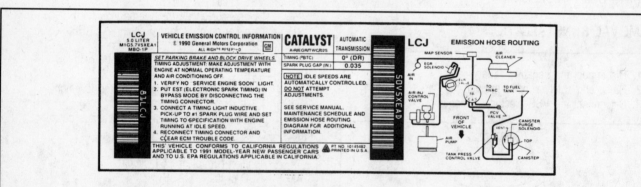

Fig. 50 Vehicle emission decal and vacuum schematic — 1991 5.0L (California) engine

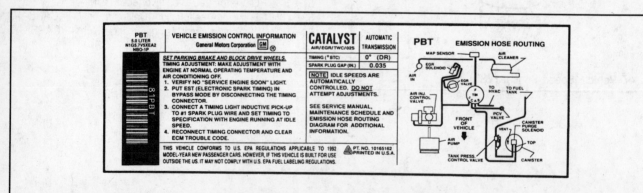

Fig. 51 Vehicle emission decal and vacuum schematic — 1992 5.0L (Federal) engine

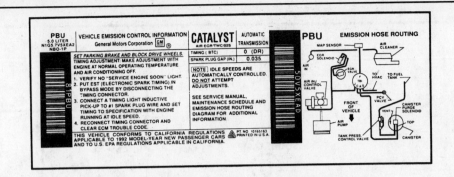

Fig. 52 Vehicle emission decal and vacuum schematic — 1992 5.0L (California) engine

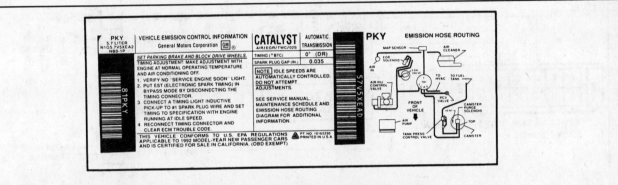

Fig. 53 Vehicle emission decal and vacuum schematic — 1992 5.7L (California) engine

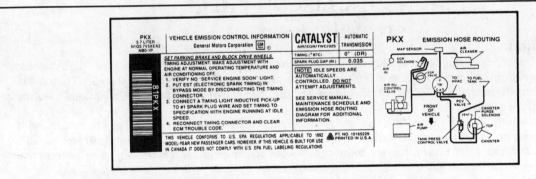

Fig. 54 Vehicle emission decal and vacuum schematic — 1992 5.7L (Federal) engine

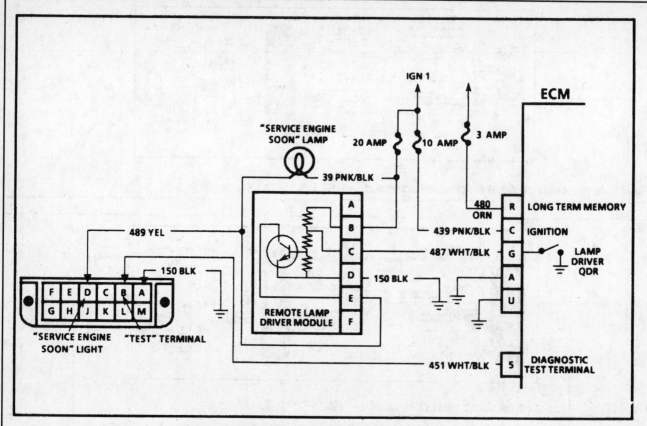

DIAGNOSTIC CIRCUIT CHECK
5.0L (VIN Y) (CARB)

Circuit Description:

   The purpose of the "Scan" diagnostic circuit check is to 1) make sure the "Service Engine Soon" light works, 2) the ECM is operating and can recognize a fault, and 3) to determine if any codes are stored. This is the starting point for any diagnosis. It is important to understand the "Scan" tool operation and limitations. See the introduction and general description.

   The "code definitions," which immediately follow the "Diagnostic Circuit Check," will help to determine if the fault is still present. From there you will be directed to the code chart or to "Symptoms" in Section "B", which explains how to check for intermittents. In most cases the facing page for a chart will also address the normal operation expected values and provide some diagnostic aids.

   When the engine is started, the ECM grounds terminal "G" to turn out the "Service Engine Soon" light. The ECM alternately grounds and opens terminal "G" to flash a code.

Test Description: Numbers below refer to circled numbers on the diagnostic chart.

1. Checks for the proper operation of the "Service Engine Soon" light. With the key "ON," "Scan" tool not connected and the engine not running, the light should be "ON" steady.
2. Grounding the test terminal will flash a Code 12 and any stored trouble codes. The light must go "ON" and "OFF" for a proper code. If the light goes from "bright" to "dim," this is not considered a code. See CHART A-6 in that case.
3. If the "Scan" tool is not operating, try it on another vehicle. If it operates on another vehicle, the cigar lighter socket should be checked for battery voltage and a good ground. If the "Scan" tool displays "No data" or "No ALDL", with the ignition "ON," see CHART A-6.
4. "No codes" at this point, indicates that the fault is intermittent and the "System Performance Check" should be performed. If a code or codes is displayed, code definitions starting on the page following this chart should be consulted.

Fig. 55 Engine controls diagnostic chart

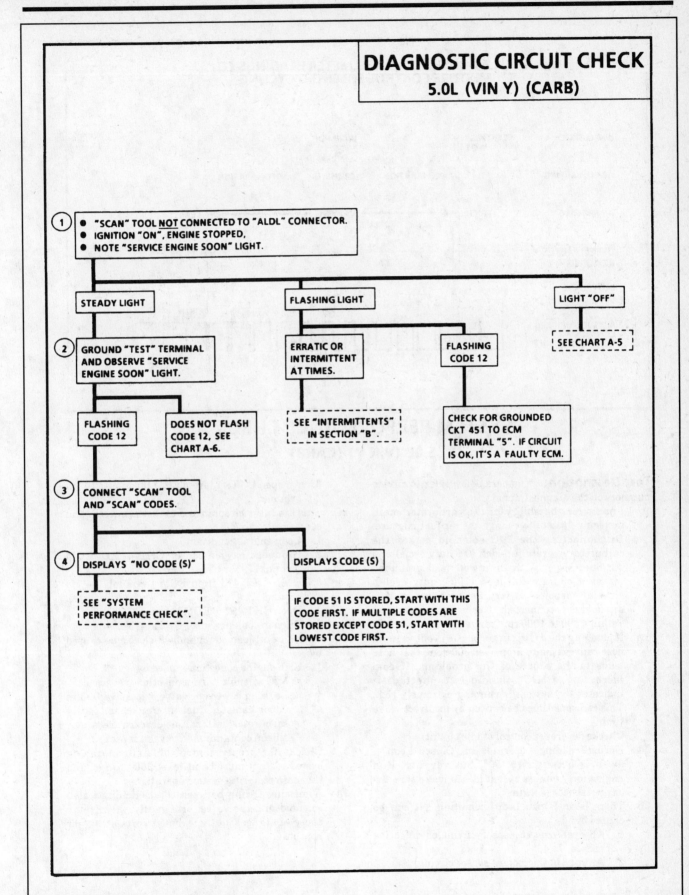

Fig. 56 Engine controls diagnostic chart

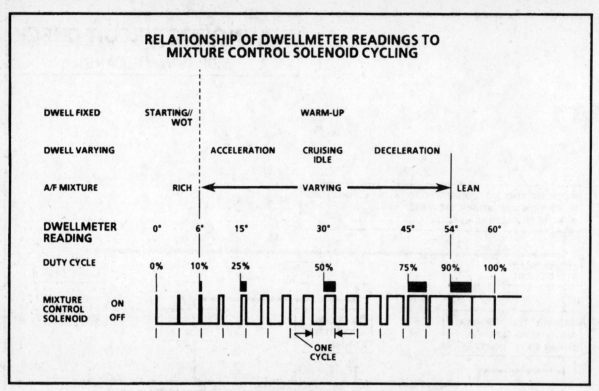

SYSTEM PERFORMANCE CHECK
5.0L (VIN Y) (CARB)

Test Description: Numbers below refer to circled numbers on the diagnostic chart.

1. Checks for the ability of the carburetor main metering system to change the air/fuel mixture. Disconnecting the M/C solenoid makes the carburetor operate full-rich (0% duty cycle) and reconnecting it with the dwell lead grounded makes it operate full-lean (100% duty cycle). Normal response is for rpm to drop, as M/C solenoid is reconnected. Normal drop should be within a 300 to 1000 rpm range.

1A. If plugging the PCV, purge, or bowl vent vacuum hose causes rpm to drop over 300 rpm, that hose leads to the source of the problem. If rpm increases as M/C solenoid is connected, it indicates the system is running extremely rich. This can sometimes be caused by incorrect valve timing.

2. Checks for proper control of idle circuit.

2A. Normal reading - operates in "Closed Loop" - dwell is between 10°-50°, but varying. Run engine for 1 minute at fast idle to make sure the oxygen sensor is warm.

2B. There is an "Open Loop" condition. It can be caused by:
   1. An open oxygen sensor circuit or defective sensor.
   2. An open in the coolant sensor circuit.

3. An open CKT 413 from ECM terminal "14" to ground.

2C. This is a full-rich command to the carburetor and can be caused by:
   1. Lean engine condition.
   2. Grounded oxygen sensor CKT 412 to ECM terminal "9" or bad sensor.
   3. Open CKT 413 from ECM terminal "14" to ground.
   4. Open CKT 452 to ECM terminal "22".
   5. Open in coolant sensor CKTs 410 or 452.

2D. This is a full lean command which can be caused by:
   1. Rich engine condition caused by:
      a. M/C solenoid wire connections reversed.
      b. Leaking bowl vent valve, excessive fuel in vapor canister, fuel in crankcase, faulty carburetor calibration or carburetor, or silicon contaminated oxygen sensor.

3. Checks for proper control of main metering system. Rpm must be at least 3000 to get into the main metering system operation.

3A. A missing O-ring between the switching valve solenoid and the valve, or a faulty valve, may cause air to leak to the exhaust ports at higher rpm only.

Fig. 57 Engine controls diagnostic chart

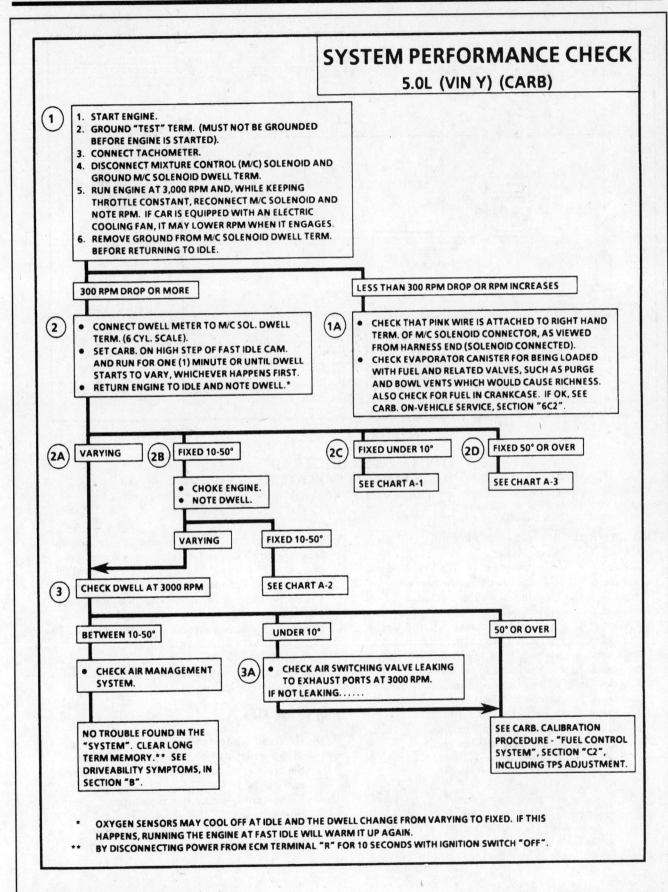

SYSTEM PERFORMANCE CHECK
5.0L (VIN Y) (CARB)

①
1. START ENGINE.
2. GROUND "TEST" TERM. (MUST NOT BE GROUNDED BEFORE ENGINE IS STARTED).
3. CONNECT TACHOMETER.
4. DISCONNECT MIXTURE CONTROL (M/C) SOLENOID AND GROUND M/C SOLENOID DWELL TERM.
5. RUN ENGINE AT 3,000 RPM AND, WHILE KEEPING THROTTLE CONSTANT, RECONNECT M/C SOLENOID AND NOTE RPM. IF CAR IS EQUIPPED WITH AN ELECTRIC COOLING FAN, IT MAY LOWER RPM WHEN IT ENGAGES.
6. REMOVE GROUND FROM M/C SOLENOID DWELL TERM. BEFORE RETURNING TO IDLE.

300 RPM DROP OR MORE

LESS THAN 300 RPM DROP OR RPM INCREASES

②
- CONNECT DWELL METER TO M/C SOL. DWELL TERM. (6 CYL. SCALE).
- SET CARB. ON HIGH STEP OF FAST IDLE CAM. AND RUN FOR ONE (1) MINUTE OR UNTIL DWELL STARTS TO VARY, WHICHEVER HAPPENS FIRST.
- RETURN ENGINE TO IDLE AND NOTE DWELL.*

①A
- CHECK THAT PINK WIRE IS ATTACHED TO RIGHT HAND TERM. OF M/C SOLENOID CONNECTOR, AS VIEWED FROM HARNESS END (SOLENOID CONNECTED).
- CHECK EVAPORATOR CANISTER FOR BEING LOADED WITH FUEL AND RELATED VALVES, SUCH AS PURGE AND BOWL VENTS WHICH WOULD CAUSE RICHNESS. ALSO CHECK FOR FUEL IN CRANKCASE. IF OK, SEE CARB. ON-VEHICLE SERVICE, SECTION "6C2".

②A VARYING   **②B** FIXED 10-50°

②C FIXED UNDER 10°   **②D** FIXED 50° OR OVER

- CHOKE ENGINE.
- NOTE DWELL.

SEE CHART A-1   SEE CHART A-3

VARYING   FIXED 10-50°

③ CHECK DWELL AT 3000 RPM   SEE CHART A-2

BETWEEN 10-50°   UNDER 10°   50° OR OVER

- CHECK AIR MANAGEMENT SYSTEM.

③A
- CHECK AIR SWITCHING VALVE LEAKING TO EXHAUST PORTS AT 3000 RPM. IF NOT LEAKING......

NO TROUBLE FOUND IN THE "SYSTEM". CLEAR LONG TERM MEMORY.** SEE DRIVEABILITY SYMPTOMS, IN SECTION "B".

SEE CARB. CALIBRATION PROCEDURE - "FUEL CONTROL SYSTEM", SECTION "C2", INCLUDING TPS ADJUSTMENT.

* OXYGEN SENSORS MAY COOL OFF AT IDLE AND THE DWELL CHANGE FROM VARYING TO FIXED. IF THIS HAPPENS, RUNNING THE ENGINE AT FAST IDLE WILL WARM IT UP AGAIN.
** BY DISCONNECTING POWER FROM ECM TERMINAL "R" FOR 10 SECONDS WITH IGNITION SWITCH "OFF".

Fig. 58 Engine controls diagnostic chart

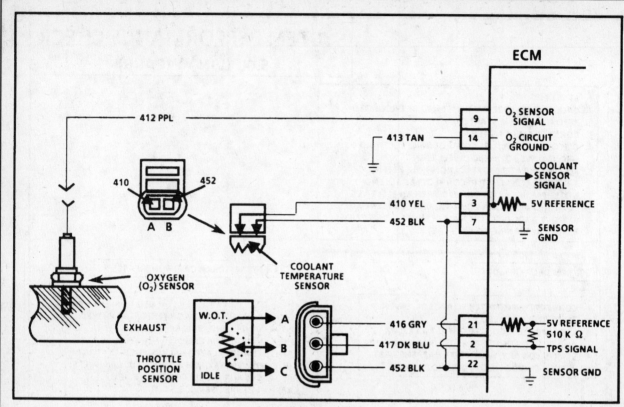

CHART A-1

DWELL FIXED UNDER 10°
(LEAN EXHAUST INDICATED)
5.0L (VIN Y) (CARB)

Test Description: Numbers below refer to circled numbers on the diagnostic chart.

1. Determines if the problem is CCC related or engine related. Dwell should start increasing as soon as engine is choked and go higher as it is choked more until it goes over 50°. With severe choking, the dwell could move up the scale momentarily even if it is not engine related, but it will move right back to a low dwell. If dwell responds the problem is a lean engine.

2. Checks for ECM response to input of O_2 sensor circuit. The voltmeter is used to put a voltage on the oxygen sensor circuit to simulate a rich condition. Dwell should increase (a lean command) if ECM and harness are good.

3. Checks for normal coolant sensor input. Coolant temperature required to enable "Closed Loop" operation varies with start-up coolant temperature, but maximum is 75°C. The engine should be above 75°C if the thermostat is open, allowing the upper radiator hose to get hot.

4. Check for O_2 sensor circuit problem or high TPS input signal which could cause a full rich command.

5. Lists causes of a lean condition which could result in a full rich command.

Diagnostic Aids:

Dwell fixed under 10° indicates a full rich command to the carburetor. This could result from:
- Severe engine misfire (refer to "Symptoms" section "B")
- False lean O_2 sensor signal voltage (low voltage).
- Very cold coolant temperature indication.
- High TPS voltage signal.

Fig. 59 Engine controls diagnostic chart

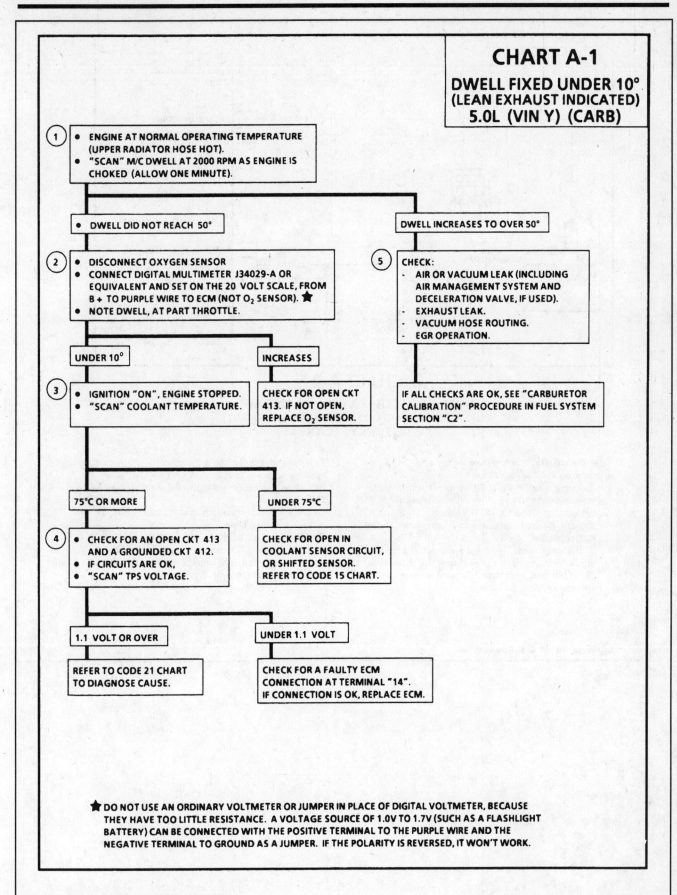

CHART A-1

DWELL FIXED UNDER 10°
(LEAN EXHAUST INDICATED)
5.0L (VIN Y) (CARB)

1
- ENGINE AT NORMAL OPERATING TEMPERATURE (UPPER RADIATOR HOSE HOT).
- "SCAN" M/C DWELL AT 2000 RPM AS ENGINE IS CHOKED (ALLOW ONE MINUTE).

- DWELL DID NOT REACH 50°

- DWELL INCREASES TO OVER 50°

2
- DISCONNECT OXYGEN SENSOR
- CONNECT DIGITAL MULTIMETER J34029-A OR EQUIVALENT AND SET ON THE 20 VOLT SCALE, FROM B + TO PURPLE WIRE TO ECM (NOT O_2 SENSOR). ★
- NOTE DWELL, AT PART THROTTLE.

5
CHECK:
- AIR OR VACUUM LEAK (INCLUDING AIR MANAGEMENT SYSTEM AND DECELERATION VALVE, IF USED).
- EXHAUST LEAK.
- VACUUM HOSE ROUTING.
- EGR OPERATION.

UNDER 10°

INCREASES

3
- IGNITION "ON", ENGINE STOPPED.
- "SCAN" COOLANT TEMPERATURE.

CHECK FOR OPEN CKT 413. IF NOT OPEN, REPLACE O_2 SENSOR.

IF ALL CHECKS ARE OK, SEE "CARBURETOR CALIBRATION" PROCEDURE IN FUEL SYSTEM SECTION "C2".

75°C OR MORE

UNDER 75°C

4
- CHECK FOR AN OPEN CKT 413 AND A GROUNDED CKT 412.
- IF CIRCUITS ARE OK,
- "SCAN" TPS VOLTAGE.

CHECK FOR OPEN IN COOLANT SENSOR CIRCUIT, OR SHIFTED SENSOR. REFER TO CODE 15 CHART.

1.1 VOLT OR OVER

UNDER 1.1 VOLT

REFER TO CODE 21 CHART TO DIAGNOSE CAUSE.

CHECK FOR A FAULTY ECM CONNECTION AT TERMINAL "14". IF CONNECTION IS OK, REPLACE ECM.

★ DO NOT USE AN ORDINARY VOLTMETER OR JUMPER IN PLACE OF DIGITAL VOLTMETER, BECAUSE THEY HAVE TOO LITTLE RESISTANCE. A VOLTAGE SOURCE OF 1.0V TO 1.7V (SUCH AS A FLASHLIGHT BATTERY) CAN BE CONNECTED WITH THE POSITIVE TERMINAL TO THE PURPLE WIRE AND THE NEGATIVE TERMINAL TO GROUND AS A JUMPER. IF THE POLARITY IS REVERSED, IT WON'T WORK.

Fig. 60 Engine controls diagnostic chart

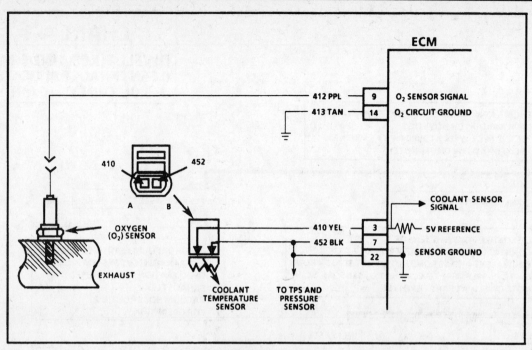

CHART A-2

DWELL FIXED BETWEEN 10° AND 50°
(OPEN COOLANT OR OXYGEN SENSOR CIRCUIT)
5.0L (VIN Y) (CARB)

Test Description: Numbers below refer to circled numbers on the diagnostic chart.
1. Running engine at 2000 rpm, for one minute, warms up the oxygen sensor. Grounding O_2 sensor input checks ECM response to a "lean" signal. Normal response; dwell decreases to full rich command.
2. This step grounds O_2 sensor circuit at the ECM to check for an open in the wiring to ECM terminal "9". Normal response; dwell decreases (rich command).

3. This step checks the coolant sensor input. Normal reading on a warm engine is over 75°C. An open circuit would cause a reading of approximately 25°C.
4. On some ECMs, an open in circuit to terminal "14" can cause "Open Loop."
5. Checks output of O_2 sensor with full rich command from ECM caused by grounding the O_2 sensor input circuit. Normal response; voltage at O_2 sensor should be over .8 volt.

Fig. 61 Engine controls diagnostic chart

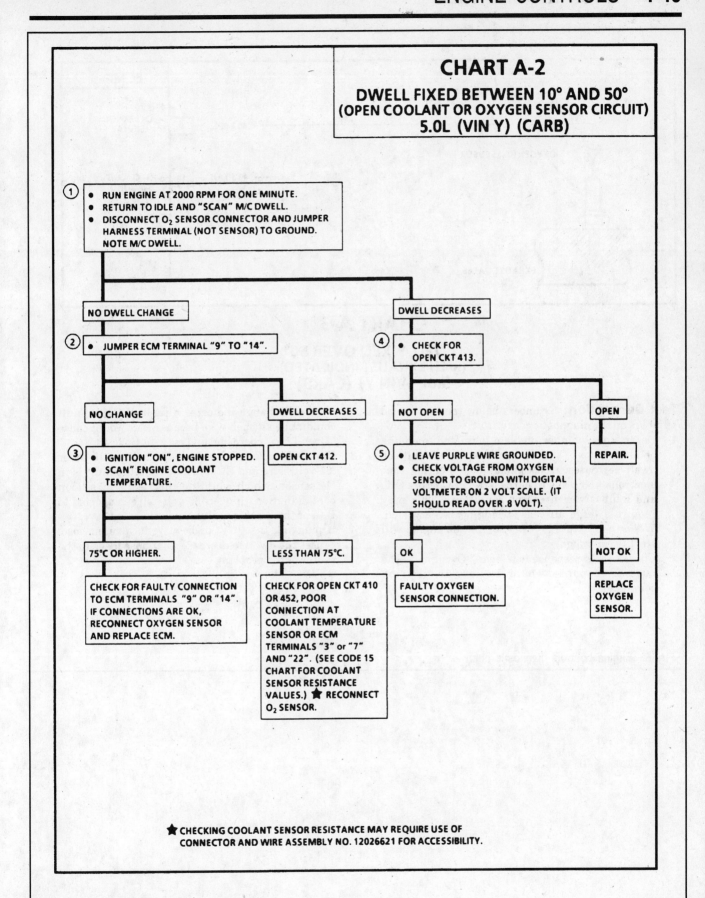

CHART A-2

DWELL FIXED BETWEEN 10° AND 50°
(OPEN COOLANT OR OXYGEN SENSOR CIRCUIT)
5.0L (VIN Y) (CARB)

① • RUN ENGINE AT 2000 RPM FOR ONE MINUTE.
• RETURN TO IDLE AND "SCAN" M/C DWELL.
• DISCONNECT O₂ SENSOR CONNECTOR AND JUMPER HARNESS TERMINAL (NOT SENSOR) TO GROUND. NOTE M/C DWELL.

NO DWELL CHANGE   DWELL DECREASES

② • JUMPER ECM TERMINAL "9" TO "14".   ④ • CHECK FOR OPEN CKT 413.

NO CHANGE   DWELL DECREASES   NOT OPEN   OPEN

③ • IGNITION "ON", ENGINE STOPPED.   OPEN CKT 412.   ⑤ • LEAVE PURPLE WIRE GROUNDED.   REPAIR.
• SCAN" ENGINE COOLANT TEMPERATURE.   • CHECK VOLTAGE FROM OXYGEN SENSOR TO GROUND WITH DIGITAL VOLTMETER ON 2 VOLT SCALE. (IT SHOULD READ OVER .8 VOLT).

75°C OR HIGHER.   LESS THAN 75°C.   OK   NOT OK

CHECK FOR FAULTY CONNECTION TO ECM TERMINALS "9" OR "14". IF CONNECTIONS ARE OK, RECONNECT OXYGEN SENSOR AND REPLACE ECM.   CHECK FOR OPEN CKT 410 OR 452, POOR CONNECTION AT COOLANT TEMPERATURE SENSOR OR ECM TERMINALS "3" or "7" AND "22". (SEE CODE 15 CHART FOR COOLANT SENSOR RESISTANCE VALUES.) ★ RECONNECT O₂ SENSOR.   FAULTY OXYGEN SENSOR CONNECTION.   REPLACE OXYGEN SENSOR.

★ CHECKING COOLANT SENSOR RESISTANCE MAY REQUIRE USE OF CONNECTOR AND WIRE ASSEMBLY NO. 12026621 FOR ACCESSIBILITY.

Fig. 62 Engine controls diagnostic chart

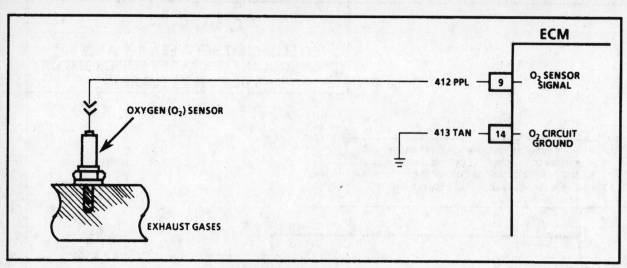

CHART A-3

DWELL FIXED OVER 50°
(RICH EXHAUST INDICATED)
5.0L (VIN Y) (CARB)

Test Description: Numbers below refer to circled numbers on the diagnostic chart.

1. Determines whether problem is related to engine or electronics. The normal response would be dwell decreases (rich command), indicating that electronics (O_2 sensor, harness, and ECM) are OK, and fault is a rich engine condition. This may require a large air leak, if engine is very rich. When the mixture is lean enough, the engine will start to run rough.
2. Checks ECM response to a "lean" O_2 signal. The normal response would be low dwell (rich command).

No dwell change indicates a faulty ECM. Fault couldn't be an open wire because that would cause "Open Loop" operation and may set Code 13.

3. Checks for excessive voltage in O_2 line. If under .55 volt, wire and ECM are OK and the fault is in O_2 sensor, which could be the result of silicon contamination. If over .55 volt, wire is shorted to B +, or the ECM is faulty.
4. If plugging the PCV, or bowl vent vacuum hose, causes the dwell to decrease, that hose leads to the source of the problem.

Fig. 63 Engine controls diagnostic chart

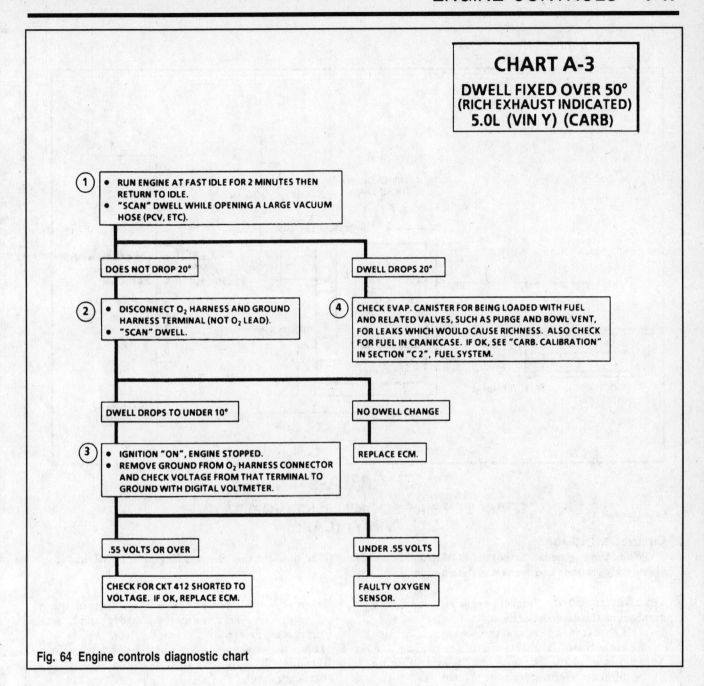

CHART A-3

DWELL FIXED OVER 50°
(RICH EXHAUST INDICATED)
5.0L (VIN Y) (CARB)

① • RUN ENGINE AT FAST IDLE FOR 2 MINUTES THEN RETURN TO IDLE.
• "SCAN" DWELL WHILE OPENING A LARGE VACUUM HOSE (PCV, ETC).

DOES NOT DROP 20°

DWELL DROPS 20°

② • DISCONNECT O_2 HARNESS AND GROUND HARNESS TERMINAL (NOT O_2 LEAD).
• "SCAN" DWELL.

④ CHECK EVAP. CANISTER FOR BEING LOADED WITH FUEL AND RELATED VALVES, SUCH AS PURGE AND BOWL VENT, FOR LEAKS WHICH WOULD CAUSE RICHNESS. ALSO CHECK FOR FUEL IN CRANKCASE. IF OK, SEE "CARB. CALIBRATION" IN SECTION "C 2", FUEL SYSTEM.

DWELL DROPS TO UNDER 10°

NO DWELL CHANGE

③ • IGNITION "ON", ENGINE STOPPED.
• REMOVE GROUND FROM O_2 HARNESS CONNECTOR AND CHECK VOLTAGE FROM THAT TERMINAL TO GROUND WITH DIGITAL VOLTMETER.

REPLACE ECM.

.55 VOLTS OR OVER

UNDER .55 VOLTS

CHECK FOR CKT 412 SHORTED TO VOLTAGE. IF OK, REPLACE ECM.

FAULTY OXYGEN SENSOR.

Fig. 64 Engine controls diagnostic chart

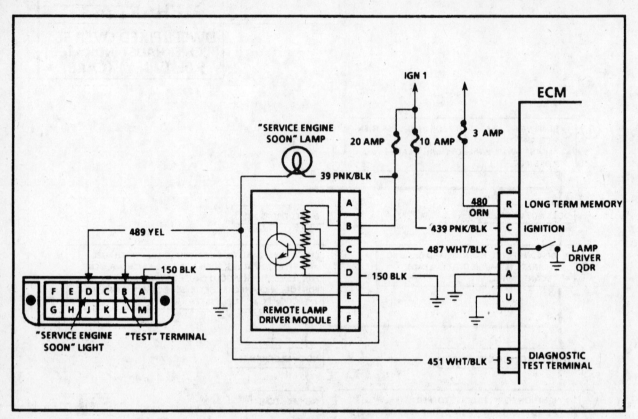

CHART A-5

"SERVICE ENGINE SOON" LIGHT INOPERATIVE
5.0L (VIN Y) (CARB)

Circuit Description:

When the engine is started, the ECM grounds terminal "G" to turn out the "Service Engine Soon" light. It alternately grounds and opens it to flash a code.

Test Description: Numbers below refer to circled numbers on the diagnostic chart.

1. This checks for open gage fuse, or open in "Service Engine Soon" light circuit, including I/P connector, printed circuit, and "Service Engine Soon" lamp. Normal response is lamp "ON."
2. This checks for a shorted ECM. Grounded ECM terminal "G" will turn the "Service Engine Soon" light "OFF." If disconnecting ECM turns light "ON," ECM is shorted. Normal response is lamp "ON."
3. This checks for grounded CKT 487 from terminal "C" of lamp driver, to ECM terminal "G", an open CKT 439 to terminal "B" of lamp driver, a bad ground or faulty lamp driver. A normal reading is about 9 to 11 volts, because of the drop through the upper resistor in the lamp driver.

Over 11 volts indicates there is no drop in the lamp driver. This indicates a bad ground, or faulty lamp driver.

4. This step checks for an open in the wire to terminal "B". Normal voltage is approximately battery voltage.
4A. This checks for an open CKT 439 to terminal "E" from the "Service Engine Soon" lamp. With terminal "E" grounded, the lamp should normally light. Lamp "OFF" indicates an open, and lamp "ON" indicates faulty lamp driver connection or lamp driver.
5. This checks for a grounded CKT 487 from driver terminal "C" to ECM terminal "G". Normal response is light "ON."

Fig. 65 Engine controls diagnostic chart

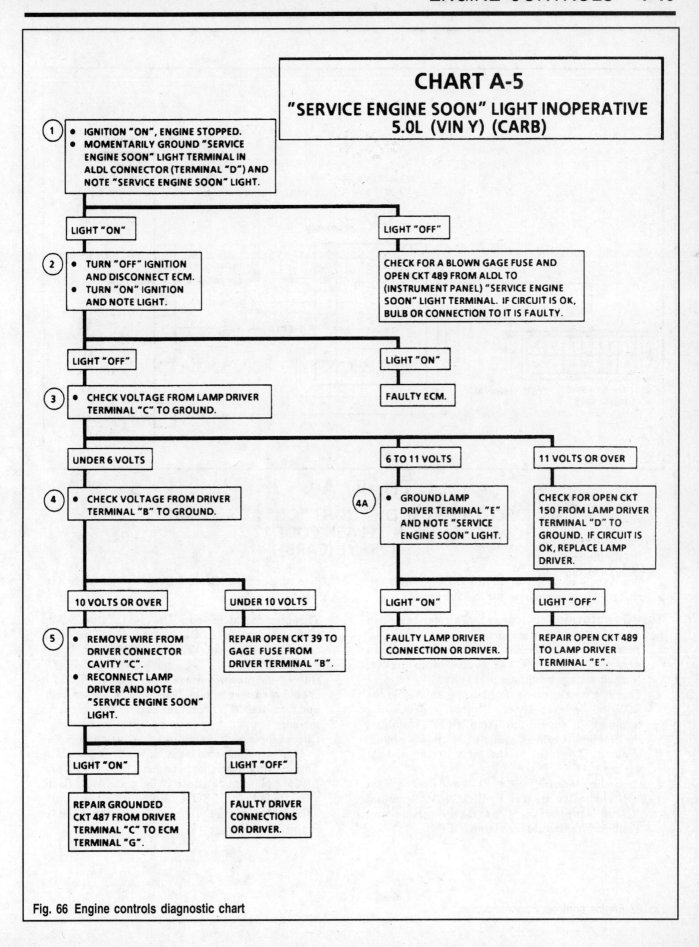

CHART A-5
"SERVICE ENGINE SOON" LIGHT INOPERATIVE
5.0L (VIN Y) (CARB)

1
- IGNITION "ON", ENGINE STOPPED.
- MOMENTARILY GROUND "SERVICE ENGINE SOON" LIGHT TERMINAL IN ALDL CONNECTOR (TERMINAL "D") AND NOTE "SERVICE ENGINE SOON" LIGHT.

LIGHT "ON"

LIGHT "OFF"

2
- TURN "OFF" IGNITION AND DISCONNECT ECM.
- TURN "ON" IGNITION AND NOTE LIGHT.

CHECK FOR A BLOWN GAGE FUSE AND OPEN CKT 489 FROM ALDL TO (INSTRUMENT PANEL) "SERVICE ENGINE SOON" LIGHT TERMINAL. IF CIRCUIT IS OK, BULB OR CONNECTION TO IT IS FAULTY.

LIGHT "OFF"

LIGHT "ON"

3
- CHECK VOLTAGE FROM LAMP DRIVER TERMINAL "C" TO GROUND.

FAULTY ECM.

UNDER 6 VOLTS

6 TO 11 VOLTS

11 VOLTS OR OVER

4
- CHECK VOLTAGE FROM DRIVER TERMINAL "B" TO GROUND.

4A
- GROUND LAMP DRIVER TERMINAL "E" AND NOTE "SERVICE ENGINE SOON" LIGHT.

CHECK FOR OPEN CKT 150 FROM LAMP DRIVER TERMINAL "D" TO GROUND. IF CIRCUIT IS OK, REPLACE LAMP DRIVER.

10 VOLTS OR OVER

UNDER 10 VOLTS

LIGHT "ON"

LIGHT "OFF"

5
- REMOVE WIRE FROM DRIVER CONNECTOR CAVITY "C".
- RECONNECT LAMP DRIVER AND NOTE "SERVICE ENGINE SOON" LIGHT.

REPAIR OPEN CKT 39 TO GAGE FUSE FROM DRIVER TERMINAL "B".

FAULTY LAMP DRIVER CONNECTION OR DRIVER.

REPAIR OPEN CKT 489 TO LAMP DRIVER TERMINAL "E".

LIGHT "ON"

LIGHT "OFF"

REPAIR GROUNDED CKT 487 FROM DRIVER TERMINAL "C" TO ECM TERMINAL "G".

FAULTY DRIVER CONNECTIONS OR DRIVER.

Fig. 66 Engine controls diagnostic chart

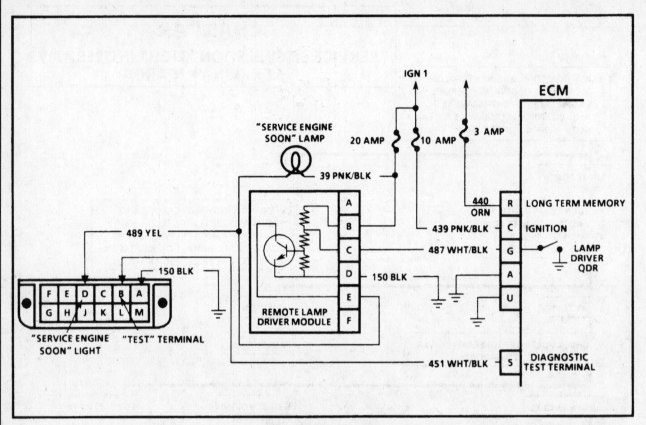

CHART A-6

"SERVICE ENGINE SOON" LIGHT "ON" AT ALL TIMES OR WON'T FLASH CODE 12
5.0L (VIN Y) (CARB)

Circuit Description:

When the engine is started, the ECM grounds terminal "G" to turn out the "Service Engine Soon" light. It alternately grounds and opens it to flash a code.

Test Description: Numbers below refer to circled numbers on the diagnostic chart.

1. This step checks for short to battery voltage in wire to terminal "C" or faulty lamp driver. Normal voltage reading is 9-11 volts.
2. This step checks to see if problem is related to the ECM or the lamp driver. Normally, grounding terminal "C" should turn lamp "OFF." If it does, the problem is related to the ECM and its wiring. If not, it is related to the lamp driver and its wiring.
3. Grounding terminal "G" at ECM and finding light "ON" indicates an open in CKT 487 to terminal "C" of lamp driver. Normally, grounding Terminal "G" should turn lamp "OFF."

4. This step checks for open CKT 451 from ECM to test terminal in ALDL connector. The lamp should flash Code 12, when terminal "5" is grounded.
5. Checks for proper voltage supply to ECM. Both should read over 9 volts. Terminal "C" is ignition, and terminal "R" is constant battery for long term memory.
6. Checks for a bad ground to ECM - terminals "A" and "U" are connected together in the ECM.
7. This step distinguishes between a faulty ECM and PROM. Normal response is for Code 51 to flash, even though the PROM is not installed in the ECM. If it doesn't, it means that the ECM is faulty.

Fig. 67 Engine controls diagnostic chart

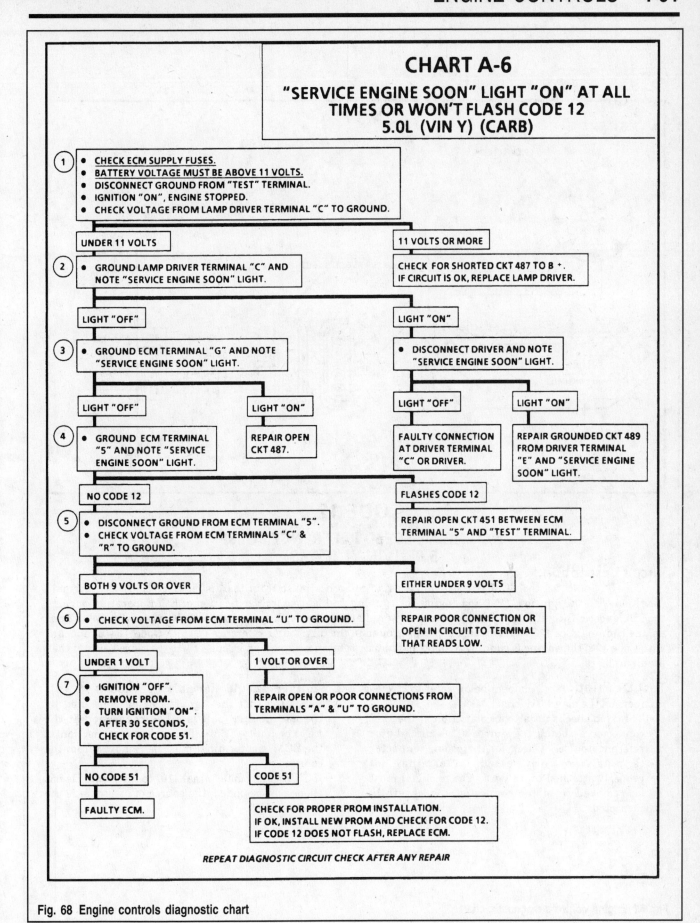

CHART A-6

"SERVICE ENGINE SOON" LIGHT "ON" AT ALL TIMES OR WON'T FLASH CODE 12
5.0L (VIN Y) (CARB)

1
- CHECK ECM SUPPLY FUSES.
- BATTERY VOLTAGE MUST BE ABOVE 11 VOLTS.
- DISCONNECT GROUND FROM "TEST" TERMINAL.
- IGNITION "ON", ENGINE STOPPED.
- CHECK VOLTAGE FROM LAMP DRIVER TERMINAL "C" TO GROUND.

UNDER 11 VOLTS	11 VOLTS OR MORE

2
- GROUND LAMP DRIVER TERMINAL "C" AND NOTE "SERVICE ENGINE SOON" LIGHT.

CHECK FOR SHORTED CKT 487 TO B +. IF CIRCUIT IS OK, REPLACE LAMP DRIVER.

LIGHT "OFF"	LIGHT "ON"

3
- GROUND ECM TERMINAL "G" AND NOTE "SERVICE ENGINE SOON" LIGHT.

- DISCONNECT DRIVER AND NOTE "SERVICE ENGINE SOON" LIGHT.

LIGHT "OFF"	LIGHT "ON"	LIGHT "OFF"	LIGHT "ON"

4
- GROUND ECM TERMINAL "5" AND NOTE "SERVICE ENGINE SOON" LIGHT.

REPAIR OPEN CKT 487.

FAULTY CONNECTION AT DRIVER TERMINAL "C" OR DRIVER.

REPAIR GROUNDED CKT 489 FROM DRIVER TERMINAL "E" AND "SERVICE ENGINE SOON" LIGHT.

NO CODE 12	FLASHES CODE 12

5
- DISCONNECT GROUND FROM ECM TERMINAL "5".
- CHECK VOLTAGE FROM ECM TERMINALS "C" & "R" TO GROUND.

REPAIR OPEN CKT 451 BETWEEN ECM TERMINAL "5" AND "TEST" TERMINAL.

BOTH 9 VOLTS OR OVER	EITHER UNDER 9 VOLTS

6
- CHECK VOLTAGE FROM ECM TERMINAL "U" TO GROUND.

REPAIR POOR CONNECTION OR OPEN IN CIRCUIT TO TERMINAL THAT READS LOW.

UNDER 1 VOLT	1 VOLT OR OVER

7
- IGNITION "OFF".
- REMOVE PROM.
- TURN IGNITION "ON".
- AFTER 30 SECONDS, CHECK FOR CODE 51.

REPAIR OPEN OR POOR CONNECTIONS FROM TERMINALS "A" & "U" TO GROUND.

NO CODE 51	CODE 51

FAULTY ECM.

CHECK FOR PROPER PROM INSTALLATION. IF OK, INSTALL NEW PROM AND CHECK FOR CODE 12. IF CODE 12 DOES NOT FLASH, REPLACE ECM.

REPEAT DIAGNOSTIC CIRCUIT CHECK AFTER ANY REPAIR

Fig. 68 Engine controls diagnostic chart

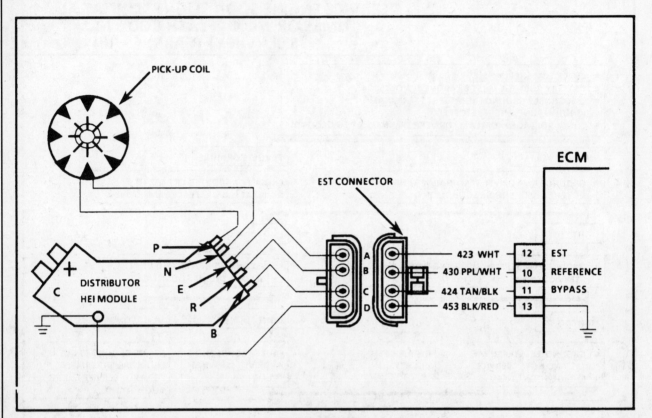

CODE 12

NO ENGINE SPEED REFERENCE PULSE
5.0L (VIN Y) (CARB)

Circuit Description:

Code 12 indicates the ECM is "ON" and sees no reference pulse from the distributor. This is a normal condition with the ignition "ON" and engine not running and is used for verification of ECM operation during the "Diagnostic Circuit Check." Code 12 is not stored and will only flash when the fault is present. With the engine running, Code 12 could mean an open or ground in the distributor reference circuit. Code 41 will appear with Code 12 if the engine is running with no distributor reference signal, and Code 41 will be stored even if the problem clears.

Test Description: Numbers below refer to circled numbers on the diagnostic chart.

1. This step checks for a poor connection at the EST connector as being the source of no distributor reference pulse. Check for corrosion, connector terminals not fully seated, or terminal not properly attached to the wire. The terminal must be removed from the connector and carefully inspected.

2. Voltage should normally be above .5 volt indicating that the signal is being generated by the module and fault is a bad connection at the ECM or faulty ECM. To check the connection at the ECM, the terminal must be removed from the connector.

3. If CKT 430 from terminal "10" to the module is not opened or grounded, the source of no signal is the module itself.

Fig. 69 Engine controls diagnostic chart

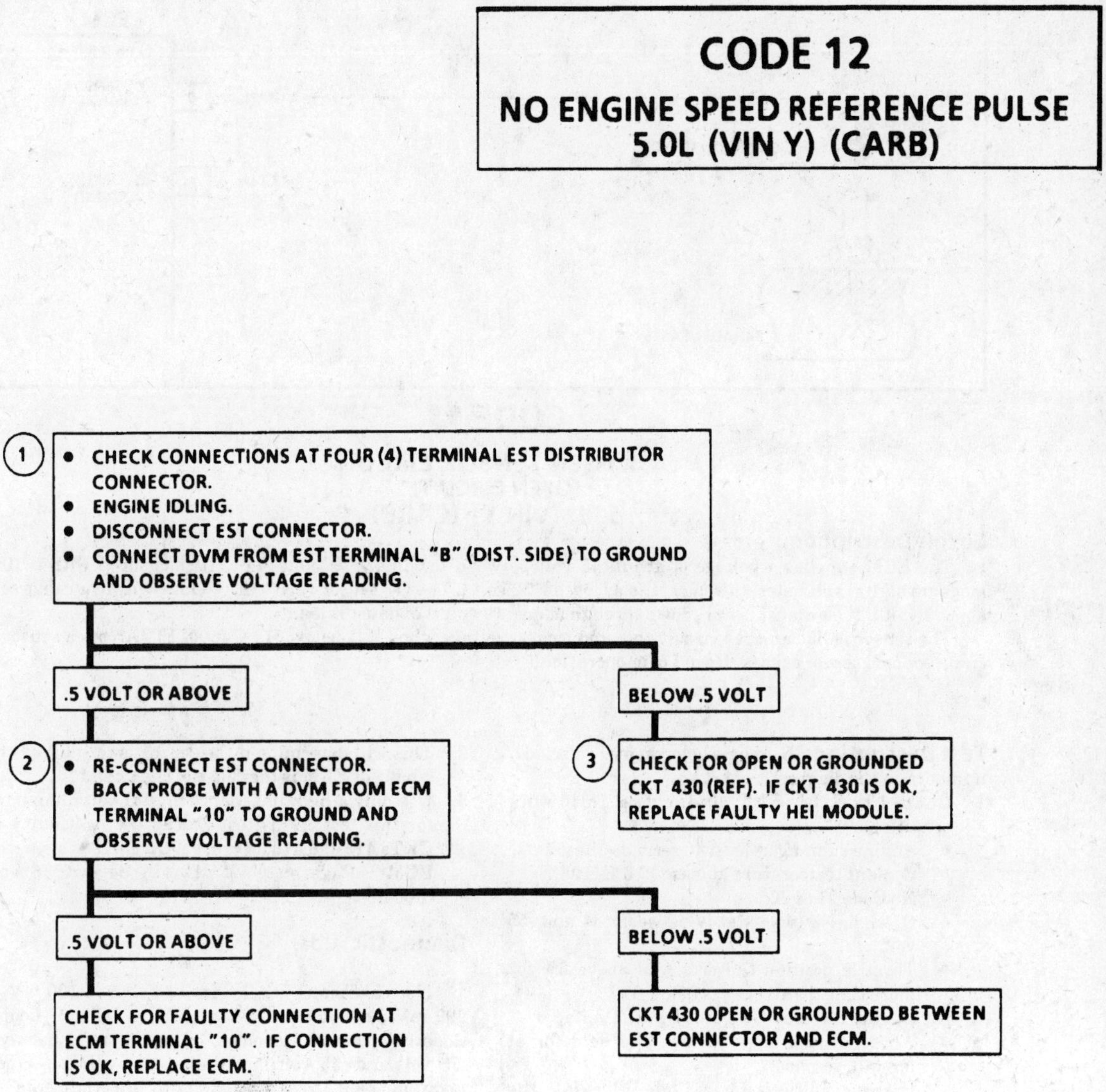

CODE 12
NO ENGINE SPEED REFERENCE PULSE
5.0L (VIN Y) (CARB)

1
- CHECK CONNECTIONS AT FOUR (4) TERMINAL EST DISTRIBUTOR CONNECTOR.
- ENGINE IDLING.
- DISCONNECT EST CONNECTOR.
- CONNECT DVM FROM EST TERMINAL "B" (DIST. SIDE) TO GROUND AND OBSERVE VOLTAGE READING.

.5 VOLT OR ABOVE

BELOW .5 VOLT

2
- RE-CONNECT EST CONNECTOR.
- BACK PROBE WITH A DVM FROM ECM TERMINAL "10" TO GROUND AND OBSERVE VOLTAGE READING.

3
CHECK FOR OPEN OR GROUNDED CKT 430 (REF). IF CKT 430 IS OK, REPLACE FAULTY HEI MODULE.

.5 VOLT OR ABOVE

BELOW .5 VOLT

CHECK FOR FAULTY CONNECTION AT ECM TERMINAL "10". IF CONNECTION IS OK, REPLACE ECM.

CKT 430 OPEN OR GROUNDED BETWEEN EST CONNECTOR AND ECM.

Fig. 70 Engine controls diagnostic chart

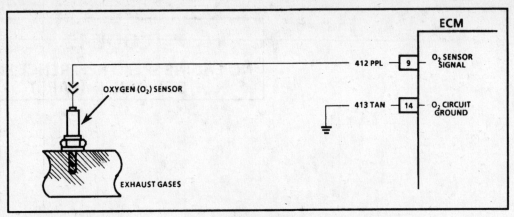

CODE 13

OXYGEN SENSOR CIRCUIT
(OPEN CIRCUIT)
5.0L (VIN Y) (CARB)

Circuit Description:

The ECM supplies a voltage of about .45 volt between terminals "9" and "14". (If measured with a 10 megohm digital voltmeter, this may read as low as .32 volt.) The O_2 sensor varies the voltage within a range of about 1 volt if the exhaust is rich, down through about .10 volt if exhaust is lean.

The sensor is like an open circuit and produces no voltage when it is below 315°C (600° F). An open sensor circuit or cold sensor causes "Open Loop" operation.

Test Description: Numbers below refer to circled numbers on the diagnostic chart.

1. Code 13 WILL SET under the following conditions:
   - Engine running at least 40 seconds after start.
   - Coolant temperature at least 42.5°C (108°F).
   - No Code 21 or 22.
   - O_2 signal voltage steady between .34 and .55 volt.
   - Throttle position sensor signal above 6% for more time than TPS was below 6%. (About .3 volt above closed throttle voltage)
   - All conditions must be met and held for at least 20 seconds.
   If the conditions for a Code 13 exist, the system will not go "Closed Loop."

2. This will determine if the sensor is at fault or the wiring or ECM is the cause of the Code 13.

3. Use only a high impedance digital volt ohmmeter for this test. This test checks the continuity of CKTs 412 and 413; because if CKT 413 is open, the ECM voltage on CKT 412 will be over .6 volt (600 mV).

Diagnostic Aids:

Normal "Scan" voltage varies between 100 mV to 999 mV (.1 volt to 1.0 volt) while in "Closed Loop." Code 13 sets in 20 seconds if voltage remains between .35 volt and .55 volt, but the system will go "Open Loop" in about 15 seconds. Refer to "Intermittents" in Section "B".

Fig. 71 Engine controls diagnostic chart

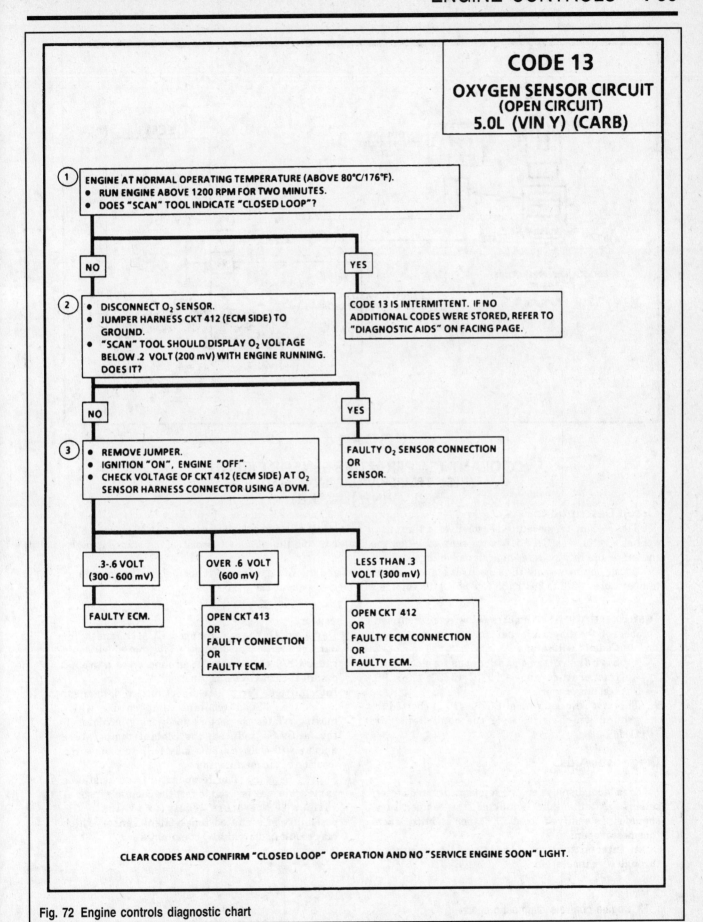

CODE 13
OXYGEN SENSOR CIRCUIT
(OPEN CIRCUIT)
5.0L (VIN Y) (CARB)

1. ENGINE AT NORMAL OPERATING TEMPERATURE (ABOVE 80°C/176°F).
   - RUN ENGINE ABOVE 1200 RPM FOR TWO MINUTES.
   - DOES "SCAN" TOOL INDICATE "CLOSED LOOP"?

NO

YES

2. - DISCONNECT O_2 SENSOR.
   - JUMPER HARNESS CKT 412 (ECM SIDE) TO GROUND.
   - "SCAN" TOOL SHOULD DISPLAY O_2 VOLTAGE BELOW .2 VOLT (200 mV) WITH ENGINE RUNNING. DOES IT?

CODE 13 IS INTERMITTENT. IF NO ADDITIONAL CODES WERE STORED, REFER TO "DIAGNOSTIC AIDS" ON FACING PAGE.

NO

YES

3. - REMOVE JUMPER.
   - IGNITION "ON", ENGINE "OFF".
   - CHECK VOLTAGE OF CKT 412 (ECM SIDE) AT O_2 SENSOR HARNESS CONNECTOR USING A DVM.

FAULTY O_2 SENSOR CONNECTION
OR
SENSOR.

.3-.6 VOLT (300 - 600 mV)	OVER .6 VOLT (600 mV)	LESS THAN .3 VOLT (300 mV)
FAULTY ECM.	OPEN CKT 413 OR FAULTY CONNECTION OR FAULTY ECM.	OPEN CKT 412 OR FAULTY ECM CONNECTION OR FAULTY ECM.

CLEAR CODES AND CONFIRM "CLOSED LOOP" OPERATION AND NO "SERVICE ENGINE SOON" LIGHT.

Fig. 72 Engine controls diagnostic chart

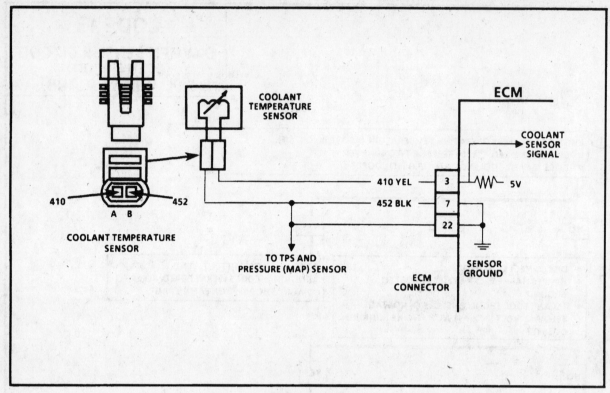

CODE 14

COOLANT TEMPERATURE SENSOR CIRCUIT
(HIGH TEMPERATURE INDICATED)
5.0L (VIN Y) (CARB)

Circuit Description:

The coolant temperature sensor uses a thermistor to control the signal voltage to the ECM. The ECM applies a voltage on CKT 410 to the sensor. When the engine is cold the sensor (thermistor) resistance is high therefore, the ECM will see high signal voltage.

As the engine warms, the sensor resistance becomes less and the voltage drops. At normal engine operating temperature 180°F to 203°F (85°C to 95°C) the voltage will measure about 1.5 to 2.0 volts.

Test Description: Numbers below refer to circled numbers on the diagnostic chart.
1.   Code 14 will set if:
   • Signal voltage indicates a coolant temperature above 167°C (333°F) for 90 seconds or more.
2.   This test will determine if CKT 410 is shorted to ground which will cause the conditions for Code 14.

Diagnostic Aids:

"Scan" tool displays engine temperature in degrees celsius. After engine is started, the temperature should rise steadily to about 90°C, then stabilize when thermostat opens.

An intermittent may be caused by a rubbed through wire insulation.

Check for:
   • Damaged Harness. Inspect ECM harness for damage or rubbed through insulation which could cause CKT 410 to short to ground or to a ground circuit such as CKT 452.
   • Intermittent Test. If connections and harness check OK, "Scan" coolant temperature while moving related connectors and wiring harness. If the failure is induced, the coolant temperature display will change. This may help to isolate the location of the malfunction.
   • Shifted Sensor. The temperature to resistance value scale may be used to test the coolant sensor at various temperature levels to evaluate the possibility of a shifted (mis-scaled) sensor which may result in driveability complaints.

Fig. 73 Engine controls diagnostic chart

CODE 14
COOLANT TEMPERATURE SENSOR CIRCUIT
(HIGH TEMPERATURE INDICATED)
5.0L (VIN Y) (CARB)

1 DOES "SCAN" TOOL DISPLAY COOLANT TEMPERATURE OF 130°C OR HIGHER?

YES

NO

2 • DISCONNECT SENSOR. "SCAN" TOOL SHOULD DISPLAY TEMPERATURE BELOW -20°C. DOES IT?

CODE 14 IS INTERMITTENT. IF NO ADDITIONAL CODES WERE STORED, REFER TO "DIAGNOSTIC AIDS" ON FACING PAGE.

YES

NO

REPLACE SENSOR.

CKT 410 SHORTED TO GROUND, OR CKT 410 SHORTED TO SENSOR GROUND CIRCUIT OR FAULTY ECM.

DIAGNOSTIC AID

COOLANT SENSOR TEMPERATURE VS. RESISTANCE VALUES (APPROXIMATE)		
°F	°C	OHMS
210	100	185
160	70	450
100	38	1,800
70	20	3,400
40	4	7,500
20	-7	13,500
0	-18	25,000
-40	-40	100,700

CLEAR CODES AND CONFIRM "CLOSED LOOP" OPERATION AND NO "SERVICE ENGINE SOON" LIGHT.

Fig. 74 Engine controls diagnostic chart

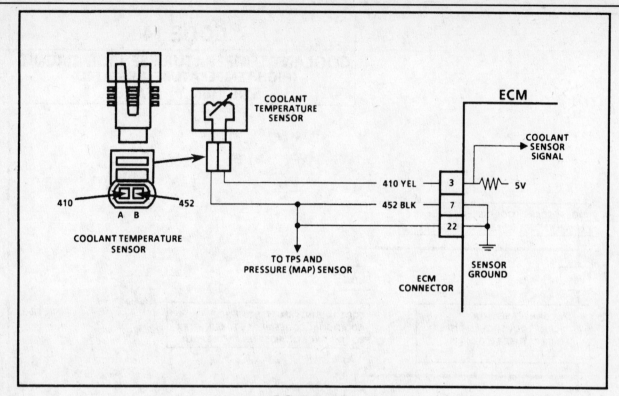

CODE 15

COOLANT TEMPERATURE SENSOR CIRCUIT
(LOW TEMPERATURE INDICATED)
5.0L (VIN Y) (CARB)

Circuit Description:

The coolant temperature sensor uses a thermistor to control the signal voltage at the ECM. The ECM applies a voltage on CKT 410 to the sensor. When the engine is cold the sensor (thermistor) resistance is high, therefore, the ECM will see high signal voltage.

As the engine warms, the sensor resistance becomes less and the voltage drops. At normal engine operating temperature 180°F to 203°F (85°C to 95°C) the voltage will measure about 1.5 to 2.0 volts.

Test Description: Numbers below refer to circled numbers on the diagnostic chart.
1. Code 15 will set if:
   - Signal voltage indicates a coolant temperature less than -1°C (-30°F) for at least 5 minutes after start.
2. This test simulates a Code 14. If the ECM recognizes the low signal voltage, (high temperature) and the "Scan" displays above 130°C, the ECM and wiring are OK.
3. This test will determine if CKT 410 is open. There should be 5 volts present at sensor connector if measured with a DVM.

Diagnostic Aids:

"Scan" tool displays engine temperature in degrees celsius. After engine is started, the temperature should rise steadily to about 90°C, then stabilize when thermostat opens.

An intermittent may be caused by a poor connection or a wire broken inside the insulation.

Check for:
- <u>Poor Connection or Damaged Harness.</u> Inspect ECM harness connectors for backed out terminals "3" or "7", improper mating, broken locks, improperly formed or damaged terminals, poor terminal to wire connection and damaged harness. A faulty connection or an open in CKT 410 or 452 will result in a Code 15. Check terminals at sensor for good contact. Refer to "Intermittents" in Section "B".
- <u>Intermittent Test.</u> If connections and harness check OK, "Scan" coolant temperature while moving related connectors and wiring harness. If the failure is induced, the coolant temperature display will change. This may help to isolate the location of the malfunction.
- <u>Shifted Sensor.</u> "Scan" coolant temperature should rise well above -1°C (30°F) within 5 minutes engine run time unless the sensor is shifted. The temperature to resistance value scale may be used to test the coolant sensor at various temperature levels to evaluate the possibility of a shifted (misscaled) sensor which may result in driveability complaints.

Fig. 75 Engine controls diagnostic chart

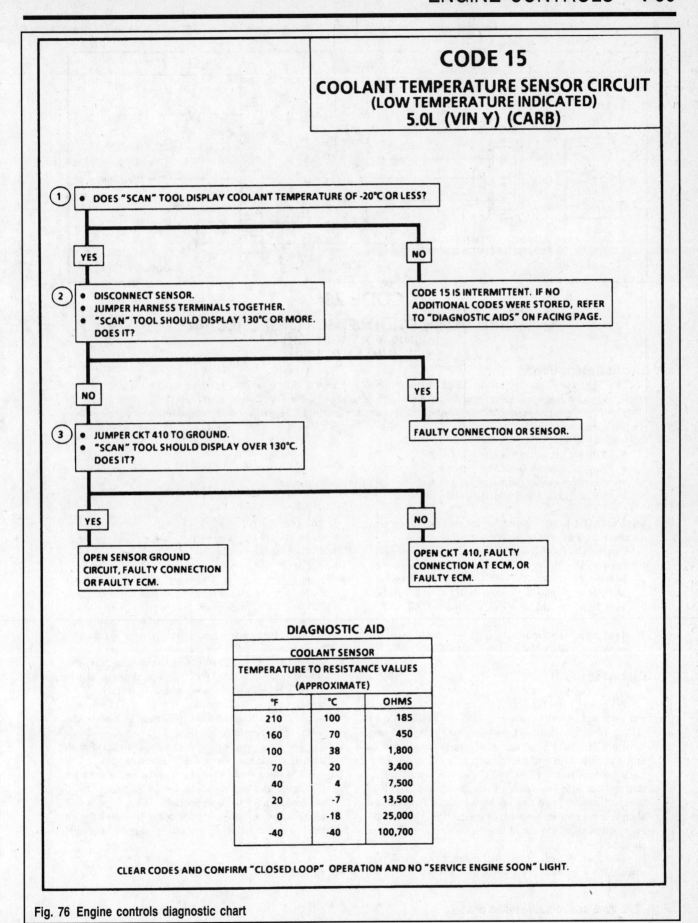

CODE 15

COOLANT TEMPERATURE SENSOR CIRCUIT
(LOW TEMPERATURE INDICATED)
5.0L (VIN Y) (CARB)

1
- DOES "SCAN" TOOL DISPLAY COOLANT TEMPERATURE OF -20°C OR LESS?

YES

NO

2
- DISCONNECT SENSOR.
- JUMPER HARNESS TERMINALS TOGETHER.
- "SCAN" TOOL SHOULD DISPLAY 130°C OR MORE. DOES IT?

CODE 15 IS INTERMITTENT. IF NO ADDITIONAL CODES WERE STORED, REFER TO "DIAGNOSTIC AIDS" ON FACING PAGE.

NO

YES

3
- JUMPER CKT 410 TO GROUND.
- "SCAN" TOOL SHOULD DISPLAY OVER 130°C. DOES IT?

FAULTY CONNECTION OR SENSOR.

YES

NO

OPEN SENSOR GROUND CIRCUIT, FAULTY CONNECTION OR FAULTY ECM.

OPEN CKT 410, FAULTY CONNECTION AT ECM, OR FAULTY ECM.

DIAGNOSTIC AID

COOLANT SENSOR		
TEMPERATURE TO RESISTANCE VALUES (APPROXIMATE)		
°F	°C	OHMS
210	100	185
160	70	450
100	38	1,800
70	20	3,400
40	4	7,500
20	-7	13,500
0	-18	25,000
-40	-40	100,700

CLEAR CODES AND CONFIRM "CLOSED LOOP" OPERATION AND NO "SERVICE ENGINE SOON" LIGHT.

Fig. 76 Engine controls diagnostic chart

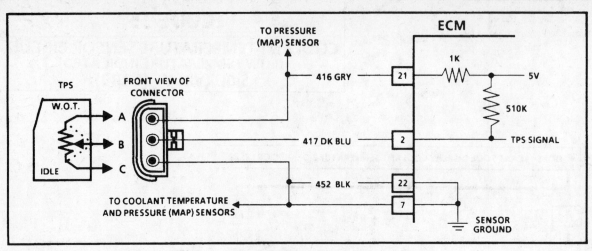

CODE 21

THROTTLE POSITION SENSOR (TPS) CIRCUIT
(SIGNAL VOLTAGE HIGH)
5.0L (VIN Y) (CARB)

Circuit Description:

The Throttle Position Sensor (TPS) provides a voltage signal that changes, relative to the throttle blade angle. Signal voltage will vary from about .4 volt at idle to about 4.9 volts at wide open throttle.

The TPS signal is one of the most important inputs used by the ECM for fuel control and for most of the ECM control outputs.

Code 21 will set if:
- TPS signal voltage is above 1.1 volts.
- Engine speed is less than 750 rpm.
- Pressure sensor indicates high manifold vacuum (closed throttle).
- All conditions met for 10 seconds.

Test Description: Numbers below refer to circled numbers on the diagnostic chart.
1. Checks CKTs 417 & 452 from the TPS connector back to the ECM. Installing a jumper between harness terminals "B" and "C" should pull voltage at ECM terminal "2" down to well below 2.5 volts.
2. Test light should be "ON" if ground CKT 452 is OK.
3. Test light "ON" indicates CKT 417 could be open, connection at ECM faulty or faulty ECM.

Diagnostic Aids:

A "Scan" tool displays TPS input voltage as an indication of throttle position. TPS voltage should be .31 to .41 volt with throttle closed, ILC retracted and ignition "ON." TPS voltage is normally between .475 and .625 volt with engine at warm idle. However, the ECM "normalizes" or "learns" the idle TPS voltage, so that an idle TPS voltage between .2 volt and .7 volt is acceptable and need not be adjusted. TPS voltage should increase at a steady rate as the throttle is opened and should reach at least 4.5 volts at wide open throttle (WOT).

Also, some "Scan" tools will display throttle angle about 10% = closed throttle, 100% = WOT.

An open in CKTs 452 or 417 will result in a Code 21 due to 510k Ω pull-up resistor inside ECM. Refer to "Intermittents" in Section "B".

Check For:
- Poor Connection or Damaged Harness Inspect ECM harness connectors for backed out terminals "2" or "22", improper mating, broken locks, improperly formed or damaged terminals, poor terminal to wire connection and damaged harness.
- Intermittent Test If connections and harness check OK, monitor TPS voltage display while moving related connectors and wiring harness. If the failure is induced, the "Scan" TPS voltage display will change. This may help to isolate the location of the malfunction.
- Skewed Pressure Sensor A false indication of high manifold vacuum from the pressure sensor could cause a false Code 21 if it occurred while throttle was open and engine speed below 750 rpm for 10 seconds. Chart C-1D in Section "6E1-C1" provides a check for the pressure sensor. Also make sure the vacuum hose or pressure sensor are not trapping vacuum.

Fig. 77 Engine controls diagnostic chart

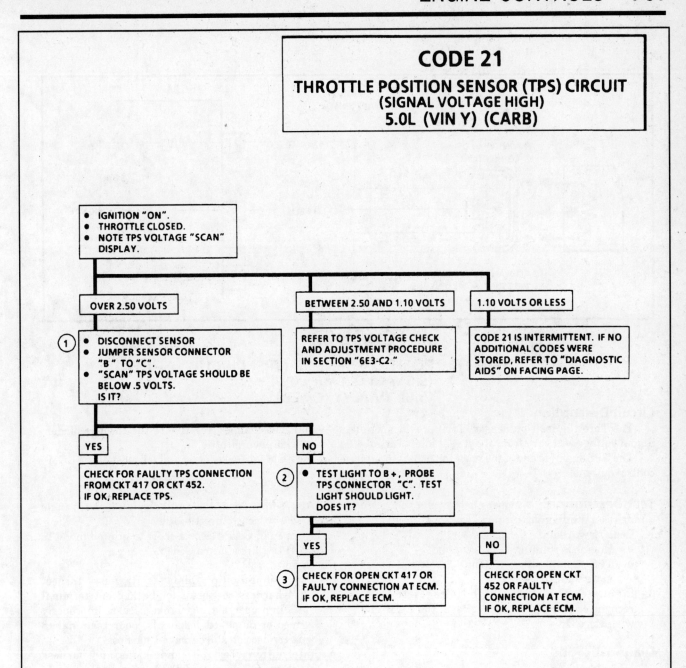

CODE 21
THROTTLE POSITION SENSOR (TPS) CIRCUIT
(SIGNAL VOLTAGE HIGH)
5.0L (VIN Y) (CARB)

- IGNITION "ON".
- THROTTLE CLOSED.
- NOTE TPS VOLTAGE "SCAN" DISPLAY.

OVER 2.50 VOLTS | BETWEEN 2.50 AND 1.10 VOLTS | 1.10 VOLTS OR LESS

① • DISCONNECT SENSOR
- JUMPER SENSOR CONNECTOR "B" TO "C".
- "SCAN" TPS VOLTAGE SHOULD BE BELOW .5 VOLTS.
  IS IT?

REFER TO TPS VOLTAGE CHECK AND ADJUSTMENT PROCEDURE IN SECTION "6E3-C2."

CODE 21 IS INTERMITTENT. IF NO ADDITIONAL CODES WERE STORED, REFER TO "DIAGNOSTIC AIDS" ON FACING PAGE.

YES | NO

CHECK FOR FAULTY TPS CONNECTION FROM CKT 417 OR CKT 452. IF OK, REPLACE TPS.

② • TEST LIGHT TO B +, PROBE TPS CONNECTOR "C". TEST LIGHT SHOULD LIGHT. DOES IT?

YES | NO

③ CHECK FOR OPEN CKT 417 OR FAULTY CONNECTION AT ECM. IF OK, REPLACE ECM.

CHECK FOR OPEN CKT 452 OR FAULTY CONNECTION AT ECM. IF OK, REPLACE ECM.

CLEAR CODES AND CONFIRM "CLOSED LOOP" OPERATION AND NO "SERVICE ENGINE SOON" LIGHT.

Fig. 78 Engine controls diagnostic chart

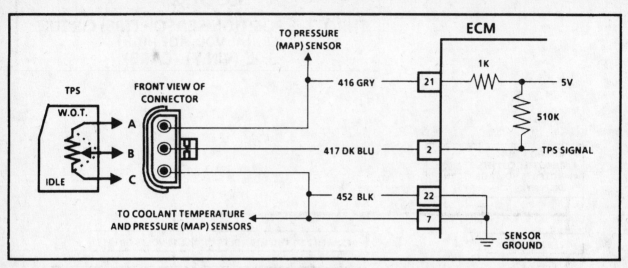

CODE 22

THROTTLE POSITION SENSOR (TPS) CIRCUIT
(SIGNAL VOLTAGE LOW)
5.0L (VIN Y) (CARB)

Circuit Description:

The Throttle Position Sensor (TPS) provides a voltage signal that changes, relative to the throttle blade. Signal voltage will vary from about .4 at idle, to about 4.9 volts at wide open throttle.

The TPS signal is one of the most important inputs used by the ECM for fuel control and for most of the ECM control outputs.

Test Description: Numbers below refer to circled numbers on the diagnostic chart.
1. Code 22 will set if:
   - Engine is running.
   - TPS signal voltage is about .2 volt or less for more than 20 seconds.
2. Simulates Code 21: (high voltage) If ECM recognizes the high signal voltage, the ECM and wiring are OK.

Diagnostic Aids:

A "Scan" tool displays TPS input voltage as an indication of throttle position. TPS voltage should be .31 to .41 volt with throttle closed, ILC retracted and ignition "ON." TPS voltage is normally between .475 and .625 volt with engine at warm idle. However, the ECM "normalizes" or "learns" the idle TPS voltage, so that an idle TPS voltage between .2 volt and .7 volt is acceptable and need not be corrected. TPS voltage should increase at a steady rate as the throttle is opened and should reach at least 4.5 volts at wide open throttle.

Also, some "Scan" tools will display throttle angle about 10% = closed throttle, 100% = WOT.

An open in CKT 416 or a short to ground in CKTs 416 or 417 will result in a Code 22.
Check For:
- Poor Connection or Damaged Harness Inspect ECM harness connector for backed out terminal "21", improper mating, broken locks, improperly formed or damaged terminals, poor terminal to wire connection and damaged harness.
- Intermittent Test If connections and harness check out OK, monitor TPS voltage display, while moving related connectors and wiring harness. If the failure is induced, the TPS display will abruptly change. This will help to isolate the location of the malfunction.
- TPS Scaling Observe TPS voltage display, while depressing accelerator pedal, with engine stopped and ignition "ON." Display should vary from closed throttle TPS voltage specification, when throttle was closed, to over 4500 mV when throttle is held at wide open throttle position.

Fig. 79 Engine controls diagnostic chart

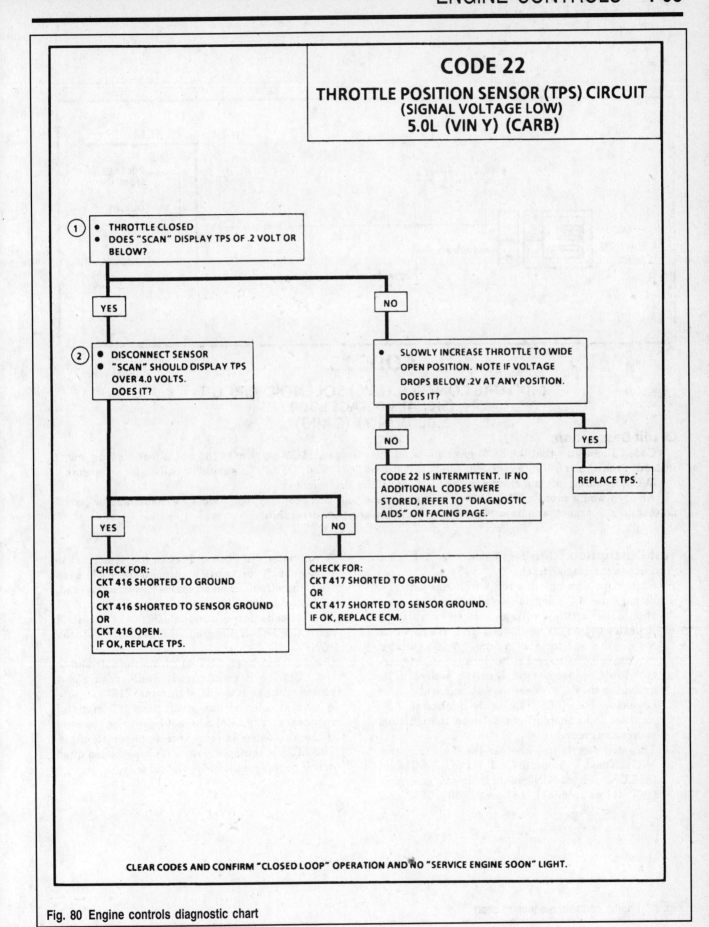

CODE 22
THROTTLE POSITION SENSOR (TPS) CIRCUIT
(SIGNAL VOLTAGE LOW)
5.0L (VIN Y) (CARB)

① • THROTTLE CLOSED
   • DOES "SCAN" DISPLAY TPS OF .2 VOLT OR BELOW?

YES

NO

② • DISCONNECT SENSOR
   • "SCAN" SHOULD DISPLAY TPS OVER 4.0 VOLTS. DOES IT?

• SLOWLY INCREASE THROTTLE TO WIDE OPEN POSITION. NOTE IF VOLTAGE DROPS BELOW .2V AT ANY POSITION. DOES IT?

NO

YES

CODE 22 IS INTERMITTENT. IF NO ADDITIONAL CODES WERE STORED, REFER TO "DIAGNOSTIC AIDS" ON FACING PAGE.

REPLACE TPS.

YES

NO

CHECK FOR:
CKT 416 SHORTED TO GROUND
OR
CKT 416 SHORTED TO SENSOR GROUND
OR
CKT 416 OPEN.
IF OK, REPLACE TPS.

CHECK FOR:
CKT 417 SHORTED TO GROUND
OR
CKT 417 SHORTED TO SENSOR GROUND.
IF OK, REPLACE ECM.

CLEAR CODES AND CONFIRM "CLOSED LOOP" OPERATION AND NO "SERVICE ENGINE SOON" LIGHT.

Fig. 80 Engine controls diagnostic chart

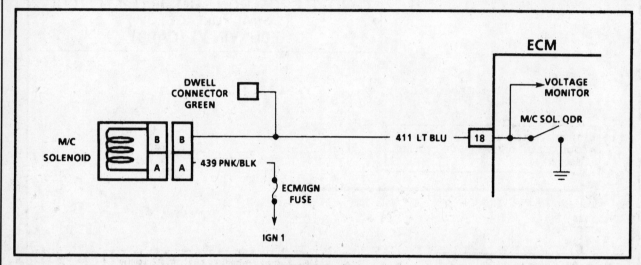

CODE 23

MIXTURE CONTROL (M/C) SOLENOID CIRCUIT
(SIGNAL VOLTAGE LOW)
5.0L (VIN Y) (CARB)

Circuit Description:

Code 23 indicates that the ECM has monitored the voltage at ECM terminal "18" and it was staying low, instead of rising and falling as the M/C solenoid is turned "ON" and "OFF." This could be caused by an open in the M/C solenoid circuit or a ground on the ECM side of the M/C solenoid.

An open would cause a full rich condition and cause poor fuel economy, odor, smoky exhaust and/or poor driveability. A ground would cause a full lean condition and poor driveability.

Test Description: Numbers below refer to circled numbers on the diagnostic chart.

1. Checks for a complete circuit from the battery through the M/C solenoid dwell lead. Voltage here should be battery voltage. Battery voltage indicates there may be an open CKT 411 between the dwell connector and ground. A "0" voltage reading could be caused either by an open between the dwell connector and ignition source or a ground on the ECM side of the M/C solenoid.

2. Checks for B+ on CKT 439 to the ignition source. The test light should light between the ignition source and ground.

3. This step determines whether the fault is in the M/C solenoid, a grounded CKT 411 to the ECM, or the ECM. A light "ON" would indicate a grounded CKT 411 to terminal "18", or a faulty ECM.

A voltmeter can't be used because it is normal to have enough current flow through the ECM even with the circuit open to make a voltmeter read, but not enough to light a test light.

4. This checks for grounded CKT 411 to ECM terminal "18". If it is grounded, the light will stay "ON."

5. Checks for an open CKT 411 from the solenoid to the ECM. A normal circuit would read about battery voltage at the ECM terminal "18".

6. A normal solenoid has about 20 to 32 ohms of resistance. The ECM does not have to be replaced if the M/C solenoid resistance is under 10 ohms. The ECM is equipped with a fault protected quad driver so replace the M/C solenoid only.

Fig. 81 Engine controls diagnostic chart

CODE 23

MIXTURE CONTROL (M/C) SOLENOID CIRCUIT
(SIGNAL VOLTAGE LOW)
5.0L (VIN Y) (CARB)

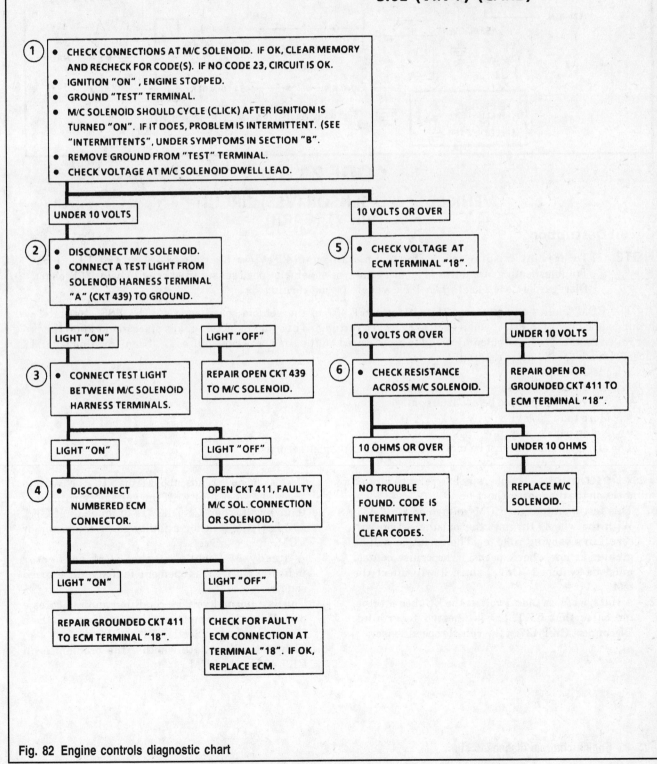

1
- CHECK CONNECTIONS AT M/C SOLENOID. IF OK, CLEAR MEMORY AND RECHECK FOR CODE(S). IF NO CODE 23, CIRCUIT IS OK.
- IGNITION "ON", ENGINE STOPPED.
- GROUND "TEST" TERMINAL.
- M/C SOLENOID SHOULD CYCLE (CLICK) AFTER IGNITION IS TURNED "ON". IF IT DOES, PROBLEM IS INTERMITTENT. (SEE "INTERMITTENTS", UNDER SYMPTOMS IN SECTION "B".
- REMOVE GROUND FROM "TEST" TERMINAL.
- CHECK VOLTAGE AT M/C SOLENOID DWELL LEAD.

UNDER 10 VOLTS

10 VOLTS OR OVER

2
- DISCONNECT M/C SOLENOID.
- CONNECT A TEST LIGHT FROM SOLENOID HARNESS TERMINAL "A" (CKT 439) TO GROUND.

5
- CHECK VOLTAGE AT ECM TERMINAL "18".

LIGHT "ON"

LIGHT "OFF"

10 VOLTS OR OVER

UNDER 10 VOLTS

3
- CONNECT TEST LIGHT BETWEEN M/C SOLENOID HARNESS TERMINALS.

REPAIR OPEN CKT 439 TO M/C SOLENOID.

6
- CHECK RESISTANCE ACROSS M/C SOLENOID.

REPAIR OPEN OR GROUNDED CKT 411 TO ECM TERMINAL "18".

LIGHT "ON"

LIGHT "OFF"

10 OHMS OR OVER

UNDER 10 OHMS

4
- DISCONNECT NUMBERED ECM CONNECTOR.

OPEN CKT 411, FAULTY M/C SOL. CONNECTION OR SOLENOID.

NO TROUBLE FOUND. CODE IS INTERMITTENT. CLEAR CODES.

REPLACE M/C SOLENOID.

LIGHT "ON"

LIGHT "OFF"

REPAIR GROUNDED CKT 411 TO ECM TERMINAL "18".

CHECK FOR FAULTY ECM CONNECTION AT TERMINAL "18". IF OK, REPLACE ECM.

Fig. 82 Engine controls diagnostic chart

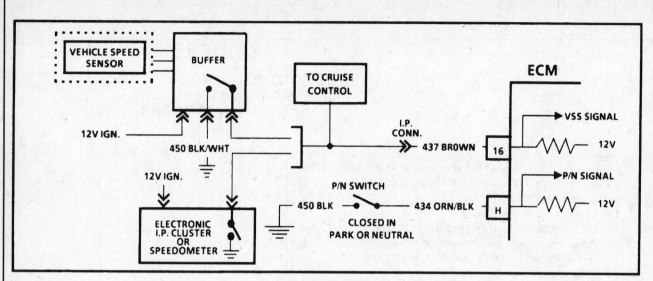

CODE 24

VEHICLE SPEED SENSOR (VSS) CIRCUIT
5.0L (VIN Y) (CARB)

Circuit Description:

NOTE: To prevent misdiagnosis, the technician should review Section "8A", or the Electrical Troubleshooting Manual, and identify the type of vehicle speed sensor used prior to using this chart. Disregard a Code 24 set when drive wheels are not turning.

The ECM applies and monitors 12 volts on CKT 437 to the vehicle speed sensor. The VSS alternately grounds and opens CKT 437, when drive wheels are turning. This pulsing action takes place about 2000 times per mile and the ECM will calculate vehicle speed based on the time between "pulses." "Scan" reading should closely match speedometer reading.

A Code 24 will set if:
- Indicated vehicle speed is less than 5 mph
- Above 1100 rpm and below 3200 rpm
- More than 20% TPS
- Not in park or neutral

The above conditions must be met for a time longer than 40 seconds.

Test Description: Numbers below refer to circled numbers on the diagnostic chart.

1. This test monitors the ECM voltage on CKT 437. With the wheels turning, the pulsing action will result in a varying voltage. The variation will be greater at low wheel speeds. The cruise control must be switched "OFF," since it will affect the test.

2. A voltage of less than 1 volt at the ECM connector, indicates that CKT 437 is shorted to ground. Disconnect CKT 437 at the vehicle speed sensor.

If voltage now reads above 10 volts, the vehicle speed sensor is faulty. If the voltage remains less than 1 volt, then CKT 437 is grounded. If CKT 437 is OK, check for a faulty ECM connector or ECM.

3. A steady 8-12 volts at the ECM connector indicates CKT 437 is open or a faulty vehicle speed sensor.

4. This is a normal voltage condition and indicates a possible intermittent condition. See "Intermittents" in Section "B".

5. This step will isolate whether the problem is in CKT 437 or the ECM.

Fig. 83 Engine controls diagnostic chart

CODE 24
VEHICLE SPEED SENSOR (VSS) CIRCUIT
5.0L (VIN Y) (CARB)

NOTE; TO PREVENT MISDIAGNOSIS, THE TECHNICIAN SHOULD REVIEW ELECTRICAL SECTION 8A, OR THE ELECTRICAL TROUBLESHOOTING SECTION SUPPLEMENT, AND IDENTIFY THE TYPE OF VEHICLE SPEED SENSOR USED PRIOR TO USING THIS CHART. DISREGARD CODE 24, IF SET WHEN DRIVE WHEELS ARE NOT TURNING.

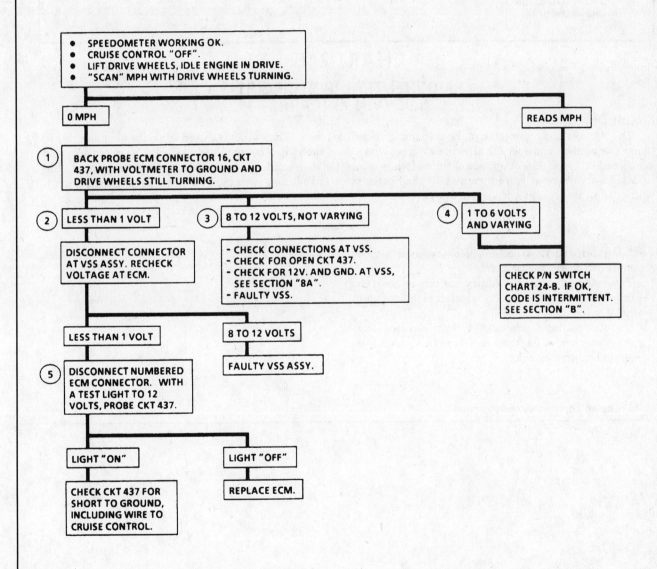

- SPEEDOMETER WORKING OK.
- CRUISE CONTROL "OFF".
- LIFT DRIVE WHEELS, IDLE ENGINE IN DRIVE.
- "SCAN" MPH WITH DRIVE WHEELS TURNING.

0 MPH

READS MPH

(1) BACK PROBE ECM CONNECTOR 16, CKT 437, WITH VOLTMETER TO GROUND AND DRIVE WHEELS STILL TURNING.

(2) LESS THAN 1 VOLT

(3) 8 TO 12 VOLTS, NOT VARYING

(4) 1 TO 6 VOLTS AND VARYING

DISCONNECT CONNECTOR AT VSS ASSY. RECHECK VOLTAGE AT ECM.

- CHECK CONNECTIONS AT VSS.
- CHECK FOR OPEN CKT 437.
- CHECK FOR 12V. AND GND. AT VSS, SEE SECTION "8A".
- FAULTY VSS.

CHECK P/N SWITCH CHART 24-B. IF OK, CODE IS INTERMITTENT. SEE SECTION "B".

LESS THAN 1 VOLT

8 TO 12 VOLTS

FAULTY VSS ASSY.

(5) DISCONNECT NUMBERED ECM CONNECTOR. WITH A TEST LIGHT TO 12 VOLTS, PROBE CKT 437.

LIGHT "ON"

LIGHT "OFF"

CHECK CKT 437 FOR SHORT TO GROUND, INCLUDING WIRE TO CRUISE CONTROL.

REPLACE ECM.

CLEAR CODES AND CONFIRM "CLOSED LOOP" OPERATION AND NO "SERVICE ENGINE SOON" LIGHT.

Fig. 84 Engine controls diagnostic chart

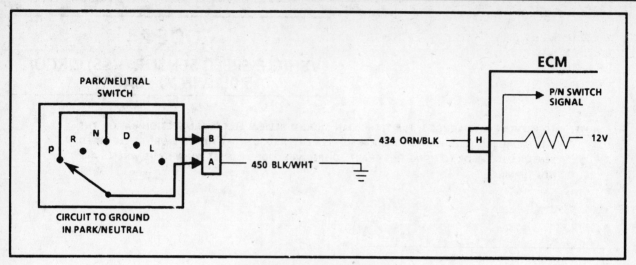

CHART 24B
PARK/NEUTRAL (P/N) CIRCUIT
5.0L (VIN Y) (CARB)

Circuit Description:

The P/N switch is connected to the transmission gear selector. The switch is closed when the gear selector is in park or neutral and open for all other ranges. One side of the switch is connected to the ECM, which supplies a buffered 12 volts. The other side of the switch is connected to ground. The P/N switch state is an input to the ECM. Low voltage at ECM terminal "H" indicates the transmission is in park or neutral range while high voltage indicates it is in a drive range or reverse.

Test Description: Numbers below refer to circled numbers on the diagnostic chart.

1. This step separates a faulty switch or switch adjustment from a faulty electrical circuit or ECM.

   Normal voltage across the terminals of the connector, removed from the P/N switch, should be about battery voltage.

Fig. 85 Engine controls diagnostic chart

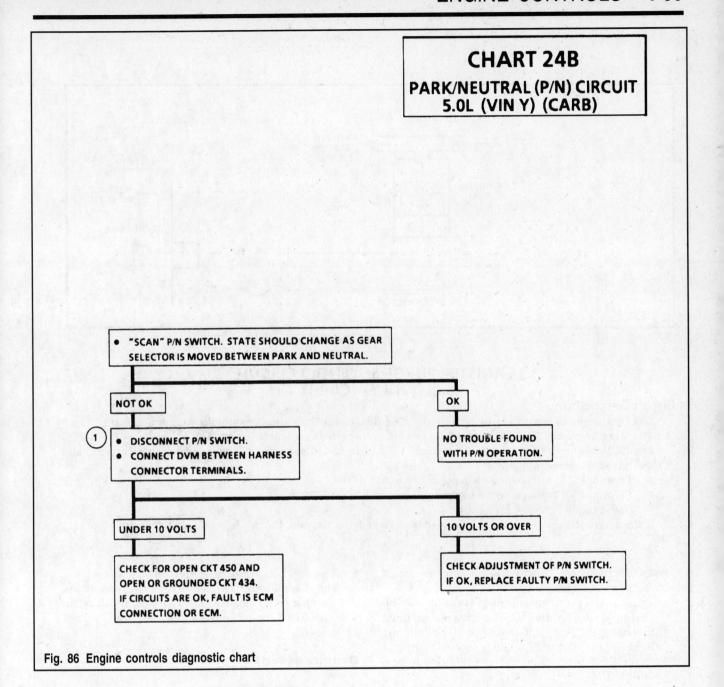

CHART 24B
PARK/NEUTRAL (P/N) CIRCUIT
5.0L (VIN Y) (CARB)

- "SCAN" P/N SWITCH. STATE SHOULD CHANGE AS GEAR SELECTOR IS MOVED BETWEEN PARK AND NEUTRAL.

NOT OK

OK

① ● DISCONNECT P/N SWITCH.
● CONNECT DVM BETWEEN HARNESS CONNECTOR TERMINALS.

NO TROUBLE FOUND WITH P/N OPERATION.

UNDER 10 VOLTS

10 VOLTS OR OVER

CHECK FOR OPEN CKT 450 AND OPEN OR GROUNDED CKT 434. IF CIRCUITS ARE OK, FAULT IS ECM CONNECTION OR ECM.

CHECK ADJUSTMENT OF P/N SWITCH. IF OK, REPLACE FAULTY P/N SWITCH.

Fig. 86 Engine controls diagnostic chart

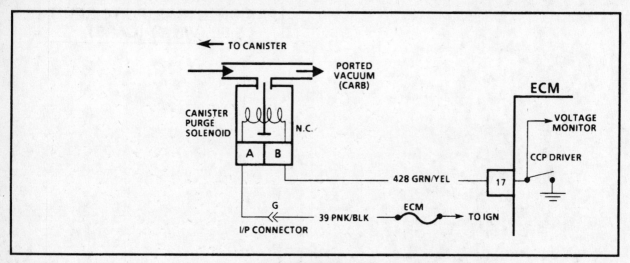

CODE 31
CANISTER PURGE SOLENOID CIRCUIT
5.0L (VIN Y) (CARB)

Circuit Description:

Canister purge is controlled by a normally closed solenoid that allows manifold vacuum to purge the canister when energized. The ECM supplies a ground to energize the solenoid (purge "ON").

The ECM monitors the voltage on terminal "17". Code 31 indicates the canister purge control, terminal "17", voltage is incorrect as follows:

- Terminal "17" voltage low when purge commanded "ON."
- Terminal "17" voltage high when purge commanded "OFF."
- Above conditions exist for a calibrated time

If the diagnostic test terminal is grounded with the engine stopped, the purge solenoid is energized (purge "ON").

Test Description: Numbers below refer to circled numbers on the diagnostic chart.

1. The canister purge solenoid should not be energized with ignition "ON," engine not running; therefore, the test light should be "OFF." If the light is "ON," either CKT 428 is shorted to ground or the ECM is providing the ground, indicating a faulty ECM.

2. This step checks for B+ at canister purge solenoid connector.

3. Grounding the diagnostic test terminal should energize the solenoid circuit, turning "ON" the test light if the ECM and wiring are OK.

4. A low resistance solenoid would allow too much current into the ECM when terminal "17" is switched to ground, causing terminal "17" voltage to be high even when the ECM is commanding it to be low.

5. The previous steps have verified that the wiring and solenoid are OK. Faulty connections at the solenoid could cause an open circuit, resulting in Code 31. If connections are OK, the problem is not present.

Diagnostic Aids:

The CCP driver is a QDR which is "protected." This means it will turn "OFF" or increase its internal resistance to limit current if too much current starts to flow into terminal "17". This would result from a shorted canister purge solenoid or a short to voltage on CKT 428, and would cause terminal "17" voltage to be high even with purge commanded "ON." Low voltage at terminal "17" with purge "OFF" would result from an open from B+.

Fig. 87 Engine controls diagnostic chart

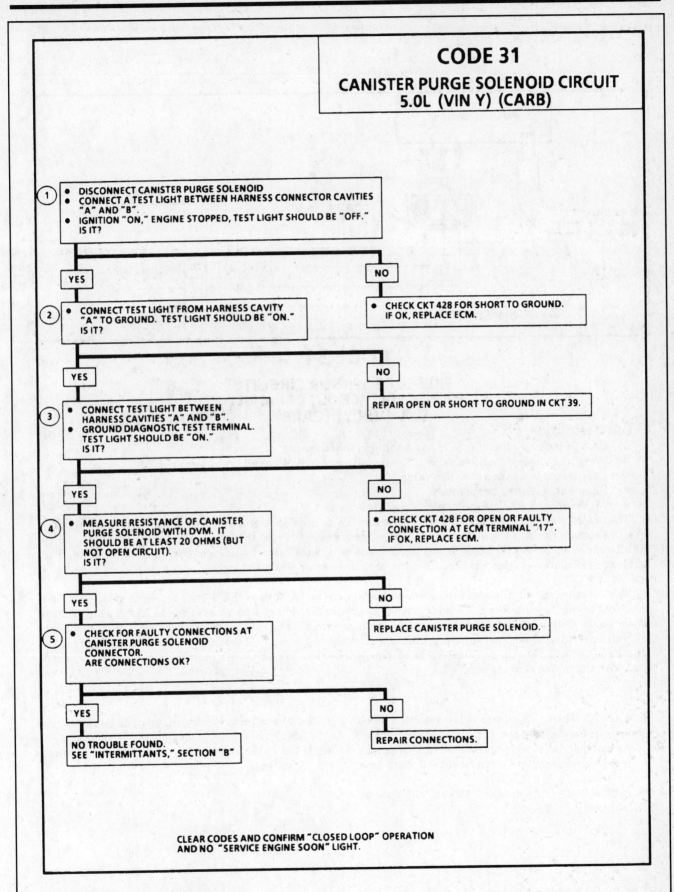

CODE 31
CANISTER PURGE SOLENOID CIRCUIT
5.0L (VIN Y) (CARB)

1.
- DISCONNECT CANISTER PURGE SOLENOID
- CONNECT A TEST LIGHT BETWEEN HARNESS CONNECTOR CAVITIES "A" AND "B".
- IGNITION "ON," ENGINE STOPPED, TEST LIGHT SHOULD BE "OFF." IS IT?

YES

2.
- CONNECT TEST LIGHT FROM HARNESS CAVITY "A" TO GROUND. TEST LIGHT SHOULD BE "ON." IS IT?

NO
- CHECK CKT 428 FOR SHORT TO GROUND. IF OK, REPLACE ECM.

YES

3.
- CONNECT TEST LIGHT BETWEEN HARNESS CAVITIES "A" AND "B".
- GROUND DIAGNOSTIC TEST TERMINAL. TEST LIGHT SHOULD BE "ON." IS IT?

NO

REPAIR OPEN OR SHORT TO GROUND IN CKT 39.

YES

4.
- MEASURE RESISTANCE OF CANISTER PURGE SOLENOID WITH DVM. IT SHOULD BE AT LEAST 20 OHMS (BUT NOT OPEN CIRCUIT). IS IT?

NO
- CHECK CKT 428 FOR OPEN OR FAULTY CONNECTION AT ECM TERMINAL "17". IF OK, REPLACE ECM.

YES

5.
- CHECK FOR FAULTY CONNECTIONS AT CANISTER PURGE SOLENOID CONNECTOR. ARE CONNECTIONS OK?

NO

REPLACE CANISTER PURGE SOLENOID.

YES

NO TROUBLE FOUND.
SEE "INTERMITTANTS," SECTION "B"

NO

REPAIR CONNECTIONS.

CLEAR CODES AND CONFIRM "CLOSED LOOP" OPERATION
AND NO "SERVICE ENGINE SOON" LIGHT.

Fig. 88 Engine controls diagnostic chart

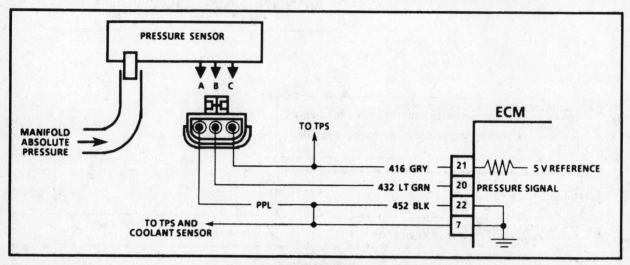

CODE 34

PRESSURE SENSOR CIRCUIT
(SIGNAL VOLTAGE OUT OF RANGE)
5.0L (VIN Y) (CARB)

Circuit Description:

Code 34 indicates that the ECM has monitored the following.
- Pressure outside a specified value range (monitored by ECM as voltage at terminal "20")
- Engine rpm less than a specified value
- Engine at operating temperature
- All the above for a time greater than specified

The pressure sensor is a dual purpose MAP sensor. When the ignition switch is turned "ON," a barometric pressure signal is sent to the ECM prior to the engine cranking. From this baro reading, the ECM calculates the altitude at which the vehicle is being operated and selects the correct spark and fuel calibration table. The ECM also calculates altitude changes from the pressure sensor while the engine is running when throttle is near or at WOT.

The pressure sensor also serves as a vacuum sensor. The ECM uses this signal to adjust spark and fuel according to engine load. The ECM inverts the pressure sensor voltage and sends it on the ALDL as a vacuum sensor value. While reading the pressure sensor voltage with a "Scan" tool with ignition "ON," it will be close to 0 volt, and with the engine running at idle, it will be above 2.5 volts. If voltage is measured at the pressure sensor and/or the ECM with a voltmeter, the voltage will be close to 5 volts with ignition "ON" and less than 2.5 volts with the engine running at idle.

Test Description: Numbers below refer to circled numbers on the diagnostic chart. (With "Scan" tool.)

1. An engine that is able to maintain 18" of intake manifold vacuum will show about 4.0 volts on a scanner.
2. If ECM and wiring are OK, .58 volt will show on scanner.
3. Low vacuum to sensor will show as low voltage on "Scan" tool.
4. If CKT 452 is open, high voltage will show on "Scan" tool.

Fig. 89 Engine controls diagnostic chart

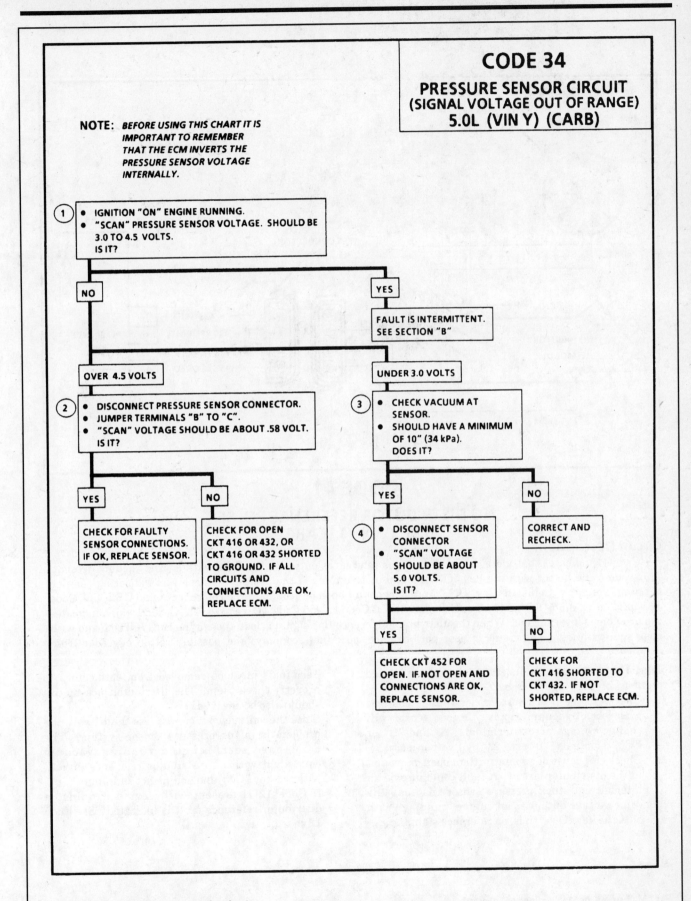

CODE 34
PRESSURE SENSOR CIRCUIT
(SIGNAL VOLTAGE OUT OF RANGE)
5.0L (VIN Y) (CARB)

NOTE: *BEFORE USING THIS CHART IT IS IMPORTANT TO REMEMBER THAT THE ECM INVERTS THE PRESSURE SENSOR VOLTAGE INTERNALLY.*

1
- IGNITION "ON" ENGINE RUNNING.
- "SCAN" PRESSURE SENSOR VOLTAGE. SHOULD BE 3.0 TO 4.5 VOLTS. IS IT?

NO

YES

FAULT IS INTERMITTENT. SEE SECTION "B"

OVER 4.5 VOLTS

UNDER 3.0 VOLTS

2
- DISCONNECT PRESSURE SENSOR CONNECTOR.
- JUMPER TERMINALS "B" TO "C".
- "SCAN" VOLTAGE SHOULD BE ABOUT .58 VOLT. IS IT?

3
- CHECK VACUUM AT SENSOR.
- SHOULD HAVE A MINIMUM OF 10" (34 kPa). DOES IT?

YES

NO

CHECK FOR FAULTY SENSOR CONNECTIONS. IF OK, REPLACE SENSOR.

CHECK FOR OPEN CKT 416 OR 432, OR CKT 416 OR 432 SHORTED TO GROUND. IF ALL CIRCUITS AND CONNECTIONS ARE OK, REPLACE ECM.

YES

NO

4
- DISCONNECT SENSOR CONNECTOR
- "SCAN" VOLTAGE SHOULD BE ABOUT 5.0 VOLTS. IS IT?

CORRECT AND RECHECK.

YES

NO

CHECK CKT 452 FOR OPEN. IF NOT OPEN AND CONNECTIONS ARE OK, REPLACE SENSOR.

CHECK FOR CKT 416 SHORTED TO CKT 432. IF NOT SHORTED, REPLACE ECM.

Fig. 90 Engine controls diagnostic chart

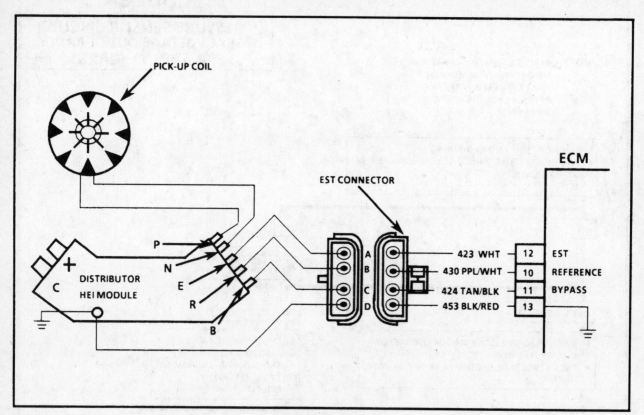

CODE 41

NO DISTRIBUTOR REFERENCE PULSE
5.0L (VIN Y) (CARB)

Circuit Description:

Code 41 indicates that there are no distributor references pulses to the ECM with engine vacuum present. This code could be set with the key "ON," engine not running if the pressure sensor was indicating "engine running" voltage with just the key "ON." With a constant open or ground in the reference signal CKT 430, Code 12 would be set along with a 41. Use Code 12 chart if Code 12 and Code 41 are both set. Code 41 alone indicates the problem is intermittent. When the distributor reference line signal is lost, the engine runs full rich and with base spark timing. The result is poor performance, poor fuel economy, and possibly rotten egg odor from exhaust.

Test Description: Numbers below refer to circled numbers on the diagnostic chart.

1. Checks to see if pressure sensor voltage changes with loss of vacuum supply. A good sensor will change voltage across terminals "A" and "B" or ECM terminals "20" and "22" by 1 volt or more.

2. Checks for cause of an intermittent open or ground in the distributor circuit. A fault could also be an intermittent stuck pressure sensor that has the same voltage output as an engine "running" with only the key "ON," thus, no reference signal.

Terminals must be removed from connectors to properly check them. The distributor pick-up coil should also be checked.

3. Since the voltage change was less than 1 volt, the problem is in the pressure sensor system. The ECM has "seen" engine running vacuum equivalent with no distributor reference signal, with the key "ON" and engine not running.

If Code 12 is present with engine running, a distributor reference fault is indicated. See Code 12 chart first.

Fig. 91 Engine controls diagnostic chart

CODE 41
NO DISTRIBUTOR REFERENCE PULSE
5.0L (VIN Y) (CARB)

(1)
- "SCAN" TOOL DISCONNECTED, ENGINE RUNNING, GROUND TEST TERMINAL AND CHECK FOR CODE 12. IF CODE 12 IS PRESENT, SEE THAT CHART FIRST.
- TEST TERMINAL NOT GROUNDED, "SCAN" PRESSURE SENSOR AS SENSOR HOSE IS DISCONNECTED.

1.0 VOLT OR MORE CHANGE

LESS THAN 1.0 VOLT CHANGE

(2) TROUBLE IS INTERMITTENT

(3) FAULT IS IN PRESSURE SENSOR CIRCUIT. SEE CHART 34.

MAKE A PHYSICAL CHECK OF WIRES AND CONNECTIONS FOR GROUNDS AND POOR CONNECTIONS. ALSO CHECK DISTRIBUTOR PICK-UP COIL RESISTANCE AND CONNECTIONS. FAULT COULD BE AN INTERMITTENT PRESSURE SENSOR. SEE "SYMPTOMS" IN SECTION "B".

Fig. 92 Engine controls diagnostic chart

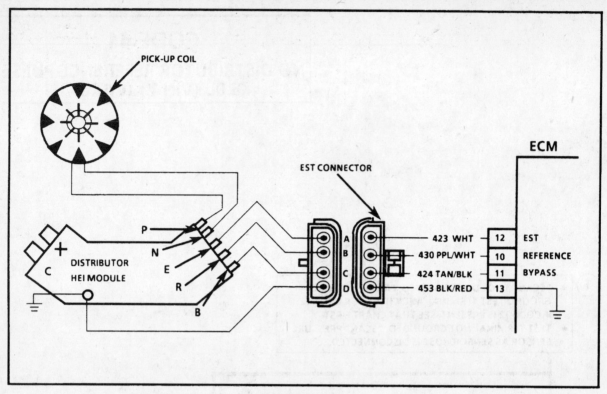

CODE 42

ELECTRONIC SPARK TIMING (EST) CIRCUIT
5.0L (VIN Y) (CARB)

Circuit Description:
Code 42 indicates that the ECM has monitored:
- Open or grounded bypass circuit (terminal "11")
- Open or grounded EST circuit (terminal "12")

A grounded EST may sometimes not set a code unless cranked 10 seconds or longer with circuit grounded.

Test Description: Numbers below refer to circled numbers on the diagnostic chart.

1. This checks operation of EST. Grounding the "test" terminal causes timing to go to a fixed value, which is normally different from that obtained with EST operating. Therefore, the timing should change. Usually, the change can be heard in engine rpm. If so, the timing change does not have to be checked. If timing varies with increase in engine rpm (module advance), a problem is indicated.

2. This step eliminates the ECM and ECM connections from the module input. By jumpering terminals "A" and "B", the distributor reference signal is fed directly into the EST line of the module. By putting voltage through the test light on terminal "C" of the harness, the module is switched to the EST mode and the vehicle should run. If the engine stops there is no EST signal reaching the module due to open or poor connections or the module is faulty.

3. By removing the jumper you are opening the EST signal and the engine should stop.

4. Since the engine ran when the module was jumpered, it says the problem is not in the distributor (if the correct HEI module is installed). The wrong HEI module can set a Code 42.

NOTE: Possible causes for intermittent Code 42.

- Loose grounds or electrical connections.
- Extended cranking time (over 10 seconds with fully charged battery).
- Abrupt re-cycling of ignition switch from "ON" to "OFF" and back "ON" again (within 5 seconds).
- EST harness routed close to plug wires or other high load electrical harness.

Fig. 93 Engine controls diagnostic chart

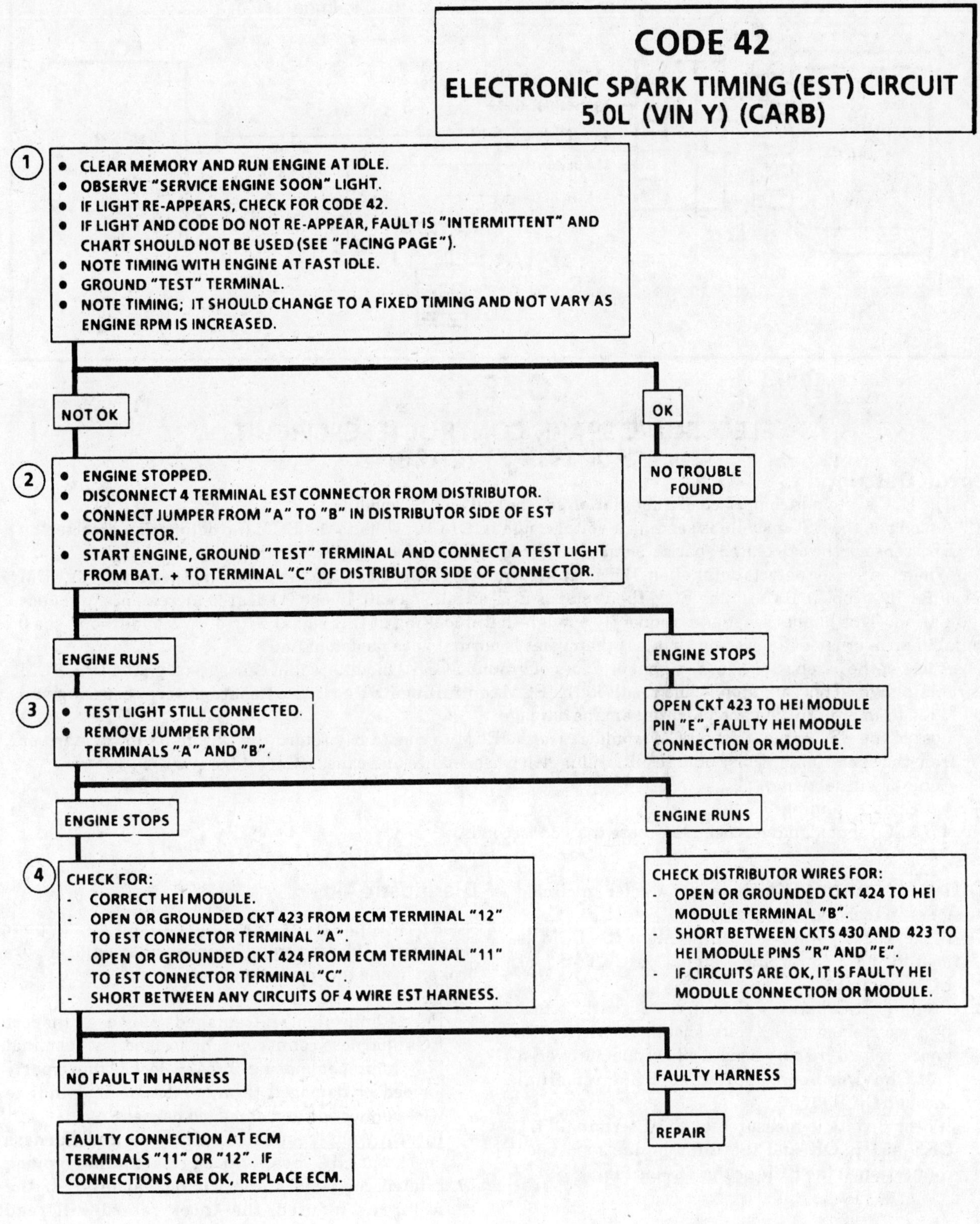

CODE 42
ELECTRONIC SPARK TIMING (EST) CIRCUIT
5.0L (VIN Y) (CARB)

1
- CLEAR MEMORY AND RUN ENGINE AT IDLE.
- OBSERVE "SERVICE ENGINE SOON" LIGHT.
- IF LIGHT RE-APPEARS, CHECK FOR CODE 42.
- IF LIGHT AND CODE DO NOT RE-APPEAR, FAULT IS "INTERMITTENT" AND CHART SHOULD NOT BE USED (SEE "FACING PAGE").
- NOTE TIMING WITH ENGINE AT FAST IDLE.
- GROUND "TEST" TERMINAL.
- NOTE TIMING; IT SHOULD CHANGE TO A FIXED TIMING AND NOT VARY AS ENGINE RPM IS INCREASED.

NOT OK | OK

OK → NO TROUBLE FOUND

2
- ENGINE STOPPED.
- DISCONNECT 4 TERMINAL EST CONNECTOR FROM DISTRIBUTOR.
- CONNECT JUMPER FROM "A" TO "B" IN DISTRIBUTOR SIDE OF EST CONNECTOR.
- START ENGINE, GROUND "TEST" TERMINAL AND CONNECT A TEST LIGHT FROM BAT. + TO TERMINAL "C" OF DISTRIBUTOR SIDE OF CONNECTOR.

ENGINE RUNS | ENGINE STOPS

ENGINE STOPS → OPEN CKT 423 TO HEI MODULE PIN "E", FAULTY HEI MODULE CONNECTION OR MODULE.

3
- TEST LIGHT STILL CONNECTED.
- REMOVE JUMPER FROM TERMINALS "A" AND "B".

ENGINE STOPS | ENGINE RUNS

4 CHECK FOR:
- CORRECT HEI MODULE.
- OPEN OR GROUNDED CKT 423 FROM ECM TERMINAL "12" TO EST CONNECTOR TERMINAL "A".
- OPEN OR GROUNDED CKT 424 FROM ECM TERMINAL "11" TO EST CONNECTOR TERMINAL "C".
- SHORT BETWEEN ANY CIRCUITS OF 4 WIRE EST HARNESS.

CHECK DISTRIBUTOR WIRES FOR:
- OPEN OR GROUNDED CKT 424 TO HEI MODULE TERMINAL "B".
- SHORT BETWEEN CKTS 430 AND 423 TO HEI MODULE PINS "R" AND "E".
- IF CIRCUITS ARE OK, IT IS FAULTY HEI MODULE CONNECTION OR MODULE.

NO FAULT IN HARNESS | FAULTY HARNESS

FAULTY CONNECTION AT ECM TERMINALS "11" OR "12". IF CONNECTIONS ARE OK, REPLACE ECM.

FAULTY HARNESS → REPAIR

Fig. 94 Engine controls diagnostic chart

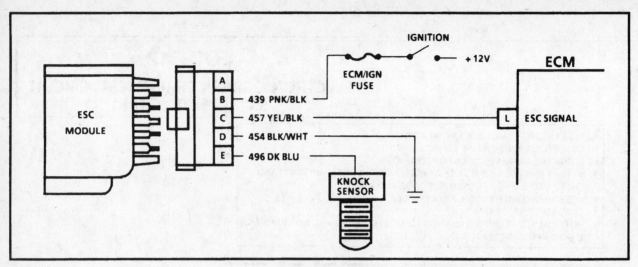

CODE 43

ELECTRONIC SPARK CONTROL (ESC) CIRCUIT
5.0L (VIN Y) (CARB)

Circuit Description:

The ESC system is comprised of a detonation sensor and an ESC module.

As long as the ESC module is sending a voltage signal (8 to 10) volts to the ECM (no detonation detected by the ESC sensor), the calculated spark advance (EST) remains unaffected by the ESC input.

When the sensor detects detonation, the module turns "OFF" the circuit to the ECM and the voltage at ECM terminal "L" drops to 0 volt. The ECM then retards EST as much as 20° in one (1) degree increments to reduce detonation. This happens fast and frequently enough that if looking at this signal with a DVM, you won't see 0 volt, but an average voltage somewhat less than what is normal with no detonation.

A loss of the detonation sensor signal or a loss of ground at ESC module would cause the signal at the ECM to remain high. This condition would result in the ECM controlling EST as if no detonation were occurring and could result in pre-ignition and potential engine damage.

Loss of the ESC signal to the ECM would cause the ECM to constantly retard the EST to its max retard or 20° from the spark table. This could result in sluggish performance and cause a Code 43 to set.

Code 43 will set when
- Engine running
- ESC input signal has been low more than 3.9 seconds.

Test Description: Numbers below refer to circled numbers on the diagnostic chart.

1. If the knock retard is reading high, the ECM is monitoring a low voltage signal on CKT 457 at ECM terminal "L".
2. Probing ESC harness terminal "C" with a test light connected to 12 volts should result in the knock retard display reading low due to over 8 volts having been applied to ECM terminal through CKT 457.
3. If over 6 volts is measured at ECM terminal "L", CKT 457 is OK and the fault is due to a poor connection at the ECM or the ECM is faulty.

Diagnostic Aids:

An intermittent may be caused by a poor connection, rubbed through wire insulation or a wire broken inside the insulation.
Check for :
- Poor Connection or Damaged Harness Inspect ECM harness connectors for backed out terminal "L", improper mating, broken locks, improperly formed or damaged terminals, poor terminal to wire connection and damaged harness.
- Intermittent Test If connections and harness check out OK, "Scan" knock retard while moving related connectors and wiring harness. If the failure is induced, the knock retard will read "LOW" to "HIGH." This will help to isolate the location of the malfunction.

Fig. 95 Engine controls diagnostic chart

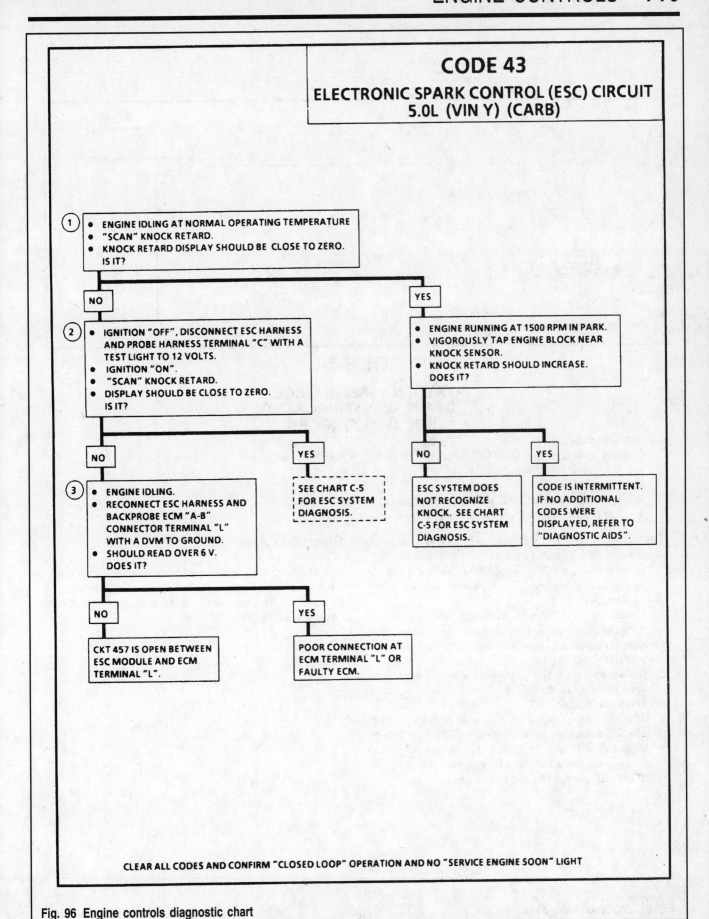

CODE 43
ELECTRONIC SPARK CONTROL (ESC) CIRCUIT
5.0L (VIN Y) (CARB)

1.
- ENGINE IDLING AT NORMAL OPERATING TEMPERATURE
- "SCAN" KNOCK RETARD.
- KNOCK RETARD DISPLAY SHOULD BE CLOSE TO ZERO. IS IT?

NO

2.
- IGNITION "OFF", DISCONNECT ESC HARNESS AND PROBE HARNESS TERMINAL "C" WITH A TEST LIGHT TO 12 VOLTS.
- IGNITION "ON".
- "SCAN" KNOCK RETARD.
- DISPLAY SHOULD BE CLOSE TO ZERO. IS IT?

YES

- ENGINE RUNNING AT 1500 RPM IN PARK.
- VIGOROUSLY TAP ENGINE BLOCK NEAR KNOCK SENSOR.
- KNOCK RETARD SHOULD INCREASE. DOES IT?

NO

3.
- ENGINE IDLING.
- RECONNECT ESC HARNESS AND BACKPROBE ECM "A-B" CONNECTOR TERMINAL "L" WITH A DVM TO GROUND.
- SHOULD READ OVER 6 V. DOES IT?

YES

SEE CHART C-5 FOR ESC SYSTEM DIAGNOSIS.

NO

ESC SYSTEM DOES NOT RECOGNIZE KNOCK. SEE CHART C-5 FOR ESC SYSTEM DIAGNOSIS.

YES

CODE IS INTERMITTENT. IF NO ADDITIONAL CODES WERE DISPLAYED, REFER TO "DIAGNOSTIC AIDS".

NO

CKT 457 IS OPEN BETWEEN ESC MODULE AND ECM TERMINAL "L".

YES

POOR CONNECTION AT ECM TERMINAL "L" OR FAULTY ECM.

CLEAR ALL CODES AND CONFIRM "CLOSED LOOP" OPERATION AND NO "SERVICE ENGINE SOON" LIGHT

Fig. 96 Engine controls diagnostic chart

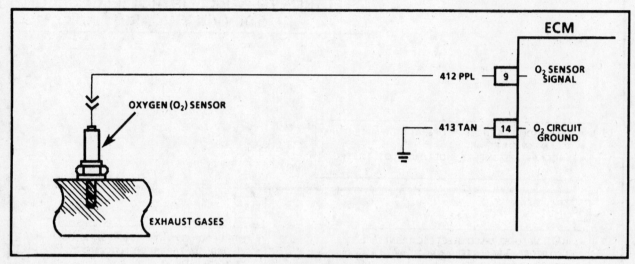

CODE 44

OXYGEN SENSOR CIRCUIT
(LEAN EXHAUST INDICATED)
5.0L (VIN Y) (CARB)

Circuit Description:

Code 44 indicates that the ECM has monitored the O_2 sensor voltage under the following conditions:
- Voltage lower than specified
- "Closed Loop"
- Within a specified TPS voltage range (part throttle).
- For a time longer than specified

Test Description: Numbers below refer to circled numbers on the diagnostic chart.

1. System will go "Open Loop" if O_2 sensor cools off while idling engine. Scan "Loop" status often during test.
2. Checks to see if the ECM is able to respond to a rich condition caused by choking the engine. If it does, the problem is a lean engine condition NOT electrical.
3. This step puts a rich O_2 signal (about 1 volt) into terminal "9" of the ECM. Dwell should increase (lean command).
4. If dwell increases to over 50°, with heavy choking, the fault is an air leak, since the ECM was able to respond. If air is going to exhaust ports, disconnect the solenoid(s) for the air control valve. If air still goes to the ports, it is a faulty valve.

Diagnostic Aids:

Verify proper TPS operation, see CHART C-2F. Check for O_2 signal wire shorted to ground. A cylinder misfire may also cause a Code 44. Refer to "Symptoms" Section "B".

Fig. 97 Engine controls diagnostic chart

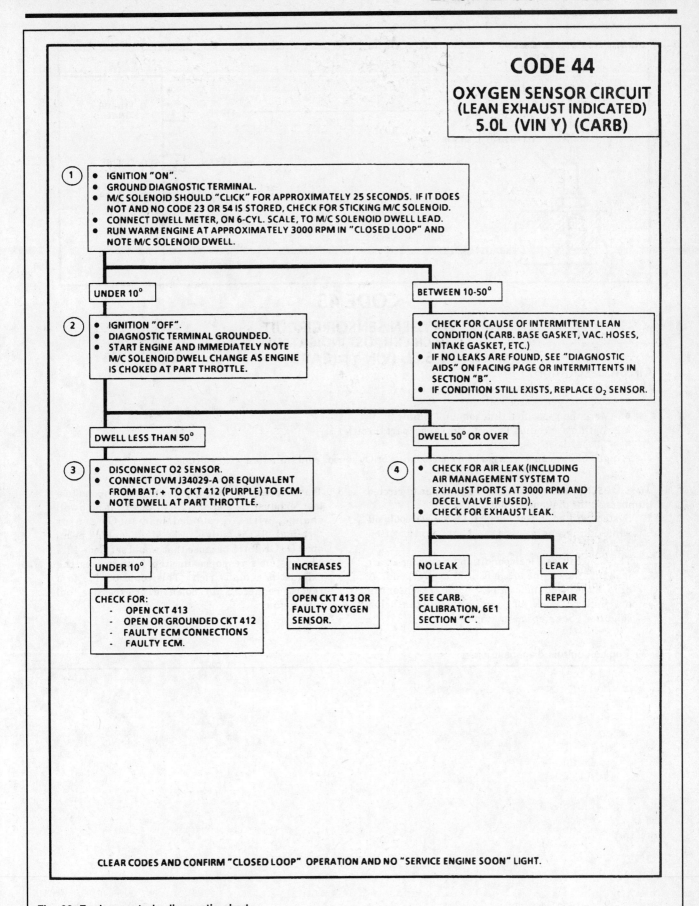

CODE 44

OXYGEN SENSOR CIRCUIT
(LEAN EXHAUST INDICATED)
5.0L (VIN Y) (CARB)

1
- IGNITION "ON".
- GROUND DIAGNOSTIC TERMINAL.
- M/C SOLENOID SHOULD "CLICK" FOR APPROXIMATELY 25 SECONDS. IF IT DOES NOT AND NO CODE 23 OR 54 IS STORED, CHECK FOR STICKING M/C SOLENOID.
- CONNECT DWELL METER, ON 6-CYL. SCALE, TO M/C SOLENOID DWELL LEAD.
- RUN WARM ENGINE AT APPROXIMATELY 3000 RPM IN "CLOSED LOOP" AND NOTE M/C SOLENOID DWELL.

UNDER 10°

BETWEEN 10-50°

2
- IGNITION "OFF".
- DIAGNOSTIC TERMINAL GROUNDED.
- START ENGINE AND IMMEDIATELY NOTE M/C SOLENOID DWELL CHANGE AS ENGINE IS CHOKED AT PART THROTTLE.

- CHECK FOR CAUSE OF INTERMITTENT LEAN CONDITION (CARB. BASE GASKET, VAC. HOSES, INTAKE GASKET, ETC.)
- IF NO LEAKS ARE FOUND, SEE "DIAGNOSTIC AIDS" ON FACING PAGE OR INTERMITTENTS IN SECTION "B".
- IF CONDITION STILL EXISTS, REPLACE O_2 SENSOR.

DWELL LESS THAN 50°

DWELL 50° OR OVER

3
- DISCONNECT O2 SENSOR.
- CONNECT DVM J34029-A OR EQUIVALENT FROM BAT. + TO CKT 412 (PURPLE) TO ECM.
- NOTE DWELL AT PART THROTTLE.

4
- CHECK FOR AIR LEAK (INCLUDING AIR MANAGEMENT SYSTEM TO EXHAUST PORTS AT 3000 RPM AND DECEL VALVE IF USED).
- CHECK FOR EXHAUST LEAK.

UNDER 10°

INCREASES

NO LEAK

LEAK

CHECK FOR:
- OPEN CKT 413
- OPEN OR GROUNDED CKT 412
- FAULTY ECM CONNECTIONS
- FAULTY ECM.

OPEN CKT 413 OR FAULTY OXYGEN SENSOR.

SEE CARB. CALIBRATION, 6E1 SECTION "C".

REPAIR

CLEAR CODES AND CONFIRM "CLOSED LOOP" OPERATION AND NO "SERVICE ENGINE SOON" LIGHT.

Fig. 98 Engine controls diagnostic chart

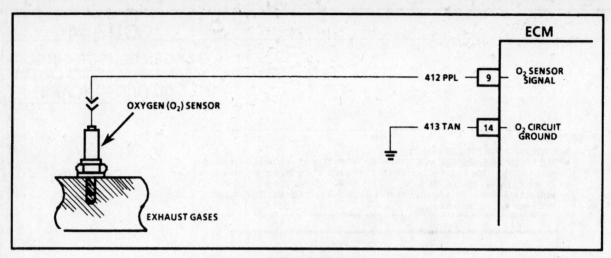

CODE 45

OXYGEN SENSOR CIRCUIT
(RICH EXHAUST INDICATED)
5.0L (VIN Y) (CARB)

Circuit Description:

Code 45 indicates that the ECM has seen:
- High oxygen sensor voltage
- More than specified time (about 2 minutes)
- Within a specified TPS voltage range (part throttle)
- "Closed Loop"

A high voltage can be caused by a rich exhaust or O_2 sensor contaminated with silicone.

Test Description: Numbers below refer to circled numbers on the diagnostic chart.

1. System will go "Open Loop" if O_2 sensor cools off while idling engine. Scan "Loop" status often during test.
2. This step causes a lean condition by putting an air leak into the engine to see if ECM can respond. A drop in the dwell indicates ECM and O_2 sensor are not faulty. Look for source of constant rich condition. See step one examples.

3. This step tests to see if ECM is able to respond to a lean exhaust O_2 signal (low voltage). If no dwell change, with a grounded lead to O_2 sensor terminal "9" the fault is in ECM. It couldn't be an open O_2 CKT 412 because that would set Code 13.
4. The system's response in step 2, indicates the exhaust is actually rich. This could be due to a reverse connected M/C solenoid, or excessive fuel into engine.

Fig. 99 Engine controls diagnostic chart

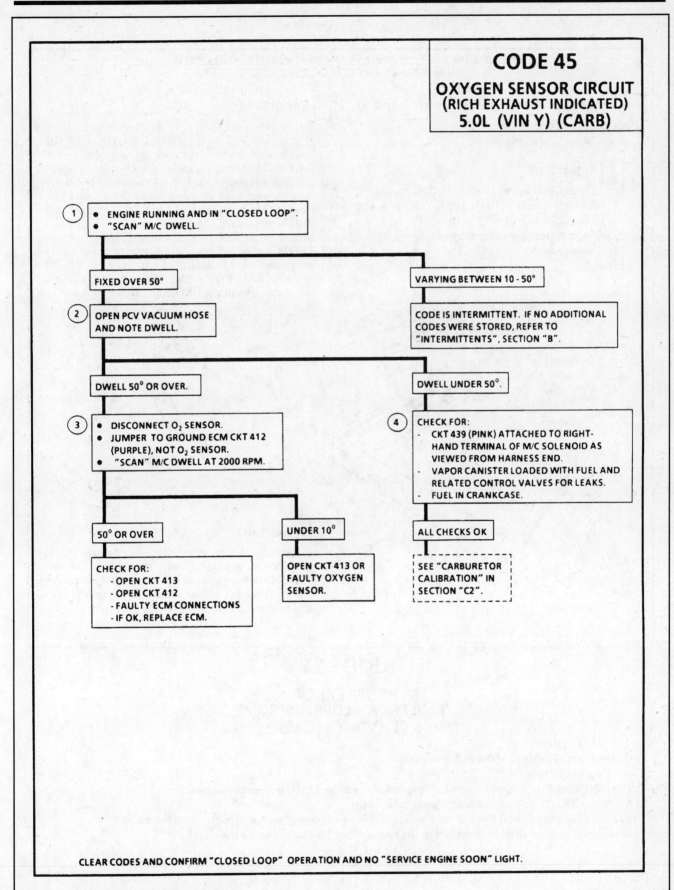

CODE 45
OXYGEN SENSOR CIRCUIT
(RICH EXHAUST INDICATED)
5.0L (VIN Y) (CARB)

1.
- ENGINE RUNNING AND IN "CLOSED LOOP".
- "SCAN" M/C DWELL.

FIXED OVER 50°

VARYING BETWEEN 10 - 50°

2. OPEN PCV VACUUM HOSE AND NOTE DWELL.

CODE IS INTERMITTENT. IF NO ADDITIONAL CODES WERE STORED, REFER TO "INTERMITTENTS", SECTION "B".

DWELL 50° OR OVER.

DWELL UNDER 50°.

3.
- DISCONNECT O₂ SENSOR.
- JUMPER TO GROUND ECM CKT 412 (PURPLE), NOT O₂ SENSOR.
- "SCAN" M/C DWELL AT 2000 RPM.

4. CHECK FOR:
- CKT 439 (PINK) ATTACHED TO RIGHT-HAND TERMINAL OF M/C SOLENOID AS VIEWED FROM HARNESS END.
- VAPOR CANISTER LOADED WITH FUEL AND RELATED CONTROL VALVES FOR LEAKS.
- FUEL IN CRANKCASE.

50° OR OVER

UNDER 10°

ALL CHECKS OK

CHECK FOR:
- OPEN CKT 413
- OPEN CKT 412
- FAULTY ECM CONNECTIONS
- IF OK, REPLACE ECM.

OPEN CKT 413 OR FAULTY OXYGEN SENSOR.

SEE "CARBURETOR CALIBRATION" IN SECTION "C2".

CLEAR CODES AND CONFIRM "CLOSED LOOP" OPERATION AND NO "SERVICE ENGINE SOON" LIGHT.

Fig. 100 Engine controls diagnostic chart

THE IGNITION SHOULD ALWAYS BE "OFF" WHEN INSTALLING OR REMOVING THE ECM CONNECTORS

⟷ Remove or Disconnect (Figures 1 and 2)

1. Connectors from ECM
2. ECM mounting hardware

⚠ Important

- Electronic Control Module (ECM) mounting hardware not illustrated. Hardware configuration will vary with car division.

3. ECM from passenger compartment
4. ECM access cover
5. PROM

⚠ Important

- Using the rocker-type PROM removal tool, engage one end of the PROM carrier with the hook end of the tool and rock the engaged end of the PROM carrier up as far as possible. Engage the opposite end of the PROM carrier in the same manner and rock this end up as far as possible. Repeat this process until the PROM carrier and PROM are free of the PROM socket. The PROM carrier with PROM in it should lift off of the PROM socket easily. PROM carrier should only be removed by using the pictured PROM removal tool (Figure 2). Other methods could cause damage to the PROM or PROM socket.

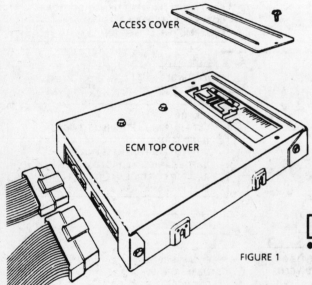

ACCESS COVER

ECM TOP COVER

FIGURE 1

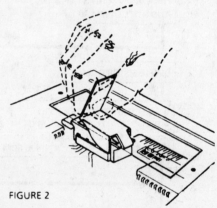

FIGURE 2

⚠ Important

- Replacement Electronic Control Module (ECM) is supplied without an engine calibration unit (PROM) so care should be taken when removing the PROM as it will be reused in the new ECM if the original ECM is found to be defective.

CODE 51

PROM ERROR
(FAULTY OR INCORRECT PROM)
5.0L (VIN Y) (CARB)

Circuit Description:

Code 51 sets if any one of the following occur:

- Faulty PROM unit
- PROM unit improperly installed (may not set a code if installed backwards)
- Some PROM pins not making contact (i.e. bent)

Always check to see that the PROM pins are not bent and are inserted properly into the ECM.

Make certain the PROM is installed in the proper direction as shown in the chart.

Fig. 101 Engine controls diagnostic chart

CHECK THAT ALL PINS ARE FULLY INSERTED IN THE SOCKET. IF OK, REPLACE PROM AND RECHECK. IF CONDITION IS NOT CORRECTED, REPLACE ECM.

CODE 51
PROM ERROR
(FAULTY OR INCORRECT PROM)
5.0L (VIN Y) (CARB)

Inspect (Figure 3)

For correct indexing of reference end of the PROM carrier and carefully set aside. Do not remove PROM from carrier to avoid incorrect reinstallation.

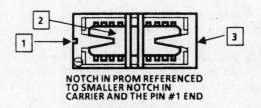

NOTCH IN PROM REFERENCED TO SMALLER NOTCH IN CARRIER AND THE PIN #1 END

1	REFERENCE END
2	PROM
3	PROM CARRIERR

Important
- (Before installing new PROM)

ANYTIME THE PROM IS INSTALLED BACKWARDS AND THE IGNITION SWITCH IS TURNED "ON", THE PROM IS DESTROYED.

NOTICE: To prevent possible Electrostatic Discharge damage to the PROM, Do Not touch the component leads, and Do Not remove integrated circuit from carrier.

Install or Connect (Figures 1 and 3)
1. PROM in PROM socket.

Important

DO NOT PRESS ON PROM - ONLY CARRIER.

- Small notch of carrier should be aligned with small notch in socket. Press on PROM carrier until it is firmly seated in the socket. Do not press on PROM; only the carrier.
2. Access cover on ECM.
3. ECM in passenger compartment.
4. Connectors to ECM.

Functional Check

1. Turn ignition "ON".
2. Enter diagnostics.
   a. Code 12 should flash four times. (No other codes present). This indicates the PROM is installed properly.
   b. If trouble Code 51 occurs or if the check engine light is "ON" constantly with no codes, the PROM is not fully seated, installed backwards, has bent pins, or is faulty.
      - If not fully seated, press firmly on PROM carrier.
      - If it is necessary to remove the PROM, follow instructions in steps "A" & "B".
      - If installed backwards, REPLACE THE PROM.
      - If pins bend, remove PROM, straighten pins, and reinstall. IF bent pins break or crack during straightening, discard PROM and replace it.

Fig. 102 Engine controls diagnostic chart

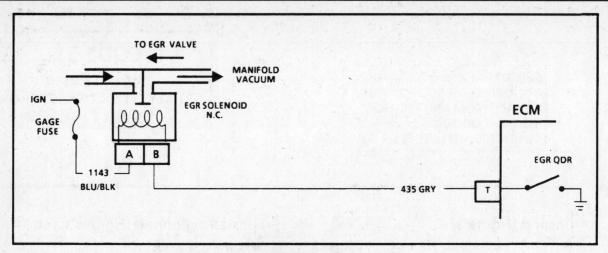

CODE 53
EGR SYSTEM MALFUNCTION
5.0L (VIN Y) (CARB)
(California only)

Circuit Description:

The ECM operates a solenoid to control the Exhaust Gas Recirculation (EGR) valve. This solenoid is normally closed. By providing a ground path, the ECM energizes the solenoid which then allows vacuum to pass to the EGR valve.

The ECM monitors EGR effectiveness by de-energizing the EGR control solenoid thereby shutting off vacuum to the EGR valve diaphragm. With the EGR valve closed, manifold vacuum will be greater than it was during normal EGR operation and this change will be relayed to the ECM by the MAP sensor. If the change is not within the calibrated window, a Code 53 will be set.

The ECM will check EGR operation when:
- Vehicle speed is above 50 mph.
- Engine vacuum is between 40 and 51 kPa.
- No change in throttle position while test is being run.
- TCC "ON."

Test Description: Numbers below refer to circled numbers on the diagnostic chart.
1. This tests for restricted valve or passage in manifold. Engine should run roughly or stall as valve is opened manually.
2. EGR valve diaphragm should begin to move as the engine speed approaches 2000 rpm.
3. This test should result in the EGR solenoid being energized, shutting off vacuum to the EGR valve diaphragm. This indicates EGR system is functioning properly.
4. Vacuum below 23.6 kPa (7" Hg) at 2000 rpm is insufficient for proper EGR operation. Lower vacuum readings require repair.

> **STEPS 1, 2 AND 3 represent an EGR system operation check.**

5. With the ignition "ON" and engine stopped, the ECM normally grounds terminal "T" to energize the EGR solenoid. This step checks for a defective (always open) solenoid or an electrical circuit problem.
6. The EGR solenoid is normally de-energized with the engine idling at normal operating temperature. This step checks for a defective (always closed) solenoid or an electrical circuit problem.
7. This step determines whether ECM is providing ground to terminal "T" or CKT 435 is shorted to ground.

Diagnostic Aids:

Vacuum lines should be thoroughly checked for internal restrictions. The ECM uses the pressure sensor for checking EGR operation. If there is a question of pressure sensor accuracy use pressure sensor check CHART C-10, in Section "6E1-C1".

If no problems are found, refer to "Intermittents" in Section "B".

Fig. 103 Engine controls diagnostic chart

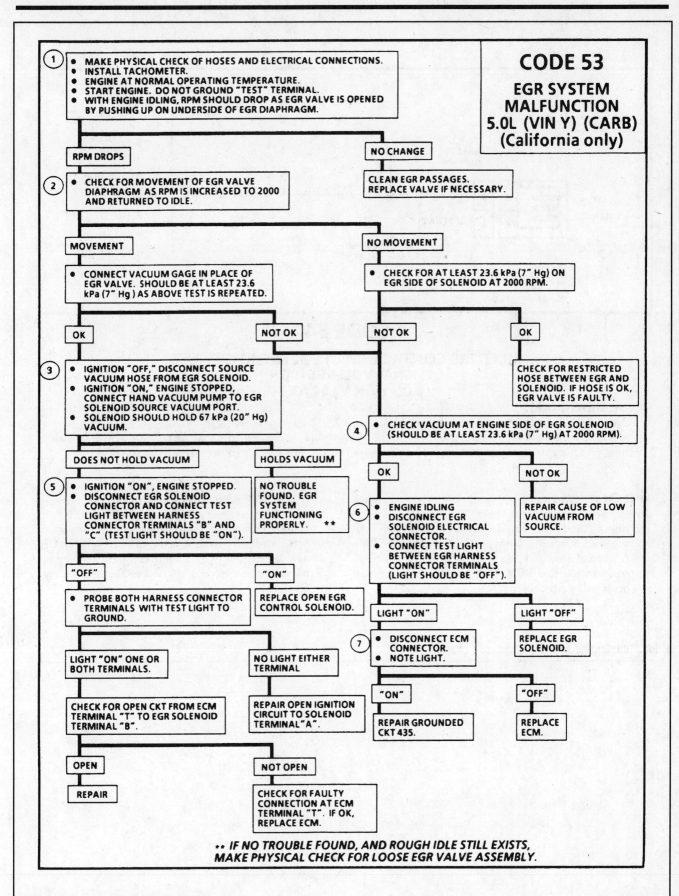

CODE 53

EGR SYSTEM MALFUNCTION 5.0L (VIN Y) (CARB) (California only)

1
- MAKE PHYSICAL CHECK OF HOSES AND ELECTRICAL CONNECTIONS.
- INSTALL TACHOMETER.
- ENGINE AT NORMAL OPERATING TEMPERATURE.
- START ENGINE. DO NOT GROUND "TEST" TERMINAL.
- WITH ENGINE IDLING, RPM SHOULD DROP AS EGR VALVE IS OPENED BY PUSHING UP ON UNDERSIDE OF EGR DIAPHRAGM.

RPM DROPS | NO CHANGE

CLEAN EGR PASSAGES. REPLACE VALVE IF NECESSARY.

2
- CHECK FOR MOVEMENT OF EGR VALVE DIAPHRAGM AS RPM IS INCREASED TO 2000 AND RETURNED TO IDLE.

MOVEMENT | NO MOVEMENT

- CONNECT VACUUM GAGE IN PLACE OF EGR VALVE. SHOULD BE AT LEAST 23.6 kPa (7" Hg) AS ABOVE TEST IS REPEATED.

- CHECK FOR AT LEAST 23.6 kPa (7" Hg) ON EGR SIDE OF SOLENOID AT 2000 RPM.

OK | NOT OK | NOT OK | OK

CHECK FOR RESTRICTED HOSE BETWEEN EGR AND SOLENOID. IF HOSE IS OK, EGR VALVE IS FAULTY.

3
- IGNITION "OFF," DISCONNECT SOURCE VACUUM HOSE FROM EGR SOLENOID.
- IGNITION "ON," ENGINE STOPPED, CONNECT HAND VACUUM PUMP TO EGR SOLENOID SOURCE VACUUM PORT.
- SOLENOID SHOULD HOLD 67 kPa (20" Hg) VACUUM.

4
- CHECK VACUUM AT ENGINE SIDE OF EGR SOLENOID (SHOULD BE AT LEAST 23.6 kPa (7" Hg) AT 2000 RPM).

DOES NOT HOLD VACUUM | HOLDS VACUUM

OK | NOT OK

5
- IGNITION "ON", ENGINE STOPPED.
- DISCONNECT EGR SOLENOID CONNECTOR AND CONNECT TEST LIGHT BETWEEN HARNESS CONNECTOR TERMINALS "B" AND "C" (TEST LIGHT SHOULD BE "ON").

NO TROUBLE FOUND. EGR SYSTEM FUNCTIONING PROPERLY. **

6
- ENGINE IDLING
- DISCONNECT EGR SOLENOID ELECTRICAL CONNECTOR.
- CONNECT TEST LIGHT BETWEEN EGR HARNESS CONNECTOR TERMINALS (LIGHT SHOULD BE "OFF").

REPAIR CAUSE OF LOW VACUUM FROM SOURCE.

"OFF" | "ON"

- PROBE BOTH HARNESS CONNECTOR TERMINALS WITH TEST LIGHT TO GROUND.

REPLACE OPEN EGR CONTROL SOLENOID.

LIGHT "ON" | LIGHT "OFF"

7
- DISCONNECT ECM CONNECTOR.
- NOTE LIGHT.

REPLACE EGR SOLENOID.

LIGHT "ON" ONE OR BOTH TERMINALS. | NO LIGHT EITHER TERMINAL

CHECK FOR OPEN CKT FROM ECM TERMINAL "T" TO EGR SOLENOID TERMINAL "B".

REPAIR OPEN IGNITION CIRCUIT TO SOLENOID TERMINAL "A".

"ON" | "OFF"

REPAIR GROUNDED CKT 435. | REPLACE ECM.

OPEN | NOT OPEN

REPAIR

CHECK FOR FAULTY CONNECTION AT ECM TERMINAL "T". IF OK, REPLACE ECM.

*** IF NO TROUBLE FOUND, AND ROUGH IDLE STILL EXISTS, MAKE PHYSICAL CHECK FOR LOOSE EGR VALVE ASSEMBLY.*

Fig. 104 Engine controls diagnostic chart

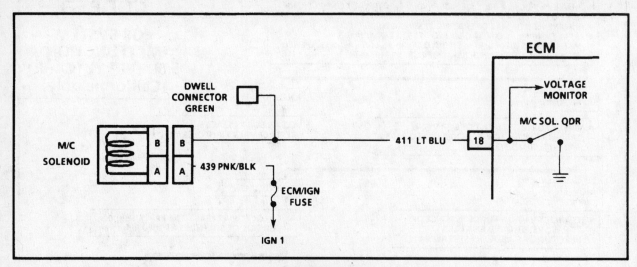

CODE 54

MIXTURE CONTROL (M/C) SOLENOID CIRCUIT
(SIGNAL VOLTAGE HIGH)
5.0L (VIN Y) (CARB)

Circuit Description:

Code 54 will be set if there is constant high voltage at ECM terminal "18".

A shorted solenoid or shorted CKT 411 to 12 volts would cause the solenoid to remain in the full rich position, resulting in potential ECM damage, excessive fuel consumption, and excessive exhaust odor.

Test Description: Numbers below refer to circled numbers on the diagnostic chart.

1. Checks the M/C solenoid resistance to determine if the fault is in the solenoid, ECM harness, or ECM. A normal solenoid has about 20 to 32 ohms of resistance. The ECM is equipped with a fault protected quad-driver.

If the M/C solenoid is under 10 ohms, only the solenoid has to be replaced, not the ECM.

2. Checks to see if reason for high voltage to terminal "18" is a faulty ECM or a short to 12 volts in CKT 411. If the test light illuminates with both ends of harness disconnected, there is a short to 12 volts in CKT 411.

Fig. 105 Engine controls diagnostic chart

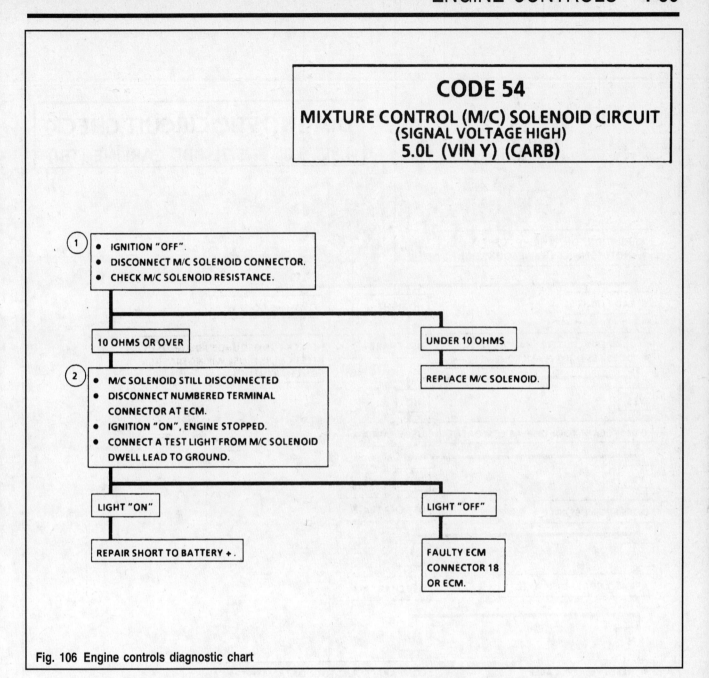

CODE 54
MIXTURE CONTROL (M/C) SOLENOID CIRCUIT
(SIGNAL VOLTAGE HIGH)
5.0L (VIN Y) (CARB)

1
- IGNITION "OFF".
- DISCONNECT M/C SOLENOID CONNECTOR.
- CHECK M/C SOLENOID RESISTANCE.

10 OHMS OR OVER

UNDER 10 OHMS

2
- M/C SOLENOID STILL DISCONNECTED
- DISCONNECT NUMBERED TERMINAL CONNECTOR AT ECM.
- IGNITION "ON", ENGINE STOPPED.
- CONNECT A TEST LIGHT FROM M/C SOLENOID DWELL LEAD TO GROUND.

REPLACE M/C SOLENOID.

LIGHT "ON"

LIGHT "OFF"

REPAIR SHORT TO BATTERY + .

FAULTY ECM CONNECTOR 18 OR ECM.

Fig. 106 Engine controls diagnostic chart

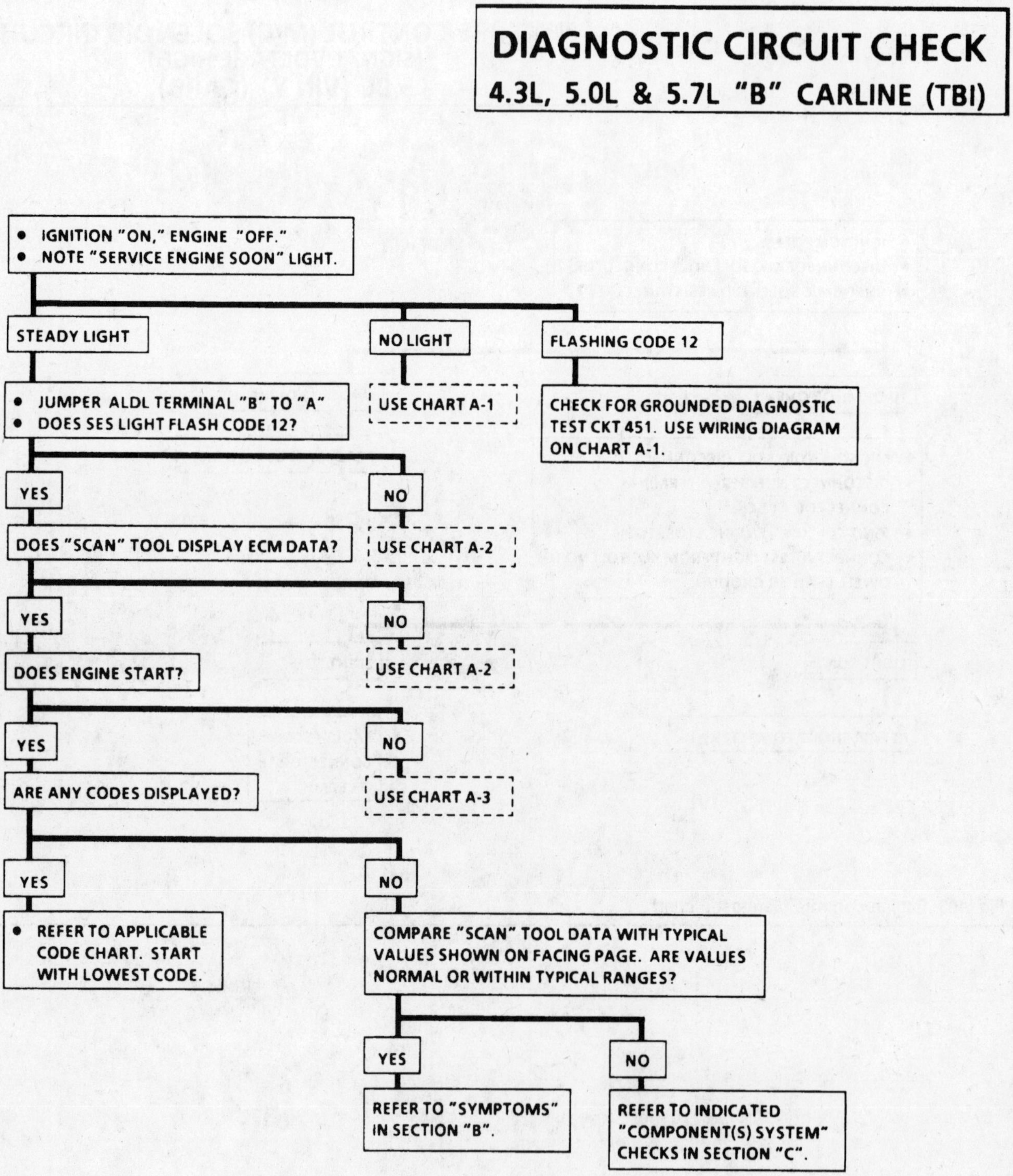

DIAGNOSTIC CIRCUIT CHECK
4.3L, 5.0L & 5.7L "B" CARLINE (TBI)

- IGNITION "ON," ENGINE "OFF."
- NOTE "SERVICE ENGINE SOON" LIGHT.

STEADY LIGHT	NO LIGHT	FLASHING CODE 12

- JUMPER ALDL TERMINAL "B" TO "A"
- DOES SES LIGHT FLASH CODE 12?

USE CHART A-1

CHECK FOR GROUNDED DIAGNOSTIC TEST CKT 451. USE WIRING DIAGRAM ON CHART A-1.

YES / NO

DOES "SCAN" TOOL DISPLAY ECM DATA?

USE CHART A-2

YES / NO

DOES ENGINE START?

USE CHART A-2

YES / NO

ARE ANY CODES DISPLAYED?

USE CHART A-3

YES / NO

- REFER TO APPLICABLE CODE CHART. START WITH LOWEST CODE.

COMPARE "SCAN" TOOL DATA WITH TYPICAL VALUES SHOWN ON FACING PAGE. ARE VALUES NORMAL OR WITHIN TYPICAL RANGES?

YES / NO

REFER TO "SYMPTOMS" IN SECTION "B".

REFER TO INDICATED "COMPONENT(S) SYSTEM" CHECKS IN SECTION "C".

Fig. 107 Engine controls diagnostic chart

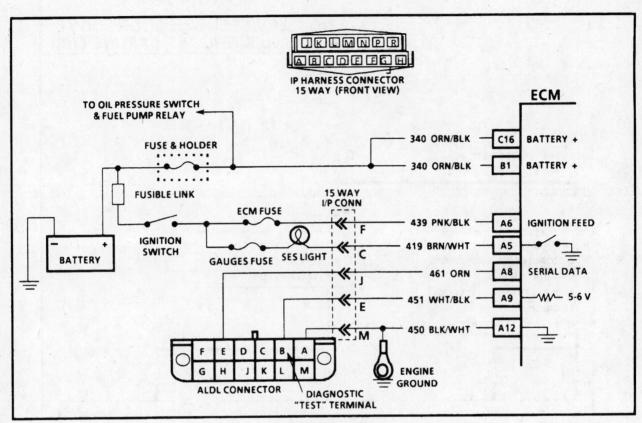

CHART A-1

NO "SERVICE ENGINE SOON" LIGHT
4.3L, 5.0L & 5.7L "B" CARLINE (TBI)

Circuit Description:

There should always be a steady "Service Engine Soon" light, when the ignition is "ON" and engine stopped. Ignition voltage is supplied directly to the light bulb. The Electronic Control Module (ECM) will control the light and turn it "ON" by providing a ground path through CKT 419 to the ECM.

Test Description: Numbers below refer to circled numbers on the diagnostic chart.

1. Battery feed CKT 340 is protected by a 20 amp in-line fuse. If this fuse was blown, refer to wiring diagram on the facing page of Code 54.
2. Using a test light connected to 12 volts, probe each of the system ground circuits to be sure a good ground is present. Refer to the ECM connector terminal end view in front of this section for ECM pin locations of ground circuits.

Diagnostic Aids:

Engine runs OK, check:
- Faulty light bulb
- CKT 419 open
- Gage fuse blown. This will result in no oil, or generator light, seat belt reminder, etc.

Engine cranks but will not run, check:
- Continuous battery - fuse or fusible link open
- ECM ignition fuse open
- Battery CKT 340 to ECM open
- Ignition CKT 439 to ECM open
- Poor connection to ECM

Fig. 108 Engine controls diagnostic chart

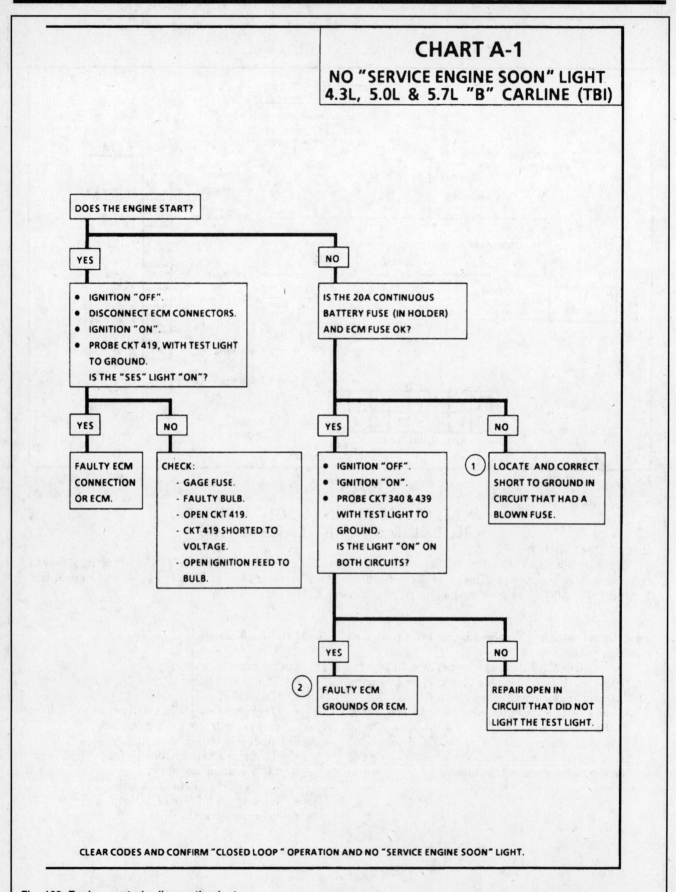

CHART A-1

NO "SERVICE ENGINE SOON" LIGHT
4.3L, 5.0L & 5.7L "B" CARLINE (TBI)

DOES THE ENGINE START?

YES

- IGNITION "OFF".
- DISCONNECT ECM CONNECTORS.
- IGNITION "ON".
- PROBE CKT 419, WITH TEST LIGHT TO GROUND.
  IS THE "SES" LIGHT "ON"?

YES

FAULTY ECM CONNECTION OR ECM.

NO

CHECK:
- GAGE FUSE.
- FAULTY BULB.
- OPEN CKT 419.
- CKT 419 SHORTED TO VOLTAGE.
- OPEN IGNITION FEED TO BULB.

NO

IS THE 20A CONTINUOUS BATTERY FUSE (IN HOLDER) AND ECM FUSE OK?

YES

- IGNITION "OFF".
- IGNITION "ON".
- PROBE CKT 340 & 439 WITH TEST LIGHT TO GROUND.
  IS THE LIGHT "ON" ON BOTH CIRCUITS?

NO

(1) LOCATE AND CORRECT SHORT TO GROUND IN CIRCUIT THAT HAD A BLOWN FUSE.

YES

(2) FAULTY ECM GROUNDS OR ECM.

NO

REPAIR OPEN IN CIRCUIT THAT DID NOT LIGHT THE TEST LIGHT.

CLEAR CODES AND CONFIRM "CLOSED LOOP" OPERATION AND NO "SERVICE ENGINE SOON" LIGHT.

Fig. 109 Engine controls diagnostic chart

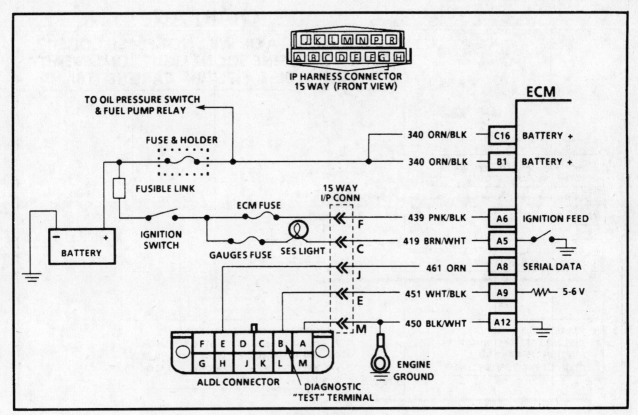

CHART A-2

NO ALDL DATA OR WILL NOT FLASH CODE 12, "SERVICE ENGINE SOON" LIGHT "ON" STEADY 4.3L, 5.0L & 5.7L "B" CARLINE (TBI)

Circuit Description:

There should always be a steady "Service Engine Soon" light, when the ignition is "ON" and engine stopped. Ignition voltage is supplied directly to the light bulb. The electronic control module (ECM) will turn the light "ON" by grounding CKT 419 in the ECM.

With the diagnostic "test" terminal grounded, the light should flash a Code 12, followed by any trouble code(s) stored in memory.

A steady light suggests a short to ground in the light control CKT 419, or an open in diagnostic CKT 451.

Test Description: Numbers below refer to circled numbers on the diagnostic chart.

1. If there is a problem with the ECM that causes a "Scan" tool to not read serial data, the ECM should not flash a Code 12. If Code 12 does flash, be sure that the "Scan" tool is working properly on another vehicle. If the "Scan" tool is functioning properly and CKT 461 is OK, the PROM or ECM may be at fault for the NO ALDL symptom.

2. If the "SES" light goes "OFF," when the ECM connector is disconnected, then CKT 419 is not shorted to ground.

3. This step will check for an open diagnostic CKT 451.

4. At this point, the "Service Engine Soon" light wiring is OK. The problem is a faulty ECM or PROM. If Code 12 does not flash, the ECM should be replaced using the original PROM. Replace the PROM only after trying an ECM, as a defective PROM is an unlikely cause of the problem.

Fig. 110 Engine controls diagnostic chart

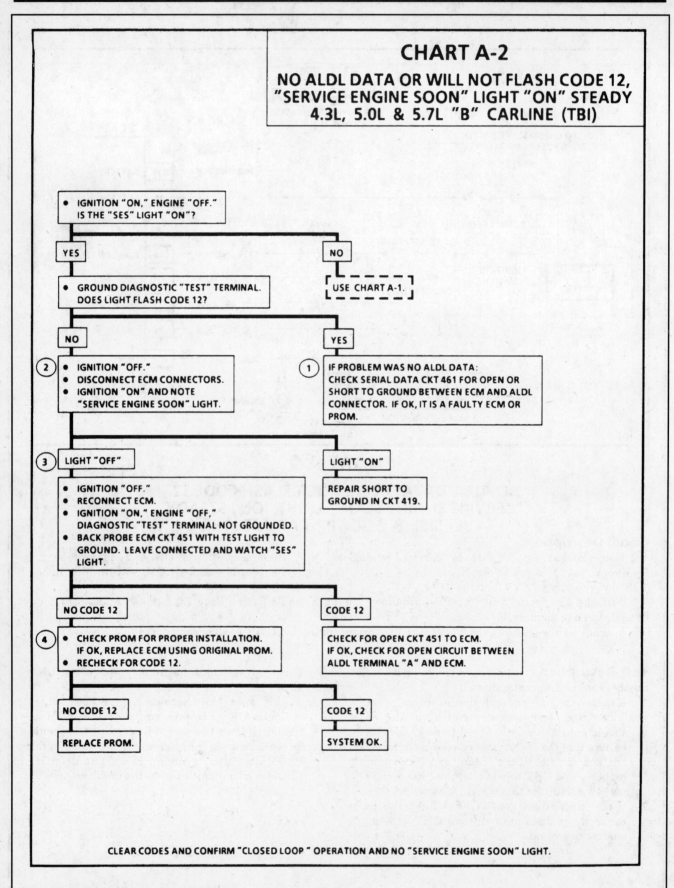

Fig. 111 Engine controls diagnostic chart

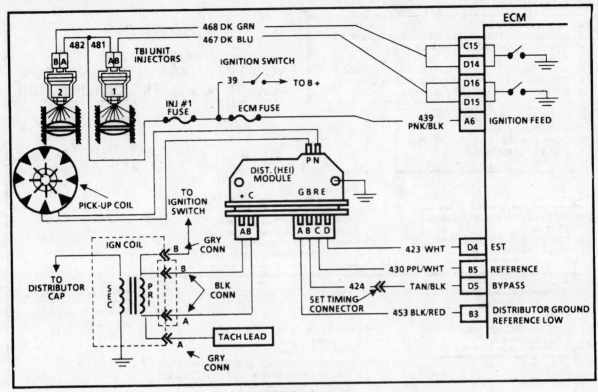

CHART A-3

(Page 1 of 2)
ENGINE CRANKS BUT WILL NOT RUN
4.3L, 5.0L & 5.7L "B" CARLINE (TBI)

Circuit Description:
   This chart assumes that battery condition and engine cranking speed are OK, and there is adequate fuel in the tank.

Test Description: Numbers below refer to circled numbers on the diagnostic chart.
1. A "Service Engine Soon" light "ON" is a basic test to determine if there is a 12 volts supply and ignition 12 volts to ECM. No ALDL may be due to an ECM problem and CHART A-2 will diagnose the ECM. If TPS is over 2.5 volts, the engine may be in the clear flood mode which will cause starting problems.
2. No spark may be caused by one of several components related to the Ignition/EST System. CHART C-4 will address all problems related to the causes of a no spark condition.
3. Fuel spray from the injector(s) indicates that fuel is available. However, the engine could be severely flooded due to too much fuel.
4. While cranking engine, there should be no fuel spray with injector disconnected. Replace an injector if it sprays fuel or drips like a leaking water faucet.
5. The fuel pressure will drop after the fuel pump stops running due to a controlled bleed in the fuel system. Use of the fuel pressure gage will determine if fuel system pressure is enough for engine to start and run. The key may have to be cycled "ON" and "OFF," 2 or more times for accurate reading.
6. No fuel spray from injector indicates a faulty fuel system or no ECM control of injector.
7. This test will determine if the ignition module is not generating the reference pulse, or if the wiring or ECM are at fault. By touching and removing a test light connected to 12 volts on CKT 430, a reference pulse should be generated. If injector test light blinks, the ECM and wiring are OK.

Diagnostic Aids:
- Water or foreign material in the fuel system can cause a no start during freezing weather.
- An EGR valve sticking open can cause a low air/fuel ratio during cranking.
- Fuel pressure: Low fuel pressure can result in a very lean air/fuel ratio. See CHART A-7.
- A grounded CKT 423 (EST) may cause a "No-Start" or a "Start then Stall" condition.

Fig. 112 Engine controls diagnostic chart

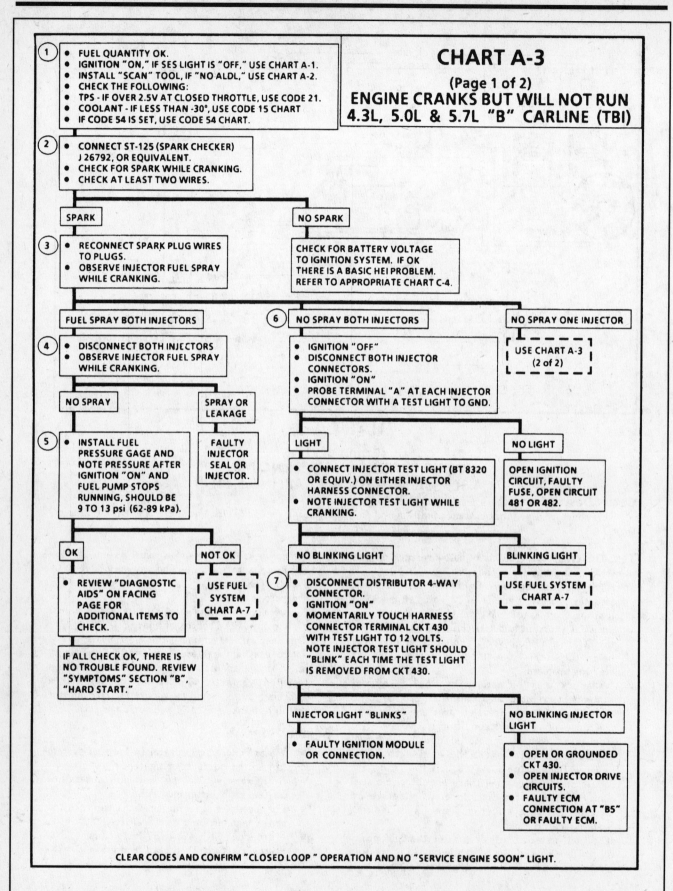

CHART A-3

(Page 1 of 2)
ENGINE CRANKS BUT WILL NOT RUN
4.3L, 5.0L & 5.7L "B" CARLINE (TBI)

①
- FUEL QUANTITY OK.
- IGNITION "ON," IF SES LIGHT IS "OFF," USE CHART A-1.
- INSTALL "SCAN" TOOL, IF "NO ALDL," USE CHART A-2.
- CHECK THE FOLLOWING:
- TPS - IF OVER 2.5V AT CLOSED THROTTLE, USE CODE 21.
- COOLANT - IF LESS THAN -30°, USE CODE 15 CHART
- IF CODE 54 IS SET, USE CODE 54 CHART.

②
- CONNECT ST-125 (SPARK CHECKER) J 26792, OR EQUIVALENT.
- CHECK FOR SPARK WHILE CRANKING.
- CHECK AT LEAST TWO WIRES.

SPARK / NO SPARK

③
- RECONNECT SPARK PLUG WIRES TO PLUGS.
- OBSERVE INJECTOR FUEL SPRAY WHILE CRANKING.

CHECK FOR BATTERY VOLTAGE TO IGNITION SYSTEM. IF OK THERE IS A BASIC HEI PROBLEM. REFER TO APPROPRIATE CHART C-4.

FUEL SPRAY BOTH INJECTORS | **⑥** NO SPRAY BOTH INJECTORS | NO SPRAY ONE INJECTOR

④
- DISCONNECT BOTH INJECTORS
- OBSERVE INJECTOR FUEL SPRAY WHILE CRANKING.

- IGNITION "OFF"
- DISCONNECT BOTH INJECTOR CONNECTORS.
- IGNITION "ON"
- PROBE TERMINAL "A" AT EACH INJECTOR CONNECTOR WITH A TEST LIGHT TO GND.

USE CHART A-3 (2 of 2)

NO SPRAY | SPRAY OR LEAKAGE

⑤
- INSTALL FUEL PRESSURE GAGE AND NOTE PRESSURE AFTER IGNITION "ON" AND FUEL PUMP STOPS RUNNING, SHOULD BE 9 TO 13 psi (62-89 kPa).

FAULTY INJECTOR SEAL OR INJECTOR.

LIGHT | NO LIGHT

- CONNECT INJECTOR TEST LIGHT (BT 8320 OR EQUIV.) ON EITHER INJECTOR HARNESS CONNECTOR.
- NOTE INJECTOR TEST LIGHT WHILE CRANKING.

OPEN IGNITION CIRCUIT, FAULTY FUSE, OPEN CIRCUIT 481 OR 482.

OK | NOT OK

- REVIEW "DIAGNOSTIC AIDS" ON FACING PAGE FOR ADDITIONAL ITEMS TO CHECK.

USE FUEL SYSTEM CHART A-7

NO BLINKING LIGHT | BLINKING LIGHT

⑦
- DISCONNECT DISTRIBUTOR 4-WAY CONNECTOR.
- IGNITION "ON"
- MOMENTARILY TOUCH HARNESS CONNECTOR TERMINAL CKT 430 WITH TEST LIGHT TO 12 VOLTS. NOTE INJECTOR TEST LIGHT SHOULD "BLINK" EACH TIME THE TEST LIGHT IS REMOVED FROM CKT 430.

USE FUEL SYSTEM CHART A-7

IF ALL CHECK OK, THERE IS NO TROUBLE FOUND. REVIEW "SYMPTOMS" SECTION "B", "HARD START."

INJECTOR LIGHT "BLINKS" | NO BLINKING INJECTOR LIGHT

- FAULTY IGNITION MODULE OR CONNECTION.

- OPEN OR GROUNDED CKT 430.
- OPEN INJECTOR DRIVE CIRCUITS.
- FAULTY ECM CONNECTION AT "B5" OR FAULTY ECM.

CLEAR CODES AND CONFIRM "CLOSED LOOP" OPERATION AND NO "SERVICE ENGINE SOON" LIGHT.

Fig. 113 Engine controls diagnostic chart

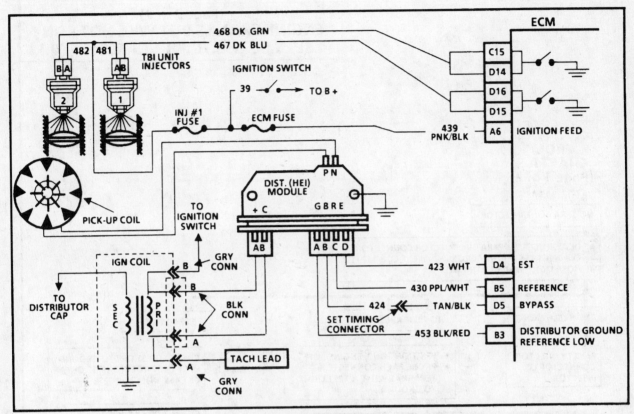

CHART A-3

(Page 2 of 2)
ENGINE CRANKS BUT WILL NOT RUN
4.3L, 5.0L & 5.7L "B" CARLINE (TBI)

Circuit Description:

This chart assumes that battery condition and engine cranking speed are OK, and there is adequate fuel in the tank.

Test Description: Numbers below refer to circled numbers on the diagnostic chart.

1. No fuel spray from one injector indicates a faulty fuel injector or no ECM control of injector. If the test light "blinks" while cranking, then ECM control should be considered OK. Be sure test light makes good contact between connector terminals during test. The light may be a little dim when "blinking." This is due to current draw of the test light. How bright it "blinks" is not important. The test light bulb should be a BT 8320 or equivalent.

2. CKT 481 and CKT 482 supply ignition voltage to the injectors. Probe each connector terminal with a test light to ground. There should be a light "ON" at one terminal of each connector. If the test light confirms ignition voltage at the connector, the ECM injector control CKT 467 or CKT 468 may be open. Reconnect the injector. Using a test light connected to ground, check for a light at the applicable ECM connector terminal. A light at this point indicates that the injector drive circuit involved is OK.

If an ECM repeat failure has occurred, the injector is shorted. Replace the injector and ECM.

Fig. 114 Engine controls diagnostic chart

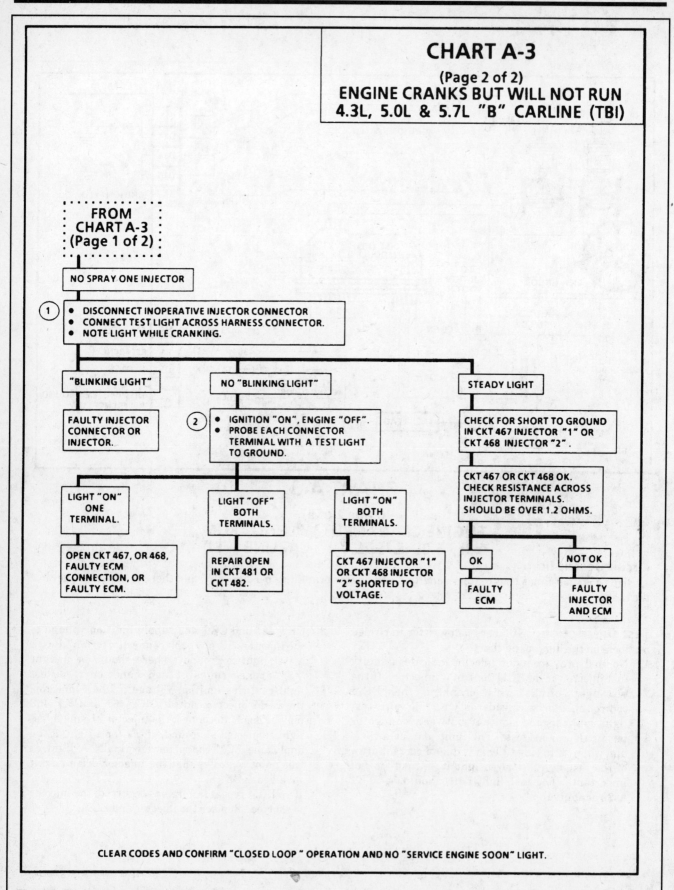

Fig. 115 Engine controls diagnostic chart

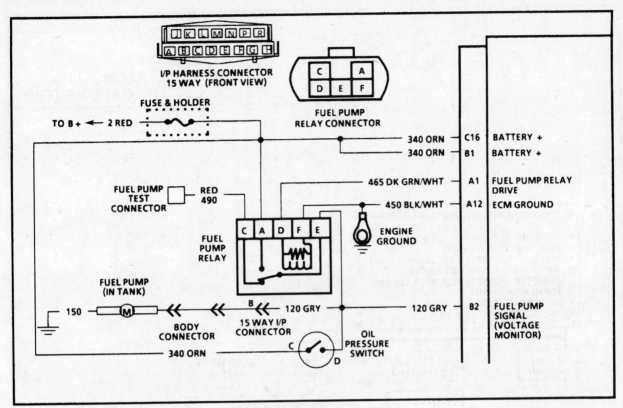

CHART A-7

(Page 1 of 3)
FUEL SYSTEM DIAGNOSIS
4.3L, 5.0L & 5.7L "B" CARLINE (TBI)

Circuit Description:

When the ignition switch is turned "ON," the Electronic Control Module (ECM) will turn "ON" the in-tank fuel pump. It will remain "ON" as long as the engine is cranking or running, and the ECM is receiving ignition reference pulses. If there are no reference pulses, the ECM will shut "OFF" the fuel pump within 2 seconds after key "ON."

The pump will deliver fuel to the TBI unit, where the system pressure is controlled from 62 to 90 kPa (9 to 13 psi). Excess fuel is then returned to the fuel tank.

When the engine is stopped, the fuel pump can be turned "ON" by applying battery voltage to the fuel pump test terminal located on the passenger side of the engine compartment.

Test Description: Numbers below refer to circled numbers on the diagnostic chart.

1. Fuel pressure should be noted while fuel pump is running. Fuel pressure will drop immediately after fuel pump stops running due to a controlled bleed in the fuel system.

The fuel pump test terminal is located on the passenger side of the engine compartment.

Diagnostic Aids:

Improper fuel system pressure can result in one of the following symptoms:
- Extended cranking time before the engine starts.
- Rough idle.
- Low idle speed.
- Cranks, but will not run.
- Code 44.
- Code 45.
- Cuts out, may feel like ignition problem.
- Poor fuel economy, loss of power.
- Hesitation.

Fig. 116 Engine controls diagnostic chart

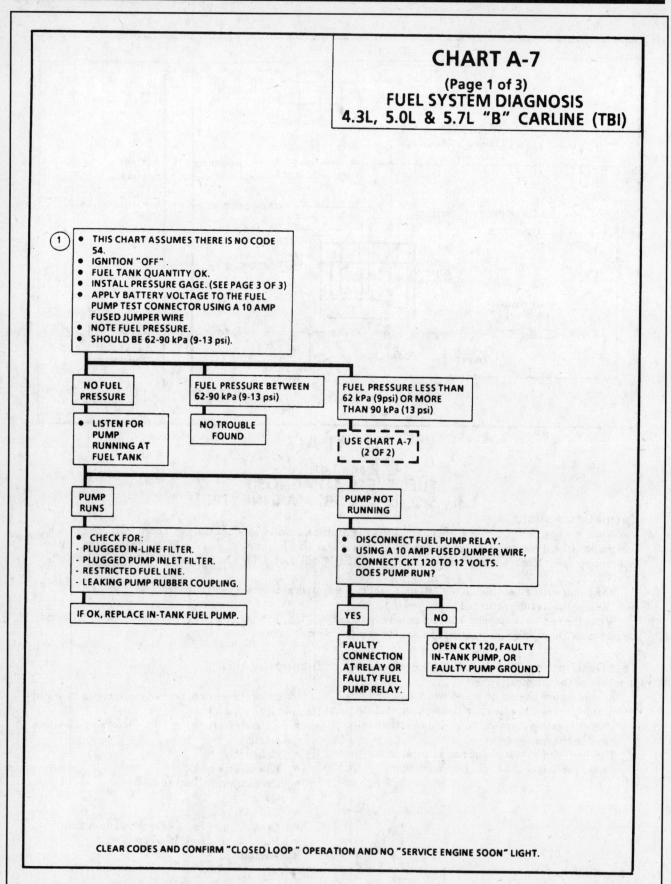

CHART A-7

(Page 1 of 3)
FUEL SYSTEM DIAGNOSIS
4.3L, 5.0L & 5.7L "B" CARLINE (TBI)

1
- THIS CHART ASSUMES THERE IS NO CODE 54.
- IGNITION "OFF".
- FUEL TANK QUANTITY OK.
- INSTALL PRESSURE GAGE. (SEE PAGE 3 OF 3)
- APPLY BATTERY VOLTAGE TO THE FUEL PUMP TEST CONNECTOR USING A 10 AMP FUSED JUMPER WIRE
- NOTE FUEL PRESSURE.
- SHOULD BE 62-90 kPa (9-13 psi).

NO FUEL PRESSURE

FUEL PRESSURE BETWEEN 62-90 kPa (9-13 psi)

FUEL PRESSURE LESS THAN 62 kPa (9psi) OR MORE THAN 90 kPa (13 psi)

- LISTEN FOR PUMP RUNNING AT FUEL TANK

NO TROUBLE FOUND

USE CHART A-7 (2 OF 2)

PUMP RUNS

PUMP NOT RUNNING

- CHECK FOR:
- PLUGGED IN-LINE FILTER.
- PLUGGED PUMP INLET FILTER.
- RESTRICTED FUEL LINE.
- LEAKING PUMP RUBBER COUPLING.

- DISCONNECT FUEL PUMP RELAY.
- USING A 10 AMP FUSED JUMPER WIRE, CONNECT CKT 120 TO 12 VOLTS. DOES PUMP RUN?

IF OK, REPLACE IN-TANK FUEL PUMP.

YES

NO

FAULTY CONNECTION AT RELAY OR FAULTY FUEL PUMP RELAY.

OPEN CKT 120, FAULTY IN-TANK PUMP, OR FAULTY PUMP GROUND.

CLEAR CODES AND CONFIRM "CLOSED LOOP" OPERATION AND NO "SERVICE ENGINE SOON" LIGHT.

Fig. 117 Engine controls diagnostic chart

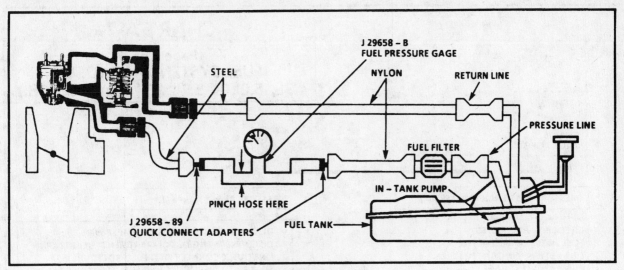

CHART A-7

(Page 2 of 3)
FUEL SYSTEM DIAGNOSIS
4.3L, 5.0L & 5.7L "B" CARLINE (TBI)

Test Description: Numbers below refer to circled numbers on the diagnostic chart.

1. Fuel Pressure less than 62 kPa (9 psi) falls into two areas:
   - Amount of fuel to injectors OK, but pressure is too low, less than 62 kPa (9 psi). System will be lean and may set Code 44. Also, hard starting cold and poor overall performance.
   - Restricted flow causing pressure drop. Normally, a vehicle with a fuel pressure of less than 62 kPa (9 psi) at idle will not be driveable. However, if the pressure drop occurs only while driving, the engine will surge then stop as pressure begins to drop rapidly.

2. Turning the fuel pump "ON" and restricting fuel flow at the fuel pressure gage (as shown) will determine if the fuel pump can supply enough fuel pressure to the injector to operate properly, above 62 kPa (9 psi).

NOTICE: Do not restrict the fuel return line as this may damage the fuel pressure regulator.

3. This test determines if the high fuel pressure is due to a restricted fuel return line or a throttle body pressure regulator problem. Apply battery voltage to the fuel pump test connector only long enough to get an accurate fuel pressure reading.

Fig. 118 Engine controls diagnostic chart

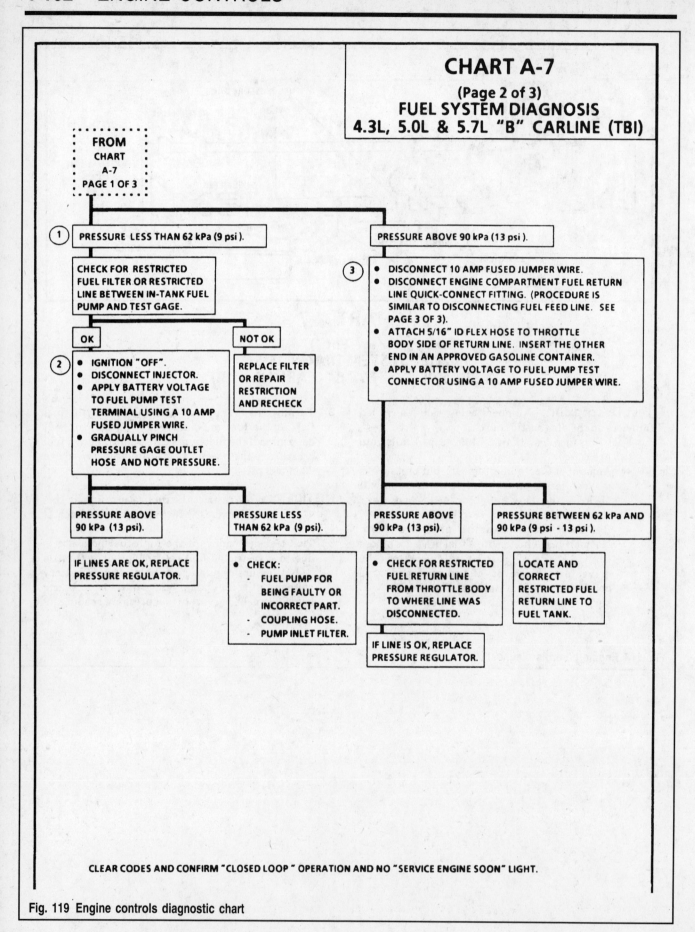

CHART A-7

(Page 2 of 3)
FUEL SYSTEM DIAGNOSIS
4.3L, 5.0L & 5.7L "B" CARLINE (TBI)

FROM CHART A-7 PAGE 1 OF 3

1 — PRESSURE LESS THAN 62 kPa (9 psi).

CHECK FOR RESTRICTED FUEL FILTER OR RESTRICTED LINE BETWEEN IN-TANK FUEL PUMP AND TEST GAGE.

OK

NOT OK

2 —
- IGNITION "OFF".
- DISCONNECT INJECTOR.
- APPLY BATTERY VOLTAGE TO FUEL PUMP TEST TERMINAL USING A 10 AMP FUSED JUMPER WIRE.
- GRADUALLY PINCH PRESSURE GAGE OUTLET HOSE AND NOTE PRESSURE.

REPLACE FILTER OR REPAIR RESTRICTION AND RECHECK

PRESSURE ABOVE 90 kPa (13 psi).

PRESSURE LESS THAN 62 kPa (9 psi).

IF LINES ARE OK, REPLACE PRESSURE REGULATOR.

- CHECK:
  - FUEL PUMP FOR BEING FAULTY OR INCORRECT PART.
  - COUPLING HOSE.
  - PUMP INLET FILTER.

PRESSURE ABOVE 90 kPa (13 psi).

3 —
- DISCONNECT 10 AMP FUSED JUMPER WIRE.
- DISCONNECT ENGINE COMPARTMENT FUEL RETURN LINE QUICK-CONNECT FITTING. (PROCEDURE IS SIMILAR TO DISCONNECTING FUEL FEED LINE. SEE PAGE 3 OF 3).
- ATTACH 5/16" ID FLEX HOSE TO THROTTLE BODY SIDE OF RETURN LINE. INSERT THE OTHER END IN AN APPROVED GASOLINE CONTAINER.
- APPLY BATTERY VOLTAGE TO FUEL PUMP TEST CONNECTOR USING A 10 AMP FUSED JUMPER WIRE.

PRESSURE ABOVE 90 kPa (13 psi).

PRESSURE BETWEEN 62 kPa AND 90 kPa (9 psi - 13 psi).

- CHECK FOR RESTRICTED FUEL RETURN LINE FROM THROTTLE BODY TO WHERE LINE WAS DISCONNECTED.

IF LINE IS OK, REPLACE PRESSURE REGULATOR.

LOCATE AND CORRECT RESTRICTED FUEL RETURN LINE TO FUEL TANK.

CLEAR CODES AND CONFIRM "CLOSED LOOP" OPERATION AND NO "SERVICE ENGINE SOON" LIGHT.

Fig. 119 Engine controls diagnostic chart

FUEL PRESSURE CHECK

Tools Required: J 29658-B - Fuel Pressure Gage
J 29658-89 - Fuel Pressure Quick Connect Adapters
J 37088 - Fuel Line Quick-Connect Separators

CAUTION: To Reduce the Risk of Fire and Personal Injury:
- It is necessary to relieve fuel system pressure before connecting a fuel pressure gage.
- A small amount of fuel may be released when disconnecting the fuel lines. Cover fuel line fittings with a shop towel before disconnecting, to catch any fuel that may leak out. Place towel in approved container when disconnect is completed.
- Do not pinch or restrict nylon fuel lines to avoid severing, which could cause a fuel leak.

NOTICE: • If nylon fuel lines become kinked, and cannot be straightened, they must be replaced.

1. Disconnect negative battery terminal.
2. Loosen fuel filler cap to relieve fuel tank pressure. (Do not tighten at this time.)
3. Locate engine compartment fuel feed quick-connect fitting.
4. Grasp both ends of fitting, twist female end $\frac{1}{4}$ turn in each direction to loosen any dirt in fitting.

CAUTION: Safety glasses must be worn when using compressed air, as flying dirt particles may cause eye injury.

5. Using compressed air, blow dirt out of quick-connect fitting.
6. Choose correct tool from separator tool set J 37088 for size of fitting. Insert tool into female end of connector, then push inward to release male connector.
7. Connect gage quick-connect adapters J 29658-89 to fuel pressure gage J 29658-B.

CAUTION: To Reduce the Risk of Fire and Personal Injury: Before connecting fuel line quick-connect fittings, always apply a few drops of clean engine oil to the male tube ends. This will ensure proper reconnection and prevent a possible fuel leak. (During normal operation, the O-rings located inside the female connector will swell and may prevent proper reconnection if not lubricated.)

8. Lubricate the male tube end of the fuel line and the gage adpater with engine oil.
9. Connect fuel pressure gage.
   - Push connectors together to cause the retaining tabs/fingers to snap into place.
   - Once installed, pull on both ends of each connection to make sure it is secure.
10. Connect negative battery terminal.
11. Check fuel pressure.
12. Disconnect negative battery terminal.
13. Disconnect fuel pressure gage.
14. Lubricate the male tube end of the fuel line, and reconnect quick-connect fitting.
   - Push connector together to cause the retaining tabs/fingers to snap into place.
   - Once installed, pull on both ends of connection to make sure it is secure.
15. Tighten fuel filler cap.
16. Connect negative battery terminal.
17. Cycle ignition "ON" and "OFF" twice, waiting ten seconds between cycles, then check for fuel leaks.

Fig. 120 Engine controls diagnostic chart

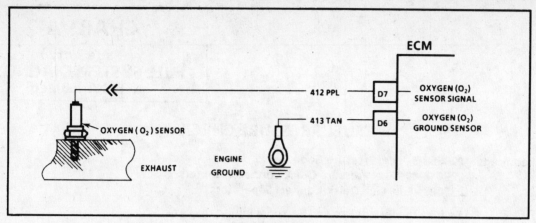

CODE 13

OXYGEN SENSOR CIRCUIT
(OPEN CIRCUIT)
4.3L, 5.0L & 5.7L "B" CARLINE (TBI)

Circuit Description:

The ECM supplies a voltage of about .45 volt between terminals "D7" and "D6". (If measured with a 10 megohm digital voltmeter, this may read as low as .32 volt). The Oxygen (O_2) sensor varies the voltage within a range of about 1 volt if the exhaust is rich, down through about .10 volt if the exhaust is lean.

The sensor is like an open circuit and produces no voltage when it is below 360°C (600°F). An open sensor circuit or cold sensor causes "Open Loop" operation.

Test Description: Numbers below refer to circled numbers on the diagnostic chart.

1. Code 13 will set:
   - Engine at normal operating temperature
   - At least 2 minutes engine time after start
   - O_2 signal voltage steady between .35 and .55 volt.
   - Rpm above 1600
   - Throttle position sensor signal above 5% (about .3 volt above closed throttle voltage).
   - All conditions must be met for about 60 seconds.
     If the conditions for a Code 13 exist, the system will not go "Closed Loop."
2. This will determine if the sensor is at fault or the wiring or ECM is the cause of the Code 13.

3. To perform this test, use only a high impedance digital volt ohmmeter. This test checks the continuity of CKT 412 and CKT 413. If CKT 413 is open, the ECM voltage on CKT 412 will be over .60 volt (600 mV).

Diagnostic Aids:

Normal "Scan" tool voltage readings varies between 100 mV to 999 mV (.1 and 1.0 volt), while in "Closed Loop." Code 13 sets in one minute if voltage remains between .35 and .55 volt, the system will go "Open Loop" in about 15 seconds.

Refer to "Intermittents" in Section "B".

Fig. 121 Engine controls diagnostic chart

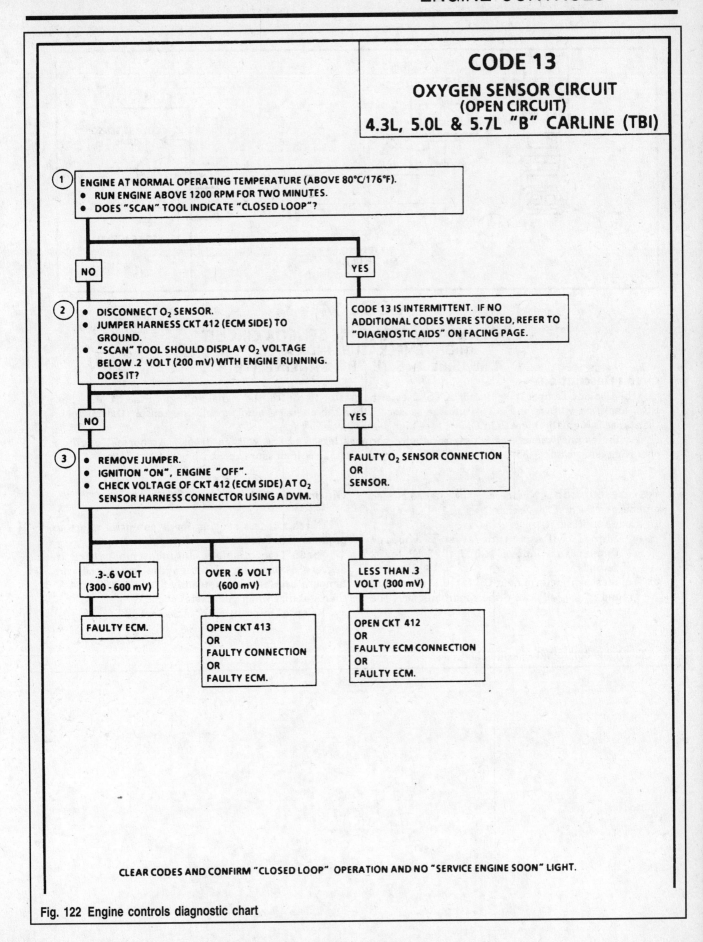

CODE 13

OXYGEN SENSOR CIRCUIT
(OPEN CIRCUIT)
4.3L, 5.0L & 5.7L "B" CARLINE (TBI)

1. ENGINE AT NORMAL OPERATING TEMPERATURE (ABOVE 80°C/176°F).
   - RUN ENGINE ABOVE 1200 RPM FOR TWO MINUTES.
   - DOES "SCAN" TOOL INDICATE "CLOSED LOOP"?

NO

YES

2. - DISCONNECT O₂ SENSOR.
   - JUMPER HARNESS CKT 412 (ECM SIDE) TO GROUND.
   - "SCAN" TOOL SHOULD DISPLAY O₂ VOLTAGE BELOW .2 VOLT (200 mV) WITH ENGINE RUNNING. DOES IT?

CODE 13 IS INTERMITTENT. IF NO ADDITIONAL CODES WERE STORED, REFER TO "DIAGNOSTIC AIDS" ON FACING PAGE.

NO

YES

3. - REMOVE JUMPER.
   - IGNITION "ON", ENGINE "OFF".
   - CHECK VOLTAGE OF CKT 412 (ECM SIDE) AT O₂ SENSOR HARNESS CONNECTOR USING A DVM.

FAULTY O₂ SENSOR CONNECTION
OR
SENSOR.

.3-.6 VOLT (300 - 600 mV)

OVER .6 VOLT (600 mV)

LESS THAN .3 VOLT (300 mV)

FAULTY ECM.

OPEN CKT 413
OR
FAULTY CONNECTION
OR
FAULTY ECM.

OPEN CKT 412
OR
FAULTY ECM CONNECTION
OR
FAULTY ECM.

CLEAR CODES AND CONFIRM "CLOSED LOOP" OPERATION AND NO "SERVICE ENGINE SOON" LIGHT.

Fig. 122 Engine controls diagnostic chart

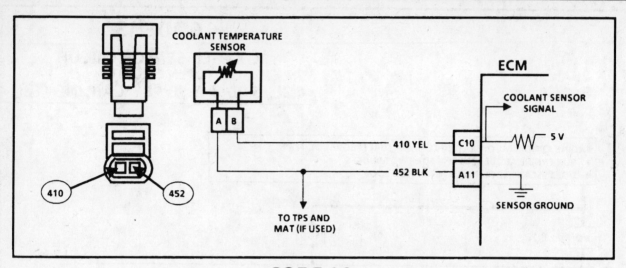

CODE 14

COOLANT TEMPERATURE SENSOR CIRCUIT
(HIGH TEMPERATURE INDICATED)
4.3L, 5.0L & 5.7L "B" CARLINE (TBI)

Circuit Description:

The Coolant Temperature Sensor (CTS) uses a thermistor to control the signal voltage to the ECM. The ECM applies a voltage on CKT 410 to the sensor. When the engine coolant is cold the sensor (thermistor) resistance is high, therefore the ECM will see high signal voltage.

As the engine warms, the sensor resistance becomes less, and the voltage drops. At normal engine operating temperature (85°C - 95°C or 185°F - 203°F) the voltage will measure about 1.5 to 2.0 volts.

Test Description: Numbers below refer to circled numbers on the diagnostic chart.
1. Code 14 will set if:
   - Signal voltage indicates a coolant temperature above 135°C (275°F) for 2 seconds.
2. This test will determine if CKT 410 is shorted to ground which will cause the conditions for Code 14.

Diagnostic Aids:

Check harness routing for a potential short to ground in CKT 410.

"Scan" tool displays engine temperature in degrees centigrade. After engine is started, the temperature should rise steadily to about 90°C (194°F) then stabilize when thermostat opens.

Refer to "Intermittents" in Section "B".

Fig. 123 Engine controls diagnostic chart

CODE 14
COOLANT TEMPERATURE SENSOR CIRCUIT
(HIGH TEMPERATURE INDICATED)
4.3L, 5.0L & 5.7L "B" CARLINE (TBI)

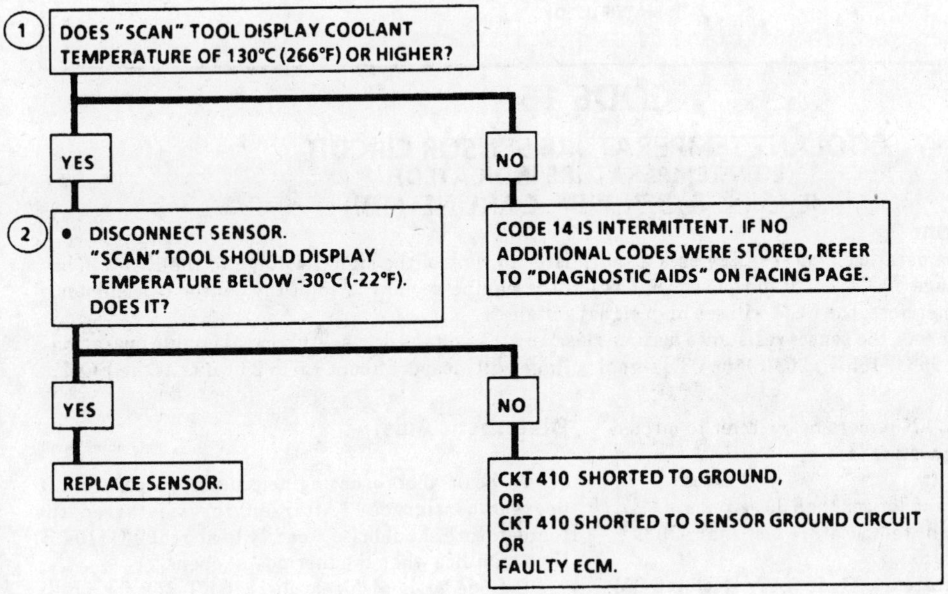

1. DOES "SCAN" TOOL DISPLAY COOLANT TEMPERATURE OF 130°C (266°F) OR HIGHER?

YES

NO

2. • DISCONNECT SENSOR. "SCAN" TOOL SHOULD DISPLAY TEMPERATURE BELOW -30°C (-22°F). DOES IT?

CODE 14 IS INTERMITTENT. IF NO ADDITIONAL CODES WERE STORED, REFER TO "DIAGNOSTIC AIDS" ON FACING PAGE.

YES

NO

REPLACE SENSOR.

CKT 410 SHORTED TO GROUND,
OR
CKT 410 SHORTED TO SENSOR GROUND CIRCUIT
OR
FAULTY ECM.

DIAGNOSTIC AID

COOLANT SENSOR TEMPERATURE VS. RESISTANCE VALUES (APPROXIMATE)		
°F	°C	OHMS
210	100	185
160	70	450
100	38	1,800
70	20	3,400
40	4	7,500
20	-7	13,500
0	-18	25,000
-40	-40	100,700

CLEAR CODES AND CONFIRM "CLOSED LOOP" OPERATION AND NO "SERVICE ENGINE SOON" LIGHT.

Fig. 124 Engine controls diagnostic chart

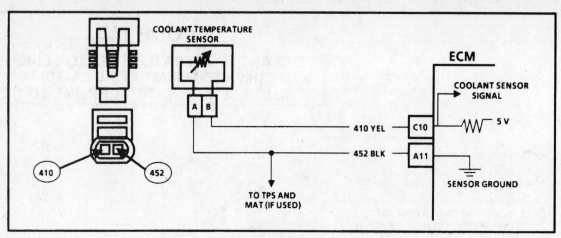

CODE 15

COOLANT TEMPERATURE SENSOR CIRCUIT
(LOW TEMPERATURE INDICATED)
4.3L, 5.0L & 5.7L "B" CARLINE (TBI)

Circuit Description:

The Coolant Temperature Sensor (CTS) uses a thermistor to control the signal voltage to the ECM. The ECM applies a voltage on CKT 410 to the sensor. When the engine coolant is cold, the sensor (thermistor) resistance is high, therefore, the ECM will see high signal voltage.

As the engine warms, the sensor resistance becomes less and the voltage drops. At normal engine operating temperature (85°C - 95°C / 185°F - 203°F) the CTS signal voltage will measure about 1.5 to 2.0 volts at the ECM.

Test Description: Numbers below refer to circled numbers on the diagnostic chart.

1. Code 15 will set if:
   - Engine running longer than 30 seconds
   - Engine coolant temperature less than -30°C (-22°F), for 3 seconds.
2. This test simulates a Code 14. If the ECM recognizes the low signal voltage, (high temperature) and "Scan" tool reads 130°C (266°F) or above, the ECM and wiring are OK.
3. This test will determine if CKT 410 is open. There should be 5 volts present at sensor connector if measured with a DVM.

Diagnostic Aids:

A "Scan" tool reads engine coolant temperature in degrees centigrade. After engine is started the temperature should rise steadily to about 90°C (194°F) then stabilize when the thermostat opens.

If Code 21 is also set, check CKT 452 for faulty wiring or connections. Check terminals at sensor for good contact.

Fig. 125 Engine controls diagnostic chart

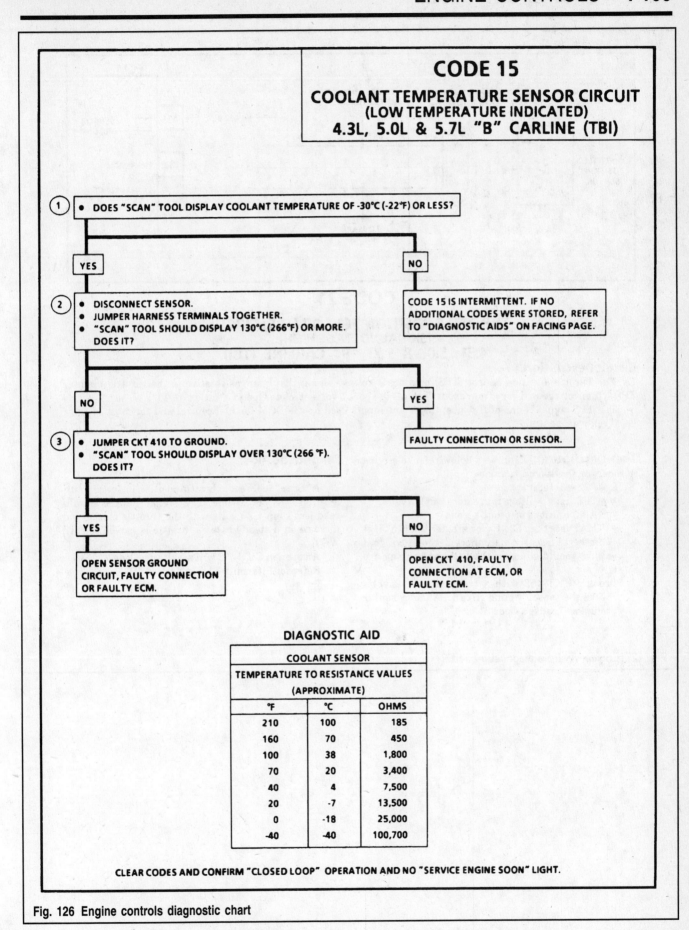

CODE 15
COOLANT TEMPERATURE SENSOR CIRCUIT
(LOW TEMPERATURE INDICATED)
4.3L, 5.0L & 5.7L "B" CARLINE (TBI)

1. • DOES "SCAN" TOOL DISPLAY COOLANT TEMPERATURE OF -30°C (-22°F) OR LESS?

YES

NO

2. • DISCONNECT SENSOR.
   • JUMPER HARNESS TERMINALS TOGETHER.
   • "SCAN" TOOL SHOULD DISPLAY 130°C (266°F) OR MORE.
     DOES IT?

CODE 15 IS INTERMITTENT. IF NO ADDITIONAL CODES WERE STORED, REFER TO "DIAGNOSTIC AIDS" ON FACING PAGE.

NO

YES

3. • JUMPER CKT 410 TO GROUND.
   • "SCAN" TOOL SHOULD DISPLAY OVER 130°C (266 °F).
     DOES IT?

FAULTY CONNECTION OR SENSOR.

YES

NO

OPEN SENSOR GROUND CIRCUIT, FAULTY CONNECTION OR FAULTY ECM.

OPEN CKT 410, FAULTY CONNECTION AT ECM, OR FAULTY ECM.

DIAGNOSTIC AID

COOLANT SENSOR		
TEMPERATURE TO RESISTANCE VALUES (APPROXIMATE)		
°F	°C	OHMS
210	100	185
160	70	450
100	38	1,800
70	20	3,400
40	4	7,500
20	-7	13,500
0	-18	25,000
-40	-40	100,700

CLEAR CODES AND CONFIRM "CLOSED LOOP" OPERATION AND NO "SERVICE ENGINE SOON" LIGHT.

Fig. 126 Engine controls diagnostic chart

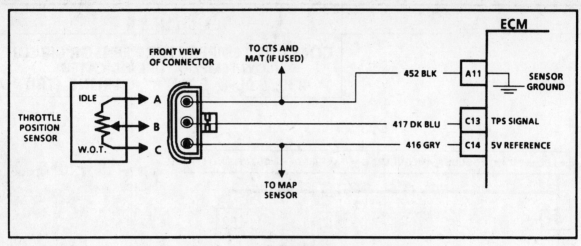

CODE 21
THROTTLE POSITION SENSOR (TPS) CIRCUIT
(SIGNAL VOLTAGE HIGH)
4.3L, 5.0L & 5.7L "B" CARLINE (TBI)

Circuit Description:

The Throttle Position Sensor (TPS) provides a voltage signal that changes relative to the throttle blade. TPS signal voltage will vary from about .5 at idle to about 5 volts at Wide Open Throttle (WOT).

The TPS signal is one of the most important inputs used by the ECM for fuel control and for most of the ECM controlled outputs.

Test Description: Numbers below refer to circled numbers on the diagnostic chart.

1. Code 21 will set if:
   - TPS signal voltage is greater than 2.5 volts
   - All conditions met for 8 seconds
   - MAP less than 52 kPa (or greater than 15" Hg)
2. With the TPS sensor disconnected, the TPS signal voltage should go low if the ECM and wiring are OK.
3. Probing CKT 452 with a test light to 12 volts checks the sensor ground circuit. A faulty sensor ground will cause a Code 21.

Diagnostic Aids:

A "Scan" tool reads throttle position in volts. With ignition "ON" or at idle, TPS signal voltage should read less than 1.25 volts with the throttle closed and increase at a steady rate as throttle is moved toward WOT.

An open in CKT 452 will result in a Code 21.
Refer to "Intermittents" in Section "B".

Fig. 127 Engine controls diagnostic chart

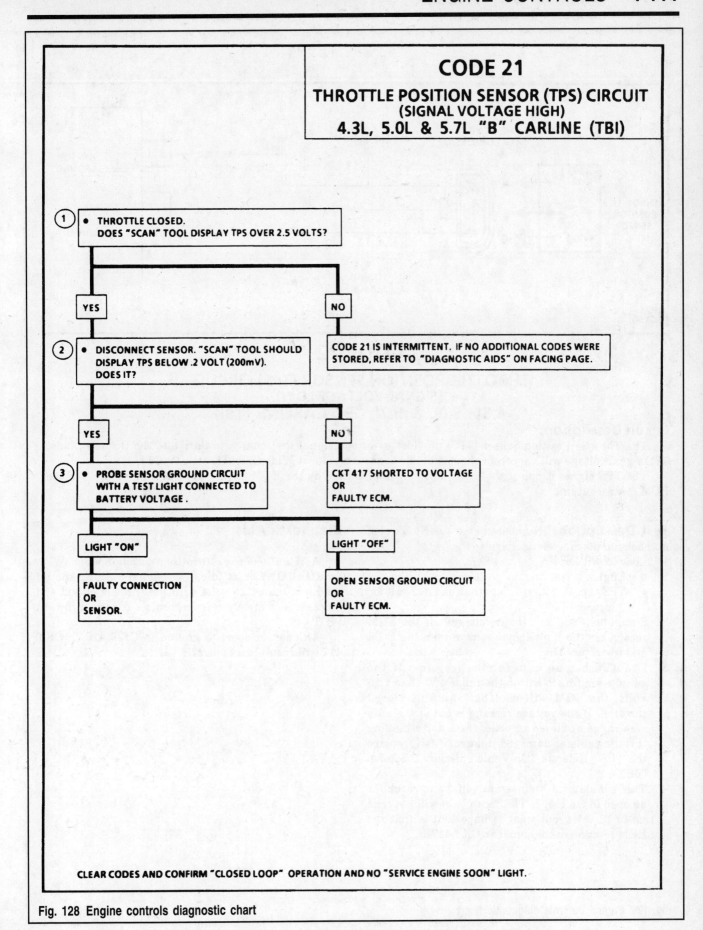

CODE 21
THROTTLE POSITION SENSOR (TPS) CIRCUIT
(SIGNAL VOLTAGE HIGH)
4.3L, 5.0L & 5.7L "B" CARLINE (TBI)

1 • THROTTLE CLOSED.
DOES "SCAN" TOOL DISPLAY TPS OVER 2.5 VOLTS?

YES

NO

2 • DISCONNECT SENSOR. "SCAN" TOOL SHOULD DISPLAY TPS BELOW .2 VOLT (200mV). DOES IT?

CODE 21 IS INTERMITTENT. IF NO ADDITIONAL CODES WERE STORED, REFER TO "DIAGNOSTIC AIDS" ON FACING PAGE.

YES

NO

3 • PROBE SENSOR GROUND CIRCUIT WITH A TEST LIGHT CONNECTED TO BATTERY VOLTAGE.

CKT 417 SHORTED TO VOLTAGE
OR
FAULTY ECM.

LIGHT "ON"

LIGHT "OFF"

FAULTY CONNECTION
OR
SENSOR.

OPEN SENSOR GROUND CIRCUIT
OR
FAULTY ECM.

CLEAR CODES AND CONFIRM "CLOSED LOOP" OPERATION AND NO "SERVICE ENGINE SOON" LIGHT.

Fig. 128 Engine controls diagnostic chart

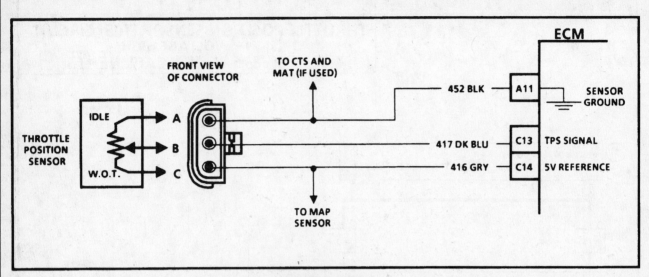

CODE 22

THROTTLE POSITION SENSOR (TPS) CIRCUIT
(SIGNAL VOLTAGE LOW)
4.3L, 5.0L & 5.7L "B" CARLINE (TBI)

Circuit Description:

The Throttle Position Sensor (TPS) provides a voltage signal that changes relative to the throttle blade. TPS signal voltage will vary from about .5 at idle to about 5 volts at Wide Open Throttle (WOT).

The TPS signal is one of the most important inputs used by the ECM for fuel control and for most of the ECM control outputs.

Test Description: Numbers below refer to circled numbers on the diagnostic chart.

1. Code 22 will set if:
   - Engine is running
   - TPS signal voltage is less than about .2 volt for 3 seconds.
2. Simulates Code 21: (high voltage). If the ECM recognizes the high signal voltage then the ECM and wiring are OK.
3. The TPS has an auto zeroing feature. If the voltage reading is within the range of 0.45 to 1.25 volts, the ECM will use that value as closed throttle. If the voltage reading is out of the auto zero range at closed throttle, check for a binding throttle cable or damaged linkage, if OK, replace the TPS. Refer to "On-Vehicle Service," Section "6E2-C1"
4. This simulates a high signal voltage to check for an open in CKT 417. The "Scan" tool will not read up to 12 volts, but what is important is that the ECM recognizes the signal on CKT 417.

Diagnostic Aids:

A "Scan" tool reads throttle position in volts. With ignition "ON" or at idle, TPS signal voltage should read less than 1.25 volts with the throttle closed and increase at a steady rate as throttle is moved toward WOT.

An open or short to ground in CKT 416 or CKT 417 will result in a Code 22.

Fig. 129 Engine controls diagnostic chart

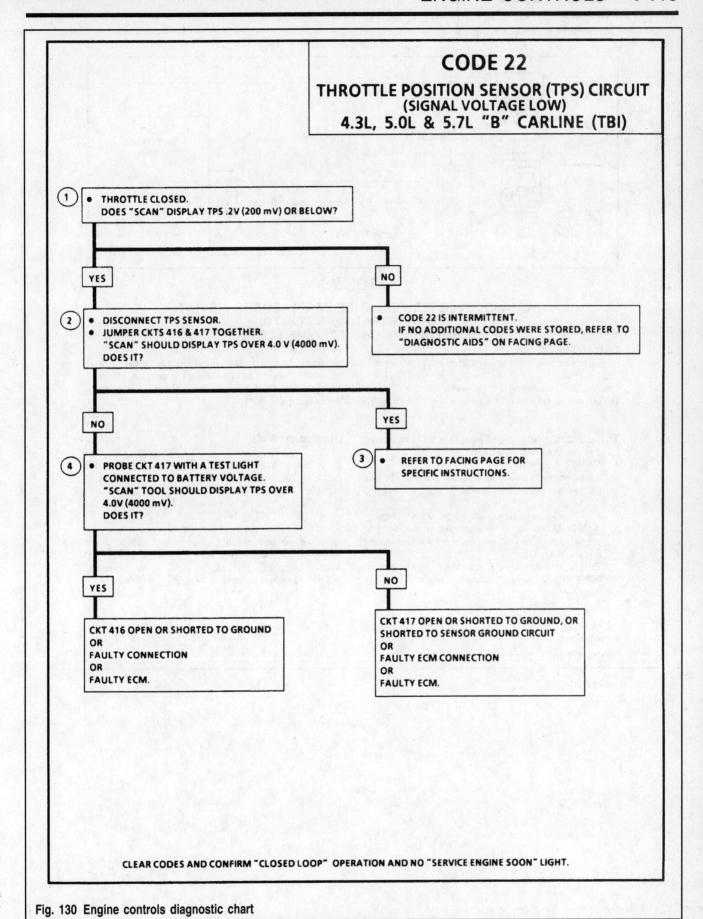

Fig. 130 Engine controls diagnostic chart

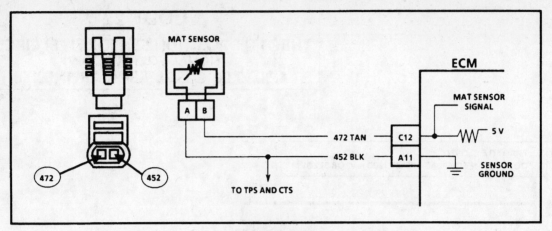

CODE 23

MANIFOLD AIR TEMPERATURE (MAT) SENSOR CIRCUIT
(LOW TEMPERATURE INDICATED)
5.0L & 5.7L "B" CARLINE (TBI)

Circuit Description:

The Manifold Air Temperature (MAT) sensor uses a thermistor to control the signal voltage to the ECM. The ECM applies a voltage (about 5 volts) on CKT 472 to the sensor. When the manifold air is cold, the sensor (thermistor) resistance is high, therefore, the ECM will see a high signal voltage. If the manifold air is warm, the sensor (thermistor) resistance is low, therefore, the ECM will see a low voltage.

Test Description: Numbers below refer to circled numbers on the diagnostic chart.

1. Code 23 will set if:
   - A signal voltage indicates a manifold air temperature below -30°C (-22°F) for 12 seconds.
   - Time since engine start is 1 minute or longer
2. A Code 23 will set, due to an open sensor, wire or connection. This test will determine if the wiring and ECM are OK.
3. This will determine if the MAT sensor signal (CKT 472) or the MAT sensor ground (CKT 452) is open.

Diagnostic Aids:

A "Scan" tool indicates the temperature of the air in the air cleaner because the MAT sensor is mounted in the air cleaner.

Carefully check harness and connections for possible open CKT 472 or CKT 452.

If the engine has been allowed to sit overnight, the manifold air temperature and coolant temperature values should read within a few degrees of each other. After the engine is started, the MAT will increase due to Thermac operation and underhood temperatures.

Fig. 131 Engine controls diagnostic chart

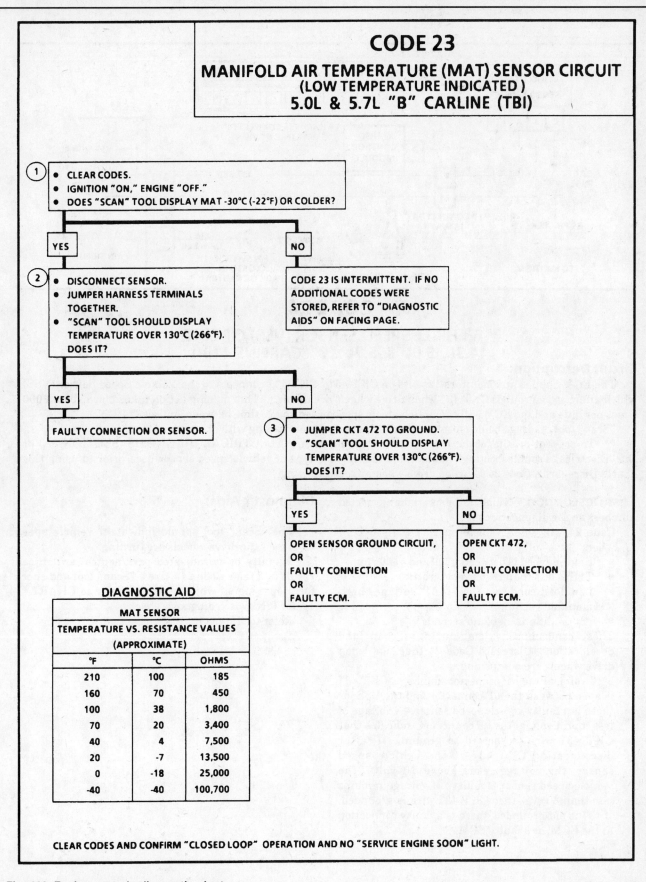

CODE 23
MANIFOLD AIR TEMPERATURE (MAT) SENSOR CIRCUIT
(LOW TEMPERATURE INDICATED)
5.0L & 5.7L "B" CARLINE (TBI)

1
- CLEAR CODES.
- IGNITION "ON," ENGINE "OFF."
- DOES "SCAN" TOOL DISPLAY MAT -30°C (-22°F) OR COLDER?

YES

NO

2
- DISCONNECT SENSOR.
- JUMPER HARNESS TERMINALS TOGETHER.
- "SCAN" TOOL SHOULD DISPLAY TEMPERATURE OVER 130°C (266°F). DOES IT?

CODE 23 IS INTERMITTENT. IF NO ADDITIONAL CODES WERE STORED, REFER TO "DIAGNOSTIC AIDS" ON FACING PAGE.

YES

NO

FAULTY CONNECTION OR SENSOR.

3
- JUMPER CKT 472 TO GROUND.
- "SCAN" TOOL SHOULD DISPLAY TEMPERATURE OVER 130°C (266°F). DOES IT?

YES

NO

OPEN SENSOR GROUND CIRCUIT,
OR
FAULTY CONNECTION
OR
FAULTY ECM.

OPEN CKT 472,
OR
FAULTY CONNECTION
OR
FAULTY ECM.

DIAGNOSTIC AID

MAT SENSOR		
TEMPERATURE VS. RESISTANCE VALUES (APPROXIMATE)		
°F	°C	OHMS
210	100	185
160	70	450
100	38	1,800
70	20	3,400
40	4	7,500
20	-7	13,500
0	-18	25,000
-40	-40	100,700

CLEAR CODES AND CONFIRM "CLOSED LOOP" OPERATION AND NO "SERVICE ENGINE SOON" LIGHT.

Fig. 132 Engine controls diagnostic chart

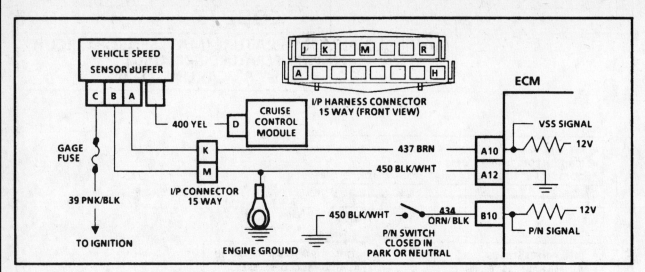

CODE 24

VEHICLE SPEED SENSOR (VSS) CIRCUIT
4.3L, 5.0L & 5.7L "B" CARLINE (TBI)

Circuit Description:

The ECM applies and monitors 12 volts on CKT 437. CKT 437 connects to the Vehicle Speed Sensor (VSS) which alternately grounds CKT 437 when drive wheels are turning. This pulsing action takes place about 2000 times per mile and the ECM will calculate vehicle speed based on the time between "pulses."

"Scan" tool reading should closely match with speedometer reading with drive wheels turning.

** To prevent misdiagnosis, the technician should review ELECTRICAL DIAGNOSIS (SECTION 8A) or the "Electrical Troubleshooting" manual and identify the type of vehicle speed sensor used prior to using this chart. Disregard a Code 24 set when drive wheels are not turning.

Test Description: Numbers below refer to circled numbers on the diagnostic chart.

1. Code 24 will set if vehicle speed equals 0 mph when:
   - Engine speed is between 1200 and 4400 rpm
   - TPS is less than 2% (closed throttle)
   - Low load condition (low MAP voltage, high manifold vacuum).
   - All conditions met for 5 seconds.

   These conditions are met during a road load deceleration. Disregard Code 24 that sets when drive wheels are not turning.

2. 8-12 volts, at the I/P connector, indicates CKT 437 is open between the I/P connector and the VSS, or there is a faulty vehicle speed sensor. A voltage of less than 1 volt, at the I/P connector, indicates that CKT 437 wire is shorted to ground. If, after disconnecting CKT 437 at the vehicle speed sensor, the voltage reads above 10 volts, the vehicle speed sensor is faulty. If voltage remains less than 8 volts, then CKT 437 wire is grounded. If 437 is not grounded, there is a faulty connection at the ECM, or a faulty ECM.

Diagnostic Aids:

The "Scan" tool should indicate a vehicle speed whenever the drive wheels are turning.

A faulty or misadjusted park/neutral switch can result in a false Code 24. Use a "Scan" tool and check for proper signal while in drive. Refer to CHART C-1A for P/N switch diagnosis check.

Refer to "Intermittents" in Section "B".

Fig. 133 Engine controls diagnostic chart

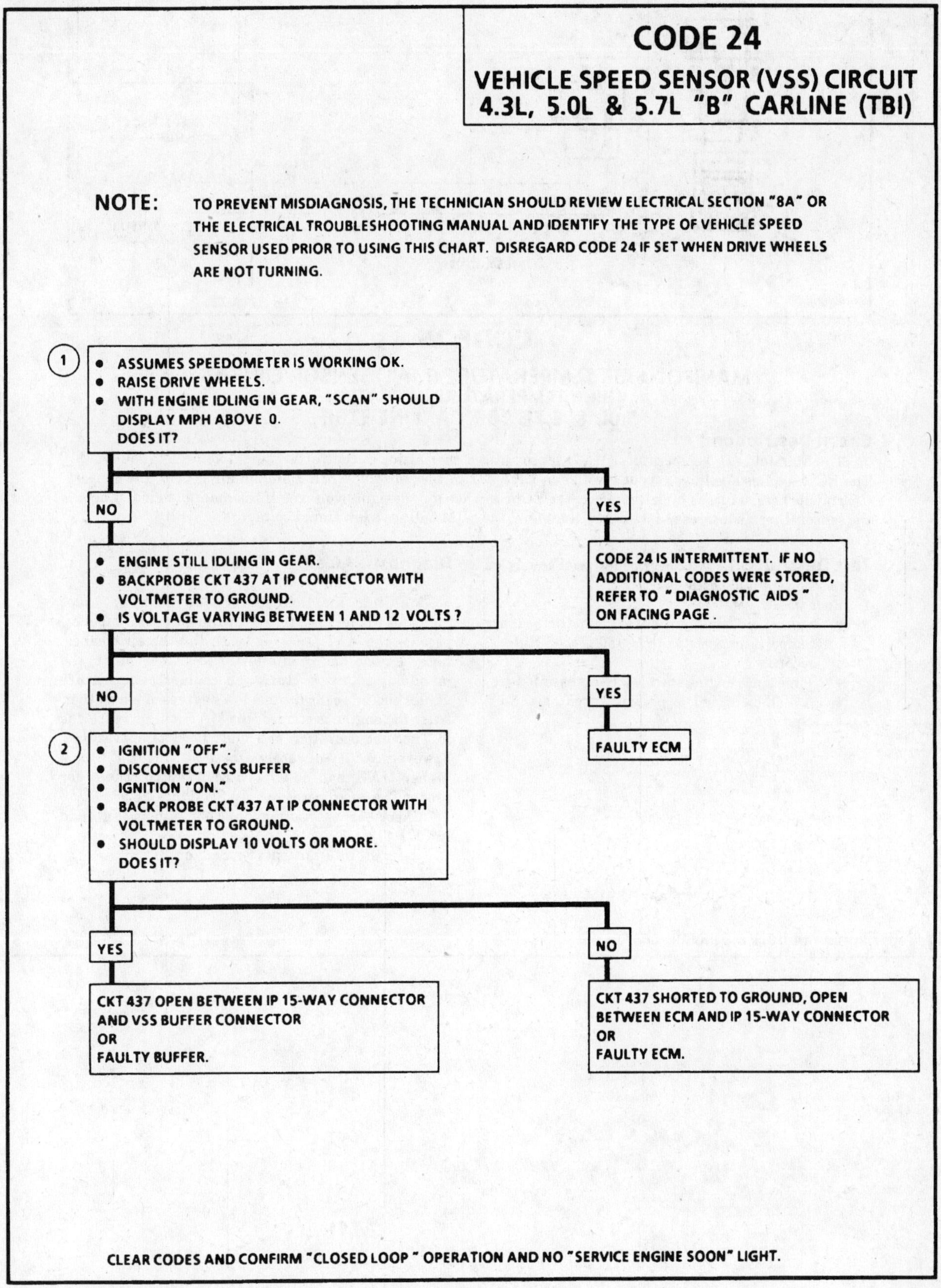

CODE 24
VEHICLE SPEED SENSOR (VSS) CIRCUIT
4.3L, 5.0L & 5.7L "B" CARLINE (TBI)

NOTE: TO PREVENT MISDIAGNOSIS, THE TECHNICIAN SHOULD REVIEW ELECTRICAL SECTION "8A" OR THE ELECTRICAL TROUBLESHOOTING MANUAL AND IDENTIFY THE TYPE OF VEHICLE SPEED SENSOR USED PRIOR TO USING THIS CHART. DISREGARD CODE 24 IF SET WHEN DRIVE WHEELS ARE NOT TURNING.

1
- ASSUMES SPEEDOMETER IS WORKING OK.
- RAISE DRIVE WHEELS.
- WITH ENGINE IDLING IN GEAR, "SCAN" SHOULD DISPLAY MPH ABOVE 0. DOES IT?

NO
- ENGINE STILL IDLING IN GEAR.
- BACKPROBE CKT 437 AT IP CONNECTOR WITH VOLTMETER TO GROUND.
- IS VOLTAGE VARYING BETWEEN 1 AND 12 VOLTS?

YES — CODE 24 IS INTERMITTENT. IF NO ADDITIONAL CODES WERE STORED, REFER TO "DIAGNOSTIC AIDS" ON FACING PAGE.

NO

YES — FAULTY ECM

2
- IGNITION "OFF".
- DISCONNECT VSS BUFFER
- IGNITION "ON."
- BACK PROBE CKT 437 AT IP CONNECTOR WITH VOLTMETER TO GROUND.
- SHOULD DISPLAY 10 VOLTS OR MORE. DOES IT?

YES — CKT 437 OPEN BETWEEN IP 15-WAY CONNECTOR AND VSS BUFFER CONNECTOR OR FAULTY BUFFER.

NO — CKT 437 SHORTED TO GROUND, OPEN BETWEEN ECM AND IP 15-WAY CONNECTOR OR FAULTY ECM.

CLEAR CODES AND CONFIRM "CLOSED LOOP" OPERATION AND NO "SERVICE ENGINE SOON" LIGHT.

Fig. 134 Engine controls diagnostic chart

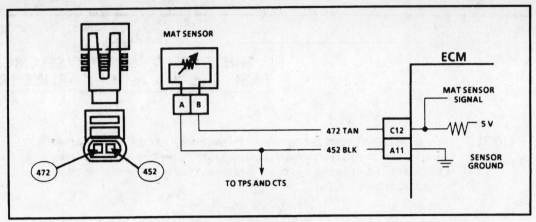

CODE 25
MANIFOLD AIR TEMPERATURE (MAT) SENSOR CIRCUIT
(HIGH TEMPERATURE INDICATED)
5.0L & 5.7L "B" CARLINE (TBI)

Circuit Description:

The Manifold Air Temperature (MAT) sensor uses a thermistor to control the signal voltage to the ECM. The ECM applies a voltage (about 5 volts) on CKT 472 to the sensor. When manifold air is cold, the sensor (thermistor) resistance is high, therefore, the ECM will see a high signal voltage. If the manifold air is warm, the sensor (thermistor) resistance is low, therefore, the ECM will see a low signal voltage.

Test Description: Numbers below refer to circled numbers on the diagnostic chart.

1. Code 25 will set if:
   - Signal voltage indicates a manifold air temperature greater than 150°C (302°F) for 2 seconds.
   - Time since engine start is 2 minutes or longer.
   - A Vehicle speed is present, greater than 5 mph.

Diagnostic Aids:

Manifold air temperature on a "Scan" tool indicates the temperature of the air in the air cleaner, because the MAT sensor is located in the air cleaner. If the engine has been allowed to sit overnight, the manifold air temperature and coolant temperature values should read within a few degrees of each other. After the engine is started, the MAT will increase due to Thermac operation and underhood temperatures, however, MAT will rarely exceed 80°C (176°F). If a higher MAT than 80°C (176°F) is noted, check for proper Thermac operation, see Section "C14".

Check harness routing for possible short to ground in CKT 472.

Refer to "Intermittents" in Section "B".

Fig. 135 Engine controls diagnostic chart

CODE 25

MANIFOLD AIR TEMPERATURE (MAT) SENSOR CIRCUIT
(HIGH TEMPERATURE INDICATED)
5.0L & 5.7L "B" CARLINE (TBI)

1
- CLEAR CODES
- IGN "ON" ENGINE "OFF"
- DOES "SCAN" TOOL DISPLAY MAT OF 145°C (293°F) OR HOTTER?

YES

- DISCONNECT SENSOR. "SCAN" TOOL SHOULD DISPLAY TEMPERATURE BELOW -30°C (-22°F). DOES IT?

NO

CODE 25 IS INTERMITTENT.
IF NO ADDITIONAL CODES WERE STORED, REFER TO "DIAGNOSTIC AIDS" ON FACING PAGE.

YES

REPLACE SENSOR.

NO

CKT 472 SHORTED TO GROUND, OR
CKT 472 SHORTED TO SENSOR GROUND OR
FAULTY ECM.

DIAGNOSTIC AID

MAT SENSOR		
TEMPERATURE VS. RESISTANCE VALUES (APPROXIMATE)		
°F	°C	OHMS
210	100	185
160	70	450
100	38	1,800
70	20	3,400
40	4	7,500
20	-7	13,500
0	-18	25,000
-40	-40	100,700

CLEAR CODES AND CONFIRM "CLOSED LOOP" OPERATION AND NO "SERVICE ENGINE SOON" LIGHT.

Fig. 136 Engine controls diagnostic chart

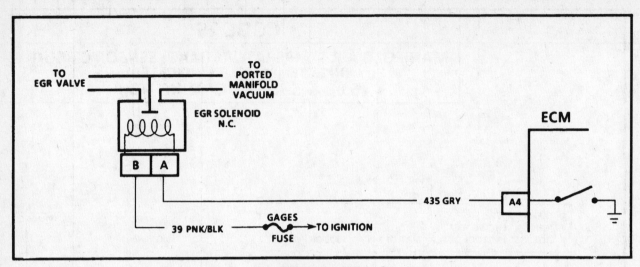

CODE 32
EXHAUST GAS RECIRCULATION (EGR) CIRCUIT
4.3L, 5.0L & 5.7L "B" CARLINE (TBI)

Circuit Description:

The ECM operates a solenoid to control the Exhaust Gas Recirculation (EGR) valve. This solenoid is normally closed. By providing a ground path, the ECM energizes the solenoid which then allows vacuum to pass to the EGR valve.

The ECM monitors EGR effectiveness by de-energizing the EGR control solenoid thereby shutting off vacuum to the EGR valve diaphragm. With the EGR valve closed, manifold vacuum will be greater than it was during normal EGR operation and this change will be relayed to the ECM by the MAP sensor. If the change is not within the calibrated window, a Code 32 will be set.

The ECM will check EGR operation when:
- Vehicle speed is above 50 mph.
- Manifold absolute pressure is between 35 and 55 kPa (10" and 16" Hg).
- No change in throttle position while test is being run.

Test Description: Numbers below refer to circled numbers on the diagnostic chart.

1. By grounding the diagnostic "test" terminal, the EGR solenoid should be energized and allow vacuum to be applied to the EGR valve and the vacuum should hold.

2. When the diagnostic "test" terminal is ungrounded, the vacuum to the EGR valve should bleed off through a vent in the solenoid and the valve should close. The gage may or may not bleed off but this does not indicate a problem.

3. This test will determine if the electrical control part of the system is at fault or if the connector or solenoid is at fault.

4. This system uses a negative backpressure EGR valve which should hold vacuum with engine "OFF."

5. When engine is started, exhaust backpressure should cause vacuum to bleed off and valve should fully close.

Diagnostic Aids:

Vacuum lines should be <u>thoroughly</u> checked for internal restrictions. The ECM uses the MAP sensor for checking EGR operation.

If there is a question of MAP sensor accuracy use CHART C-1D MAP output check in Section "C".

If no problems are found refer to "Intermittents" in Section "B".

Fig. 137 Engine controls diagnostic chart

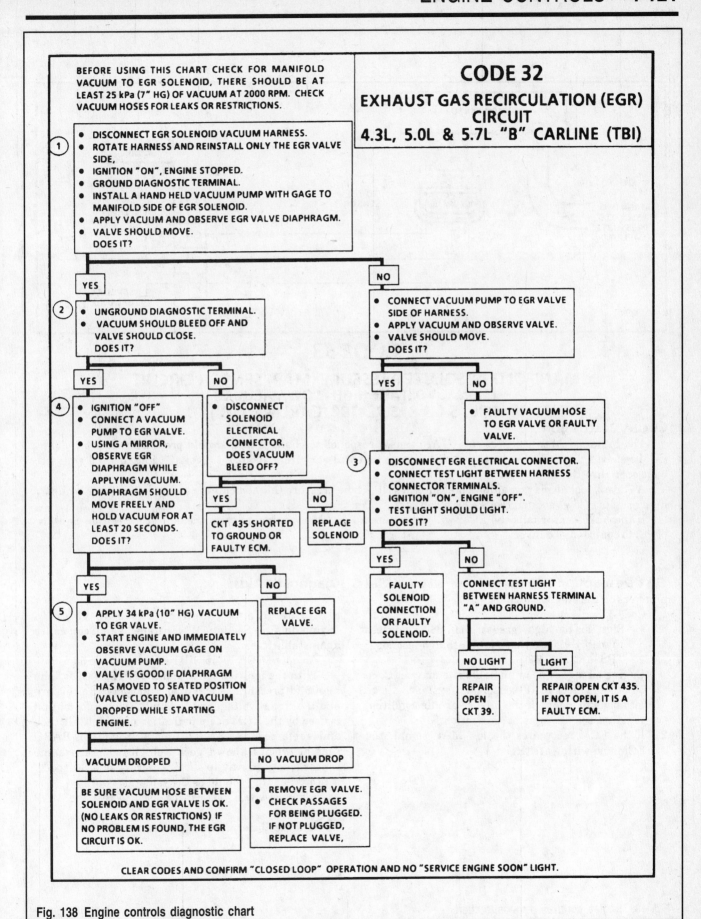

BEFORE USING THIS CHART CHECK FOR MANIFOLD VACUUM TO EGR SOLENOID, THERE SHOULD BE AT LEAST 25 kPa (7" HG) OF VACUUM AT 2000 RPM. CHECK VACUUM HOSES FOR LEAKS OR RESTRICTIONS.

CODE 32
EXHAUST GAS RECIRCULATION (EGR) CIRCUIT
4.3L, 5.0L & 5.7L "B" CARLINE (TBI)

1
- DISCONNECT EGR SOLENOID VACUUM HARNESS.
- ROTATE HARNESS AND REINSTALL ONLY THE EGR VALVE SIDE,
- IGNITION "ON", ENGINE STOPPED.
- GROUND DIAGNOSTIC TERMINAL.
- INSTALL A HAND HELD VACUUM PUMP WITH GAGE TO MANIFOLD SIDE OF EGR SOLENOID.
- APPLY VACUUM AND OBSERVE EGR VALVE DIAPHRAGM.
- VALVE SHOULD MOVE. DOES IT?

YES

NO

2
- UNGROUND DIAGNOSTIC TERMINAL.
- VACUUM SHOULD BLEED OFF AND VALVE SHOULD CLOSE. DOES IT?

- CONNECT VACUUM PUMP TO EGR VALVE SIDE OF HARNESS.
- APPLY VACUUM AND OBSERVE VALVE.
- VALVE SHOULD MOVE. DOES IT?

YES

NO

YES

NO

4
- IGNITION "OFF"
- CONNECT A VACUUM PUMP TO EGR VALVE.
- USING A MIRROR, OBSERVE EGR DIAPHRAGM WHILE APPLYING VACUUM.
- DIAPHRAGM SHOULD MOVE FREELY AND HOLD VACUUM FOR AT LEAST 20 SECONDS. DOES IT?

- DISCONNECT SOLENOID ELECTRICAL CONNECTOR. DOES VACUUM BLEED OFF?

- FAULTY VACUUM HOSE TO EGR VALVE OR FAULTY VALVE.

YES

NO

3
- DISCONNECT EGR ELECTRICAL CONNECTOR.
- CONNECT TEST LIGHT BETWEEN HARNESS CONNECTOR TERMINALS.
- IGNITION "ON", ENGINE "OFF".
- TEST LIGHT SHOULD LIGHT. DOES IT?

CKT 435 SHORTED TO GROUND OR FAULTY ECM.

REPLACE SOLENOID

YES

NO

YES

NO

REPLACE EGR VALVE.

FAULTY SOLENOID CONNECTION OR FAULTY SOLENOID.

CONNECT TEST LIGHT BETWEEN HARNESS TERMINAL "A" AND GROUND.

5
- APPLY 34 kPa (10" HG) VACUUM TO EGR VALVE.
- START ENGINE AND IMMEDIATELY OBSERVE VACUUM GAGE ON VACUUM PUMP.
- VALVE IS GOOD IF DIAPHRAGM HAS MOVED TO SEATED POSITION (VALVE CLOSED) AND VACUUM DROPPED WHILE STARTING ENGINE.

NO LIGHT

LIGHT

REPAIR OPEN CKT 39.

REPAIR OPEN CKT 435. IF NOT OPEN, IT IS A FAULTY ECM.

VACUUM DROPPED

NO VACUUM DROP

BE SURE VACUUM HOSE BETWEEN SOLENOID AND EGR VALVE IS OK. (NO LEAKS OR RESTRICTIONS) IF NO PROBLEM IS FOUND, THE EGR CIRCUIT IS OK.

- REMOVE EGR VALVE.
- CHECK PASSAGES FOR BEING PLUGGED. IF NOT PLUGGED, REPLACE VALVE,

CLEAR CODES AND CONFIRM "CLOSED LOOP" OPERATION AND NO "SERVICE ENGINE SOON" LIGHT.

Fig. 138 Engine controls diagnostic chart

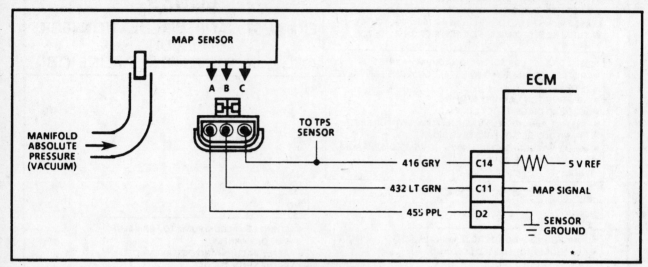

CODE 33

MANIFOLD ABSOLUTE PRESSURE (MAP) SENSOR CIRCUIT
(SIGNAL VOLTAGE HIGH - LOW VACUUM)
4.3L, 5.0L & 5.7L "B" CARLINE (TBI)

Circuit Description:

The Manifold Absolute Pressure (MAP) sensor responds to changes in manifold pressure (vacuum). The ECM receives this information as a signal voltage that will vary from about 1-1.5 volts at idle to 4-4.5 volts at wide open throttle.

A "Scan" tool displays manifold pressure in volts. Low pressure (high vacuum) reads a low voltage while a high pressure (low vacuum) reads a high voltage.

If the MAP sensor fails the ECM will substitute a fixed MAP value and use the Throttle Position Sensor (TPS) to control fuel delivery.

Test Description: Numbers below refer to circled numbers on the diagnostic chart.

1. Code 33 will set when:
   - Signal is too high, (greater than 68 kPa or less than 9" Hg) for a time greater than 5 seconds.
   - TPS less than 4%

   Engine misfire or a low unstable idle may set Code 33. Disconnect MAP sensor and system will go into backup mode. If the misfire or idle condition remains, see "Symptoms" in Section "B".

2. If the ECM recognizes the low MAP signal, the ECM and wiring are OK.

Diagnostic Aids:

If the idle is rough or unstable refer to "Symptoms" in Section "B" for items which can cause an unstable idle.

An open in CKT 455 will result in a Code 33.

With the ignition "ON" and the engine "OFF," the manifold pressure is equal to atmospheric pressure and the signal voltage will be high. This information is used by the ECM as an indication of vehicle altitude and is referred to as BARO. Comparison of this BARO reading with a known good vehicle with the same sensor is a good way to check accuracy of a "suspect" sensor. Reading should be the same ± .4 volt.

Also CHART C-1D can be used to test the MAP sensor.

Refer to "Intermittents" in Section "B".

Fig. 139 Engine controls diagnostic chart

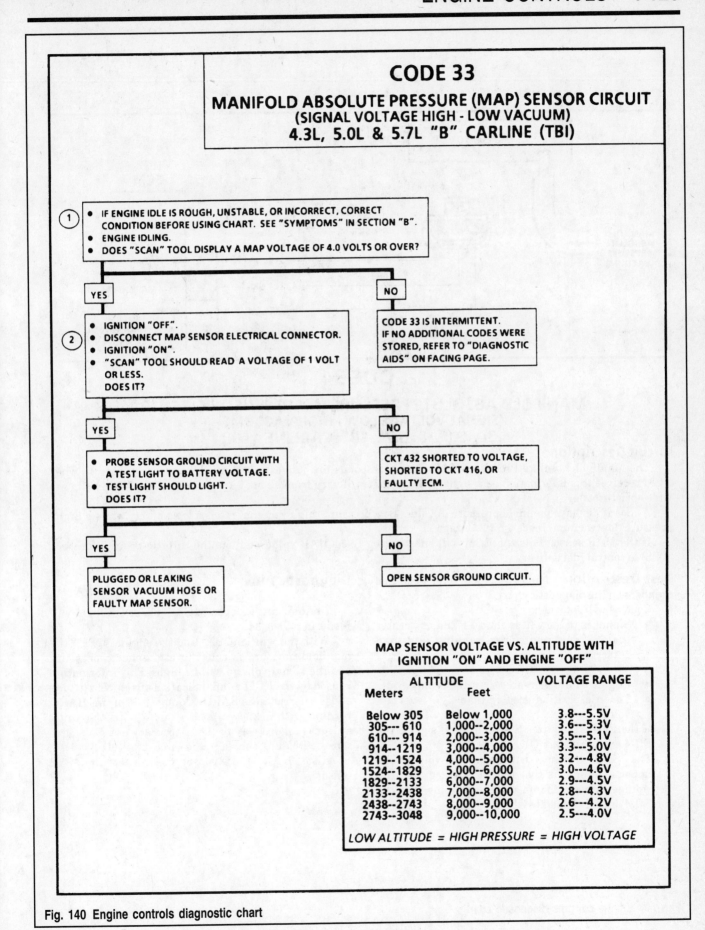

CODE 33

MANIFOLD ABSOLUTE PRESSURE (MAP) SENSOR CIRCUIT
(SIGNAL VOLTAGE HIGH - LOW VACUUM)
4.3L, 5.0L & 5.7L "B" CARLINE (TBI)

① • IF ENGINE IDLE IS ROUGH, UNSTABLE, OR INCORRECT, CORRECT CONDITION BEFORE USING CHART. SEE "SYMPTOMS" IN SECTION "B".
• ENGINE IDLING.
• DOES "SCAN" TOOL DISPLAY A MAP VOLTAGE OF 4.0 VOLTS OR OVER?

YES

NO

② • IGNITION "OFF".
• DISCONNECT MAP SENSOR ELECTRICAL CONNECTOR.
• IGNITION "ON".
• "SCAN" TOOL SHOULD READ A VOLTAGE OF 1 VOLT OR LESS. DOES IT?

CODE 33 IS INTERMITTENT. IF NO ADDITIONAL CODES WERE STORED, REFER TO "DIAGNOSTIC AIDS" ON FACING PAGE.

YES

NO

• PROBE SENSOR GROUND CIRCUIT WITH A TEST LIGHT TO BATTERY VOLTAGE.
• TEST LIGHT SHOULD LIGHT. DOES IT?

CKT 432 SHORTED TO VOLTAGE, SHORTED TO CKT 416, OR FAULTY ECM.

YES

NO

PLUGGED OR LEAKING SENSOR VACUUM HOSE OR FAULTY MAP SENSOR.

OPEN SENSOR GROUND CIRCUIT.

MAP SENSOR VOLTAGE VS. ALTITUDE WITH IGNITION "ON" AND ENGINE "OFF"

ALTITUDE		VOLTAGE RANGE
Meters	Feet	
Below 305	Below 1,000	3.8---5.5V
305--- 610	1,000--2,000	3.6---5.3V
610--- 914	2,000--3,000	3.5---5.1V
914--1219	3,000--4,000	3.3---5.0V
1219--1524	4,000--5,000	3.2---4.8V
1524--1829	5,000--6,000	3.0---4.6V
1829--2133	6,000--7,000	2.9---4.5V
2133--2438	7,000--8,000	2.8---4.3V
2438--2743	8,000--9,000	2.6---4.2V
2743--3048	9,000--10,000	2.5---4.0V
LOW ALTITUDE = HIGH PRESSURE = HIGH VOLTAGE		

Fig. 140 Engine controls diagnostic chart

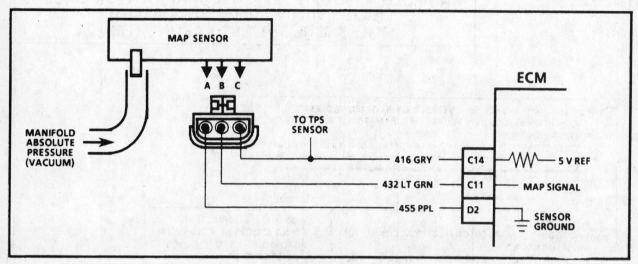

CODE 34

MANIFOLD ABSOLUTE PRESSURE (MAP) SENSOR CIRCUIT
(SIGNAL VOLTAGE LOW - HIGH VACUUM)
4.3L, 5.0L & 5.7L "B" CARLINE (TBI)

Circuit Description:

The Manifold Absolute Pressure (MAP) sensor responds to changes in manifold pressure (vacuum). The ECM receives this information as a signal voltage that will vary from about 1-1.5 volts at idle to 4-4.5 volts at wide open throttle.

A "Scan" displays manifold pressure in volts. Low pressure (high vacuum) reads a low voltage while a high pressure (low vacuum) reads a high voltage.

If the MAP sensor fails the ECM will substitute a fixed MAP value and use the throttle position sensor (TPS) to control fuel delivery.

Test Description: Numbers below refer to circled numbers on the diagnostic chart.

1. Code 34 will set when:
   - Signal is too low (less than 14 kPa or greater than 28" Hg) and engine running less than 1200 rpm.

   OR
   - Engine running greater than 1200 rpm
   - Throttle position greater than 21% (over 1.5 volts).
2. If the ECM recognizes the high MAP signal, the ECM and wiring are OK.
3. The "Scan" tool may not display 12 volts. The important thing is that the ECM recognizes the voltage as more than 4 volts, indicating that the ECM and CKT 432 are OK.

Diagnostic Aids:

An intermittent open in CKT 432 or CKT 416 will result in a Code 34.

With the ignition "ON" and the engine "OFF," the manifold pressure is equal to atmospheric pressure and the signal voltage will be high. This information is used by the ECM as an indication of vehicle altitude and is referred to as BARO. Comparison of this BARO reading with a known good vehicle with the same sensor is a good way to check accuracy of a "suspect" sensor. Reading should be the same ± .4 volt.

Also CHART C-1D can be used to test the MAP sensor.

Fig. 141 Engine controls diagnostic chart

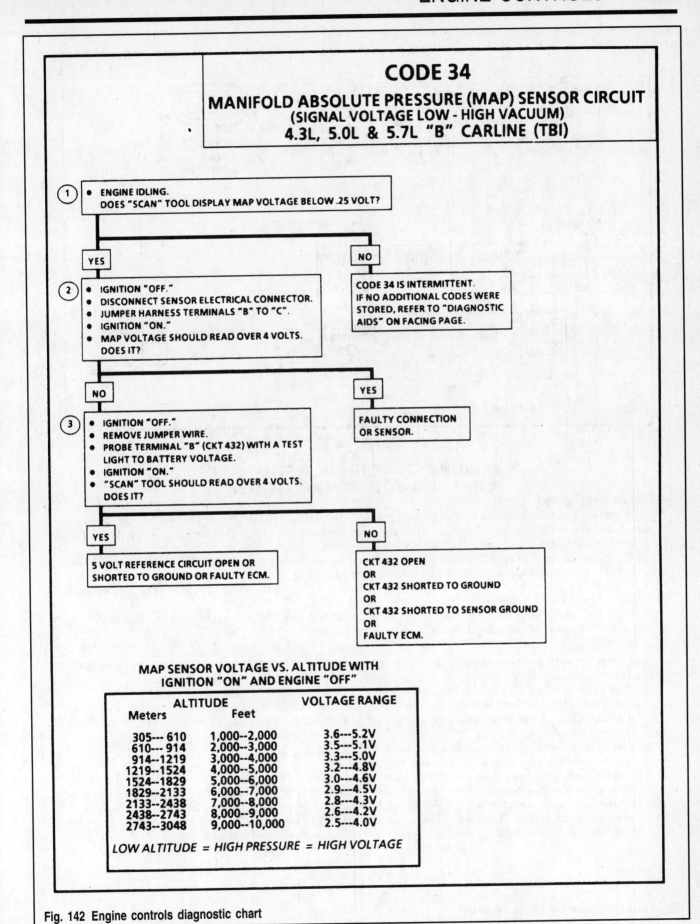

CODE 34
MANIFOLD ABSOLUTE PRESSURE (MAP) SENSOR CIRCUIT
(SIGNAL VOLTAGE LOW - HIGH VACUUM)
4.3L, 5.0L & 5.7L "B" CARLINE (TBI)

1
- ENGINE IDLING.
  DOES "SCAN" TOOL DISPLAY MAP VOLTAGE BELOW .25 VOLT?

YES

NO

2
- IGNITION "OFF."
- DISCONNECT SENSOR ELECTRICAL CONNECTOR.
- JUMPER HARNESS TERMINALS "B" TO "C".
- IGNITION "ON."
- MAP VOLTAGE SHOULD READ OVER 4 VOLTS.
  DOES IT?

CODE 34 IS INTERMITTENT.
IF NO ADDITIONAL CODES WERE STORED, REFER TO "DIAGNOSTIC AIDS" ON FACING PAGE.

NO

YES

3
- IGNITION "OFF."
- REMOVE JUMPER WIRE.
- PROBE TERMINAL "B" (CKT 432) WITH A TEST LIGHT TO BATTERY VOLTAGE.
- IGNITION "ON."
- "SCAN" TOOL SHOULD READ OVER 4 VOLTS.
  DOES IT?

FAULTY CONNECTION
OR SENSOR.

YES

NO

5 VOLT REFERENCE CIRCUIT OPEN OR SHORTED TO GROUND OR FAULTY ECM.

CKT 432 OPEN
OR
CKT 432 SHORTED TO GROUND
OR
CKT 432 SHORTED TO SENSOR GROUND
OR
FAULTY ECM.

MAP SENSOR VOLTAGE VS. ALTITUDE WITH IGNITION "ON" AND ENGINE "OFF"

ALTITUDE		VOLTAGE RANGE
Meters	Feet	
305--- 610	1,000--2,000	3.6---5.2V
610--- 914	2,000--3,000	3.5---5.1V
914--1219	3,000--4,000	3.3---5.0V
1219--1524	4,000--5,000	3.2---4.8V
1524--1829	5,000--6,000	3.0---4.6V
1829--2133	6,000--7,000	2.9---4.5V
2133--2438	7,000--8,000	2.8---4.3V
2438--2743	8,000--9,000	2.6---4.2V
2743--3048	9,000--10,000	2.5---4.0V

LOW ALTITUDE = HIGH PRESSURE = HIGH VOLTAGE

Fig. 142 Engine controls diagnostic chart

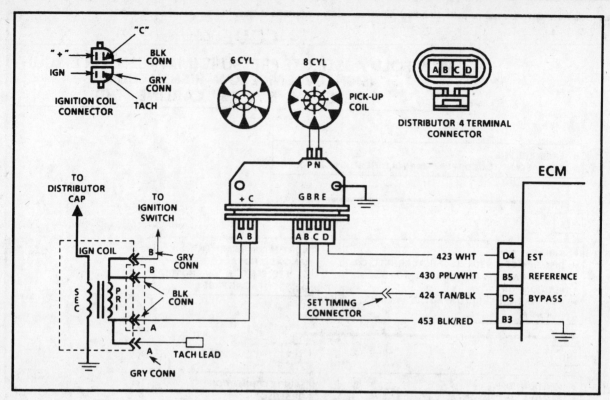

CODE 42

ELECTRONIC SPARK TIMING (EST) CIRCUIT
4.3L, 5.0L & 5.7L "B" CARLINE (TBI)

Circuit Description:

When the system is running on the ignition module, that is, no voltage on the bypass line, the ignition module grounds the EST signal. The ECM expects to see no voltage on the EST line during this condition. If it sees a voltage, it sets Code 42 and will not go into the EST mode.

When the rpm for EST is reached (about 400 rpm), and bypass voltage applied, the EST should no longer be grounded in the ignition module so the EST voltage should be varying.

If the bypass line is open or grounded, the ignition module will not switch to EST mode so the EST voltage will be low and Code 42 will be set.

If the EST line is grounded, the ignition module will switch to EST, but because the line is grounded there will be no EST signal. A Code 42 will be set.

Test Description: Numbers below refer to circled numbers on the diagnostic chart.

1. Code 42 means the ECM has seen an open or short to ground in the EST or bypass circuits. This test confirms Code 42 and that the fault causing the code is present.
2. Checks for a normal EST ground path through the ignition module. An EST CKT 423 shorted to ground will also read less than 500 ohms; however, this will be checked later.
3. As the test light voltage touches CKT 424, the module should switch. The important thing is that the module "switched."

4. The module did not switch and this step checks for:
   - EST CKT 423 shorted to ground
   - Bypass CKT 424 open
   - Faulty ignition module connection or module
5. Confirms that Code 42 is a faulty ECM and not an intermittent in CKT 423 or CKT 424.

Diagnostic Aids:

If a Code 42 was stored and the customer complains of a "Hard Start," the problem is most likely a grounded EST line (CKT 423).

The "Scan" tool does not have any ability to help diagnose a Code 42 problem.

A PROM not fully seated in the ECM can result in a Code 42.

Fig. 143 Engine controls diagnostic chart

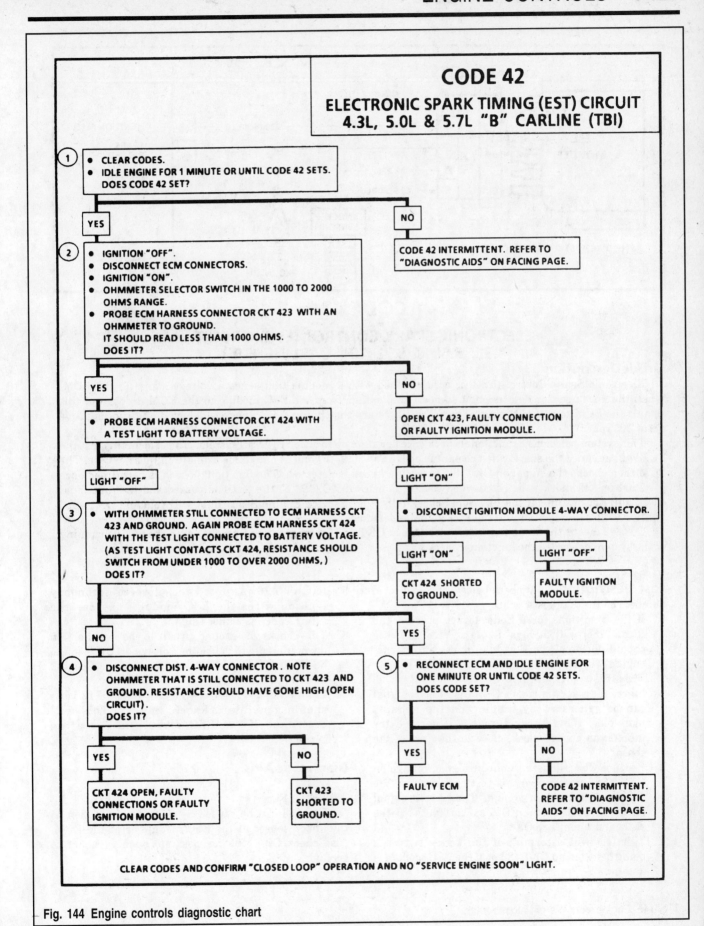

CODE 42
ELECTRONIC SPARK TIMING (EST) CIRCUIT
4.3L, 5.0L & 5.7L "B" CARLINE (TBI)

1
- CLEAR CODES.
- IDLE ENGINE FOR 1 MINUTE OR UNTIL CODE 42 SETS. DOES CODE 42 SET?

YES

NO

CODE 42 INTERMITTENT. REFER TO "DIAGNOSTIC AIDS" ON FACING PAGE.

2
- IGNITION "OFF".
- DISCONNECT ECM CONNECTORS.
- IGNITION "ON".
- OHMMETER SELECTOR SWITCH IN THE 1000 TO 2000 OHMS RANGE.
- PROBE ECM HARNESS CONNECTOR CKT 423 WITH AN OHMMETER TO GROUND. IT SHOULD READ LESS THAN 1000 OHMS. DOES IT?

YES

NO

OPEN CKT 423, FAULTY CONNECTION OR FAULTY IGNITION MODULE.

- PROBE ECM HARNESS CONNECTOR CKT 424 WITH A TEST LIGHT TO BATTERY VOLTAGE.

LIGHT "OFF"

LIGHT "ON"

3
- WITH OHMMETER STILL CONNECTED TO ECM HARNESS CKT 423 AND GROUND. AGAIN PROBE ECM HARNESS CKT 424 WITH THE TEST LIGHT CONNECTED TO BATTERY VOLTAGE. (AS TEST LIGHT CONTACTS CKT 424, RESISTANCE SHOULD SWITCH FROM UNDER 1000 TO OVER 2000 OHMS,) DOES IT?

- DISCONNECT IGNITION MODULE 4-WAY CONNECTOR.

LIGHT "ON"

LIGHT "OFF"

CKT 424 SHORTED TO GROUND.

FAULTY IGNITION MODULE.

NO

YES

4
- DISCONNECT DIST. 4-WAY CONNECTOR . NOTE OHMMETER THAT IS STILL CONNECTED TO CKT 423 AND GROUND. RESISTANCE SHOULD HAVE GONE HIGH (OPEN CIRCUIT) . DOES IT?

5
- RECONNECT ECM AND IDLE ENGINE FOR ONE MINUTE OR UNTIL CODE 42 SETS. DOES CODE SET?

YES

NO

YES

NO

CKT 424 OPEN, FAULTY CONNECTIONS OR FAULTY IGNITION MODULE.

CKT 423 SHORTED TO GROUND.

FAULTY ECM

CODE 42 INTERMITTENT. REFER TO "DIAGNOSTIC AIDS" ON FACING PAGE.

CLEAR CODES AND CONFIRM "CLOSED LOOP" OPERATION AND NO "SERVICE ENGINE SOON" LIGHT.

Fig. 144 Engine controls diagnostic chart

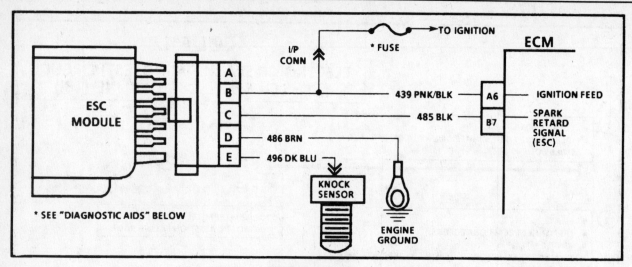

CODE 43
ELECTRONIC SPARK CONTROL (ESC) CIRCUIT
4.3L, 5.0L & 5.7L "B" CARLINE (TBI)

Circuit Description:

Electronic Spark Control (ESC) is accomplished with a module that sends a voltage signal to the ECM. When the knock sensor detects engine knock, the voltage from the ESC module to the ECM drops, and this signals the ECM to retard timing. The ECM will retard the timing when knock is detected and rpm is above about 900 rpm.

This system performs a functional check once per start up to check the ESC system. To perform this test the ECM will advance the spark when coolant is above 95°C (194°F) and at a high load condition (near WOT). The ECM then checks the signal on CKT 485 to see if a knock is detected. The functional check is performed once per start up. If knock is detected when coolant is below 95°C (194°F) the test has passed and the functional check will not be run. If the functional check fails, the "Service Engine Soon" light will remain "ON" until ignition is turned "OFF" or until a knock signal is detected.

Code 43 means the ECM has read low voltage at CKT 485 for longer than 5 seconds with the engine running or the system has failed the functional check.

Test Description: Numbers below refer to circled numbers on the diagnostic chart.

1. If the conditions for a Code 43 are present the "Scan" tool will always display "YES." There should not be a knock at idle unless an internal engine problem, or a system problem exists.
2. This test will determine if the system is functioning at this time. Usually a knock signal can be generated by tapping on the exhaust manifold. If no knock signal is generated try tapping on engine block, close to the area of the sensor.
3. Because Code 43 sets when the signal voltage on CKT 485 remains low this test should cause the signal on CKT 485 to go high. The 12 volts signal should be seen by the ECM as "no knock" if the ECM and wiring are OK.
4. This test will determine if the knock signal is being detected on CKT 496 or if the ESC module is at fault.

5. If CKT 496 is routed too close to secondary ignition wires the ESC module may see the interference as a knock signal.
6. This checks the ground circuit to the module. An open ground will cause the voltage on CKT 485 to be about 12 volts which would cause the Code 43 functional test to fail.
7. Contacting CKT 496 with a test light to 12 volts should generate a knock signal. This will determine if the ESC module is operating correctly.

Diagnostic Aids:

* ECM Fuse

Code 43 can be caused by a faulty connection at the knock sensor at the ESC module or at the ECM. Also check CKT 485 for possible open or short to ground.

Fig. 145 Engine controls diagnostic chart

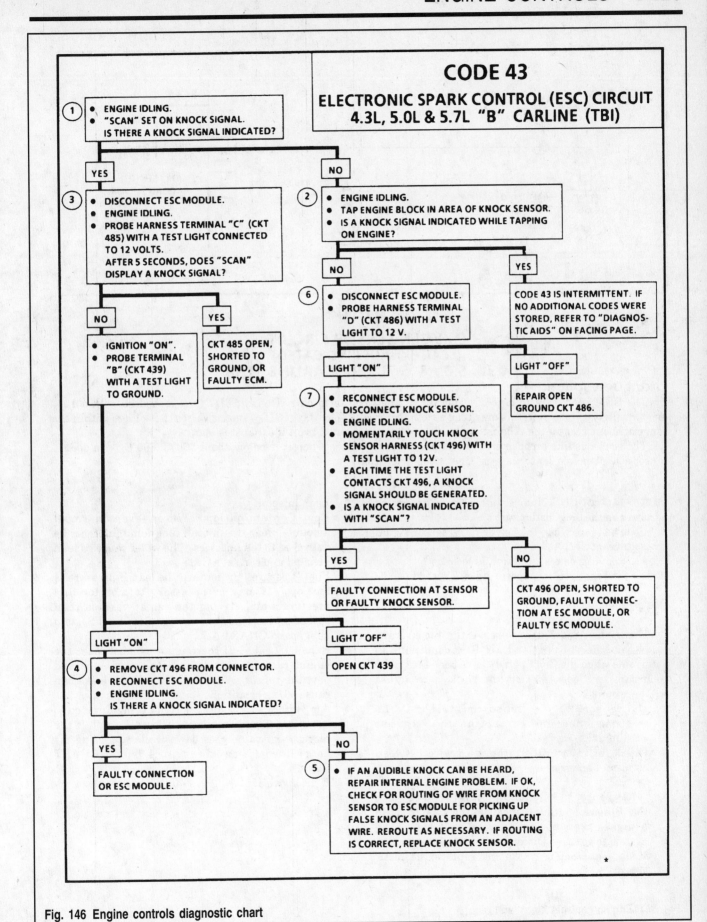

CODE 43
ELECTRONIC SPARK CONTROL (ESC) CIRCUIT
4.3L, 5.0L & 5.7L "B" CARLINE (TBI)

① • ENGINE IDLING.
• "SCAN" SET ON KNOCK SIGNAL.
  IS THERE A KNOCK SIGNAL INDICATED?

YES

③ • DISCONNECT ESC MODULE.
• ENGINE IDLING.
• PROBE HARNESS TERMINAL "C" (CKT 485) WITH A TEST LIGHT CONNECTED TO 12 VOLTS.
  AFTER 5 SECONDS, DOES "SCAN" DISPLAY A KNOCK SIGNAL?

NO

• IGNITION "ON".
• PROBE TERMINAL "B" (CKT 439) WITH A TEST LIGHT TO GROUND.

YES

CKT 485 OPEN, SHORTED TO GROUND, OR FAULTY ECM.

NO

② • ENGINE IDLING.
• TAP ENGINE BLOCK IN AREA OF KNOCK SENSOR.
• IS A KNOCK SIGNAL INDICATED WHILE TAPPING ON ENGINE?

NO

⑥ • DISCONNECT ESC MODULE.
• PROBE HARNESS TERMINAL "D" (CKT 486) WITH A TEST LIGHT TO 12 V.

YES

CODE 43 IS INTERMITTENT. IF NO ADDITIONAL CODES WERE STORED, REFER TO "DIAGNOSTIC AIDS" ON FACING PAGE.

LIGHT "ON"

⑦ • RECONNECT ESC MODULE.
• DISCONNECT KNOCK SENSOR.
• ENGINE IDLING.
• MOMENTARILY TOUCH KNOCK SENSOR HARNESS (CKT 496) WITH A TEST LIGHT TO 12V.
• EACH TIME THE TEST LIGHT CONTACTS CKT 496, A KNOCK SIGNAL SHOULD BE GENERATED.
• IS A KNOCK SIGNAL INDICATED WITH "SCAN"?

LIGHT "OFF"

REPAIR OPEN GROUND CKT 486.

YES

FAULTY CONNECTION AT SENSOR OR FAULTY KNOCK SENSOR.

NO

CKT 496 OPEN, SHORTED TO GROUND, FAULTY CONNECTION AT ESC MODULE, OR FAULTY ESC MODULE.

LIGHT "ON"

④ • REMOVE CKT 496 FROM CONNECTOR.
• RECONNECT ESC MODULE.
• ENGINE IDLING.
  IS THERE A KNOCK SIGNAL INDICATED?

LIGHT "OFF"

OPEN CKT 439

YES

FAULTY CONNECTION OR ESC MODULE.

NO

⑤ • IF AN AUDIBLE KNOCK CAN BE HEARD, REPAIR INTERNAL ENGINE PROBLEM. IF OK, CHECK FOR ROUTING OF WIRE FROM KNOCK SENSOR TO ESC MODULE FOR PICKING UP FALSE KNOCK SIGNALS FROM AN ADJACENT WIRE. REROUTE AS NECESSARY. IF ROUTING IS CORRECT, REPLACE KNOCK SENSOR.

Fig. 146 Engine controls diagnostic chart

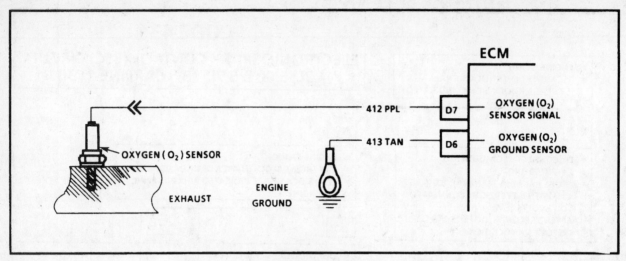

CODE 44

OXYGEN SENSOR CIRCUIT
(LEAN EXHAUST INDICATED)
4.3L, 5.0L & 5.7L "B" CARLINE (TBI)

Circuit Description:

The ECM supplies a voltage of about .45 volt between terminals "D6" and "D7". (If measured with a 10 megohm digital voltmeter, this may read as low as .32 volt). The Oxygen (O_2) sensor varies the voltage within a range of about 1 volt if the exhaust is rich, down through about .10 volt if exhaust is lean.

The sensor is like an open circuit and produces no voltage when it is below about 360°C (600°F). An open sensor circuit or cold sensor causes "Open Loop" operation.

Test Description: Numbers below refer to circled numbers on the diagnostic chart.
1. Code 44 is set when the Oxygen (O_2) sensor signal voltage on CKT 412.
   - Remains below .2 volt for 50 seconds
   - And the system is operating in "Closed Loop."

Diagnostic Aids:

Using the "Scan" tool observe the block learn values at different rpm and air flow conditions to determine when the Code 44 may have been set. If the conditions for Code 44 exists the block learn values will be around 150.
- O_2 Sensor Wire. Sensor pigtail may be mispositioned and contacting the exhaust manifold.
- Check for intermittent ground in wire between connector and sensor.

- MAP Sensor. A Manifold Absolute Pressure (MAP) sensor output that causes the ECM to sense a higher than normal vacuum will cause the system to go lean. Disconnect the MAP sensor and if the lean condition is gone, replace the MAP sensor.

- Lean Injector(s).
- Fuel Contamination. Water, even in small amounts, near the in-tank fuel pump inlet can be delivered to the injectors. The water causes a lean exhaust and can set a Code 44.
- Fuel Pressure. System will be lean if pressure is too low. It may be necessary to monitor fuel pressure while driving the car at various road speeds and/or loads to confirm. See "Fuel System Diagnosis" CHART A-7.
- Exhaust Leaks. If there is an exhaust leak, the engine can pull outside air into the exhaust and past the sensor. Vacuum or crankcase leaks can cause a lean condition.
- Air System. Be sure air is not being directed to the exhaust parts while in "Closed Loop." If the block learn value goes down while squeezing air hose to the left side exhaust ports, refer to CHART C-6.
- If the above are OK, it is a faulty oxygen sensor.

Fig. 147 Engine controls diagnostic chart

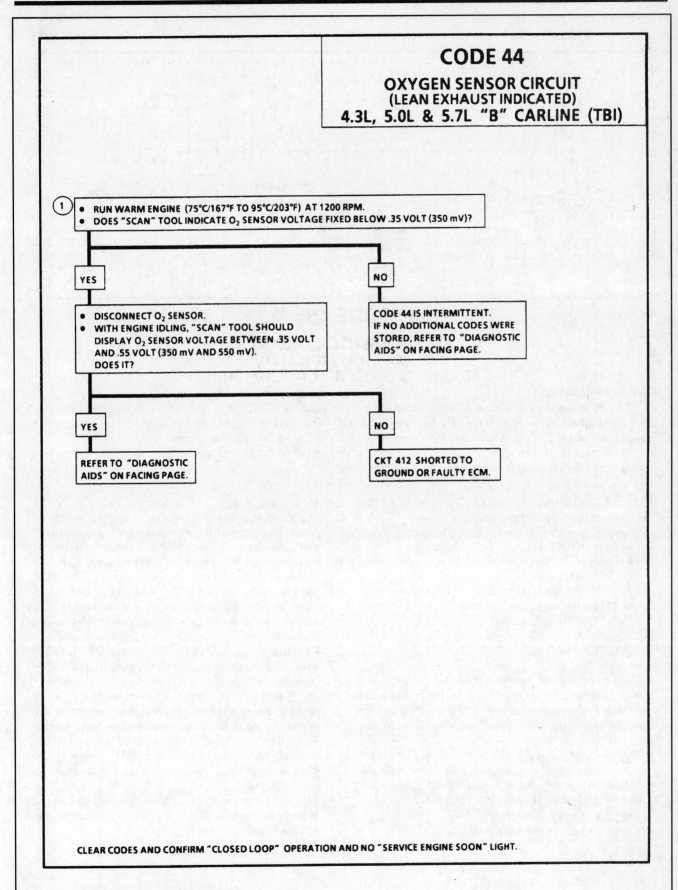

Fig. 148 Engine controls diagnostic chart

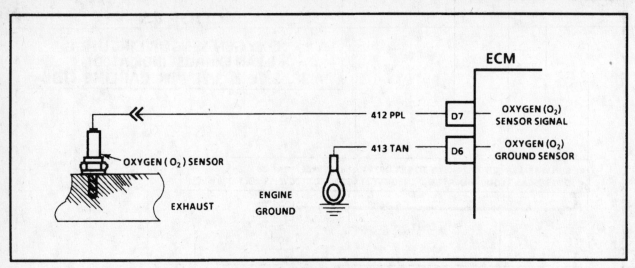

CODE 45
OXYGEN SENSOR CIRCUIT
(RICH EXHAUST INDICATED)
4.3L, 5.0L & 5.7L "B" CARLINE (TBI)

Circuit Description:

The ECM supplies a voltage of about .45 volt between terminals "D6" and "D7". (If measured with a 10 megohm digital voltmeter, this may read as low as .32 volt). The Oxygen (O_2) sensor varies the voltage within a range of about 1 volt if the exhaust is rich, down through about .10 volt if exhaust is lean.

The sensor is like an open circuit and produces no voltage when it is below about 360°C (600°F). An open sensor circuit or cold sensor causes "Open Loop" operation.

Test Description: Numbers below refer to circled numbers on the diagnostic chart.
1. Code 45 is set when the Oxygen (O_2) sensor signal voltage on CKT 412.
   - Remains above .7 volt for 30 seconds; and in "Closed Loop."
   - Engine time after start is 1 minute or more.
   - Throttle angle greater than 2% (about .2 volt above idle voltage) but less than 20%.

Diagnostic Aids:

Using the "Scan" tool observe the block learn values at different rpm conditions to determine when the Code 45 may have been set. If the conditions for Code 45 exists, the block learn values will be around 115.
- Fuel Pressure. System will go rich if pressure is too high. The ECM can compensate for some increase. However, if it gets too high, a Code 45 may be set. See "Fuel System Diagnosis" CHART A-7.
- Leaking injector. See CHART A-7.
- Check for fuel contaminated oil.

- HEI Shielding. An open ground CKT 453 (distributor ground, reference low) may result in Electromagnetic Interference (EMI), or induced electrical "noise." The ECM looks at this "noise" as reference pulses. The additional pulses result in a higher than actual engine speed signal. The ECM then delivers too much fuel, causing system to go rich. Engine tachometer will also show higher than actual engine speed, which can help in diagnosing this problem.
- Canister purge. Check for fuel saturation. If full of fuel, check canister control and hoses. See "Canister Purge" Section "C3".
- MAP sensor. An output that causes the ECM to sense a lower than normal vacuum can cause the system to go rich. Disconnecting the MAP sensor will allow the ECM to set a fixed value for the sensor. Substitute a different MAP sensor if the rich condition is gone while the sensor is disconnected.
- TPS. An intermittent TPS output will cause the system to go rich, due to a false indication of the engine accelerating.

Fig. 149 Engine controls diagnostic chart

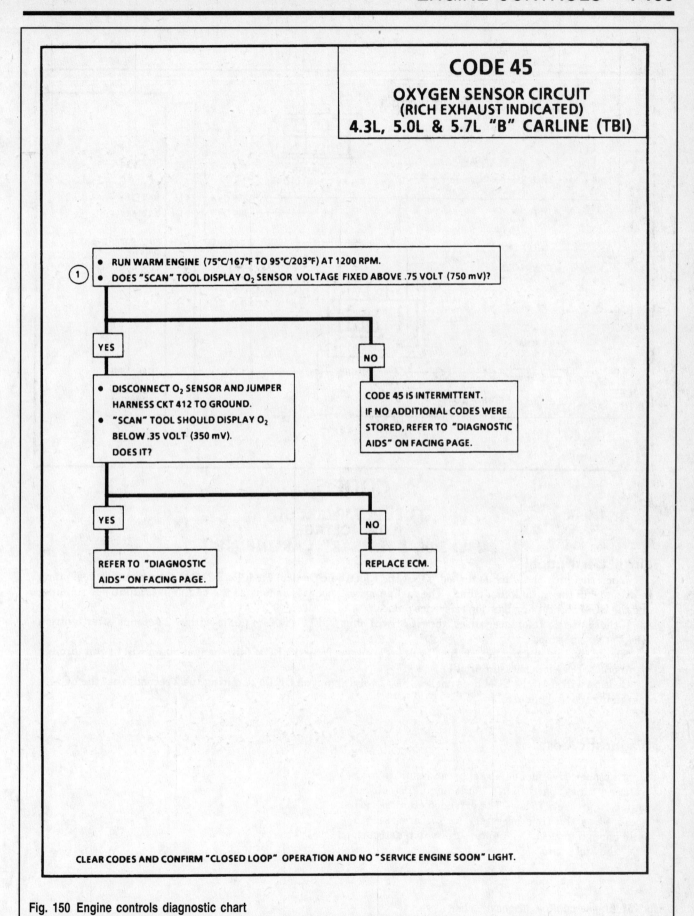

CODE 45

OXYGEN SENSOR CIRCUIT
(RICH EXHAUST INDICATED)
4.3L, 5.0L & 5.7L "B" CARLINE (TBI)

1
- RUN WARM ENGINE (75°C/167°F TO 95°C/203°F) AT 1200 RPM.
- DOES "SCAN" TOOL DISPLAY O₂ SENSOR VOLTAGE FIXED ABOVE .75 VOLT (750 mV)?

YES

- DISCONNECT O₂ SENSOR AND JUMPER HARNESS CKT 412 TO GROUND.
- "SCAN" TOOL SHOULD DISPLAY O₂ BELOW .35 VOLT (350 mV). DOES IT?

NO

CODE 45 IS INTERMITTENT.
IF NO ADDITIONAL CODES WERE STORED, REFER TO "DIAGNOSTIC AIDS" ON FACING PAGE.

YES

REFER TO "DIAGNOSTIC AIDS" ON FACING PAGE.

NO

REPLACE ECM.

CLEAR CODES AND CONFIRM "CLOSED LOOP" OPERATION AND NO "SERVICE ENGINE SOON" LIGHT.

Fig. 150 Engine controls diagnostic chart

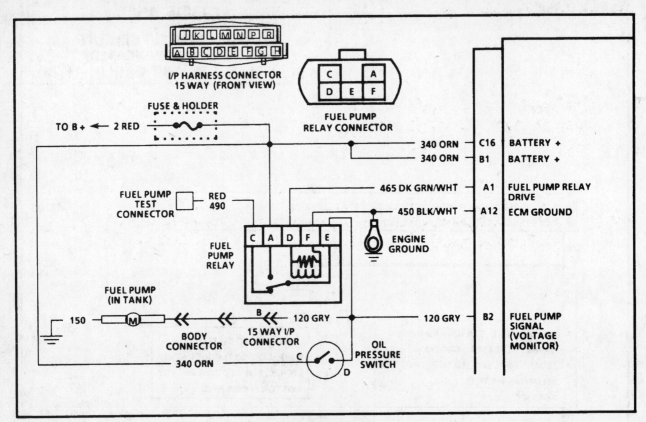

CODE 54

FUEL PUMP CIRCUIT
(LOW VOLTAGE)
4.3L, 5.0L & 5.7L "B" CARLINE (TBI)

Circuit Description:

When the ignition switch is turned "ON," the Electronic Control Module (ECM) will activate the fuel pump relay and run the in-tank fuel pump. The fuel pump will operate as long as the engine is cranking or running, and the ECM is receiving ignition reference pulses.

If there are no reference pulses, the ECM will shut "OFF" the fuel pump within 2 seconds after ignition "ON," or engine stops.

Should the fuel pump relay, or the 12 volts relay drive from the ECM fail, the fuel pump will be run through an oil pressure switch back-up circuit.

Code 54 will set if the ECM does not see the 12 volts signal on CKT 120 during the 2 seconds that the ECM is energizing the fuel pump relay.

Diagnostic Aids:

An inoperative fuel pump relay can result in long cranking times, particularly if the engine is cold or engine oil pressure is low. The extended crank period is caused by the time necessary for oil pressure to build enough to close the oil pressure switch and turn "ON" the fuel pump.

Fig. 151 Engine controls diagnostic chart

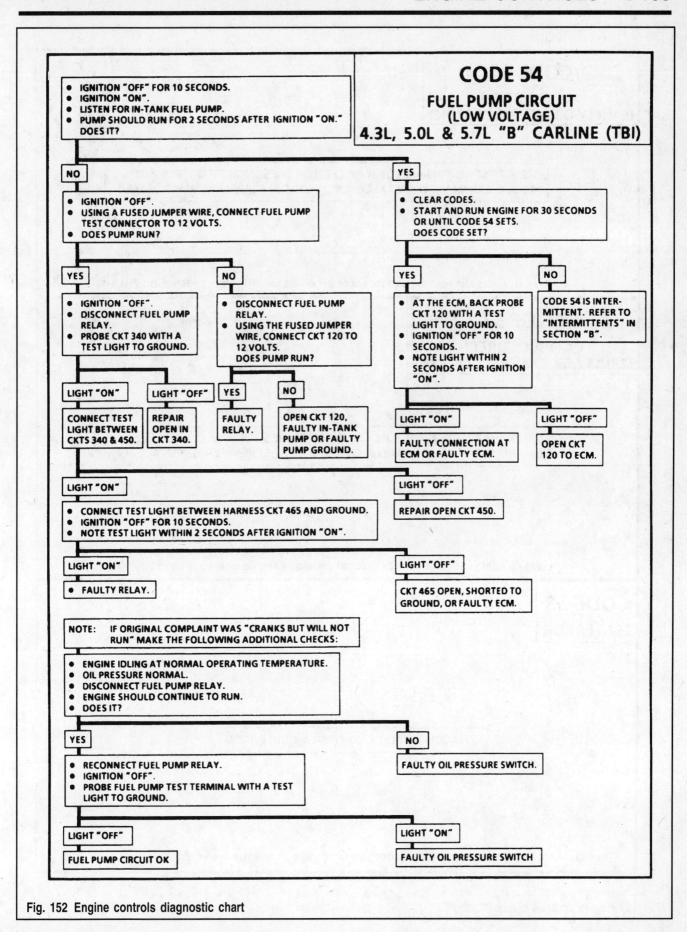

CODE 54

FUEL PUMP CIRCUIT
(LOW VOLTAGE)
4.3L, 5.0L & 5.7L "B" CARLINE (TBI)

- IGNITION "OFF" FOR 10 SECONDS.
- IGNITION "ON".
- LISTEN FOR IN-TANK FUEL PUMP.
- PUMP SHOULD RUN FOR 2 SECONDS AFTER IGNITION "ON." DOES IT?

NO

- IGNITION "OFF".
- USING A FUSED JUMPER WIRE, CONNECT FUEL PUMP TEST CONNECTOR TO 12 VOLTS.
- DOES PUMP RUN?

YES

- IGNITION "OFF".
- DISCONNECT FUEL PUMP RELAY.
- PROBE CKT 340 WITH A TEST LIGHT TO GROUND.

NO

- DISCONNECT FUEL PUMP RELAY.
- USING THE FUSED JUMPER WIRE, CONNECT CKT 120 TO 12 VOLTS. DOES PUMP RUN?

LIGHT "ON"

CONNECT TEST LIGHT BETWEEN CKTS 340 & 450.

LIGHT "OFF"

REPAIR OPEN IN CKT 340.

YES

FAULTY RELAY.

NO

OPEN CKT 120, FAULTY IN-TANK PUMP OR FAULTY PUMP GROUND.

LIGHT "ON"

- CONNECT TEST LIGHT BETWEEN HARNESS CKT 465 AND GROUND.
- IGNITION "OFF" FOR 10 SECONDS.
- NOTE TEST LIGHT WITHIN 2 SECONDS AFTER IGNITION "ON".

LIGHT "ON"

- FAULTY RELAY.

NOTE: IF ORIGINAL COMPLAINT WAS "CRANKS BUT WILL NOT RUN" MAKE THE FOLLOWING ADDITIONAL CHECKS:

- ENGINE IDLING AT NORMAL OPERATING TEMPERATURE.
- OIL PRESSURE NORMAL.
- DISCONNECT FUEL PUMP RELAY.
- ENGINE SHOULD CONTINUE TO RUN.
- DOES IT?

YES

- RECONNECT FUEL PUMP RELAY.
- IGNITION "OFF".
- PROBE FUEL PUMP TEST TERMINAL WITH A TEST LIGHT TO GROUND.

LIGHT "OFF"

FUEL PUMP CIRCUIT OK

NO

FAULTY OIL PRESSURE SWITCH.

LIGHT "ON"

FAULTY OIL PRESSURE SWITCH

YES

- CLEAR CODES.
- START AND RUN ENGINE FOR 30 SECONDS OR UNTIL CODE 54 SETS. DOES CODE SET?

YES

- AT THE ECM, BACK PROBE CKT 120 WITH A TEST LIGHT TO GROUND.
- IGNITION "OFF" FOR 10 SECONDS.
- NOTE LIGHT WITHIN 2 SECONDS AFTER IGNITION "ON".

NO

CODE 54 IS INTERMITTENT. REFER TO "INTERMITTENTS" IN SECTION "B".

LIGHT "ON"

FAULTY CONNECTION AT ECM OR FAULTY ECM.

LIGHT "OFF"

OPEN CKT 120 TO ECM.

LIGHT "OFF"

REPAIR OPEN CKT 450.

LIGHT "OFF"

CKT 465 OPEN, SHORTED TO GROUND, OR FAULTY ECM.

Fig. 152 Engine controls diagnostic chart

CODE 51

PROM ERROR
(FAULTY OR INCORRECT PROM)

> CHECK THAT ALL PINS ARE FULLY INSERTED IN THE SOCKET. IF OK, REPLACE PROM, CLEAR MEMORY AND RECHECK. IF CODE 51 REAPPEARS, REPLACE ECM.

CLEAR ALL CODES AND CONFIRM "CLOSED LOOP" OPERATION AND NO "SERVICE ENGINE SOON" LIGHT

CODE 52

CALPAK ERROR
(FAULTY OR INCORRECT CALPAK)

> CHECK THAT ALL PINS ARE FULLY INSERTED IN THE SOCKET. IF OK, REPLACE CALPAK, CLEAR MEMORY AND RECHECK. IF CODE 52 REAPPEARS, REPLACE ECM.

CLEAR ALL CODES AND CONFIRM "CLOSED LOOP" OPERATION AND NO "SERVICE ENGINE SOON" LIGHT

CODE 55

ECM ERROR

> REPLACE ELECTRONIC CONTROL MODULE (ECM).

CLEAR ALL CODES AND CONFIRM "CLOSED LOOP" OPERATION AND NO "SERVICE ENGINE SOON" LIGHT

Fig. 153 Engine controls diagnostic chart

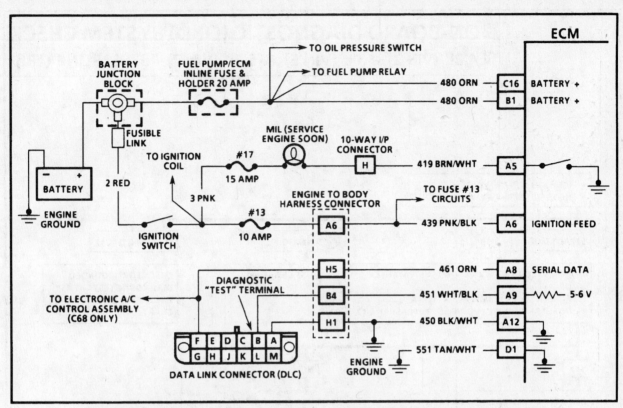

ON-BOARD DIAGNOSTIC (OBD) SYSTEM CHECK
4.3L (VIN Z), 5.0L (VIN E) & 5.7L (VIN 7) "B" CARLINE (TBI)

Circuit Description:

The On-Board Diagnostic (OBD) system check is an organized approach to identifying a problem created by an electronic engine control system malfunction. It must be the starting point for any driveability complaint diagnosis, because it directs the service technician to the next logical step in diagnosing the complaint. Understanding the chart and using it correctly will reduce diagnostic time and prevent the unnecessary replacement of good parts.

Test Description: Number(s) below refer to circled number(s) on the diagnostic chart.

1. This step is a check for the proper operation of the Malfunction Indicator Lamp (MIL) "Service Engine Soon." The MIL should be "ON" steady.

2. No MIL at this point indicates that there is a problem with the MIL circuit or the ECM control of that circuit.

3. This test checks the ability of the ECM to control the MIL. With the diagnostic terminal grounded, the MIL should flash a DTC 12 three times, followed by any DTC stored in memory.

4. Most of the 6E procedures use a scan tool to aid diagnosis, therefore, serial data must be available. If a PROM error is present, the ECM may have been able to flash DTC 12/51, but not enable serial data.

5. Although the ECM is powered up, a "Cranks But Will Not Run" symptom could exist because of an ECM or system problem.

6. This step will isolate if the customer complaint is a MIL or a driveability problem with no MIL. An invalid DTC may be the result of a faulty scan tool.

7. Comparison of actual control system data with the typical values is a quick check to determine if any parameter is not within limits. Keep in mind that a base engine problem (i.e., advanced cam timing) may substantially alter sensor values.

8. Installation of a scan tool will provide a good ground path for the ECM and may hide a driveability complaint due to poor ECM grounds.

9. If the actual data is not within the typical values established, the charts in "Component Systems," Section "6E2-C" will provide a functional check of the suspect component or system.

Fig. 154 Engine controls diagnostic chart

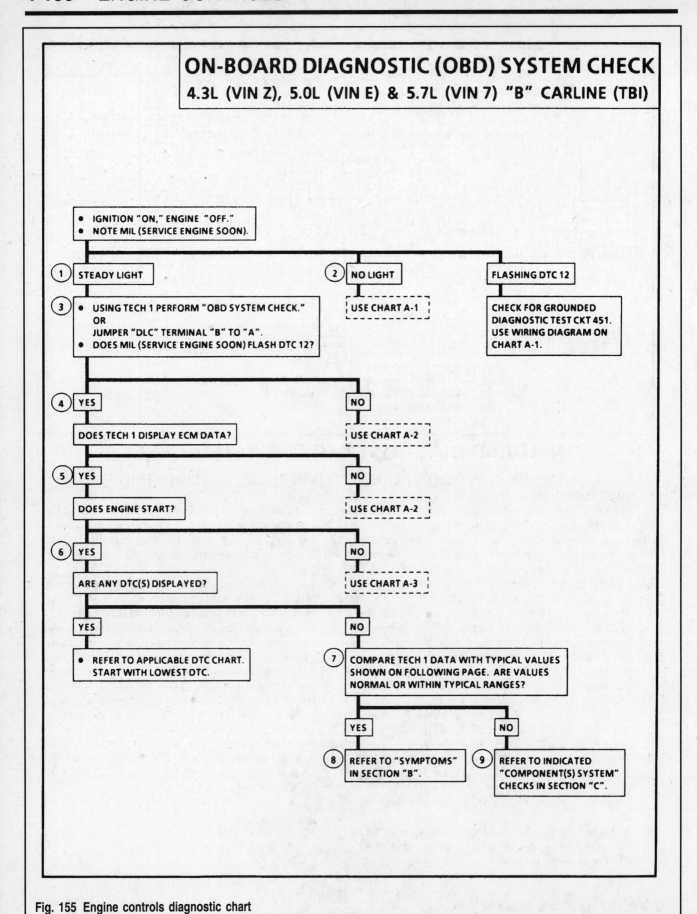

ON-BOARD DIAGNOSTIC (OBD) SYSTEM CHECK
4.3L (VIN Z), 5.0L (VIN E) & 5.7L (VIN 7) "B" CARLINE (TBI)

- IGNITION "ON," ENGINE "OFF."
- NOTE MIL (SERVICE ENGINE SOON).

1 STEADY LIGHT

2 NO LIGHT

FLASHING DTC 12

3
- USING TECH 1 PERFORM "OBD SYSTEM CHECK." OR
  JUMPER "DLC" TERMINAL "B" TO "A".
- DOES MIL (SERVICE ENGINE SOON) FLASH DTC 12?

USE CHART A-1

CHECK FOR GROUNDED DIAGNOSTIC TEST CKT 451. USE WIRING DIAGRAM ON CHART A-1.

4 YES

NO

DOES TECH 1 DISPLAY ECM DATA?

USE CHART A-2

5 YES

NO

DOES ENGINE START?

USE CHART A-2

6 YES

NO

ARE ANY DTC(S) DISPLAYED?

USE CHART A-3

YES

NO

- REFER TO APPLICABLE DTC CHART. START WITH LOWEST DTC.

7 COMPARE TECH 1 DATA WITH TYPICAL VALUES SHOWN ON FOLLOWING PAGE. ARE VALUES NORMAL OR WITHIN TYPICAL RANGES?

YES

NO

8 REFER TO "SYMPTOMS" IN SECTION "B".

9 REFER TO INDICATED "COMPONENT(S) SYSTEM" CHECKS IN SECTION "C".

Fig. 155 Engine controls diagnostic chart

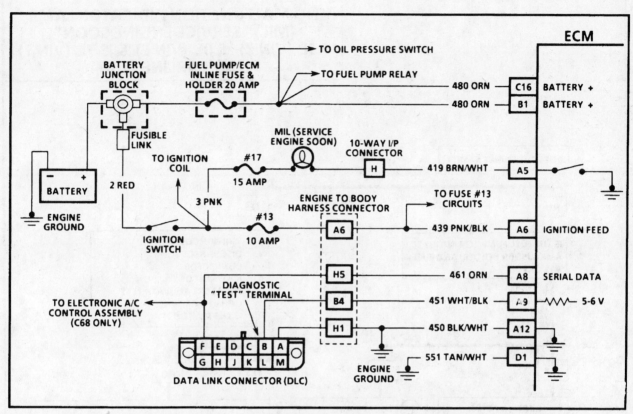

CHART A-1

NO MALFUNCTION INDICATOR LAMP (MIL) "SERVICE ENGINE SOON"
4.3L (VIN Z), 5.0L (VIN E) & 5.7L (VIN 7) "B" CARLINE (TBI)

Circuit Description:

There should always be a steady Malfunction Indicator Lamp (MIL) "Service Engine Soon," when the ignition is "ON" and engine stopped. Ignition voltage is supplied directly to the light bulb. The Engine Control Module (ECM) will control the light and turn it "ON" by providing a ground path through CKT 419 to the ECM.

Test Description: Number(s) below refer to circled number(s) on the diagnostic chart.

1. Battery feed CKT 480 is protected by a 20 amp in-line fuse. If this fuse was open, refer to wiring diagram on the facing page of DTC 54.
2. Using a test light connected to 12 volts, probe each of the system ground circuits to be sure a good ground is present. Refer to the ECM connector terminal end view in front of this section for ECM pin locations and ground circuits.

Diagnostic Aids:

Engine runs OK, check:
- Faulty light bulb.
- CKT 419 open.
- Fuse #17 open. This will result in no MIL operation.

Engine cranks but will not run, check:
- Continuous battery - fuse or fusible link open.
- ECM ignition fuse open. (Fuse #13)
- Battery CKT 480 to ECM open.
- Ignition CKT 439 to ECM open.
- Poor connection to ECM.

Fig. 156 Engine controls diagnostic chart

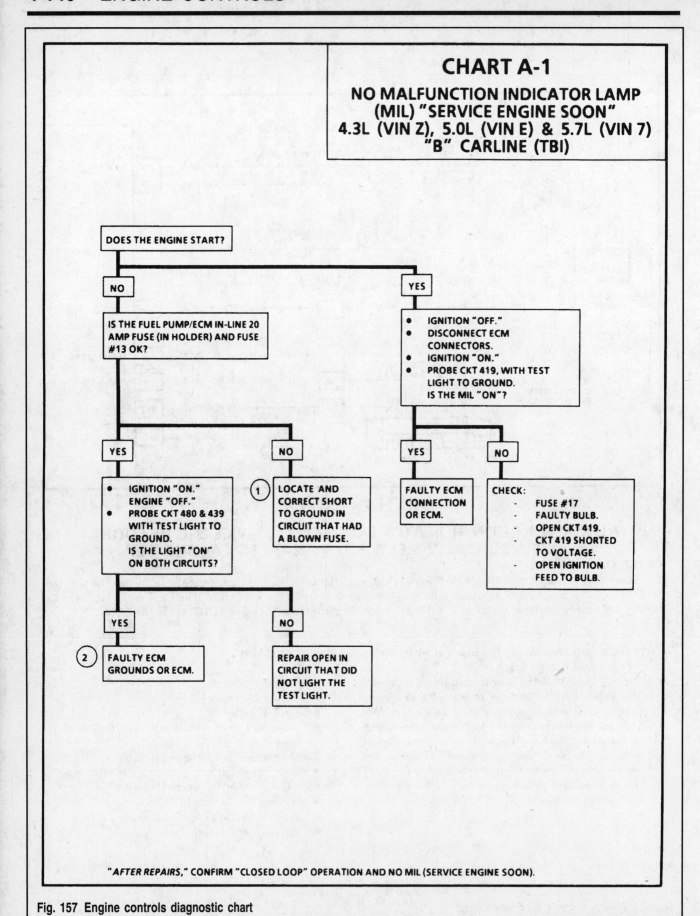

CHART A-1

**NO MALFUNCTION INDICATOR LAMP
(MIL) "SERVICE ENGINE SOON"
4.3L (VIN Z), 5.0L (VIN E) & 5.7L (VIN 7)
"B" CARLINE (TBI)**

DOES THE ENGINE START?

NO

YES

IS THE FUEL PUMP/ECM IN-LINE 20 AMP FUSE (IN HOLDER) AND FUSE #13 OK?

- IGNITION "OFF."
- DISCONNECT ECM CONNECTORS.
- IGNITION "ON."
- PROBE CKT 419, WITH TEST LIGHT TO GROUND. IS THE MIL "ON"?

YES

NO

YES

NO

- IGNITION "ON." ENGINE "OFF."
- PROBE CKT 480 & 439 WITH TEST LIGHT TO GROUND. IS THE LIGHT "ON" ON BOTH CIRCUITS?

1 LOCATE AND CORRECT SHORT TO GROUND IN CIRCUIT THAT HAD A BLOWN FUSE.

FAULTY ECM CONNECTION OR ECM.

CHECK:
- FUSE #17
- FAULTY BULB.
- OPEN CKT 419.
- CKT 419 SHORTED TO VOLTAGE.
- OPEN IGNITION FEED TO BULB.

YES

NO

2 FAULTY ECM GROUNDS OR ECM.

REPAIR OPEN IN CIRCUIT THAT DID NOT LIGHT THE TEST LIGHT.

"AFTER REPAIRS," CONFIRM "CLOSED LOOP" OPERATION AND NO MIL (SERVICE ENGINE SOON).

Fig. 157 Engine controls diagnostic chart

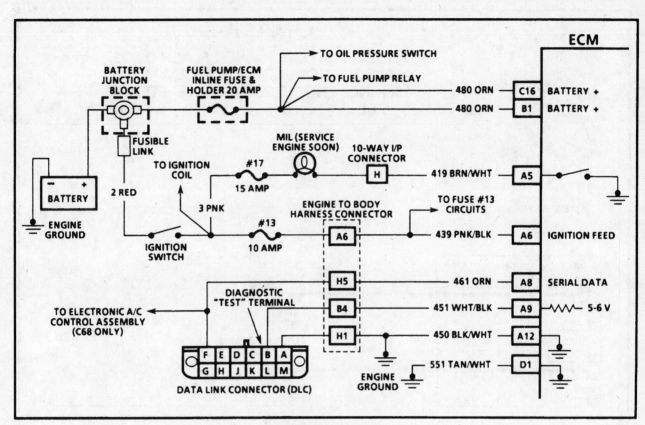

CHART A-2

NO DLC DATA OR WILL NOT FLASH DTC 12, MALFUNCTION INDICATOR LAMP (MIL) "SERVICE ENGINE SOON" "ON" STEADY
4.3L (VIN Z), 5.0L (VIN E) & 5.7L (VIN 7) "B" CARLINE (TBI)

Circuit Description:

There should always be a steady MIL (Service Engine Soon), when the ignition is "ON" and engine stopped. Ignition voltage is supplied directly to the light bulb. The Engine Control Module (ECM) will control the light and turn it "ON" by providing a ground path through CKT 419 to the ECM.

With the diagnostic "test" terminal grounded, the light should flash a DTC 12, followed by any DTC(S) stored in memory.

A steady light suggests a short to ground in the light control CKT 419, or an open in diagnostic CKT 451.

Test Description: Number(s) below refer to circled number(s) on the diagnostic chart.

1. If the scan tool is unable to display serial data due to an ECM problem, then the ECM will not flash a DTC 12. If DTC 12 does flash, check to see if the scan tool works properly on another vehicle. If the scan tool is functioning properly, and CKT 461 is OK, then a faulty PROM or ECM may be causing the NO DLC data.

2. If the MIL goes "OFF," when the ECM connector is disconnected, then CKT 419 is not shorted to ground.

3. This step will check for an open diagnostic CKT 451.

4. At this point, the MIL (Service Engine Soon) wiring is OK. The problem is a faulty ECM or PROM. If DTC 12 does not flash, the ECM should be replaced using the original PROM. Replace the PROM only after trying an ECM, as a defective PROM is an unlikely cause of the problem.

Fig. 158 Engine controls diagnostic chart

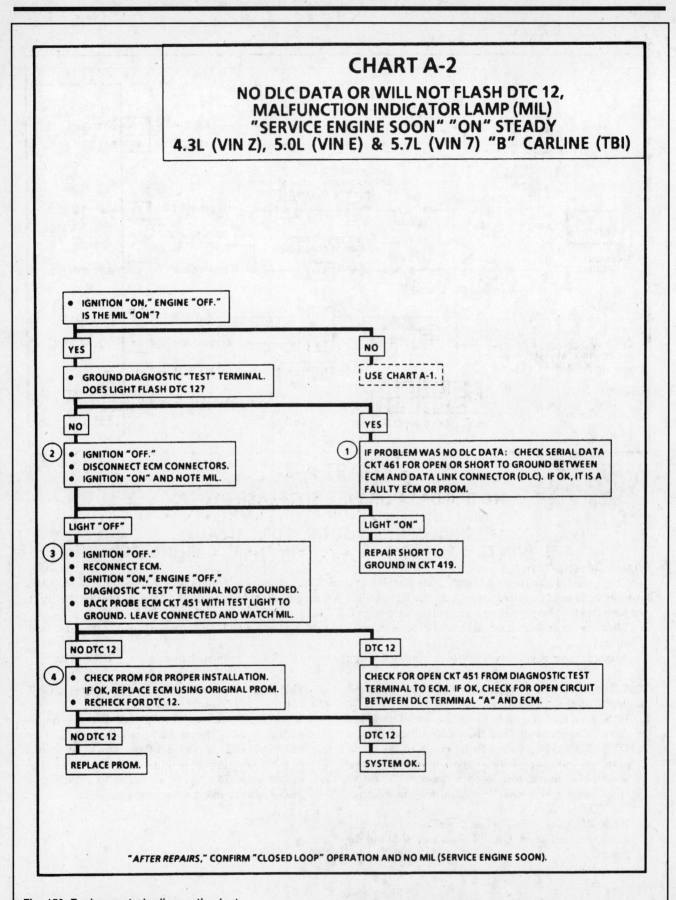

CHART A-2

NO DLC DATA OR WILL NOT FLASH DTC 12,
MALFUNCTION INDICATOR LAMP (MIL)
"SERVICE ENGINE SOON" "ON" STEADY
4.3L (VIN Z), 5.0L (VIN E) & 5.7L (VIN 7) "B" CARLINE (TBI)

- IGNITION "ON," ENGINE "OFF."
  IS THE MIL "ON"?

YES

- GROUND DIAGNOSTIC "TEST" TERMINAL.
  DOES LIGHT FLASH DTC 12?

NO

USE CHART A-1.

NO

②
- IGNITION "OFF."
- DISCONNECT ECM CONNECTORS.
- IGNITION "ON" AND NOTE MIL.

YES

① IF PROBLEM WAS NO DLC DATA: CHECK SERIAL DATA
CKT 461 FOR OPEN OR SHORT TO GROUND BETWEEN
ECM AND DATA LINK CONNECTOR (DLC). IF OK, IT IS A
FAULTY ECM OR PROM.

LIGHT "OFF"

LIGHT "ON"

③
- IGNITION "OFF."
- RECONNECT ECM.
- IGNITION "ON," ENGINE "OFF,"
  DIAGNOSTIC "TEST" TERMINAL NOT GROUNDED.
- BACK PROBE ECM CKT 451 WITH TEST LIGHT TO
  GROUND. LEAVE CONNECTED AND WATCH MIL.

REPAIR SHORT TO
GROUND IN CKT 419.

NO DTC 12

DTC 12

④
- CHECK PROM FOR PROPER INSTALLATION.
  IF OK, REPLACE ECM USING ORIGINAL PROM.
- RECHECK FOR DTC 12.

CHECK FOR OPEN CKT 451 FROM DIAGNOSTIC TEST
TERMINAL TO ECM. IF OK, CHECK FOR OPEN CIRCUIT
BETWEEN DLC TERMINAL "A" AND ECM.

NO DTC 12

DTC 12

REPLACE PROM.

SYSTEM OK.

"AFTER REPAIRS," CONFIRM "CLOSED LOOP" OPERATION AND NO MIL (SERVICE ENGINE SOON).

Fig. 159 Engine controls diagnostic chart

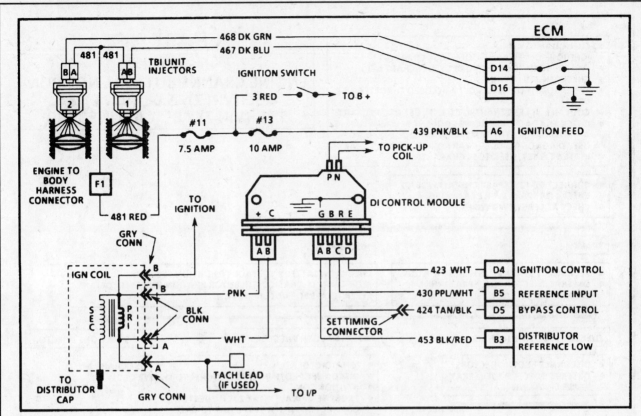

CHART A-3

(Page 1 of 2)
ENGINE CRANKS BUT WILL NOT RUN
4.3L (VIN Z), 5.0L (VIN E) & 5.7L (VIN 7) "B" CARLINE (TBI)

Circuit Description:
   This chart assumes that battery condition and engine cranking speed are OK, and there is adequate fuel in the tank.

Test Description: Number(s) below refer to circled number(s) on the diagnostic chart.

1. A MIL (Service Engine Soon) "ON" is a basic test to determine if there is a 12 volts supply and ignition 12 volts to ECM. No DLC data may be due to an ECM problem and CHART A-2 will diagnose the ECM. If TP sensor is over 2.5 volts, the engine may be in the clear flood mode which will cause starting problems. A "slewed" or "shifted" ECT that indicates coolant temperature less than actual may flood the engine during hot restarts. A ECT that indicates coolant temperature greater than actual may result in a "no start" in cold weather.
2. No spark may be caused by one of several components related to the Distributor Ignition (DI) system. CHART C-4 will address all problems related to the causes of a no spark condition.
3. Fuel spray from the injector(s) indicates that fuel is available. However, the engine could be severely flooded due to an excessive amount of fuel.
4. While cranking engine, there should be no fuel spray with injector disconnected. Replace an injector if it sprays fuel or drips.

5. The fuel pressure will drop after the fuel pump stops running due to a controlled bleed in the fuel system. Use of the fuel pressure gage will determine if fuel system pressure is enough for engine to start and run. The key may have to be cycled "ON" and "OFF," 2 or more times for accurate reading.
6. No fuel spray from injector indicates a faulty fuel system, no ECM control of injectors, or no ignition feed.
7. This test will determine if the ignition control module is not generating the reference pulse, or if the wiring or ECM are at fault. By touching and removing a test light connected to 12 volts on CKT 430, a reference pulse should be generated. If injector test light blinks, the ECM and wiring are OK.

Diagnostic Aids:
- Water or foreign material in the fuel system can cause a no start during freezing weather.
- An EGR valve sticking open can cause a low air/fuel ratio during cranking.
- Fuel pressure: Low fuel pressure can result in a very lean air/fuel ratio. Use CHART A-7.
- A grounded CKT 423 (IC) may cause a "No-Start" or a "Start" then "Stall" condition.

Fig. 160 Engine controls diagnostic chart

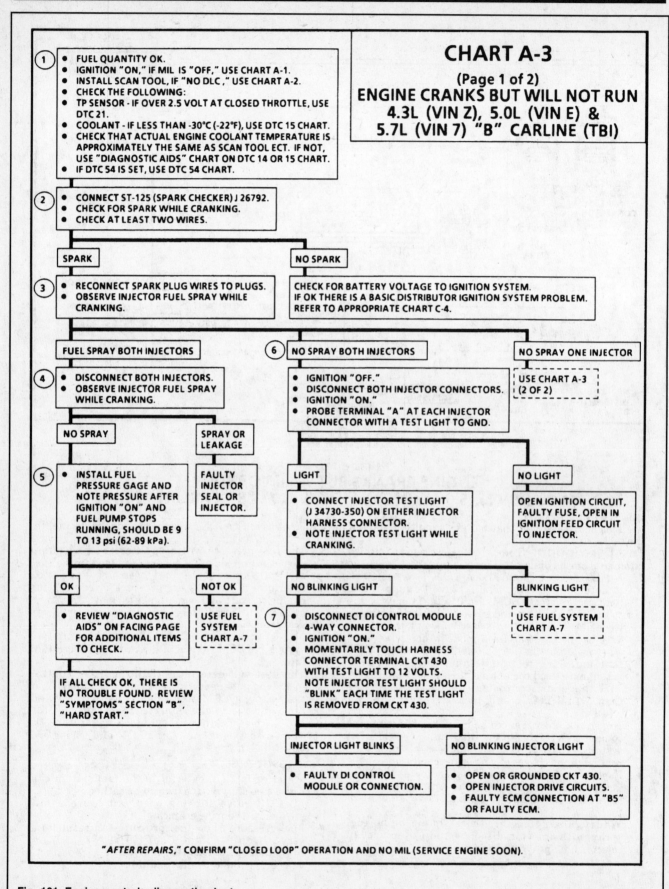

CHART A-3
(Page 1 of 2)
ENGINE CRANKS BUT WILL NOT RUN
4.3L (VIN Z), 5.0L (VIN E) &
5.7L (VIN 7) "B" CARLINE (TBI)

1
- FUEL QUANTITY OK.
- IGNITION "ON," IF MIL IS "OFF," USE CHART A-1.
- INSTALL SCAN TOOL, IF "NO DLC," USE CHART A-2.
- CHECK THE FOLLOWING:
- TP SENSOR - IF OVER 2.5 VOLT AT CLOSED THROTTLE, USE DTC 21.
- COOLANT - IF LESS THAN -30°C (-22°F), USE DTC 15 CHART.
- CHECK THAT ACTUAL ENGINE COOLANT TEMPERATURE IS APPROXIMATELY THE SAME AS SCAN TOOL ECT. IF NOT, USE "DIAGNOSTIC AIDS" CHART ON DTC 14 OR 15 CHART.
- IF DTC 54 IS SET, USE DTC 54 CHART.

2
- CONNECT ST-125 (SPARK CHECKER) J 26792.
- CHECK FOR SPARK WHILE CRANKING.
- CHECK AT LEAST TWO WIRES.

SPARK | **NO SPARK**

3
- RECONNECT SPARK PLUG WIRES TO PLUGS.
- OBSERVE INJECTOR FUEL SPRAY WHILE CRANKING.

CHECK FOR BATTERY VOLTAGE TO IGNITION SYSTEM.
IF OK THERE IS A BASIC DISTRIBUTOR IGNITION SYSTEM PROBLEM.
REFER TO APPROPRIATE CHART C-4.

FUEL SPRAY BOTH INJECTORS | **6 NO SPRAY BOTH INJECTORS** | **NO SPRAY ONE INJECTOR**

4
- DISCONNECT BOTH INJECTORS.
- OBSERVE INJECTOR FUEL SPRAY WHILE CRANKING.

6
- IGNITION "OFF."
- DISCONNECT BOTH INJECTOR CONNECTORS.
- IGNITION "ON."
- PROBE TERMINAL "A" AT EACH INJECTOR CONNECTOR WITH A TEST LIGHT TO GND.

USE CHART A-3 (2 OF 2)

NO SPRAY | **SPRAY OR LEAKAGE**

LIGHT | **NO LIGHT**

5
- INSTALL FUEL PRESSURE GAGE AND NOTE PRESSURE AFTER IGNITION "ON" AND FUEL PUMP STOPS RUNNING, SHOULD BE 9 TO 13 psi (62-89 kPa).

FAULTY INJECTOR SEAL OR INJECTOR.

- CONNECT INJECTOR TEST LIGHT (J 34730-350) ON EITHER INJECTOR HARNESS CONNECTOR.
- NOTE INJECTOR TEST LIGHT WHILE CRANKING.

OPEN IGNITION CIRCUIT, FAULTY FUSE, OPEN IN IGNITION FEED CIRCUIT TO INJECTOR.

OK | **NOT OK** | **NO BLINKING LIGHT** | **BLINKING LIGHT**

- REVIEW "DIAGNOSTIC AIDS" ON FACING PAGE FOR ADDITIONAL ITEMS TO CHECK.

USE FUEL SYSTEM CHART A-7

7
- DISCONNECT DI CONTROL MODULE 4-WAY CONNECTOR.
- IGNITION "ON."
- MOMENTARILY TOUCH HARNESS CONNECTOR TERMINAL CKT 430 WITH TEST LIGHT TO 12 VOLTS. NOTE INJECTOR TEST LIGHT SHOULD "BLINK" EACH TIME THE TEST LIGHT IS REMOVED FROM CKT 430.

USE FUEL SYSTEM CHART A-7

IF ALL CHECK OK, THERE IS NO TROUBLE FOUND. REVIEW "SYMPTOMS" SECTION "B", "HARD START."

INJECTOR LIGHT BLINKS | **NO BLINKING INJECTOR LIGHT**

- FAULTY DI CONTROL MODULE OR CONNECTION.

- OPEN OR GROUNDED CKT 430.
- OPEN INJECTOR DRIVE CIRCUITS.
- FAULTY ECM CONNECTION AT "B5" OR FAULTY ECM.

"AFTER REPAIRS," CONFIRM "CLOSED LOOP" OPERATION AND NO MIL (SERVICE ENGINE SOON).

Fig. 161 Engine controls diagnostic chart

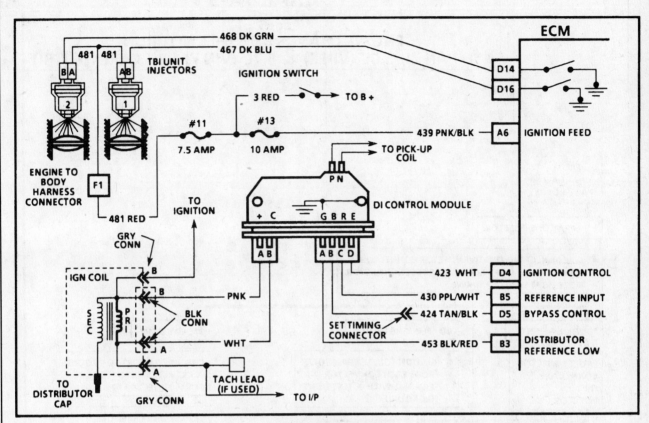

CHART A-3

(Page 2 of 2)
ENGINE CRANKS BUT WILL NOT RUN
4.3L (VIN Z), 5.0L (VIN E) & 5.7L (VIN 7) "B" CARLINE (TBI)

Circuit Description:

This chart assumes that battery condition and engine cranking speed are OK, and there is adequate fuel in the tank.

Test Description: Number(s) below refer to circled number(s) on the diagnostic chart.

1. No fuel spray from one injector indicates a faulty fuel injector or no ECM control of injector. If the test light "blinks" while cranking, then ECM control should be considered OK. Be sure test light makes good contact between connector terminals during test. The test light bulb should be a J 34730-350.

2. Check resistance of both injectors. Resistance of injectors should be above 1.2 ohms. Replace injector(s) that are below 1.2 ohms.

3. CKT 481 supplies ignition voltage to the injectors. Probe each connector terminal with a test light to ground. There should be a light "ON" at one terminal of each connector. If the test light confirms ignition voltage at the connector, the ECM injector control CKT 467 or CKT 468 may be open. Reconnect the injector. Using a test light connected to ground, check for a light at the applicable ECM connector terminal. A light at this point indicates that the injector drive circuit involved is OK.

If an ECM repeat failure has occurred, the injector is shorted. Replace the injector and ECM.

Fig. 162 Engine controls diagnostic chart

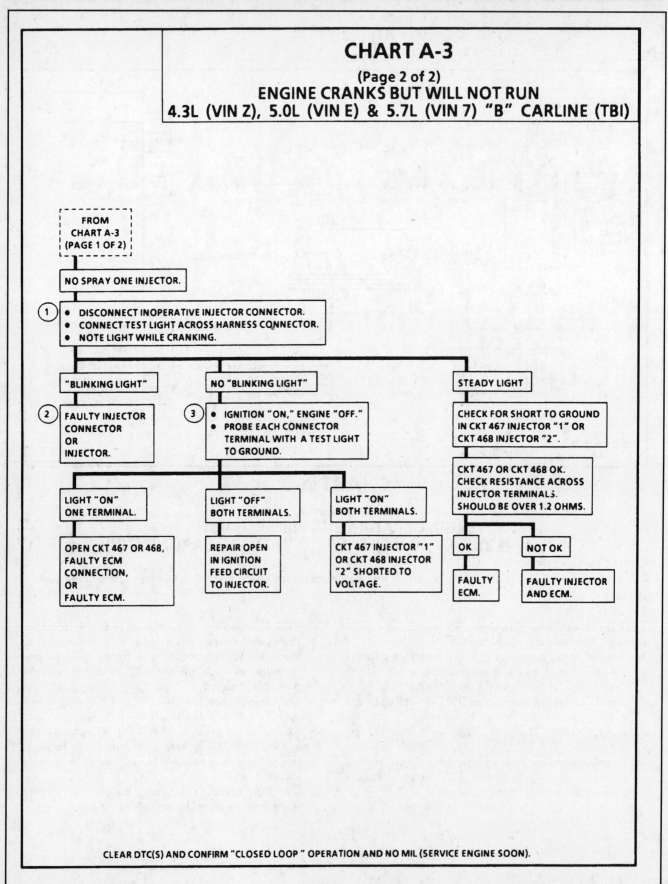

CHART A-3
(Page 2 of 2)
ENGINE CRANKS BUT WILL NOT RUN
4.3L (VIN Z), 5.0L (VIN E) & 5.7L (VIN 7) "B" CARLINE (TBI)

FROM CHART A-3 (PAGE 1 OF 2)

NO SPRAY ONE INJECTOR.

1
- DISCONNECT INOPERATIVE INJECTOR CONNECTOR.
- CONNECT TEST LIGHT ACROSS HARNESS CONNECTOR.
- NOTE LIGHT WHILE CRANKING.

"BLINKING LIGHT"

NO "BLINKING LIGHT"

STEADY LIGHT

2 FAULTY INJECTOR CONNECTOR OR INJECTOR.

3
- IGNITION "ON," ENGINE "OFF."
- PROBE EACH CONNECTOR TERMINAL WITH A TEST LIGHT TO GROUND.

CHECK FOR SHORT TO GROUND IN CKT 467 INJECTOR "1" OR CKT 468 INJECTOR "2".

CKT 467 OR CKT 468 OK. CHECK RESISTANCE ACROSS INJECTOR TERMINALS. SHOULD BE OVER 1.2 OHMS.

LIGHT "ON" ONE TERMINAL.

LIGHT "OFF" BOTH TERMINALS.

LIGHT "ON" BOTH TERMINALS.

OK

NOT OK

OPEN CKT 467 OR 468, FAULTY ECM CONNECTION, OR FAULTY ECM.

REPAIR OPEN IN IGNITION FEED CIRCUIT TO INJECTOR.

CKT 467 INJECTOR "1" OR CKT 468 INJECTOR "2" SHORTED TO VOLTAGE.

FAULTY ECM.

FAULTY INJECTOR AND ECM.

CLEAR DTC(S) AND CONFIRM "CLOSED LOOP " OPERATION AND NO MIL (SERVICE ENGINE SOON).

Fig. 163 Engine controls diagnostic chart

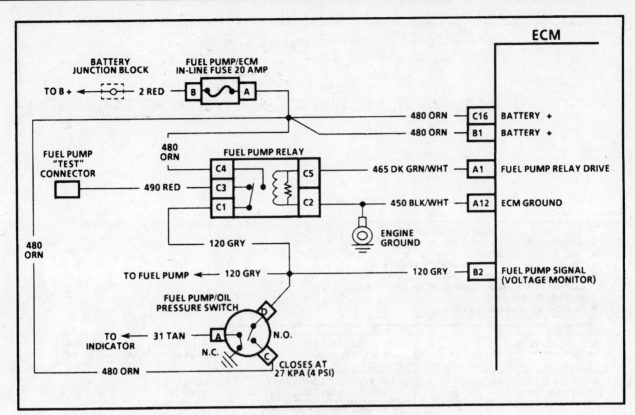

CHART A-7

(Page 1 of 3)
FUEL SYSTEM DIAGNOSIS
4.3L (VIN Z), 5.0L (VIN E) & 5.7L (VIN 7) "B" CARLINE (TBI)

Circuit Description:

When the ignition switch is turned "ON," the Engine Control Module (ECM) will turn "ON" the in-tank fuel pump. It will remain "ON" as long as the engine is cranking or running, and the ECM is receiving ignition reference pulses. If there are no reference pulses, the ECM will shut "OFF" the fuel pump within 2 seconds after key "ON."

The pump will deliver fuel to the TBI unit, where the system pressure is controlled from 62 to 90 kPa (9 to 13 psi) by the pressure regulator. Excess fuel is then returned to the fuel tank.

When the engine is stopped, the fuel pump can be turned "ON" by applying battery voltage to the fuel pump "test" terminal located near the passenger side cowl of the engine compartment.

Test Description: Number(s) below refer to the circled number(s) on the diagnostic chart.

1. Fuel pressure should be noted while fuel pump is running. Fuel pressure will drop immediately after fuel pump stops running due to a controlled bleed in the fuel system.

   The fuel pump test terminal is located near the passenger side cowl of the engine compartment.

2. This check will verify the operation of the fuel pump check valve. A leaking check valve will cause fuel in the pressure (feed) line to drain back to the tank and result in long crank times. The amount of pressure is not important as long as some pressure is maintained.

Diagnostic Aids:

Improper fuel system pressure can result in one of the following symptoms:

- Extended cranking time before the engine starts.
- Rough idle.
- Low idle speed.
- Cranks, but will not run.
- DTC 44.
- DTC 45.
- Cuts out, may feel like ignition problem.
- Poor fuel economy, loss of power.
- Hesitation.

Fig. 164 Engine controls diagnostic chart

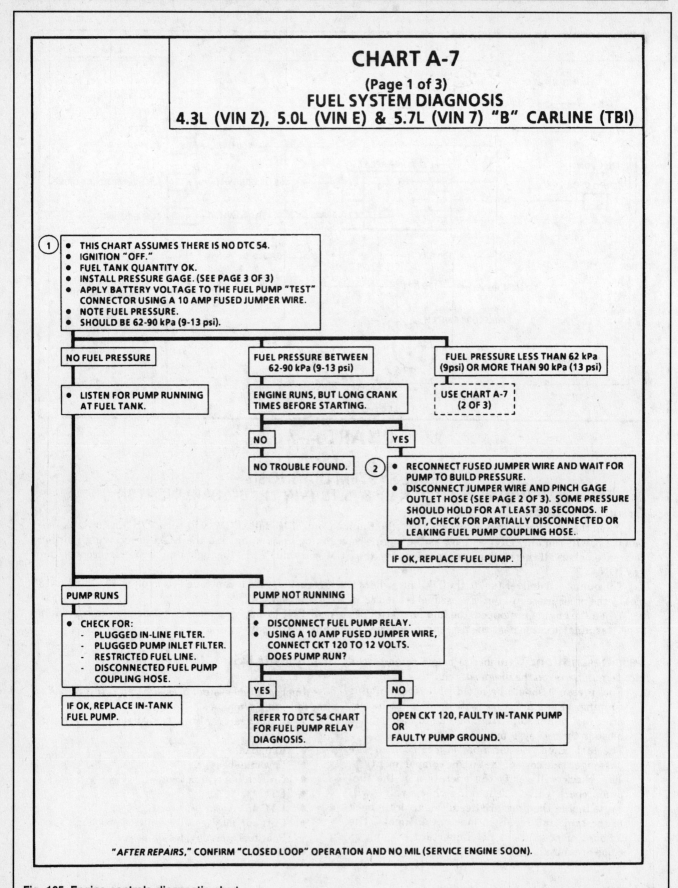

CHART A-7

(Page 1 of 3)
FUEL SYSTEM DIAGNOSIS
4.3L (VIN Z), 5.0L (VIN E) & 5.7L (VIN 7) "B" CARLINE (TBI)

1
- THIS CHART ASSUMES THERE IS NO DTC 54.
- IGNITION "OFF."
- FUEL TANK QUANTITY OK.
- INSTALL PRESSURE GAGE. (SEE PAGE 3 OF 3)
- APPLY BATTERY VOLTAGE TO THE FUEL PUMP "TEST" CONNECTOR USING A 10 AMP FUSED JUMPER WIRE.
- NOTE FUEL PRESSURE.
- SHOULD BE 62-90 kPa (9-13 psi).

NO FUEL PRESSURE

FUEL PRESSURE BETWEEN 62-90 kPa (9-13 psi)

FUEL PRESSURE LESS THAN 62 kPa (9psi) OR MORE THAN 90 kPa (13 psi)

- LISTEN FOR PUMP RUNNING AT FUEL TANK.

ENGINE RUNS, BUT LONG CRANK TIMES BEFORE STARTING.

USE CHART A-7 (2 OF 3)

NO

YES

NO TROUBLE FOUND.

2
- RECONNECT FUSED JUMPER WIRE AND WAIT FOR PUMP TO BUILD PRESSURE.
- DISCONNECT JUMPER WIRE AND PINCH GAGE OUTLET HOSE (SEE PAGE 2 OF 3). SOME PRESSURE SHOULD HOLD FOR AT LEAST 30 SECONDS. IF NOT, CHECK FOR PARTIALLY DISCONNECTED OR LEAKING FUEL PUMP COUPLING HOSE.

IF OK, REPLACE FUEL PUMP.

PUMP RUNS

PUMP NOT RUNNING

- CHECK FOR:
  - PLUGGED IN-LINE FILTER.
  - PLUGGED PUMP INLET FILTER.
  - RESTRICTED FUEL LINE.
  - DISCONNECTED FUEL PUMP COUPLING HOSE.

- DISCONNECT FUEL PUMP RELAY.
- USING A 10 AMP FUSED JUMPER WIRE, CONNECT CKT 120 TO 12 VOLTS. DOES PUMP RUN?

IF OK, REPLACE IN-TANK FUEL PUMP.

YES

NO

REFER TO DTC 54 CHART FOR FUEL PUMP RELAY DIAGNOSIS.

OPEN CKT 120, FAULTY IN-TANK PUMP OR FAULTY PUMP GROUND.

"AFTER REPAIRS," CONFIRM "CLOSED LOOP" OPERATION AND NO MIL (SERVICE ENGINE SOON).

Fig. 165 Engine controls diagnostic chart

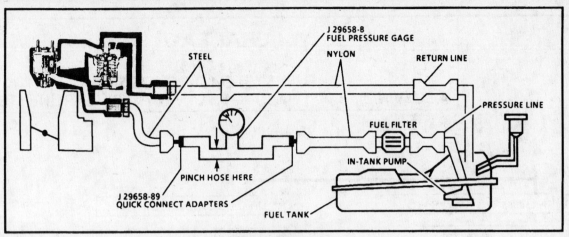

CHART A-7

(Page 2 of 3)
FUEL SYSTEM DIAGNOSIS
4.3L (VIN Z), 5.0L (VIN E) & 5.7L (VIN 7) "B" CARLINE (TBI)

Test Description: Number(s) below refer to circled number(s) on the diagnostic chart.

1. Fuel pressure less than 62 kPa (9 psi) falls into two areas:
   - Amount of fuel to injectors OK, but pressure is less than 62 kPa (9 psi). In this case the fuel injection system will be lean and may set DTC 44. Also, hard starting cold and poor overall performance.
   - Restricted flow causing pressure drop. Normally, a vehicle with a fuel pressure of less than 62 kPa (9 psi) at idle will not be driveable. However, if the pressure drop occurs only while driving, the engine will surge then stop as pressure begins to drop rapidly.

2. Turning the fuel pump "ON" and restricting fuel flow at the fuel pressure gage (as shown) will determine if the fuel pump can supply enough fuel pressure to the injector to operate properly, above 62 kPa (9 psi).

   NOTICE: Do not restrict the fuel return line as this may damage the fuel pressure regulator.

3. This test determines if the high fuel pressure is due to a restricted fuel return line or a throttle body pressure regulator problem. Apply battery voltage to the fuel pump test connector only long enough to get an accurate fuel pressure reading.

Fig. 166 Engine controls diagnostic chart

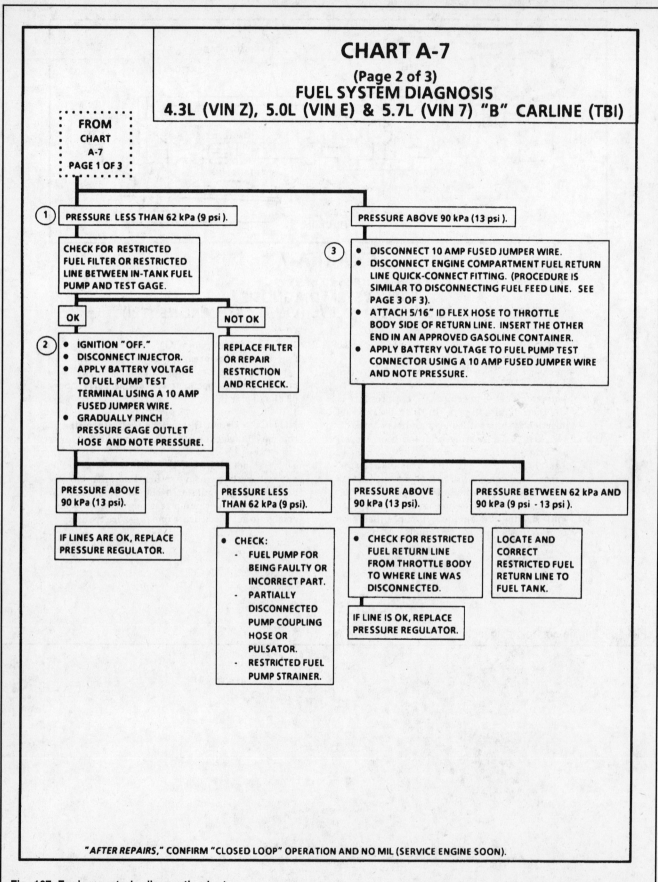

CHART A-7

(Page 2 of 3)
FUEL SYSTEM DIAGNOSIS
4.3L (VIN Z), 5.0L (VIN E) & 5.7L (VIN 7) "B" CARLINE (TBI)

FROM CHART A-7 PAGE 1 OF 3

1 | PRESSURE LESS THAN 62 kPa (9 psi).

PRESSURE ABOVE 90 kPa (13 psi).

CHECK FOR RESTRICTED FUEL FILTER OR RESTRICTED LINE BETWEEN IN-TANK FUEL PUMP AND TEST GAGE.

3
- DISCONNECT 10 AMP FUSED JUMPER WIRE.
- DISCONNECT ENGINE COMPARTMENT FUEL RETURN LINE QUICK-CONNECT FITTING. (PROCEDURE IS SIMILAR TO DISCONNECTING FUEL FEED LINE. SEE PAGE 3 OF 3).
- ATTACH 5/16" ID FLEX HOSE TO THROTTLE BODY SIDE OF RETURN LINE. INSERT THE OTHER END IN AN APPROVED GASOLINE CONTAINER.
- APPLY BATTERY VOLTAGE TO FUEL PUMP TEST CONNECTOR USING A 10 AMP FUSED JUMPER WIRE AND NOTE PRESSURE.

OK | NOT OK

2
- IGNITION "OFF."
- DISCONNECT INJECTOR.
- APPLY BATTERY VOLTAGE TO FUEL PUMP TEST TERMINAL USING A 10 AMP FUSED JUMPER WIRE.
- GRADUALLY PINCH PRESSURE GAGE OUTLET HOSE AND NOTE PRESSURE.

REPLACE FILTER OR REPAIR RESTRICTION AND RECHECK.

PRESSURE ABOVE 90 kPa (13 psi).

PRESSURE LESS THAN 62 kPa (9 psi).

PRESSURE ABOVE 90 kPa (13 psi).

PRESSURE BETWEEN 62 kPa AND 90 kPa (9 psi - 13 psi).

IF LINES ARE OK, REPLACE PRESSURE REGULATOR.

- CHECK:
  - FUEL PUMP FOR BEING FAULTY OR INCORRECT PART.
  - PARTIALLY DISCONNECTED PUMP COUPLING HOSE OR PULSATOR.
  - RESTRICTED FUEL PUMP STRAINER.

- CHECK FOR RESTRICTED FUEL RETURN LINE FROM THROTTLE BODY TO WHERE LINE WAS DISCONNECTED.

LOCATE AND CORRECT RESTRICTED FUEL RETURN LINE TO FUEL TANK.

IF LINE IS OK, REPLACE PRESSURE REGULATOR.

"AFTER REPAIRS," CONFIRM "CLOSED LOOP" OPERATION AND NO MIL (SERVICE ENGINE SOON).

Fig. 167 Engine controls diagnostic chart

CHART A-7

(Page 3 of 3)
FUEL SYSTEM DIAGNOSIS
4.3L (VIN Z), 5.0L (VIN E) & 5.7L (VIN 7) "B" CARLINE (TBI)

FUEL PRESSURE CHECK

Tools Required: J 29658-B - Fuel Pressure Gage
J 29658-89 - Fuel Pressure Quick Connect Adapters
J 37088 - Fuel Line Quick-Connect Separators

CAUTION: To Reduce the Risk of Fire and Personal Injury:
- It is necessary to relieve fuel system pressure before connecting a fuel pressure gage.
- A small amount of fuel may be released when disconnecting the fuel lines. Cover fuel line fittings with a shop towel before disconnecting, to catch any fuel that may leak out. Place towel in approved container when disconnect is completed.
- Do not pinch or restrict nylon fuel lines to avoid severing, which could cause a fuel leak.

NOTICE:
- If nylon fuel lines become kinked, and cannot be straightened, they must be replaced.

1. Disconnect negative battery terminal.
2. Loosen fuel filler cap to relieve fuel tank pressure. (Do not tighten at this time.)
3. Locate engine compartment fuel feed quick-connect fitting.
4. Grasp both ends of fitting, twist female end ¼ turn in each direction to loosen any dirt in fitting.

CAUTION: Safety glasses must be worn when using compressed air, as flying dirt particles may cause eye injury.

5. Using compressed air, blow dirt out of quick-connect fitting.
6. Choose correct tool from separator tool set J 37088 for size of fitting. Insert tool into female end of connector, then push inward to release male connector.
7. Connect gage quick-connect adapters J 29658-89 to fuel pressure gage J 29658-B.

CAUTION: To Reduce the Risk of Fire and Personal Injury: Before connecting fuel line quick-connect fittings, always apply a few drops of clean engine oil to the male tube ends. This will ensure proper reconnection and prevent a possible fuel leak. (During normal operation, the O-rings located inside the female connector will swell and may prevent proper reconnection if not lubricated.)

8. Lubricate the male tube end of the fuel line and the gage adapter with engine oil.
9. Connect fuel pressure gage.
   - Push connectors together to cause the retaining tabs/fingers to snap into place.
   - Once installed, pull on both ends of each connection to make sure it is secure.
10. Connect negative battery terminal.
11. Check fuel pressure.
12. Disconnect negative battery terminal.
13. Disconnect fuel pressure gage.
14. Lubricate the male tube end of the fuel line, and reconnect quick-connect fitting.
   - Push connector together to cause the retaining tabs/fingers to snap into place.
   - Once installed, pull on both ends of connection to make sure it is secure.
15. Tighten fuel filler cap.
16. Connect negative battery terminal.
17. Cycle ignition "ON" and "OFF" twice, waiting ten seconds between cycles, then check for fuel leaks.

"AFTER REPAIRS," CONFIRM "CLOSED LOOP" OPERATION AND NO MIL (SERVICE ENGINE SOON).

Fig. 168 Engine controls diagnostic chart

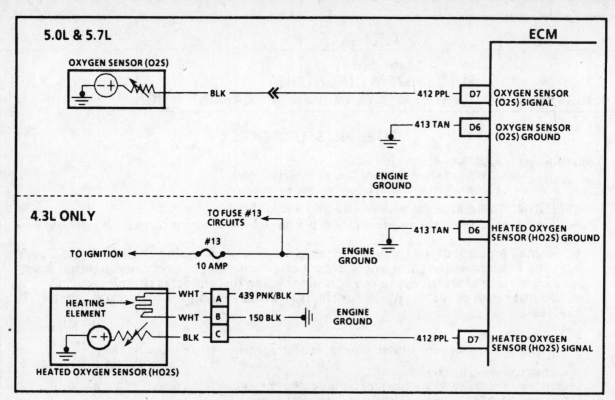

DTC 13

O2S AND HO2S CIRCUIT
(OPEN CIRCUIT)
4.3L (VIN Z), 5.0L (VIN E) & 5.7L (VIN 7) "B" CARLINE (TBI)

Circuit Description:

The ECM supplies a voltage of about .45 volt (450 mV) between terminals "D7" and "D6". (If measured with a 10 megohm digital voltmeter, this may read as low as .32 volt). The O2S or HO2S varies the voltage within a range of about 1 volt if the exhaust is rich, down through about 10 mV if the exhaust is lean.

The sensor is like an open circuit and produces no voltage when it is below 315°C (600°F). An open sensor circuit or cold sensor causes "Open Loop" operation.

Test Description: Number(s) below refer to circled number(s) on the diagnostic chart.
1. DTC 13 will set:
   - Engine at normal operating temperature 70°C (158°F).
   - At least 2 minutes engine time after start.
   - O2S/HO2S signal voltage steady between .35 and .55 volt.
   - Throttle Position (TP) sensor signal above 5% (about .3 volt above closed throttle voltage).
   - All conditions must be met for about 60 seconds.
2. This test checks the heated oxygen sensor's heating element. The heating element resistance should be 3.5 ohms at 20°C (68°F) or 14 ohms at 350°C (662°F). This will determine if the sensor is at fault.
3. This will determine if the sensor is at fault.
4. For this test use only a high impedance Digital Volt Ohmmeter (J 39200). This test checks the continuity of CKT 412 and CKT 413. If CKT 413 is open, the ECM voltage on CKT 412 will be over .6 volt (600 mV).

5. If the #13 fuse was open, check the #13 fuse circuits for shorts.

Diagnostic Aids:

If the heated oxygen sensor heater on the 4.3L engine is not operating properly, system may go into "Open Loop" after extended idle.

Normal scan tool voltage varies between 10 mV to 1000 mV (.01 and 1.0 volt), while in "Closed Loop." DTC 13 sets in one minute if voltage remains between .35 and .55 volt, however the system will go "Open Loop" in about 15 seconds.

Refer to "Intermittents" in "Symptoms," Section "6E2-B".

An O2S/HO2S supply inside the O2S/HO2S is necessary for proper O2S/HO2S operation. This supply of oxygen is supplied through the O2S/HO2S wires. All O2S/HO2S wires and connections should be inspected for breaks or contamination that could prevent reference oxygen from reaching the O2S/HO2S.

Fig. 169 Engine controls diagnostic chart

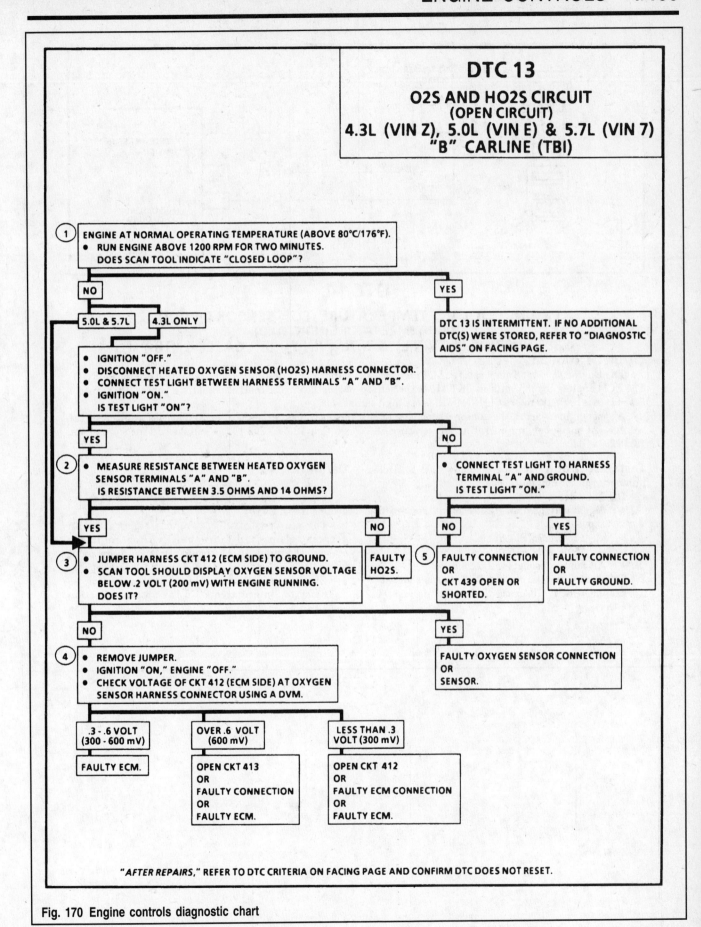

DTC 13

O2S AND HO2S CIRCUIT
(OPEN CIRCUIT)
4.3L (VIN Z), 5.0L (VIN E) & 5.7L (VIN 7)
"B" CARLINE (TBI)

1 ENGINE AT NORMAL OPERATING TEMPERATURE (ABOVE 80°C/176°F).
• RUN ENGINE ABOVE 1200 RPM FOR TWO MINUTES.
  DOES SCAN TOOL INDICATE "CLOSED LOOP"?

NO

YES → DTC 13 IS INTERMITTENT. IF NO ADDITIONAL DTC(S) WERE STORED, REFER TO "DIAGNOSTIC AIDS" ON FACING PAGE.

5.0L & 5.7L | **4.3L ONLY**

• IGNITION "OFF."
• DISCONNECT HEATED OXYGEN SENSOR (HO2S) HARNESS CONNECTOR.
• CONNECT TEST LIGHT BETWEEN HARNESS TERMINALS "A" AND "B".
• IGNITION "ON."
  IS TEST LIGHT "ON"?

YES

NO → • CONNECT TEST LIGHT TO HARNESS TERMINAL "A" AND GROUND.
  IS TEST LIGHT "ON."

2 • MEASURE RESISTANCE BETWEEN HEATED OXYGEN SENSOR TERMINALS "A" AND "B".
  IS RESISTANCE BETWEEN 3.5 OHMS AND 14 OHMS?

YES | **NO** → FAULTY HO2S.

NO | **YES**

5 FAULTY CONNECTION OR CKT 439 OPEN OR SHORTED. | FAULTY CONNECTION OR FAULTY GROUND.

3 • JUMPER HARNESS CKT 412 (ECM SIDE) TO GROUND.
• SCAN TOOL SHOULD DISPLAY OXYGEN SENSOR VOLTAGE BELOW .2 VOLT (200 mV) WITH ENGINE RUNNING.
  DOES IT?

NO

YES → FAULTY OXYGEN SENSOR CONNECTION OR SENSOR.

4 • REMOVE JUMPER.
• IGNITION "ON," ENGINE "OFF."
• CHECK VOLTAGE OF CKT 412 (ECM SIDE) AT OXYGEN SENSOR HARNESS CONNECTOR USING A DVM.

.3 - .6 VOLT (300 - 600 mV) | **OVER .6 VOLT (600 mV)** | **LESS THAN .3 VOLT (300 mV)**

FAULTY ECM. | OPEN CKT 413 OR FAULTY CONNECTION OR FAULTY ECM. | OPEN CKT 412 OR FAULTY ECM CONNECTION OR FAULTY ECM.

"AFTER REPAIRS," REFER TO DTC CRITERIA ON FACING PAGE AND CONFIRM DTC DOES NOT RESET.

Fig. 170 Engine controls diagnostic chart

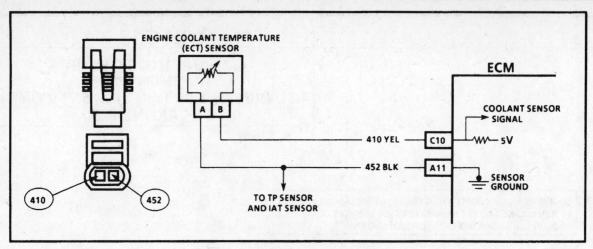

DTC 14
ENGINE COOLANT TEMPERATURE (ECT) SENSOR CIRCUIT
(HIGH TEMPERATURE INDICATED)
4.3L (VIN Z), 5.0L (VIN E) & 5.7L (VIN 7) "B" CARLINE (TBI)

Circuit Description:

The Engine Coolant Temperature (ECT) sensor uses a thermistor to control the signal voltage to the ECM. The ECM applies about 5 volts on CKT 410 to the sensor. When the engine coolant is cold, the sensor (thermistor) resistance is high, therefore the ECM will sense high signal voltage.

As the engine warms, the sensor (thermistor) resistance becomes less, and the ECM senses a lower signal voltage. At normal engine operating temperature (85°C - 95°C or 185°F - 203°F) the voltage will measure about 1.5 to 2.0 volts.

Test Description: Number(s) below refer to circled number(s) on the diagnostic chart.

1. DTC 14 will set if:
   - Signal voltage indicates a coolant temperature above:
     - 135°C (275°F) 4.3L.
     - 150°C (302°F) 5.0L & 5.7L.
   - All conditions met for 2 seconds.
2. This test will determine if CKT 410 is shorted to ground which will cause the conditions for DTC 14.

Diagnostic Aids:

Check harness routing for a potential short to ground in CKT 410.

The scan tool displays engine temperature in degrees celsius and fahrenheit. After engine is started, the temperature should rise steadily to about 90°C (194°F) then stabilize when the thermostat opens.

Check terminals at sensor for a good connection.

Refer to "Intermittents" in "Symptoms," Section "6E2-B".

Fig. 171 Engine controls diagnostic chart

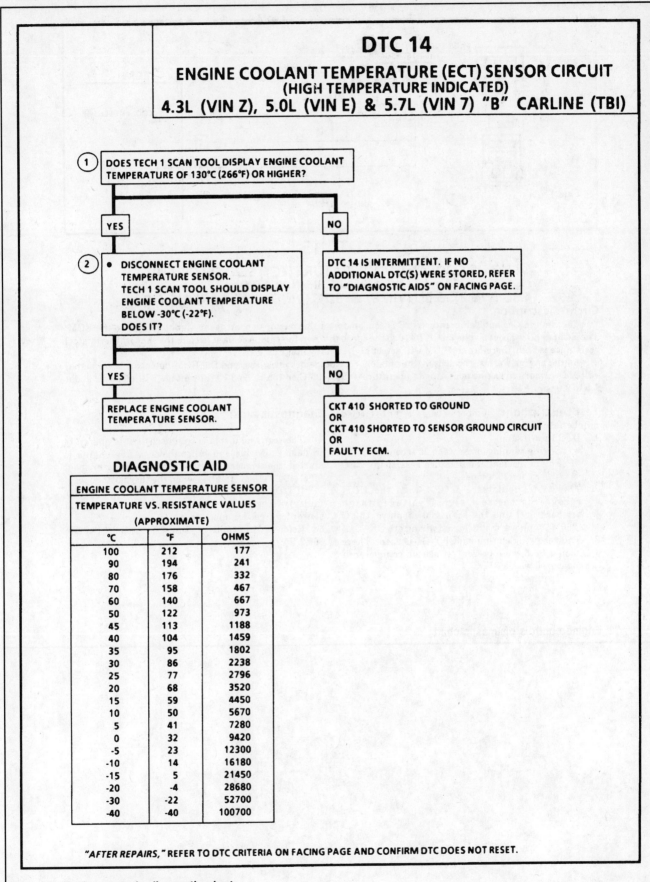

DTC 14

ENGINE COOLANT TEMPERATURE (ECT) SENSOR CIRCUIT
(HIGH TEMPERATURE INDICATED)
4.3L (VIN Z), 5.0L (VIN E) & 5.7L (VIN 7) "B" CARLINE (TBI)

1 DOES TECH 1 SCAN TOOL DISPLAY ENGINE COOLANT TEMPERATURE OF 130°C (266°F) OR HIGHER?

YES

NO

2
- DISCONNECT ENGINE COOLANT TEMPERATURE SENSOR.
  TECH 1 SCAN TOOL SHOULD DISPLAY ENGINE COOLANT TEMPERATURE BELOW -30°C (-22°F).
  DOES IT?

DTC 14 IS INTERMITTENT. IF NO ADDITIONAL DTC(S) WERE STORED, REFER TO "DIAGNOSTIC AIDS" ON FACING PAGE.

YES

NO

REPLACE ENGINE COOLANT TEMPERATURE SENSOR.

CKT 410 SHORTED TO GROUND
OR
CKT 410 SHORTED TO SENSOR GROUND CIRCUIT
OR
FAULTY ECM.

DIAGNOSTIC AID

ENGINE COOLANT TEMPERATURE SENSOR		
TEMPERATURE VS. RESISTANCE VALUES (APPROXIMATE)		
°C	°F	OHMS
100	212	177
90	194	241
80	176	332
70	158	467
60	140	667
50	122	973
45	113	1188
40	104	1459
35	95	1802
30	86	2238
25	77	2796
20	68	3520
15	59	4450
10	50	5670
5	41	7280
0	32	9420
-5	23	12300
-10	14	16180
-15	5	21450
-20	-4	28680
-30	-22	52700
-40	-40	100700

"AFTER REPAIRS," REFER TO DTC CRITERIA ON FACING PAGE AND CONFIRM DTC DOES NOT RESET.

Fig. 172 Engine controls diagnostic chart

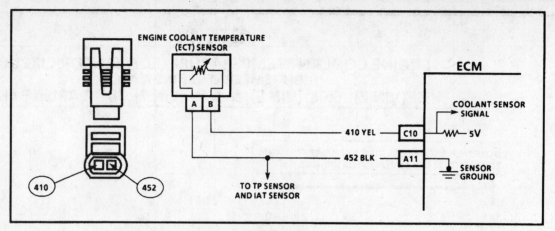

DTC 15

ENGINE COOLANT TEMPERATURE (ECT) SENSOR CIRCUIT
(LOW TEMPERATURE INDICATED)
4.3L (VIN Z), 5.0L (VIN E) & 5.7L (VIN 7) "B" CARLINE (TBI)

Circuit Description:

The Engine Coolant Temperature (ECT) sensor uses a thermistor to control the signal voltage to the ECM. The ECM applies about 5 volts on CKT 410 to the sensor. When the engine coolant is cold, the sensor (thermistor) resistance is high, therefore the ECM will detect high signal voltage.

As the engine warms, the sensor (thermistor) resistance becomes less, and the ECM detects a lower signal voltage. At normal engine operating temperature (85°C - 95°C or 185°F - 203°F) the voltage will measure about 1.5 to 2.0 volts.

Test Description: Number(s) below refer to circled number(s) on the diagnostic chart.

1. DTC 15 will set if:
   - Engine running longer than 30 seconds.
   - Engine coolant temperature less than -33°C (-27°F), for 30 seconds.
2. This test simulates a DTC 14. If the ECM recognizes the low signal voltage, (high temperature) and the scan tool displays 130°C (266°F) or above, the ECM and wiring are OK.
3. This test will determine if CKT 410 is open. There should be 5 volts present at sensor connector if measured with a DVM.

Diagnostic Aids:

The scan tool displays engine coolant temperature in degrees celsius and fahrenheit. After engine is started, the temperature should rise steadily to about 90°C (194°F) then stabilize when the thermostat opens.

If DTC 21 or 23 is also set, check CKT 452 for faulty wiring or connections. Check terminals at sensor for a good connection.

Refer to "Intermittents" in "Symptoms," Section "6E2-B".

Fig. 173 Engine controls diagnostic chart

DTC 15
ENGINE COOLANT TEMPERATURE (ECT) SENSOR CIRCUIT
(LOW TEMPERATURE INDICATED)
4.3L (VIN Z), 5.0L (VIN E) & 5.7L (VIN 7) "B" CARLINE (TBI)

1 • DOES TECH 1 SCAN TOOL DISPLAY ENGINE COOLANT TEMPERATURE OF -30°C (-22°F) OR LESS?

YES

NO

2 • DISCONNECT ENGINE COOLANT TEMPERATURE SENSOR.
• JUMPER HARNESS TERMINALS TOGETHER.
• TECH 1 SCAN TOOL SHOULD DISPLAY 130°C (266°F) OR MORE. DOES IT?

DTC 15 IS INTERMITTENT. IF NO ADDITIONAL DTCs WERE STORED, REFER TO "DIAGNOSTIC AIDS" ON FACING PAGE.

NO

YES

3 • JUMPER CKT 410 TO GROUND.
• TECH 1 SCAN TOOL SHOULD DISPLAY OVER 130°C (266°F). DOES IT?

FAULTY CONNECTION OR ENGINE COOLANT TEMPERATURE SENSOR.

YES

NO

OPEN ENGINE COOLANT TEMPERATURE SENSOR GROUND CIRCUIT, FAULTY CONNECTION OR FAULTY ECM.

OPEN CKT 410, FAULTY CONNECTION AT ECM, OR FAULTY ECM.

DIAGNOSTIC AID

ENGINE COOLANT TEMPERATURE SENSOR		
TEMPERATURE VS. RESISTANCE VALUES		
(APPROXIMATE)		
°C	°F	OHMS
100	212	177
90	194	241
80	176	332
70	158	467
60	140	667
50	122	973
45	113	1188
40	104	1459
35	95	1802
30	86	2238
25	77	2796
20	68	3520
15	59	4450
10	50	5670
5	41	7280
0	32	9420
-5	23	12300
-10	14	16180
-15	5	21450
-20	-4	28680
-30	-22	52700
-40	-40	100700

"AFTER REPAIRS," REFER TO DTC CRITERIA ON FACING PAGE AND CONFIRM DTC DOES NOT RESET.

Fig. 174 Engine controls diagnostic chart

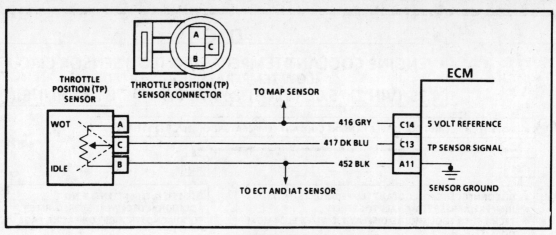

DTC 21

THROTTLE POSITION (TP) SENSOR CIRCUIT
(SIGNAL VOLTAGE HIGH)
4.3L (VIN Z), 5.0L (VIN E) & 5.7L (VIN 7) "B" CARLINE (TBI)

Circuit Description:

The Throttle Position (TP) sensor provides a voltage signal that changes relative to the throttle blade position. TP sensor signal voltage will vary from about .2 to .95 at idle to about 5 volts at Wide Open Throttle (WOT).

The TP sensor signal is one of the most important inputs used by the ECM for fuel control and for most of the ECM controlled outputs.

Test Description: Number(s) below refer to circled number(s) on the diagnostic chart.

1. DTC 21 will set if:
   - TP sensor signal voltage is greater than 2.5 volts.
   - MAP less than 52 kPa pressure (or greater than 15" of Hg vacuum).
   - All conditions met for 8 seconds.
2. With the TP sensor disconnected, the TP sensor signal voltage should go low if the ECM and wiring are OK.
3. Probing CKT 452 with a test light to 12 volts checks the sensor ground circuit. A faulty sensor ground will cause a DTC 21.

Diagnostic Aids:

A scan tool displays throttle position in volts. With ignition "ON" or at idle, TP sensor signal voltage should read between about .2 to .95 volts with the throttle closed and increase at a steady rate as throttle is moved toward WOT.

An open in CKT 452 will result in a DTC 21.

Refer to "Intermittents" in "Symptoms," Section "6E2-B".

Fig. 175 Engine controls diagnostic chart

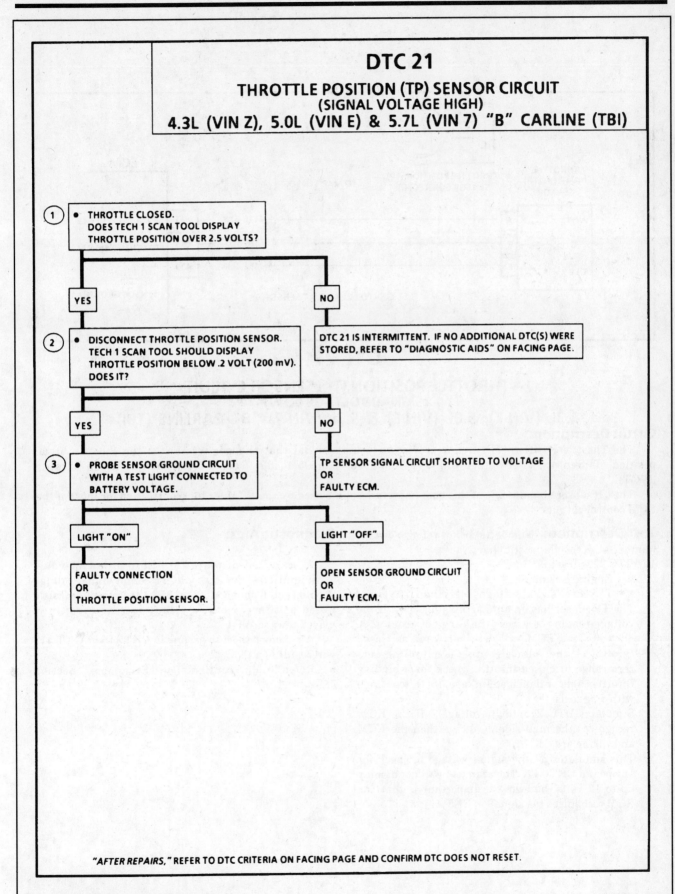

DTC 21
THROTTLE POSITION (TP) SENSOR CIRCUIT
(SIGNAL VOLTAGE HIGH)
4.3L (VIN Z), 5.0L (VIN E) & 5.7L (VIN 7) "B" CARLINE (TBI)

1. • THROTTLE CLOSED.
   DOES TECH 1 SCAN TOOL DISPLAY
   THROTTLE POSITION OVER 2.5 VOLTS?

   YES

   NO

2. • DISCONNECT THROTTLE POSITION SENSOR.
   TECH 1 SCAN TOOL SHOULD DISPLAY
   THROTTLE POSITION BELOW .2 VOLT (200 mV).
   DOES IT?

   DTC 21 IS INTERMITTENT. IF NO ADDITIONAL DTC(S) WERE
   STORED, REFER TO "DIAGNOSTIC AIDS" ON FACING PAGE.

   YES

   NO

3. • PROBE SENSOR GROUND CIRCUIT
   WITH A TEST LIGHT CONNECTED TO
   BATTERY VOLTAGE.

   TP SENSOR SIGNAL CIRCUIT SHORTED TO VOLTAGE
   OR
   FAULTY ECM.

   LIGHT "ON"

   LIGHT "OFF"

   FAULTY CONNECTION
   OR
   THROTTLE POSITION SENSOR.

   OPEN SENSOR GROUND CIRCUIT
   OR
   FAULTY ECM.

"AFTER REPAIRS," REFER TO DTC CRITERIA ON FACING PAGE AND CONFIRM DTC DOES NOT RESET.

Fig. 176 Engine controls diagnostic chart

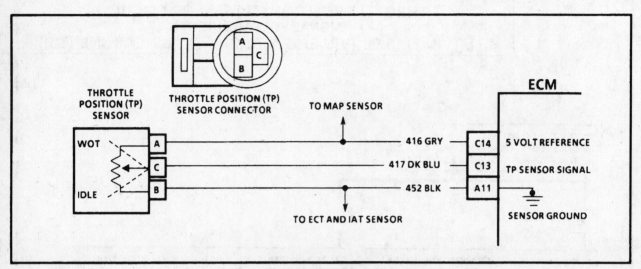

DTC 22

THROTTLE POSITION (TP) SENSOR CIRCUIT
(SIGNAL VOLTAGE LOW)
4.3L (VIN Z), 5.0L (VIN E) & 5.7L (VIN 7) "B" CARLINE (TBI)

Circuit Description:

The Throttle Position (TP) sensor provides a voltage signal that changes relative to the throttle blade position. TP sensor signal voltage will vary from about .2 to .95 at idle to about 5 volts at Wide Open Throttle (WOT).

The TP sensor signal is one of the most important inputs used by the ECM for fuel control and for most of the ECM control outputs.

Test Description: Number(s) below refer to circled number(s) on the diagnostic chart.

1. DTC 22 will set if:
   - Engine is running.
   - TP sensor signal voltage is less than .20 volt.
   The TP sensor has an auto zeroing feature. If the voltage reading is within the range of about .2 to .95 volts, the ECM will use that value as closed throttle. If the voltage reading is out of the auto zero range at closed throttle, check for a binding throttle cable or damaged linkage, if OK, continue with diagnosis.
2. Simulates DTC 21: (high voltage). If the ECM recognizes the high signal voltage then the ECM and wiring are OK.
3. This simulates a high signal voltage to check for an open in CKT 417. The scan tool will not display up to 12 volts, but what is important is that the ECM recognizes the signal on CKT 417.

Diagnostic Aids:

A scan tool displays throttle position in volts. With ignition "ON" or at idle, TP sensor signal voltage should read from about .2 to .95 volts with the throttle closed and increase at a steady rate as throttle is moved toward WOT.

An open or short to ground in CKT 416 or CKT 417 will result in a DTC 22.

Refer to "Intermittents" in "Symptoms," Section "6E2-B".

Fig. 177 Engine controls diagnostic chart

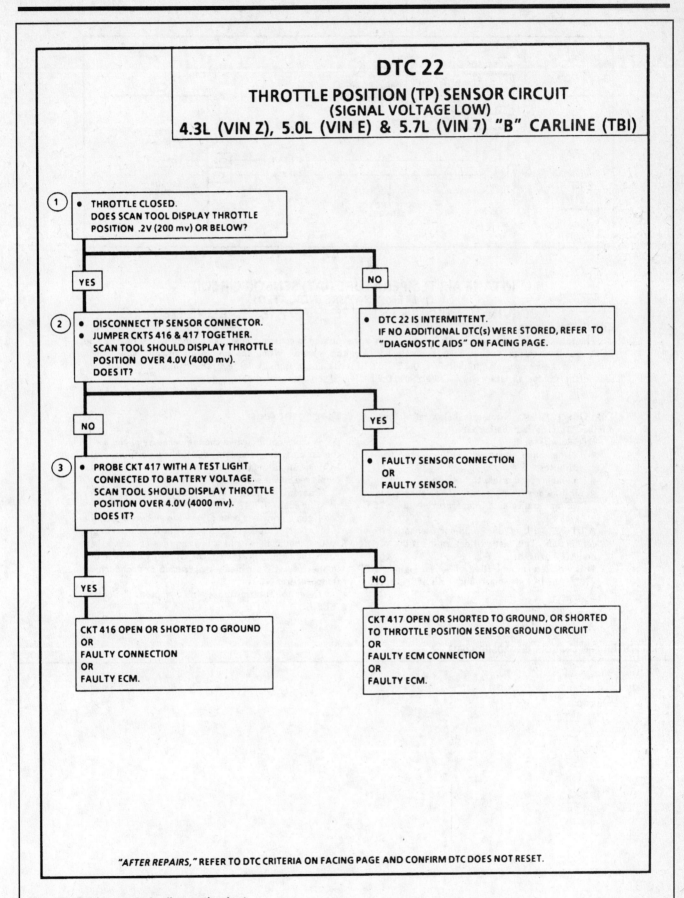

DTC 22

THROTTLE POSITION (TP) SENSOR CIRCUIT
(SIGNAL VOLTAGE LOW)
4.3L (VIN Z), 5.0L (VIN E) & 5.7L (VIN 7) "B" CARLINE (TBI)

1
- THROTTLE CLOSED.
  DOES SCAN TOOL DISPLAY THROTTLE
  POSITION .2V (200 mv) OR BELOW?

YES

NO

2
- DISCONNECT TP SENSOR CONNECTOR.
- JUMPER CKTS 416 & 417 TOGETHER.
  SCAN TOOL SHOULD DISPLAY THROTTLE
  POSITION OVER 4.0V (4000 mv).
  DOES IT?

- DTC 22 IS INTERMITTENT.
  IF NO ADDITIONAL DTC(s) WERE STORED, REFER TO
  "DIAGNOSTIC AIDS" ON FACING PAGE.

NO

YES

3
- PROBE CKT 417 WITH A TEST LIGHT
  CONNECTED TO BATTERY VOLTAGE.
  SCAN TOOL SHOULD DISPLAY THROTTLE
  POSITION OVER 4.0V (4000 mv).
  DOES IT?

- FAULTY SENSOR CONNECTION
  OR
  FAULTY SENSOR.

YES

NO

CKT 416 OPEN OR SHORTED TO GROUND
OR
FAULTY CONNECTION
OR
FAULTY ECM.

CKT 417 OPEN OR SHORTED TO GROUND, OR SHORTED
TO THROTTLE POSITION SENSOR GROUND CIRCUIT
OR
FAULTY ECM CONNECTION
OR
FAULTY ECM.

"AFTER REPAIRS," REFER TO DTC CRITERIA ON FACING PAGE AND CONFIRM DTC DOES NOT RESET.

Fig. 178 Engine controls diagnostic chart

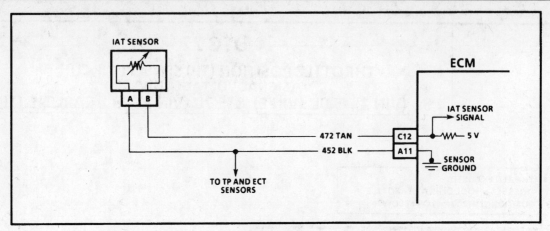

DTC 23

INTAKE AIR TEMPERATURE (IAT) SENSOR CIRCUIT
(LOW TEMPERATURE INDICATED)
4.3L (VIN Z), 5.0L (VIN E) & 5.7L (VIN 7) "B" CARLINE (TBI)

Circuit Description:

The Intake Air Temperature (IAT) sensor uses a thermistor to control the signal voltage to the ECM. The ECM applies a voltage (about 5 volts) on CKT 472 to the sensor. When the intake air is cold, the sensor (thermistor) resistance is high, therefore, the ECM will sense a high signal voltage. If the intake air is warm, the sensor (thermistor) resistance is low, therefore, the ECM will sense a low signal voltage.

Test Description: Number(s) below refer to circled number(s) on the diagnostic chart.

1. DTC 23 will set if:
   - Time since engine start is longer than 5 minutes.
   - Vehicle speed is less than 45 mph.
   - Intake Air Temperature (IAT) sensor signal voltage indicates a temperature below -25°C (-13°F).
2. A DTC 23 will set, due to an open sensor, wire or connection. This test will determine if the wiring and ECM are OK.
3. This will determine if the IAT sensor signal (CKT 472) or the IAT sensor ground (CKT 452) is open.

Diagnostic Aids:

A scan tool indicates the temperature of the air in the air cleaner. When the ECM detects a fault in the IAT circuit, a default value of 40°C (104°F) will be displayed on the scan tool.

Carefully check harness and connections for possible open CKT 472 or CKT 452.

If the engine has been allowed to sit overnight, the intake air temperature and coolant temperature values should be within a few degrees of each other. After the engine is started, the IAT will increase due to thermostatic air cleaner operation and underhood temperatures.

Refer to "Intermittents" in "Symptoms," Section "6E2-B".

Fig. 179 Engine controls diagnostic chart

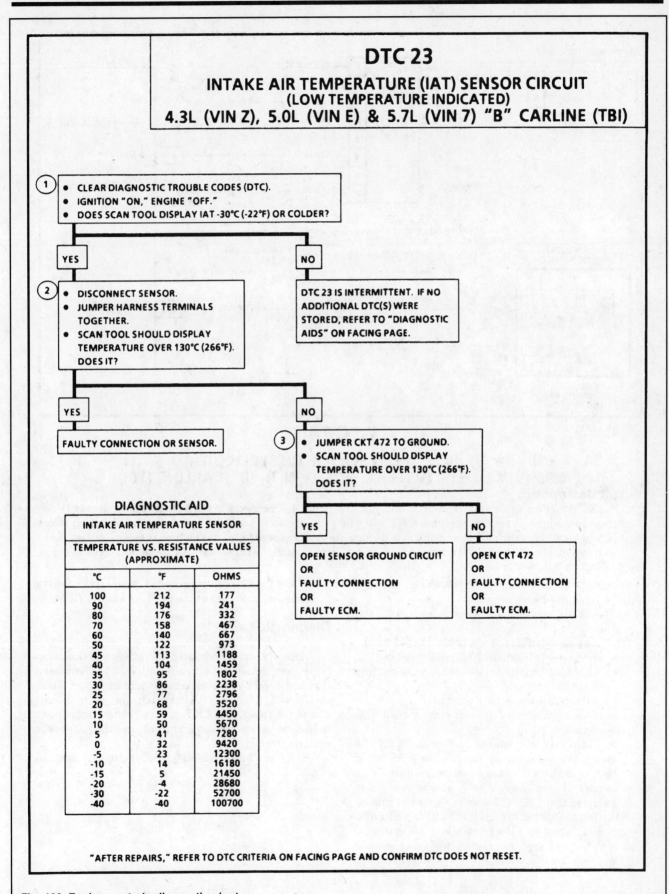

DTC 23
INTAKE AIR TEMPERATURE (IAT) SENSOR CIRCUIT
(LOW TEMPERATURE INDICATED)
4.3L (VIN Z), 5.0L (VIN E) & 5.7L (VIN 7) "B" CARLINE (TBI)

①
- CLEAR DIAGNOSTIC TROUBLE CODES (DTC).
- IGNITION "ON," ENGINE "OFF."
- DOES SCAN TOOL DISPLAY IAT -30°C (-22°F) OR COLDER?

YES

NO

②
- DISCONNECT SENSOR.
- JUMPER HARNESS TERMINALS TOGETHER.
- SCAN TOOL SHOULD DISPLAY TEMPERATURE OVER 130°C (266°F). DOES IT?

DTC 23 IS INTERMITTENT. IF NO ADDITIONAL DTC(S) WERE STORED, REFER TO "DIAGNOSTIC AIDS" ON FACING PAGE.

YES

NO

FAULTY CONNECTION OR SENSOR.

③
- JUMPER CKT 472 TO GROUND.
- SCAN TOOL SHOULD DISPLAY TEMPERATURE OVER 130°C (266°F). DOES IT?

YES

NO

OPEN SENSOR GROUND CIRCUIT
OR
FAULTY CONNECTION
OR
FAULTY ECM.

OPEN CKT 472
OR
FAULTY CONNECTION
OR
FAULTY ECM.

DIAGNOSTIC AID

INTAKE AIR TEMPERATURE SENSOR		
TEMPERATURE VS. RESISTANCE VALUES (APPROXIMATE)		
°C	°F	OHMS
100	212	177
90	194	241
80	176	332
70	158	467
60	140	667
50	122	973
45	113	1188
40	104	1459
35	95	1802
30	86	2238
25	77	2796
20	68	3520
15	59	4450
10	50	5670
5	41	7280
0	32	9420
-5	23	12300
-10	14	16180
-15	5	21450
-20	-4	28680
-30	-22	52700
-40	-40	100700

"AFTER REPAIRS," REFER TO DTC CRITERIA ON FACING PAGE AND CONFIRM DTC DOES NOT RESET.

Fig. 180 Engine controls diagnostic chart

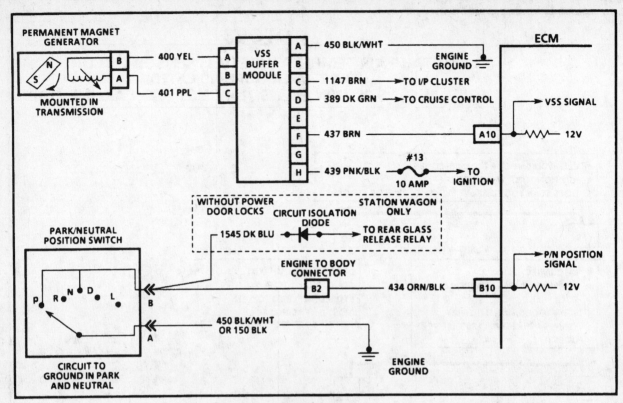

DTC 24

VEHICLE SPEED SENSOR (VSS) CIRCUIT
4.3L (VIN Z), 5.0L (VIN E) & 5.7L (VIN 7) "B" CARLINE (TBI)

Circuit Description:

The ECM applies and monitors 12 volts on CKT 437. CKT 437 connects to the Vehicle Speed Sensor (VSS) buffer module which alternately grounds CKT 437 when drive wheels are turning. This pulsing action takes place about 2000 times per mile and the ECM will calculate vehicle speed based on the time between "pulses."

Scan tool display should closely match speedometer display with the drive wheels turning and vehicle speed approximately 3 mph or greater.

Test Description: Number(s) below refer to circled number(s) on the diagnostic chart.

1. DTC 24 will set if vehicle speed is less than 5 mph when:
   - Engine speed is between 1200 and 4400 RPM.
   - TP sensor is less than 3% (closed throttle).
   - Low load condition (low MAP voltage, high manifold vacuum).
   - All conditions met for 5 seconds.

   These conditions are met during a road load deceleration.

2. 8-12 volts, at the connector, indicates CKT 437 is open between the connector and the VSS buffer module, or there is a faulty vehicle speed sensor. A voltage of less than 1 volt, at the connector, indicates that CKT 437 wire is shorted to ground. If, after disconnecting CKT 437 at the VSS buffer module, and the voltage is above 10 volts, the vehicle speed sensor is faulty. If voltage remains less than 8 volts, then CKT 437 wire is grounded.

If CKT 437 is not grounded, there is a faulty connection or open at the ECM, or a faulty ECM.

Diagnostic Aids:

A faulty or misadjusted Park/Neutral Position (PNP) switch can result in a false DTC 24. Use a scan tool and check for proper signal while in drive. Refer to CHART C-1A for PNP switch diagnosis check. Check CKTs 400 and CKT 401 for proper connections to be sure they are clean and tight, and the harness is routed correctly.

Refer to "Intermittents" in "Symptoms," Section "6E2-B".

Fig. 181 Engine controls diagnostic chart

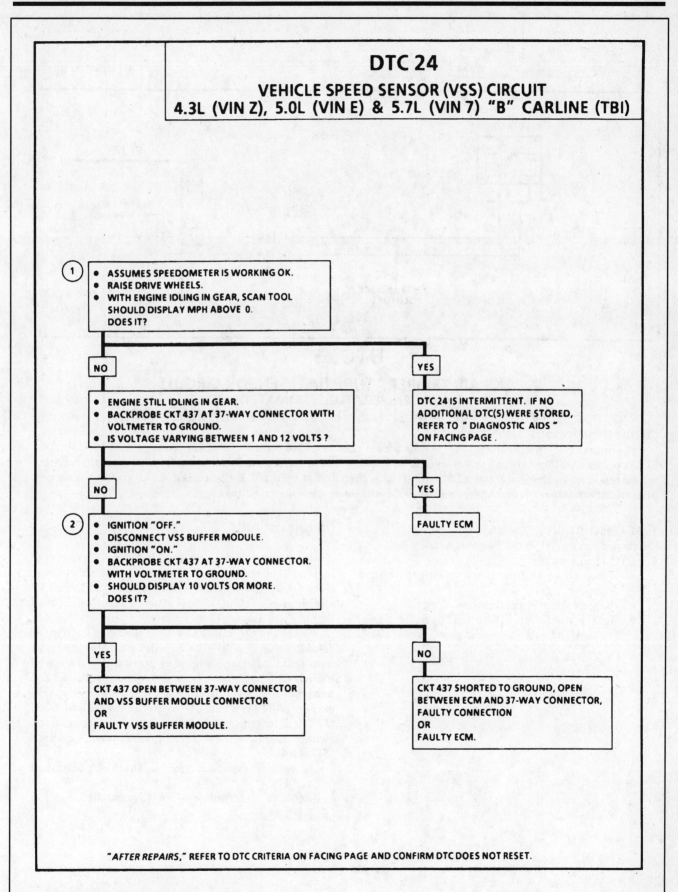

Fig. 182 Engine controls diagnostic chart

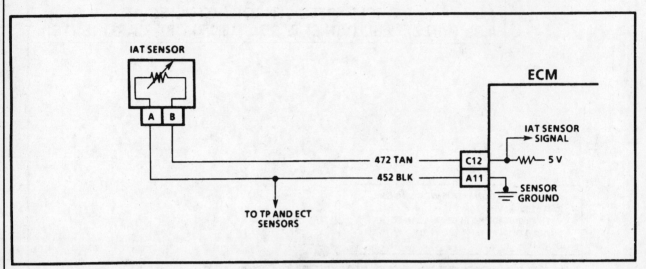

DTC 25

INTAKE AIR TEMPERATURE (IAT) SENSOR CIRCUIT
(HIGH TEMPERATURE INDICATED)
4.3L (VIN Z), 5.0L (VIN E) & 5.7L (VIN 7) "B" CARLINE (TBI)

Circuit Description:

The Intake Air Temperature (IAT) sensor uses a thermistor to control the signal voltage to the ECM. The ECM applies a voltage (about 5 volts) on CKT 472 to the sensor. When intake air is cold, the sensor (thermistor) resistance is high, therefore, the ECM will sense a high signal voltage. If the intake air is warm, the sensor (thermistor) resistance is low, therefore, the ECM will sense a low signal voltage.

Test Description: The number(s) below refers to the circled number(s) on the diagnostic chart.
1. DTC 25 will set if:
   - Time since engine start is longer than 5 minutes.
   - Vehicle speed is greater than 45 mph.
   - Intake Air Temperature (IAT) sensor signal voltage indicates a temperature above 135°C (275°F).

Diagnostic Aids:

Intake Air Temperature (IAT) on a scan tool indicates the temperature of the air in the air cleaner. If the engine has been allowed to sit overnight, the IAT and engine coolant temperature values should be within a few degrees of each other.

When the ECM detects a fault in the IAT circuit, a default value of 40°C (104°F) will be displayed on the scan tool. After the engine is started, the IAT will increase due to thermostatic air cleaner operation and underhood temperatures, however, IAT will rarely exceed 80°C (176°F). If a higher IAT than 80°C (176°F) is noted, check for proper thermostatic air cleaner operation, see "Air Intake System," Section "6E2-C14".

Check harness routing for possible short to ground in CKT 472.

Refer to "Intermittents" in "Symptoms," Section "6E2-B".

Fig. 183 Engine controls diagnostic chart

DTC 25
INTAKE AIR TEMPERATURE (IAT) SENSOR CIRCUIT
(HIGH TEMPERATURE INDICATED)
4.3L (VIN Z), 5.0L (VIN E) & 5.7L (VIN 7) "B" CARLINE (TBI)

1
- CLEAR DIAGNOSTIC TROUBLE CODES (DTC).
- IGNITION "ON," ENGINE "OFF."
- DOES SCAN TOOL DISPLAY IAT OF 145°C (293°F) OR HOTTER?

YES
- DISCONNECT SENSOR. SCAN TOOL SHOULD DISPLAY TEMPERATURE BELOW -30°C (-22°F). DOES IT?

NO
DTC 25 IS INTERMITTENT. IF NO ADDITIONAL DTC(S) WERE STORED, REFER TO "DIAGNOSTIC AIDS" ON FACING PAGE.

YES
REPLACE SENSOR.

NO
CKT 472 SHORTED TO GROUND
OR
CKT 472 SHORTED TO SENSOR GROUND
OR
FAULTY ECM.

DIAGNOSTIC AID

INTAKE AIR TEMPERATURE SENSOR

TEMPERATURE VS. RESISTANCE VALUES (APPROXIMATE)

°C	°F	OHMS
100	212	177
90	194	241
80	176	332
70	158	467
60	140	667
50	122	973
45	113	1188
40	104	1459
35	95	1802
30	86	2238
25	77	2796
20	68	3520
15	59	4450
10	50	5670
5	41	7280
0	32	9420
-5	23	12300
-10	14	16180
-15	5	21450
-20	-4	28680
-30	-22	52700
-40	-40	100700

"AFTER REPAIRS," REFER TO DTC CRITERIA ON FACING PAGE AND CONFIRM DTC DOES NOT RESET.

Fig. 184 Engine controls diagnostic chart

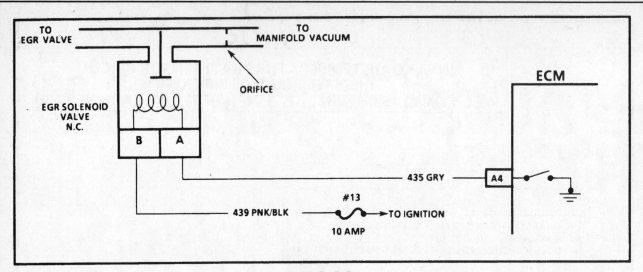

DTC 32

(Page 1 of 3)
EXHAUST GAS RECIRCULATION (EGR) CIRCUIT
4.3L (VIN Z), 5.0L (VIN E) & 5.7L (VIN 7) "B" CARLINE (TBI)

Circuit Description:

The ECM operates a solenoid valve to control the Exhaust Gas Recirculation (EGR) valve. This solenoid valve is normally closed. By providing a ground path, the ECM energizes the solenoid valve which then allows vacuum to pass to the EGR valve.

The ECM monitors EGR effectiveness by de-energizing the EGR control solenoid valve, thereby, shutting "OFF" vacuum to the EGR valve diaphragm. With the EGR valve closed, manifold vacuum will be greater than it was during normal EGR operation and this change will be relayed to the ECM by the MAP sensor. If the vacuum change is not within the calibrated window, a DTC 32 will be set.

The ECM will check EGR operation when:
- Vehicle speed is above 80 km/h (50 mph).
- MAP is as listed in table (depends on altitude).
- TP is between 9% and 20% (5.0L & 5.7L).
- TP is between 5% and 20% (4.3L).
- No change in Throttle Position (TP) while test is being run.

Test Description: Number(s) below refer to circled number(s) on the diagnostic chart.

1. **Intake Passage:** Shut "OFF" engine and remove the EGR valve from the manifold. Plug the exhaust side hole with a shop rag or suitable stopper. Leaving the intake side hole open, attempt to start the engine. If the engine runs at a very high idle (up to 3000 RPM is possible) or starts and stalls, the EGR passages are not restricted. If the engine starts and idles normally, the EGR intake side passage in the intake manifold is restricted.
   Exhaust Passage: With EGR valve still removed, plug the intake side hole with a suitable stopper. With the exhaust side hole open, check for the presence of exhaust gas. If no exhaust gas is present, the EGR exhaust side passage in the intake manifold is restricted.
2. By grounding the diagnostic "test" terminal, the EGR solenoid valve should be energized and allow vacuum to be applied to the gage. The vacuum at the gage may or may not slowly bleed off. It is important that the gage is able to read the amount of vacuum being applied.

MAP WITH KEY "ON" ENGINE "OFF" (BARO)

	100	90	80	70	
MAP	49	39	29	19	V-6
RANGE	60	50	40	30	
FOR					
TEST	45	35	25	15	V-8
	65	55	45	35	

3. When the diagnostic "test" terminal is ungrounded, the vacuum gage should bleed off through a vent in the solenoid valve. The pump gage may or may not bleed off but this does not indicate a problem.
4. This test will determine if the electrical control part of the system is at fault or if the connector or solenoid is at fault.
5. EGR valves used with this engine are stamped on the top side of the valve with: (P) for Positive backpressure valves or, (N) for Negative backpressure valves. Refer to "EGR Valve Identification," in "Exhaust Gas Recirculation (EGR) System," Section "6E2-C7" for more information.

Diagnostic Aids:

Vacuum lines should be thoroughly checked for proper routing.

Suction from shop exhaust hoses can alter exhaust backpressure and may affect the functional check of the EGR valve, during in-stall testing.

Fig. 185 Engine controls diagnostic chart

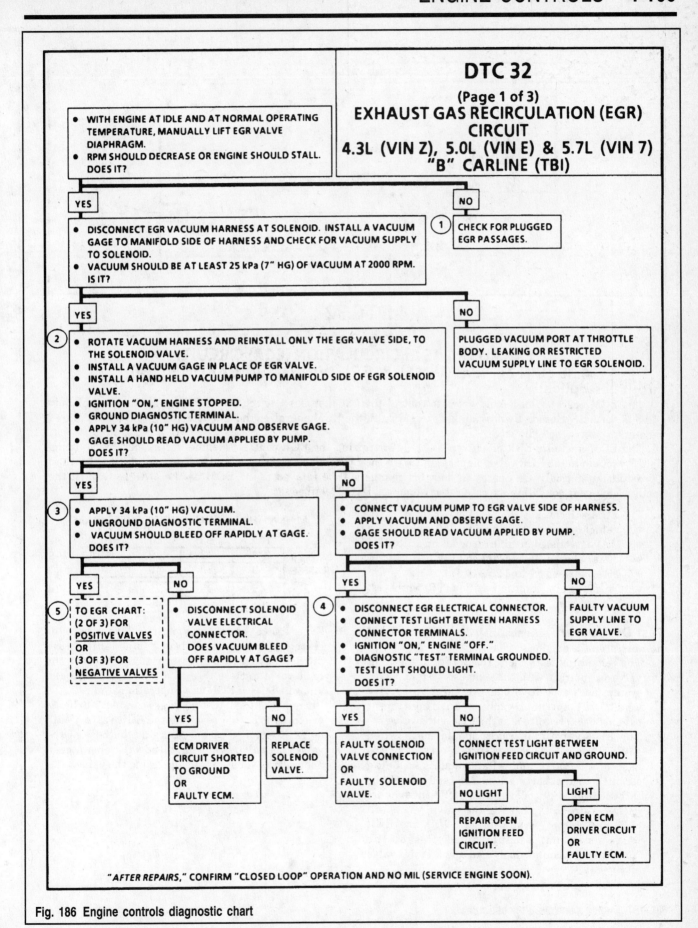

Fig. 186 Engine controls diagnostic chart

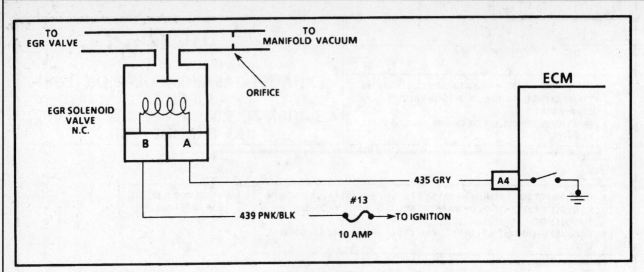

DTC 32

(Page 2 of 3)
EXHAUST GAS RECIRCULATION (EGR) CIRCUIT
4.3L (VIN Z), 5.0L (VIN E) & 5.7L (VIN 7) "B" CARLINE (TBI)

Circuit Description:

The ECM operates a solenoid valve to control the Exhaust Gas Recirculation (EGR) valve. This solenoid valve is normally closed. By providing a ground path, the ECM energizes the solenoid valve which then allows vacuum to pass to the EGR valve.

The ECM monitors EGR effectiveness by de-energizing the EGR control solenoid valve, thereby, shutting "OFF" vacuum to the EGR valve diaphragm. With the EGR valve closed, manifold vacuum will be greater than it was during normal EGR operation and this change will be relayed to the ECM by the MAP sensor. If the vacuum change is not within the calibrated window, a DTC 32 will be set.

The ECM will check EGR operation when:
- Vehicle speed is above 80 km/h (50 mph).
- MAP is as listed in table (depends on altitude).
- TP is between 9% and 20% (5.0L & 5.7L).
- TP is between 5% and 20% (4.3L).
- No change in Throttle Position (TP) while test is being run.

MAP WITH KEY "ON" ENGINE "OFF" (BARO)

	100	90	80	70	
MAP RANGE FOR TEST	49	39	29	19	V-6
	60	50	40	30	
	45	35	25	15	V-8
	65	55	45	35	

Test Description: Number(s) below refer to circled number(s) on the diagnostic chart.

6. The remaining tests check the ability of the EGR valve to interact with the exhaust system. This system uses a positive backpressure EGR valve which will not hold vacuum until sufficient exhaust backpressure is at the base of the valve.

7. The EGR valve diaphragm should move when sufficient exhaust backpressure is present at the base of the valve <u>and</u> when vacuum is being supplied to the valve. Rapidly "snapping" the throttle from idle should provide sufficient exhaust backpressure to the base of the valve which will close an internal vacuum bleed. With the EGR valve's internal vacuum bleed closed, the "jumpered" vacuum supply can now lift the valve off its seat.

8. Excessive exhaust backpressure from bent or restricted exhaust system components could provide enough backpressure at the base of the EGR valve to close the valve's internal bleed and allow undesired EGR valve operation at idle.

9. Plugged EGR exhaust passages can block exhaust backpressure from reaching the EGR valve. With no EGR exhaust backpressure at the base of the valve, the valve's internal bleed will remain open and prevent vacuum from operating the valve.

Fig. 187 Engine controls diagnostic chart

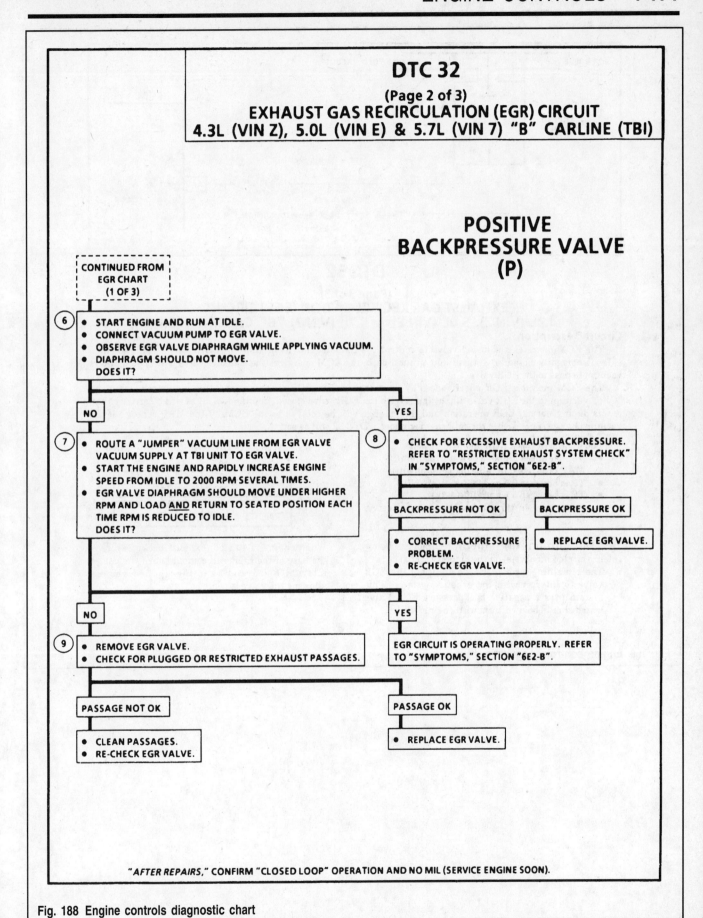

DTC 32
(Page 2 of 3)
EXHAUST GAS RECIRCULATION (EGR) CIRCUIT
4.3L (VIN Z), 5.0L (VIN E) & 5.7L (VIN 7) "B" CARLINE (TBI)

POSITIVE BACKPRESSURE VALVE (P)

CONTINUED FROM EGR CHART (1 OF 3)

6
- START ENGINE AND RUN AT IDLE.
- CONNECT VACUUM PUMP TO EGR VALVE.
- OBSERVE EGR VALVE DIAPHRAGM WHILE APPLYING VACUUM.
- DIAPHRAGM SHOULD NOT MOVE. DOES IT?

NO

YES

7
- ROUTE A "JUMPER" VACUUM LINE FROM EGR VALVE VACUUM SUPPLY AT TBI UNIT TO EGR VALVE.
- START THE ENGINE AND RAPIDLY INCREASE ENGINE SPEED FROM IDLE TO 2000 RPM SEVERAL TIMES.
- EGR VALVE DIAPHRAGM SHOULD MOVE UNDER HIGHER RPM AND LOAD <u>AND</u> RETURN TO SEATED POSITION EACH TIME RPM IS REDUCED TO IDLE. DOES IT?

8
- CHECK FOR EXCESSIVE EXHAUST BACKPRESSURE. REFER TO "RESTRICTED EXHAUST SYSTEM CHECK" IN "SYMPTOMS," SECTION "6E2-B".

BACKPRESSURE NOT OK

- CORRECT BACKPRESSURE PROBLEM.
- RE-CHECK EGR VALVE.

BACKPRESSURE OK

- REPLACE EGR VALVE.

NO

YES

9
- REMOVE EGR VALVE.
- CHECK FOR PLUGGED OR RESTRICTED EXHAUST PASSAGES.

EGR CIRCUIT IS OPERATING PROPERLY. REFER TO "SYMPTOMS," SECTION "6E2-B".

PASSAGE NOT OK

- CLEAN PASSAGES.
- RE-CHECK EGR VALVE.

PASSAGE OK

- REPLACE EGR VALVE.

"AFTER REPAIRS," CONFIRM "CLOSED LOOP" OPERATION AND NO MIL (SERVICE ENGINE SOON).

Fig. 188 Engine controls diagnostic chart

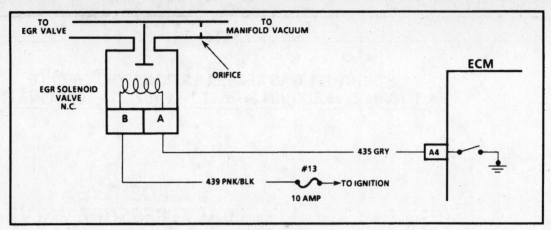

DTC 32

(Page 3 of 3)
EXHAUST GAS RECIRCULATION (EGR) CIRCUIT
4.3L (VIN Z), 5.0L (VIN E) & 5.7L (VIN 7) "B" CARLINE (TBI)

Circuit Description:

The ECM operates a solenoid valve to control the Exhaust Gas Recirculation (EGR) valve. This solenoid valve is normally closed. By providing a ground path, the ECM energizes the solenoid valve which then allows vacuum to pass to the EGR valve.

The ECM monitors EGR effectiveness by de-energizing the EGR control solenoid valve, thereby, shutting "OFF" vacuum to the EGR valve diaphragm. With the EGR valve closed, manifold vacuum will be greater than it was during normal EGR operation and this change will be relayed to the ECM by the MAP sensor. If the vacuum change is not within the calibrated window, a DTC 32 will be set.

The ECM will check EGR operation when:
- Vehicle speed is above 80 km/h (50 mph).
- MAP is as listed in table (depends on altitude).
- TP is between 9% and 20% (5.0L & 5.7L).
- TP is between 5% and 20% (4.3L).
- No change in throttle position while test is being run.

MAP WITH KEY "ON" ENGINE "OFF" (BARO)

	100	90	80	70	
MAP RANGE FOR TEST	49	39	29	19	**V-6**
	60	50	40	30	
	45	35	25	15	**V-8**
	65	55	45	35	

Test Description (continued): Number(s) below refer to circled number(s) on the diagnostic chart.

6. The remaining tests check the ability of the EGR valve to interact with the exhaust system. This system uses a negative backpressure EGR valve which should hold vacuum with engine "OFF."

7. When engine is started, exhaust backpressure at the base of the EGR valve should open the valve's internal bleed and vent the applied vacuum allowing the valve to seat.

Fig. 189 Engine controls diagnostic chart

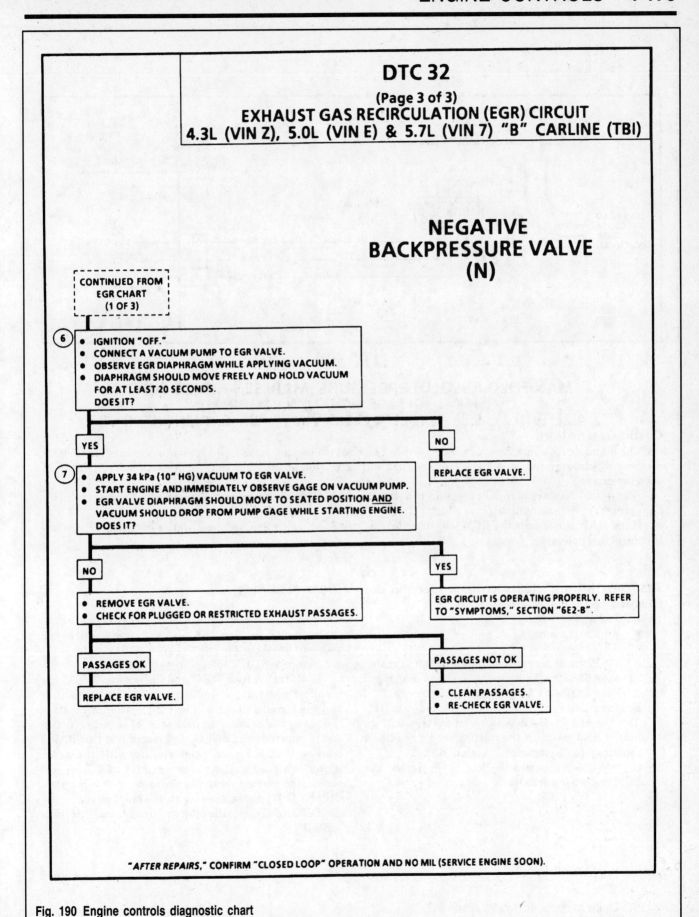

DTC 32

(Page 3 of 3)
EXHAUST GAS RECIRCULATION (EGR) CIRCUIT
4.3L (VIN Z), 5.0L (VIN E) & 5.7L (VIN 7) "B" CARLINE (TBI)

NEGATIVE BACKPRESSURE VALVE (N)

CONTINUED FROM
EGR CHART
(1 OF 3)

6
- IGNITION "OFF."
- CONNECT A VACUUM PUMP TO EGR VALVE.
- OBSERVE EGR DIAPHRAGM WHILE APPLYING VACUUM.
- DIAPHRAGM SHOULD MOVE FREELY AND HOLD VACUUM FOR AT LEAST 20 SECONDS. DOES IT?

YES

NO

REPLACE EGR VALVE.

7
- APPLY 34 kPa (10" HG) VACUUM TO EGR VALVE.
- START ENGINE AND IMMEDIATELY OBSERVE GAGE ON VACUUM PUMP.
- EGR VALVE DIAPHRAGM SHOULD MOVE TO SEATED POSITION <u>AND</u> VACUUM SHOULD DROP FROM PUMP GAGE WHILE STARTING ENGINE. DOES IT?

NO

YES

- REMOVE EGR VALVE.
- CHECK FOR PLUGGED OR RESTRICTED EXHAUST PASSAGES.

EGR CIRCUIT IS OPERATING PROPERLY. REFER TO "SYMPTOMS," SECTION "6E2-B".

PASSAGES OK

PASSAGES NOT OK

REPLACE EGR VALVE.

- CLEAN PASSAGES.
- RE-CHECK EGR VALVE.

"AFTER REPAIRS," CONFIRM "CLOSED LOOP" OPERATION AND NO MIL (SERVICE ENGINE SOON).

Fig. 190 Engine controls diagnostic chart

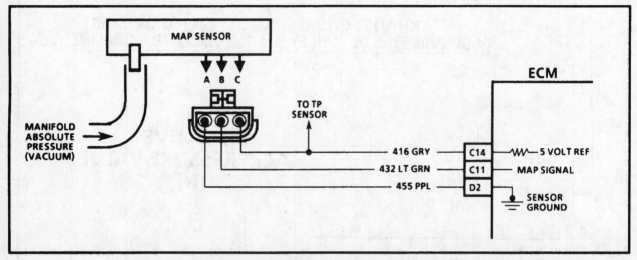

DTC 33

MANIFOLD ABSOLUTE PRESSURE (MAP) SENSOR CIRCUIT
(SIGNAL VOLTAGE HIGH - LOW VACUUM)
4.3L (VIN Z), 5.0L (VIN E) & 5.7L (VIN 7) "B" CARLINE (TBI)

Circuit Description:

The Manifold Absolute Pressure (MAP) sensor responds to changes in manifold pressure (vacuum). The ECM receives this information as a signal voltage that will vary from about 1-1.5 volts at idle to 4-4.5 volts at wide open throttle.

A scan tool displays manifold pressure in volts. Low pressure (high vacuum) displays a low voltage while a high pressure (low vacuum) displays a high voltage.

If the MAP sensor fails the ECM will substitute a fixed MAP value and use the Throttle Position (TP) sensor to control fuel delivery.

Test Description: Number(s) below refer to circled number(s) on the diagnostic chart.

1. DTC 33 will set when:
   - Engine is running.
   - TP less than 4%.
   - MAP sensor signal voltage is too high, (greater than 68 kPa of pressure or less than 9.5" Hg of vacuum) for a time greater than 5 seconds.

   Engine misfire or a low unstable idle may set DTC 33. Disconnect MAP sensor and system will go into backup mode. If the misfire or idle condition remains, see "Symptoms," Section "6E2-B".

2. If the ECM recognizes the low MAP signal, the ECM and wiring are OK.

Diagnostic Aids:

If the idle is rough or unstable refer to "Symptoms," Section "6E2-B" for items which can cause an unstable idle.

An open in CKT 455 will result in a DTC 33.

With the ignition "ON" and the engine "OFF," the manifold pressure is equal to atmospheric pressure and the signal voltage will be high. This information is used by the ECM as an indication of vehicle altitude and is referred to as BARO. Comparison of this BARO reading with a known good vehicle with the same sensor is a good way to check accuracy of a "suspect" sensor, the reading should be the same ± .4 volt. Also, CHART C-1D can be used to test the MAP sensor.

Refer to "Intermittents" in "Symptoms," Section "6E2-B".

Fig. 191 Engine controls diagnostic chart

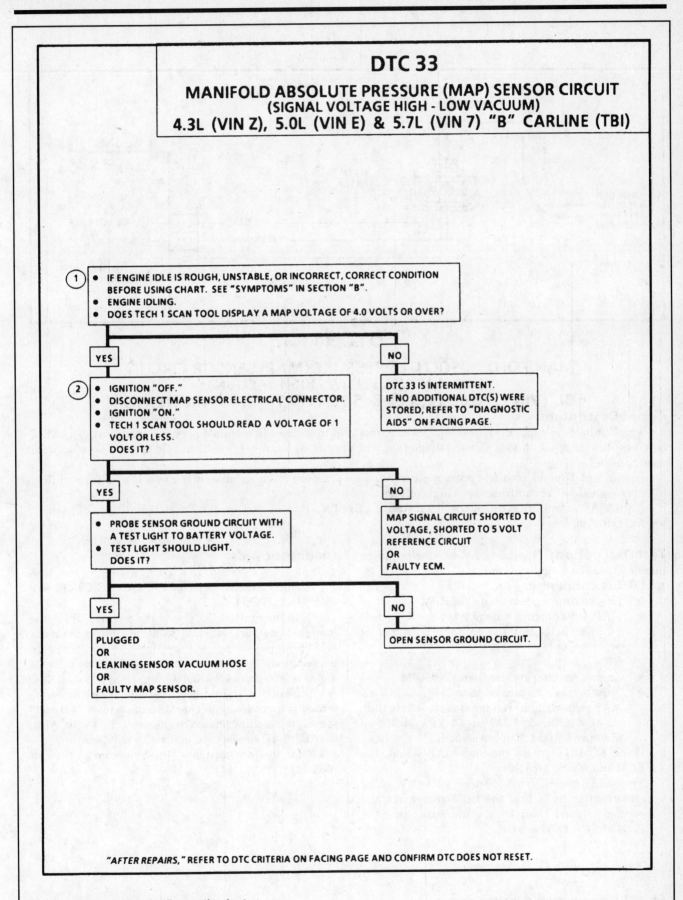

DTC 33

MANIFOLD ABSOLUTE PRESSURE (MAP) SENSOR CIRCUIT
(SIGNAL VOLTAGE HIGH - LOW VACUUM)
4.3L (VIN Z), 5.0L (VIN E) & 5.7L (VIN 7) "B" CARLINE (TBI)

1
- IF ENGINE IDLE IS ROUGH, UNSTABLE, OR INCORRECT, CORRECT CONDITION BEFORE USING CHART. SEE "SYMPTOMS" IN SECTION "B".
- ENGINE IDLING.
- DOES TECH 1 SCAN TOOL DISPLAY A MAP VOLTAGE OF 4.0 VOLTS OR OVER?

YES

2
- IGNITION "OFF."
- DISCONNECT MAP SENSOR ELECTRICAL CONNECTOR.
- IGNITION "ON."
- TECH 1 SCAN TOOL SHOULD READ A VOLTAGE OF 1 VOLT OR LESS. DOES IT?

NO

DTC 33 IS INTERMITTENT. IF NO ADDITIONAL DTC(S) WERE STORED, REFER TO "DIAGNOSTIC AIDS" ON FACING PAGE.

YES

- PROBE SENSOR GROUND CIRCUIT WITH A TEST LIGHT TO BATTERY VOLTAGE.
- TEST LIGHT SHOULD LIGHT. DOES IT?

NO

MAP SIGNAL CIRCUIT SHORTED TO VOLTAGE, SHORTED TO 5 VOLT REFERENCE CIRCUIT OR FAULTY ECM.

YES

PLUGGED OR LEAKING SENSOR VACUUM HOSE OR FAULTY MAP SENSOR.

NO

OPEN SENSOR GROUND CIRCUIT.

"AFTER REPAIRS," REFER TO DTC CRITERIA ON FACING PAGE AND CONFIRM DTC DOES NOT RESET.

Fig. 192 Engine controls diagnostic chart

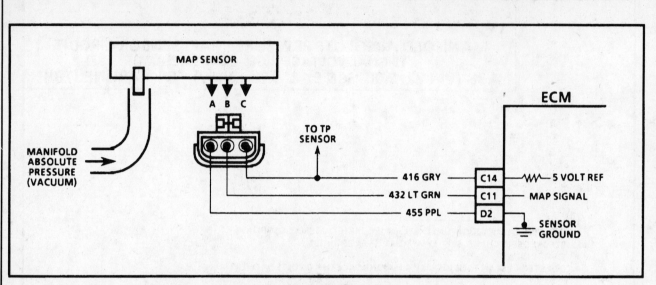

DTC 34

MANIFOLD ABSOLUTE PRESSURE (MAP) SENSOR CIRCUIT
(SIGNAL VOLTAGE LOW - HIGH VACUUM)
4.3L (VIN Z), 5.0L (VIN E) & 5.7L (VIN 7) "B" CARLINE (TBI)

Circuit Description:

The Manifold Absolute Pressure (MAP) sensor responds to changes in manifold pressure (vacuum). The ECM receives this information as a signal voltage that will vary from about 1-1.5 volts at idle to 4-4.5 volts at wide open throttle.

A scan tool displays manifold pressure in volts. Low pressure (high vacuum) displays a low voltage while a high pressure (low vacuum) displays a high voltage.

If the MAP sensor fails the ECM will substitute a fixed MAP value and use the Throttle Position (TP) sensor to control fuel delivery.

Test Description: Number(s) below refer to circled number(s) on the diagnostic chart.

1. DTC 34 will set when:
   - Engine running less than 1200 RPM.
   - MAP sensor signal voltage is too low (less than 12 kPa (5.0L & 5.7L) or 14 kPa (4.3L) of pressure for less than one second).
     OR
   - Engine running greater than 1200 RPM.
   - Throttle position greater than 21%.
   - MAP sensor signal voltage is too low (less than 12 kPa (5.0L & 5.7L) or 14 kPa (4.3L) of pressure for less than one second).
2. If the ECM recognizes the high MAP signal, the ECM and wiring are OK.
3. The scan tool may not display 12 volts. The important thing is that the ECM recognizes the voltage as more than 4 volts, indicating that the ECM and CKT 432 are OK.

Diagnostic Aids:

An intermittent open in CKT 432 or CKT 416 will result in a DTC 34.

With the ignition "ON" and the engine "OFF," the manifold pressure is equal to atmospheric pressure and the signal voltage will be high. This information is used by the ECM as an indication of vehicle altitude and is referred to as BARO. Comparison of this BARO reading with a known good vehicle with the same sensor is a good way to check accuracy of a "suspect" sensor, the reading should be the same ± .4 volt. Also, CHART C-1D can be used to test the MAP sensor.

Refer to "Intermittents" in "Symptoms," Section "6E2-B".

Fig. 193 Engine controls diagnostic chart

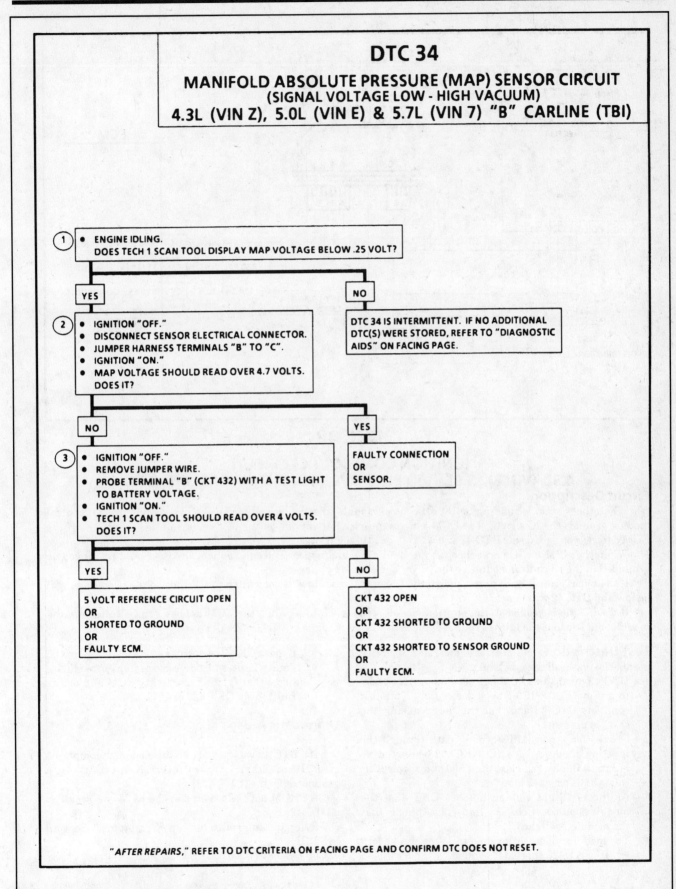

DTC 34

MANIFOLD ABSOLUTE PRESSURE (MAP) SENSOR CIRCUIT
(SIGNAL VOLTAGE LOW - HIGH VACUUM)
4.3L (VIN Z), 5.0L (VIN E) & 5.7L (VIN 7) "B" CARLINE (TBI)

1
- ENGINE IDLING.
  DOES TECH 1 SCAN TOOL DISPLAY MAP VOLTAGE BELOW .25 VOLT?

YES

NO

2
- IGNITION "OFF."
- DISCONNECT SENSOR ELECTRICAL CONNECTOR.
- JUMPER HARNESS TERMINALS "B" TO "C".
- IGNITION "ON."
- MAP VOLTAGE SHOULD READ OVER 4.7 VOLTS. DOES IT?

DTC 34 IS INTERMITTENT. IF NO ADDITIONAL DTC(S) WERE STORED, REFER TO "DIAGNOSTIC AIDS" ON FACING PAGE.

NO

YES

3
- IGNITION "OFF."
- REMOVE JUMPER WIRE.
- PROBE TERMINAL "B" (CKT 432) WITH A TEST LIGHT TO BATTERY VOLTAGE.
- IGNITION "ON."
- TECH 1 SCAN TOOL SHOULD READ OVER 4 VOLTS. DOES IT?

FAULTY CONNECTION
OR
SENSOR.

YES

NO

5 VOLT REFERENCE CIRCUIT OPEN
OR
SHORTED TO GROUND
OR
FAULTY ECM.

CKT 432 OPEN
OR
CKT 432 SHORTED TO GROUND
OR
CKT 432 SHORTED TO SENSOR GROUND
OR
FAULTY ECM.

"AFTER REPAIRS," REFER TO DTC CRITERIA ON FACING PAGE AND CONFIRM DTC DOES NOT RESET.

Fig. 194 Engine controls diagnostic chart

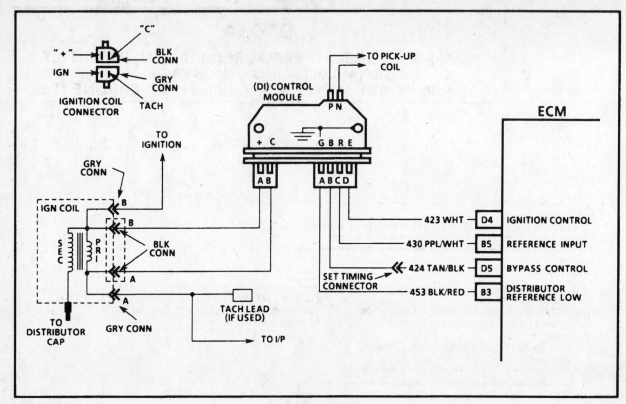

DTC 42

IGNITION CONTROL (IC) CIRCUIT
4.3L (VIN Z), 5.0L (VIN E) & 5.7L (VIN 7) "B" CARLINE (TBI)

Circuit Description:

When the system is running on the DI control module, that is, no voltage on the bypass line, the DI control module grounds the IC signal. The ECM expects to sense low voltage on the IC line during this condition. If the ECM detects voltage, it sets DTC 42 and will not go into the IC mode.

When the RPM for IC is reached (about 400 RPM), and bypass voltage applied, the IC should no longer be grounded in the DI control module so the IC voltage should be varying.

If the bypass line is open or grounded, the DI control module will not switch to IC mode so the IC voltage will be low and DTC 42 will be set.

If the IC line is grounded, the ignition module will switch to IC when the ECM applies bypass voltage to the module, but because the line is grounded, there will be no IC signal. A DTC 42 will be set.

Test Description: Number(s) below refer to circled number(s) on the diagnostic chart.

1. DTC 42 means the ECM has seen an open or short to ground in the IC or bypass circuits. This test confirms DTC 42 and that the fault causing the DTC is present.
2. Checks for a normal IC ground path through the ignition module. An IC CKT 423 shorted to ground will also read less than 500 ohms; however, this will be checked later.
3. As the test light voltage touches CKT 424, the module should switch. The important thing is that the module "switched."
4. The module did not switch and this step checks for:
   - IC CKT 423 shorted to ground.

- Bypass CKT 424 open.
- Faulty ignition module connection or module.
5. Confirms that DTC 42 is a faulty ECM and not an intermittent in CKT 423 or CKT 424.

Diagnostic Aids:

If a DTC 42 was stored and the customer complains of a "Hard Start," the problem is most likely a grounded IC line (CKT 423).

A PROM not fully seated in the ECM can result in a DTC 42.

Refer to "Intermittents" in "Symptoms," Section "6E2-B".

Fig. 195 Engine controls diagnostic chart

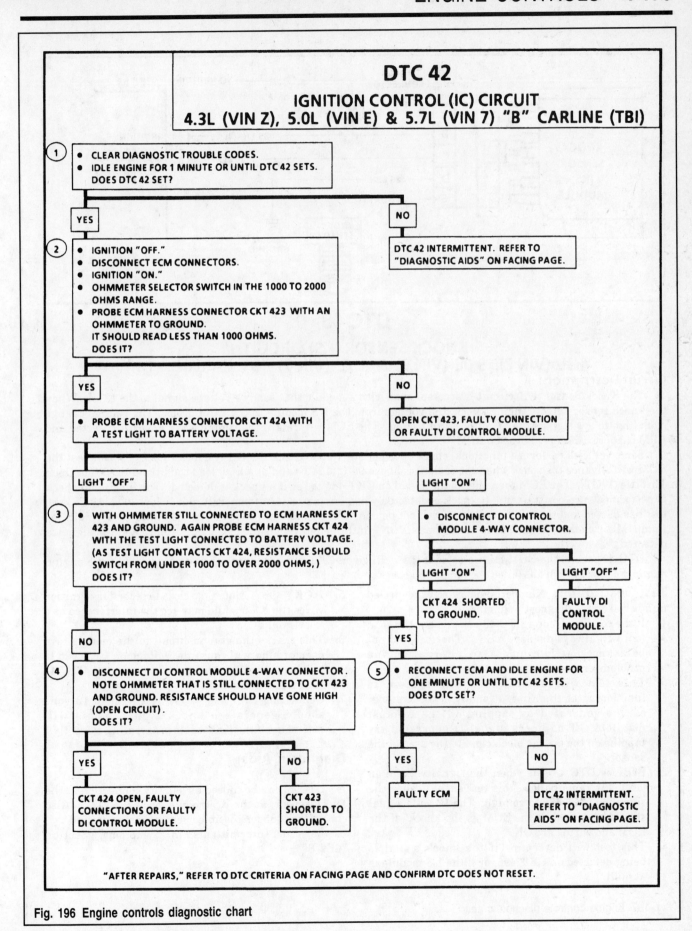

DTC 42
IGNITION CONTROL (IC) CIRCUIT
4.3L (VIN Z), 5.0L (VIN E) & 5.7L (VIN 7) "B" CARLINE (TBI)

1
- CLEAR DIAGNOSTIC TROUBLE CODES.
- IDLE ENGINE FOR 1 MINUTE OR UNTIL DTC 42 SETS.
  DOES DTC 42 SET?

YES

NO

DTC 42 INTERMITTENT. REFER TO "DIAGNOSTIC AIDS" ON FACING PAGE.

2
- IGNITION "OFF."
- DISCONNECT ECM CONNECTORS.
- IGNITION "ON."
- OHMMETER SELECTOR SWITCH IN THE 1000 TO 2000 OHMS RANGE.
- PROBE ECM HARNESS CONNECTOR CKT 423 WITH AN OHMMETER TO GROUND.
  IT SHOULD READ LESS THAN 1000 OHMS.
  DOES IT?

YES

NO

- PROBE ECM HARNESS CONNECTOR CKT 424 WITH A TEST LIGHT TO BATTERY VOLTAGE.

OPEN CKT 423, FAULTY CONNECTION OR FAULTY DI CONTROL MODULE.

LIGHT "OFF"

LIGHT "ON"

3
- WITH OHMMETER STILL CONNECTED TO ECM HARNESS CKT 423 AND GROUND. AGAIN PROBE ECM HARNESS CKT 424 WITH THE TEST LIGHT CONNECTED TO BATTERY VOLTAGE. (AS TEST LIGHT CONTACTS CKT 424, RESISTANCE SHOULD SWITCH FROM UNDER 1000 TO OVER 2000 OHMS,)
  DOES IT?

- DISCONNECT DI CONTROL MODULE 4-WAY CONNECTOR.

LIGHT "ON"

LIGHT "OFF"

CKT 424 SHORTED TO GROUND.

FAULTY DI CONTROL MODULE.

NO

YES

4
- DISCONNECT DI CONTROL MODULE 4-WAY CONNECTOR. NOTE OHMMETER THAT IS STILL CONNECTED TO CKT 423 AND GROUND. RESISTANCE SHOULD HAVE GONE HIGH (OPEN CIRCUIT).
  DOES IT?

5
- RECONNECT ECM AND IDLE ENGINE FOR ONE MINUTE OR UNTIL DTC 42 SETS.
  DOES DTC SET?

YES

NO

YES

NO

CKT 424 OPEN, FAULTY CONNECTIONS OR FAULTY DI CONTROL MODULE.

CKT 423 SHORTED TO GROUND.

FAULTY ECM

DTC 42 INTERMITTENT. REFER TO "DIAGNOSTIC AIDS" ON FACING PAGE.

"AFTER REPAIRS," REFER TO DTC CRITERIA ON FACING PAGE AND CONFIRM DTC DOES NOT RESET.

Fig. 196 Engine controls diagnostic chart

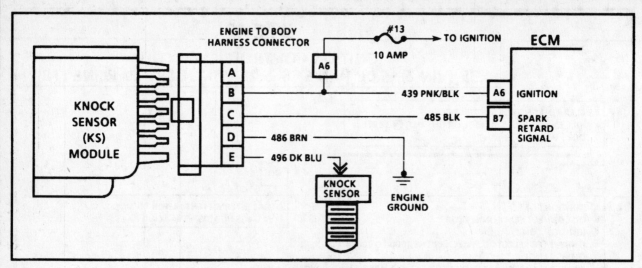

DTC 43

KNOCK SENSOR (KS) CIRCUIT
4.3L (VIN Z), 5.0L (VIN E) & 5.7L (VIN 7) "B" CARLINE (TBI)

Circuit Description:

The Knock Sensor (KS) circuit is accomplished with a module that sends a voltage signal to the ECM. When the knock sensor detects engine knock, the voltage from the KS module to the ECM drops. The voltage change from high to low signals the ECM to retard timing. The ECM will retard the timing when knock is detected and RPM is approximately above 900 RPM.

Some vehicles perform a functional check once per start up to check the KS system. To perform this test the ECM will advance the spark when the coolant is above 90°C (194°F) and at a high load condition near Wide Open Throttle (WOT). The ECM then checks the signal on CKT 485 to see if a knock is detected. The functional check is performed once per start up. If knock is detected when engine coolant temperature is below 90°C (194°F) the test has passed and the functional check will not be run. If the functional check fails, the Malfunction Indicator Lamp (MIL) "Service Engine Soon" will remain "ON" until the ignition is turned "OFF" or until a knock signal is detected.

DTC 43 means the ECM has detected a low voltage on CKT 485 for longer than 4 seconds with the engine running or the system has failed the functional check.

Test Description: Number(s) below refer to circled number(s) on the diagnostic chart.

1. If the conditions for a DTC 43 are present the scan tool will always display "YES." There should not be a knock at idle unless an internal engine problem, or a system problem exists.

2. This test will determine if the system is functioning at this time. Usually a knock signal can be generated by tapping on the exhaust manifold. If no knock signal is generated try tapping on the engine block close to the area of the sensor.

3. Because DTC 43 sets when the signal voltage on CKT 485 remains low, this test should cause the signal on CKT 485 to go high. The 12 volts signal should be sensed by the ECM as "no knock" if the ECM and wiring are OK.

4. This test will determine if the knock signal is being detected on CKT 496, or if the KS module is at fault.

5. If CKT 496 is routed too close to secondary ignition wires the KS module may see the interference as a knock signal.

6. This checks the ground circuit to the module. An open ground will cause the voltage on CKT 485 to be about 12 volts which would cause the DTC 43 functional test to fail.

7. Contacting CKT 496 with a test light to 12 volts should generate a knock signal. This will determine if the KS module is operating correctly.

Diagnostic Aids:

DTC 43 can be caused by a faulty connection at the knock sensor, at the KS module, or at the ECM. Also check CKT 485 for possible open or short to ground.

Refer to "Intermittents" in "Symptoms," Section "6E2-B".

Fig. 197 Engine controls diagnostic chart

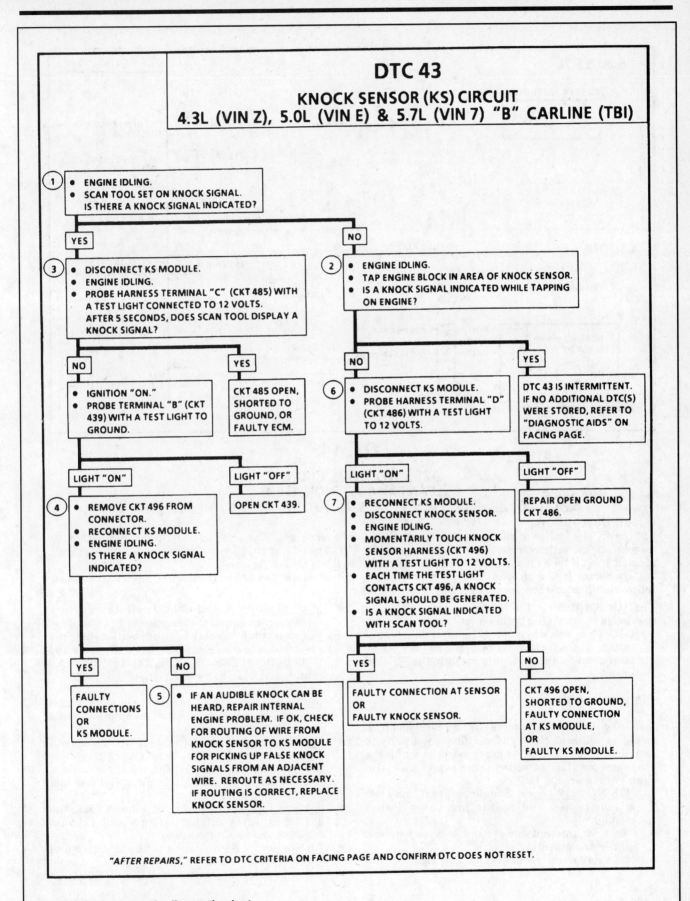

DTC 43

KNOCK SENSOR (KS) CIRCUIT
4.3L (VIN Z), 5.0L (VIN E) & 5.7L (VIN 7) "B" CARLINE (TBI)

1
- ENGINE IDLING.
- SCAN TOOL SET ON KNOCK SIGNAL.
  IS THERE A KNOCK SIGNAL INDICATED?

YES

NO

3
- DISCONNECT KS MODULE.
- ENGINE IDLING.
- PROBE HARNESS TERMINAL "C" (CKT 485) WITH
  A TEST LIGHT CONNECTED TO 12 VOLTS.
  AFTER 5 SECONDS, DOES SCAN TOOL DISPLAY A
  KNOCK SIGNAL?

2
- ENGINE IDLING.
- TAP ENGINE BLOCK IN AREA OF KNOCK SENSOR.
- IS A KNOCK SIGNAL INDICATED WHILE TAPPING
  ON ENGINE?

NO

YES

- IGNITION "ON."
- PROBE TERMINAL "B" (CKT
  439) WITH A TEST LIGHT TO
  GROUND.

CKT 485 OPEN,
SHORTED TO
GROUND, OR
FAULTY ECM.

NO

YES

6
- DISCONNECT KS MODULE.
- PROBE HARNESS TERMINAL "D"
  (CKT 486) WITH A TEST LIGHT
  TO 12 VOLTS.

DTC 43 IS INTERMITTENT.
IF NO ADDITIONAL DTC(S)
WERE STORED, REFER TO
"DIAGNOSTIC AIDS" ON
FACING PAGE.

LIGHT "ON"

LIGHT "OFF"

LIGHT "ON"

LIGHT "OFF"

4
- REMOVE CKT 496 FROM
  CONNECTOR.
- RECONNECT KS MODULE.
- ENGINE IDLING.
  IS THERE A KNOCK SIGNAL
  INDICATED?

OPEN CKT 439.

7
- RECONNECT KS MODULE.
- DISCONNECT KNOCK SENSOR.
- ENGINE IDLING.
- MOMENTARILY TOUCH KNOCK
  SENSOR HARNESS (CKT 496)
  WITH A TEST LIGHT TO 12 VOLTS.
- EACH TIME THE TEST LIGHT
  CONTACTS CKT 496, A KNOCK
  SIGNAL SHOULD BE GENERATED.
- IS A KNOCK SIGNAL INDICATED
  WITH SCAN TOOL?

REPAIR OPEN GROUND
CKT 486.

YES

NO

YES

NO

FAULTY
CONNECTIONS
OR
KS MODULE.

5
- IF AN AUDIBLE KNOCK CAN BE
  HEARD, REPAIR INTERNAL
  ENGINE PROBLEM. IF OK, CHECK
  FOR ROUTING OF WIRE FROM
  KNOCK SENSOR TO KS MODULE
  FOR PICKING UP FALSE KNOCK
  SIGNALS FROM AN ADJACENT
  WIRE. REROUTE AS NECESSARY.
  IF ROUTING IS CORRECT, REPLACE
  KNOCK SENSOR.

FAULTY CONNECTION AT SENSOR
OR
FAULTY KNOCK SENSOR.

CKT 496 OPEN,
SHORTED TO GROUND,
FAULTY CONNECTION
AT KS MODULE,
OR
FAULTY KS MODULE.

"AFTER REPAIRS," REFER TO DTC CRITERIA ON FACING PAGE AND CONFIRM DTC DOES NOT RESET.

Fig. 198 Engine controls diagnostic chart

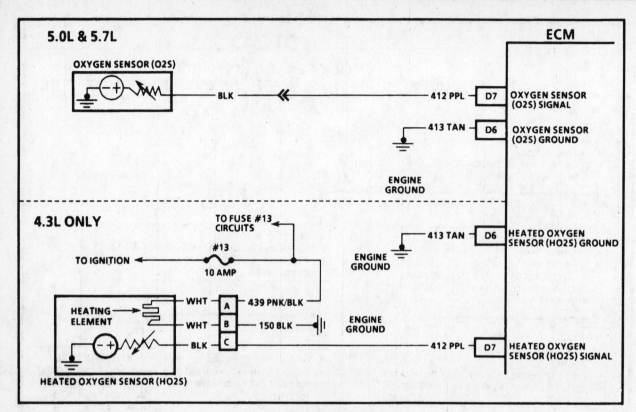

DTC 44

O2S AND HO2S CIRCUIT
(LEAN EXHAUST INDICATED)
4.3L (VIN Z), 5.0L (VIN E) & 5.7L (VIN 7) "B" CARLINE (TBI)

Circuit Description:

The ECM supplies a voltage of about .45 volt between terminals "D6" and "D7". (If measured with a 10 megohm digital voltmeter, this may read as low as 320 mV). The O2S or HO2S varies the voltage within a range of about 1 volt if the exhaust is rich, down through about 10 mV if exhaust is lean.

The sensor is like an open circuit and produces no voltage when it is below about 315°C (600°F). An open sensor circuit or cold sensor causes "Open Loop" operation.

Test Description: The number(s) below refers to the circled number(s) on the diagnostic chart.

1. DTC 44 is set when the O2S or HO2S signal voltage on CKT 412 remains below 250 mV for 50 seconds while the system is operating in "Closed Loop."

Diagnostic Aids:

Using the scan tool observe the long term fuel trim values at different RPM and air flow conditions to determine when the DTC 44 may have been set. If the conditions for DTC 44 exist the long term fuel trim values will be around 150.

- O2S/HO2S Wires. Sensor pigtail may be mispositioned and contacting the exhaust manifold.
- Check for intermittent ground in wire between connector and sensor.
- Make sure sensor ground is clean and tight.

- MAP Sensor. A Manifold Absolute Pressure (MAP) sensor output that causes the ECM to sense a higher than normal vacuum will cause the system to go lean. Disconnect the MAP sensor and if the lean condition is gone, replace the MAP sensor.
- Lean Injector(s).
- Fuel Contamination. Water, even in small amounts, near the in-tank fuel pump inlet can be delivered to the injectors.
- Fuel Pressure. The fuel system will be lean if pressure is too low. It may be necessary to monitor fuel pressure while driving the vehicle at various road speeds and/or loads to confirm that low fuel pressure does exist.
- Exhaust Leaks. If there is an exhaust leak, the engine can pull outside air into the exhaust manifold and past the sensor.
- Air System. Be sure air is not being directed to the exhaust ports while in "Closed Loop."
- If the above are OK, the O2S or HO2S is faulty.

Fig. 199 Engine controls diagnostic chart

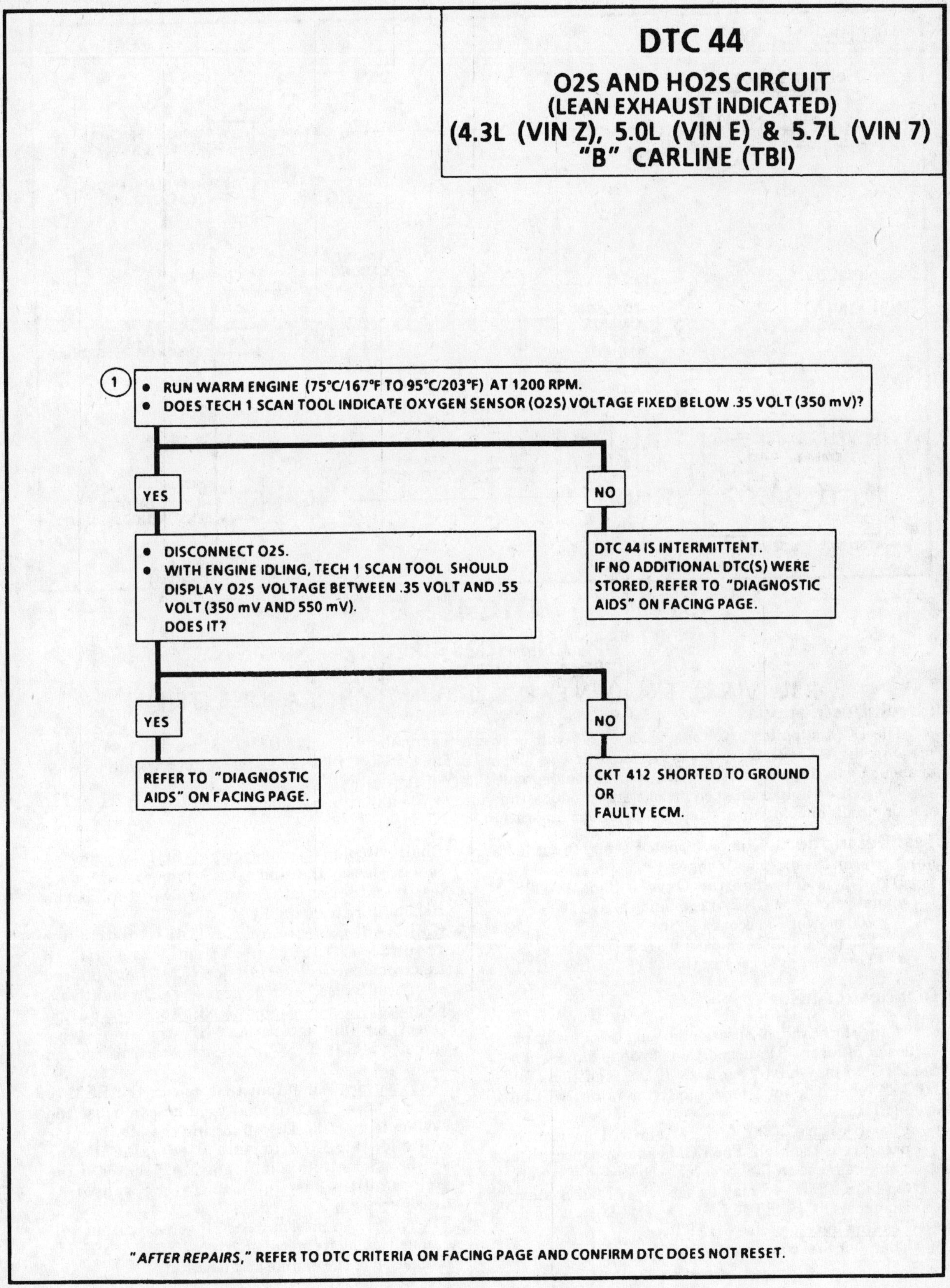

DTC 44

O2S AND HO2S CIRCUIT
(LEAN EXHAUST INDICATED)
(4.3L (VIN Z), 5.0L (VIN E) & 5.7L (VIN 7)
"B" CARLINE (TBI)

1
- RUN WARM ENGINE (75°C/167°F TO 95°C/203°F) AT 1200 RPM.
- DOES TECH 1 SCAN TOOL INDICATE OXYGEN SENSOR (O2S) VOLTAGE FIXED BELOW .35 VOLT (350 mV)?

YES
- DISCONNECT O2S.
- WITH ENGINE IDLING, TECH 1 SCAN TOOL SHOULD DISPLAY O2S VOLTAGE BETWEEN .35 VOLT AND .55 VOLT (350 mV AND 550 mV). DOES IT?

NO
DTC 44 IS INTERMITTENT. IF NO ADDITIONAL DTC(S) WERE STORED, REFER TO "DIAGNOSTIC AIDS" ON FACING PAGE.

YES
REFER TO "DIAGNOSTIC AIDS" ON FACING PAGE.

NO
CKT 412 SHORTED TO GROUND OR FAULTY ECM.

"AFTER REPAIRS," REFER TO DTC CRITERIA ON FACING PAGE AND CONFIRM DTC DOES NOT RESET.

Fig. 200 Engine controls diagnostic chart

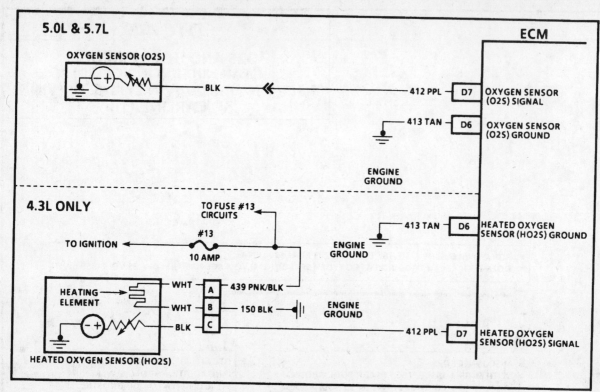

DTC 45

O2S AND HO2S CIRCUIT
(RICH EXHAUST INDICATED)
4.3L (VIN Z), 5.0L (VIN E) & 5.7L (VIN 7) "B" CARLINE (TBI)

Circuit Description:

The ECM supplies a voltage of about .45 volt between terminals "D6" and "D7". (If measured with a 10 megohm digital voltmeter, this may read as low as 320 mV.) The O2S or HO2S varies the voltage within a range of about 1 volt if the exhaust is rich, down through about 10 mV if exhaust is lean.

The sensor is like an open circuit and produces no voltage when it is below about 315°C (600°F). An open sensor circuit or cold sensor causes "Open Loop" operation.

Test Description: Number(s) below refers to circled number(s) on the diagnostic chart.
1. DTC 45 is set when the Oxygen Sensor (O2S) signal voltage on CKT 412 remains above:
   - 700 mV for 70 seconds (4.3L).
   - 750 mV for 30 seconds (5.0L & 5.7L).
   - Throttle angle greater than 20% (5.0L & 5.7L).

Diagnostic Aids:

Using the scan tool observe the long term fuel trim values at different RPM conditions to determine when the DTC 45 may have been set. If the conditions for DTC 45 exist, the long term fuel trim values will be around 110.
- Fuel Pressure. The fuel system will go rich if pressure is too high. The ECM can compensate for some increase in fuel pressure, however, if it gets too high a DTC 45 may be set. See "Fuel System Diagnosis," CHART A-7.
- Leaking injector. Use CHART A-7.
- Check for fuel contaminated oil.

- Engine Coolant Temperature (ECT) sensor. A coolant sensor that indicates a temperature much less than the actual temperature will command a rich mixture from the ECM.
- EMI. An open ground CKT 453 (distributor ground, reference low) may result in Electromagnetic Interference (EMI), or induced electrical "noise," and may cause a rich condition.
- Evaporative Emission (EVAP) canister purge. Check for fuel saturation. If the fuel vapor canister is full of fuel, check canister control and hoses.
- MAP sensor. An output that causes the ECM to sense a lower than normal vacuum can cause the system to go rich. Disconnecting the MAP sensor will allow the ECM to set a fixed value for the sensor. Substitute a different MAP sensor if the rich condition is gone while the sensor is disconnected.
- TP sensor. An intermittent TP sensor output will cause the system to go rich, due to a false indication of the engine accelerating.

Fig. 201 Engine controls diagnostic chart

DTC 45

O2S AND HO2S CIRCUIT
(RICH EXHAUST INDICATED)
4.3L (VIN Z), 5.0L (VIN E) & 5.7L (VIN 7) "B" CARLINE (TBI)

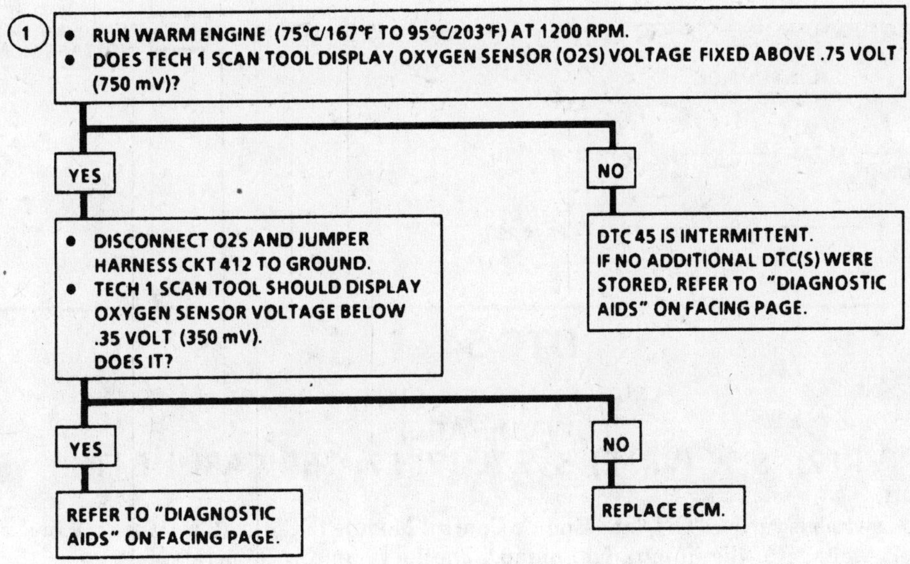

1
- RUN WARM ENGINE (75°C/167°F TO 95°C/203°F) AT 1200 RPM.
- DOES TECH 1 SCAN TOOL DISPLAY OXYGEN SENSOR (O2S) VOLTAGE FIXED ABOVE .75 VOLT (750 mV)?

YES
- DISCONNECT O2S AND JUMPER HARNESS CKT 412 TO GROUND.
- TECH 1 SCAN TOOL SHOULD DISPLAY OXYGEN SENSOR VOLTAGE BELOW .35 VOLT (350 mV). DOES IT?

NO
DTC 45 IS INTERMITTENT. IF NO ADDITIONAL DTC(S) WERE STORED, REFER TO "DIAGNOSTIC AIDS" ON FACING PAGE.

YES
REFER TO "DIAGNOSTIC AIDS" ON FACING PAGE.

NO
REPLACE ECM.

"AFTER REPAIRS," REFER TO DTC CRITERIA ON FACING PAGE AND CONFIRM DTC DOES NOT RESET.

Fig. 202 Engine controls diagnostic chart

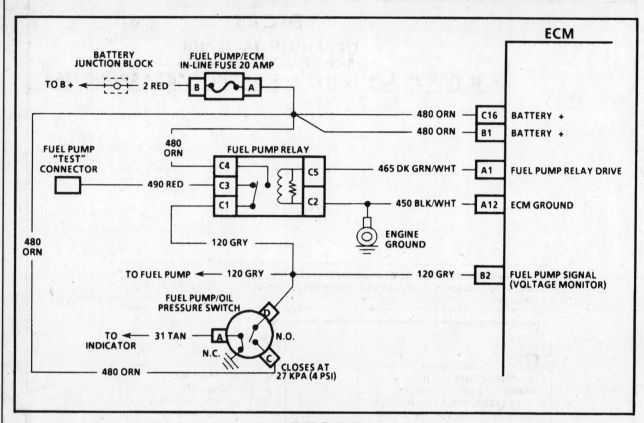

DTC 54

FUEL PUMP CIRCUIT
(LOW VOLTAGE)
4.3L (VIN Z), 5.0L (VIN E) & 5.7L (VIN 7) "B" CARLINE (TBI)

Circuit Description:

When the ignition switch is turned "ON," the Engine Control Module (ECM) will activate the fuel pump relay which supplies battery voltage to the in-tank fuel pump. The fuel pump will operate as long as the engine is cranking or running, and the ECM is receiving ignition reference pulses.

If there are no reference pulses, the ECM will shut "OFF" the fuel pump within 2 seconds after ignition "ON," or the engine stops.

Should the fuel pump relay, or the 12 volts relay drive from the ECM fail, the fuel pump will be run through an oil pressure switch back-up circuit.

DTC 54 will set if the ECM does not sense the 12 volts signal on CKT 120 during the 2 seconds that the ECM is energizing the fuel pump relay.

Diagnostic Aids:

An inoperative fuel pump relay can result in long cranking times, particularly if the engine is cold or engine oil pressure is low. The extended crank period is caused by the time necessary for oil pressure to build enough to close the oil pressure switch and turn "ON" the fuel pump.

Fig. 203 Engine controls diagnostic chart

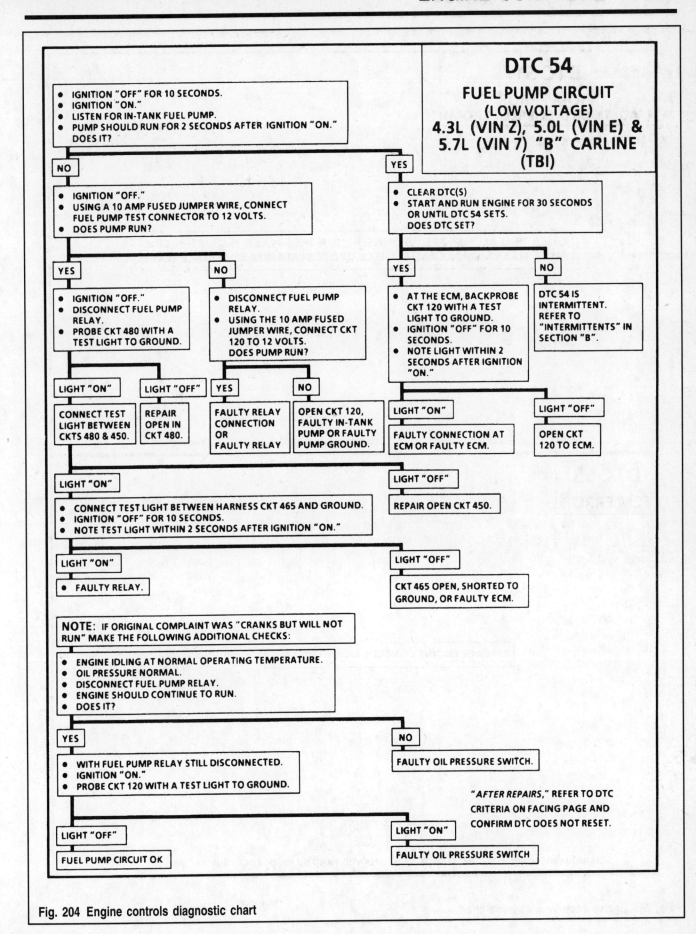

Fig. 204 Engine controls diagnostic chart

DTC 51
PROM ERROR
(FAULTY OR INCORRECT PROM)

CHECK THAT ALL PINS ARE FULLY INSERTED IN THE SOCKET. IF OK, REPLACE PROM, CLEAR MEMORY AND RECHECK. IF DTC 51 REAPPEARS, REPLACE ECM.

CLEAR ALL DTC(S) AND CONFIRM "CLOSED LOOP" OPERATION AND NO MIL (SERVICE ENGINE SOON).

DTC 55
ECM ERROR

REPLACE ENGINE CONTROL MODULE (ECM).

CLEAR ALL DTC(S) AND CONFIRM "CLOSED LOOP" OPERATION AND NO MIL (SERVICE ENGINE SOON).

Fig. 205 Engine controls diagnostic chart

5

FUEL SYSTEM

CARBURETED FUEL SYSTEM

Mechanical Fuel Pump

The fuel pump is a single diaphragm type. The mechanical fuel pump used on the 5.0L (VIN Y) engine is of the diaphragm type and because of the design is serviced by replacement only. No adjustments or repairs are possible.

The fuel pump is mounted on the right front of the engine. The fuel pumps is operated by an eccentric on the front of the camshaft sprocket. The spring loaded fuel pump rocker arm is in constant contact with eccentric on the camshaft sprocket.

REMOVAL & INSTALLATION

▶ See Figure 1

❊❊CAUTION

Do not use a droplight around work area when disconnecting fuel lines. If fuel contacts a droplight, the bulb may explode causing serious personal injury not to mention material damage. Instead a flashlight may be used.

1. Disconnect the fuel intake and outlet lines at the pump and plug the pump intake line.

➡**When disconnecting the fuel pump outlet fitting, always use 2 wrenches to avoid twisting the line.**

2. Remove the two pump mounting bolts and lockwashers; remove the pump and its gasket.
3. Install the fuel pump with a new gasket reversing the removal procedure. Coat the mating surfaces with sealer.
4. Connect the fuel lines and check for leaks.

TESTING

To determine if the pump is in good condition, tests for both volume and pressure should be performed. The tests are made with the pump installed, and the engine at normal operating temperature and idle speed. Verify the fuel tank has

Fig. 1 Carbureted engine fuel pump — 5.0L (VIN Y) engine

a sufficient quantity of fuel to perform the test. Never replace a fuel pump without first performing these simple tests.

Ensure the fuel filter has been changed at the specified interval. If in doubt, install a new filter first. Always check for broken or deteriorated fuel hoses. If a line has a crack or split, the pump may be operating properly, but the pump will only draw air, not fuel.

Pressure Test

1. Disconnect the fuel line at the carburetor and connect a fuel pump pressure gauge. Ensure the carburetor float bowl has a sufficient amount of gasoline.
2. Start the engine and check the pressure with the engine at idle. If the pump has a vapor return hose, squeeze it off so that an accurate reading can be obtained. Pressure should be $5\frac{1}{2}$-$6\frac{1}{2}$ psi.
3. If the pressure is incorrect, replace the pump. If it is OK, go on to the volume test.

Volume Test

1. Disconnect the pressure gauge. Run the fuel line into a graduated container.
2. Run the engine at idle until a ½ pint of gasoline has been pumped. A ½ pint should be delivered in approximately 15 seconds or less. There is normally enough fuel in the carburetor float bowl to perform this test, but refill it if necessary.
3. If the delivery rate is below the minimum, check the lines for restrictions, cracks or leaks, then replace the pump.

Carburetors

▶ See Figure 2

The 5.0L (VIN Y) engine uses the E4MC. This carburetor is of the downdraft design used in conjunction with the CCC system of fuel control. They have special design features for optimum air/fuel mixture control during all ranges of engine operation.

An electric solenoid in the carburetor controls the air/fuel ratio. The solenoid is connected to an Electronic Control Module (ECM) which is an on board computer. The ECM provides a controlling signal to the solenoid. The solenoid controls the metering rod(s) and an idle air bleed valve to closely control the air/fuel ratio throughout the operating range of the engine.

MODEL IDENTIFICATION

▶ See Figure 3

General Motors Rochester carburetors are identified by their model code. The first number indicates the number of barrels, while one of the last letters indicates the type of choke used. These are V for the manifold mounted choke coil, C for the choke coil mounted in the carburetor body, and E for electric

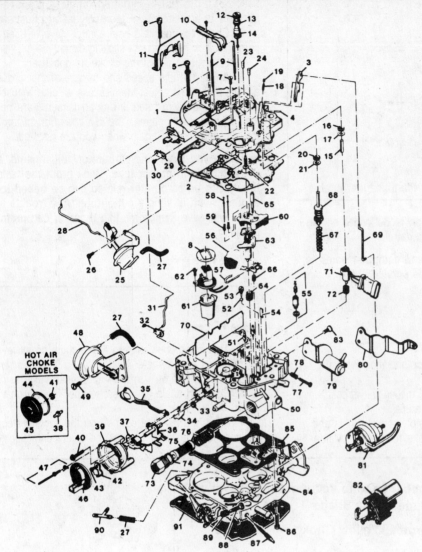

HOT AIR CHOKE MODELS

1. Air horn assembly
2. Gasket—air horn
3. Lever—pump actuating
4. Roll pin—pump lever hinge
5. Screw—air horn, long (2)
6. Screw—air horn, short
7. Screw—air horn, countersunk (2)
8. Gasket—solenoid connector to air horn
9. Metering rod—secondary (2)
10. Holder & screw—secondary metering rod
11. Baffle—secondary air
12. Valve—idle air bleed
13. "O" ring (thick)—idle air bleed valve
14. "O" ring (thin)—idle air bleed valve
15. Plunger—TPS actuator
16. Seal—TPS plunger
17. Retainer—TPS seal
18. Screw—TPS adjusting

19. Plug—TPS screw
20. Seal—pump plunger
21. Retainer—pump seal
22. Screw—solenoid plunger stop (rich mixture stop)
23. Plug—plunger stop screw (rich mixture stop)
24. Plug—solenoid adjusting screw (lean mixture)
25. Vacuum break & bracket—front
26. Screw—vacuum break attaching (2)
27. Hose—vacuum
28. Rod—air valve
29. Lever—choke rod (upper)
30. Screw—choke lever
31. Rod—choke
32. Lever—choke rod (lower)
33. Seal—intermediate choke shaft
34. Lever—secondary lockout

35. Link—rear vacuum break
36. Intermediate choke shaft & lever
37. Cam—fast idle
38. Seal—choke housing to bowl (hot air choke)
39. Choke housing
40. Screw—choke housing to bowl
41. Seal—intermediate choke shaft (hot air choke)
42. Lever—choke coil
43. Screw—choke coil lever
44. Gasket—Stat cover (hot air choke)
45. Stat cover & coil assembly (hot air choke)
46. Stat cover & coil assembly (electric choke)
47. Kit—stat cover attaching
48. Vacuum break assembly—rear

49. Screw—vacuum break attaching (2)
50. Float Bowl Assembly
51. Jet—primary metering (2)
52. Ball—pump discharge
53. Retainer—pump discharge ball
54. Baffle—pump well
55. Needle & seat assembly
56. Float assembly
57. Hinge pin—float assembly
58. Rod—primary metering (2)
59. Spring—primary metering rod (2)
60. Insert—float bowl
61. Insert—bowl cavity
62. Screw—connector attaching
63. Mixture control (M/C) solenoid & plunger assembly
64. Spring—solenoid tension
65. Screw—solenoid adjusting (lean mixture)
66. Spring—solenoid adjusting screw
67. Spring—pump return
68. Pump assembly
69. Link—pump
70. Baffle—secondary bores
71. Throttle position sensor (TPS)
72. Spring—TPS Tension
73. Filter nut—fuel inlet
74. Gasket—filter nut
75. Filter—fuel inlet
76. Spring—fuel filter
77. Screw—idle stop
78. Spring—idle stop screw
79. Idle speed solenoid & bracket assembly
80. Bracket—throttle return spring
81. Idle load compensator & bracket assembly
82. Idle speed control & bracket assembly
83. Screw—bracket attaching
84. Throttle body assembly
85. Gasket—throttle body
86. Screw—throttle body
87. Idle needle & spring assembly (2)
88. Screw—fast idle adjusting
89. Spring fast idle screw
90. Tee—vacuum hose
91. Gasket—flange

Fig. 2 Exploded view of the E4MC/E4ME carburetor

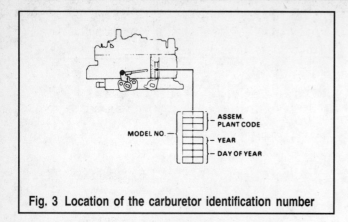

Fig. 3 Location of the carburetor identification number

choke, also mounted on the carburetor. Model codes ending in A indicate an altitude-compensating carburetor.

➡Because of the intricate nature and computer controls, the E4M carburetors should only be serviced by a qualified technician.

PRELIMINARY CHECK

The following should be observed before attempting any adjustments.

1. Thoroughly warm the engine. If the engine is cold, be sure that it reaches operating temperature.

2. Check the torque of all carburetor mounting nuts and assembly screws. Also check the intake manifold-to-cylinder head bolts. If air is leaking at any of these points, any attempts at adjustment will inevitably lead to frustration.

3. Check the manifold heat control valve (if used) to be sure that it is free and not sticking closed.

4. Check and adjust the choke as necessary.

5. Adjust the idle speed and mixture. If the mixture screws are capped, don't adjust them unless all other causes of rough idle have been eliminated. If any adjustments are performed that might possibly change the idle speed or mixture, adjust the idle and mixture again when you are finished.

➡Before you make any carburetor adjustments, ensure the engine is in proper tune. Many problems which are thought to be carburetor related can be traced to an engine which is simply out-of-tune. Any trouble in these areas will have symptoms like those of carburetor problems.

ADJUSTMENTS

Fast Idle
▶ See Figure 4

1. Attach a rubber band to the vacuum break lever of the intermediate choke shaft.

2. Open the throttle to allow the choke valve to close.

3. Place an angle gauge set to specification on the choke valve.

4. Place the fast idle cam 'A' on the second step against the cam follower lever 'B', with the lever contacting the rise of

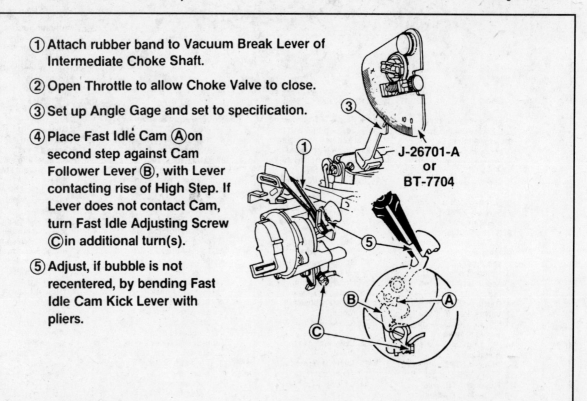

① Attach rubber band to Vacuum Break Lever of Intermediate Choke Shaft.

② Open Throttle to allow Choke Valve to close.

③ Set up Angle Gage and set to specification.

④ Place Fast Idle Cam Ⓐ on second step against Cam Follower Lever Ⓑ, with Lever contacting rise of High Step. If Lever does not contact Cam, turn Fast Idle Adjusting Screw Ⓒ in additional turn(s).

⑤ Adjust, if bubble is not recentered, by bending Fast Idle Cam Kick Lever with pliers.

J-26701-A or BT-7704

Fig. 4 Fast idle adjustment — E4M carburetor

the High Step. If the lever does not contact the Cam, turn the fast idle adjusting screw 'C' in additional turn(s).

5. Adjust, if bubble is not recentered, by bending fast idle cam kick lever with a suitable tool.

Float and Fuel Level
▶ See Figure 5

1. Remove the air horn and gasket from the float bowl. Hold the float retainer down firmly. Push the float down (lightly) against the needle.

2. Position a T-scale over the toe of the float 3/16 inch from the end of the float toe.

3. If the float level varies more than 1/16 inch from the specified setting, it must be reset.

FLOAT LEVEL TOO HIGH

1. Hold the float retainer in place.

2. Push down on the center of the float until the correct level is obtained.

FLOAT LEVEL TOO LOW

1. Lift out the metering rods and remove the solenoid connector screws.

2. Turn the lean mixture solenoid screw clockwise, counting and recording the number of turns required to seat the screw in the float bowl.

3. Turn the screw counterclockwise and remove it. Lift the solenoid and the connector from the float bowl.

4. Remove the float and bend the arm up to adjust. The float must be correctly aligned after adjustment.

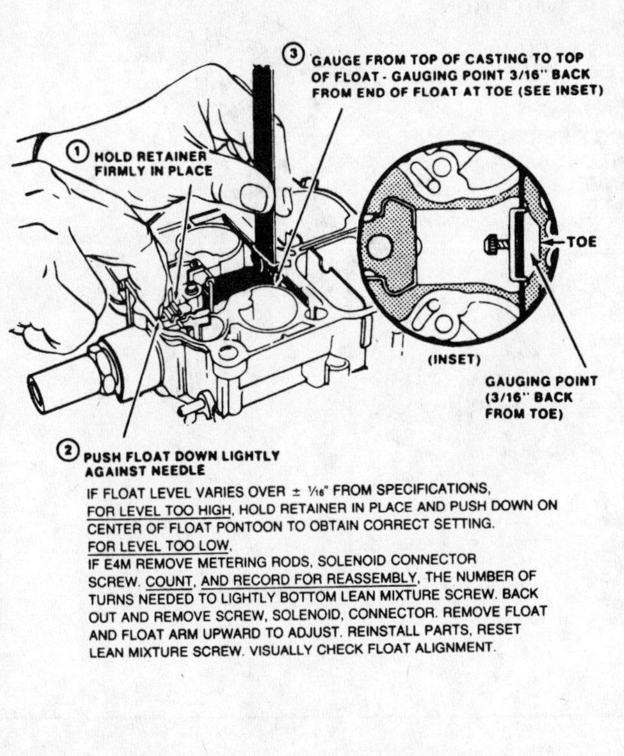

5. To install the components, reverse the order of removal. Back out the solenoid mixture screw the number of turns that were recorded in step 2.

Throttle Linkage

Due to the design of the throttle cable for the carburetor systems, no adjustments of the throttle linkage can be made.

Choke Unloader (Primary)
▶ See Figures 6 and 7

1. Connect a rubber band to the green tang of the intermediate choke shaft.

2. Open the throttle to allow the choke valve to close.

3. Set up the angle gauge and set to specifications.

4. Using a vacuum source, retract the vacuum break plunger. The air valve rod must not restrict the breaker plunger from fully retracting.

5. With the vacuum applied, turn the adjusting screw until the centering bubble of the angle gauge is level.

Choke Unloader (Secondary)
▶ See Figure 8

1. Connect a rubber band to the vacuum break lever of the intermediate choke shaft.

2. Open the throttle to allow the choke valve to close.

3. Set up the angle gauge and set the angle to specification.

4. Using a vacuum source, retract the vacuum break plunger.

➡ The air valve rod must not restrict the vacuum break plunger from fully retracting.

5. With the vacuum applied, turn the adjusting screw or bend the vacuum break rod until the bubble of the angle gauge is centered.

Air Valve Spring Adjustment
▶ See Figure 9

1. Loosen the lock screw and turn the tension adjusting screw counterclockwise until the air valve partly opens.

2. Turn the tension adjusting screw clockwise until the air valve just closes, then turn the screw clockwise a specified number of turns.

3. Tighten the lock screw and apply lithium grease to the spring contact area.

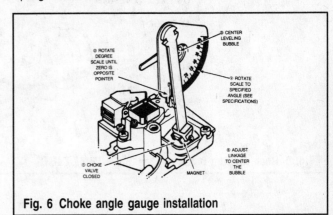

③ GAUGE FROM TOP OF CASTING TO TOP OF FLOAT - GAUGING POINT 3/16" BACK FROM END OF FLOAT AT TOE (SEE INSET)

① HOLD RETAINER FIRMLY IN PLACE

TOE

(INSET)

GAUGING POINT (3/16" BACK FROM TOE)

② PUSH FLOAT DOWN LIGHTLY AGAINST NEEDLE

IF FLOAT LEVEL VARIES OVER ± 1/16" FROM SPECIFICATIONS, FOR LEVEL TOO HIGH, HOLD RETAINER IN PLACE AND PUSH DOWN ON CENTER OF FLOAT PONTOON TO OBTAIN CORRECT SETTING. FOR LEVEL TOO LOW. IF E4M REMOVE METERING RODS, SOLENOID CONNECTOR SCREW. COUNT, AND RECORD FOR REASSEMBLY, THE NUMBER OF TURNS NEEDED TO LIGHTLY BOTTOM LEAN MIXTURE SCREW. BACK OUT AND REMOVE SCREW, SOLENOID, CONNECTOR. REMOVE FLOAT AND FLOAT ARM UPWARD TO ADJUST. REINSTALL PARTS, RESET LEAN MIXTURE SCREW. VISUALLY CHECK FLOAT ALIGNMENT.

Fig. 5 Float level adjustment — E4ME/E4MC

① ROTATE DEGREE SCALE UNTIL ZERO IS OPPOSITE POINTER

② CENTER LEVELING BUBBLE

② ROTATE SCALE TO SPECIFIED ANGLE (SEE SPECIFICATIONS)

③ ADJUST LINKAGE TO CENTER THE BUBBLE

① CHOKE VALVE CLOSED

MAGNET

Fig. 6 Choke angle gauge installation

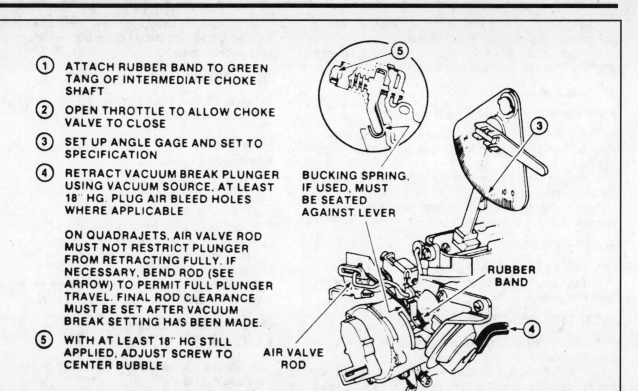

① ATTACH RUBBER BAND TO GREEN TANG OF INTERMEDIATE CHOKE SHAFT

② OPEN THROTTLE TO ALLOW CHOKE VALVE TO CLOSE

③ SET UP ANGLE GAGE AND SET TO SPECIFICATION

④ RETRACT VACUUM BREAK PLUNGER USING VACUUM SOURCE, AT LEAST 18" HG. PLUG AIR BLEED HOLES WHERE APPLICABLE

ON QUADRAJETS, AIR VALVE ROD MUST NOT RESTRICT PLUNGER FROM RETRACTING FULLY. IF NECESSARY, BEND ROD (SEE ARROW) TO PERMIT FULL PLUNGER TRAVEL. FINAL ROD CLEARANCE MUST BE SET AFTER VACUUM BREAK SETTING HAS BEEN MADE.

⑤ WITH AT LEAST 18" HG STILL APPLIED, ADJUST SCREW TO CENTER BUBBLE

BUCKING SPRING, IF USED, MUST BE SEATED AGAINST LEVER

RUBBER BAND

AIR VALVE ROD

Fig. 7 Front vacuum break adjustment — E4ME/E4MC

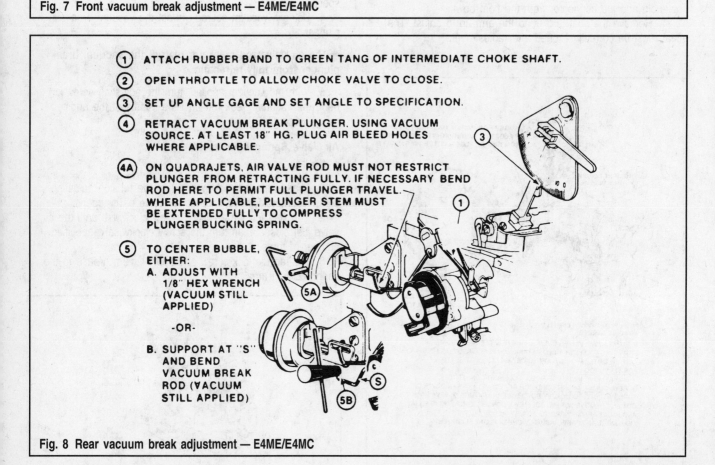

① ATTACH RUBBER BAND TO GREEN TANG OF INTERMEDIATE CHOKE SHAFT.

② OPEN THROTTLE TO ALLOW CHOKE VALVE TO CLOSE.

③ SET UP ANGLE GAGE AND SET ANGLE TO SPECIFICATION.

④ RETRACT VACUUM BREAK PLUNGER. USING VACUUM SOURCE. AT LEAST 18" HG. PLUG AIR BLEED HOLES WHERE APPLICABLE.

④A ON QUADRAJETS, AIR VALVE ROD MUST NOT RESTRICT PLUNGER FROM RETRACTING FULLY. IF NECESSARY BEND ROD HERE TO PERMIT FULL PLUNGER TRAVEL. WHERE APPLICABLE, PLUNGER STEM MUST BE EXTENDED FULLY TO COMPRESS PLUNGER BUCKING SPRING.

⑤ TO CENTER BUBBLE, EITHER:
A. ADJUST WITH 1/8" HEX WRENCH (VACUUM STILL APPLIED)

-OR-

B. SUPPORT AT "S" AND BEND VACUUM BREAK ROD (VACUUM STILL APPLIED)

Fig. 8 Rear vacuum break adjustment — E4ME/E4MC

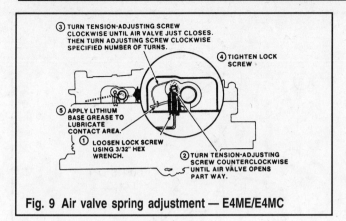

Fig. 9 Air valve spring adjustment — E4ME/E4MC

Air Valve Rod Adjustment

▶ See Figure 10

1. Using a vacuum source, seat the vacuum break plunger. The air valve must be closed.
2. Insert a 0.025 inch plug gauge between the rod and the end of the slot.
3. To adjust, bend the air valve rod.

Choke Lever Adjustment

▶ See Figure 11

1. If the choke cover plate is riveted, drill out the rivets and remove the plate assembly.
2. Place the fast idle cam follower on the high step of the fast idle cam.

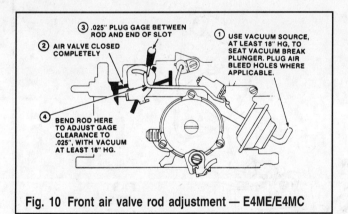

Fig. 10 Front air valve rod adjustment — E4ME/E4MC

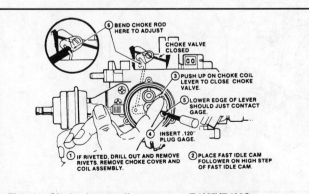

Fig. 11 Choke lever adjustment — E4ME/E4MC

3. Lift up on the choke lever to close the choke valve and insert a 0.120 inch plug gauge into the choke housing hole. The choke lever should just touch the gauge.
4. To adjust, bend the choke rod.
5. To replace the cover plate, rivet in place.

Choke Rod Fast Idle Cam Adjustment

▶ See Figure 12

1. Connect a rubber band to the green tang of the intermediate choke shaft.
2. Open the throttle to allow the choke valve to close.
3. Set up the angle gauge and set the angle to specifications.
4. Place the cam follower on the second step of the fast idle cam, against the rise of the first step. If the cam follower does not contact the cam, turn the fast idle screw additional turns.
5. To adjust, bend the tang of the fast idle cam until the gauge bubble is centered.

➡ **The final fast idle speed adjustment must be performed according to the emission control label.**

Unloader Adjustment

▶ See Figure 13

1. Connect a rubber band to the green tang of the intermediate shaft.
2. Open the throttle to allow the choke valve to close.
3. Set up the angle gauge and set the angle to specification.
4. Hold the secondary lockout lever away from the pin.
5. Hold the throttle lever in the wide-open position.
6. To adjust, bend the tang of the fast idle lever until the bubble of the angle gauge is centered.

Secondary Lockout Adjustment

▶ See Figure 14

1. With the choke and the throttle valves closed, insert a 0.015 inch plug gauge between the lockout lever and the pin. To establish clearance, bend the pin.
2. Push down on the fast idle cam and hold the choke valve wide open.
3. Insert a 0.015 inch plug gauge sideways between the lockout lever and the pin. To adjust, file the end of the pin.

Mixture Control Solenoid

▶ See Figures 15 and 16

Travel Test

Before checking the mixture control solenoid travel, it may be necessary to modify the float gauge J-9789-130 or equivalent (used to externally check the float level).

This should be done by filing or grinding the sufficient material off the gauge to allow for insertion down the vertical D-shaped hole in the air horn casting (located next to the idle air bleed valve cover).

Check that the gauge freely enters the D-shaped vent hole and does not bind. The gauge will also be used to determine the total mixture control solenoid travel.

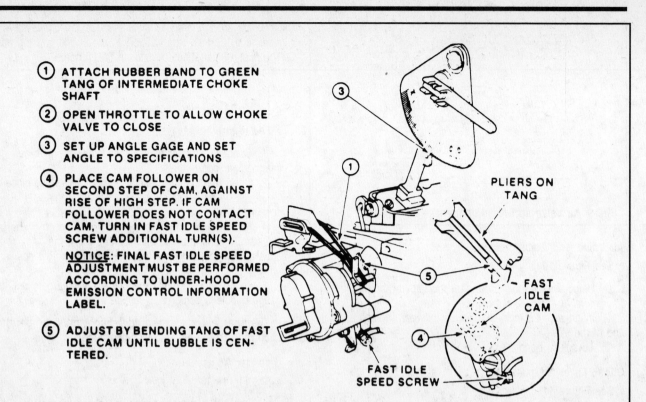

① ATTACH RUBBER BAND TO GREEN TANG OF INTERMEDIATE CHOKE SHAFT

② OPEN THROTTLE TO ALLOW CHOKE VALVE TO CLOSE

③ SET UP ANGLE GAGE AND SET ANGLE TO SPECIFICATIONS

④ PLACE CAM FOLLOWER ON SECOND STEP OF CAM, AGAINST RISE OF HIGH STEP. IF CAM FOLLOWER DOES NOT CONTACT CAM, TURN IN FAST IDLE SPEED SCREW ADDITIONAL TURN(S).

NOTICE: FINAL FAST IDLE SPEED ADJUSTMENT MUST BE PERFORMED ACCORDING TO UNDER-HOOD EMISSION CONTROL INFORMATION LABEL.

⑤ ADJUST BY BENDING TANG OF FAST IDLE CAM UNTIL BUBBLE IS CENTERED.

Fig. 12 Choke rod fast idle cam adjustment — E4ME/E4MC

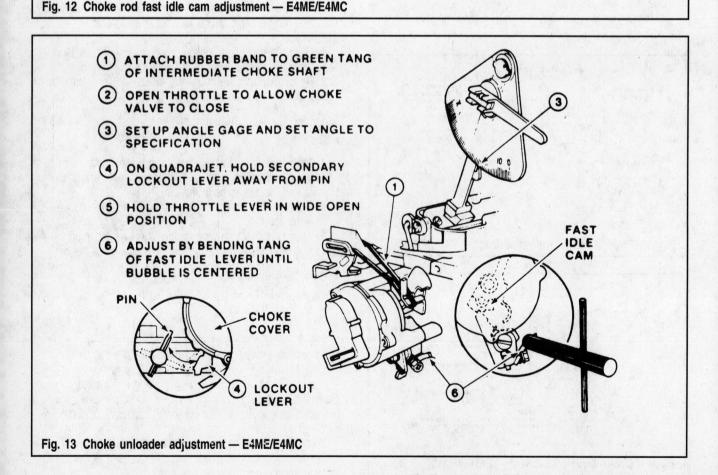

① ATTACH RUBBER BAND TO GREEN TANG OF INTERMEDIATE CHOKE SHAFT

② OPEN THROTTLE TO ALLOW CHOKE VALVE TO CLOSE

③ SET UP ANGLE GAGE AND SET ANGLE TO SPECIFICATION

④ ON QUADRAJET, HOLD SECONDARY LOCKOUT LEVER AWAY FROM PIN

⑤ HOLD THROTTLE LEVER IN WIDE OPEN POSITION

⑥ ADJUST BY BENDING TANG OF FAST IDLE LEVER UNTIL BUBBLE IS CENTERED

Fig. 13 Choke unloader adjustment — E4ME/E4MC

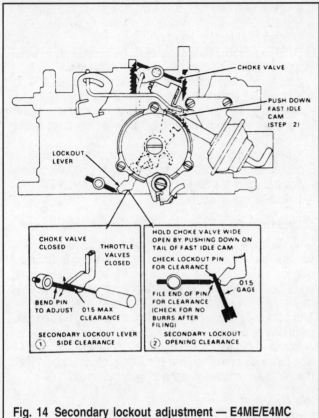

Fig. 14 Secondary lockout adjustment — E4ME/E4MC

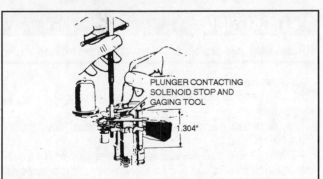

Fig. 15 Adjusting the solenoid stop screw — E4MC/E4ME carburetor

A. Tool J-34935-1 or BT-8420A
B. Tool J-28696-10 or BT-7928
C. Solenoid stop screw hole

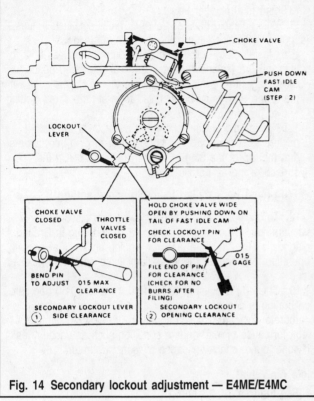

Fig. 16 Adjusting the lean mixture solenoid screw — E4MC/E4ME carburetor

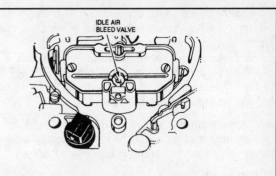

Fig. 17 Idle air bleed adjustment — E4MC/E4ME carburetor

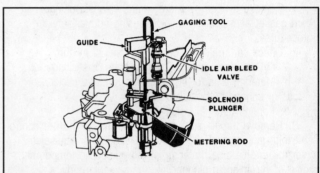

Fig. 18 Installing the air bleed valve gauging tool — E4MC/E4ME carburetor

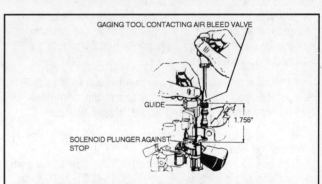

Fig. 19 Setting the idle air bleed valve until it just contacts the gauging tool — E4MC/E4ME carburetor

With the engine off and the air cleaner removed, measure the control solenoid travel as follows:

1. Insert a modified float gauge J-9789-130 or equivalent down the D-shaped vent hole. Press down on the gauge and release it.

2. Observe that the gauge moves freely and does not bind. With the gauge released (solenoid in the up position), be sure to read it at eye level and record the mark on the gauge (in inches) that lines up with the top of the air horn casting (upper edge).

3. Lightly press down on the gauge until bottomed (solenoid in the down position). Record (in inches) the mark on the gauge that lines up with the top of the air horn casting.

4. Subtract the gauge up dimension from gauge dimension. Record the difference (in inches). This difference is total solenoid travel.

5. If total solenoid travel is not within $3/32$-$5/32$ inch (2.4-3.9mm), perform the mixture control solenoid adjustments. If the difference is within $3/32$-$5/32$ inch (2.4-3.9mm), proceed to the idle air bleed valve adjustment.

➡**If adjustment is required, it will be necessary to remove the air horn and drive out the mixture control solenoid screw plug from the under side of the air horn.**

Adjustments

Before making adjustment to mixture control solenoid, verify that the plunger travel is not correct.

1. Remove air horn, mixture control solenoid plunger, air horn gasket and plastic filler block, using normal service procedures.

2. Check carburetor for cause of incorrect mixture:

   a. M/C solenoid bore or plunger worn or sticking

   b. Metering rods for incorrect part number, sticking or rods or springs not installed properly

   c. Foreign material in jets

3. Remove throttle side metering rod. Install mixture control solenoid gauging tool, J-33815-1, BT-8253-A, or equivalent, over the throttle side metering jet rod guide and temporarily reinstall the solenoid plunger into the solenoid body.

4. Holding the solenoid plunger in the **DOWN** position, use tool J-28696-10, BT-7928, or equivalent, to turn lean mixture solenoid screw counterclockwise until the plunger breaks contact with the gauging tool. Turn slowly clockwise until the plunger makes contact with the gauging tool. The adjustment is correct when the solenoid plunger is contacting both the solenoid stop and the gauging tool.

➡**If the total difference in adjustment required less than $3/4$ turn of the lean mixture solenoid screw, the original setting was within the manufacturer's specifications.**

5. Remove solenoid plunger and gauging tool and reinstall metering rod and plastic filler block.

6. Invert air horn and remove rich mixture stop screw from bottom side of air horn, using tool J-28696-4, BT-7967-A, or equivalent.

7. Remove lean mixture screw plug and the rich mixture stop screw plug from air horn, using a suitable sized punch.

8. Reinstall rich mixture stop screw in air horn and bottom lightly, then back screw out $1/4$ turn.

9. Reinstall air horn gasket, mixture control solenoid plunger and air horn to carburetor.

10. Adjust M/C Solenoid Plunger travel as follows:

   a. Insert float gauge down D-shaped vent hole. Press down on gauge and release, observing that the gauge moves freely and does not bind. With gauge released, (plunger UP position), read at eye level and record the reading of the gauge mark (in inches) that lines up with the top of air horn casting, (upper edge).

   b. Lightly press down on gauge until bottomed, (plunger DOWN position). Read and record (in inches) the reading of the gauge mark that lines up with top of air horn casting.

   c. Subtract gauge **UP** position (Step 1) from gauge **DOWN** position (Step 2) and record the difference. This difference is the total plunger travel. Insert external float

gauge in vent hole and, with tool J-28696-10, BT-7928, or equivalent, adjust rich mixture stop screw to obtain $5/32$ inch (3.9mm) total plunger travel.

11. With solenoid plunger travel correctly set, install plugs (supplied in service kits) in the air horn, as follows:

   a. Install plug, hollow end down, into the access hole to lean mixture (solenoid) screw. Use suitably sized punch to drive plug into the air horn until the top of plug is even with the lower. Plug must be installed to retain the screw setting and to prevent fuel vapor loss.

   b. Install plug, with hollow end down, over the rich mixture stop screw access hole and drive plug into place so that the top of the plug is $3/16$ inch (4.7mm) below the surface of the air horn casting.

➡**Plug must be installed to retain screw setting.**

12. To check the M/C solenoid dwell, first disconnect vacuum line to the canister purge valve and plug it. Ground diagnostic TEST terminal and run engine until it is at normal operation temperature (upper radiator hose hot) and in closed loop.

13. Check M/C dwell at 3000 rpm. If within 10-50 degrees, calibration is complete. If higher than 50 degrees, check carburetor for cause of rich condition. If below 10 degrees, look for cause of lean engine condition such as vacuum leaks. If none found, check for cause of lean carburetor.

Idle Air Valve

▶ **See Figures 17, 18 and 19**

A cover is in place over the idle air bleed valve and the access holes to the idle mixture needles are sealed with hardened plugs, to seal the factory settings, during original equipment production. These items are NOT to be removed unless required for cleaning, part replacement, improper dwell readings or if the System Performance Check indicates the carburetor is the cause of the trouble.

1. With engine **OFF**, cover the internal bowl vents and inlet to bleed valve and the carburetor air intakes with masking tape, to prevent metal chips from entering.

2. Carefully drill rivet head of idle air bleed cover, with 0.110 in. drill bit.

3. Remove rivet head and all pieces of rivet.

4. Lift cover off air bleed valve and blow out any metal shavings, or use a magnet to remove excess metal.

✳✳CAUTION

Always wear eye protection when using compressed air.

5. Remove masking tape.

6. Start engine allow to reach normal operating temperature.

7. Disconnect the vacuum hose from the canister purge valve and plug it.

8. While idling in **D** for automatic transmission or **N** for manual transmission, slowly turn the valve counterclockwise or clockwise, until the dwell reading varies within the 25-35 degree range, attempting to be as close to 30 degrees as possible.

➡**Perform this step carefully. The air bleed valve is very sensitive and should be turned in $1/8$ turn increments only.**

9. If the dwell reading does not vary and is not within the 25-35 degree range, it will be necessary to remove the plugs and to adjust the idle mixture needles.

Idle Mixture

▶ See Figures 20 and 21

1. Using tool J-29030-B, BT-7610-B, or equivalent, turn each idle mixture needle clockwise until lightly seated, then turn each mixture needle counterclockwise 3 turns.

2. Reinstall carburetor on engine, using a new flange mounting gasket, but do not install air cleaner or gasket at this time.

3. Disconnect vacuum hose to canister purge valve and plug it.

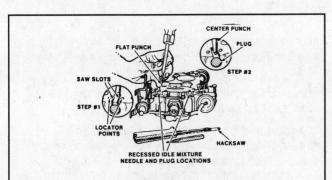

Fig. 20 Removing the idle mixture needle plugs — E4MC/E4ME carburetor

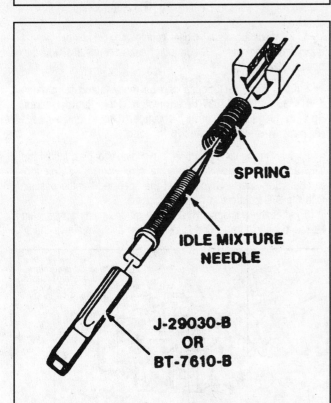

Fig. 21 Idle mixture needle assembly — E4MC/E4ME carburetor

4. Start engine and allow it to reach normal operating temperature.

5. While idling in **D** (**N** for manual transmission), adjust both mixture needles equally, in ⅛ turn increments, until dwell reading varies within the 25-35 degree range, attempting to be as close to 30 degrees as possible.

6. If reading is too low, turn mixture needles counterclockwise. If reading is too high, turn mixture needles clockwise. Allow time for dwell reading to stabilize after each adjustment.

➡ **After adjustments are complete, seal the idle mixture needle openings in the throttle body, using silicone sealant, RTV rubber, or equivalent. The sealer is required to discourage unnecessary readjustment of the setting and prevent fuel vapor loss in that area.**

7. On vehicles without a carburetor-mounted Idle Load Compensator, adjust curb idle speed if necessary.

8. Check, and if necessary, adjust fast idle speed, as described on the Vehicle Emission Control Information label.

Idle Load Compensator

▶ See Figure 22

The idle load compensator is adjusted at the factory. Do not make any adjustments unless diagnosis or curb idle speed is not to specification.

1. Make certain ignition timing, mixture adjustment, vacuum hoses, fuel pressure and CCC system meets specifications.

2. Remove air cleaner and plug hose to thermal vacuum valve.

3. Connect a tachometer.

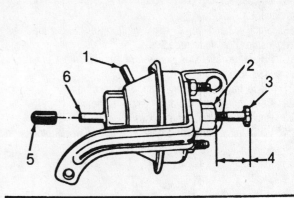

1. Vacuum inlet tube
2. Jam nut
3. ILC plunger (do not use to set curb idle speed)
4. Dimension "A" distance must not exceed 1 in. (25mm) after plunger adj.
5. Rubber cap
6. Idle speed adj. screw

Fig. 22 Idle Load Compensator (ILC) — E4MC/E4ME carburetor

4. Disconnect and plug hose to EGR valve.

5. Disconnect and plug hose to canister purge port.

6. Disconnect and plug hose to idle load compensator.

7. Back out idle stop screw on carburetor 3 turns.

8. Turn air conditioning **OFF**.

9. Block drive wheels, set parking brake, place transmission in **P**, start and warm engine to normal operating temperature. Make certain choke is **OPEN**.

10. With engine **RUNNING** place transmission in **D** and idle load compensator fully extended (no vacuum applied). Using tool J-29607, or equivalent, adjust plunger to obtain 650-750 rpm. Locknut on plunger must be held with a wrench to prevent damage to guide tabs.

11. Measure distance from the locknut to tip of the plunger. This distance must not exceed 1 inch (25mm). If it does check for low idle condition.

12. Reconnect vacuum hose to idle load compensator and observe idle speed.

13. Idle speed should be 425-475 rpm in **D**.

14. If idle speed is correct no further adjustment is necessary, proceed with Step 18. If idle speed is still incorrect continue with Step 15.

➡**It may be necessary to remove the idle load compensator from the engine unless a hex key wrench is modified to clear obstructions.**

15. Stop engine, remove rubber cap from the center outlet tube.

16. Using a 0.90 inch hex wrench, insert through open center tube to engage idle speed adjusting screw.

17. If idle speed in Step 13, was low turn the adjusting screw counterclockwise 1 turn for every 85 rpm low. If idle speed was high turn screw 1 turn for every 85 rpm high.

18. Disconnect and plug vacuum hose to the idle load compensator.

19. Using a hand pump, apply vacuum to the idle load compensator until fully retracted.

20. Adjust the idle stop screw on carburetor float bowl to obtain 450 rpm in **D**.

21. Place transmission in **P** and stop engine.

22. Reconnect the idle load compensator.

23. Reconnect all vacuum hoses.

24. Install air cleaner and gasket. Remove wheel blocks.

Throttle Position Sensor (TPS)

◗ **See Figures 23 and 24**

Before the throttle position sensor voltage output setting can be accurately checked or adjusted the idle rpm must be within specifications. The plug covering the TPS adjustment screw is used to provide a tamper-resistant design and retain the factory setting during vehicle operation. Do not remove the plug unless diagnosis indicates the TPS is not adjusted correctly, or it is necessary to replace the air horn assembly, float bowl, TPS, or TPS adjustment screw. This is a critical adjustment that must be performed accurately to ensure proper vehicle performance and control of exhaust emissions. Remove TPS plug if not already removed.

➡**Adjustment is required only if voltage is above the following readings, as the ECM automatically zeros below 0.70 Volts.**

1. Using a ⁵⁄₆₄ inch (2 mm) drill bit, carefully drill a hole in the steel or aluminum plug. Be sure to drill only far enough to start a self tapping screw, the approximate drilling depth is ¹⁄₁₆ -¹⁄₈ inch.

➡**Use care in drilling so as not to damage the TPS adjustment screw head.**

2. Start a long self tapping screw (No. 8 **x** ½ inch) into the drilled pilot hole in the plug. Turn the screw in only enough to ensure a good thread engagement in the drilled hole.

3. Place a suitable tool between the screw head and the air horn casting. Then pry against the screw head to remove the plug. A small slide hammer may also be used in this procedure. Be sure to discard the plug when it has been removed.

4. Connect a suitable digital voltmeter (J-29125 or equivalent) from the TPS connector center terminal (B) to the bottom terminal (C).

➡**Jumper wires for access can be made using terminals 12014836 and 12014837 or equivalent. Make jumper wires up with 16 gauge (1.0mm), 18 gauge (0.8mm) or 20 gauge (0.5mm) wire approximately 6 in. long.**

5. With the ignition **ON** and the engine stopped, install the TPS adjustment screw and turn the screw with a suitable tool to obtain the specified voltage at the specified throttle position with the A/C controls in the **OFF** position.

6. After the adjustment has been made, install a new plug kit (supplied in the service kits), into the air horn. Drive the

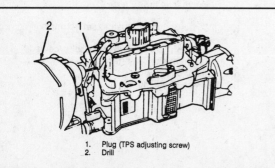

1. Plug (TPS adjusting screw)
2. Drill

Fig. 23 Removing the Throttle Positioning Sensor (TPS) plug — E4MC/E4ME carburetor

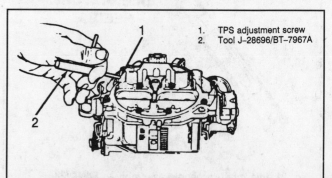

1. TPS adjustment screw
2. Tool J–28696/BT–7967A

Fig. 24 Adjusting the TPS using the proper tool — E4MC/E4ME carburetor

plug into place until it is flush with the raised pump lever boss on the casting. Clear trouble code memory after adjustment.

➡**The plug must be installed to retain the TPS adjustment screw setting. If a plug kit is not available, remove the TPS adjusting screw and apply thread sealer adhesive X-10 or equivalent to the screw threads. Now repeat the TPS adjustment procedure to obtain the correct TPS voltage.**

REMOVAL & INSTALLATION

▶ **See Figure 25**

Always replace all internal gaskets that are removed. Base gasket should be inspected and replaced only if damaged. Flooding, stumble on acceleration and other performance complaints are in many instances, caused by presence of dirt, water, or other foreign matter in carburetor. To aid in diagnosis, carburetor should be carefully removed from engine without draining fuel from bowl. Contents of fuel bowl may then be examined for contamination as carburetor is disassembled. Check fuel filter.

1. Disconnect the battery and remove the air cleaner.
2. Disconnect the accelerator linkage.
3. Disconnect the transmission detent cable.
4. If equipped, remove the cruise control.
5. Disconnect all of the necessary vacuum lines.
6. Disconnect the fuel line at the carburetor inlet. Place a rag beneath the line to soak up any fuel that spills, then dispose of the rag properly.
7. Remove the attaching bolts and remove the carburetor.
8. To install, position the carburetor onto the manifold and install the attaching bolts.
9. Connect the fuel line at the carburetor inlet.
10. Connect all of the vacuum lines.
11. If equipped, install the cruise control cable.
12. Connect the transmission detent cable.
13. Connect the accelerator linkage.
14. Install the air cleaner and connect the battery.

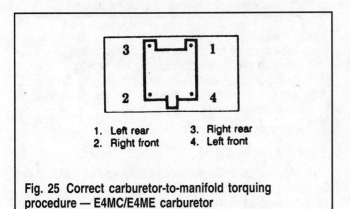

Fig. 25 Correct carburetor-to-manifold torquing procedure — E4MC/E4ME carburetor

OVERHAUL

▶ **See Figure 26**

Efficient carburetion depends greatly on careful cleaning and inspection during overhaul, since dirt, gum, water, or varnish in or on the carburetor parts are often responsible for poor performance.

Overhaul your carburetor in a clean, dust-free area. Carefully disassemble the carburetor, referring often to the exploded views and directions packaged with the rebuilding kit. Keep all similar and look-alike parts separated during disassembly and cleaning to avoid accidental interchange during assembly. Make a note of all jet sizes.

When the carburetor is disassembled, wash all parts (except diaphragms, electric components, pump plunger, and any other plastic, leather, fiber, or rubber parts) in clean carburetor solvent. Do not leave parts in the solvent any longer than is necessary to sufficiently loosen the deposits. Excessive cleaning may remove the special finish from the float bowl and choke valve bodies, leaving these parts unfit for service. Rinse all parts in clean solvent and blow them dry with compressed air or allow them to air dry. Wipe clean all cork, plastic, leather, and fiber parts with a clean, lint-free cloth.

Blow out all passages and jets with compressed air and be sure that there are no restrictions or blockages. Never use wire or similar tools to clean jets, fuel passages, or air bleeds. Clean all jets and valves separately to avoid accidental interchange.

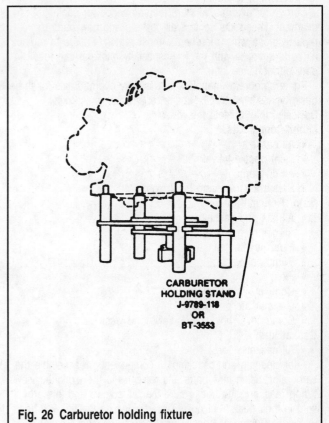

Fig. 26 Carburetor holding fixture

Check all parts for wear or damage. If wear or damage is found, replace the defective parts. Especially check the following:

1. Check the float needle and seat for wear. If wear is found, replace the complete assembly.

2. Check the float hinge pin for wear and the float(s) for dents or distortion. Replace the float if fuel has leaked into it.

3. Check the throttle and choke shaft bores for wear or an out-of-round condition. Damage or wear to the throttle arm, shaft, or shaft bore will often require replacement of the throttle body. These parts require a close tolerance of fit; wear may allow air leakage, which could affect starting and idling.

➡**Throttle shafts and bushings are not included in overhaul kits. They can be purchased separately or repaired by a qualified carburetor overhaul shop.**

4. Inspect the idle mixture adjusting needles for burrs or grooves. Any such condition requires replacement of the needle, since you will not be able to obtain a satisfactory idle.

5. Test the accelerator pump check valves. They should pass air one way but not the other. Test for proper seating by blowing and sucking on the valve. Replace the valve check ball and spring as necessary. If the valve is satisfactory, wash the valve parts again to remove breath moisture.

6. Check the bowl cover for warped surfaces with a straightedge.

7. Closely inspect the accelerator pump plunger for wear and damage, replacing as necessary.

8. After the carburetor is assembled, check the choke valve for freedom of operation.

Carburetor overhaul kits are recommended for each overhaul. These kits contain all gaskets and new parts to replace those which deteriorate most rapidly. Failure to replace all parts supplied with the kit (especially gaskets) can result in poor performance later.

Some carburetor manufacturers supply overhaul kits for three basic types: minor repair; major repair; and gasket kits. Basically, they contain the following:

Minor Repair Kits:
- All gaskets
- Float needle valve
- All diagrams
- Spring for the pump diaphragm

Major Repair Kits:
- All jets and gaskets
- All diaphragms
- Float needle valve
- Pump ball valve
- Float
- Complete intermediate rod
- Intermediate pump lever
- Some cover holddown screws and washers

Gasket kits:
- All gaskets

After cleaning and checking all components, reassemble the carburetor, using new parts and referring to the exploded view. When reassembling, make sure that all screws and jets are tight in their seats, but do not overtighten as the tips will be distorted. Tighten all screws gradually, in rotation. Do not tighten needle valves into their seats; uneven jetting will result.

Always use new gaskets. Be sure to follow all assembly and adjustment procedures.

➡**Before performing any service on the carburetor, it is essential that it be placed on a suitable holding fixture, such as tool J-9789-118, BY-30-15 or equivalent. Without the use of the holding fixture, it is possible to damage throttle valves or other parts of the carburetor.**

Carburetor Disassembly

IDLE SPEED CONTROL (ISC) SOLENOID REMOVAL

Remove the attaching screws, then remove the Idle Speed Control solenoid (ISC). The ISC should not be immersed in any carburetor cleaner. They must always be removed before complete carburetor overhaul, as carburetor cleaner will damage the internal components.

IDLE MIXTURE NEEDLE PLUG REMOVAL

1. Use a hacksaw to make 2 parallel cuts in the throttle body, 1 on each side of the locator points near an idle mixture needle plug. The distance between the cuts will depend on the size of the punch to be used. Cuts should reach down to the steel plug, but should but extend more than $\frac{1}{8}$ inch beyond the locator points.

2. Place a flat punch at a point near the ends of the saw marks in the throttle body. Hold the punch at a 45 degree angle and drive it into the throttle body until the casting breaks away, exposing the hardened steel plug. The plug will break, rather than remaining intact. Remove all the loose pieces.

3. Repeat the procedure for the other idle mixture needle plug.

IDLE AIR BLEED VALVE REMOVAL

1. Cover internal bowl vents and air inlets to the bleed valve with masking tape.

2. Carefully align a $\frac{7}{64}$ inch drill bit on rivet head. Drill only enough to remove head of each rivet holding the idle air bleed valve cover.

3. Use a suitably sized punch to drive out the remainder of the rivet from the castings. Repeat procedure with other rivet.

✳✳CAUTION

For the next operation, safety glasses must be worn to protect eyes from possible metal shaving damage.

4. Lift off cover and remove any pieces of rivet still inside tower. Use shop air to blow out any remaining chips.

5. Remove idle air bleed valve from the air horn.

6. Remove and discard O-ring seals from valve. New O-ring seals are required for reassembly. The idle air bleed valve is serviced as a complete assembly only.

AIR HORN REMOVAL

▶ **See Figures 27 and 28**

1. Remove upper choke lever from the end of choke shaft by removing retaining screw. Rotate upper choke lever to remove choke rod from slot in lever.

2. Remove choke rod from lower lever inside the float bowl casting. Remove rod by holding lower lever outward with small suitable tool and twisting rod counterclockwise.

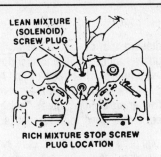

Fig. 27 Removing the lean and rich mixture screw plugs from the top of the air horn — E4MC/E4ME carburetor

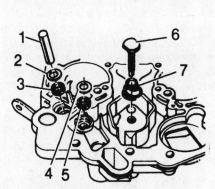

1. Senor actuator plunger
2. TPS seal retainer
3. TPS plunger seal
4. Pump stem seal retainer
5. Pump stem seal
6. Rich mixture solenoid stop screw (some models)
7. Rich authority adjusting spring (some models)

Fig. 28 Bottom view of the air horn assembly — E4MC/E4ME carburetor

3. Remove secondary metering rods by removing the small screw in the top of the metering rod hanger. Lift upward on the metering rod hanger until the secondary metering rods are completely out of the air horn. Metering rods may be disassembled from the hanger by rotating the ends out of the holes in the end of the hanger.

4. Remove pump link retainer and remove link from pump lever.

➡Do not attempt to remove the lever, as damage to the air horn could result.

5. Remove the front vacuum break hose from tube on float bowl.

6. Remove 11 air horn-to-bowl screws; then remove the 2 countersunk attaching screws located next to the venturi. If

used, remove secondary air baffle deflector from beneath the 2 center air horn screws.

7. Remove air horn from float bowl by lifting it straight up. The air horn gasket should remain on the float bowl for removal later.

➡When removing air horn from float bowl, use care to prevent damaging the mixture control solenoid connector, Throttle Position Sensor (TPS) adjustment lever and the small tubes protruding from the air horn. These tubes are permanently pressed into the air horn casting. Do not remove them. Do not place vacuum break assembly in carburetor cleaner, as damage to vacuum break will occur.

8. Remove front vacuum break bracket attaching screws. The vacuum break assembly may now be removed from the air valve dashpot rod and the dashpot rod from the air valve lever.

9. Remove TPS plunger by pushing plunger down through seal in air horn.

10. Remove TPS seal and pump plunger stem seal by inverting air horn and using a small suitable tool to remove staking holding seal retainers in place. Remove and discard retainers and seals.

➡Use care in removing the TPS plunger seal retainer and pump plunger stem seal retainer to prevent damage to air horn casting. New seals and retainers are required for reassembly.

11. Invert air horn and use tool J-28696-4, BT-7967A, or equivalent, to remove rich mixture stop screw and spring.

12. Use a suitable punch to drive the lean mixture screw plug and rich mixture stop screw plug out of the air horn. Discard the plugs.

13. Further disassembly of the air horn is not required for cleaning purposes.

➡The choke valve and choke valve screws, the air valves and air valve shaft should not be removed. However, if it is necessary to replace the air valve closing springs or center plastic eccentric cam, a repair kit is available. Instructions for assembly are included in the repair kit.

FLOAT BOWL DISASSEMBLY
▶ See Figures 29 and 30

1. Remove solenoid metering rod plunger by lifting straight up.

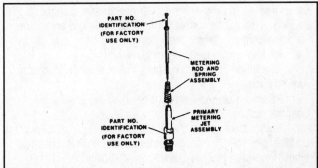

Fig. 29 Metering rod and jet identification — E4MC/E4ME carburetor

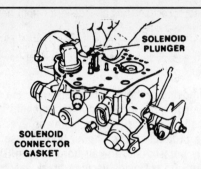

Fig. 30 Removing the solenoid plunger — E4MC/E4ME carburetor

2. Remove air horn gasket by lifting it from the dowel locating pins on float bowl. Discard gasket.

3. Remove pump plunger from pump well.

4. Remove staking holding Throttle Position Sensor (TPS) in bowl as follows:

   a. Lay a flat tool or metal piece across bowl casting to protect gasket sealing surface.

   b. Use a small suitable tool to depress TPS sensor lightly and hold against spring tension.

   c. Observing safety precautions, pry upward with a small prybar, or other suitable tool, to remove bowl staking, making sure prying force is exerted against the metal piece and not against the bowl casting. Use care not to damage the TPS sensor.

   d. Push up from bottom on electrical connector and remove TPS and connector assembly from bowl. Use care in removing sensor and connector assembly to prevent damage to this critical electrical part.

   e. Remove spring from bottom of TPS well in float bowl.

5. Remove plastic bowl insert from float bowl.

6. Carefully lift each metering rod out of the guided metering jet, checking to be sure the return spring is removed with each metering rod.

➡**Use extreme care when handling these critical parts to avoid damage to the metering rod and spring.**

7. Remove the mixture control solenoid from the float bowl as follows:

   a. Remove screw attaching solenoid connector to float bowl. Do not remove solenoid connector from float bowl until called for in text.

   b. Use tool J-28696-10, BT-7928, or equivalent, to remove lean mixture (solenoid) screw. Do not remove plunger return spring or connector and wires from the solenoid body. The mixture control solenoid, with plunger and connector, is only serviced as a complete assembly.

   c. Remove rubber gasket from top of solenoid connector and discard.

   d. Remove solenoid screw tension spring (next to float hanger pin).

8. Remove float assembly and float needle by pulling up on retaining pin. Remove needle and seat and gasket using set remover tool J-22769, BT-3006M, or equivalent.

9. Remove large mixture control solenoid tension spring from boss on bottom of float bowl located between guided metering jets.

10. If necessary, remove the primary main metering jets using special tool J-28696-4, BT-7928, or equivalent.

➡**Use care installing tool on jet, to prevent damage to the metering rod guide (upper area), and locating tool over vertical float sections on lower area of jet. Also, no attempt should be made to remove the secondary metering jets (metering orifice plates). These jets are fixed and, if damaged, entire bowl replacement is required.**

11. Remove pump discharge check ball retainer and turn bowl upside down, catching discharge ball as it falls.

12. Remove secondary air baffle, if replacement is required.

13. Remove pump well fill slot baffle only if necessary.

CHOKE DISASSEMBLY

The tamper-resistant choke cover is used to discourage unnecessary readjustment of the choke thermostatic cover and coil assembly. However, if it is necessary to remove the cover and coil assembly during normal carburetor disassembly for cleaning and normal carburetor disassembly for cleaning and overhaul, the procedures below should be followed.

1. Support float bowl and throttle body, as an assembly, on a suitable holding fixture such as tool J-9789-118, BT-30-15, or equivalent.

2. Carefully align a ⁵/₃₂ inch drill (0.159 inch) on rivet head and drill only enough to remove rivet head. Drill the 2 remaining rivet heads, then use a drift and small hammer to drive the remainder of the rivets out of the choke housing.

➡**Use care in drilling to prevent damage to the choke cover or housing.**

3. Remove the 2 conventional retainers, retainer with tab and choke cover assembly from choke housing.

4. Remove choke housing assembly from float bowl by removing retaining screw and washer inside the choke housing. The complete choke assembly can be removed from the float bowl by sliding outward.

5. Remove secondary throttle valve lock-out lever from float bowl.

6. Remove lower choke lever from inside float bowl cavity by inverting bowl.

7. To disassemble intermediate choke shaft from choke housing, remove coil lever retaining screw at end of shaft inside the choke housing. Remove thermostatic coil lever from flats on intermediate choke shaft.

8. Remove intermediate choke shaft from the choke housing by sliding it outward. The fast idle cam can now be removed from the intermediate choke shaft. Remove the cup seal from the float bowl cleaning purposes. Do not attempt to remove the insert.

9. Remove fuel inlet nut, gasket, check valve, filter assembly and spring. Discard check valve filter assembly and gasket.

10. Remove 3 throttle body-to-bowl attaching screws and lockwashers and remove throttle body assembly.

11. Remove throttle body-to-bowl insulator gasket.

THROTTLE BODY DISASSEMBLY

Place throttle body assembly on carburetor holding fixture to avoid damage to throttle valves.

1. Remove pump rod from the throttle lever by rotating the rod until the tang on the rod aligns with the slot in the lever.

2. Use tool J-29030-B, BT-7610B, or equivalent, to remove idle mixture needles for thorough throttle body cleaning.

3. Further disassembly of the throttle body is not required for cleaning purposes. The throttle valve screws are permanently staked in place and should not be removed. The throttle body is serviced as a complete assembly.

CLEANING AND INSPECTION

The carburetor parts should be cleaned in a cold immersion-type cleaner such as Carbon X (X-55) or equivalent.

➡**The idle speed solenoid, the mixture control solenoid, the throttle position sensor, the electric choke, the rubber parts, the plastic parts, the diaphragms, the pump plunger, the plastic filler block, should not be immersed in carburetor cleaner as they will hardened, swell or distort. The plastic busing in the throttle lever will withstand normal cleaning in the carburetor cleaner. Thoroughly clean all of the metal parts and blow dry with shop air. Make sure all the fuel passages and metering parts are free of burrs and dirt. Do not pass the drills or wires through the jets and passages.**

1. Inspect the upper and lower surface of the carburetor castings for damage.

2. Inspect the holes in the levers for excessive wear or out of round conditions. If worn, the levers should be replaced. Inspect the plastic bushings in the levers for damage and excessive wear, replace as required.

3. Check, repair or replace parts, if the following problems are encountered:

A. Flooding

1. Inspect the float valve and seat for dirt, deep wear grooves, scores and improper sealing.

2. Inspect the float valve pull clip for proper installation; be careful not to bend the pull clip.

3. Inspect the float, the float arms and the hinge pin for distortion, binds, and burrs. Check the density of the material in the float; if heavier than normal, replace the float.

4. Clean or replace the fuel inlet filter and check the valve assembly.

B. Hesitation

1. Inspect the pump plunger for cracks, scores or cup excessive wear. A used pump cup will shrink when dry. If dried out, soak in fuel for 8 hours before testing.

2. Inspect the pump duration and return springs for weakness or distortion.

3. Check the pump passages and the jet(s) for dirt, improper seating of the discharge checkball or the temperature bypass disc and/or scores in the pumpwell. Check the condition of the pump discharge check ball spring, replace as necessary.

4. Check the pump linkage for excessive wear; repair or replace as necessary.

C. Hard Starting-Poor Cold Operation

1. Check the choke valve and linkage for excessive wear, binds or distortion.

2. Test the vacuum break diaphragm(s) for leaks.

3. Clean or replace the fuel filter.

4. Inspect the float valve for sticking, dirt, etc.

5. Also check the items under 'Flooding'.

D. Poor Performance-Poor Gas Mileage

1. Clean all fuel and vacuum passages in the castings.

2. Check the choke valve for freedom of movement.

3. Check the Mixture Control solenoid for sticking or binding.

4. Inspect the metering jet for dirt, loose parts or damage.

➡**Do not attempt to readjust the mixture screw located inside the metering jet. The screw if factory adjusted and a change can upset the fuel system calibration. No attempt should be made to change this adjustment in the field except as the result of a Computer Command Control system performance check.**

5. Check the air valve and secondary metering rod for binding conditions. If the air valve or metering rod is damaged or the metering rod adjustment is changed from the factory setting, the air horn assembly must be replaced. Also check the air valve lever spring for proper installation (tension against the air valve shaft pin.

E. Rough Idle

1. Inspect the gasket and gasket mating surfaces on the casting for nicks, burrs or damage to the sealing beads.

2. Check the operation and sealing of the mixture control solenoid.

3. Clean all of the idle field passages.

4. If removed, inspect the idle mixture needle for ridges, burrs or being bent.

5. Check the throttle lever and valves for binds, nicks. or other damage.

6. Check all of the diaphragms for possible ruptures or leaks.

Carburetor Reassembly

▶ **See Figures 15, 16, 17, 18, 19, 31, 32 and 33**

1. Install the lower end of the pump rod in the throttle lever by aligning the tang on the rod with the slot in the lever. The end of the rod should point outward toward the throttle lever.

2. Install idle mixture needles and springs using tool J-29030-B, BT-07610B, or equivalent. Lightly seat each needle and then turn counterclockwise the number of specified turns, the final idle mixture adjustment is made on the vehicle.

3. If a new float bowl assembly is used, stamp or engrave the model number on the new float bowl. Install new throttle body-to-bowl insulator gasket over 2 locating dowels on bowl.

4. Install throttle body making certain throttle body is properly located over dowels on float bowl. Install 3 throttle body-to-bowl screws and lockwashers and tighten evenly and securely.

5. Place carburetor on proper holding fixture such as J-9789-118, BT-30-15 or equivalent.

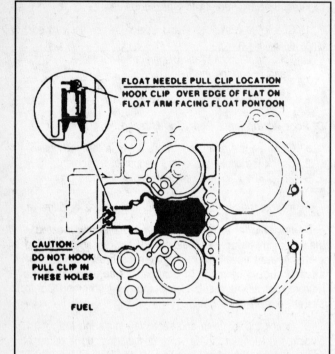

Fig. 31 Float needle pull clip installation — E4MC/E4ME carburetor

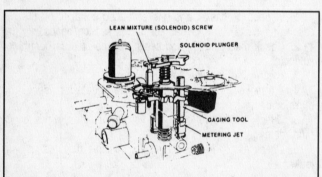

Fig. 32 Installing the mixture control solenoid gauging tool — E4MC/E4ME carburetor

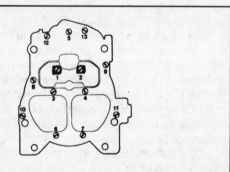

Fig. 33 Air horn screw location and tightening sequence — E4MC/E4ME carburetor

6. Install fuel inlet filter spring, a new check valve filter assembly, new gasket and inlet nut. Tighten nut to 18 ft. lbs. (24 Nm).

➡ **When installing a service replacement filter, make sure the filter is the type that includes the check valve to meet government safety standard. New service replacement filters with check valve meet this requirement. When properly installed, the hole in the filter faces toward the inlet nut. Ribs on the closed end of the filter element prevent it from being installed incorrectly, unless forced. Tightening beyond the specified torque can damage the nylon gasket.**

7. Install a new cup seal into the insert on the side of the float bowl for the intermediate choke shaft. The lip on the cup seal faces outward.

8. Install the secondary throttle valve lock-out lever on the boss of the float bowl, with the recess hole in the lever facing inward.

9. Install the fast idle cam on the intermediate choke shaft (steps on cam face downward).

10. Carefully install fast idle cam and intermediate choke shaft assembly in the choke housing. Install the thermostatic coil lever on the flats on the intermediate choke shaft. Inside thermostatic choke coil lever is properly aligned when both inside and outside levers face toward the fuel inlet. Install inside lever retaining screw into the end of the intermediate choke shaft.

11. Install lower choke rod (inner) lever into cavity in float bowl.

12. Install choke housing to bowl, sliding intermediate choke shaft into lower (inner) lever. tool J-23417, BT-6911 or equivalent, can be used to hold the lower choke lever in correct position while installing the choke housing. The intermediate choke shaft lever and fast idle cam are in correct position when the tang on lever is beneath the fast idle cam.

13. Install choke housing retaining screws and washers. Check linkage for freedom of movement. Do not install choke cover and coil assembly until inside coil lever is adjusted.

14. If removed, install air baffle in secondary side of float bowl with notches toward the top. Top edge of baffle must be flush with bowl casting.

15. If removed, install baffle inside of the pump well with slot toward the bottom.

16. Install pump discharge check ball and retainer screw in the passage next to the pump well.

17. If removed, carefully install primary main metering jets in bottom of float bowl using tool J-28696-4, BT-7928, or equivalent.

➡ **Use care in installing jets to prevent damage to metering rod guide.**

18. Install large mixture control solenoid tension spring over boss on bottom of float bowl.

19. Install needle seat assembly, with gasket, using seat installer J-22769, BT-3006M, or equivalent.

20. To make adjustment easier, carefully bend float arm before assembly.

21. Install float needle onto float arm by sliding float lever under needle pull clip. Proper installation of the needle pull clip is to hook the clip over the edge of the float on the float arm facing the float pontoon.

22. Install float hinge pin into float arm with end of loop of pin facing pump well. Install float assembly by aligning needle in the seat and float hinge pin into locating channels in float bowl. Do not install float needle pull clip into holes in float arm.

23. Perform a float level adjustment, as necessary.

24. Install mixture control solenoid screw tension spring between raised bosses next to float hanger pin.

25. Install mixture control solenoid and connector assembly as follows:

a. Install new rubber gasket on top of solenoid connector.

b. Install solenoid carefully in the float chamber, aligning pin on end of solenoid with hole in raised boss at bottom of bowl. Align solenoid connector wires to fit in slot in bowl.

c. Install lean mixture (solenoid) screw through hole in solenoid bracket and tension spring in bowl, engaging first 6 screw threads to assure proper thread engagement.

d. Install mixture control solenoid gauging tool J-33815-1, BT-8253-A, or equivalent over the throttle side metering jet rod guide and temporarily install solenoid plunger.

e. Holding the solenoid plunger against the solenoid stop, use tool J-28696-10, BT-7928, or equivalent, to turn the lean mixture (solenoid) screw slowly clockwise, until the solenoid plunger just contacts the gauging tool. The adjustment is correct when the solenoid plunger is contacting both the solenoid stop and the gauging tool.

f. Remove solenoid plunger and gauging tool.

26. Install connector attaching screw, but do not overtighten, as that could cause damage to the connector.

27. Install Throttle Position Sensor (TPS) return spring in bottom of well in float bowl.

28. Install the TPS and connector assembly in float bowl by aligning groove in electrical connector with slot in float bowl casting. Push down on connector and sensor assembly so that connector and wires are located below bowl casting surface.

29. Install plastic bowl insert over float valve, pressing downward until properly seated (flush with bowl casting surface).

30. Slide metering rod return spring over metering rod tip until small end of spring stops against shoulder on rod. Carefully install metering rod and spring assembly through holding in plastic bowl insert and gently lower the metering rod into the guided metering jet, until large end of spring seats on the recess on end of jet guide.

➡**Do not force metering rod down in jet. Use extreme care when handling these critical parts to avoid damage to rod and spring. If service replacement metering rods, springs and jets are installed, they must be installed in matched sets.**

31. Install pump return spring in pump well.

32. Install pump plunger assembly in pump well.

33. Holding down on pump plunger assembly against return spring tension, install air horn gasket by aligning pump plunger stem with hole in gasket and aligning holes in gasket over TPS plunger, solenoid plunger return spring metering rods, solenoid attaching screw and electrical connector. Position gasket over the 2 dowel locating pins on the float bowl.

34. Holding down on air horn gasket and pump plunger assembly, install the solenoid-metering rod plunger in the solenoid, aligning slot in end of plunger with solenoid attaching screw. Be sure plunger arms engage top of each metering.

35. If a service replacement mixture control solenoid package is installed, the solenoid and plunger MUST be installed as a matched set.

Air Horn Assembly

1. If removed, install Throttle Position Sensor (TPS) adjustment screw in air horn using tool J-28696-10, BT-7967A, or equivalent. Final adjustment of the TPS is made on the vehicle.

2. Inspect the air valve shaft pin for lubrication. Apply a liberal quantity of lithium base grease to the air valve shaft pin, especially in the area contacted by the air valve spring.

3. Install new pump plunger and TPS plunger seals and retainers in air horn casting. The lip on the seal faces outward, away from the air horn mounting surface. Lightly stake seal retainer in 3 places, choosing locations different from the original stakings.

4. Install rich mixture stop screw and rich authority adjusting spring from bottom side of the air horn. Use tool J-2869-4, BT-7967A, or equivalent, to bottom the stop screw lightly, then back out 1/4 turn. Final adjustment procedure will be covered later in this section.

5. Install TPS actuator plunger in the seal.

6. Carefully lower the air horn assembly onto the float bowl while positioning the TPS adjustment lever over the TPS sensor and guiding pump plunger stem through the seal in the air horn casting. To ease installation, insert a thin suitable tool between the air horn gasket and float bowl to raise the TPS Adjustment Lever, positioning it over the TPS sensor.

7. Make sure that the bleed tubes and accelerating well tubes are positioned properly through the holes in the air horn gasket. Do not force the air horn assembly onto the bowl, but lower it lightly into place over the 2 dowel locating pins.

8. Install 2 long air horn screws and lockwashers, 9 short screws and lockwashers and 2 countersunk screws located next to the carburetor venturi area. Install secondary air baffle beneath the No. 3 and 4 screws. Tighten all screws evenly and securely.

9. Install air valve rod into slot in the lever on the end of the air valve shaft. Install the other end of the rod in hole in front vacuum break plunger. Install front vacuum break and bracket assembly on the air horn, using 2 attaching screws. Tighten screw securely. Connect pump link to pump lever and install retainer.

➡**Use care installing the roll pin to prevent damage to the pump lever bearing surface and casting bosses.**

10. Install 2 secondary metering rods into the secondary metering rod hanger (upper end of rods point toward each other). Install secondary metering rod holder, with rods, onto air valve cam follower. Install retaining screw and tighten securely. Work air valves up and down several times to make sure they remove freely in both directions.

11. Connect choke rod into lower choke lever inside bowl cavity. Install choke rod in slot in upper choke lever. Position the lever on end of choke shaft, making sure flats on end of shaft align with flats in lever. Install attaching screw and tighten securely. When properly installed, the number on the lever will face outward.

12. Adjust the rich mixture stop screw:

a. Insert external float gauging tool J-34935-1, BT-8420A, or equivalent, in the vertical D-shaped vent hole in the air horn casting (next to the idle air bleed valve) and allow it to float freely.

b. Read (at eye level) the mark on the gauge, in inches, that lines up with the tip of the air horn casting.

c. Lightly press down on gauge, reading and recording the mark on the gauge that lines up with the top of the air horn casting.

d. Subtract gauge **UP** dimension, found in Step b, from gauge **DOWN** dimension, found in Step c and record the difference in inches. This difference in dimension is the total solenoid plunger travel.

e. Insert tool J-28696-10, BT-7928, or equivalent, in the access hole in the air horn and adjust the rich mixture stop screw to obtain $1/8$ inch total solenoid plunger travel.

13. With the solenoid plunger travel correctly set, install the plugs supplied in the service kit into the air horn to retain the setting and prevent fuel vapor loss:

a. Install the plug, hollow end down, into the access hole to the lean mixture (solenoid) screw and use a suitably sized punch to drive the plug into the air horn until top of plug is even with the lower edge of the hole chamber.

b. In a similar manner, install the plug over the rich mixture screw access hole and drive the plug into place so that the tip of the plug is $1/16$ inch below the surface of the air horn casting.

14. Install the idle air bleed valve as follows:

a. Lightly coat 2 new O-ring seals with automatic transmission fluid, to aid in their installation on the idle air bleed valve body. The thick seal goes in the upper groove and the thin seal goes in the lower groove.

b. Install the idle air bleed valve in the air horn, making sure that there is proper thread engagement.

c. Insert idle air bleed valve gauging tool J-33815-2, BT-8353B, or equivalent, in throttle side D-shaped vent hole of the air horn casting. The upper end of the tool should be positioned over the open cavity next to the idle air bleed valve.

d. Hold the gauging tool down lightly so that the solenoid plunger is against the solenoid stop, then adjust the idle air bleed valve so that the gauging tool will pivot over and just contact the top of the valve.

e. Remove the gauging tool.

f. The final adjustment of the idle air bleed valve is made on the vehicle to obtain idle mixture control.

15. Perform the air valve spring adjustment and choke coil Lever Adjustment.

16. Install the cover and coil assembly in the choke housing, as follows:

a. Place the cam follower on the highest step of the fast idle cam.

b. Install the thermostatic cover and coil assembly in the choke housing, making sure the coil tang engages the inside coil pickup lever. Ground contact for the electric choke is provided by a metal plate located at the rear of the choke cover assembly. Do not install a choke cover gasket between the electric choke assembly and the choke housing.

c. A choke cover retainer kit is required to attach the choke cover to the choke housing. Follow the instructions found in the kit and install the proper retainer and rivets using a suitable blind rivet tool.

d. It may be necessary to use an adapter (tube) if the installing tool interferes with the electrical connector tower on the choke cover.

17. Install the hose on the front vacuum brake and on the tube on the float bowl.

18. Position the idle speed solenoid and bracket assembly on the float bowl, retaining it with 2 large countersunk screws.

19. Perform the choke rod-fast idle cam adjustment, primary (front) vacuum break adjustment, air valve rod adjustment-front, unloader adjustment and the secondary lockout adjustment.

20. Reinstall the carburetor on the vehicle with a new flange gasket.

GASOLINE FUEL INJECTION SYSTEM

Description of System

The TBI unit equipped on the 4.3L, 5.0L (VIN E) and 5.7L engines is made up of 2 major casting assemblies: (1) a throttle body with a valve to control airflow and (2) a fuel body assembly with an integral pressure regulator and fuel injector to supply the required fuel. An electronically operated device to control the idle speed and a device to provide information regarding throttle valve position are included as part of the TBI unit.

The fuel injector(s) is a solenoid-operated device controlled by the ECM. The incoming fuel is directed to the lower end of the injector assembly which has a fine screen filter surrounding the injector inlet. The ECM actuates the solenoid, which lifts a normally closed ball valve off a seat. The fuel under pressure is injected in a conical spray pattern at the walls of the throttle body bore above the throttle valve. The excess fuel passes through a pressure regulator before being returned to the vehicle's fuel tank.

The pressure regulator is a diaphragm-operated relief valve with injector pressure on one side and air cleaner pressure on the other. The function of the regulator is to maintain a constant pressure drop across the injector throughout the operating load and speed range of the engine.

The throttle body portion of the TBI may contain ports located at, above, or below the throttle valve. These ports generate the vacuum signals for the EGR valve, MAP sensor, and the canister purge system.

The Throttle Position Sensor (TPS) is a variable resistor used to convert the degree of throttle plate opening to an electrical signal to the ECM. The ECM uses this signal as a reference point of throttle valve position. In addition, an Idle Air Control (IAC) assembly, mounted in the throttle body s used to control idle speeds. A cone-shaped valve in the IAC assembly is located in an air passage in the throttle body that leads from the point beneath the air cleaner to below the throttle valve. The ECM monitors idle speeds and, depending on engine load, moves the IAC cone in the air passage to increase or decrease air bypassing the throttle valve to the intake manifold for control of idle speeds.

Cranking Mode

During engine crank, for each distributor reference pulse the ECM will deliver an injector pulse (synchronized). The crank air/fuel ratio will be used if the throttle position is less than 80% open. Crank air fuel is determined by the ECM and ranges from 1.5:1 at -33°F (-36°C) to 14.7:1 at 201°F (94°C).

The lower the coolant temperature, the longer the pulse width (injector on-time) or richer the air/fuel ratio. The higher the coolant temperature, the less pulse width (injector on-time) or the leaner the air/fuel ratio.

Clear Flood Mode

If for some reason the engine should become flooded, provisions have been made to clear this condition. To clear the flood, the driver must depress the accelerator pedal enough to open to wide-open throttle position. The ECM then issues injector pulses at a rate that would be equal to an air/fuel ratio of 20:1. The ECM maintains this injector rate as long as the throttle remains wide open and the engine rpm is below 600. If the throttle position becomes less than 80%, the ECM then would immediately start issuing crank pulses to the injector calculated by the ECM based on the coolant temperature.

Run Mode

There are 2 different run modes. When the engine rpm is above 400, the system goes into open loop operation. In open loop operation, the ECM will ignore the signal from the oxygen (O_2) sensor and calculate the injector on-time based upon inputs from the coolant and manifold absolute pressure sensors.

During open loop operation, the ECM analyzes the following items to determine when the system is ready to go to the closed loop mode:

1. The oxygen sensor varying voltage output. (This is dependent on temperature).
2. The coolant sensor must be above specified temperature.
3. A specific amount of time must elapse after starting the engine. These values are stored in the PROM.

When these conditions have been met, the system goes into closed loop operation In closed loop operation, the ECM will modify the pulse width (injector on-time) based upon the signal from the oxygen sensor. The ECM will decrease the on-time if the air/fuel ratio is too rich, and will increase the on-time if the air/fuel ratio is too lean.

The pulse width, thus the amount of enrichment, is determined by manifold pressure change, throttle angle change, and coolant temperature. The higher the manifold pressure and the wider the throttle opening, the wider the pulse width. The acceleration enrichment pulses are delivered nonsynchronized.Any reduction in throttle angle will cancel the enrichment pulses. This way, quick movements of the accelerator will not over-enrich the mixture.

Acceleration Enrichment Mode

When the engine is required to accelerate, the opening of the throttle valve(s) causes a rapid increase in Manifold

Absolute Pressure (MAP). This rapid increase in the manifold pressure causes fuel to condense on the manifold walls. The ECM senses this increase in throttle angle and MAP, and supplies additional fuel for a short period of time. This prevents the engine from stumbling due to too lean a mixture.

Deceleration Leanout Mode

Upon deceleration, a leaner fuel mixture is required to reduce emission of hydrocarbons (HC) and carbon monoxide (CO). To adjust the injection on-time, the ECM uses the decrease in manifold pressure and the decrease in throttle position to calculate a decrease in pulse width. To maintain an idle fuel ratio of 14.7:1, fuel output is momentarily reduced. This is done because of the fuel remaining in the intake manifold during deceleration.

Deceleration Fuel Cut-Off Mode

The purpose of deceleration fuel cut-off is to remove fuel from the engine during extreme deceleration conditions. Deceleration fuel cut-off is based on values of manifold pressure, throttle position, and engine rpm stored in the calibration PROM. Deceleration fuel cut-off overrides the deceleration enleanment mode.

Battery Voltage Correction Mode

The purpose of battery voltage correction is to compensate for variations in battery voltage to fuel pump and injector response. The ECM modifies the pulse width by a correction factor in the PROM. When battery voltage decreases, pulse width increases.

Battery voltage correction takes place in all operating modes. When battery voltage is low, the spark delivered by the distributor may be low. To correct this low battery voltage problem, the ECM can do any or all of the following:

1. Increase injector pulse width (increase fuel)
2. Increase idle rpm
3. Increase ignition dwell time

Fuel Cut-Off Mode

When the ignition is **OFF**, the ECM will not energize the injector. Fuel will also be cut off if the ECM does not receive a reference pulse from the distributor. To prevent dieseling, fuel delivery is completely stopped as soon as the engine is stopped. The ECM will not allow any fuel supply until it receives distributor reference pulses which prevents flooding.

Backup Mode

When in this mode, the ECM is operating on the fuel backup logic calibrated by the CalPak. The CalPak is used to control the fuel delivery if the ECM fails. This mode verifies that the backup feature is working properly. The parameters that can be read on a scan tool in this mode are not much use for service.

Highway Mode

When driven at highway speeds the system may enter highway or semi-closed loop mode. This improves fuel economy by leaning out fuel mixture slightly. The ECM must see correct engine temperature, ignition timing, canister activity and a constant vehicle speed before if will enter this mode.

The system will switch back to closed loop periodically to check all system functions.

A scan tool scan determine highway mode by looking at the integrator/block learn values and oxygen sensor voltage. Integrator and block learn will show very little change and the oxygen sensor voltage is be less than 100 millivolts.

ALCL/ALDL Connector

The Assembly Line Communication Link (ALCL) or Assembly Line Diagnostic Link (ALDL) is a diagnostic connector located in the passenger compartment. It has terminals which are used in the assembly plant to check that the engine is operating properly before it leaves the plant. This connector is a very useful tool in diagnosing EFI engines. Important information from the ECM is available at this terminal and can be read with one of the many popular scanner tools.

Relieving Fuel System Pressure

The TBI unit is equipped with a constant bleed feature, therefore when the engine is turned OFF and the fuel filler cap is loosened the system pressure is automatically released. No further pressure relief is necessary.

➡ Both Section 4 and this Section contain simple testing and service procedures for your fuel injection system.

Electric Fuel Pump

REMOVAL & INSTALLATION

✳✳CAUTION

To reduce the risk of fire and personal injury the fuel pressure must be relieved.

1. Disconnect the negative battery cable and relieve the fuel system pressure.
2. Raise and support the vehicle safely.
3. Remove the fuel tank.
4. Remove the fuel tank sending unit and pump assembly as follows:
   a. On 1990 models, use tool J-24187 or equivalent to remove the assembly retaining cam, assembly and O-ring from fuel tank. Discard the O-ring.
   b. On 1991-93 models, remove the assembly attaching nuts, retaining flag, assembly and O-ring from the tank. Discard the O-ring.
To install:
5. Install fuel sending unit in fuel tank as follows:
   a. On 1990 models, install a new O-ring on fuel tank. Use tool J-24187, or equivalent, to connect fuel meter assembly and assembly retaining cam and fuel tank.
   b. On 1991-93 models, position a new O-ring on fuel tank. Install fuel sender assembly, retaining flag, and attaching nuts to fuel tank. Tighten attaching nuts to 27 inch lbs. (3 Nm).
6. Install fuel tank.
7. Lower vehicle.

8. Turn the ignition **ON** for 2 seconds, **OFF** for 10 seconds, the **ON** and inspect the system for leaks.

TESTING

➡ For more complete Fuel Injection Testing and Diagnosis, refer to Section 4 Diagnostic Charts.

When the ignition switch is turned **ON**, the ECM will turn the in-tank fuel pump **ON**. It will remain on as long as the engine is cranking or running and the ECM is receiving ignition reference pulses. If there are no reference pulses, the ECM will shut the fuel pump **OFF** within 2 seconds after the key is turned **ON**. The pump will deliver fuel to the TBI unit at a pressure controlled by the internal regulator to approximately 9-13 psi. Excess fuel is then returned to the fuel tank.

While the engine is stopped, the fuel pump can be activated by applying battery voltage to the fuel pump test terminal located near the passenger side cowl of the engine compartment.

➡ Fuel pressure should be noted while the fuel pump is running. Fuel pressure will drop immediately after the fuel pump stops running due to the controlled bleed in the fuel system.

1. Turn the ignition **OFF** and relieve fuel system pressure by removing fuel filler cap.
2. Locate the engine compartment fuel feed quick-connect fitting. Uncouple the fuel supply flexible hose as follows:
   a. Grasp both ends of the fitting and twist female end ¼ turn in each direction to loosen any dirt in fitting.
   b. Wearing proper safety glasses, use compressed air to blow dirt out of the quick-connect fitting.
3. Separate the male and female leads of the connector by inserting tool into female end of the connector to release the male end.
4. Install a fuel pressure gauge between the two ends of the connector. Be sure to always lubricate the male end with a few drops of engine oil to ensure proper connection and prevent a fuel leak.
5. Apply battery voltage to the fuel pump test connector.
6. The fuel pressure should be 9-13 psi.

Throttle Body Assembly

▸ **See Figures 34 and 35**

The throttle body injection used the 4.3L, 5.0L (VIN E) and 5.7L engines is centrally located on the intake manifold. Its function is to supply an air/fuel mixture to the intake manifold, which is controlled by the ECM.

The assembly is simple. It consists of two casting assemblies: a throttle body and a fuel metering assembly. The assembly contains a pressure regulator, idle air control valve, electrical solenoid that activates the fuel injector, throttle position sensor, fuel inlet and a fuel return fitting.

The Throttle Body Injection identification number is stamped on the lower mounting flange located near the TPS. The number is in alphabetical code and should be noted before servicing the unit.

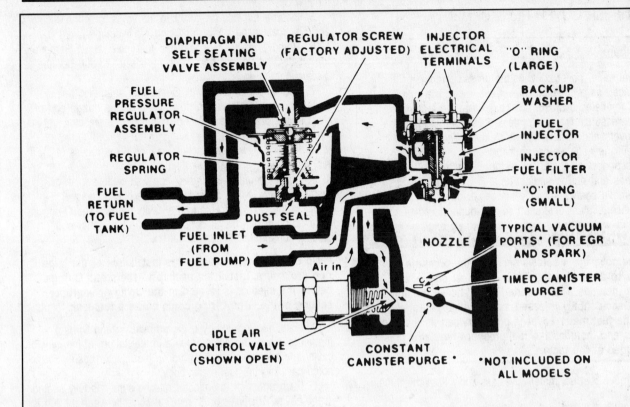

DIAPHRAGM AND SELF SEATING VALVE ASSEMBLY

REGULATOR SCREW (FACTORY ADJUSTED)

INJECTOR ELECTRICAL TERMINALS

"O" RING (LARGE)

BACK-UP WASHER

FUEL INJECTOR

INJECTOR FUEL FILTER

"O" RING (SMALL)

FUEL PRESSURE REGULATOR ASSEMBLY

REGULATOR SPRING

FUEL RETURN (TO FUEL TANK)

DUST SEAL

FUEL INLET (FROM FUEL PUMP)

Air in

NOZZLE

TYPICAL VACUUM PORTS* (FOR EGR AND SPARK)

TIMED CANISTER PURGE *

IDLE AIR CONTROL VALVE (SHOWN OPEN)

CONSTANT CANISTER PURGE *

*NOT INCLUDED ON ALL MODELS

Fig. 34 TBI fuel and air mixture schematic

1. Bolt—tighten to 16 N·m (12 ft. lbs.)
2. TBI unit
3. Gasket (must be installed with stripe facing up)
5. Engine intake manifold

Fig. 35 Throttle Body assembly removal

An oxygen sensor in the main exhaust system functions to provide feedback information to the ECM as to oxygen content, lean or rich in the exhaust. The ECM then uses this information to modify fuel delivery to achieve as near as possible to the ideal air/fuel ratio of 14.7:1. This ratio permits the catalytic converter to become more effective in reducing emissions while providing acceptable driveability.

Trouble diagnosis of the injection system is nearly impossible for the novice mechanic to perform, because of the interaction between the injection, emissions, and ignition systems; all of which are controlled by the ECM. Should you encounter any type of engine performance problem, have a complete system test performed by a qualified, professional technician. If the fault lies in the injection system, you can use the following procedures to remove the TBI unit(s) and replace the defective component(s).

REMOVAL & INSTALLATION

1. Disconnect the THERMAC hose from the engine fitting and remove the air cleaner.
2. Disconnect the electrical connectors at the idle air control, throttle position sensor, and the injector.
3. Disconnect the throttle linkage, return spring, and cruise control (if equipped).
4. Disconnect the throttle body vacuum hoses, fuel supply and fuel return lines.
5. Disconnect the 3 bolts securing the throttle body and remove the throttle body.
6. To install, reverse the removal procedures. Replace the manifold gasket and O-rings.

FUEL METER COVER REPLACEMENT

▶ **See Figure 36**

The fuel meter cover contains the pressure regulator and is only serviced as a complete preset assembly. The fuel pressure regulator is preset and plugged at the factory.

1. Depressurize the fuel system. Raise the hood, install fender covers and remove the air cleaner assembly. Disconnect the negative battery cable.
2. Disconnect electrical connector to injector by squeezing on tow tabs and pulling straight up.
3. Remove screws securing fuel meter cover to fuel meter body. Notice location of 2 short screws during removal.

✳✳CAUTION

Do not remove the 4 screws securing the pressure regulator to the fuel meter cover. The fuel pressure regulator includes a large spring under heavy tension which, if accidentally released, could cause personal injury. The fuel meter cover is only serviced as a complete assembly and includes the fuel pressure regulator preset and plugged at the factor.

4. Remove the fuel meter cover assembly from the throttle body.

➡**Do not immerse the fuel meter cover (with pressure regulator) in any type of cleaner. Immersion of cleaner will damage the internal fuel pressure regulator diaphragms and gaskets.**

5. Installation is the reverse order of the removal procedure. Be sure to use new gaskets and torque the fuel meter cover attaching screws to 27 inch lbs. (3.0 Nm).

➡**The service kits include a small vial of thread locking compound with directions for use. If the material is not available, use part number 1052624, Loctite® 262, or equivalent. Do not use a higher strength locking compound than recommended, as this may prevent attaching screw removal or breakage of the screwhead if removal is again required.**

FUEL INJECTOR REPLACEMENT

Use care in removing the injector to prevent damage to the electrical connector pins on top of the injector, the injector fuel filter and the nozzle. The fuel injector is serviced as a complete assembly only. The fuel injector is an electrical component and should not be immersed in any type of cleaner.

1. Depressurize the fuel system. Raise the hood, install fender covers and remove the air cleaner assembly. Disconnect the negative battery cable.
2. Disconnect electrical connector to injector by squeezing on tow tabs and pulling straight up.
3. Remove the fuel meter cover assembly.
4. With the fuel meter cover gasket in place to prevent damage to the casting, use a suitable dowel rod and lay the dowel rod on top of the fuel meter body.

5. Insert a suitable pry tool into the small lip of the injector and pry against the dowel rod lifting the injector straight up.
6. Remove the injector from the fuel meter body. Remove the small O-ring at the bottom of the injector cavity. Be sure to discard both O-rings.
7. Lubricate the new small O-ring with automatic transmission fluid. Push the new O-ring on the nozzle end of the injector, pressing the O-ring up against the injector fuel filter.
8. Install a new steel backup washer in the recess of the fuel meter body.
9. Lubricate the new large O-ring with clean engine oil. Install the new O-ring directly above the backup washer, pressing the O-ring down into the cavity recess. The O-ring is installed properly when it is flush with the fuel meter body casting surface.

➡**Do not attempt to reverse the installation of the large O-ring procedure. Install the backup washers and O-rings before the injector is located in the cavity or improper seating of the large O-ring could cause a fuel leak.**

10. Install the injector by using as pushing and twisting motion to center the nozzle O-ring in the bottom of the injector cavity and aligning the raised lug on the injector base with the notch cast into the fuel meter body.
11. Push down on the injector making sure it is fully seated in the cavity. The injector is installed correctly when the lug is seated in the notch and the electrical terminals are parallel to the throttle shaft in the throttle body.
12. Install the fuel meter cover. Install the injector electrical connector and all electrical and vacuum lines. Install the air cleaner assembly.
13. With the engine **OFF** and the ignition **ON** check for fuel leaks.

FUEL METER BODY REPLACEMENT

1. Depressurize the fuel system. Raise the hood, install fender covers and remove the air cleaner assembly. Disconnect the negative battery cable.
2. Remove the fuel meter cover assembly. Remove the fuel meter cover gasket, fuel meter outlet gasket and pressure regulator seal.
3. Remove the fuel injectors. Remove the fuel inlet and fuel outlet nuts and gaskets from the fuel meter body. Take note that the inlet has a larger passage than the outlet nut.
4. Remove the screws and lockwashers, then remove the fuel meter body from the throttle assembly.

➡**Do not remove the center screw and staking at each end holding the fuel distribution skirt in the throttle body. The skirt is an integral part of the throttle body and is not serviced separately.**

5. Remove the fuel meter body insulator gasket.
To install:
6. Install the new throttle body to fuel meter body gasket. Match the cut portions in the gasket with the opening in the throttle body.
7. Install the fuel meter body assembly onto the throttle body assembly.

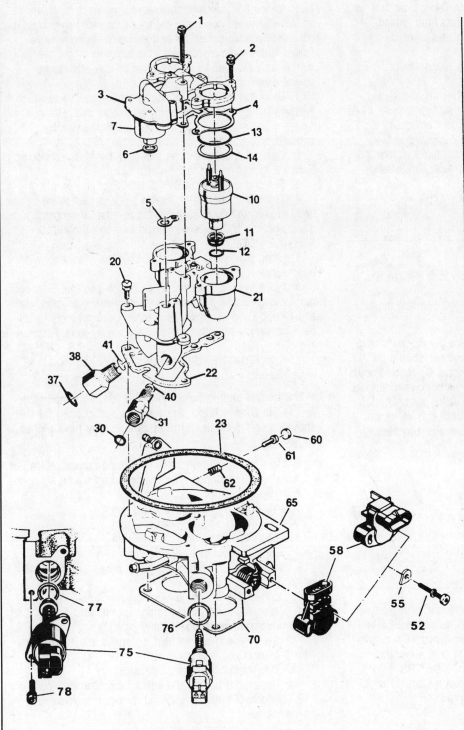

1	Screw Assembly - Fuel Meter Cover Attaching - Long
2	Screw Assembly - Fuel Meter Cover Attaching - Short
3	Fuel Meter Cover Assembly
4	Gasket - Fuel Meter Cover
5	Gasket - Fuel Meter Outlet
6	Seal - Pressure Regulator
7	Pressure Regulator
10	Injector - Fuel
11	Filter - Fuel Injector Inlet
12	O-ring - Fuel Injector - Lower
13	O-ring - Fuel Injector - Upper
14	Washer - Fuel Injector
20	Screw Assembly - Fuel Meter Body - Throttle Body Attaching
21	Fuel Meter Body Assembly
22	Gasket - Throttle Body to Fuel Meter Body
23	Gasket - Air Cleaner
30	O-ring - Fuel Return Line
31	Nut - Fuel Outlet
37	O-ring - Fuel Inlet Line
38	Nut - Fuel Inlet
40	Gasket - Fuel Outlet Nut
41	Gasket - Fuel Inlet Nut
52	Screw Assembly - TPS Attaching
55	Retainer - TPS Attaching Screw
58	Sensor - Throttle Position
60	Plug - Idle Stop Screw
61	Screw Assembly - Idle Stop
62	Spring - Idle Stop Screw
65	Throttle Body Assembly
70	Gasket - Flange
75	Valve Assembly - Idle Air Control
76	Gasket - Idle Air Control Valve Assembly
77	O-Ring - IAC Valve
78	Screw Assembly - IAC Valve Attaching

Fig. 36 TBI assembly exploded view

8. Install the fuel meter body to the throttle body attaching screw assemblies, precoated with a suitable thread sealer.

9. Torque the screw assemblies to 32 inch lbs. (5 Nm). Install the fuel inlet and outlet nuts with new gaskets to the fuel meter body assembly. Torque the inlet nut to 30 ft. lbs. (40 Nm) and the outlet nut to 21 ft. lbs (29 Nm).

10. Fuel inlet and return lines and new O-rings. Be sure to use a back-up wrench to keep the TBI nuts from turning.

11. Install the injectors with new upper and lower O-rings in the fuel meter body assembly.

12. Install the fuel meter cover gasket, fuel meter outlet gasket and pressure regulator seal.

13. Install the fuel meter cover assembly. Install the long and short fuel meter cover attaching screws assemblies, coated with a suitable thread sealer. Torque the screws to 27 inch lbs. (4 Nm).

14. Install the electrical connectors to the fuel injectors. With the engine **OFF** and the ignition **ON** check for fuel leaks.

IDLE AIR CONTROL ASSEMBLY (IAC) REPLACEMENT

1. Remove the air cleaner.
2. Disconnect the electrical connection from the idle air control assembly.
3. Using a 1¼" wrench, remove the IAC from the throttle body.

➡**Before installing a NEW IAC measure the distance that the conical valve is extended. Measurement should be made from motor housing to end of cone. Distance should be no greater than 1.259" (28mm). If the cone is extended too far, damage may result when the valve is installed. If necessary push on the end of cone, until it is retracted. Don not adjust a used IAC valve or damage may result.**

4. Installation is the reverse of removal. Torque the motor bolts to 13 ft. lbs. (17 Nm).

Adjustments

No internal adjustments of the TBI unit are possible.

THROTTLE POSITION SENSOR (TPS) ADJUSTMENT

The TPS has the ability to auto-zero the sensor voltage as long as the reading is between 0.20-0.95 volts. The ECM will determine any reading within these parameters as 0% throttle opening. Scan tools have the capability to read either the actual voltage or throttle opening percent. If the TPS is not within the specified range, the ECM will set a Code 21 or 22. The TPS can only be replaced, not adjusted.

MINIMUM IDLE ADJUSTMENT

The minimum idle speed should only be adjusted when installing a replacement throttle body. The idle stop screw is used to regulate the minimum idle speed of the engine. On original equipment throttle bodies, it is adjusted at the factory, then covered with a a plug to discourage unnecessary readjustment. If necessary to remove the plug, pierce the idle stop screw plug with an awl, and apply leverage to remove it.

The minimum idle speed adjustment is critical to vehicle performance and component durability. Incorrect minimum idle speed adjustment (too high) will cause the IAC valve pintle to constantly bottom out on its seat and result in early valve failure. If the minimum idle speed is adjusted to low, the vehicle may not start in cold weather or may stall during engine warm up.

1. Block the drive wheels and apply the parking brake. Remove the air cleaner assembly and or air duct. Remove and plug any vacuum hoses on the tube manifold assembly, if equipped.

2. Connect a suitable scan tool onto the ALDL connector. Turn the ignition switch to the **ON** position.

3. Select the **FIELD SERVICE MODE** on the scan tool.

4. This will cause the IAC valve pintle to seat in the throttle body (closing the air passage). Wait at least 20 seconds, disconnect the IAC valve connector, then exit the **FIELD SERVICE MODE**.

5. Using the ROAD TEST MODE on the scan tool, select engine rpm.

6. Place the transmission in the **P** or **N** position. Start and run the engine until it reaches normal operating temperature and Closed Loop operation as read on the scan tool. It may be necessary to hold the throttle open slightly to maintain an idle.

7. Select **ENGINE RPM** on the scan tool and read the engine speed.

➡**The engine should be at normal operating temperature and in the Closed Loop. Accessories and cooling fan should be off. Vehicles at high altitude may have higher engine rpm.**

8. Make sure that the throttle and cruise control cables do not hold the throttle open. The idle speed should be set at the following specifications:
   3.1L (VIN D) engine — 600±50 rpm.
   4.3L (VIN Z) engine — 425±25 rpm.
   5.0L (VIN E) engine — 475±25 rpm.
   5.7L (VIN 7) engine — 475±25 rpm.

9. Adjust the minimum idle speed if necessary. Turn the ignition switch to the **OFF** position.

10. Connect the IAC valve electrical connector.

11. Reset IAC valve pintle position as follows:
   a. Depress accelerator slightly.
   b. Start the engine and hold the speed above 2000 rpm for 5 seconds.
   c. Turn ignition **OFF** for 10 seconds.
   d. Restart the engine and check for proper idle operation.

12. Disconnect the scan tool and remove the blocks from the drive wheels.

13. Install air cleaner assembly.

FUEL TANK

▶ See Figures 37, 38, 39, 40 and 41

REMOVAL & INSTALLATION

1990-91

SEDAN

1. Disconnect the negative battery cable.
2. Relieve fuel system pressure, drain the fuel tank and store the fuel in a safe location.
3. Raise and support the vehicle safely.
4. Clean and disconnect fuel feed and return line quick-connect fittings at fuel level meter.
5. Clean and disconnect vapor hose connection at fuel level meter.
6. Disconnect the fuel level meter electrical connector and free it from the routing clip on the fuel tank strap.
7. With the aid of an assistant, support the fuel tank and remove the fuel tank retaining straps, nuts and bolts.
8. Remove the fuel tank and place in a safe well ventilated area.
   To install:
9. With the aid of an assistant, support the fuel tank in the correct position and attach the fuel tank retaining strap, nuts and bolts. Tighten front fuel tank retaining strap bolts to 26 ft. lbs. (35 Nm) and rear tank retaining strap nuts to 97 inch lbs. (11 Nm).
10. Connect the fuel level meter electrical connector to the routing clip at the fuel tank strap and to the fuel level meter.
11. Connect vapor hose.
12. Connect fuel feed and return line quick-connect fittings to fuel level meter. Be sure to apply a few drops of clean engine oil to the male connector tube ends.
13. Lower vehicle, add fuel and install fuel filler cap.
14. Connect the negative battery cable. Turn ignition **ON** for 2 seconds, **OFF** for 10 seconds, then **ON** again and inspect the tank and lines for leaks.

WAGON

1. Disconnect the negative battery cable.
2. Drain the fuel tank and store the fuel in a safe location.
3. Remove filler neck stone shield attaching screws and shield.
4. Remove filler neck attaching screw from body bracket and remove the filler neck.
5. Raise and support the vehicle safely.
6. Disconnect fuel level meter electrical connector, free connector from routing clip at body and remove.
7. Remove ground lead from body.
8. Clean and remove fuel feed and return pipe connecting hoses from fuel level meter.
9. Clean and remove fuel vapor hose from fuel level meter.

10. With the aid of an assistant, support the fuel tank and remove the retaining straps, nuts and bolts.
11. Remove the fuel tank and store in a safe well ventilated area.
    To install:
12. With the aid of an assistant, support the fuel tank in the correct position and attach the fuel tank retaining strap, nuts and bolts. Tighten front retaining strap bolts to 26 ft. lbs. (35 Nm) and rear retaining strap nuts to 97 inch lbs. (11 Nm).
13. Connect fuel vapor, return and feed pipe hoses.
14. Connect fuel level meter electrical connector to the fuel level meter and snap electrical connector into routing clip at body.
15. Attach the ground lead to body.
16. Lower vehicle and attach filler neck to body bracket with filler neck attaching screw.
17. Attach filler neck stone shield and attaching screws.
18. Connect the negative battery cable and add fuel.
19. Start engine and inspect the tank and lines for leaks.

1992-93

1. Disconnect the negative battery cable.
2. Relieve fuel system pressure.
3. Drain the fuel tank and store the fuel in a safe location.
4. Raise and support the vehicle safely.
5. Disconnect lower fuel tank shield attaching screws and shield.
6. Clean and disconnect vapor hose at the fuel sender, vent hose at fuel filler neck vent pipe, and fuel filler tube at fuel tank.
7. Clean and disconnect fuel feed and return line quick-connect fittings at fuel sender assembly.
8. Disconnect fuel sender assembly electrical connector.
9. With the aid of an assistant, support the fuel tank and remove the fuel tank retaining straps, nuts and bolts.
10. Remove the fuel tank and place in a safe well ventilated area.
    To install:
11. With the aid of an assistant, support the fuel tank in the correct position and attach the fuel tank retaining straps, nuts and bolts. Tighten front strap retaining bolts to 24 ft. lbs. (31 Nm) and rear retaining nuts to 18 ft. lbs. (24 Nm).
12. Connect fuel filler tube, vent hose, vapor hose, and clamps.
13. Connect fuel sender assembly electrical connector.
14. Attach fuel feed and return pipe quick-connect fittings. Be sure to apply a few drops of clean engine oil to the male connector tube ends.
15. Connect lower fuel tank shield and attaching screws. Tighten to 18 inch lbs. (2.0 Nm).
16. Lower vehicle, add fuel and attach filler cap.
17. Attach negative battery cable.
18. Turn the ignition **ON** for 2 seconds, **OFF** for 10 seconds, then **ON** and inspect the tank and lines for leaks.

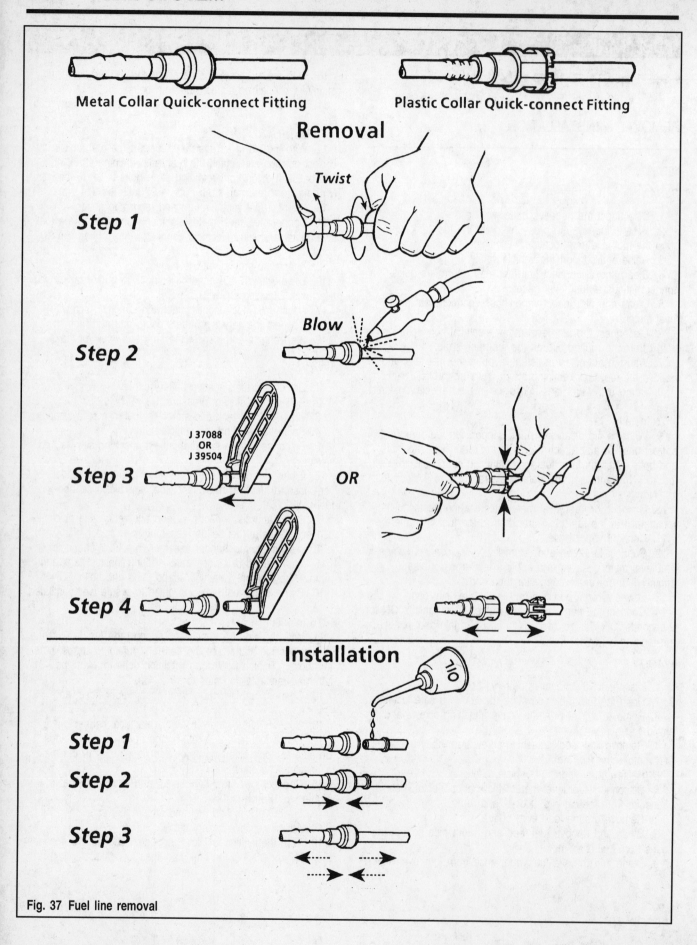

Metal Collar Quick-connect Fitting   Plastic Collar Quick-connect Fitting

Removal

Twist

Step 1

Blow

Step 2

J 37088
OR
J 39504

Step 3   **OR**

Step 4

Installation

OIL

Step 1

Step 2

Step 3

Fig. 37 Fuel line removal

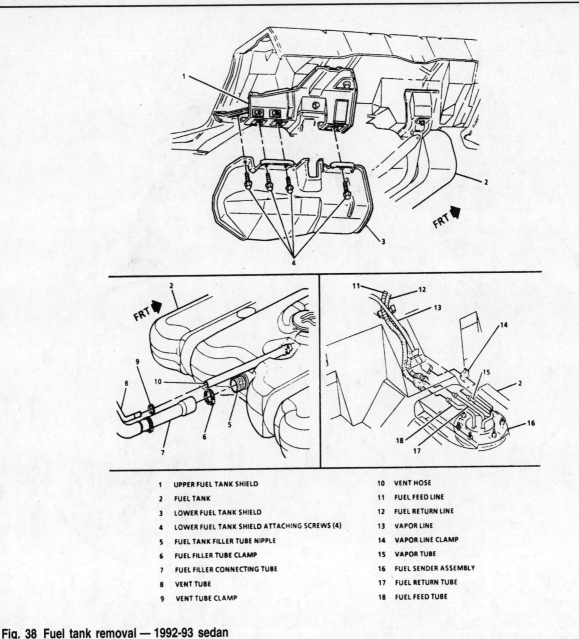

1	UPPER FUEL TANK SHIELD	10	VENT HOSE
2	FUEL TANK	11	FUEL FEED LINE
3	LOWER FUEL TANK SHIELD	12	FUEL RETURN LINE
4	LOWER FUEL TANK SHIELD ATTACHING SCREWS (4)	13	VAPOR LINE
5	FUEL TANK FILLER TUBE NIPPLE	14	VAPOR LINE CLAMP
6	FUEL FILLER TUBE CLAMP	15	VAPOR TUBE
7	FUEL FILLER CONNECTING TUBE	16	FUEL SENDER ASSEMBLY
8	VENT TUBE	17	FUEL RETURN TUBE
9	VENT TUBE CLAMP	18	FUEL FEED TUBE

Fig. 38 Fuel tank removal — 1992-93 sedan

SENDING UNIT AND FUEL PUMP ASSEMBLY REPLACEMENT

The electric fuel pump and sensing unit are an assembly, which is located inside the fuel tank.

1. Disconnect the negative battery cable and relieve the fuel system pressure.

2. Raise and support the vehicle safely.

3. Remove the fuel tank.

4. Remove the fuel tank sending unit and pump assembly as follows:

   a. On 1990 models, use tool J-24187 or equivalent to remove the assembly retaining cam, assembly and O-ring from fuel tank. Discard the O-ring.

   b. On 1991-93 models, remove the assembly attaching nuts, retaining flag, assembly and O-ring from the tank. Discard the O-ring.

To install:

5. Install fuel sending unit in fuel tank as follows:

   a. On 1990 models, install a new O-ring on fuel tank. Use tool J-24187, or equivalent, to connect fuel meter assembly and assembly retaining cam and fuel tank.

   b. On 1991-93 models, position a new O-ring on fuel tank. Install fuel sender assembly, retaining flag, and attaching nuts to fuel tank. Tighten attaching nuts to 27 inch lbs. (3 Nm).

6. Install fuel tank.

7. Lower vehicle.

8. Turn the ignition **ON** for 2 seconds, **OFF** for 10 seconds, the **ON** and inspect the system for leaks.

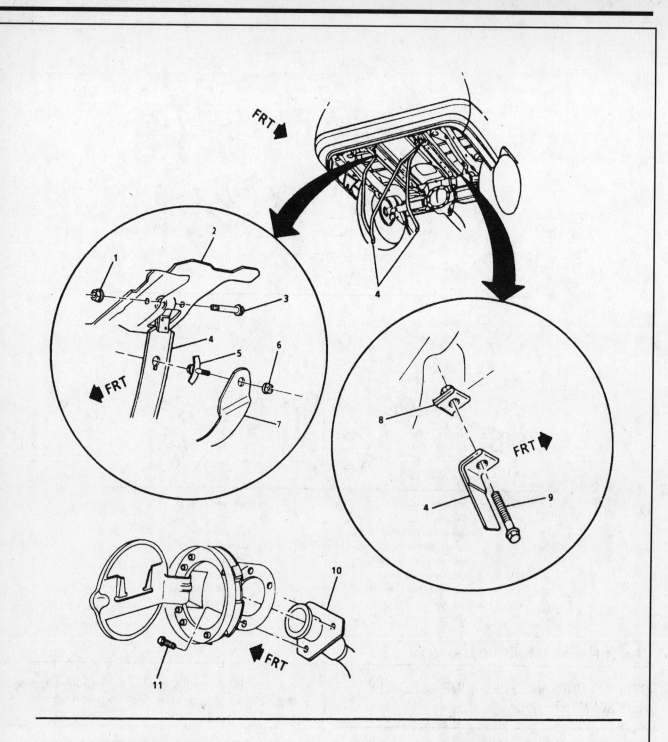

1 REAR FUEL TANK RETAINING STRAP NUTS (2)	7 FUEL TANK CROSS STRAP
2 UNDER BODY	8 FRONT FUEL TANK RETAINING STRAP BODY NUTS (2)
3 REAR FUEL TANK RETAINING STRAP BOLTS (2)	9 FRONT FUEL TANK RETAINING STRAP BOLTS (2)
4 FUEL TANK RETAINING STRAPS (2)	10 FUEL FILLER TUBE
5 FUEL TANK CROSS STRAP ATTACHING SCREW	11 FUEL FILLER TUBE ATTACHING SCREWS (3)
6 FUEL TANK CROSS STRAP ATTACHING NUT	

Fig. 39 Fuel tank removal — 1992-93 station wagon

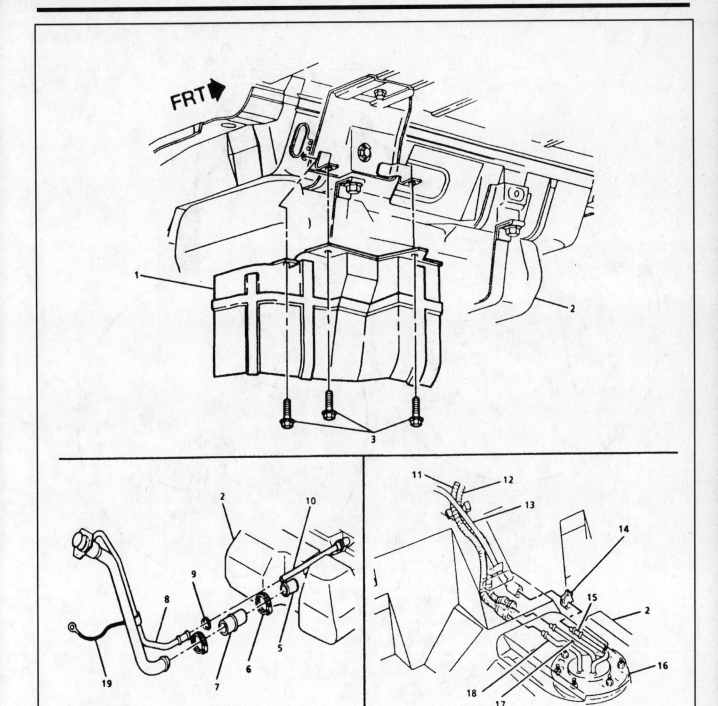

1	FUEL TANK SHIELD	**10**	FUEL FEED PIPE
2	FUEL TANK	**11**	FUEL RETURN PIPE
3	FUEL TANK SHIELD ATTACHING SCREWS (3)	**12**	VAPOR PIPE
4	FUEL TANK FILLER TUBE NIPPLE	**13**	VAPOR PIPE CLAMP
5	FUEL FILLER TUBE CLAMP	**14**	VAPOR TUBE
6	FUEL FILLER CONNECTING TUBE	**15**	FUEL SENDER ASSEMBLY
7	VENT TUBE	**16**	FUEL RETURN TUBE
8	VENT TUBE CLAMP	**17**	FUEL FEED TUBE
9	VENT HOSE	**18**	GROUNDING STRAP

Fig. 40 Fuel tank removal — 1992-93 station wagon

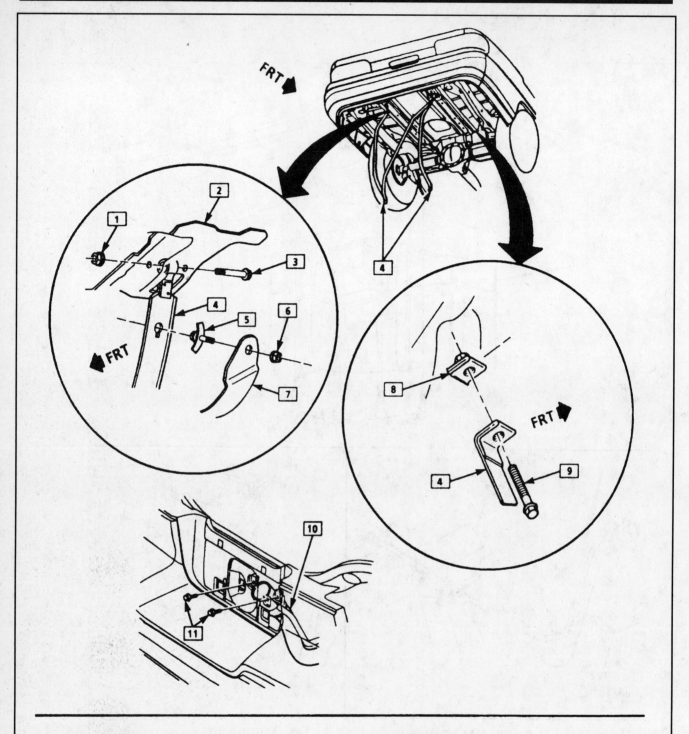

1	REAR FUEL TANK RETAINING STRAP NUTS (2) · 25 N·m (18 lb. ft.)	**7**	FUEL TANK CROSS STRAP
2	UNDER BODY	**8**	FRONT FUEL TANK RETAINING STRAP BODY NUTS (2)
3	REAR FUEL TANK RETAINING STRAP BOLTS (2)	**9**	FRONT FUEL TANK RETAINING STRAP BOLTS (2) · 32 N·m (24 lb. ft.)
4	FUEL TANK RETAINING STRAPS (2)	**10**	FUEL FILLER TUBE
5	FUEL TANK CROSS STRAP ATTACHING SCREW	**11**	FUEL FILLER TUBE ATTACHING SCREWS (2) · 2 N·m (18 lb. in.)
6	FUEL TANK CROSS STRAP ATTACHING NUT · 15 N·m (11 lb. ft.)		

Fig. 41 Fuel tank removal — 1992-93 sedan

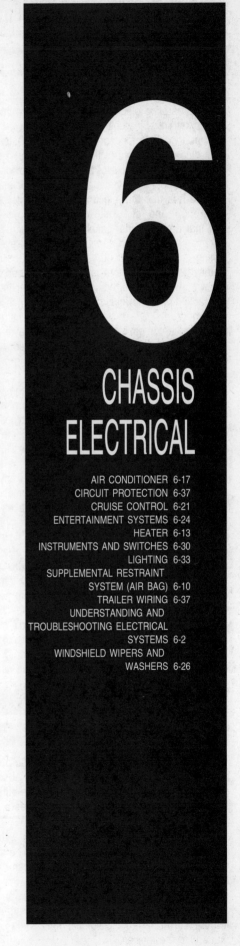

6

CHASSIS ELECTRICAL

UNDERSTANDING AND TROUBLESHOOTING ELECTRICAL SYSTEMS

At the rate which both import and domestic manufacturers are incorporating electronic control systems into their production lines, it won't be long before every new vehicle is equipped with one or more on-board computer. These electronic components (with no moving parts) should theoretically last the life of the vehicle, provided nothing external happens to damage the circuits or memory chips.

While it is true that electronic components should never wear out, in the real world malfunctions do occur. It is also true that any computer-based system is extremely sensitive to electrical voltages and cannot tolerate careless or haphazard testing or service procedures. An inexperienced individual can literally do major damage looking for a minor problem by using the wrong kind of test equipment or connecting test leads or connectors with the ignition switch **ON**. When selecting test equipment, make sure the manufacturers instructions state that the tester is compatible with whatever type of electronic control system is being serviced. Read all instructions carefully and double check all test points before installing probes or making any test connections.

The following section outlines basic diagnosis techniques for dealing with computerized automotive control systems. Along with a general explanation of the various types of test equipment available to aid in servicing modern electronic automotive systems, basic repair techniques for wiring harnesses and connectors is given. Read the basic information before attempting any repairs or testing on any computerized system, to provide the background of information necessary to avoid the most common and obvious mistakes that can cost both time and money. Although the replacement and testing procedures are simple in themselves, the systems are not, and unless one has a thorough understanding of all components and their function within a particular computerized control system, the logical test sequence these systems demand cannot be followed. Minor malfunctions can make a big difference, so it is important to know how each component affects the operation of the overall electronic system to find the ultimate e cause of a problem without replacing good components unnecessarily. It is not enough to use the correct test equipment; the test equipment must be used correctly.

Safety Precautions

✳✳CAUTION

Whenever working on or around any computer based microprocessor control system, always observe these general precautions to prevent the possibility of personal injury or damage to electronic components.

• Never install or remove battery cables with the key ON or the engine running. Jumper cables should be connected with the key OFF to avoid power surges that can damage electronic control units. Engines equipped with computer controlled systems should avoid both giving and getting jump starts due to the possibility of serious damage to components from arcing in the engine compartment when connections are made with the ignition ON.

• Always remove the battery cables before charging the battery. Never use a high output charger on an installed battery or attempt to use any type of 'hot shot' (24 volt) starting aid.

• Exercise care when inserting test probes into connectors to insure good connections without damaging the connector or spreading the pins. Always probe connectors from the rear (wire) side, NOT the pin side, to avoid accidental shorting of terminals during test procedures.

• Never remove or attach wiring harness connectors with the ignition switch ON, especially to an electronic control unit.

• Do not drop any components during service procedures and never apply 12 volts directly to any component (like a solenoid or relay) unless instructed specifically to do so. Some component electrical windings are designed to safely handle only 4 or 5 volts and can be destroyed in seconds if 12 volts are applied directly to the connector.

• Remove the electronic control unit if the vehicle is to be placed in an environment where temperatures exceed approximately 176°F (80°C), such as a paint spray booth or when arc or gas welding near the control unit location in the car.

ORGANIZED TROUBLESHOOTING

When diagnosing a specific problem, organized troubleshooting is a must. The complexity of a modern automobile demands that you approach any problem in a logical, organized manner. There are certain troubleshooting techniques that are standard:

1. Establish when the problem occurs. Does the problem appear only under certain conditions? Were there any noises, odors, or other unusual symptoms?

2. Isolate the problem area. To do this, make some simple tests and observations; then eliminate the systems that are working properly. Check for obvious problems such as broken wires, dirty connections or split or disconnected vacuum hoses. Always check the obvious before assuming something complicated is the cause.

3. Test for problems systematically to determine the cause once the problem area is isolated. Are all the components functioning properly? Is there power going to electrical switches and motors? Is there vacuum at vacuum switches and/or actuators? Is there a mechanical problem such as bent linkage or loose mounting screws? Doing careful, systematic checks will often turn up most causes on the first inspection without wasting time checking components that have little or no relationship to the problem.

4. Test all repairs after the work is done to make sure that the problem is fixed. Some causes can be traced to more than one component, so a careful verification of repair work is important to pick up additional malfunctions that may cause a problem to reappear or a different problem to arise. A blown fuse, for example, is a simple problem that may require more than another fuse to repair. If you don't look for a problem that caused a fuse to blow, for example, a shorted wire may go undetected.

Experience has shown that most problems tend to be the result of a fairly simple and obvious cause, such as loose or corroded connectors or air leaks in the intake system; making careful inspection of components during testing essential to quick and accurate troubleshooting. Special, hand held computerized testers designed specifically for diagnosing the system are available from a variety of aftermarket sources, as well as from the vehicle manufacturer, but care should be taken that any test equipment being used is designed to diagnose that particular computer controlled system accurately without damaging the control unit (ECM) or components being tested.

➡️**Pinpointing the exact cause of trouble in an electrical system can sometimes only be accomplished by the use of special test equipment. The following describes commonly used test equipment and explains how to put it to best use in diagnosis. In addition to the information covered below, the manufacturer's instructions booklet provided with the tester should be read and clearly understood before attempting any test procedures.**

TEST EQUIPMENT

Jumper Wires

Jumper wires are simple, yet extremely valuable, pieces of test equipment. Jumper wires are merely wires that are used to bypass sections of a circuit. The simplest type of jumper wire is merely a length of multi-strand wire with an alligator clip at each end. Jumper wires are usually fabricated from lengths of standard automotive wire and whatever type of connector (alligator clip, spade connector or pin connector) that is required for the particular vehicle being tested. The well equipped tool box will have several different styles of jumper wires in several different lengths. Some jumper wires are made with three or more terminals coming from a common splice for special purpose testing. In cramped, hard-to-reach areas it is advisable to have insulated boots over the jumper wire terminals in order to prevent accidental grounding, sparks, and possible fire, especially when testing fuel system components.

Jumper wires are used primarily to locate open electrical circuits, on either the ground (-) side of the circuit or on the hot (+) side. If an electrical component fails to operate, connect the jumper wire between the component and a good ground. If the component operates only with the jumper installed, the ground circuit is open. If the ground circuit is good, but the component does not operate, the circuit between the power feed and component is open. You can sometimes connect the jumper wire directly from the battery to the hot terminal of the component, but first make sure the component uses 12 volts in operation. Some electrical components, such as fuel injectors, are designed to operate on about 4 volts and running 12 volts directly to the injector terminals can burn out the wiring. By inserting an in-line fuseholder between a set of test leads, a fused jumper wire can be used for bypassing open circuits. Use a 5 amp fuse to provide protection against voltage spikes. When in doubt, use a voltmeter to check the voltage input to the component and measure how much voltage is being applied normally. By moving the jumper wire

successively back from the lamp toward the power source, you can isolate the area of the circuit where the open is located. When the component stops functioning, or the power is cut off, the open is in the segment of wire between the jumper and the point previously tested.

✳✳CAUTION

Never use jumpers made from wire that is of lighter gauge than used in the circuit under test. If the jumper wire is of too small gauge, it may overheat and possibly melt. Never use jumpers to bypass high resistance loads in a circuit. Bypassing resistances, in effect, creates a short circuit which may, in turn, cause damage and fire. Never use a jumper for anything other than temporary bypassing of components in a circuit.

12 Volt Test Light

The 12 volt test light is used to check circuits and components while electrical current is flowing through them. It is used for voltage and ground tests. Twelve volt test lights come in different styles but all have three main parts; a ground clip, a probe, and a light. The most commonly used 12 volt test lights have pick-type probes. To use a 12 volt test light, connect the ground clip to a good ground and probe wherever necessary with the pick. The pick should be sharp so that it can penetrate wire insulation to make contact with the wire, without making a large hole in the insulation. The wrap-around light is handy in hard to reach areas or where it is difficult to support a wire to push a probe pick into it. To use the wrap around light, hook the wire to probed with the hook and pull the trigger. A small pick will be forced through the wire insulation into the wire core.

✳✳CAUTION

Do not use a test light to probe electronic ignition spark plug or coil wires. Never use a pick-type test light to probe wiring on computer controlled systems unless specifically instructed to do so. Any wire insulation that is pierced by the test light probe should be taped and sealed with silicone after testing.

Like the jumper wire, the 12 volt test light is used to isolate opens in circuits. But, whereas the jumper wire is used to bypass the open to operate the load, the 12 volt test light is used to locate the presence of voltage in a circuit. If the test light glows, you know that there is power up to that point; if the 12 volt test light does not glow when its probe is inserted into the wire or connector, you know that there is an open circuit (no power). Move the test light in successive steps back toward the power source until the light in the handle does glow. When it does glow, the open is between the probe and point previously probed.

➡️**The test light does not detect that 12 volts (or any particular amount of voltage) is present; it only detects that some voltage is present. It is advisable before using the test light to touch its terminals across the battery posts to make sure the light is operating properly.**

Self-Powered Test Light

The self-powered test light usually contains a 1.5 volt penlight battery. One type of self-powered test light is similar in design to the 12 volt test light. This type has both the battery and the light in the handle and pick-type probe tip. The second type has the light toward the open tip, so that the light illuminates the contact point. The self-powered test light is dual purpose piece of test equipment. It can be used to test for either open or short circuits when power is isolated from the circuit (continuity test). A powered test light should not be used on any computer controlled system or component unless specifically instructed to do so. Many engine sensors can be destroyed by even this small amount of voltage applied directly to the terminals.

Open Circuit Testing

To use the self-powered test light to check for open circuits, first isolate the circuit from the vehicle's 12 volt power source by disconnecting the battery or wiring harness connector. Connect the test light ground clip to a good ground and probe sections of the circuit sequentially with the test light. (start from either end of the circuit). If the light is out, the open is between the probe and the circuit ground. If the light is on, the open is between the probe and end of the circuit toward the power source.

Short Circuit Testing

By isolating the circuit both from power and from ground, and using a self-powered test light, you can check for shorts to ground in the circuit. Isolate the circuit from power and ground. Connect the test light ground clip to a good ground and probe any easy-to-reach test point in the circuit. If the light comes on, there is a short somewhere in the circuit. To isolate the short, probe a test point at either end of the isolated circuit (the light should be on). Leave the test light probe connected and open connectors, switches, remove parts, etc., sequentially, until the light goes out. When the light goes out, the short is between the last circuit component opened and the previous circuit opened.

➡**The 1.5 volt battery in the test light does not provide much current. A weak battery may not provide enough power to illuminate the test light even when a complete circuit is made (especially if there are high resistances in the circuit). Always make sure that the test battery is strong. To check the battery, briefly touch the ground clip to the probe; if the light glows brightly the battery is strong enough for testing. Never use a self-powered test light to perform checks for opens or shorts when power is applied to the electrical system under test. The 12 volt vehicle power will quickly burn out the 1.5 volt light bulb in the test light.**

Voltmeter

A voltmeter is used to measure voltage at any point in a circuit, or to measure the voltage drop across any part of a circuit. It can also be used to check continuity in a wire or circuit by indicating current flow from one end to the other. Voltmeters usually have various scales on the meter dial and a selector switch to allow the selection of different voltages. The voltmeter has a positive and a negative lead. To avoid damage to the meter, always connect the negative lead to the negative (-) side of circuit (to ground or nearest the ground side of the circuit) and connect the positive lead to the positive (+) side of the circuit (to the power source or the nearest power source). Note that the negative voltmeter lead will always be black and that the positive voltmeter will always be some color other than black (usually red). Depending on how the voltmeter is connected into the circuit, it has several uses.

A voltmeter can be connected either in parallel or in series with a circuit and it has a very high resistance to current flow. When connected in parallel, only a small amount of current will flow through the voltmeter current path; the rest will flow through the normal circuit current path and the circuit will work normally. When the voltmeter is connected in series with a circuit, only a small amount of current can flow through the circuit. The circuit will not work properly, but the voltmeter reading will show if the circuit is complete or not.

Available Voltage Measurement

Set the voltmeter selector switch to the 20V position and connect the meter negative lead to the negative post of the battery. Connect the positive meter lead to the positive post of the battery and turn the ignition switch ON to provide a load. Read the voltage on the meter or digital display. A well charged battery should register over 12 volts. If the meter reads below 11.5 volts, the battery power may be insufficient to operate the electrical system properly. This test determines voltage available from the battery and should be the first step in any electrical trouble diagnosis procedure. Many electrical problems, especially on computer controlled systems, can be caused by a low state of charge in the battery. Excessive corrosion at the battery cable terminals can cause a poor contact that will prevent proper charging and full battery current flow.

Normal battery voltage is 12 volts when fully charged. When the battery is supplying current to one or more circuits it is said to be 'under load'. When everything is off the electrical system is under a 'no-load' condition. A fully charged battery may show about 12.5 volts at no load; will drop to 12 volts under medium load; and will drop even lower under heavy load. If the battery is partially discharged the voltage decrease under heavy load may be excessive, even though the battery shows 12 volts or more at no load. When allowed to discharge further, the battery's available voltage under load will decrease more severely. For this reason, it is important that the battery be fully charged during all testing procedures to avoid errors in diagnosis and incorrect test results.

Voltage Drop

When current flows through a resistance, the voltage beyond the resistance is reduced (the larger the current, the greater the reduction in voltage). When no current is flowing, there is no voltage drop because there is no current flow. All points in the circuit which are connected to the power source are at the same voltage as the power source. The total voltage drop always equals the total source voltage. In a long circuit with many connectors, a series of small, unwanted voltage drops due to corrosion at the connectors can add up to a total loss of voltage which impairs the operation of the normal loads in the circuit.

INDIRECT COMPUTATION OF VOLTAGE DROPS

1. Set the voltmeter selector switch to the 20 volt position.
2. Connect the meter negative lead to a good ground.
3. Probe all resistances in the circuit with the positive meter lead.
4. Operate the circuit in all modes and observe the voltage readings.

DIRECT MEASUREMENT OF VOLTAGE DROPS

1. Set the voltmeter switch to the 20 volt position.
2. Connect the voltmeter negative lead to the ground side of the resistance load to be measured.
3. Connect the positive lead to the positive side of the resistance or load to be measured.
4. Read the voltage drop directly on the 20 volt scale.

Too high a voltage indicates too high a resistance. If, for example, a blower motor runs too slowly, you can determine if there is too high a resistance in the resistor pack. By taking voltage drop readings in all parts of the circuit, you can isolate the problem. Too low a voltage drop indicates too low a resistance. If, for example, a blower motor runs too fast in the MED and/or LOW position, the problem can be isolated in the resistor pack by taking voltage drop readings in all parts of the circuit to locate a possibly shorted resistor. The maximum allowable voltage drop under load is critical, especially if there is more than one high resistance problem in a circuit because all voltage drops are cumulative. A small drop is normal due to the resistance of the conductors.

HIGH RESISTANCE TESTING

1. Set the voltmeter selector switch to the 4 volt position.
2. Connect the voltmeter positive lead to the positive post of the battery.
3. Turn on the headlights and heater blower to provide a load.
4. Probe various points in the circuit with the negative voltmeter lead.
5. Read the voltage drop on the 4 volt scale. Some average maximum allowable voltage drops are:

    FUSE PANEL: 7 volts
    IGNITION SWITCH: 5 volts
    HEADLIGHT SWITCH: 7 volts
    IGNITION COIL (+): 5 volts
    ANY OTHER LOAD: 1.3 volts

➡**Voltage drops are all measured while a load is operating; without current flow, there will be no voltage drop.**

Ohmmeter

The ohmmeter is designed to read resistance (ohms) in a circuit or component. Although there are several different styles of ohmmeters, all will usually have a selector switch which permits the measurement of different ranges of resistance (usually the selector switch allows the multiplication of the meter reading by 10, 100, 1,000, and 10,000). A calibration knob allows the meter to be set at zero for accurate measurement. Since all ohmmeters are powered by an internal battery (usually 9 volts), the ohmmeter can be used as a self-powered test light. When the ohmmeter is connected, current from the ohmmeter flows through the circuit or component

being tested. Since the ohmmeter's internal resistance and voltage are known values, the amount of current flow through the meter depends on the resistance of the circuit or component being tested.

The ohmmeter can be used to perform continuity test for opens or shorts (either by observation of the meter needle or as a self-powered test light), and to read actual resistance in a circuit. It should be noted that the ohmmeter is used to check the resistance of a component or wire while there is no voltage applied to the circuit. Current flow from an outside voltage source (such as the vehicle battery) can damage the ohmmeter, so the circuit or component should be isolated from the vehicle electrical system before any testing is done. Since the ohmmeter uses its own voltage source, either lead can be connected to any test point.

➡**When checking diodes or other solid state components, the ohmmeter leads can only be connected one way in order to measure current flow in a single direction. Make sure the positive (+) and negative (-) terminal connections are as described in the test procedures to verify the one-way diode operation.**

In using the meter for making continuity checks, do not be concerned with the actual resistance readings. Zero resistance, or any resistance readings, indicate continuity in the circuit. Infinite resistance indicates an open in the circuit. A high resistance reading where there should be none indicates a problem in the circuit. Checks for short circuits are made in the same manner as checks for open circuits except that the circuit must be isolated from both power and normal ground. Infinite resistance indicates no continuity to ground, while zero resistance indicates a dead short to ground.

RESISTANCE MEASUREMENT

The batteries in an ohmmeter will weaken with age and temperature, so the ohmmeter must be calibrated or 'zeroed' before taking measurements. To zero the meter, place the selector switch in its lowest range and touch the two ohmmeter leads together. Turn the calibration knob until the meter needle is exactly on zero.

➡**All analog (needle) type ohmmeters must be zeroed before use, but some digital ohmmeter models are automatically calibrated when the switch is turned on. Self-calibrating digital ohmmeters do not have an adjusting knob, but its a good idea to check for a zero readout before use by touching the leads together. All computer controlled systems require the use of a digital ohmmeter with at least 10 megohms impedance for testing. Before any test procedures are attempted, make sure the ohmmeter used is compatible with the electrical system or damage to the on-board computer could result.**

To measure resistance, first isolate the circuit from the vehicle power source by disconnecting the battery cables or the harness connector. Make sure the key is OFF when disconnecting any components or the battery. Where necessary, also isolate at least one side of the circuit to be checked to avoid reading parallel resistances. Parallel circuit resistances will always give a lower reading than the actual resistance of either of the branches. When measuring the resistance of parallel circuits, the total resistance will always be lower than the smallest resistance in the circuit. Connect the meter leads to both sides of the circuit (wire or component) and read the actual measured ohms on the meter scale. Make sure the selector switch is set to the proper ohm scale for the circuit being tested to avoid misreading the ohmmeter test value.

✳✳WARNING

Never use an ohmmeter with power applied to the circuit. Like the self-powered test light, the ohmmeter is designed to operate on its own power supply. The normal 12 volt automotive electrical system current could damage the meter!

Ammeters

An ammeter measures the amount of current flowing through a circuit in units called amperes or amps. Amperes are units of electron flow which indicate how fast the electrons are flowing through the circuit. Since Ohms Law dictates that current flow in a circuit is equal to the circuit voltage divided by the total circuit resistance, increasing voltage also increases the current level (amps). Likewise, any decrease in resistance will increase the amount of amps in a circuit. At normal operating voltage, most circuits have a characteristic amount of amperes, called 'current draw' which can be measured using an ammeter. By referring to a specified current draw rating, measuring the amperes, and comparing the two values, one can determine what is happening within the circuit to aid in diagnosis. An open circuit, for example, will not allow any current to flow so the ammeter reading will be zero. More current flows through a heavily loaded circuit or when the charging system is operating.

An ammeter is always connected in series with the circuit being tested. All of the current that normally flows through the circuit must also flow through the ammeter; if there is any other path for the current to follow, the ammeter reading will not be accurate. The ammeter itself has very little resistance to current flow and therefore will not affect the circuit, but it will measure current draw only when the circuit is closed and electricity is flowing. Excessive current draw can blow fuses and drain the battery, while a reduced current draw can cause motors to run slowly, lights to dim and other components to not operate properly. The ammeter can help diagnose these conditions by locating the cause of the high or low reading.

Multimeters

Different combinations of test meters can be built into a single unit designed for specific tests. Some of the more common combination test devices are known as Volt/Amp testers, Tach/Dwell meters, or Digital Multimeters. The Volt/Amp tester is used for charging system, starting system or battery tests and consists of a voltmeter, an ammeter and a variable resistance carbon pile. The voltmeter will usually have at least two ranges for use with 6, 12 and 24 volt systems. The ammeter also has more than one range for testing various levels of battery loads and starter current draw and the carbon pile can be adjusted to offer different amounts of resistance. The Volt/Amp tester has heavy leads to carry large amounts of current and many later models have an inductive ammeter pickup that clamps around the wire to simplify test

connections. On some models, the ammeter also has a zero-center scale to allow testing of charging and starting systems without switching leads or polarity. A digital multimeter is a voltmeter, ammeter and ohmmeter combined in an instrument which gives a digital readout. These are often used when testing solid state circuits because of their high input impedance (usually 10 megohms or more).

The tach/dwell meter combines a tachometer and a dwell (cam angle) meter and is a specialized kind of voltmeter. The tachometer scale is marked to show engine speed in rpm and the dwell scale is marked to show degrees of distributor shaft rotation. In most electronic ignition systems, dwell is determined by the control unit, but the dwell meter can also be used to check the duty cycle (operation) of some electronic engine control systems. Some tach/dwell meters are powered by an internal battery, while others take their power from the car battery in use. The battery powered testers usually require calibration much like an ohmmeter before testing.

Special Test Equipment

A variety of diagnostic tools are available to help troubleshoot and repair computerized engine control systems. The most sophisticated of these devices are the console type engine analyzers that usually occupy a garage service bay, but there are several types of aftermarket electronic testers available that will allow quick circuit tests of the engine control system by plugging directly into a special connector located in the engine compartment or under the dashboard. Several tool and equipment manufacturers offer simple, hand held testers that measure various circuit voltage levels on command to check all system components for proper operation. Although these testers usually cost about $300-500, consider that the average computer control unit (or ECM) can cost just as much and the money saved by not replacing perfectly good sensors or components in an attempt to correct a problem could justify the purchase price of a special diagnostic tester the first time it's used.

These computerized testers can allow quick and easy test measurements while the engine is operating or while the car is being driven. In addition, the on-board computer memory can be read to access any stored trouble codes; in effect allowing the computer to tell you where it hurts and aid trouble diagnosis by pinpointing exactly which circuit or component is malfunctioning. In the same manner, repairs can be tested to make sure the problem has been corrected. The biggest advantage these special testers have is their relatively easy hookups that minimize or eliminate the chances of making the wrong connections and getting false voltage readings or damaging the computer accidentally.

➡**It should be remembered that these testers check voltage levels in circuits; they don't detect mechanical problems or failed components if the circuit voltage falls within the preprogrammed limits stored in the tester PROM unit. Also, most of the hand held testers are designed to work only on one or two systems made by a specific manufacturer.**

A variety of aftermarket testers are available to help diagnose different computerized control systems. Owatonna Tool Company (OTC), for example, markets a device called the OTC Monitor which plugs directly into the assembly line diagnostic link (ALDL). The OTC tester makes diagnosis a simple matter of pressing the correct buttons and, by changing the internal PROM or inserting a different diagnosis cartridge, it will work on any model from full size to subcompact, over a wide range of years. An adapter is supplied with the tester to allow connection to all types of ALDL links, regardless of the number of pin terminals used. By inserting an updated PROM into the OTC tester, it can be easily updated to diagnose any new modifications of computerized control systems.

Wiring Harnesses

The average automobile contains about ½ mile of wiring, with hundreds of individual connections. To protect the many wires from damage and to keep them from becoming a confusing tangle, they are organized into bundles, enclosed in plastic or taped together and called wire harnesses. Different wiring harnesses serve different parts of the vehicle. Individual wires are color coded to help trace them through a harness where sections are hidden from view.

A loose or corroded connection or a replacement wire that is too small for the circuit will add extra resistance and an additional voltage drop to the circuit. A ten percent voltage drop can result in slow or erratic motor operation, for example, even though the circuit is complete. Automotive wiring or circuit conductors can be in any one of three forms:

1. Single strand wire
2. Multi-strand wire
3. Printed circuitry

Single strand wire has a solid metal core and is usually used inside such components as alternators, motors, relays and other devices. Multi-strand wire has a core made of many small strands of wire twisted together into a single conductor. Most of the wiring in an automotive electrical system is made up of multi-strand wire, either as a single conductor or grouped together in a harness. All wiring is color coded on the insulator, either as a solid color or as a colored wire with an identification stripe. A printed circuit is a thin film of copper or other conductor that is printed on an insulator backing. Occasionally, a printed circuit is sandwiched between two sheets of plastic for more protection and flexibility. A complete printed circuit, consisting of conductors, insulating material and connectors for lamps or other components is called a printed circuit board. Printed circuitry is used in place of individual wires or harnesses in places where space is limited, such as behind instrument panels.

Wire Gauge

Since computer controlled automotive electrical systems are very sensitive to changes in resistance, the selection of properly sized wires is critical when systems are repaired. The wire gauge number is an expression of the cross section area of the conductor. The most common system for expressing wire size is the American Wire Gauge (AWG) system.

Wire cross section area is measured in circular mils. A mil is ¹/₁₀₀₀ (0.001 inch); a circular mil is the area of a circle one mil in diameter. For example, a conductor ¼ inch in diameter is 0.250 inch or 250 mils. The circular mil cross section area of the wire is 250 squared (250^2) or 62,500 circular mils. Imported car models usually use metric wire gauge

designations, which is simply the cross section area of the conductor in square millimeters (mm^2).

Gauge numbers are assigned to conductors of various cross section areas. As gauge number increases, area decreases and the conductor becomes smaller. A 5 gauge conductor is smaller than a 1 gauge conductor and a 10 gauge is smaller than a 5 gauge. As the cross section area of a conductor decreases, resistance increases and so does the gauge number. A conductor with a higher gauge number will carry less current than a conductor with a lower gauge number.

➡**Gauge wire size refers to the size of the conductor, not the size of the complete wire. It is possible to have two wires of the same gauge with different diameters because one may have thicker insulation than the other.**

12 volt automotive electrical systems generally use 10, 12, 14, 16 and 18 gauge wire. Main power distribution circuits and larger accessories usually use 10 and 12 gauge wire. Battery cables are usually 4 or 6 gauge, although 1 and 2 gauge wires are occasionally used. Wire length must also be considered when making repairs to a circuit. As conductor length increases, so does resistance. An 18 gauge wire, for example, can carry a 10 amp load for 10 feet without excessive voltage drop; however if a 15 foot wire is required for the same 10 amp load, it must be a 16 gauge wire.

An electrical schematic shows the electrical current paths when a circuit is operating properly. It is essential to understand how a circuit works before trying to figure out why it doesn't. Schematics break the entire electrical system down into individual circuits and show only one particular circuit. In a schematic, no attempt is made to represent wiring and components as they physically appear on the vehicle; switches and other components are shown as simply as possible. Face views of harness connectors show the cavity or terminal locations in all multi-pin connectors to help locate test points.

If you need to backprobe a connector while it is on the component, the order of the terminals must be mentally reversed. The wire color code can help in this situation, as well as a keyway, lock tab or other reference mark.

WIRING REPAIR

▶ **See Figure 1**

Soldering is a quick, efficient method of joining metals permanently. Everyone who has the occasion to make wiring

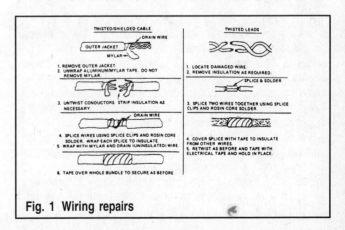

Fig. 1 Wiring repairs

repairs should know how to solder. Electrical connections that are soldered are far less likely to come apart and will conduct electricity much better than connections that are only 'pig-tailed' together. The most popular (and preferred) method of soldering is with an electrical soldering gun. Soldering irons are available in many sizes and wattage ratings. Irons with higher wattage ratings deliver higher temperatures and recover lost heat faster. A small soldering iron rated for no more than 50 watts is recommended, especially on electrical systems where excess heat can damage the components being soldered.

There are three ingredients necessary for successful soldering; proper flux, good solder and sufficient heat. A soldering flux is necessary to clean the metal of tarnish, prepare it for soldering and to enable the solder to spread into tiny crevices. When soldering, always use a resin flux or resin core solder which is non-corrosive and will not attract moisture once the job is finished. Other types of flux (acid core) will leave a residue that will attract moisture and cause the wires to corrode. Tin is a unique metal with a low melting point. In a molten state, it dissolves and alloys easily with many metals. Solder is made by mixing tin with lead. The most common proportions are 40/60, 50/50 and 60/40, with the percentage of tin listed first. Low priced solders usually contain less tin, making them very difficult for a beginner to use because more heat is required to melt the solder. A common solder is 40/60 which is well suited for all-around general use, but 60/40 melts easier, has more tin f or a better joint and is preferred for electrical work.

Soldering Techniques

Successful soldering requires that the metals to be joined be heated to a temperature that will melt the solder, usually 360-460°F (182-238°C). Contrary to popular belief, the purpose of the soldering iron is not to melt the solder itself, but to heat the parts being soldered to a temperature high enough to melt the solder when it is touched to the work. Melting flux-cored solder on the soldering iron will usually destroy the effectiveness of the flux.

➡**Soldering tips are made of copper for good heat conductivity, but must be 'tinned' regularly for quick transference of heat to the project and to prevent the solder from sticking to the iron. To 'tin' the iron, simply heat it and touch the flux-cored solder to the tip; the solder will flow over the hot tip. Wipe the excess off with a clean rag, but be careful as the iron will be hot.**

After some use, the tip may become pitted. If so, simply dress the tip smooth with a smooth file and 'tin' the tip again. An old saying holds that 'metals well cleaned are half soldered.' Flux-cored solder will remove oxides but rust, bits of insulation and oil or grease must be removed with a wire brush or emery cloth. For maximum strength in soldered parts, the joint must start off clean and tight. Weak joints will result in gaps too wide for the solder to bridge.

If a separate soldering flux is used, it should be brushed or swabbed on only those areas that are to be soldered. Most solders contain a core of flux and separate fluxing is unnecessary. Hold the work to be soldered firmly. It is best to solder on a wooden board, because a metal vise will only rob the piece to be soldered of heat and make it difficult to melt the solder. Hold the soldering tip with the broadest face against the work to be soldered. Apply solder under the tip close to the work, using enough solder to give a heavy film between the iron and the piece being soldered, while moving slowly and making sure the solder melts properly. Keep the work level or the solder will run to the lowest part and favor the thicker parts, because these require more heat to melt the solder. If the soldering tip overheats (the solder coating on the face of the tip burns up), it should be retinned. Once the soldering is completed, let the soldered joint stand until cool. Tape and seal all soldered wire splices after the repair has cooled.

Wire Harness and Connectors

The on-board computer (ECM) wire harness electrically connects the control unit to the various solenoids, switches and sensors used by the control system. Most connectors in the engine compartment or otherwise exposed to the elements are protected against moisture and dirt which could create oxidation and deposits on the terminals. This protection is important because of the very low voltage and current levels used by the computer and sensors. All connectors have a lock which secures the male and female terminals together, with a secondary lock holding the seal and terminal into the connector. Both terminal locks must be released when disconnecting ECM connectors.

These special connectors are weather-proof and all repairs require the use of a special terminal and the tool required to service it. This tool is used to remove the pin and sleeve terminals. If removal is attempted with an ordinary pick, there is a good chance that the terminal will be bent or deformed. Unlike standard blade type terminals, these terminals cannot be straightened once they are bent. Make certain that the connectors are properly seated and all of the sealing rings in place when connecting leads. On some models, a hinge-type flap provides a backup or secondary locking feature for the terminals. Most secondary locks are used to improve the connector reliability by retaining the terminals if the small terminal lock tangs are not positioned properly.

Molded-on connectors require complete replacement of the connection. This means splicing a new connector assembly into the harness. All splices in on-board computer systems should be soldered to insure proper contact. Use care when probing the connections or replacing terminals in them as it is possible to short between opposite terminals. If this happens to the wrong terminal pair, it is possible to damage certain components. Always use jumper wires between connectors for circuit checking and never probe through weatherproof seals.

Open circuits are often difficult to locate by sight because corrosion or terminal misalignment are hidden by the connectors. Merely wiggling a connector on a sensor or in the wiring harness may correct the open circuit condition. This should always be considered when an open circuit or a failed sensor is indicated. Intermittent problems may also be caused by oxidized or loose connections. When using a circuit tester for diagnosis, always probe connections from the wire side. Be careful not to damage sealed connectors with test probes.

All wiring harnesses should be replaced with identical parts, using the same gauge wire and connectors. When signal wires are spliced into a harness, use wire with high temperature insulation only. With the low voltage and current levels found in the system, it is important that the best possible connection at all wire splices be made by soldering the splices together. It is seldom necessary to replace a complete harness. If replacement is necessary, pay close attention to insure proper harness routing. Secure the harness with suitable plastic wire clamps to prevent vibrations from causing the harness to wear in spots or contact any hot components.

➡**Weatherproof connectors cannot be replaced with standard connectors. Instructions are provided with replacement connector and terminal packages. Some wire harnesses have mounting indicators (usually pieces of colored tape) to mark where the harness is to be secured.**

In making wiring repairs, it's important that you always replace damaged wires with wires that are the same gauge as the wire being replaced. The heavier the wire, the smaller the gauge number. Wires are color-coded to aid in identification and whenever possible the same color coded wire should be used for replacement. A wire stripping and crimping tool is necessary to install solderless terminal connectors. Test all crimps by pulling on the wires; it should not be possible to pull the wires out of a good crimp.

Wires which are open, exposed or otherwise damaged are repaired by simple splicing. Where possible, if the wiring harness is accessible and the damaged place in the wire can be located, it is best to open the harness and check for all possible damage. In an inaccessible harness, the wire must be bypassed with a new insert, usually taped to the outside of the old harness.

When replacing fusible links, be sure to use fusible link wire, NOT ordinary automotive wire. Make sure the fusible segment is of the same gauge and construction as the one being replaced and double the stripped end when crimping the terminal connector for a good contact. The melted (open) fusible link segment of the wiring harness should be cut off as close to the harness as possible, then a new segment spliced in as described. In the case of a damaged fusible link that feeds two harness wires, the harness connections should be replaced with two fusible link wires so that each circuit will have its own separate protection.

➡**Most of the problems caused in the wiring harness are due to bad ground connections. Always check all vehicle ground connections for corrosion or looseness before performing any power feed checks to eliminate the chance of a bad ground affecting the circuit.**

Repairing Hard Shell Connectors

Unlike molded connectors, the terminal contacts in hard shell connectors can be replaced. Weatherproof hard-shell connectors with the leads molded into the shell have non-replaceable terminal ends. Replacement usually involves the use of a special terminal removal tool that depress the locking tangs (barbs) on the connector terminal and allow the connector to be removed from the rear of the shell. The connector shell should be replaced if it shows any evidence of burning, melting, cracks, or breaks. Replace individual terminals that are burnt, corroded, distorted or loose.

➡**The insulation crimp must be tight to prevent the insulation from sliding back on the wire when the wire is pulled. The insulation must be visibly compressed under the crimp tabs, and the ends of the crimp should be turned in for a firm grip on the insulation.**

The wire crimp must be made with all wire strands inside the crimp. The terminal must be fully compressed on the wire strands with the ends of the crimp tabs turned in to make a firm grip on the wire. Check all connections with an ohmmeter to insure a good contact. There should be no measurable resistance between the wire and the terminal when connected.

Mechanical Test Equipment

Vacuum Gauge

Most gauges are graduated in inches of mercury (in. Hg.), although a device called a manometer reads vacuum in inches of water (in. Hg.). The normal vacuum reading usually varies between 18 and 22 in.Hg at sea level. To test engine vacuum, the vacuum gauge must be connected to a source of manifold vacuum. Many engines have a plug in the intake manifold which can be removed and replaced with an adapter fitting. Connect the vacuum gauge to the fitting with a suitable rubber hose or, if no manifold plug is available, connect the vacuum gauge to any device using manifold vacuum, such as EGR valves, etc. The vacuum gauge can be used to determine if enough vacuum is reaching a component to allow its actuation.

Hand Vacuum Pump

Small, hand-held vacuum pumps come in a variety of designs. Most have a built-in vacuum gauge and allow the component to be tested without removing it from the vehicle. Operate the pump lever or plunger to apply the correct amount of vacuum required for the test specified in the diagnosis routines. The level of vacuum in inches of Mercury (in.Hg) is indicated on the pump gauge. For some testing, an additional vacuum gauge may be necessary.

Intake manifold vacuum is used to operate various systems and devices on late model vehicles. To correctly diagnose and solve problems in vacuum control systems, a vacuum source is necessary for testing. In some cases, vacuum can be taken from the intake manifold when the engine is running, but vacuum is normally provided by a hand vacuum pump. These hand vacuum pumps have a built-in vacuum gauge that allow testing while the device is still attached to the component. For some tests, an additional vacuum gauge may be necessary.

Fuse Link

The fuse link is a short length of special, Hypalon (high temperature) insulated wire, integral with the engine compartment wiring harness and should not be confused with standard wire. It is several wire gauges smaller than the circuit which it protects. Under no circumstances should a fuse link replacement repair be made using a length of standard wire cut from bulk stock or from another wiring harness.

To repair any blown fuse link use the following procedure:

1. Determine which circuit is damaged, its location and the cause of the open fuse link. If the damaged fuse link is one of three fed by a common No. 10 or 12 gauge feed wire, determine the specific affected circuit.

2. Disconnect the negative battery cable.

3. Cut the damaged fuse link from the wiring harness and discard it. If the fuse link is one of three circuits fed by a single feed wire, cut it out of the harness at each splice end and discard it.

4. Identify and procure the proper fuse link and butt connectors for attaching the fuse link to the harness.

5. To repair any fuse link in a 3-link group with one feed:

a. After cutting the open link out of the harness, cut each of the remaining undamaged fuse links close to the feed wire weld.

b. Strip approximately ½ inch (13mm) of insulation from the detached ends of the two good fuse links, Then insert two wire ends into one end of a butt connector and carefully push one stripped end of the replacement fuse link into the same end of the butt connector and crimp all three firmly together.

➡**Care must be taken when fitting the three fuse links into the butt connector as the internal diameter is a snug fit for three wires. Make sure to use a proper crimping tool. Pliers, side cutter, etc. will not apply the proper crimp to retain the wires and withstand a pull test.**

c. After crimping the butt connector to the three fuse links, cut the weld portion from the feed wire and strip approximately ½ inch (13mm) of insulation from the cut end. Insert the stripped end into the open end of the butt connector and crimp very firmly.

d. To attach the remaining end of the replacement fuse link, strip approximately ½ inch (13mm) of insulation from the wire end of the circuit from which the blown fuse link was removed, and firmly crimp a butt connector or equivalent to the stripped wire. Then, insert the end of the replacement link into the other end of the butt connector and crimp firmly.

e. Using rosin core solder with a consistency of 60 percent tin and 40 percent lead, solder the connectors and the wires at the repairs and insulate with electrical tape.

6. To replace any fuse link on a single circuit in a harness, cut out the damaged portion, strip approximately ½ inch (13mm) of insulation from the two wire ends and attach the appropriate replacement fuse link to the stripped wire ends with two proper size butt connectors. Solder the connectors and wires and insulate with tape.

7. To repair any fuse link which has an eyelet terminal on one end such as the charging circuit, cut off the open fuse link behind the weld, strip approximately ½ inch (13mm) of insulation from the cut end and attach the appropriate new eyelet fuse link to the cut stripped wire with an appropriate size butt connector. Solder the connectors and wires at the repair and insulate with tape.

8. Connect the negative battery cable to the battery and test the system for proper operation.

➡**Do not mistake a resistor wire for a fuse link. The resistor wire is generally longer and has print stating, 'Resistor-don't cut or splice'.**

When attaching a single No. 16, 17, 18 or 20 gauge fuse link to a heavy gauge wire, always double the stripped wire end of the fuse link before inserting and crimping it into the butt connector for positive wire retention.

SUPPLEMENTAL RESTRAINT SYSTEM (AIR BAG)

General Information

SYSTEM OPERATION

The air bag system used on many vehicles is referred to as the Supplemental Inflatable Restraint (SIR) system. The air bag is designed to deploy when the vehicle is involved in a front end collision of sufficient force, up to 30 degrees off center line of the vehicle. The steering column still continues to be collapsible, the same as vehicle without an air bag.

The SIR system contains a deployment loop and a Diagnostic Energy Reserve Module (DERM). The function of the deployment loop is to supply current through the inflator module in the steering wheel, which will cause air bag deployment during a severe accident. The DERM supplies the necessary power, even if the battery has been damaged.

The deployment loop is made up of the arming sensors, coil assembly, inflator module and the discriminating sensors. The inflator module is only supplied sufficient current to deploy the air bag, when the arming sensors and at least 1 of the discriminating sensors close simultaneously. The function of the DERM is to supply the deployment loop a 36 Volt Loop

Reserve (36 VLR) to assure air bag deployment for seconds after ignition voltage is lost during an accident.

The DERM in conjunction with the resistors make it possible to detect circuit and component faults within the deployment loop. If the voltages monitored by the DERM fall outside expected limits, the DERM will indicate a fault code through the storage of a malfunction code and turning ON the INFLATABLE RESTRAINT lamp.

SYSTEM COMPONENTS

Diagnostic Energy Reserve Module (DERM)

The DERM is designed to perform 5 main functions. It maintains an energy reserve of 36 volts for several seconds. The DERM performs diagnostic monitoring of the SIR system and records malfunction codes, which can be obtained from a hand scan tool or the INFLATABLE RESTRAINT lamp. It warns the driver of a malfunction by controlling the INFLATABLE RESTRAINT lamp and keeps a record of the SIR system during a vehicle accident. Air bag deployment can still take place without the DERM connected, if adequate voltage is present at the arming sensor or dual pole sensor.

The DERM is connected to the system with a 24-way connector. This harness has a shorting bar across certain terminals in the contact areas. The shorting bar connects the INFLATABLE RESTRAINT lamp input to ground when the DERM is disconnected causing the lamp to light when the ignition switch is **ON**.

The DERM does not need to be replaced after each air bag deployment. After 4 deployments the DERM will register a Code 52. The Code 52 informs that the accident memory is full and the DERM must be replaced.

Inflatable Restraint Indicator

The INFLATABLE RESTRAINT indicator lamp is used to verify the DERM operation by flashing 7-9 times when the ignition is first turned **ON**. It is also used to warn the driver of a SIR malfunction. For certain tests it can provide diagnostic information by flashing the fault code when the fault code diagnostic mode is enabled.

Discriminating Sensor

There can be 2, 3 or 4 discriminating sensors. The forward, left or right sensors are located in the engine compartment. The passenger sensor, if equipped, is located behind the right side of the instrument panel or the center of the console. These sensors are calibrated to close with velocity changes which are severe enough to warrant air bag deployment.

The sensors consist of a sensing element, a normally open switch and a diagnostic resistor. The diagnostic resistor is wired in parallel with the switch within each sensor. They provide a ground for current to pass during normal non-deployment operation. The DERM measures this current to determine component faults.

When the arming sensor is located in the same housing as the passenger compartment discriminating sensor, the assembly is referred known as a dual sensor.

Arming Sensor

This sensor is found on vehicles with a single air bag.

➡**All sensors are specifically calibrated to each series vehicle and keyed to the mounting brackets. Great care must be taken to mount the correct sensors on the vehicle being serviced. The sensors, mounting brackets and wiring harness must never be modified from original design.**

The arming sensor is a protective switch in the power feed side of the deployment loop. It is calibrated to close at low level velocity changes. This insures that the inflator module is connect to the 36 VLR output of the DERM or ignition 1 voltage.

The sensor consists of a sensing element, normally open switch a diagnostic resistor and 2 steering diodes. The resistor is connected in parallel with the switch and allows a small amount of current to flow through the deployment loop during normal non-deployment operation. The DERM monitors this voltage to determine component faults.

The arming sensor is located in the same housing as the passenger compartment discriminating sensor. The assembly is referred to as the dual sensor and is located behind the right side of the instrument panel.

Dual Sensor

On single air bag vehicles so equipped, the dual sensor is a sensor that combines the arming sensor and the passenger compartment discriminating sensor into the same unit.

SIR Coil Assembly

The coil assembly consists of 2 current carrying coils. They are attached to the steering column and allow rotation of the steering wheel, while maintaining continuous contact of the deployment loop through the inflator module.

There is a shorting bar on the lower steering column connector, which connects the SIR coil to the SIR harness. The shorting bar shorts the circuit when the connector is disconnected. The circuit to the module is shorted in this way to help prevent unwanted deployment of the air bag, while performing service.

Inflator Module

The inflator module is located in the steering wheel hub under the vinyl trim. It includes the air bag, inflator and initiator. When the vehicle is in an accident, current is passed through the deployment loop. This current passing through the deployment loop ignites the squib in the inflator module. The gas produced rapidly inflates the air bag.

There is a shorting bar on the lower steering column connector, which connects the SIR coil to the SIR harness. The shorting bar shorts the circuit when the connector is disconnected. The circuit to the module is shorted in this way to help prevent unwanted deployment of the air bag, while performing service.

Resistor Module

The resistor module is in the SIR harness between the inflator module and DERM. This allows the DERM to monitor the deployment loop for faults and also allows the DERM to detect if the air bag has been deployed.

The resistors in the resistor module are balanced with the resistors in the arming and discriminating sensors to allow the DERM to monitor voltage drops across the circuits. These resistors also help reduce the possibility of unwanted deployment in the case of wiring harness damage.

Knee Bolster

The knee bolster is used to absorb energy and control the driver's forward movement during an accident by limiting leg movement.

Wiring Harness and Connectors

The wiring harness and connectors for the SIR system are of special design. Any wiring repairs should be done using tool kit J-38125, or equivalent. Always use the crimp and seal splice sleeves contained in this wiring repair kit. If damage is done to a component pigtail the component must be replaced.

SERVICE PRECAUTIONS

❋❋CAUTION

To avoid personal injury when servicing the SIR system or components in the immediate area, do not use electrical test equipment such as battery or A.C. powered voltmeter, ohmmeter, etc. or any type of tester other than specified. Do not use a non-powered probe tester. Instructions must be followed in detail to avoid deployment.

• Never disconnect any electrical connection with the ignition switch **ON** unless instructed to do so in a test.
• Always wear a grounded wrist static strap when servicing any control module or component labeled with a Electrostatic Discharge (ESD) sensitive device symbol.
• Avoid touching module connector pins.
• Leave new components and modules in the shipping package until ready to install them.
• Always touch a vehicle ground after sliding across a vehicle seat or walking across vinyl or carpeted floors to avoid static charge damage.
• The DERM can maintain sufficient voltage to cause a deployment for up to 10 minute, even if the battery is disconnected.
• Sensor mounting and wiring must never be modified.
• Never strike or jar a sensor, or deployment could occur.
• Never power up the SIR system when any sensor is not rigidly attached to the vehicle.
• Always carry an inflator module with the trim cover away from your body.
• Always place an inflator module on the workbench with the trim cover facing UP, away from loose objects.
• The inflator module is to be stored and shipped under DOT E-8236 flammable solid regulations.
• The inflator module must be deployed before it is discarded.
• After deployment the air bag surface may contain sodium hydroxide dust. Always wear gloves and safety glasses when handling the assembly. Wash hands with mild soap and water afterwards.
• A Code 51 requires, at minimum, replacement of the arming sensor, passenger compartment discriminating sensor, forward discriminating sensor and the inflator module.
• Any visible damage to sensors requires component replacement.
• Wire and connector repair must be performed using kit J-38125-A, or equivalent. Use special crimping tools, heat torch and seals.
• Absolutely no wire connector, or terminal repair is to be attempted on the arming sensor, passenger compartment discriminating sensor, forward discriminating sensor, inflator module or SIR coil assembly
• Never use a battery or A.C. powered test light or tester on the SIR system or deployment could occur.
• Never use an ohmmeter on the SIR system, unless instructed to do so, or deployment could occur.

• Never bake dry paint on vehicle or allow to exceed temperatures over 300°F, without disabling the SIR system and removing the inflator module.
• Sensors are not interchangeable between models or years.
• Never allow welding cables to lay on, near or across any vehicle electrical wiring.
• Avoid extension cords for power tools or droplights to lay on, near or across any vehicle electrical wiring.

DISARMING THE SYSTEM

▶ See Figure 2

1. Read all service precautions.
2. Turn the steering wheel so wheels are facing straight ahead and turn the ignition switch to **LOCK**.
3. Disconnect the negative battery cable and tape the end of cable to avoid possible terminal contact. Remove the SIR fuse.
4. Remove the left side sound insulator and courtesy lamp, as needed.
5. Remove the Connector Positive Assurance (CPA) lockpin on the yellow 2-way connector at the base of the steering column.
6. Disconnect the yellow 2-way connector.
7. The inflator module or steering can now be serviced.

ENABLING THE SYSTEM

1. Reconnect the yellow connector at the base of the steering column.
2. Reinstall the CPA lockpin on the yellow connector.
3. Install the sound insulator and lamp, if removed.
4. Install the SIR fuse and connect the battery cable.
5. Turn ignition switch to **ON** and check that the INFLATABLE RESTRAINT lamp flashes 7-9 times and then goes out.

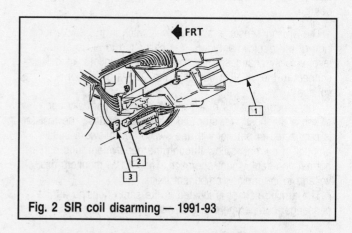

Fig. 2 SIR coil disarming — 1991-93

HEATER

Blower Motor

REMOVAL & INSTALLATION

1990

▶ See Figure 3

1. Disconnect the negative battery cable.
2. Disconnect the blower motor wiring harness.
3. Remove the blower motor cooling tube.
4. Remove the blower motor retaining screws and lift the blower motor and fan straight up and out of the upper case of the air conditioning module.

To install:

5. Clean and replace sealer as necessary.
6. Lower blower motor into upper case of the air conditioning module and tighten motor retaining screws.
7. Connect the blower motor cooling tube.
8. Connect blower motor wiring harness.
9. Connect the negative battery cable and check for proper motor operation.

1991-93

▶ See Figure 4

1. Disconnect the negative battery cable.

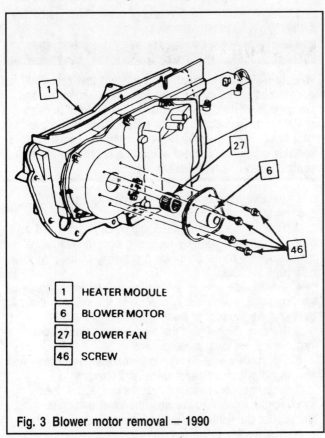

1	HEATER MODULE
6	BLOWER MOTOR
27	BLOWER FAN
46	SCREW

Fig. 3 Blower motor removal — 1990

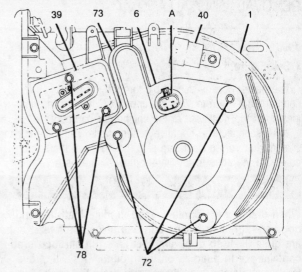

A CONNECTOR, BLOWER MOTOR
1 MODULE ASSEMBLY, HEATER AND AIR CONDITIONING EVAPORATOR
6 MOTOR ASSEMBLY, BLOWER
39 RESISTOR ASSEMBLY, BLOWER MOTOR
40 RELAY, AIR CONDITIONING POWER
72 BOLT/SCREW, BLOWER MOTOR, 1.9 N·m (17 LB. IN.)
73 SEAL, MOTOR
78 BOLT/SCREW, POWER MODULE, 1.9 N·m (17 LB. IN.)

Fig. 4 Blower motor removal — 1991-93

2. Remove the 4 retaining screws and remove the right side instrument panel sound insulator.
3. Disconnect the blower motor electrical connector.
4. Remove the right side hinge pillar trim finish panel by pulling it away from the front body hinge pillar.
5. Remove the screw from the secondary ECM bracket and swing the ECM module and bracket aside to provide access to the blower motor.
6. Remove the blower mounting screws, leaving the screw closest to the relay for last. Carefully lower the blower motor fan assembly and remove.

To install:

7. Align the blower motor and fan assembly, making sure the ECM module and retainer are out of the way, and carefully raise the assembly into place.
8. Insert and tighten the 3 mounting screws.
9. Swing the ECM module and bracket back into place and tighten the retaining screw to 17 inch lbs. (1.9 Nm).
10. Snap the right side hinge pillar trim finish panel into place on the front body hinge pillar.
11. Connect the blower motor electrical connector.
12. Insert the right side instrument panel sound insulator and attach the 4 retaining screws. Tighten the sound insulator retaining screws to 17 inch lbs. (1.9 Nm).
13. Connect the negative battery cable and check motor operation.

Heater Core

REMOVAL & INSTALLATION

1990
▶ **See Figure 5**

The heater core is accessible through the engine compartment, by removing the upper A/C housing assembly located in the right rear of the engine compartment.

1. Disconnect the negative battery cable. Drain the cooling system then, disconnect and plug the hoses at the heater core. Cut the hose to facilitate removal, if necessary.

❋❋CAUTION

When draining the coolant, keep in mind that cats and dogs are attracted by the ethylene glycol antifreeze, and are quite likely to drink any that is left in an uncovered container or in puddles on the ground. This will prove fatal in sufficient quantity. Always drain the coolant into a sealable container. Coolant should be reused unless it is contaminated or several years old.

2. Remove the blower motor assembly.
3. Remove the hood-to-cowl seal in the area of the A/C module.
4. Remove both halves of the air inlet screen (fresh air vent screen).
5. Remove the right side wiper arm.

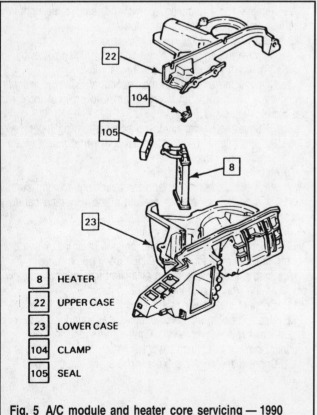

8	HEATER
22	UPPER CASE
23	LOWER CASE
104	CLAMP
105	SEAL

Fig. 5 A/C module and heater core servicing — 1990

6. Remove the module ground strap.
7. Disconnect and tag the connectors from the blower motor, resistor, blower relay and the thermostatic switch.
8. Remove the upper case half to lower case half cowl attaching screws.
9. Remove the heater core to case attaching screw and pull up firmly to release the core from the spring loaded clip. Remove the heater core from the vehicle.

   To install:
10. Line up the core base with the clip at the bottom of the case before you insert the core. The top retaining bracket will line up with the hole at the top of the core when properly seated.
11. Install the new core in the spring loaded clip and install the core to case mounting screws.
12. Install the case cover making sure that cover is completely seated in the sealer.
13. Install the upper case half to the lower half and tighten the mounting screws.
14. Install the leaf screen. Install the wiring harness in the retainer on the casing.
15. Connect the wiring and diagnostic connector at the casing.
16. Connect the heater hoses to the core and fill the cooling system.
17. Connect the negative battery cable, run the engine and check the heater operation.

1991-93
▶ **See Figure 6**

1. Disconnect the negative battery cable. Drain the cooling system into a suitable container.

❋❋CAUTION

When draining the coolant, keep in mind that cats and dogs are attracted by the ethylene glycol antifreeze, and are quite likely to drink any that is left in an uncovered container or in puddles on the ground. This will prove fatal in sufficient quantity. Always drain the coolant into a sealable container. Coolant should be reused unless it is contaminated or several years old.

2. Remove the screw holding the hose assembly to the cowl panel.
3. Release the quick connect fittings, on the inlet and outlet pipes of the heater core, by squeezing both release tabs at the base of the heater core tube and pulling on the pipe to disengage the fitting.
4. From inside vehicle, remove the four retaining screws on the upper right side sound insulator. Pull the insulator straight back until the two locator studs are disengaged.
5. Remove the nut from the shroud panel stud on the Instrument panel lower reinforcement.
6. Remove the screw from the instrument panel carrier and remove the instrument panel lower reinforcement.
7. Disconnect both vacuum harness connectors, then remove the connector halves from the lower evaporator case and position the harnesses out of the way.
8. Remove the right side hinge pillar finish (kick) panel by pulling it away from the body pillar.

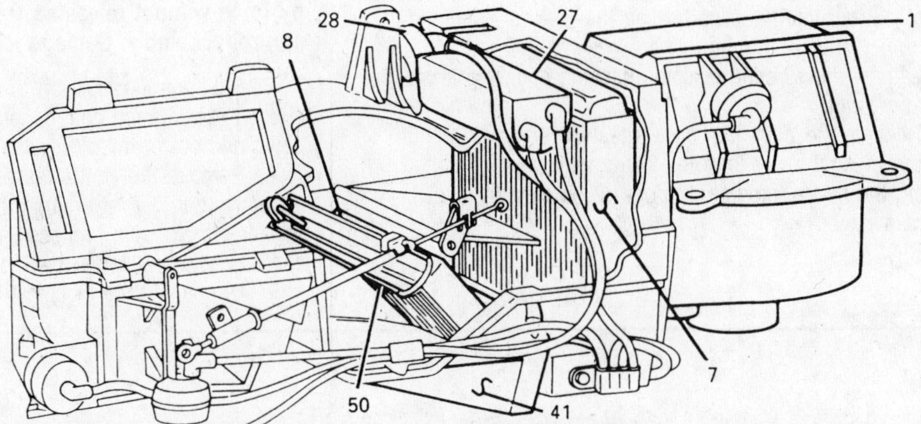

Fig. 6 A/C module and heater core servicing — 1991-93

1 MODULE ASSEMBLY, HEATER AND AIR CONDITIONING
   EVAPORATOR
7 EVAPORATOR, AIR CONDITIONING
8 CORE, HEATER

27 TANK, VACUUM
28 ACTUATOR, HEATER SHUT-OFF VALVE
41 CASE, LOWER EVAPORATOR MODULE
50 VALVE, HEATER SHUT-OFF

9. Roll the carpeting back enough to provide access to the lower area of the A/C module.

10. Remove the seven screws attaching the lower case to the module.

➡ **The forward center attaching screw may be difficult find. It is located almost directly below the lower right side heater core tube, the screw head is straight down from the A/C vacuum tank, using a ¼ in. drive 7mm socket with a swivel adaptor and short extension on a ratchet handle will aid in the removal.**

11. Remove the lower evaporator case.

12. Remove the heater core mounting straps and screws.

13. Carefully pull the heater core rearward, working the heater core tubes out of the seal.

To install:

14. Transfer the quick connect tabs to the new heater core.

15. Insert heater core into position, carefully pushing the tubes through the seal. Install the mounting straps and screws.

16. Install the lower evaporator case and tighten attaching screws evenly.

17. Fit the carpeting back into place.

18. Connect both vacuum connectors and install assembled connectors to the lower case.

19. With the instrument panel lower reinforcement held into position, install the nut to the shroud panel stud (tighten to 89 inch lbs.) and install the screw to the instrument panel carrier (tighten to 89 inch lbs.).

20. Snap the right side hinge pillar finish trim (kick) panel into place.

21. Slide the sound insulator forward into position engaging both locator tabs, and install the four attaching screws.

22. Hold the control valve and hose assembly into position, align the quick connect fitting tabs with the grooves in the fitting sleeve.

23. Push the sleeve into place on the heater core tube, then pull back on the sleeve to check for proper connection. Repeat for other connector.

24. Install the heater outlet pipe retaining screw. Fill with coolant, start engine and check for leaks and proper heater operation.

Control Head

REMOVAL & INSTALLATION

1990

1. Disconnect the negative battery cable.

2. Remove the air condition/radio console trim plate.

3. Remove the control head retaining screws.

4. Pull the assembly forward, disconnect the electrical and vacuum connections. Remove the temperature control cable.

5. Remove the control assembly from the vehicle.

6. To install, position the control head into the vehicle.

7. Install the temperature control cable.

8. Connect the electrical and vacuum connections and push the assembly rearward.

9. Install the air condition control retaining screws.

10. Install the console trim plate.

11. Connect the negative battery cable.

1991-93

▶ **See Figure 7**

1. Remove the steering column opening filler by removing the two screws near the lower edge of the filler. Pull down to unsnap the four integral clips holding the filler to instrument panel.

2. Loosen the steering column attaching nuts and lower the steering column.

3. Remove the eight trim plate attaching screws. Pull the trim plate straight away from the instrument panel carrier, snapping the seven integral clips out of the slots in the instrument panel.

4. Remove the temperature control cable push-on retainer and cable loop from the pin at the bottom of the control assembly.

➡**Do not attempt to remove the temperature control cable by force without releasing the lock tab in the slot of the control assembly. Damage to the lock tab will result.**

5. Squeeze the lock tab toward the left side of vehicle to release temperature control cable retainer and clip the retainer down and out of the slot in the control assembly.

6. Remove the control assembly attaching screws and pull assembly out just far enough to reach the electrical connectors, vacuum harness connectors and temperature control cable end at the back of the control assembly.

7. Disconnect the electrical connectors.

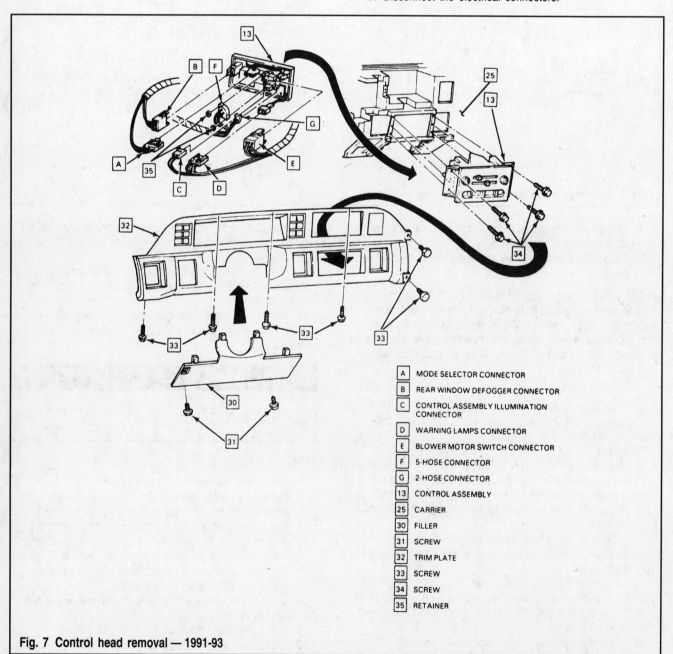

A	MODE SELECTOR CONNECTOR
B	REAR WINDOW DEFOGGER CONNECTOR
C	CONTROL ASSEMBLY ILLUMINATION CONNECTOR
D	WARNING LAMPS CONNECTOR
E	BLOWER MOTOR SWITCH CONNECTOR
F	5-HOSE CONNECTOR
G	2-HOSE CONNECTOR
13	CONTROL ASSEMBLY
25	CARRIER
30	FILLER
31	SCREW
32	TRIM PLATE
33	SCREW
34	SCREW
35	RETAINER

Fig. 7 Control head removal — 1991-93

8. Remove the two push-on retainers holding the circular 5-hose connector, and pull the connector off the vacuum switch.

9. Pull the 2-hose connector off the hot water valve vacuum switch, and remove the control assembly.

To install:

10. Install the vacuum harness assembly and push-on retainers to the back of the control assembly.

11. Connect the electrical connectors to the back of control head assembly.

12. Install the temperature control cable retainer and clip the retainer in the slot in the control assembly.

AIR CONDITIONER

→ **Refer to Section 1 for proper Discharging, etc. of the air conditioning system.**

Compressor

▶ **See Figure 8**

REMOVAL & INSTALLATION

1. Discharge the A/C system following all precautions. Refer to Section 1 for discharging the A/C system.

2. Remove fitting block (coupled hose assembly) bolt at rear of compressor.

3. Remove mounting bracket bolts, nuts, washers and spacers. It may be necessary to remove the front bracket.

4. Remove the drive belt.

5. Remove the compressor assembly.

6. To install, use new O-rings lubricated with refrigerant oil.

7. Install the compressor.

8. Install the drive belt.

9. Install the mounting bracket and bolts, nuts, washers and spacers.

10. Install the fitting block, new O-ring seal and bolt at the rear of the compressor.

11. Evacuate and recharge system. Inspect for proper operation and/or system leaks.

Condenser

REMOVAL & INSTALLATION

▶ **See Figure 9**

1. Discharge the A/C system following all precaution.

2. Disconnect coupled hose and liquid line fittings. Cap all open lines immediately.

3. Remove the radiator assembly.

4. Remove top condenser retaining screws.

5. Carefully lift the condenser out of radiator support.

6. To install, use new O-rings lubricated with refrigerant oil.

7. Install the condenser onto the radiator support.

8. Install the top condenser retaining screws.

9. Install the radiator and shroud.

10. Connect the coupled hose and liquid line fittings.

13. Install the control assembly and attaching screws.

14. Install the trim plate and attaching screws.

15. Raise the steering column and tighten the steering column attaching nuts.

16. Install the steering column opening filler and the two screws near the lower edge of the filler.

Blower Switch

With the control head removed from the vehicle remove the blower switch knob attaching screw and remove the switch.

11. Evacuate and recharge system. Test for proper operation and inspect for system leaks.

Evaporator Core

REMOVAL & INSTALLATION

1990

▶ **See Figure 10**

1. Discharge the A/C system. Refer to Section 1 for discharging.

2. Remove the evaporator inlet and outlet pipes.

3. Remove the expansion tube from the evaporator inlet pipe (thinner pipe).

4. Remove the A/C upper case screws.

5. Remove the upper case and lift the evaporator core out of the case (retain the foam wedge).

To install:

6. Position the evaporator core into place with the foam wedge and seals; install the evaporator clamp.

7. Install the upper case.

8. Install the expansion (orifice) tube into the evaporator inlet with a light coat of refrigerant oil.

9. Add 3 ounces of fresh refrigerant oil to the system.

10. Install new O-rings coated with refrigerant oil onto the inlet and outlet pipes. Tighten the inlet and outlet lines.

11. Recharge the system and inspect for proper operation and leaks.

1991-93

1. Discharge the A/C system. Refer to Section 1 for discharging.

2. Remove the evaporator inlet and outlet pipes.

3. Plug all open lines to prevent moisture and/or dirt from contaminating the system.

4. From inside vehicle, remove the four retaining screws on the upper right side sound insulator. Pull the insulator straight back until the two locator studs are disengaged.

5. Remove the nut from the shroud panel stud on the Instrument panel lower reinforcement.

6. Remove the screw from the instrument panel carrier and remove the instrument panel lower reinforcement.

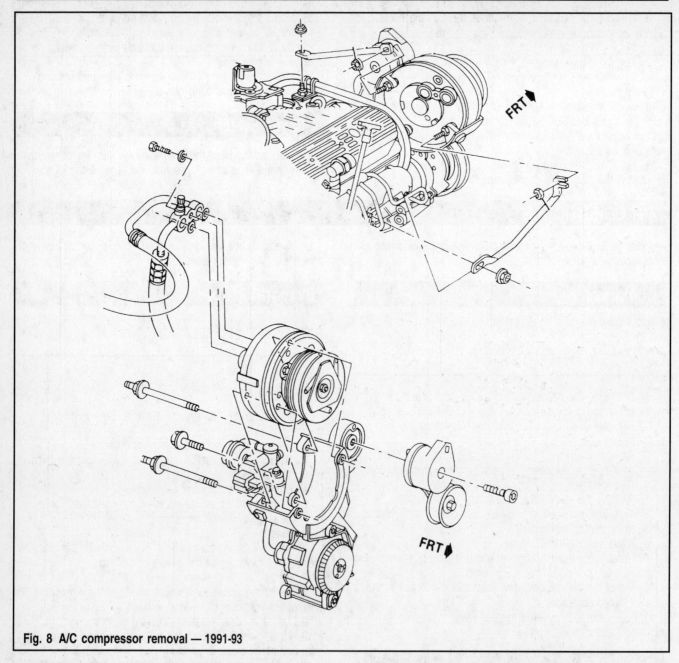

Fig. 8 A/C compressor removal — 1991-93

7. Disconnect both vacuum harness connectors, then remove the connector halves from the lower evaporator case and position the harnesses out of the way.

8. Remove the right side hinge pillar finish (kick) panel by pulling it away from the body pillar.

9. Roll the carpeting back enough to provide access to the lower area of the A/C module.

10. Remove the seven screws attaching the lower case to the module.

➡**The forward center attaching screw may be difficult find. It is located almost directly below the lower right side heater core tube, the screw head is straight down from the A/C vacuum tank, using a ¼ inch drive 7mm socket with a swivel adaptor and short extension on a ratchet handle will aid in the removal.**

11. Remove the lower evaporator case.

12. Remove the evaporator mounting bracket and screw.

13. Remove the evaporator assembly by sliding it rearward, then down.

To install:

14. Install the evaporator assembly, bracket and screw.

15. Install the lower evaporator case.

16. Add 3 ounces of fresh refrigerant oil to the system.

17. Install the evaporator inlet and outlet pipes with new seals. Coat the seals with refrigerant oil. Tighten the nuts to 12 ft. lbs. (16 Nm).

18. Recharge the system and inspect for proper operation and leaks.

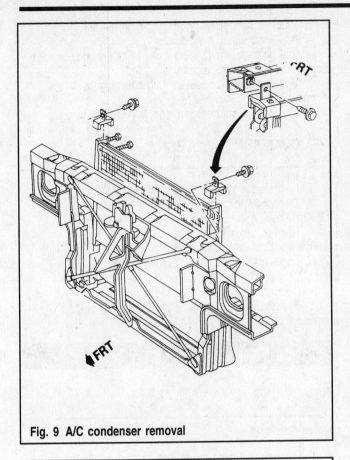

Fig. 9 A/C condenser removal

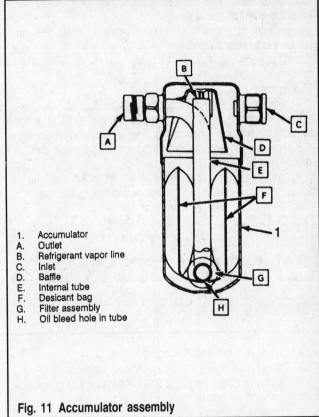

1. Accumulator
A. Outlet
B. Refrigerant vapor line
C. Inlet
D. Baffle
E. Internal tube
F. Desicant bag
G. Filter assembly
H. Oil bleed hole in tube

Fig. 11 Accumulator assembly

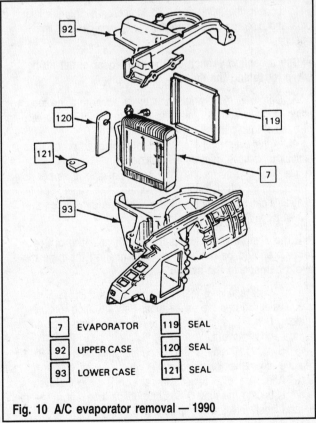

7	EVAPORATOR	119	SEAL
92	UPPER CASE	120	SEAL
93	LOWER CASE	121	SEAL

Fig. 10 A/C evaporator removal — 1990

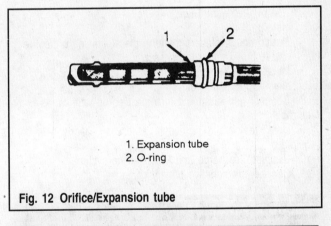

1. Expansion tube
2. O-ring

Fig. 12 Orifice/Expansion tube

Accumulator

REMOVAL & INSTALLATION

▶ See Figure 11

1. Disconnect the negative battery cable.
2. Properly discharge the air conditioning system.
3. Disconnect the low-pressure lines at the inlet and outlet fittings on the accumulator.

➡ Cap the refrigerant lines when opening the system to prevent the entry of dirt and moisture and the loss of refrigerant lubricant.

4. Disconnect the pressure cycling switch connection and remove the switch, as required.

5. Loosen the lower strap bolt and spread the strap. Turn the accumulator and remove.

6. Drain and measure the oil in the accumulator. Discard the old oil.

To install:

7. Add new oil equivalent to the amount drained from the old accumulator. Add an additional 2-3 oz. (60-90ml) of oil to compensate for the oil retained by the accumulator desiccant.

8. Position the accumulator in the securing bracket and tighten the clamp bolt.

9. Install new O-rings at the inlet and outlet connections on the accumulator. Lubricate the O-rings with refrigerant oil.

10. Connect the low-pressure inlet and outlet lines.

11. Evacuate, charge and leak test the system.

12. Connect the negative battery cable.

Refrigerant Lines

REMOVAL & INSTALLATION

1. Disconnect the negative battery cable.
2. Properly discharge the air conditioning system.
3. Disconnect the refrigerant line connectors, using a backup wrench as required.
4. Remove refrigerant line support or routing brackets, as required.
5. Remove refrigerant line.

To install:

6. Position new refrigerant line in place, leaving protective caps installed until ready to connect.
7. Install new O-rings on refrigerant line connector fittings. Lubricate with refrigerant oil.
8. Connect refrigerant line, using a backup wrench, as required.
9. Install refrigerant line support or routing brackets, as required.
10. Evacuate, recharge and leak test the system.
11. Connect the negative battery cable.

Vacuum Actuator

OPERATION

Used on certain heating and air conditioning systems, the vacuum actuators operate the air doors determining the different modes. The actuator consists of a spring loaded diaphragm connected to a lever. When vacuum is applied to the diaphragm, the lever moves the control door to its appropriate position. When the lever on the control panel is moved to another position, vacuum is cut off and the spring returns the actuator lever to its normal position.

TESTING

1. Disconnect the vacuum line from the actuator.

2. Attach a hand-held vacuum pump to the actuator.
3. Apply vacuum to the actuator.
4. The actuator lever should move to its engaged position and remain there while vacuum is applied.
5. When vacuum is released it should move back to its normal position.
6. The lever should operate smoothly and not bind.

REMOVAL & INSTALLATION

1. Remove the vacuum lines from the actuator.
2. Disconnect the linkage from the actuator.
3. Remove the hardware attaching the actuator.
4. Remove the actuator.

To install:

5. Install the actuator and attaching hardware.
6. Connect the linkage to the actuator.
7. Connect the vacuum lines to the actuator.
8. Test system to confirm proper functioning of the actuator.

Orifice Tube

REMOVAL & INSTALLATION

▶ See Figure 12

1. Properly discharge the air conditioning system.
2. Loosen the fitting at the liquid line on evaporator inlet pipe and disconnect. Discard the O-ring and cap the line opening.

➡**Use a backup wrench on the condenser outlet fitting when loosening the lines.**

3. Carefully, remove the fixed orifice tube from the tube fitting in the evaporator inlet line using tool J-26549E or a pair of needle nose pliers.
4. In the event that the restricted or plugged orifice tube is difficult to remove, perform the following:
   a. Remove as much of the impacted residue as possible.
   b. Using a hair dryer, epoxy drier or equivalent, carefully apply heat approximately ¼ inch from the dimples on the inlet pipe. Do not overheat the pipe.

➡**If the system has a pressure switch near the orifice tube, it should be removed prior to heating the pipe to avoid damage to the switch.**

   c. While applying heat, use special tool J-26549-E or equivalent to grip the orifice tube. Use a turning motion along with a push-pull motion to loosen the impacted orifice tube and remove it.
5. Swab the inside of the evaporator inlet pipe with R-11 to remove any remaining residue.
6. Add 1 oz. of 525 viscosity refrigerant oil to the system.
7. Lubricate the new O-ring and orifice tube with refrigerant oil and insert into the inlet pipe.

➡**Ensure that the new orifice tube is inserted in the inlet tube with the smaller screen end first.**

8. Connect the evaporator inlet pipe with the condenser outlet fitting.

➡**Use a backup wrench on the condenser outlet fitting when tightening the lines.**

CRUISE CONTROL

Electric and Vacuum Brake Release Switch

▶ **See Figure 13**

REMOVAL & INSTALLATION

1. At the brake switch, remove either the 2 electrical connectors or the electrical connector and the vacuum hose.
2. Remove the switch from the retainer.
3. Remove the tubular retainer from the brake pedal mounting bracket.

To install:

1. Install the tubular retainer to the brake pedal mounting bracket.
2. Press the brake pedal and install the release switch into the retainer until fully seated in the clips.
3. Connect the wiring and/or vacuum lines. Adjust the switch.

Adjustment

1. Depress the brake pedal and check that the release switch is fully seated in the clips.
2. Slowly pull the brake pedal back to the at-rest position; the switch and valve assembly will move within the clips to the adjusted position.
3. Measure pedal travel and check switch engagement. The electric brake release switch contacts must open at ⅛-½ inch of pedal travel when measured at the centerline of the pedal pad. The brake lights should illuminate after another 1/16 inch of travel. The vacuum release should engage at ⅝-1 inch of pedal travel.

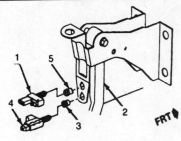

1. Release switch— cruise control
2. Brake pedal
3. Retainer
4. Stoplight switch
5. Retainer—cruise control switch

Fig. 13 Cruise control brake release switch — 1991-93

9. Evacuate, recharge and leak test the system.

Vacuum Servo Unit

▶ **See Figures 14 and 15**

REMOVAL & INSTALLATION

1. Disconnect the electrical connector and vacuum hoses at the servo.
2. Disconnect the actuating chain, cable or rod from the servo.
3. Remove the screws holding the vacuum servo and solenoid unit to the bracket and remove the unit.

To install:

1. Connect the large diameter brake release vacuum line to the servo unit. Connect the vacuum hose from the vacuum control valve to the servo unit.
2. Connect the actuating chain, rod or cable to the servo.
3. Install the servo unit to the bracket; tighten the screws to 12 inch lbs. (1.4 Nm).
4. Install the electrical connector to the servo.
5. Adjust the cable, rod or chain.

Vacuum System Linkage Adjustment

➡**Do not stretch cables or chains to make pins fit or holes align. This will prevent the engine from returning to idle.**

1. Check that the cable is properly installed and that the throttle is closed to the idle position.
2. Pull the servo end of the cable toward the linkage bracket of the servo. Place the servo connector in one of the 6 holes in the bracket which allows the least amount of slack and does not move the throttle linkage.
3. Install the retainer clip. Check that the throttle linkage is still in the idle position.

Multi-Function Lever with Set/Coast and Resume/Accel

REMOVAL & INSTALLATION

1990

1. Disconnect the negative battery terminal.
2. Disconnect cruise control switch connector at the base of steering column. it may be necessary to remove an under dash panel or trim piece for access.
3. Make sure lever is in **CENTER** or **OFF** position.

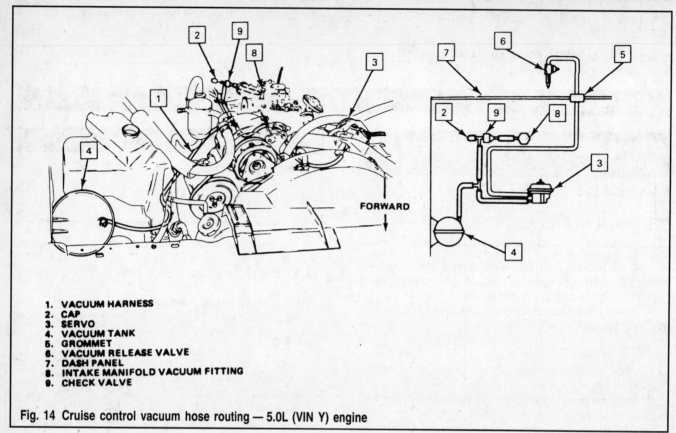

1. VACUUM HARNESS
2. CAP
3. SERVO
4. VACUUM TANK
5. GROMMET
6. VACUUM RELEASE VALVE
7. DASH PANEL
8. INTAKE MANIFOLD VACUUM FITTING
9. CHECK VALVE

Fig. 14 Cruise control vacuum hose routing — 5.0L (VIN Y) engine

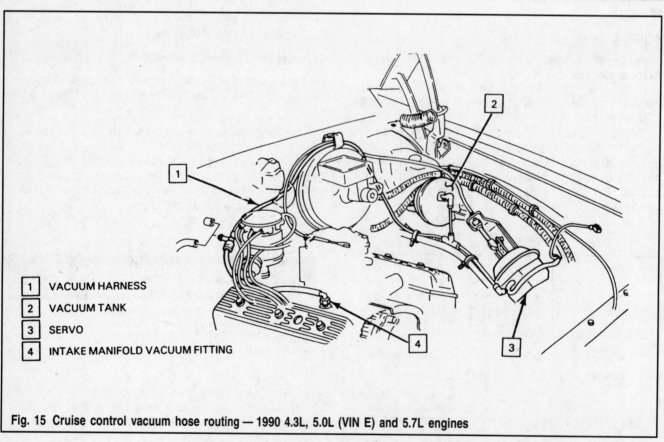

1	VACUUM HARNESS
2	VACUUM TANK
3	SERVO
4	INTAKE MANIFOLD VACUUM FITTING

Fig. 15 Cruise control vacuum hose routing — 1990 4.3L, 5.0L (VIN E) and 5.7L engines

4. Pull lever straight out of retaining clip within the steering column.

5. Attach mechanic's wire or similar to the end of the harness connector; gently pull the harness through the column, guiding the pull wire through the column.

To install:

1. Place the transmission selector in **LOW** or **1**. Attach the mechanic's wire to the new switch harness connector. Gently pull the harness into place, checking that the harness is completely clear of any moving or movable components such as tilt-column, telescoping column, brake pedal linkage, etc.

2. Position the lever and push it squarely into the retainer until it snaps in place.

3. Remove the mechanics' wire and connect the cruise control harness connector.

4. Reinstall any panels or insulation which were removed for access.

5. Connect the negative battery terminal.

1991-93

1. Disconnect the negative battery terminal.
2. Remove the steering column cover at the switch.
3. Disconnect switch connector behind the steering column cover.
4. Make sure the windshield wiper is in **OFF** position.
5. Pull lever straight out of retaining clip within the steering column.

To install:

6. Install the lever by pushing it in firmly.
7. Connect the switch wire connector.
8. Install the steering column cover.

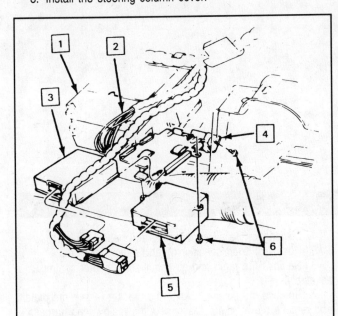

1. RADIO
2. RADIO LEADS
3. CRUISE MODULE
4. MOUNTING BRACKET
5. TONE GENERATOR
6. FULLY DRIVEN, SEATED AND NOT STRIPPED

Fig. 16 Cruise control module removal — 1990

9. Connect the negative battery cable.

Cruise Control Module

REMOVAL & INSTALLATION

1990

▶ **See Figure 16**

The module is located under the left side of the instrument panel inside the vehicle.

1. Disconnect the negative battery cable.
2. Remove the left side instrument panel undercover.
3. Slide the cruise control module from the mounting bracket.
4. Disconnect the connector and remove the module assembly.
5. Installation is the reverse of the removal procedure.

1991-93

▶ **See Figures 17 and 18**

The module is located on the left wheelhouse in the engine compartment.

1. Disconnect the negative battery cable.
2. Disconnect the module wire connector.
3. Compress the cable conduit tangs and pull the cable out of the housing.
4. Disconnect the cable bead from the cruise motor band end fitting on the module assembly.
5. Remove the module mounting bolts.
6. Remove the module assembly.

To install:

7. Install the module assembly and secure with mounting bolts.
8. Attach the cable bead to the cruise motor band end fitting on the module.
9. Pull the engine end of cable until taunt.
10. Turn the engine end of the cable assembly until band is flat. The band must not be twisted.
11. Slide the cable conduit over the band until the tangs of the conduit engage the holes in the module housing.
12. Connect the module wiring harness.
13. Connect the negative battery cable. Check for proper cruise control action, adjust the cable as necessary.

ADJUSTMENT

▶ **See Figure 19**

1. Remove the air cleaner and resonator.
2. Unlock the cable conduit at the support bracket.
3. With the throttle lever closed, lock the cable conduit by pressing down on the lock tab.

➡ **When the lock tab is in the UP unlocked position and the throttle is closed, the spring loaded cable adjuster takes up the appropriate amount of cable slack. The lock tab must be fully UP to allow cable to be properly adjusted.**

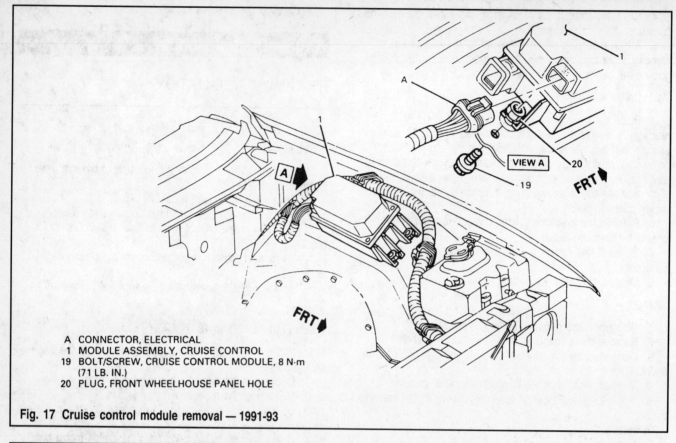

A   CONNECTOR, ELECTRICAL
1   MODULE ASSEMBLY, CRUISE CONTROL
19 BOLT/SCREW, CRUISE CONTROL MODULE, 8 N·m
    (71 LB. IN.)
20 PLUG, FRONT WHEELHOUSE PANEL HOLE

Fig. 17 Cruise control module removal — 1991-93

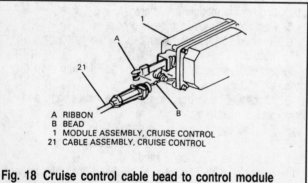

A   RIBBON
B   BEAD
1   MODULE ASSEMBLY, CRUISE CONTROL
21 CABLE ASSEMBLY, CRUISE CONTROL

Fig. 18 Cruise control cable bead to control module
removal — 1991-93

4. Install the air cleaner and resonator. Check for proper cruise control operation

ENTERTAINMENT SYSTEMS

Radio

REMOVAL & INSTALLATION

▶ See Figure 20

1990

1. Disconnect the negative battery cable.
2. Remove the ash tray.
3. Remove the instrument panel compartment.

4. Disconnect the air conditioning and heater cables.
5. Remove the air conditioning and radio trim plate.
6. Remove the radio and air conditioning heater control assembly.
7. Remove the screws holding the bracket to the trim plate and remove the bracket. Disconnect the radio wiring harness and antenna.
8. Remove the screws holding the radio to the bracket and remove the radio.
   To install:
9. Position the radio in the bracket and attach with screws.

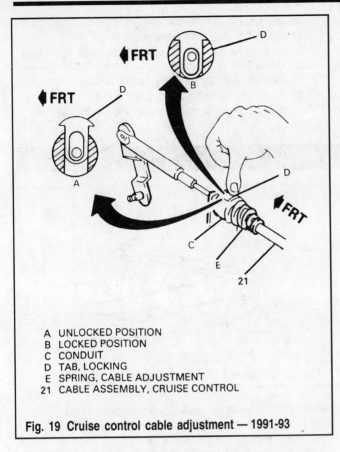

A UNLOCKED POSITION
B LOCKED POSITION
C CONDUIT
D TAB, LOCKING
E SPRING, CABLE ADJUSTMENT
21 CABLE ASSEMBLY, CRUISE CONTROL

Fig. 19 Cruise control cable adjustment — 1991-93

10. Connect the radio wiring harness and antenna. Attach the trim plate to the bracket with screws.

11. Connect the radio and air conditioning heater control assembly.

12. Connect the air conditioning and heater cables.

13. Attach the instrument panel compartment and insert the ash tray.

14. Connect the negative battery cable.

1991-93

1. Disconnect the negative battery cable.

→**This vehicle is equipped with an air bag system, make certain to follow the recommended disarming procedure before, or arming procedure after, repairs.**

2. Remove the left hand trim plate:

a. Remove the steering column opening filler.

b. Open the instrument panel compartment door and carefully unsnap the right side molding from the carrier.

c. Loosen the capsule nuts attaching the steering column support bracket to the carrier, to the end of the threads but do not remove from the bolts. Gently lower the steering column.

d. Remove the 6 screws attaching the trim plate to the carrier and carefully unsnap and pull away.

3. Remove the 3 screws attaching the bracket to the carrier and remove the bracket and the attached radio from the carrier.

4. Disconnect the body harness connector and the antenna lead from the radio.

5. Remove the 3 nuts attaching the bracket to the radio and if necessary remove the 3 bolts from the radio.

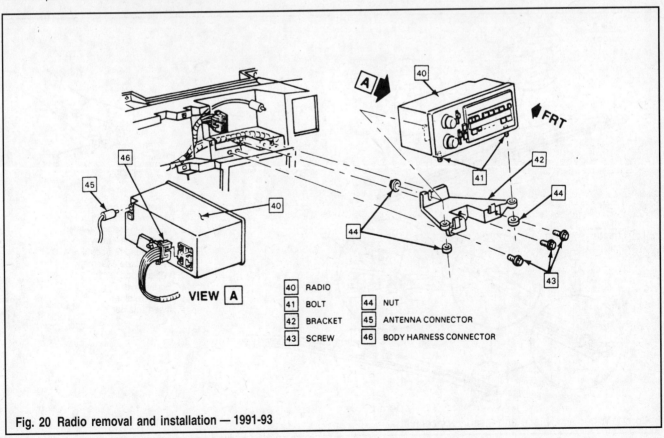

40	RADIO			
41	BOLT		44	NUT
42	BRACKET		45	ANTENNA CONNECTOR
43	SCREW		46	BODY HARNESS CONNECTOR

Fig. 20 Radio removal and installation — 1991-93

To install:

6. Attach the bolts to radio, if necessary, and use nuts to attach the radio to the bracket. Tighten nuts to 27 inch lbs. (3 Nm).

7. Attach the body harness and antenna connectors to the radio.

8. Use screws to attach the bracket to the carrier. Tighten screws to 17 inch lbs. (1.9 Nm).

9. Attach the left hand trim plate:

a. Attach trim plate with screws and snaps.

b. Gently raise the steering column into place and attach with capsule nuts to the carrier.

c. Snap the right side molding to the carrier.

d. Attach the steering column opening filler.

10. Attach the negative battery cable and enable the SIR system.

WINDSHIELD WIPERS AND WASHERS

Blade and Arm

▶ **See Figures 21, 22 and 23**

REMOVAL & INSTALLATION

If the wiper assembly has a press type release tab at the center, simply depress the tab and remove the blade. If the blade has no release tab, use a screwdriver to depress the spring at the center. This will release the assembly. To install the assembly, position the blade over the pin at the tip of the arm and press until the spring retainer engages the groove in the pin.

To remove the element, either depress the release button or squeeze the spring type retainer clip at the outer end together, and slide the blade element out. Just slide the new element in until it latches.

Removal of the wiper arms on 1990 vehicles requires the use of a special tool, G.M. J-8966 or its equivalent. Versions

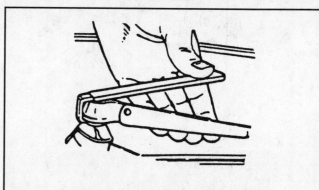

Fig. 22 Windshield wiper removal tool — 1990

of this tool are generally available in auto parts stores. Removal of wiper arms on 1991 — 93 vehicles requires removing the protective cap and mounting nut, then use a battery terminal puller to remove the arm from the knurled shaft.

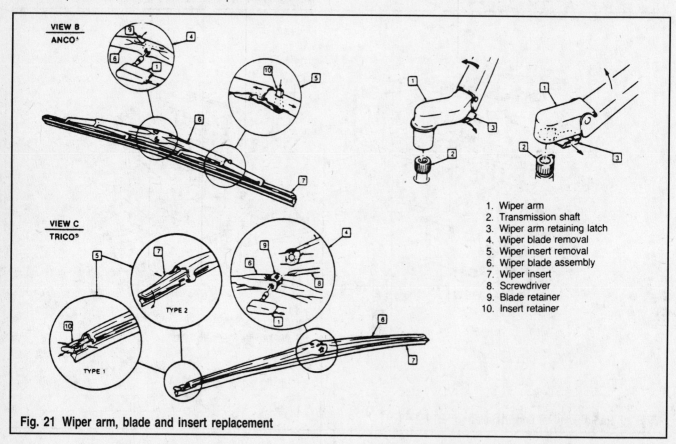

1. Wiper arm
2. Transmission shaft
3. Wiper arm retaining latch
4. Wiper blade removal
5. Wiper insert removal
6. Wiper blade assembly
7. Wiper insert
8. Screwdriver
9. Blade retainer
10. Insert retainer

Fig. 21 Wiper arm, blade and insert replacement

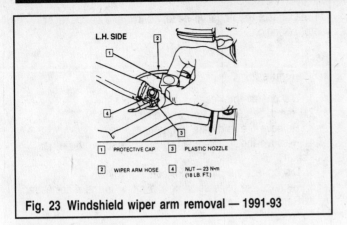

1	PROTECTIVE CAP	3	PLASTIC NOZZLE
2	WIPER ARM HOSE	4	NUT — 23 N·m (18 LB. FT.)

Fig. 23 Windshield wiper arm removal — 1991-93

1990 WIPER ARMS

1. Insert the tool under the wiper arm and lever the arm off the shaft.

➡**Raising the hood on most later models will facilitate easier wiper arm removal.**

2. Disconnect the washer hose from the arm (if so equipped). Remove the arm.
3. Installation is in the reverse order of removal. Be sure that the motor is in the park position before installing the arms.

1991-93

Front

1. Disconnect the washer hose from the plastic nozzle.
2. Remove the wiper arm protective cap.

3. Lift the wiper blade and insert a pin or pop rivet through the holes next to the wiper arm pivot. The pin will hold the wiper blade UP and OFF the windshield so that the blade has no pressure on it.
4. Remove the wiper arm mounting nut.
5. Remove the wiper arm using a battery terminal puller or suitable tool.
6. Installation is in the reverse order of removal. Be sure that the motor is in the park position before installing the arms.

Rear

7. Disconnect the washer hose.
8. Lift the wiper arm and insert a suitable tool to push the retaining latch outward.
9. Remove the arm.
10. Installation is in the reverse order of removal. Be sure that the motor is in the park position before installing the arm.

Windshield Wiper Motor

REMOVAL & INSTALLATION

Front

▶ **See Figure 24**

1. Disconnect the negative battery cable.
2. Raise the hood and on 1991-93, remove the right side wiper arm and hose.

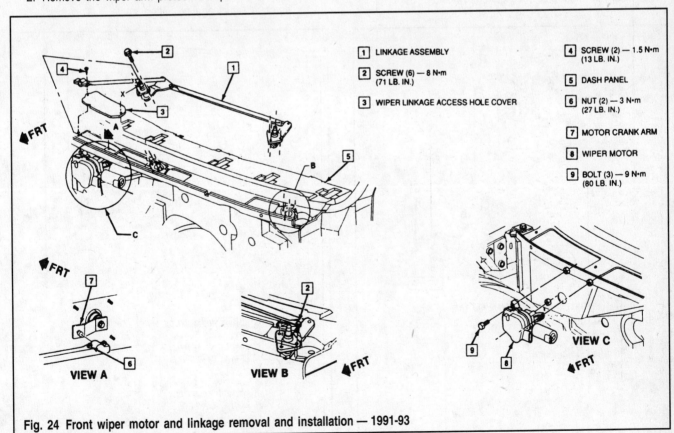

1	LINKAGE ASSEMBLY	4	SCREW (2) — 1.5 N·m (13 LB. IN.)
2	SCREW (6) — 8 N·m (71 LB. IN.)	5	DASH PANEL
3	WIPER LINKAGE ACCESS HOLE COVER	6	NUT (2) — 3 N·m (27 LB. IN.)
		7	MOTOR CRANK ARM
		8	WIPER MOTOR
		9	BOLT (3) — 9 N·m (80 LB. IN.)

VIEW A   VIEW B   VIEW C

Fig. 24 Front wiper motor and linkage removal and installation — 1991-93

3. Remove cowl screen, beginning with the left side on 1991-93.

➡ On 1991-93 vehicles, the left side cowl screen must be removed before the right side cowl screen to prevent possible windshield damage.

4. Remove the linkage access hole cover, if equipped.
5. Loosen the transmission drive link to crank arm retaining bolts. Remove the drive link from the motor crank arm.
6. Disconnect the electrical wiring and any remaining washer hoses from the motor assembly.
7. Remove the motor retaining screws. Remove the windshield wiper motor while guiding the crank arm through the hole.

To install:
8. Guide the wiper motor guiding crank arm through the hole.
9. Insert and tighten wiper motor attaching bolts to 80 inch lbs. (9 Nm).
10. Attach electrical connectors.
11. Place the motor in the **P** position and attach the motor crank arm to the drive link. Tighten drive link nuts to 27 inch lbs. (3 Nm).
12. Attach wiper linkage access hole cover with screws. Tighten hole cover screws to 13 inch lbs. (1.5 Nm).
13. Install right and left side cowl screens.

➡ On 1991-93 vehicles, the right side cowl screen must be installed before the left side cowl screen to prevent possible windshield damage.

14. Attach the right side wiper arm and hose.

15. Connect the negative battery cable and check wiper motor operation.

Rear
◆ See Figure 25

1. Disconnect the negative battery cable.
2. Remove the wiper arm and blade assembly.
3. Remove the end gate trim panel.
4. Remove the motor retaining nut located on the wiper arm shaft.
5. Disconnect the motor wire connector.
6. Remove the bolts securing the motor to the rear header.
7. Remove the motor assembly.
To install:
8. Install the motor assembly.
9. Install the bolts securing the motor to the rear header.
10. Connect the motor wire connector.
11. Install the motor retaining nut located on the wiper arm shaft.
12. Install the end gate trim panel.
13. Install the wiper arm and blade assembly.
14. Connect the negative battery cable.

Park Switch

◆ See Figures 26 and 27

REMOVAL & INSTALLATION

1. Disconnect the negative battery cable.

A	SERRATED TRANSMISSION SHAFT
2	MOTOR
6	NUT
7	REAR HEADER
8	BOLT

Fig. 25 Rear wiper motor removal — 1991-93

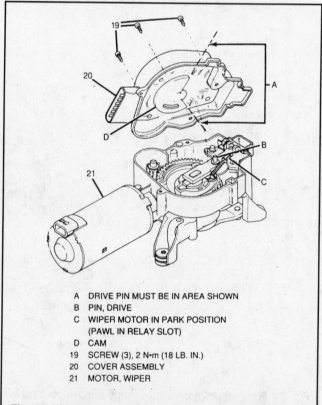

A	DRIVE PIN MUST BE IN AREA SHOWN
B	PIN, DRIVE
C	WIPER MOTOR IN PARK POSITION (PAWL IN RELAY SLOT)
D	CAM
19	SCREW (3), 2 N•m (18 LB. IN.)
20	COVER ASSEMBLY
21	MOTOR, WIPER

Fig. 26 Washer pump/cover removal and installation

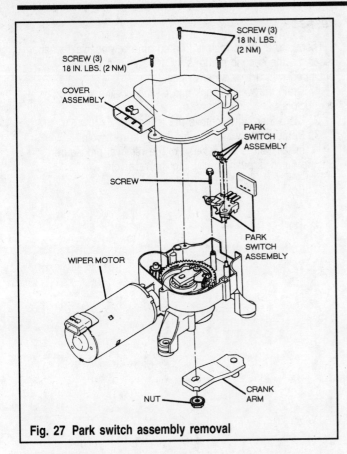

Fig. 27 Park switch assembly removal

2. Remove the windshield wiper cover retaining screws and remove the cover.

3. If the wiper motor is in the **PARK** position, operate the motor as required to take it out of this position.

4. Remove the park switch retaining screws and remove the assembly.

5. Installation is the reverse of the removal procedure. Ensure the motor is in the **PARK** position with the drive pin in the open area of the cam before installing the cover assembly.

Wiper Linkage

REMOVAL & INSTALLATION

1. Remove the wiper arms and blades. Remove the lower windshield reveal molding, cowl vent screen and access hole cover as required.

2. Disconnect the transmission drive link to the motor crank arm.

3. Remove the transmission-to-body attaching screws from both the right and left sides of the car.

4. Guide the transmissions and linkage out through the cowl opening.

5. To install, guide the transmissions and linkage in through the cowl opening.

6. Install the transmission-to-body attaching screws to both the right and left sides of the car.

7. Connect the drive link to the arm.

8. Install the access hole cover, cowl vent screen and lower windshield reveal molding, as required.

9. Install the wiper arms and blades.

Washer Pump

▶ **See Figures 28 and 29**

REMOVAL & INSTALLATION

1990

1. Remove the washer hoses from the pump.

2. Disconnect the pump wire connector.

3. Remove the pump plastic cover.

4. Remove the screws securing the pump to the wiper motor and remove the pump assembly.

To install:

5. With the plastic pump cover removed locate the indexing hole in the pump cam and plate. Align these holes using a pin or drill bit. This is the PARK position.

6. Position the pump cover on the wiper motor. Ensure the slot in the 4-lobe cam of the pump is aligned with the drive pin on the wiper motor assembly.

7. Secure the assembly with the retaining screws. Remove the aligning pin and install the pump plastic cover.

8. Turn the pump motor ON to check operation. A loud knocking noise indicates the pump is misaligned.

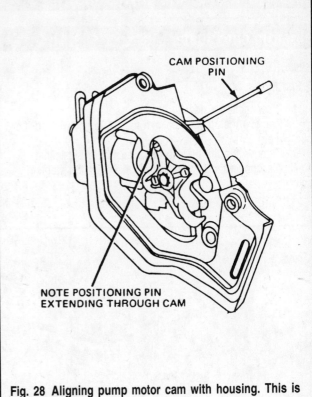

Fig. 28 Aligning pump motor cam with housing. This is the park position

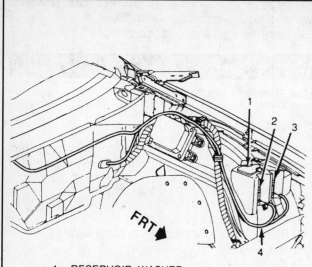

1 RESERVOIR, WASHER
2 PUMP, WINDSHIELD WASHER
3 PUMP, REAR WINDOW WASHER (REF.)
4 HOSE, WASHER

Fig. 29 Washer pump motor identification for front and rear wiper systems — 1991-93

1991-93

There are 2 pump motors located on the windshield washer reservoir, the second pump is for 1993 station wagons equipped with a rear wiper system.

1. Drain the washer tank and disconnect the wire connectors.
2. Disconnect and remove the reservoir
3. Remove the washer pump from the reservoir.
4. Installation is the reverse of the removal procedure. Ensure pump is pushed fully into the reservoir.

INSTRUMENTS AND SWITCHES

Instrument Cluster

1990

▶ See Figure 30

1. Disconnect the negative battery cable.
2. Remove the steering column trim plate screws and the trim plate.
3. Remove the left hand sound insulator, if applicable.
4. Disconnect the shift indicator cable from the steering column.

5. Remove the steering column to instrument panel screws. Lower the steering column.

➡**Use extreme care when lowering the steering column in order to prevent damage to column assembly.**

6. Remove the screws and the snap in fasteners from the perimeter of the instrument cluster lens.
7. Reach behind the instrument panel and remove the stud nuts from the lower corner of the cluster.
8. Reach behind the instrument panel and disconnect the speedometer cable, if applicable, and wiring harness connections.
9. Remove the assembly from the vehicle.

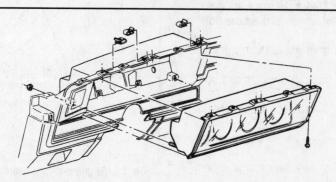

Fig. 30 Instrument panel cluster and bezel — 1990

To install:

10. Position instrument assembly to the instrument panel and connect the speedometer cable.

11. Attach the wiring harness connections.

12. Install nuts attaching 2 rear lower corner studs to the instrument panel carrier.

13. Attach cluster to carrier with screws.

14. Carefully raise the steering column and attach with screws to the instrument panel.

15. Connect the shift indicator cable to the steering column.

16. If removed, connect the left hand sound insulator.

17. Connect the steering column trim plate and screws.

18. Connect the negative battery cable.

1991-93

▶ **See Figure 31**

These vehicles are equipped with an instrument cluster assembly which is not repairable. The entire assembly must be replaced as a unit.

➡**This vehicle is equipped with an air bag system, make certain to follow the recommended disarming procedures before, and arming procedures after, repairs.**

1. Disconnect the negative battery cable.

2. Remove the left side trim plate:

  a. Remove the steering column opening filler.

  b. Open the instrument panel compartment door and unsnap the right side molding from the carrier.

  c. Loosen the capsule nuts attaching the steering column support bracket to the carrier, to the end of the threads but do not remove from the bolts. Gently lower the steering column.

  d. Remove the 6 screws attaching the trim plate to the carrier and carefully unsnap and pull away.

3. Remove the 4-5 screws attaching the cluster to carrier.

4. Disconnect the shift indicator cable from the steering column.

5. Gently pull the cluster from the electrical connector and remove the cluster from the vehicle.

To install:

6. Position the cluster in the vehicle and gently snap onto the connector.

7. Attach the shift indicator cable to the steering column.

8. Attach cluster to the carrier with the 4-5 carrier screws and tighten to 17 inch lbs. (1.9 Nm).

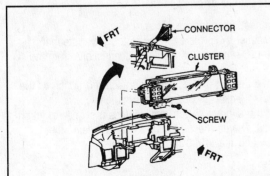

Fig. 31 Instrument panel cluster and bezel — 1991-93

9. Attach the left side trim plate and, if necessary, adjust the shift indicator as follows:

  a. Remove the steering column opening filler.

  b. The shift lever should be in the **N** gate notch.

  c. Position the guide clip on the edge of the gearshift lever bowl to centrally position the pointer on **N**. Push the guide clip onto the gearshift lever bowl.

10. Connect negative battery cable and enable the SIR system.

Speedometer

Only 1990 vehicles have a replaceable speedometer, all 1991-93 vehicle instrument clusters must be replaced as an assembly.

REMOVAL & INSTALLATION

1. Disconnect the negative battery cable.

2. Remove the left hand sound insulators.

3. Remove the steering column and left side trim plate.

4. Remove the trip odometer knob, if equipped.

5. Remove the screws and unsnap the speedometer lens-to-instrument cluster carrier.

6. Remove the screws attaching the face and adapter plates to the cluster carrier. Remove the face and adapter plates.

7. Remove the screws attaching the speedometer to the cluster carrier.

8. Disconnect the speedometer cable at the speedometer assembly.

9. Remove the screws securing the speed sensor pick-up to the speedometer head. Remove the speedometer assembly.

To install:

10. Install the screws securing the speed sensor pick-up to the speedometer head. Install the speedometer assembly.

11. Connect the speedometer cable at the speedometer assembly.

12. Install the screws attaching the speedometer to the cluster carrier.

13. Install the screws attaching the face and adapter plates to the cluster carrier.

14. Install the screws and snap-in the speedometer lens-to-instrument cluster carrier.

15. Install the trip odometer knob, if equipped.

16. Install the steering column and left side trim plate.

17. Install the left hand sound insulators.

18. Connect the negative battery cable.

Wiper Switch

REMOVAL & INSTALLATION

▶ **See Figure 32**

➡**The wiper switch is part of the multi-function lever, located on the steering wheel column.**

1. Disconnect the negative battery cable.

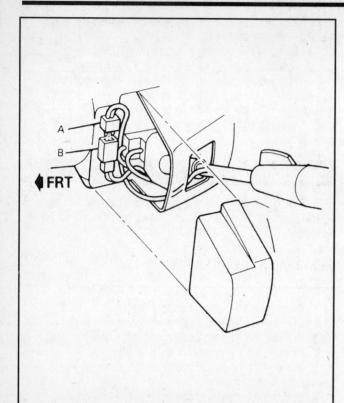

Fig. 32 Multi-Function (windshield wiper switch) lever removal and installation

2. Remove the tilt wheel lever by turning clockwise, if equipped. Remove the turn signal protective cover, on 1991-93 vehicles.

3. With the turn signal lever in the center position, grasp the lever firmly; twist and pull the lever straight out.

4. If equipped with cruise control, disconnect the wire at the base of the steering column and connect a piece of mechanics wire to the connector, on 1990 vehicles. On 1991-93 vehicles disconnect the wire at the lever assembly.

To install:

5. Use the mechanics wire to pull the cruise control connector harness down through the steering column and connect the connector at the base of the column.

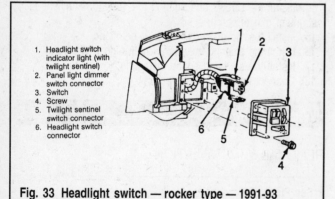

1. Headlight switch indicator light (with twilight sentinel)
2. Panel light dimmer switch connector
3. Switch
4. Screw
5. Twilight sentinel switch connector
6. Headlight switch connector

Fig. 33 Headlight switch — rocker type — 1991-93

6. Push the control lever into the spring loaded socket (be sure to align the tang).

7. Install the turn signal lever protective cover, if removed.

8. Install the tilt wheel lever, if removed. Connect the negative battery cable.

Headlight Switch

REMOVAL & INSTALLATION

ROCKER TYPE SWITCH

▶ See Figure 33

1. Disconnect the negative battery cable.

➡If equipped with an air bag system, make certain to follow the recommended disarming procedure or arming procedure after repairs.

2. Remove the left side trim plate:
   a. Remove the steering column opening filler.
   b. Open the instrument panel compartment door and unsnap the right side molding from the carrier.
   c. Loosen the capsule nuts attaching the steering column support bracket to the carrier, to the end of the threads but do not remove from the bolts. Gently lower the steering column.
   d. Remove the 6 screws attaching the trim plate to the carrier and carefully unsnap and pull away.

3. Remove the 3 screws attaching the switch to the instrument carrier and remove the switch.

To install:

4. Place switch in instrument carrier and attach with screws.

5. Attach left side trim plate.

6. Enable SIR system and connect the negative battery cable.

Dimmer Switch

REMOVAL & INSTALLATION

➡If equipped with an air bag system, make certain to follow the recommended disarming procedure before, and rearming procedure after, repairs.

1. Disconnect the negative battery cable.

2. The dimmer switch is attached to the lower steering column jacket. Disconnect all electrical connections from the switch.

3. Remove the nut and screw that attach the switch to the steering column jacket and remove the switch.

4. Install the dimmer switch and depress it slightly to insert a 3/32 inch drill. Force the switch up to remove lash, then tighten screw and nut to 4.0 ft. lbs.

Back-up Light Switch

REMOVAL & INSTALLATION

▶ See Figure 34

1. Disconnect the negative battery cable.

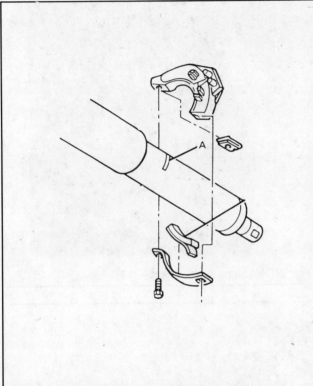

Fig. 34 Neutral safety and back-up Light switch — 1991-93

2. Remove the left sound insulator. Disconnect the wiring at the switch assembly.

3. Disconnect the parking brake vacuum actuator hose assembly, if equipped.

4. Remove the switch assembly retainer and sealing strip, if equipped. Remove the switch assembly.

To install:

5. Block the drive wheels and place the transmission in **N**.

6. Align the actuator on the switch assembly with the hole on the shaft tube.

7. Position the connector side of the switch assembly to fit into the cutout on the steering column shaft.

8. Push down on the switch assembly to lock the tangs into place in the steering shaft.

9. If a used switch was reinstalled, move the switch assembly to the right, the **LOW** gear position. Then, place the transmission in **P**, the switch assembly will ratchet as it adjusts itself.

10. If a new switch being installed, simply place the transmission in **P** and the switch assembly will ratchet as it adjusts itself automatically.

11. Verify the switch is adjusted properly.

12. Install the switch retainer, if equipped.

13. Install the parking brake vacuum actuator.

14. Connect the switch wire connector.

15. Install the instrument panel sound insulator.

16. Connect the negative battery cable.

LIGHTING

Headlights

REMOVAL & INSTALLATION

1990

▶ See Figure 35

1. Remove headlamp bezel retaining screws and remove bezel.

2. Disengage spring from the retaining ring with a cotter pin removal tool and remove the retaining ring attaching screws.

3. Remove retaining ring, disconnect sealed beam unit at wiring connector and remove the unit.

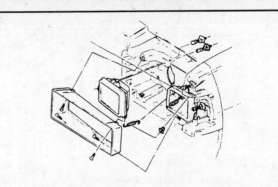

Fig. 35 Headlamp and bezel assembly — 1990

4. To install, attach the connector to replacement unit and position the unit in place making sure the number molded into the lens face is at the top.

➡In the dual headlamp installation the inboard unit (No. 1) takes a double connector plug, the outboard unit (No. 2) takes a triple connector plug.

5. Position retaining ring into place and install the retaining ring attaching screws and spring.
6. Check operation of unit and install the headlamp bezel.

1991-1993

▶ See Figures 36, 37 and 38

✳✳CAUTION

These vehicles use a halogen bulb which contains gas under pressure. To avoid personal injury, use care when handling the bulb and avoid contacting the glass portion of the assembly.

1. From the back of the headlamp assembly, twist the bulb retainer clockwise.
2. Remove the bulb assembly.
3. Disconnect the wire connector from the bulb.
4. Installation is the reverse of the removal procedure. Do not touch the new halogen bulbs glass when installing.

Fig. 37 Headlamp replacement — 1991-93

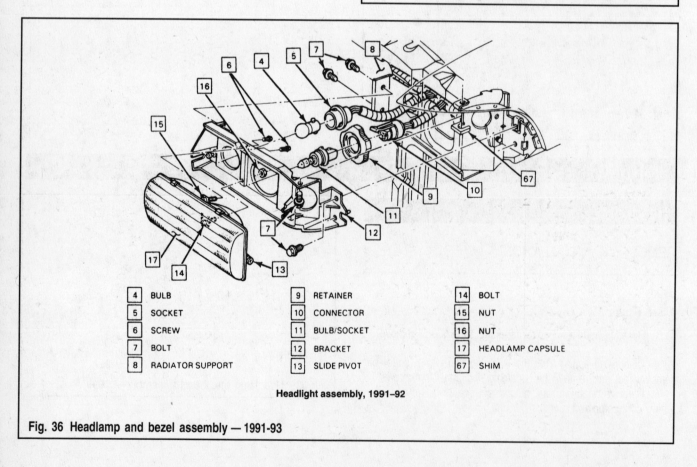

4	BULB	9	RETAINER	14	BOLT
5	SOCKET	10	CONNECTOR	15	NUT
6	SCREW	11	BULB/SOCKET	16	NUT
7	BOLT	12	BRACKET	17	HEADLAMP CAPSULE
8	RADIATOR SUPPORT	13	SLIDE PIVOT	67	SHIM

Headlight assembly, 1991–92

Fig. 36 Headlamp and bezel assembly — 1991-93

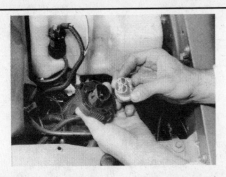

Fig. 38 When installing the new halogen headlamp bulb avoid touching the glass — 1991-93

AIMING

▶ **See Figures 39 and 40**

The use of SAE approved equipment is preferred to achieve exact adjustment of the headlamps, although a fairly accurate method of adjustment is as follows:

1. Position the vehicle approximately 25 ft. from a screen or wall, ensure the vehicle is facing the wall straight.

2. Measure the height from the ground to the center of each headlamp.

3. Next measure from the ground-up the same distance as previously measured and mark the appropriate spot on the screen or wall with chalk or tape, ensuring the marks are straight ahead of each headlamp.

4. Turn the headlamps on and note the marks previously made.

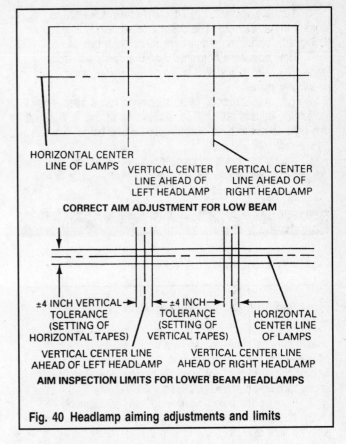

HORIZONTAL CENTER LINE OF LAMPS   VERTICAL CENTER LINE AHEAD OF LEFT HEADLAMP   VERTICAL CENTER LINE AHEAD OF RIGHT HEADLAMP

CORRECT AIM ADJUSTMENT FOR LOW BEAM

±4 INCH VERTICAL TOLERANCE (SETTING OF HORIZONTAL TAPES)   ±4 INCH TOLERANCE (SETTING OF VERTICAL TAPES)   HORIZONTAL CENTER LINE OF LAMPS

VERTICAL CENTER LINE AHEAD OF LEFT HEADLAMP   VERTICAL CENTER LINE AHEAD OF RIGHT HEADLAMP

AIM INSPECTION LIMITS FOR LOWER BEAM HEADLAMPS

Fig. 40 Headlamp aiming adjustments and limits

5. The vertical aim, if properly adjusted, should be 4 in. up or down from your center mark previously made.

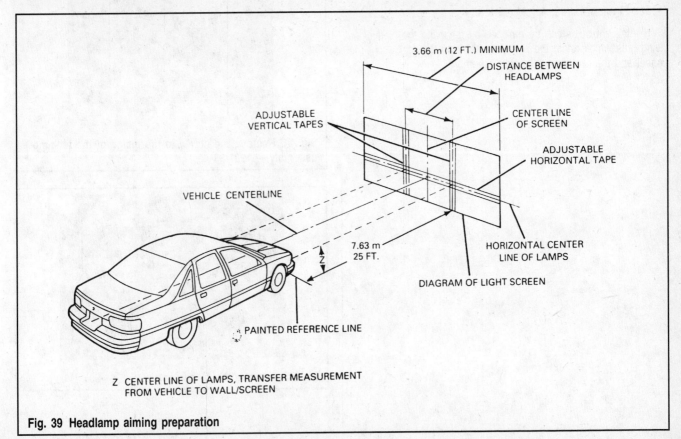

3.66 m (12 FT.) MINIMUM

DISTANCE BETWEEN HEADLAMPS

CENTER LINE OF SCREEN

ADJUSTABLE HORIZONTAL TAPE

ADJUSTABLE VERTICAL TAPES

VEHICLE CENTERLINE

7.63 m 25 FT.

HORIZONTAL CENTER LINE OF LAMPS

DIAGRAM OF LIGHT SCREEN

PAINTED REFERENCE LINE

Z CENTER LINE OF LAMPS, TRANSFER MEASUREMENT FROM VEHICLE TO WALL/SCREEN

Fig. 39 Headlamp aiming preparation

6. Turn the vertical (top) adjusting screw if needed to correct the adjustment. The best overall setting is 2 in. up for low beams and 0 in. (straight ahead) for high beams.

7. Next check the horizontal aim, if properly adjusted, should be 4 in. to the right or left of the center mark previously made.

8. Turn the horizontal (side) adjuster screw if needed to obtain the correct setting. The best overall setting is ½ inch to the right as not to blind oncoming traffic and better illumination of the sidewalk and curb.

9. After adjustment is complete, recheck previous adjustment, the headlamps will change slightly (up or down) when turning the opposite adjuster.

Signal and Marker Lights

REMOVAL & INSTALLATION

Front Park/Turn and Side Marker Lights

1. Reach around to the back side of the light assembly and unlock the bulb holder/wiring harness by grasping the bulb holder/wiring harness and turning it counterclockwise approximately ¼ turn. Remove the cornering lamp assembly screw to gain access to bulbs, on 1991-93.

2. Remove the bulb holder/wiring harness assembly.

3. To install, insert the bulb holder/wiring harness assembly into the light assembly and locking the holder by turning it ¼ turn clockwise.

Rear Brake, Park & Turn Lights
▶ See Figures 41, 42, 43, 44, 45 and 46

The taillight bulbs can be replaced by removing the plastic wing nuts which retain the light assemblies to the rear end panel and then removing the light assembly.

Fig. 43 Remove the taillamp retaining screws — 1991-93

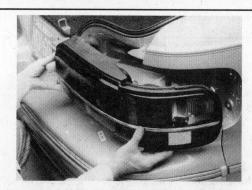
Fig. 44 Remove the taillamp assembly — 1991-93

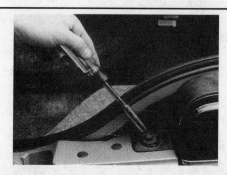
Fig. 41 Remove the screw to the inside of the taillamp assembly — 1991-93

Fig. 42 Remove the plastic screw — 1991-93

Fig. 46 Squeeze the bulb connector and rotate to remove the socket from the taillamp assembly — 1991-93

Fig. 45 Turn the assembly over to access bulbs — 1991-93

TRAILER WIRING

Wiring the vehicle for towing is fairly easy. There are a number of good wiring kits available and these should be used, rather than trying to design your own. All trailers will need brake lights and turn signals as well as tail lights and side marker lights. Most states require extra marker lights for overly wide trailers. Also, most states have recently required back-up lights for trailers, and most trailer manufacturers have been building trailers with back-up lights for several years.Additionally, some Class I, most Class II and just about all Class III trailers will have electric brakes.

Add to this number an accessories wire, to operate trailer internal equipment or to charge the trailer's battery, and you can have as many as seven wires in the harness.

Determine the equipment on your trailer and buy the wiring kit necessary. The kit will contain all the wires needed, plus a plug adapter set which included the female plug, mounted on the bumper or hitch, and the male plug, wired into, or plugged into the trailer harness.

When installing the kit, follow the manufacturer's instructions. The color coding of the wires is standard throughout the industry.

One point to note, some domestic vehicles, and most imported vehicles, have separate turn signals. On most domestic vehicles, the brake lights and rear turn signals operate with the same bulb. For those vehicles with separate turn signals, you can purchase an isolation unit so that the brake lights won't blink whenever the turn signals are operated, or, you can go to your local electronics supply house and buy four diodes to wire in series with the brake and turn signal bulbs. Diodes will isolate the brake and turn signals. The choice is yours. The isolation units are simple and quick to install, but far more expensive than the diodes. The diodes, however, require more work to install properly, since they require the cutting of each bulb's wire and soldering in place of the diode.

One final point, the best kits are those with a spring loaded cover on the vehicle mounted socket. This cover prevents dirt and moisture from corroding the terminals. Never let the vehicle socket hang loosely. Always mount it securely to the bumper or hitch.

➥For more information on towing a trailer please refer to Section 1.

CIRCUIT PROTECTION

Fusible Links

▶ See Figure 47

In addition to circuit breakers and fuses, the wiring harness incorporates fusible links to protect the wiring. Links are used rather than a fuse, in wiring circuits that are not normally fused, such as the ignition circuit. Camaro fusible links are color coded red in the charging and load circuits to match the color coding of the circuits they protect. Each link is four gauges smaller than the cable it protects, and is marked on the insulation with the gauge size because the insulation makes it appear heavier than it really is.

The engine compartment wiring harness has several fusible links. The same size wire with a special Hypalon insulation must be used when replacing a fusible link.

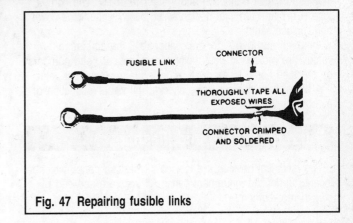

Fig. 47 Repairing fusible links

The links are located in the following areas:

1. A molded splice at the starter solenoid **Bat** terminal, usually a 14 gauge red wire.

2. A fusible link at the junction block to protect the unfused wiring of 12 gauge or larger wire. This link stops at the bulkhead connector.

3. The alternator warning light and field circuitry is protected by a fusible link used in the battery feed-to-voltage regulator terminal. The link is installed as a molded splice in the circuit at the junction block.

REPLACEMENT

1. Determine the circuit that is damaged.
2. Disconnect the negative battery terminal.
3. Cut the damaged fuse link from the harness and discard it.
4. Identify and procure the proper fuse link and butt connectors.
5. Strip the wire about ½ inch on each end.
6. Connect the fusible link and crimp the butt connectors making sure that the wires are secure.
7. Solder each connection with resin core solder, and wrap the connections with plastic electrical tape.
8. Reinstall the wire in the harness.
9. Connect the negative battery terminal and test the system for proper operation.

Circuit Breakers

Various circuit breakers are located under the instrument panel. In order to gain access to these components, it may be necessary to first remove the under dash padding. Most of the circuit breakers are located in the fuse panel.

Fuse Block

▶ **See Figures 48 and 49**

The fuse block is located under the instrument panel next to the drivers door. The 1991-93 Caprice fuse panel is accessible with the drivers door opened.

Each fuse block uses miniature fuses which are designed for increased circuit protection and greater reliability. The compact fuse is a blade terminal design which allows fingertip removal and replacement.

Although the fuses are interchangeable, the amperage values are molded in bold, color coded, easy to read numbers on the fuse body. Use only fuses of equal replacement value.

A blown fuse can easily be checked by visual inspection or by continuity checking.

Buzzers, Relays and Flashers

The electrical devices are located in the fuse panel, which is located under the instrument panel. All units are serviced by plug-in replacements.

TURN SIGNAL FLASHER

The turn signal flasher is located in the fuse block. In order to gain access to the turn signal flasher, it may be necessary to first remove the under dash padding.

HAZARD FLASHER

The hazard flasher is located in the fuse panel. In order to gain access to the turn signal flasher, it may be necessary to first remove the under dash padding.

RELAYS

ABS Solenoid valve relay — integrated into the brake pressure modulator located in the left side of the engine compartment left of the generator.

A/C Blower Relay — integrated into the brake pressure modulator located in the left side of the engine compartment left of the generator.

A/C Blower Relay — located in the right rear of the engine compartment, near the blower motor on 1989-90 vehicles. For 1991-93 vehicles, it is near the blower which has been relocated to access from under the right hand side of the dash.

A/C Compressor Relay — located in the right rear of the engine compartment on the multi-use relay bracket.

Antenna Relay — located under the instrument panel compartment near the convenience center.

Choke Heater Relay — located on the left side front of the firewall, beside the brake booster.

Early Fuel Evaporation Relay — located in the right side of the engine compartment, top of the wheel house.

Electronic Level Control Relay — located in the engine compartment, on the fender next to the electronic level control compressor.

Fuel Pump Relay — located on a bracket in the right side of the engine compartment.

Headlight Relay — located at the front side of the engine compartment, near the headlight.

Horn Relay — is in the convenience center, behind the instrument panel to the left of the steering column.

Power Door Locks Relay — located behind the lower right kick panel.

Power Seat Relay — located on under the right or left seat.

Rear Glass Release Relay — located in the convenience center under the dash, left of the steering column.

Tailgate Release Relay — located at the base of the left side A pillar.

Theft Deterrent Relay — located behind the instrument panel to the left of the steering column.

Wiper Motor Relay — incorporated in the connector, on the wiper/washer assembly.

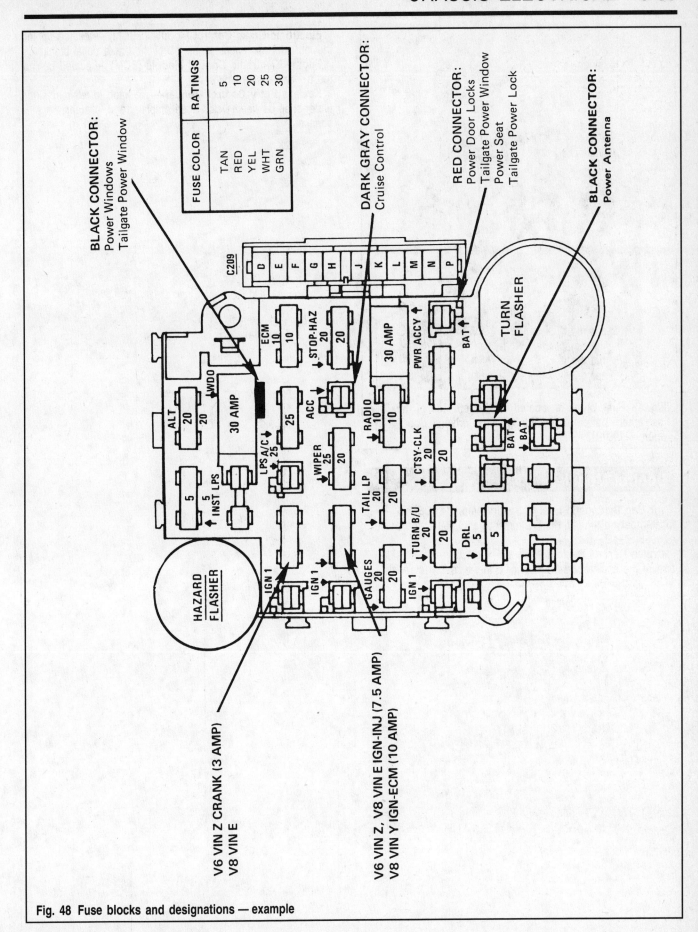

Fig. 48 Fuse blocks and designations — example

Fig. 49 Fuse block is located on the left side of the instrument panel, accessible with the drivers' door open — 1991-93

Control Modules

Air Bag Diagnostic Energy Reserve Module (DERM) — located behind the left side instrument panel, left of the brake pedal bracket.

Cruise Control System Module — located in the left side rear of the engine compartment next to the master cylinder.

Electronic Brake Control Module (EBCM) — located behind the left side instrument panel, left of the brake pedal bracket.

Engine Electronic Control Module (ECM) — located behind the front right side kick panel.

Keyless Entry Control Module — mounted to left rear side under-shelf between Delco-Bose amplifier and left rear speaker.

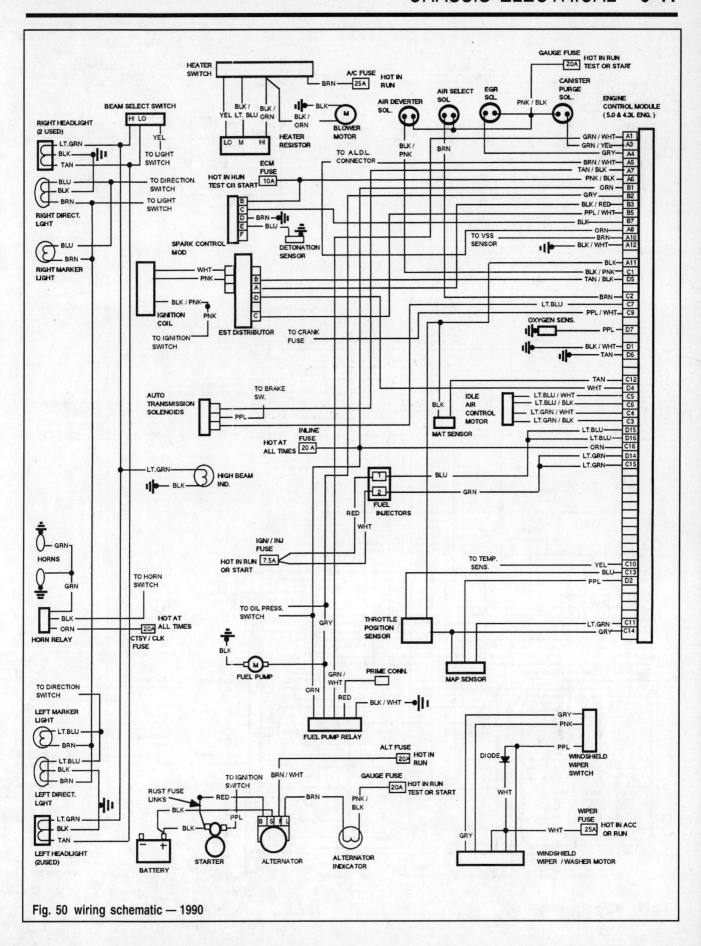

Fig. 50 wiring schematic — 1990

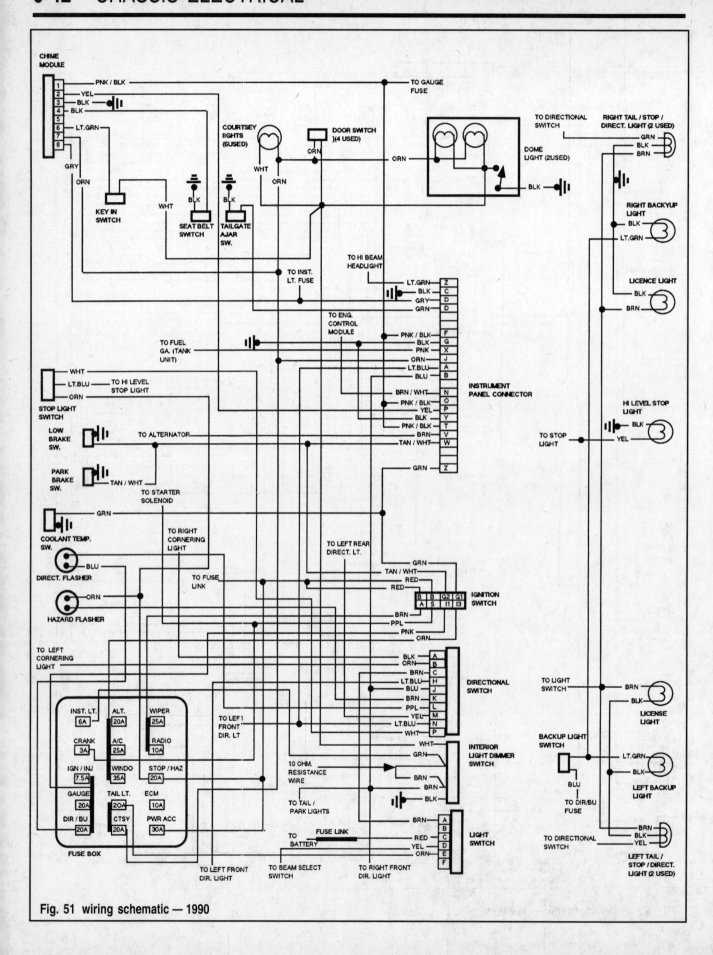

Fig. 51 wiring schematic — 1990

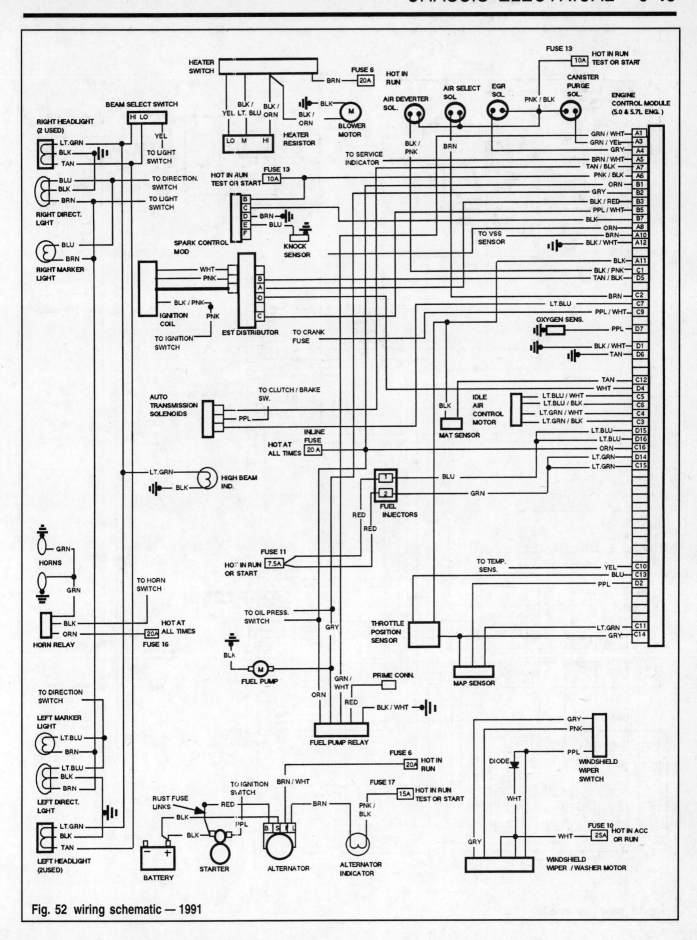

Fig. 52 wiring schematic — 1991

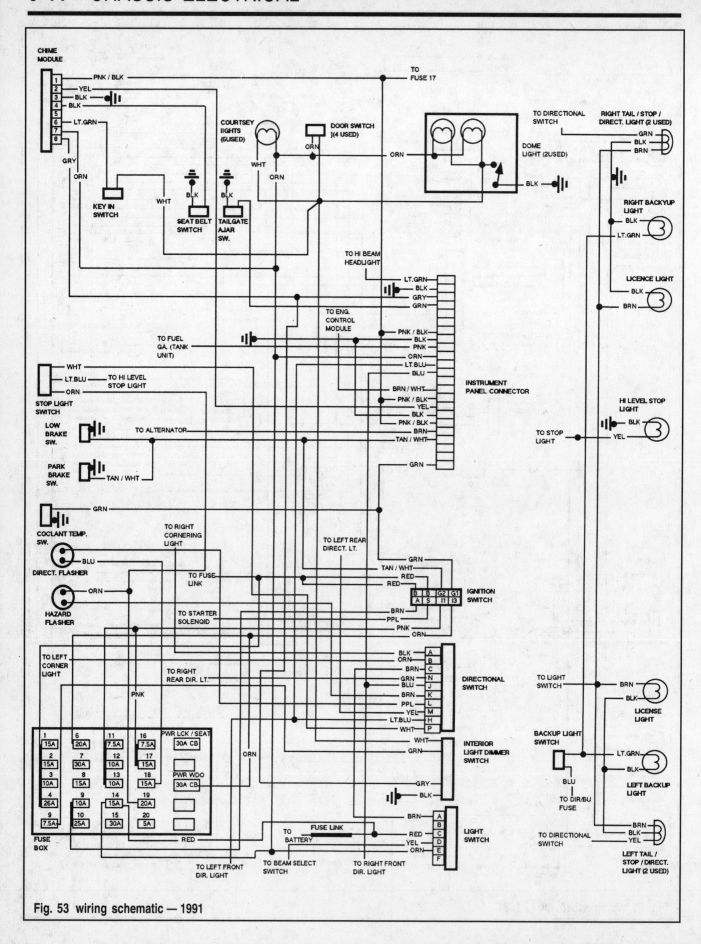

Fig. 53 wiring schematic – 1991

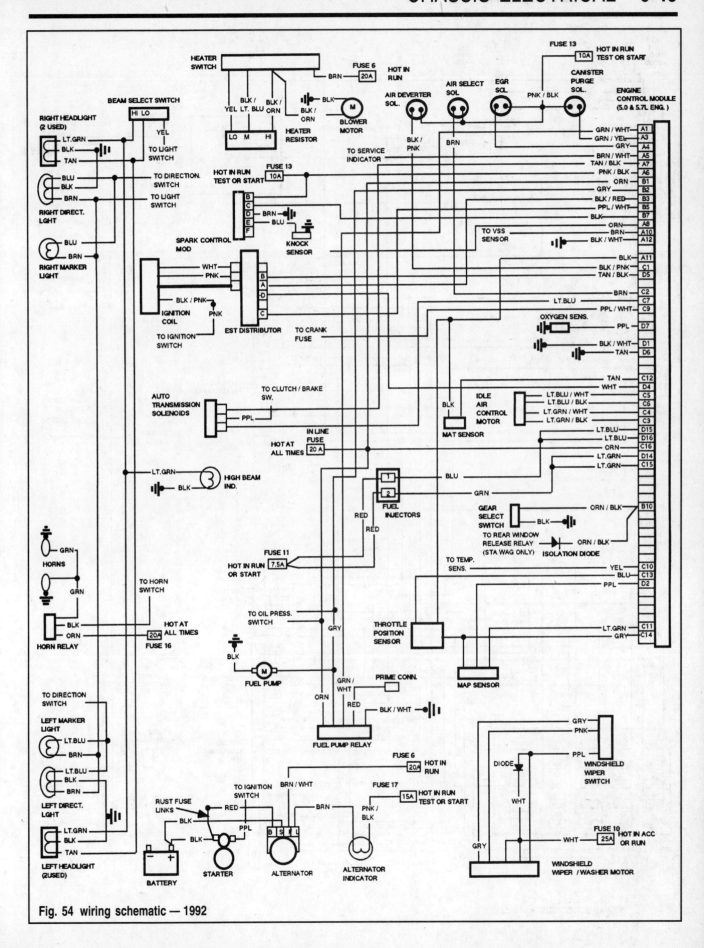

Fig. 54 wiring schematic — 1992

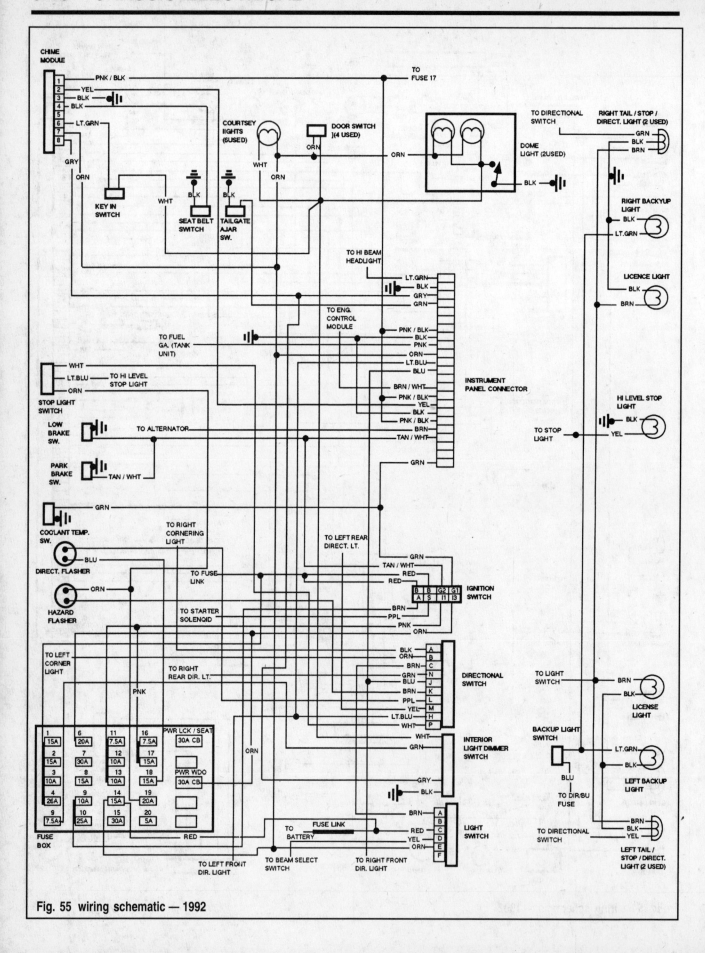

Fig. 55 wiring schematic — 1992

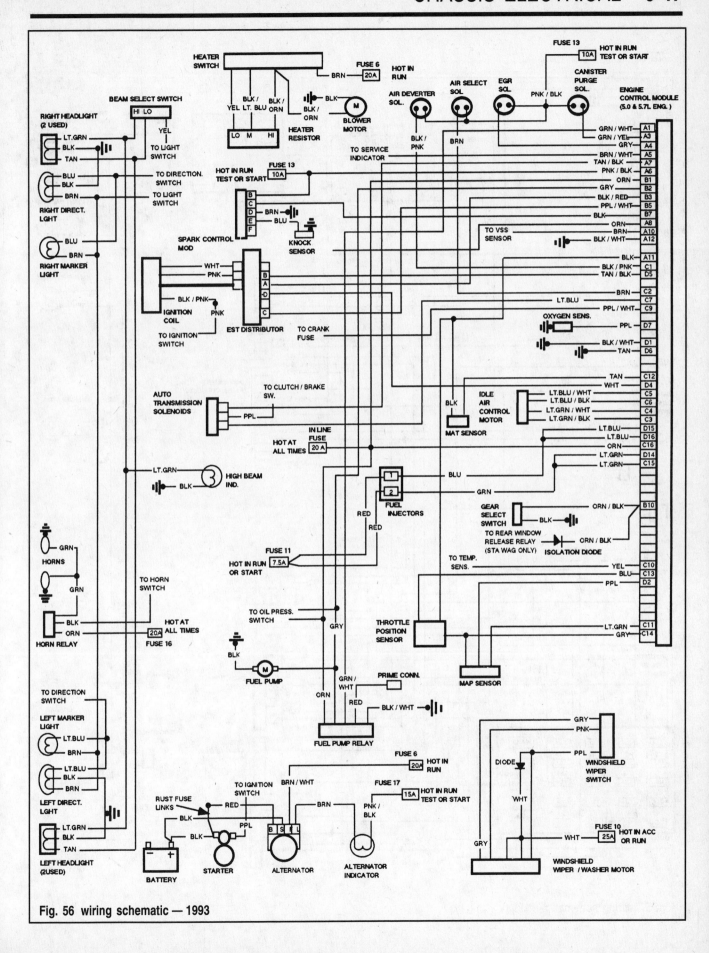

Fig. 56 wiring schematic — 1993

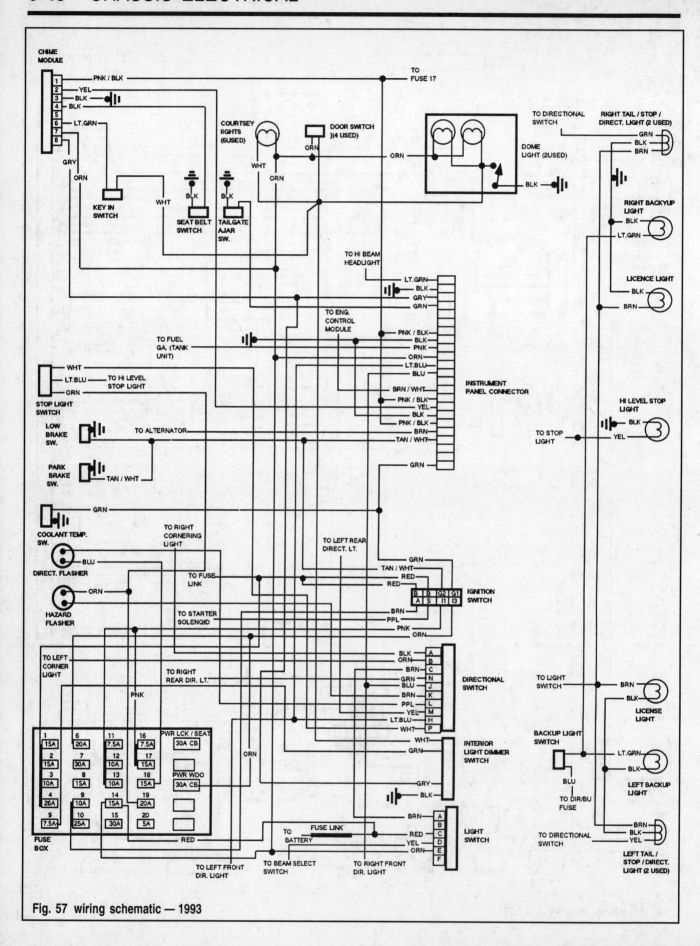

Fig. 57 wiring schematic — 1993

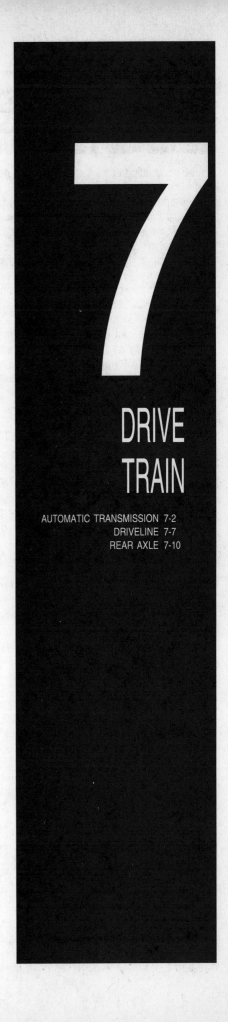

7

DRIVE
TRAIN

AUTOMATIC TRANSMISSION

Understanding Automatic Transmissions

The automatic transmission allows engine torque and power to be transmitted to the rear wheels within a narrow range of engine operating speeds. The transmission will allow the engine to turn fast enough to produce plenty of power and torque at very low speeds, while keeping it at a sensible rpm at high vehicle speeds. The transmission performs this job entirely without driver assistance. The transmission uses a light fluid as the medium for the transmission of power. This fluid also works in the operation of various hydraulic control circuits and as a lubricant. Because the transmission fluid performs all of these three functions, trouble within the unit can easily travel from one part to another. For this reason, and because of the complexity and unusual operating principles of the transmission, a very sound understanding of the basic principles of operation will simplify troubleshooting.

THE TORQUE CONVERTER

The torque converter replaces the conventional clutch. It has three functions:

1. It allows the engine to idle with the vehicle at a standstill, even with the transmission in gear.
2. It allows the transmission to shift from range to range smoothly, without requiring that the driver close the throttle during the shift.
3. It multiplies engine torque to an increasing extent as vehicle speed drops and throttle opening is increased. This has the effect of making the transmission more responsive and reduces the amount of shifting required.

The torque converter is a metal case which is shaped like a sphere that has been flattened on opposite sides. It is bolted to the rear end of the engine's crankshaft. Generally, the entire metal case rotates at engine speed and serves as the engine's flywheel.

The case contains three sets of blades. One set is attached directly to the case. This set forms the torus or pump. Another set is directly connected to the output shaft, and forms the turbine. The third set is mounted on a hub which, in turn, is mounted on a stationary shaft through a one-way clutch. This third set is known as the stator.

A pump, which is driven by the converter hub at engine speed, keeps the torque converter full of transmission fluid at all times. Fluid flows continuously through the unit to provide cooling.

Under low speed acceleration, the torque converter functions as follows:

The torus is turning faster than the turbine. It picks up fluid at the center of the converter and, through centrifugal force, slings it outward. Since the outer edge of the converter moves faster than the portions at the center, the fluid picks up speed.

The fluid then enters the outer edge of the turbine blades. It then travels back toward the center of the converter case along the turbine blades. In impinging upon the turbine blades, the fluid loses the energy picked up in the torus.

If the fluid were now to immediately be returned directly into the torus, both halves of the converter would have to turn at approximately the same speed at all times, and torque input and output would both be the same.

In flowing through the torus and turbine, the fluid picks up two types of flow, or flow in two separate directions. It flows through the turbine blades, and it spins with the engine. The stator, whose blades are stationary when the vehicle is being accelerated at low speeds, converts one type of flow into another. Instead of allowing the fluid to flow straight back into the torus, the stator's curved blades turn the fluid almost 90° toward the direction of rotation of the engine. Thus the fluid does not flow as fast toward the torus, but is already spinning when the torus picks it up. This has the effect of allowing the torus to turn much faster than the turbine. This difference in speed may be compared to the difference in speed between the smaller and larger gears in any gear train. The result is that engine power output is higher, and engine torque is multiplied.

As the speed of the turbine increases, the fluid spins faster and faster in the direction of engine rotation. As a result, the ability of the stator to redirect the fluid flow is reduced. Under cruising conditions, the stator is eventually forced to rotate on its one-way clutch in the direction of engine rotation. Under these conditions, the torque converter begins to behave almost like a solid shaft, with the torus and turbine speeds being almost equal.

THE PLANETARY GEARBOX

The ability of the torque converter to multiply engine torque is limited. Also, the unit tends to be more efficient when the turbine is rotating at relatively high speeds. Therefore, a planetary gearbox is used to carry the power output of the turbine to the driveshaft.

Planetary gears function very similarly to conventional transmission gears. However, their construction is different in that three elements make up one gear system, and, in that all three elements are different from one another. The three elements are: an outer gear that is shaped like a hoop, with teeth cut into the inner surface; a sun gear, mounted on a shaft and located at the very center of the outer gear; and a set of three planet gears, held by pins in a ring-like planet carrier, meshing with both the sun gear and the outer gear. Either the outer gear or the sun gear may be held stationary, providing more than one possible torque multiplication factor for each set of gears. Also, if all three gears are forced to rotate at the same speed, the gearset forms, in effect, a solid shaft.

Most modern automatics use the planetary gears to provide either a single reduction ratio of about 1.8:1, or two reduction gears: a low of about 2.5:1, and an intermediate of about 1.5:1. Bands and clutches are used to hold various portions of the gearsets to the transmission case or to the shaft on which they are mounted. Shifting is accomplished, then, by changing the portion of each planetary gearset which is held to the transmission case or to the shaft.

THE SERVOS AND ACCUMULATORS

The servos are hydraulic pistons and cylinders. They resemble the hydraulic actuators used on many familiar machines, such as bulldozers. Hydraulic fluid enters the cylinder, under pressure, and forces the piston to move to engage the band or clutches.

The accumulators are used to cushion the engagement of the servos. The transmission fluid must pass through the accumulator on the way to the servo. The accumulator housing contains a thin piston which is sprung away from the discharge passage of the accumulator. When fluid passes through the accumulator on the way to the servo, it must move the piston against spring pressure, and this action smooths out the action of the servo.

THE HYDRAULIC CONTROL SYSTEM

The hydraulic pressure used to operate the servos comes from the main transmission oil pump. This fluid is channeled to the various servos through the shift valves. There is generally a manual shift valve which is operated by the transmission selector lever and an automatic shift valve for each automatic upshift the transmission provides: i.e., 2-speed automatics have a low/high shift valve, while 3-speeds have a 1-2 valve, and a 2-3 valve.

There are two pressures which effect the operation of these valves. One is the governor pressure which is affected by vehicle speed. The other is the modulator pressure which is affected by intake manifold vacuum or throttle position. Governor pressure rises with an increase in vehicle speed, and modulator pressure rises as the throttle is opened wider. By responding to these two pressures, the shift valves cause the upshift points to be delayed with increased throttle opening to make the best use of the engine's power output.

Most transmissions also make use of an auxiliary circuit for down shifting. This circuit may be actuated by the throttle linkage or the vacuum line which actuates the modulator, or by a cable or solenoid. It applies pressure to a special downshift surface on the shift valve or valves.

The transmission modulator also governs the line pressure, used to actuate the servos. In this way, the clutches and bands will be actuated with a force matching the torque output of the engine.

Identification

▶ **See Figure 1**

Two types of transmissions are used on this vehicle; Turbo Hydra-Matic 200-4R and Turbo Hydra-Matic 700-R4 which became the Hydra-Matic 4L60 in 1990. Both transmissions incorporate 4 forward speeds (3 plus overdrive) and reverse. A picture of the pan gaskets used is shown in the illustration.

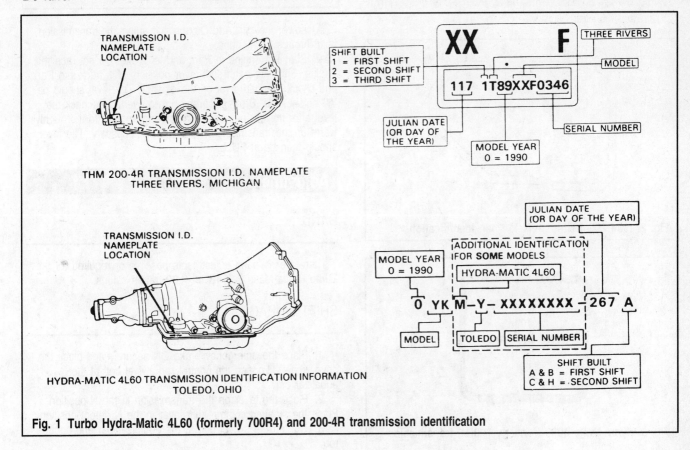

Fig. 1 Turbo Hydra-Matic 4L60 (formerly 700R4) and 200-4R transmission identification

Fluid Pan

▶ See Figures 2, 3 and 4

REMOVAL & INSTALLATION/FLUID & FILTER CHANGE

➡To remove the oil pan which has been installed with sealant, refer to the oil pan removal section of Section 1. The fluid should be changed with the transmission warm. A 20 minute drive at highway speeds should accomplish this.

1. Raise and safely support the vehicle. Safely support the transmission and remove the transmission crossmember, as required.

2. Place a large pan under the transmission pan. Remove all the front and side pan bolts. Loosen the rear bolts about four turns.

3. Tap the pan loose with a rubber mallet and let the pan drain.

4. Remove the pan and gasket. Clean the pan thoroughly with solvent and air dry it. Be very careful not to get any lint from rags in the pan.

5. Remove the filter and filter neck seal.

6. Install a new filter and seal.

7. Reinstall the pan with a new gasket. Torque the pan bolts to 97 inch lbs. (11 Nm) on the 200-4R or 12 ft. lbs. (16 Nm) on the 4L60 transmission.

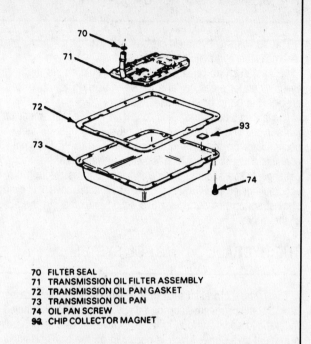

70 FILTER SEAL
71 TRANSMISSION OIL FILTER ASSEMBLY
72 TRANSMISSION OIL PAN GASKET
73 TRANSMISSION OIL PAN
74 OIL PAN SCREW
93 CHIP COLLECTOR MAGNET

Fig. 4 Replacing the transmission filter, pan gasket and filter neck seal — Hydra-Matic 4L60

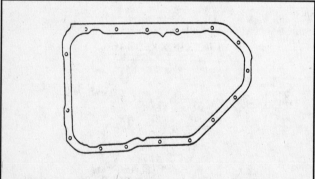

Fig. 2 THM 200-4R transmission pan identification

700
Turbo-Hydramatic

Fig. 3 Hydra-Matic 4L60 (formerly 700R4) transmission pan identification

8. Lower the car. Add Dexron® II automatic transmission fluid through the fill tube.

9. Start the engine in Park and let it idle. Do not race the engine. Shift into each shift lever position, shift back into Park, and check the fluid level on the dipstick. The level should be 1/4" below ADD. Be very careful not to overfill. Recheck the level after the car has been driven long enough to thoroughly warm up the transmission. Add fluid as necessary. The level should then be at FULL.

Adjustments

BAND

There are no band adjustments possible or required for the Turbo Hydra-Matic 200-4R or 4L60 transmissions.

SHIFT LINKAGE

1. Place the emergency brake ON securely and block the drive wheels. Loosen the control rod swivel bolt at the equalizer bar.

2. Place the lever on the transmission in the **N** position. Place the steering column shift lever in the **N** detent position.

3. Tighten the swivel bolt at the equalizer bar and control rod.

4. Check the shifter for proper operation.

THROTTLE VALVE (TV) CABLE

The TV cable controls transmission line pressure which in turn controls the shift and kick down points of the transmission.

▶ **See Figures 5 and 6**

1. After installation of the cable to the transmission, engine bracket, and the cable actuating lever, check to assure that the cable slider is in the zero or fully re-adjusted position.

2. If cable slider is not in the zero or fully re-adjusted, depress and hold the metal re-adjust tab. Move the slider back through the fitting in the direction away from the cable actuating (throttle) lever until the slider stops against the fitting. Release the metal re-adjust tab.

3. Rotate the cable actuating (throttle) lever to its full travel position.

4. The slider must move (ratchet) forward when the lever is rotated to the full travel position.

5. Release the lever. Check the adjustment by road testing the vehicle.

Neutral Start/Back-Up Light Switch

REPLACEMENT AND ADJUSTMENT

1. Disconnect the negative battery cable.

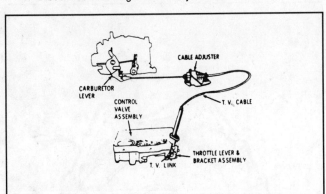

Fig. 5 Throttle Valve (TV) cable and linkage assembly

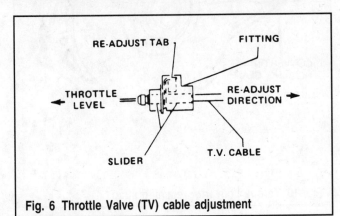

Fig. 6 Throttle Valve (TV) cable adjustment

2. Remove the left sound insulator. Disconnect the wiring at the switch assembly.

3. Disconnect the parking brake vacuum actuator hose assembly, if equipped.

4. Remove the switch assembly retainer and sealing strip, if equipped. Remove the switch assembly.

To install:

5. Block the drive wheels and place the transmission in **N**.

6. Align the actuator on the switch assembly with the hole on the shaft tube.

7. Position the connector side of the switch assembly to fit into the cutout on the steering column shaft.

8. Push down on the switch assembly to lock the tangs into place in the steering shaft.

9. If a used switch was reinstalled, move the switch assembly to the right, the **LOW** gear position. Then, place the transmission in **P**, the switch assembly will ratchet as it adjusts itself.

10. If a new switch being installed, simply place the transmission in **P** and the switch assembly will ratchet as it adjusts itself automatically.

11. Verify the switch is adjusted properly.

12. Install the switch retainer, if equipped.

13. Install the parking brake vacuum actuator.

14. Connect the switch wire connector.

15. Install the instrument panel sound insulator.

16. Connect the negative battery cable.

Extension Housing Seal (in Vehicle)

REMOVAL & INSTALLATION

This seal controls transmission oil leakage around the drive shaft. Continued failure of this seal usually indicates a worn output shaft bushing. If so, there will be signs of the same wear on the driveshaft where it contacts the seal and bushing. The seal is available and is fairly simple to install, with the proper tool.

1. Raise and safely support rear of the vehicle to minimize transmission oil loss when the driveshaft is removed.

2. Unbolt the driveshaft from the differential. Wrap tape around the bearing cups to keep them in place on the universal joint and slide the shaft out of the transmission.

3. Remove the floorpan reinforcement.

4. Use a suitable tool to carefully pry out the old seal. Be careful not to insert the tool too far into the housing or the bushing will be damaged.

5. Coat the outside surface of the seal with a non-hardening sealer. Use a suitable oil seal installation tool to evenly drive the new seal into the housing. Make sure the tool only contacts the outer metal portion of the seal.

6. Install the driveshaft and floorpan reinforcement. Torque the universal bearing cup retainer bolts to 15 ft. lbs. (20 Nm). Recheck fluid level.

Transmission

REMOVAL & INSTALLATION

▶ See Figures 7, 8, 9, 10 and 11

1. Disconnect the negative battery cable at the battery.
2. Remove the air cleaner assembly.
3. Disconnect the throttle valve (TV) control cable at the carburetor.
4. Remove the transmission oil dipstick. Unbolt and remove the dipstick tube.
5. Raise the vehicle and support it safely with jackstands.

➡ In order to provide adequate clearance for transmission removal, it may be necessary to raise both the front and the rear of the vehicle.

6. Mark the relationship between the driveshaft and the rear pinion flange so that the driveshaft may be reinstalled in its original position.
7. Unbolt the universal joint straps from the pinion flange (use care to keep the universal joint caps in place), lower and remove the driveshaft from the vehicle. Place a transmission tailshaft plug or rag in place of the driveshaft to keep the transmission fluid from draining out.
8. Remove the floorpan reinforcement.
9. Disconnect the catalytic converter support bracket at the transmission.

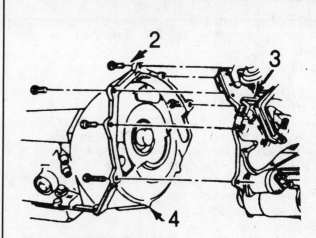

1. Transmission
2. Bolts
3. Engine

Fig. 9 Transmission-to-engine attaching bolts

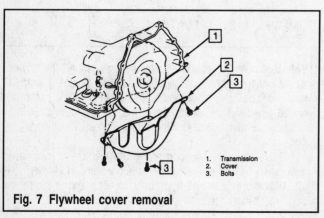

1. Transmission
2. Cover
3. Bolts

Fig. 7 Flywheel cover removal

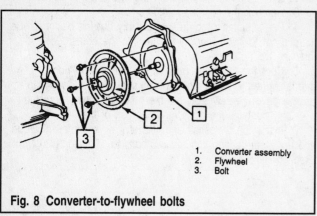

1. Converter assembly
2. Flywheel
3. Bolt

Fig. 8 Converter-to-flywheel bolts

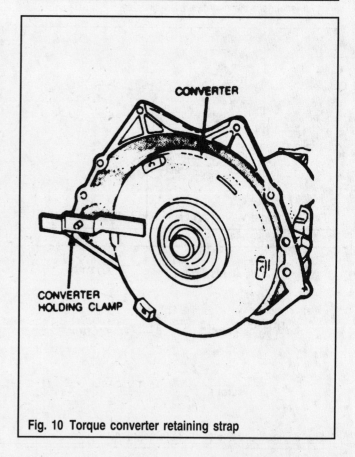

Fig. 10 Torque converter retaining strap

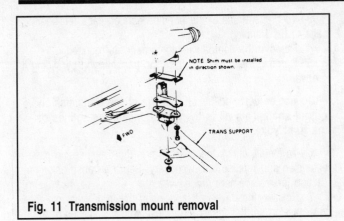

NOTE Shim must be installed in direction shown.

FWD

TRANS SUPPORT

Fig. 11 Transmission mount removal

10. Disconnect the speedometer cable, electrical connectors and the shift control cable from the transmission.

11. Remove the flywheel cover, then mark the relationship between the torque converter and the flywheel so that these parts may be reassembled in the same relationship.

12. Remove the 3 torque converter-to-flywheel attaching bolts. Remove the bolts by rotating the flywheel to access each bolt.

13. Support the transmission with a jack, then remove the transmission mount bolt.

14. Unbolt and remove the transmission crossmember.

15. Lower the transmission slightly. Disconnect the throttle valve cable and oil cooler lines from the transmission. Plug the transmission cooler lines to prevent leakage and dirt from entering.

16. Support the engine using Chevrolet special tool BT-6424 or its equivalent. Remove the transmission-to-engine mounting bolts. Install a suitable converter holding strap to retain the converter in position.

❋❋CAUTION

The transmission must be secured to the transmission jack.

17. Remove the transmission from the vehicle. Be careful not to damage the oil cooler lines, throttle valve cable, or the shift control cable. Also, keep the rear of the transmission lower than the front to avoid the possibility of the torque converter disengaging from the transmission.

To install:

18. To install, position the transmission and converter into place.

19. Install the transmission-to-engine mounting bolts.

20. Connect the throttle valve cable and oil cooler lines to the transmission.

21. Install the transmission crossmember and secure with bolts.

22. Install the transmission mount bolt.

23. Align the match mark on the torque converter and flywheel. Install the torque converter-to-flywheel attaching bolts.

➡**Before installing the converter-to-flywheel bolts, be sure that the weld nuts on the converter are flush with the flywheel, and that the converter rotates freely by hand in this position. This will ensure that the converter is properly engaged to the front pump of the transmission.**

24. Install the flywheel cover.

25. Connect the speedometer cable, electrical connectors and the shift control cable from the transmission.

26. Connect the catalytic converter support bracket at the transmission.

27. Install the driveshaft to the match mark made earlier to the driveshaft and axle pinion. Bolt the universal joint straps to the pinion flange.

28. Install the floorpan reinforcement.

29. Lower the vehicle.

30. Install the dipstick tube using a new dipstick tube O-ring and secure with the bolt. Install the transmission oil dipstick.

31. Connect the throttle valve (TV) control cable at TBI assembly.

32. Install the air cleaner assembly.

33. Connect the negative battery cable at the battery.

DRIVELINE

Driveshaft and U-Joints

The driveshaft (propeller shaft) is a long steel tube that transmits engine power from the transmission to the rear axle assembly. It is connected to, and revolves with, the transmission output shaft (remember, the transmission shaft is connected to and revolves with the engine crankshaft) whenever the transmission is put into gear. With the transmission in neutral, the driveshaft does not move. Located at each end of the driveshaft is a flexible joint that rotates with the shaft. These flexible joints, known as U-joints (universal joints) perform an important function. The rear axle assembly moves with the car. It moves up and down with every bump or dip in the road. The driveshaft by itself is a rigid tube incapable of bending. When combined with the flexing capabilities of the U-joints, however, it can do so.

A slip joint is coupled to the front of the driveshaft by a universal joint. This U-joint allows the yoke (slip joint) to move up and down with the car. The yoke is a cylinder containing splines that slide over the meshes with splines on the transmission output shaft. When the rear axle moves up and down, the yoke slides back and forth a small amount on the transmission shaft. Therefore, it combines with the U-joints in allowing the driveshaft to move with the movements of the car. The rear universal joint is secured to a companion flange which is attached to, and revolves with, the rear axle drive pinion.

A U-joint consists of a cross piece (trunnion) and, on each of the four ends, a dust seal and a series of needle bearings that fit into a bearing cup. Each U-joint connects one yoke with another and the bearings allow the joints to revolve within each yoke.

The U-joint is secured to the yoke in one of two ways. Dana and Cleveland shafts use a conventional snapring to hold each bearing cup in the yoke. The snapring fits into a groove located in each yoke end just on top of each bearing cup. The Saginaw design shaft secures its U-joints in another way. Nylon material is injected through a small hole in the yoke and flows along a circular groove between the U-joint and the yoke, creating a synthetic snapring. Disassembly of the Saginaw U-joint requires the joint to be pressed from the yoke. This results in damage to the bearing cups and destruction of the nylon rings.

Replacement kits include new bearing cups and conventional snaprings to replace the original nylon rings. These replacement rings must go inboard of the yoke in contrast to outboard mounting of the Dana and Cleveland designs. Previous service to the Saginaw U-joints can be recognized by the presence of snaprings inboard of the yoke.

Bad U-joints, requiring replacement, will produce a clunking sound when the car is put into gear. This is due to worn needle bearings or a scored trunnion end possibly caused by improper lubrication during assembly. U-joints require no periodic maintenance and therefore have no lubrication fittings. The replacement U-joints generally have lubrication fitting.

Driveshaft

▶ **See Figure 12**

REMOVAL & INSTALLATION

1. Raise the vehicle and safely support it on jackstands. Paint a reference line from the rear end of the driveshaft to the companion (axle) flange so they can be reassembled in the same position.
2. Disconnect the rear universal joint by removing the U-bolts, retaining straps, or the flange bolts.

3. To prevent loss of the needle bearings, tape the bearing caps to the trunnion.
4. Remove the floorpan reinforcement, as required.
5. Remove the driveshaft from the transmission by sliding it rearward.

➡**Do not be alarmed by oil leakage at the transmission output shaft. This oil is there to lubricate the splines of the front yoke.**

6. To install, check the yoke seal in the transmission case extension and replace it if necessary. See the transmission section for replacement procedures.
7. Position the driveshaft and insert the front yoke into the transmission so that the splines mesh with the splines of the transmission shaft.
8. Using reference marks made during removal, align the driveshaft with the companion flange and secure it with U-bolts or, retaining straps.
9. Install the floorpan reinforcement.

U-JOINT REPLACEMENT

▶ **See Figures 13, 14, 15, 16 and 17**

1. Support the driveshaft horizontally in line with the base plate of a press.
2. Place the U-joint so the lower ear of the shaft yoke is supported on a 1⅛ inch socket.
3. Remove the lower bearing cap out of the yoke ear by placing tool J-9522-3 or equivalent, on the open horizontal

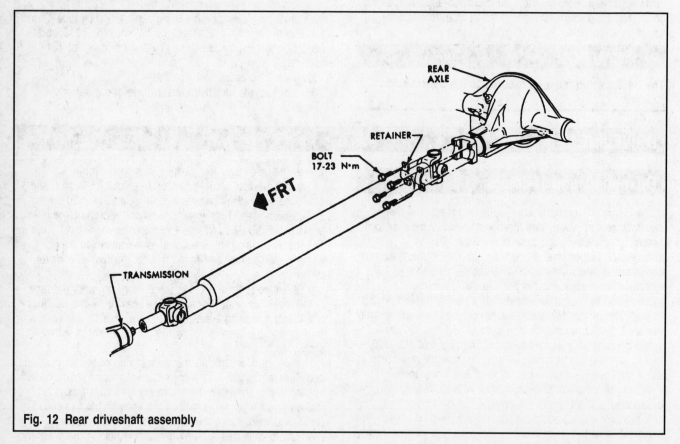

Fig. 12 Rear driveshaft assembly

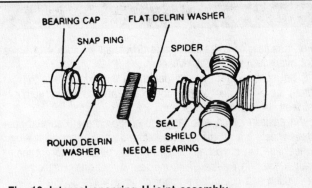

Fig. 13 Internal snapring U-joint assembly

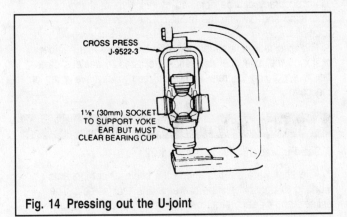

Fig. 14 Pressing out the U-joint

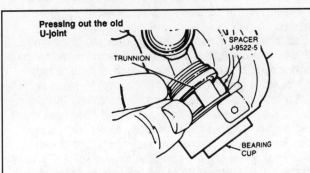

Fig. 15 Insert spacer tool to push cup out of joint all the way

bearing caps and pressing the lower bearing cap out of the yoke ear.

➡This will shear the nylon injector ring, if the original U-joint is being removed. There are no bearing retaining grooves in the production bearing caps, therefore they cannot be reused. If a replacement U-joint is being removed, ensure to remove the retaining clips from the U-joint.

4. If the bearing cap is not completely removed, lift tool J-9522-3 and insert tool J-9522-5 or equivalent between the bearing cap and seal and continue pressing the U-joint out of the yoke.

5. Repeat the procedure for the opposite side.
6. Remove the spider from the yoke.
To install:
7. Install 1 bearing cap part way into 1 side of the yoke. Turn this yoke ear to the bottom.
8. Using tool J-9522-3 or equivalent, seat the trunnion into the bearing cap.
9. Install the opposite bearing cap partially onto the trunnion.
10. Ensure both trunnions are straight and true in the bearing caps.
11. Press the spider against the opposite bearing cap, while working the spider back and forth to ensure free movement of the trunnions in the bearing caps.
12. If trunnion is binding, the needle bearings have tipped over under the end of the cap.
13. Stop pressing when 1 bearing cap clears the retainer groove inside the yoke.
14. Install a retaining ring.
15. Repeat the procedure for the remaining bearing caps and U-joints.
16. Installation of the driveshaft is the reverse of the removal procedure. Tighten the strap bolts to 16 ft. lbs. (22 Nm).

➡Some Saginaw shafts use two different sizes of bearing cups at the differential end. The larger cups (the ones with the groove) fit into the driveshaft yoke.

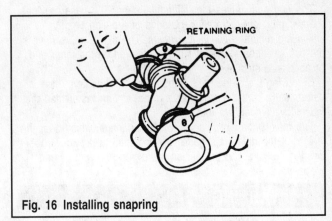

Fig. 16 Installing snapring

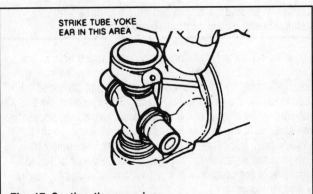

Fig. 17 Seating the snapring

REAR AXLE

Identification

The rear axle code and the manufacturers code, plus the date built, is stamped on the right axle tube on the forward side. Any reports made on the rear axle assemblies must include the full code letters and the date built numbers. The Limited-slip differentials are identified by a tag attached to the lower right section of the axle.

Understanding Drive Axles

The drive axle is a special type of transmission that reduces the speed of the drive from the engine and transmission and divides the power to the wheels. Power enters the axle from the driveshaft via the companion flange. The flange is mounted on the drive pinion shaft. The drive pinion shaft and gear which carry the power into the differential turn at engine speed. The gear on the end of the pinion shaft drives a large ring gear the axis of rotation of which is 90 degrees away from the of the pinion. The pinion and gear reduce the gear ratio of the axle, and change the direction of rotation to turn the axle shafts which drive both wheels. The axle gear ratio is found by dividing the number of pinion gear teeth into the number of ring gear teeth.

The ring gear drives the differential case. The case provides the two mounting points for the ends of a pinion shaft on which are mounted two pinion gears. The pinion gears drive the two side gears, one of which is located on the inner end of each axle shaft.

By driving the axle shafts through the arrangement, the differential allows the outer drive wheel to turn faster than the inner drive wheel in a turn.

The main drive pinion and the side bearings, which bear the weight of the differential case, are shimmed to provide proper bearing preload, and to position the pinion and ring gears properly.

✳✳WARNING

The proper relationship of the ring and pinion gears is critical. It should be attempted only by those with extensive equipment and/or experience.

Limited-slip differentials include clutches which tend to link each axle shaft to the differential case. Clutches may be engaged either by spring action or by pressure produced by the torque on the axles during a turn. During turning on a dry pavement, the effects of the clutches are overcome, and each wheel turns at the required speed. When slippage occurs at either wheel, however, the clutches will transmit some of the power to the wheel which has the greater amount of traction. Because of the presence of clutches, limited-slip units require a special lubricant.

Determining Axle Ratio

An axle ratio is obtained by dividing the number of teeth on the drive pinion gear into the number of teeth on the ring gear.

For instance, on a 4.11 ratio, the driveshaft will turn 4.11 times for every turn of the rear wheel.

The most accurate way to determine the axle ratio is to drain the differential, remove the cover, and count the number of teeth on the ring and pinion.

An easier method is to jack and support the car so that both rear wheels are off the ground. Make a chalk mark on the rear wheel and the driveshaft. Block the front wheels and put the transmission in Neutral. Turn the rear wheel one complete revolution and count the number of turns made by the driveshaft. The number of driveshaft rotations is the axle ratio. More accuracy can be obtained by going more than one tire revolution and dividing the result by the number of tire rotations.

The axle ratio is also identified by the axle serial number prefix on the axle; the axle ratios are listed in dealer's parts books according to prefix number. Some axles have a tag on the cover.

Axle Shaft, Bearing and Seal

▶ **See Figures 18, 19, 20, 21 and 22**

Axle shafts are the last link in the chain of components working to transmit engine power to the rear wheels. The splined end of each shaft meshes with the internal splines of each differential side gear. As the side gears turn, so do the axle shafts, and, since they are also connected, so do the wheels.

Each shaft passes through the side gear and is locked into place by a C-lock located inside the differential cover. As the name implies, the C-lock is a flat, C-shaped piece of metal that fits into a groove at the end of the shaft. A round pinion shaft is wedged in between the end of the shafts. This pinion shaft prevents the shafts from sliding inward and makes the C-locks functional by pushing them tightly against each side gear. Removing this pinion shaft allows the shafts to slide inward making the C-locks accessible for removal. Once the C-locks are removed, the axle shafts can be pulled from the car.

The wheel end of each shaft is flanged and pressed into it are five wheel lug bolts serving to hold on the wheel. Each axle shaft is supported by an axle bearing (wheel bearing) and oil seal located within the axle shaft housing just to the outside of the brake backing plate.

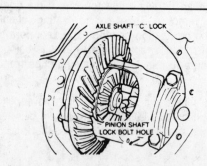

Fig. 18 Removing the pinion shaft lock bolt, pin and C-Locks

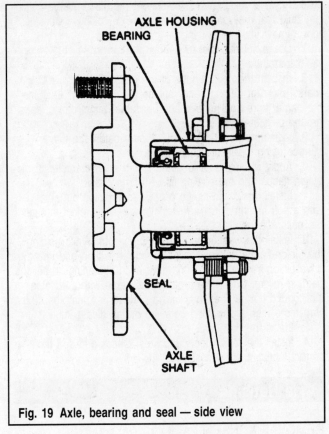

Fig. 19 Axle, bearing and seal — side view

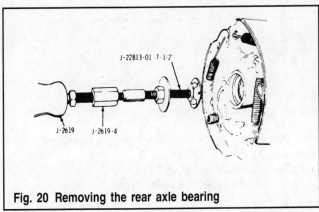

Fig. 20 Removing the rear axle bearing

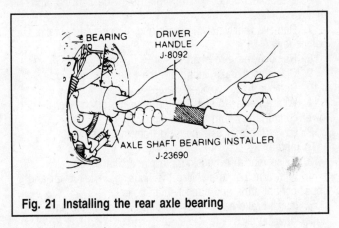

Fig. 21 Installing the rear axle bearing

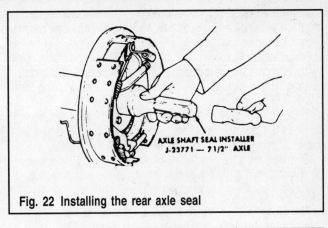

Fig. 22 Installing the rear axle seal

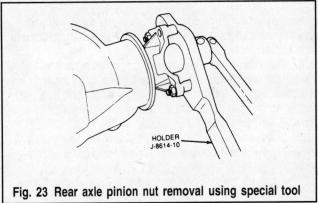

Fig. 23 Rear axle pinion nut removal using special tool

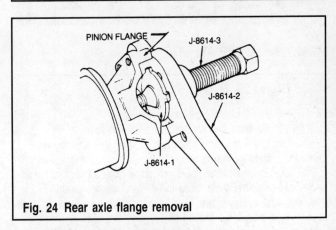

Fig. 24 Rear axle flange removal

REMOVAL & INSTALLATION

1. Raise vehicle and support it safely. Remove the tire and wheel assembly. Remove the brake drum.

2. Drain the fluid. Clean all dirt from the rear carrier cover and remove. Discard the gasket.

3. Remove the pinion shaft lock bolt and the pinion gear shaft.

4. Push flanged end of axle shaft toward center of the vehicle and remove C-lock from button end of shaft.

5. Remove axle shaft from housing, being careful not to damage oil seal.

6. Remove seal from housing with a prybar behind steel case of seal, being careful not to damage housing.

7. Insert tool J-23689 or equivalent, into bore and position it behind bearing so tangs on tool engage bearing outer race. Remove bearing, using slide hammer.

To install:

8. Lubricate the new bearing with gear lubricant and install bearing so tool bottoms against shoulder in housing, using tool J-23690 or equivalent.

9. Lubricate seal lips with gear lubricant. Position seal on tool J-21128 or equivalent, and position seal into housing bore. Tap seal into place so it is flush with axle tube.

10. Insert the axle into the place while engaging the splines on the end of the shaft with the splines of the rear axle side gear. Be careful not to damage the seal.

➡**The 30-spline 8 ½ in. ring gear axle shaft is not interchangeable with any pre-1989 axle shaft.**

11. Install the C-lock on the bottom of the axle shaft and push the shaft outward so the lock seats in the counterbore of the rear axle side gear.

12. Install the rear axle pinion gear shaft through the differential case, thrust washers and pinions, align the hole in the shaft with the lock bolt hole. Install the lock bolt and tighten to 24 ft. lbs. (31 Nm) for 7½ inch ring gears or 20 ft. lbs. (27 Nm) for 8½ inch ring gears.

13. Install the carrier cover and bolts using a new gasket.

14. Fill the rear assembly with the proper grade and type gear oil.

15. Install the brake drum and wheel and lower the vehicle.

Pinion Seal

REMOVAL & INSTALLATION

▶ **See Figures 23, 24 and 25**

1. Raise and safely support the vehicle.
2. Remove both rear wheel and tire assemblies.
3. Matchmark the driveshaft and pinion yoke so they may be reassembled in the same position. Remove the driveshaft.
4. Using a suitable inch pound torque wrench on the pinion yoke nut, measure and record the pinion bearing, axle bearings and seal preload.
5. Using a suitable tool to hold the pinion yoke in place, remove the pinion yoke nut and washer.

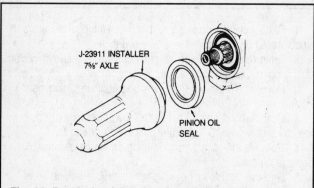

J-23911 INSTALLER
7⅝" AXLE

PINION OIL
SEAL

Fig. 25 Rear axle pinion seal installation

6. Place a suitable container under the differential to catch any fluid that may drain from the rear axle. Using a suitable tool, remove the pinion flange.

7. Use a suitable tool to remove the pinion seal.

To install:

8. Inspect the seal surface of the pinion flange for tool marks, nicks or damage and replace, as necessary. Examine the carrier bore and remove any burrs that might cause leaks around the outside of the seal.

9. Install the seal 0.010 in. (0.25mm) below the flange surface using a suitable seal installer.

10. Apply suitable seal lubricant to the outer diameter of the pinion flange and the sealing lip of the new seal.

11. Install the pinion flange on the drive pinion by taping with a soft hammer until a few pinion threads project through the pinion flange.

12. Install the washer and pinion flange nut. While holding the pinion flange, tighten the nut a little at a time and turn the drive pinion several revolutions after each tightening, to set the bearing rollers. Check the preload each time with a suitable inch pound torque wrench until the preload is 5 inch lbs. (0.6 Nm) more then the reading obtained during disassembly.

13. Install the driveshaft.

14. Install the rear wheels and tires. Check and add the correct lubricant, as necessary.

Axle Housing

REMOVAL & INSTALLATION

1990

▶ **See Figure 26**

1. Raise the vehicle and support it safely. Be sure the rear axle assembly is supported safely.
2. Disconnect the ABS rear axle speed sensor connector, if equipped.
3. Remove the shock absorbers from axle housing, if applicable.
4. Remove the driveshaft.
5. Remove the brake line junction block bolt at axle housing, disconnect brake lines at junction block.
6. Disconnect upper control arms from axle housing, and remove springs.
7. Remove rear wheels, drums and, if necessary, brake components.
8. Remove the axle shaft.
9. Disconnect brake lines from the axle housing clips.
10. Remove brake backing plates.
11. With a helper to stabilize the housing, disconnect the lower control arms from the axle housing.
12. Lower the rear axle housing from the hoist.

To install:

13. Raise rear axle housing into place with a hoist.
14. With a helper to stabilize the housing, install lower and upper control arms and hand tighten bolts.
15. Install brake backing plates and position brake lines under housing clips.
16. Install the axle shaft.

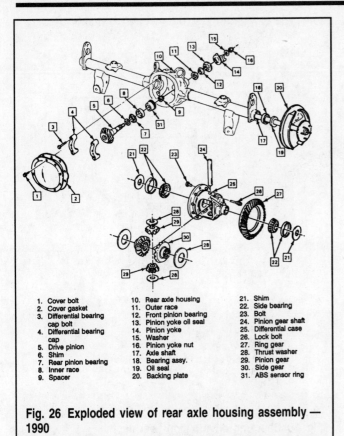

1. Cover bolt
2. Cover gasket
3. Differential bearing cap bolt
4. Differential bearing cap
5. Drive pinion
6. Shim
7. Rear pinion bearing
8. Inner race
9. Spacer
10. Rear axle housing
11. Outer race
12. Front pinion bearing
13. Pinion yoke oil seal
14. Pinion yoke
15. Washer
16. Pinion yoke nut
17. Axle shaft
18. Bearing assy.
19. Oil seal
20. Backing plate
21. Shim
22. Side bearing
23. Bolt
24. Pinion gear shaft
25. Differential case
26. Lock bolt
27. Ring gear
28. Thrust washer
29. Pinion gear
30. Side gear
31. ABS sensor ring

Fig. 26 Exploded view of rear axle housing assembly — 1990

17. Install brake components, if removed, rear drums and wheels.

18. Install springs.

19. Connect brake lines to the junction block and the junction block to the rear axle housing.

20. Install the driveshaft.

21. Install the ABS sensor connector.

22. Install shock absorbers, where applicable.

23. Fill axle with suitable gear oil.

24. Torque upper and lower control arms with the weight of the vehicle on the axle.

25. Remove supports and lower vehicle, bleed the brake system as necessary.

1991-93

1. Raise the vehicle and support it safely. Be sure the rear axle assembly is supported safely.

2. Disconnect the ABS rear axle speed sensor connector.

3. Disconnect the automatic level sensor control link, if equipped.

4. Remove the driveshaft.

5. Remove rear wheels, drums and, if necessary, brake components.

6. Remove axle shaft.

7. Disconnect the parking brake cables. Remove the brake backing plate and rear brake pipes from the rear hose fittings. Plug brake pipes to prevent fluid loss and to protect from dirt.

8. Disconnect bolts attaching rear brake hose fitting to housing and remove hose fitting.

9. If replacing housing, remove rear brake pipes from housing.

10. With a helper, remove rear springs and disconnect upper and lower control arms.

11. Lower rear axle housing from hoist.

To install:

12. Raise rear axle housing into place with a hoist.

13. With a helper to stabilize the housing, install lower and upper control arms.

14. Install rear springs.

15. Attach rear brake pipes to housing with retaining clips or straps, if housing was replaced.

16. Connect rear brake fitting and attaching bolt to housing. Tighten bolt to 20 ft. lbs. (27 Nm).

17. Unplug and connect rear brake pipes to rear brake hose fitting. Tighten fitting to 18 ft. lbs. (24 Nm).

18. Connect parking brake cable and brake backing plate.

19. Install axle shaft.

20. Install brake components, drums and rear wheels.

21. Install the driveshaft.

22. Connect the automatic level control sensor link and the ABS rear axle speed sensor connector.

23. Fill axle housing with suitable gear oil.

24. Remove support from the housing and lower the vehicle.

25. Be sure to bleed the brake system, as required.

Differential Assembly

REMOVAL & INSTALLATION

1. Raise and safely support the vehicle.

2. Place a suitable container under the differential. Remove the carrier cover and drain the gear oil.

3. Remove the drive axles.

4. Mark the differential bearing caps **L** and **R** to make sure they will be reassembled in their original location.

5. Using a suitable tool, remove the differential carrier. Be careful not to damage the gasket sealing surface when removing the unit. Place the right and left bearing outer races of the side bearing assemblies and shims in sets with the marked differential bearings caps so they can be reinstalled in their original positions.

To install:

6. Inspect the differential carrier housing for foreign material. Check the ring and pinion for chipped teeth, excessive wear and scoring. Check the carrier bearings visually and by feel. Clean the differential housing and replace components, as necessary.

7. Install the differential carrier. Check the carrier bearing preload and ring and pinion backlash and adjust, as necessary. Tighten the differential bearing cap bolts to 55 ft. lbs. (75 Nm).

8. Install the axles.

9. Install the carrier cover using a new gasket. Tighten the carrier cover bolts to 20 ft. lbs. (27 Nm). Add the proper type and quantity of gear oil to axle assembly.

Differential Overhaul

◆ See Figures 27, 28, 29, 30 and 31

➡The Auburn limited slip differential case is non-serviceable and must be replaced as an assembly. Removal and replacement of the limited slip differential case and service on the side bearings and ring gear is the same as for the standard rear axle.

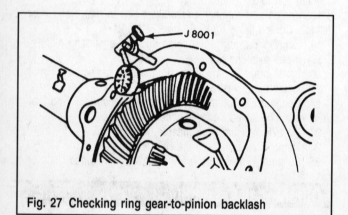

Fig. 27 Checking ring gear-to-pinion backlash

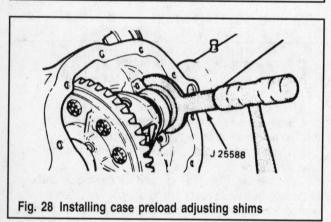

Fig. 28 Installing case preload adjusting shims

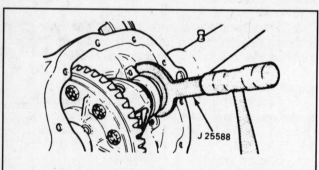

Fig. 29 Pinion gage installed in carrier — Standard & Auburn limited slip rear axle

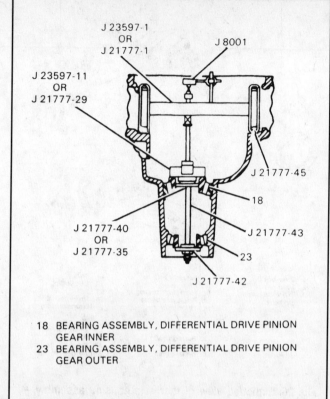

18 BEARING ASSEMBLY, DIFFERENTIAL DRIVE PINION GEAR INNER
23 BEARING ASSEMBLY, DIFFERENTIAL DRIVE PINION GEAR OUTER

Fig. 30 Checking drive pinion gear depth

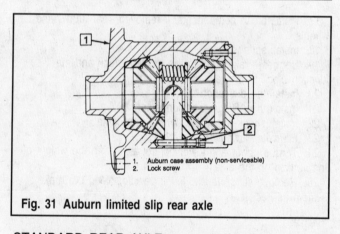

1. Auburn case assembly (non-serviceable)
2. Lock screw

Fig. 31 Auburn limited slip rear axle

STANDARD REAR AXLE

❋❋WARNING

Several special tools are required to disassemble, assemble and adjust the rear axle. Listed here are some of the tools required for disassembly. Overhaul of the rear axle assembly is not suggested for the novice mechanic who do not have access to all special tools. The adjustments and set-up procedure of the rear assembly is crucial for dependability, wear characteristics and silent operation.

- J-2619-01 Slide Hammer
- J-22813-01 Axle Bearing Puller
- J-8107-2/-4 Differential Side Bearing Remover Plug
- J-22888 Side Bearing Remover
- J-8614-01 Pinion Flange Remover
- J-25320 Rear Pinion Bearing Remover

➡**Before disassembly, there are some things to check. First drain the oil and examine it. If there is heavy gear or bearing wear in the axle, usually the oil takes on a metal-flake appearance from the worn metal being suspended in the oil. Also check the backlash, described later in this procedure. This information can be useful in determining the cause of axle problems and in deciding on the shim packs to be used for assembly.**

1. With the axle properly supported and the brake drums removed, remove the rear cover.
2. Remove the pinion shaft lock bolt, pinion shaft and C locks from the button end of the axle shaft.
3. Remove the axle shafts and carefully pry out the oil seal from each end of the housing.
4. Use the bearing removal tools to remove the axle be.
5. Make sure the tool engages the outer race of the bearing.
6. Roll the pinion gears out of the case with their thrust washers. Label their position.
7. Remove the side gears and thrust washers and label their position.
8. Mark the differential bearing caps left and right and remove them.
9. Insert a pry bar into the differential window and carefully pry the differential out of the axle housing. Be careful not to damage the gasket surface of the housing.
10. When removing the differential bearing races, keep the shims and spacers together with the race and label them left and right.
11. Install the puller on the differential side bearing, making sure the jaws contact the inner race of the bearing, not the cage. Remove the bearings.
12. Remove the ring gear from the differential case, using a brass drift and hammer. The 10 bolts are left hand thread. DO NOT pry the gear off, this will damage the gear and the case.
13. Before removing the drive pinion, use an inch pound torque wrench to see how much torque is required to turn the pinion. This checks the bearing preload.
14. Install the pinion flange holding tool remove the pinion flange nut.
15. To remove the pinion flange use the special puller.
16. To remove the drive pinion, put the rear housing cover on with 2 screws so the pinion doesn't fall to the floor.
17. Put the flange nut onto the pinion a few thread and use a hammer and soft drift pin to drive the pinion out of the housing.
18. With the pinion out, remove the collapsible spacer.
19. Remove the oil seal and outer pinion bearing.
20. To remove the inner pinion bearing, use the bearing pulling tool J-25320 and a press. Keep track of the shims under the bearing. If equipped with anti-lock brakes, remove the rear speed sensor ring using puller tool J-22912-01.
21. Remove the pinion drive bearing races from the case with a hammer and brass drift pin.

Inspection

Clean all parts in a clean solvent and dry with air. Carefully inspect the housing for damage to the sealing areas and the bearing areas for burrs or nicks that may interfere with assembly. Remove any imperfections that are found. Thoroughly clean the housing using solvent, not steam or water. Any metal chips or rust left in the housing will damage the gears and bearings. Check the housing for cracks.

Check the differential gears, shafts and thrust washers for uneven or heavy wear patterns. Check the differential case for cracks and signs of heat damage or scoring. Check the fit of the gears on the axle shafts and in the differential case. If in doubt, replace the parts.

Inspect the pinion shaft splines for wear and check the fit with the pinion flange. If the sealing surface on the flange is nicked or worn, replace the flange. Compare the wear patterns on the ring and pinion gears for excessive wear or signs of heat damage. A ring and pinion gear are a matched set and must be replaced together.

Inspect the bearings for signs of heat damage or contamination. The big end of tapered rollers is where signs of wear or damage will appear first. Low mileage units will show some scratches on the bearings from initial preload. If the (oiled) bearing still feels smooth, it need not be replaced. If the axle was used for an extended period with very loose bearings, the ring and pinion should be replaced. When replacing bearings, also replace the outer race.

Assembly

➡**Several special assembly tools are required for correct measurement and positioning of the ring and pinion.**

PINION DEPTH ADJUSTMENT

1. Clean all gage parts.
2. Lubricate the front and rear pinion bearings with gear oil.
3. With the outer races installed into the axle housing, place the bearings into the outer races and secure them in place with the pilot washers and stud assembly tool and gage plate as shown.
4. Torque the J-21777-43 stud assembly to 20 inch lbs. (2.2 Nm).
5. Rotate the gage plate and bearings several revolutions to seat the bearings.
6. Torque the stud assembly.
7. Install the arbor, side bearing disks and dial indicator as shown.
8. Install the side bearing caps and finger tighten the bolts.
9. Rotate the gage plate until the gaging areas are parallel with the disks.
10. Position the gage plate shaft assembly in the carrier so that the dial indicator rod is centered on the gage area of the gage block.
11. Set the dial indicator at zero and preload the dial to about ¾ turn of the needle.
12. Rotate the gage shaft to find the high point and zero the dial.
13. Rotate the gage shaft until the dial indicator rod does not touch the gage block.
14. Record the actual number on the dial indicator, not the number which represents how far the needle traveled. This is the nominal pinion setting. Example: If the indicator moved left

0.067 inch (1.7mm) to a reading of 0.033 inch (0.84mm), record the reading of 0.033 inch (0.84mm), not the travel of 0.067 inch (1.7mm). At this point the indicator should be in the 0.020-0.050 inch (0.050-1.27mm) range.

15. Check the pinion face for a pinion adjustment mark. This mark is the best running position for the pinion from the nominal setting.

16. Remove the measuring tools and install the pinion shim according to the measurements taken.

DIFFERENTIAL ASSEMBLY

1. Lubricate all parts with gear oil.
2. Install the side gear thrust washers to the side gears.
3. Install the side gears into the same side that they were removed from.
4. Install the pinion gears without the thrust washers. To do this, place one pinion gear onto the side gears and rotate the side gears until the pinion is opposite the differential window. Install the second pinion gear so the pinion holes line up and rotate the gears into place in the differential housing.
5. Install the pinion gear thrust washers by rotating the pinion gears just enough to slide the washer into place.
6. Install the pinion shaft and pinion shaft screw.
7. Install the ring gear to the differential case by putting two studs into the ring gear on opposite sides. Place the gear onto the case and align the holes with the studs.
8. Use new bolts to secure the ring gear. Tighten each one in stages, gradually pulling the gear into place. When the gear is fully seated, torque the bolts in 2 or 3 steps to 90 ft. lbs. (120 Nm).
9. Install the differential side bearings using the proper tools. Support the differential when driving the bearing on the opposite side so the bearing does not take the load.

SETTING SIDE BEARING PRE-LOAD ADJUSTMENT

The adjustment is to position the differential properly side-to-side in the axle housing so the bearing are properly loaded. This is done by changing the shim thickness on both sides equally so the original backlash is maintained. Productions shims are made of case iron and must not be reused. Measure the shims and spacers one at a time and add the numbers to obtain the original shim thickness. The new service spacer thickness is 0.170 inch (4.32mm). The shims are available in increments of 0.004 inch (0.10mm) in sizes from 0.040-0.100 inch (1.0-2.5mm)

1. With the bearing races installed and lubricated, set the differential case into the axle housing to set the side bearing pre-load adjustment.
2. Insert the gaging tool between the axle housing and the left bearing cup.
3. Move the tool back and forth in the bore while turning the adjusting nut to the right until a noticeable drag is produced. Tighten the lock bolt on the side of the tool and leave the tool in place.
4. Install a new spacer and a shim between the right bearing race and the axle housing.
5. Determine the bearing preload by inserting progressively larger feeler gages between the carrier and the shim. Push the gage down so it contacts the shim at the top and bottom, then contacts the axle housing. The point just before additional drag begins is the correct feeler gage thickness. This is the zero setting without preload.

6. Remove the gaging tool, spacer, shim, feeler gage and differential from the axle housing.
7. Measure the gaging tool in 3 places using a micrometer and average the readings.
8. Add the dimensions of the right side spacer, shim and feeler gage.
9. For an initial backlash setting, move the ring gear away from the pinion by subtracting 0.010 in. (0.04mm) from the ring gear side of the shim pack and adding the same to the opposite side.
10. To obtain the proper preload on the side bearings, add 0.010 inch (0.04mm) to the measurement of each shim pack.
11. The differential is ready for installation.

PINION INSTALLATION

1. The bearing races should already be installed from the pinion depth adjustment done earlier. Install the pinion inner bearing onto the pinion; drive the inner race until it is seated on the shims.
2. Install a new collapsible spacer.
3. Install the pinion into the axle housing.
4. While holding the pinion in place, carefully drive the outer bearing onto the pinion shaft.
5. Install a new pinion oil seal.
6. Install the pinion flange by tapping it with a soft mallet until enough threads show to start the nut.
7. Install the flange holding tool and install the washer and a new nut. DO NOT tighten the nut. The bearing preload must be adjusted.

PINION BEARING PRELOAD ADJUSTMENT

1. Tighten the pinion nut just until the end play is taken out.
2. Remove the holding tool and use an inch pound torque wrench to determine how much torque is required to turn the pinion. This is bearing preload. Some of the resistance to turning the pinion shaft comes from the seal, so make sure it is properly lubricated. Turn the pinion several times to seat the bearings before taking a reading.
3. The preload should be 20-25 inch lbs. (2.3-2.8 Nm) on new bearings. On used bearings the preload should be 10-15 inch lbs. (1.1-1.7 Nm).
4. If the preload is low, tighten the nut in small increments and check the preload again. If the preload is exceeded, the collapsible spacer must be replaced.
5. Once the preload is correct, install the differential and set the backlash.

BACKLASH ADJUSTMENT

1. With the side bearing preload properly adjusted and the differential installed, install the bearing caps and torque the bolts to 55 ft. lbs. (75 Nm). Rotate the pinion and differential several times to seat the bearings.
2. Install a dial indicator to the axle housing. A unit with a magnetic base is acceptable.
3. Touch the stem to the heel of a tooth on the ring gear. That's the outer edge of the convex or drive side.
4. Hold the pinion fast and rock the ring gear to see how much play there is between the gear teeth; backlash. Record the reading and check 3 or 4 more places.

5. The readings should all be within 0.002 in. (0.05mm). If the readings vary more than this, check for burrs, a distorted case flange or uneven torque of the ring gear bolts.

6. The correct backlash is 0.005-0.009 in. (0.13-0.23mm) for new gear sets.

7. To adjust backlash, remove shim thickness from one side of the differential and add the same amount to the other side. This moves the ring gear to one side while maintaining the side bearing preload. Moving 0.002 inch (0.05mm) of shim changes the backlash by 0.001 inch (0.03mm).

8. When the backlash is correctly adjusted, remove the side bearing caps and shim packs.

9. Add 0.004 inch (0.10mm) of shim to the right side shim pack and drive the shim pack into place. Install the bearing cap and torque the bolts to 55 ft. lbs. (75 Nm).

10. Add 0.004 inch (0.10mm) of shim to the right side shim pack and install it. Install the left bearing cap but do not tighten the bolts yet.

11. Recheck the backlash and adjust as needed.

FINAL ASSEMBLY

1. Install new axle bearings and oil them with gear oil.

2. Install new axle seals and oil the lips with gear oil.

3. Install the axle shafts and engage the splines with the side gears in the differential.

4. Install the C locks on the end of the shafts. Pull out on the shafts to seat the C locks in the side gears.

5. Install the pinion shaft into the differential gears and install the lock bolt. DO NOT over tighten the lock bolt. Torque it to 25 ft. lbs. (34 Nm).

6. Install the rear cover with a new gasket and torque the bolts to 20 ft. lbs. (27 Nm). Refill with lubricant.

TORQUE SPECIFICATIONS

Component	English	Metric
Driveshaft retaining clamps:	15 ft. lbs.	20 Nm
Driveshaft retaining clamps:	15 ft. lbs.	20 Nm
Transmission-to-engine bolts:	55 ft. lbs.	74 Nm
Mount-to-transmission bolts:	35 ft. lbs.	47 Nm
Mount-to-crossmember bolts:	35 ft. lbs.	47 Nm
Transmission shift cable:	11 ft. lbs.	15 Nm
Pinion shaft lock screw:	27 ft. lbs.	36 Nm
Rear axle cover bolts:	22 ft. lbs.	30 Nm
Differential caps:	55 ft. lbs.	75 Nm

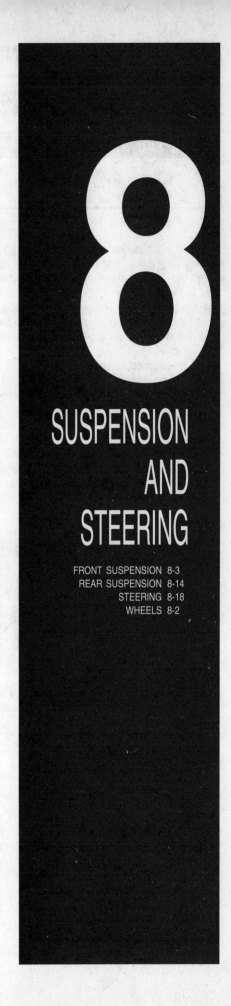

8

SUSPENSION AND STEERING

WHEELS

Front and Rear

REMOVAL & INSTALLATION

▶ **See Figures 1 and 2**

These vehicles use a variety of wheel styles, but from the factory they are all one piece rims with 5 bolt holes. Standard sizes are 15 in., although an aluminum wheel or steel wheel are available with the Caprice. A space saver spare for emergency use only comes with the vehicle also.

1. When removing a wheel, loosen all the lug nuts 2 turns with the wheel on the ground, then raise and safely support the vehicle.

2. If the wheel is stuck or rusted on the hub, make all the lug nuts finger tight, then back each one off 2 turns. Put the vehicle back on the ground and rock it side to side. Get another person to help if necessary. This is far safer then hitting a stuck wheel with the vehicle on a jack or lift.

3. When installing a wheel, tighten the lug nuts in a rotation skipping every other one. If the nuts are numbered 1 through 5 in a circle, the tightening sequence will be 1-3-5-2-4.

4. Always use a torque wrench to avoid uneven tightening, which will distort the brake drum or disc. Torque the nuts to 100 ft. lbs. (140 Nm).

INSPECTION

▶ **See Figure 3**

Wheels can be distorted or bent and not effect dry road handling to a noticeable degree. Out of round wheels will show up as uneven tire wear, a thumping noise or will make it difficult to balance the tire. Runout can be checked using a suitable dial indicator with the wheel on or off the vehicle, with the tire on or off the rim.

1. If the tire is on the wheel, set a dial indicator to touch the wheel in position 'A" in the illustration to measure lateral runout.

2. To measure radial runout, set the dial indicator to position 'B".

3. If the tire is not on the wheel, use the same positions on the inside of the rim. This is usually more accurate and easier to get a clean surface for the indicator stem.

4. For steel wheels, the radial runout limit is 1mm (0.040 inch), the lateral runout limit is 1.1mm (0.045 inch).

5. For aluminum alloy wheels, the limit for both runout directions is 0.8mm (0030 inch).

Fig. 2 Tire information decal, which is located on the left front door, may be used for determining correct tire pressures and sizes

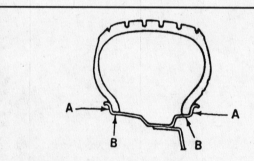

Fig. 3 Use a dial indicator to measure lateral or radial runout

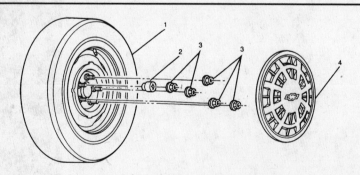

Fig. 1 Removing the wheel

Wheel Lug Studs

REMOVAL & INSTALLATION

Front

▶ See Figure 4

1. Raise and safely support the vehicle and remove the wheel.

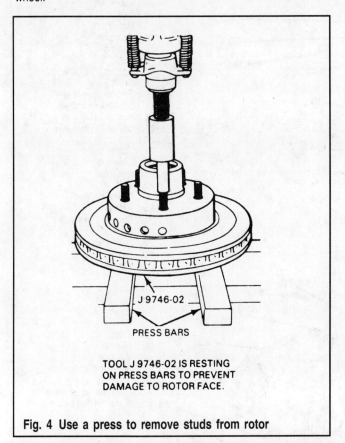

J 9746-02

PRESS BARS

TOOL J 9746-02 IS RESTING ON PRESS BARS TO PREVENT DAMAGE TO ROTOR FACE.

Fig. 4 Use a press to remove studs from rotor

2. Remove the brake pads and caliper. Refer to the Section 9 on brakes, if necessary.

3. Remove the rotor from the spindle. Refer to Front Wheel Bearings later in this section, if necessary.

4. Properly support the rotor and press the stud out.

5. Clean the stud hole with a wire brush and start the new stud with a hammer and drift pin. Do not use any lubricant or thread sealer.

6. Finish installing the stud with the press.

7. Install the rotor, adjust the wheel bearing and install the brake caliper and pads.

Rear

1. Raise and safely support the vehicle and remove the wheel.

2. Remove the brake drum or rotor. Refer to the Section 9 on brakes, if necessary.

3. Do not hammer the wheel stud to remove it. This will ruin the wheel bearing. Use the press tool to press the stud out of the hub.

4. Clean the hole with a wire brush and start the new stud into the hole. Do not use any lubricant or thread sealer.

5. Stack 4 or 5 washers onto the stud and then put the nut on. Tighten the nut to draw the stud into place. It should be easy to feel when the stud is seated.

6. Reinstall the rotor and caliper or drum and use a torque wrench when installing the wheel.

FRONT SUSPENSION

▶ See Figures 5 and 6

The front suspension is designed to allow each wheel to compensate for changes in the road surface level without appreciably affecting the opposite wheel. Each wheel is independently connected to the frame by a steering knuckle, upper and lower ball joint, and upper and lower control arm. The steering knuckles move in a prescribed three dimensional arc. The front wheels are held in proper relationship to each other by steering linkage, which includes the inner and outer tie rods, center link, idler arm and pitman arm.

Coil chassis springs are mounted between the spring housings on the frame and the lower control arms. Ride control is provided by double, direct acting shock assemblies. The upper portion of each shock assembly extends through the center of the coil spring and attached to the top of the frame housing with a nut. The lower portion of the shock is connected to the lower control arm.

Side roll of the front suspension is controlled by a spring steel stabilizer shaft. It is mounted in rubber bushings which are held to the frame side rails by brackets. The ends of the stabilizer are connected to the lower control arms by link bolts isolated by rubber grommets.

The upper control arm is attached to a cross shaft through isolating rubber bushings. The cross shaft is in turn bolted to the frame brackets. Shims are generally installed between the frame brackets and cross shaft to aid front end alignment, thus controlling the caster and camber adjustment. A ball joint is riveted to the outer end of the upper control arm. The upper ball joint is attached to the steering knuckle by a castellated nut and cotter pin.

The inner ends of the lower control arm have pressed-in bushings. Bolts, passing through the bushings, attach the arm to the suspension crossmember. The lower ball joint assembly

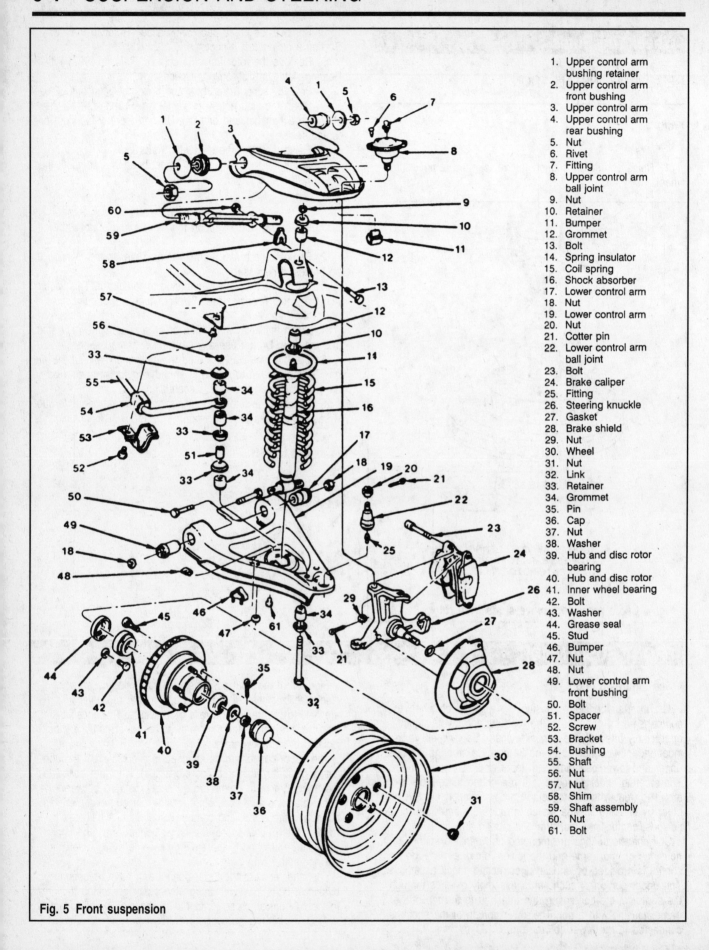

Fig. 5 Front suspension

1. Upper control arm bushing retainer
2. Upper control arm front bushing
3. Upper control arm
4. Upper control arm rear bushing
5. Nut
6. Rivet
7. Fitting
8. Upper control arm ball joint
9. Nut
10. Retainer
11. Bumper
12. Grommet
13. Bolt
14. Spring insulator
15. Coil spring
16. Shock absorber
17. Lower control arm
18. Nut
19. Lower control arm
20. Nut
21. Cotter pin
22. Lower control arm ball joint
23. Bolt
24. Brake caliper
25. Fitting
26. Steering knuckle
27. Gasket
28. Brake shield
29. Nut
30. Wheel
31. Nut
32. Link
33. Retainer
34. Grommet
35. Pin
36. Cap
37. Nut
38. Washer
39. Hub and disc rotor bearing
40. Hub and disc rotor
41. Inner wheel bearing
42. Bolt
43. Washer
44. Grease seal
45. Stud
46. Bumper
47. Nut
48. Nut
49. Lower control arm front bushing
50. Bolt
51. Spacer
52. Screw
53. Bracket
54. Bushing
55. Shaft
56. Nut
57. Nut
58. Shim
59. Shaft assembly
60. Nut
61. Bolt

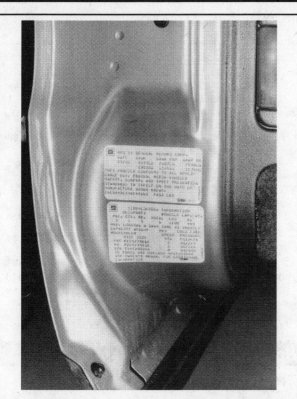

Fig. 6 View of front suspension with vehicle safely supported

is a press fit in the arm and attaches to the steering knuckle with a castellated nut and cotter pin.

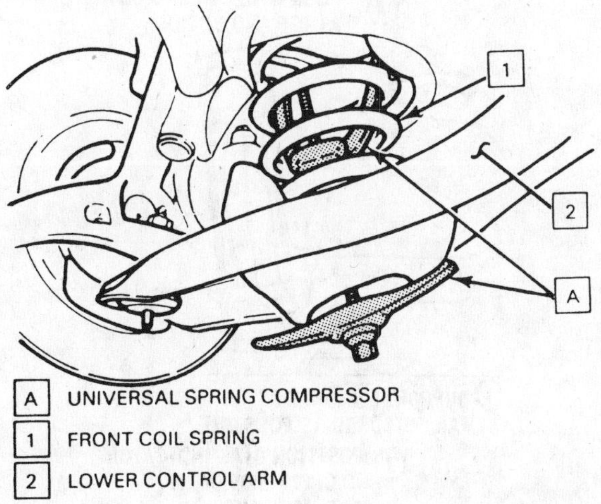

Rubber grease seals are provided at all of ball socket assemblies to keep dirt and moisture from entering the joint and damaging bearing surfaces.

Coil Springs

▶ See Figures 7 and 8

REMOVAL & INSTALLATION

1. Raise and support the vehicle safely.
2. Disconnect the ABS wheel speed sensor, if equipped, and secure aside.
3. Remove the wheel and shock absorber.
4. Remove the stabilizer linkage nut, retainer and linkage from the lower control arm.
5. Remove the steering knuckle from the tie rod end, using a suitable puller tool.
6. Install a universal spring compressor and compress the spring.
7. Support the lower control arm and remove the lower control arm to frame bolts.
8. Pivot the lower control arm rearward and remove the compressor and spring.

To install:

9. Properly position the spring onto the lower control arm, using spring compressor tool.
10. Position the control arm into the frame and install the pivot bolts but wait until the suspension is fully loaded (wheels on the ground) before tightening the pivot bolts. With the front bolt installed continue from front to rear.

A	UNIVERSAL SPRING COMPRESSOR
1	FRONT COIL SPRING
2	LOWER CONTROL ARM

Fig. 7 Removing and installing coil spring using compressor

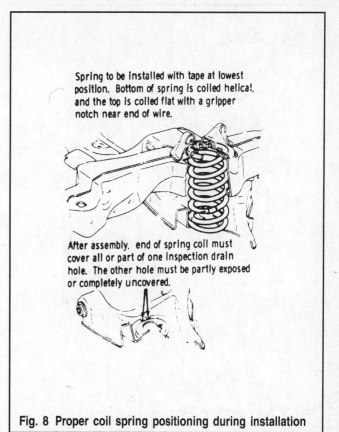

Spring to be installed with tape at lowest position. Bottom of spring is coiled helical, and the top is coiled flat with a gripper notch near end of wire.

After assembly, end of spring coil must cover all or part of one inspection drain hole. The other hole must be partly exposed or completely uncovered.

Fig. 8 Proper coil spring positioning during installation

11. Remove the spring compressor tool, install the steering knuckle to tie rod end and tighten the nut to 35 ft. lbs. (47 Nm). Install a new cotter pin.

12. Remove the support from the lower control arm and install the stabilizer linkage and tighten the bolt/nut to 13 ft. lbs. (17 Nm).

13. Install the shock absorber. Tighten the lower attaching bolts to 20 ft. lbs. (27 Nm) and the upper attaching nut to 97 inch lbs. (11 Nm).

14. Install the ABS wheel speed sensor, if equipped.

15. Install the wheel and lower the vehicle.

16. Tighten the wheel lug nuts to 100 ft. lbs. (140 Nm) and the lower control arm nuts to 92 ft. lbs. (125 Nm).

Shock Absorbers

INSPECTION

There are several ways to check shock absorbers, they are as follows:

1. Bounce the vehicle up and down. The vehicle should rebound approximately 2 times.

2. Look at the shock and check for oil leakage around the stem area.

3. Check the shock mounts for looseness or the rubber grommets being deteriorated or missing.

4. If any of the above items are found, shock should be replaced, preferably in pairs.

REMOVAL & INSTALLATION

▶ **See Figure 9**

1. Raise and support the vehicle safely.

2. Hold the shock absorber upper stem from turning and remove the upper nut, retainer and grommet.

➡**There are several tools available to hold the shock stem from turning while removing the stem nut.**

3. Remove the 2 bolts and lock washers securing the shock to the lower control arm.

To install:

4. With the lower retainer and grommet in place over the upper stem, install the fully extended shock up through the lower control arm and spring.

5. Install the upper rubber insulator, retainer and attaching nut over the shock. Tighten the nut to 97 inch lbs. (11 Nm).

6. Install the shock lower pivot to the lower control arm with the 2 attaching bolts and tighten to 20 ft. lbs. (27 Nm).

7. Lower the vehicle.

Upper Ball Joints

▶ **See Figures 10, 11 and 12**

INSPECTION

1. Raise the vehicle and position floor stands under the left and right lower control arm as near as possible to each lower

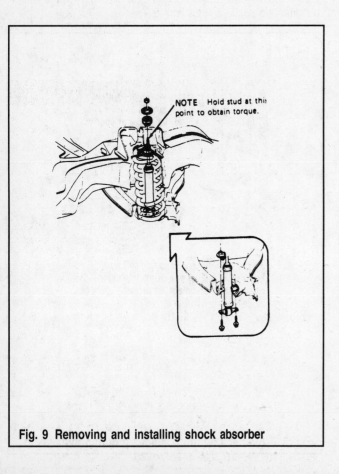

Fig. 9 Removing and installing shock absorber

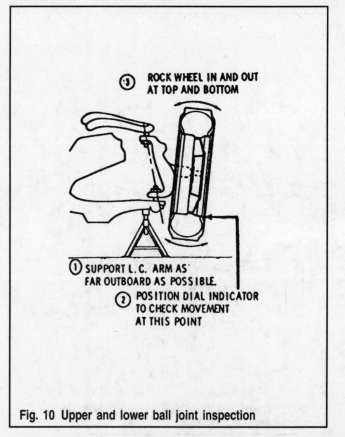

Fig. 10 Upper and lower ball joint inspection

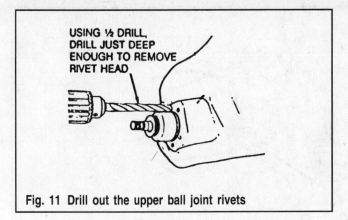

Fig. 11 Drill out the upper ball joint rivets

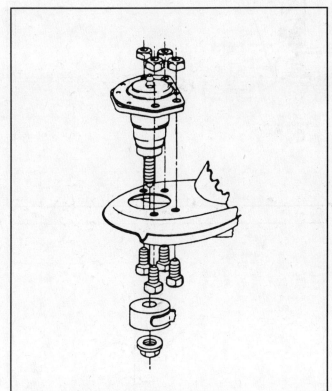

Fig. 12 Install the new upper ball joint using nuts and bolts; ensure the nuts are on top

ball joint. There should be sufficient space between the upper control arm bumper and frame.

2. Position a dial indicator against the wheel rim.

3. Grasp the front wheel and push in on bottom of the tire while pulling out at the top. Read the gauge, then reverse the push-pull procedure. Horizontal deflection on the dial indicator should not exceed 0.125 inch (3.18mm).

4. If the indicator exceeds 0.125 inch (3.18mm) or if the ball stud, when disconnected from the knuckle assembly, can be twisted in its socket by hand, replace the ball joint.

REMOVAL & INSTALLATION

1. Raise and safely support the vehicle; place floor stands under the lower control arm between the spring seats and the ball joints.

➡**Leave the jack under the spring seat during removal and installation, in order to compress the coil spring and relieve spring tension from the upper control arm.**

2. Remove the wheel.

3. Remove the cotter pin and nut from the upper ball joint.

4. Using a ball joint splitter tool, break the stud loose and pull the stud out of the knuckle. Support the steering knuckle to prevent damage to the brake line.

5. Using a ⅛ inch diameter drill bit, drill into each of the 4 rivet heads to a depth of ¼ inch

6. Drill off the rivet heads with a ½ inch diameter bit.

7. Punch out the rivets with a suitable tool and remove the ball joint.

To install:

8. Place the new ball joint in the upper control arm and secure it with 4 bolts and nuts in place of rivets. Torque the nuts to specifications.

9. Connect the ball joint to steering knuckle. Torque the nut to 60 ft. lbs. (82 Nm) and insert a new cotter pin.

➡**When replacing the ball joints, use only high-quality replacement parts; bolts and nuts specified to be strong enough to endure the stress. Always turn the ball stud nut to align the cotter pin hole.**

10. Install the grease fitting and lubricate until grease appears at the seal.

11. Install the wheel and road test the vehicle. Align the vehicle front end as necessary.

Lower Ball Joint

▶ **See Figures 13, 14, 15 and 16**

INSPECTION

The lower ball joints contain a visual wear indicator and are checked in this fashion alone. The lower ball joint grease plug is threaded into the wear indicator protruding from the bottom of the ball joint housing. As long as the wear indicator extends out of the ball joint housing, the ball joint is not worn. If the tip of the wear indicator is parallel with or recessed into the ball joint housing, the ball joint is defective.

REMOVAL & INSTALLATION

1. Raise the vehicle and support the frame safely.

2. Remove the tire and wheel.

3. Place a floor jack or axle stand under the control arm spring seat.

➡**Leave the jack or axle stand under the spring seat during removal and installation, in order to keep the spring and control arm positioned.**

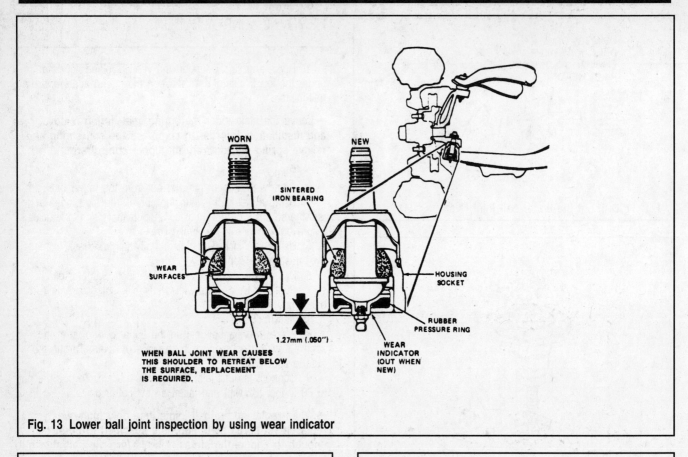

Fig. 13 Lower ball joint inspection by using wear indicator

Fig. 14 Disconnecting lower ball joint from steering knuckle using special tool

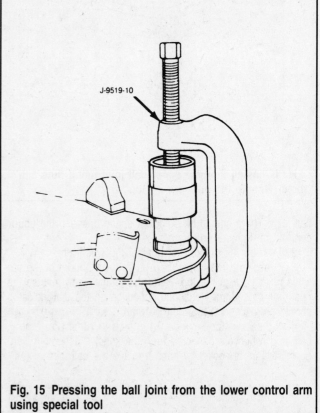

Fig. 15 Pressing the ball joint from the lower control arm using special tool

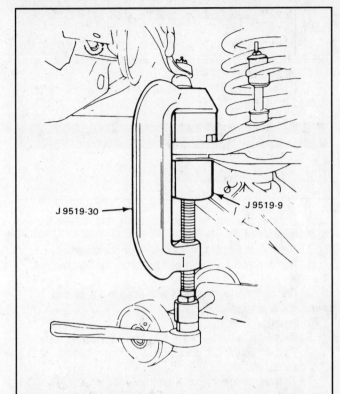

Fig. 16 Pressing the ball joint into the lower control arm using special tool

4. Remove the cotter pin from the ball joint stud. Using a ball joint splitter tool, separate the ball joint from the steering knuckle.

5. When the stud comes loose, remove the stud nut.

6. With a small suitable tool, guide the control arm to a position where the ball joint is accessible.

7. Block the steering knuckle aside by using a block of wood between the frame and the upper control arm.

8. Remove the grease fittings.

9. Using a ball joint remover, remove the lower ball joint from the control arm.

To install:

10. Using a ball joint installer, press in a new ball joint until it bottoms on the lower control arm.

➡**Make sure the grease purge on the seal faces away from the brakes.**

11. Assemble the suspension and torque the lower ball joint nut to 83 ft. lbs. (112 Nm) on 1990 vehicles or 79 ft. lbs. (107 Nm) for 1991-93 vehicles. Install the cotter pin and bend it to the side, not over the top of the nut.

12. Install the ball joint fitting and lubricate until grease appears at the seal.

13. Install the tire and wheel assembly.

14. Adjust wheel alignment, if necessary, and road test the vehicle.

Stabilizer Shaft

REMOVAL & INSTALLATION

1. Raise the car and support the car on jackstands.

2. Remove the link bolt, nut, grommet, spacer and retainers.

3. Remove the insulators and brackets.

4. Remove the stabilizer shaft.

5. To install, position the stabilizer shaft into place and install the insulators and brackets.

6. Hold the stabilizer shaft approximately 55mm from the bottom of the side rail and torque the bracket bolts to 37 ft. lbs. (50 Nm).

7. Install the bolt, nut, grommets, spacer and retainers.

8. Lower the car.

Upper Control Arms

REMOVAL & INSTALLATION

▶ **See Figure 17**

1. If removing the left side control arm on 1991-93 vehicles, remove the air cleaner and resonator.

2. Raise and support the vehicle safely and remove the tire and wheel assembly.

3. Place a floor jack or axle stand under the lower control arm spring seat.

➡**Leave the floor jack or axle stand under the spring seat during removal and installation, in order to keep the spring and control arm positioned.**

4. Disconnect the wheel speed sensor, if equipped with ABS.

5. Loosen the pivot shaft to frame nuts and remove alignment shims. Tape shims together and mark for installation in the original positions.

6. Remove the cotter pin and upper ball joint nut. Remove the ball joint from the steering knuckle, with suitable tool. Support the hub assembly to prevent damage to the brake line.

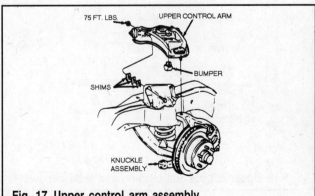

Fig. 17 Upper control arm assembly

7. Remove the upper control arm shaft attaching nuts and remove the control arm.

To install:

8. Install the pivot shaft on the attaching bolts.

9. Install alignment shims in the same position from which they were removed and tighten upper control arm attaching nuts to 72 ft. lbs. (98 Nm).

10. Remove the temporary support from the hub and connect the ball joint to the steering knuckle. Tighten the upper nut to 60 ft. lbs. (82 Nm) and install a new cotter pin.

11. Connect the ABS wheel speed sensor, if equipped.

12. Install the tire and wheel assembly.

13. Remove the jackstands and lower the vehicle.

14. Install the air cleaner and resonator, if removed.

15. Check the wheel alignment.

CONTROL ARM BUSING REPLACEMENT

▶ **See Figures 18, 19 and 20**

1. Remove the upper control arm assembly from the vehicle.

2. Remove the nuts and washers from the ends of the pivot shaft.

3. Using tool J-22269-1, press the bushings from the shaft and control arm.

To install:

4. Position pivot shaft in control arm with the depression in the shaft facing inboard.

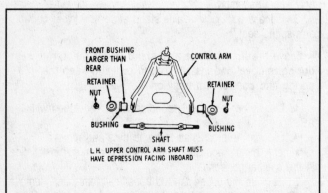

Fig. 18 Upper control arm bushing and shaft assembly

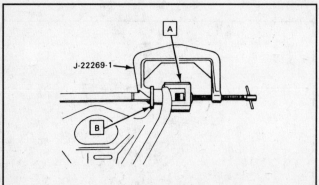

Fig. 19 Upper control arm bushing and shaft removal

5. Push the new bushings over the shaft and into the control arm.

6. Install the washer and nut finger tight onto the shaft. Do not tighten the shaft nuts until the suspension is loaded.

7. Install the control arm onto the vehicle.

8. Lower the vehicle and torque the control arm pivot shaft nuts to 85 ft. lbs. (115 Nm).

Lower Control Arm

REMOVAL & INSTALLATION

1. Raise and support the vehicle safely and remove the tire and wheel assembly.

2. Remove the front coil spring and shock absorber.

3. Remove and the lower ball joint from the steering knuckle.

4. Remove the lower control arm attaching bolts and remove the assembly.

To install:

5. Install the lower ball joint stud into the steering knuckle.

6. Position spring and shock absorber in place and install the lower control arm.

7. Tighten the lower control arm bolt/nuts to 92 ft. lbs. (125 Nm), the lower ball joint stud nut to 83 ft. lbs. (112 Nm) on 1990-91 vehicles or 79 ft. lbs. (107 Nm) for 1992-93 vehicles, and the shock absorber lower attaching bolts to 20 ft. lbs. (27 Nm).

8. Install new cotter pins on all appropriate nuts.

9. Install wheel and tire assembly.

10. Lower the vehicle and check alignment.

CONTROL ARM BUSHING REPLACEMENT

Front Bushing

▶ **See Figures 21, 22, 23 and 24**

1. Remove the lower control arm assembly from the vehicle.

2. Using a blunt chisel, drive the bushing flare located on the inside of the control arm, down flush with the bushing. This will enable the bushing to be pressed from the control arm easier.

3. Using the tools as shown in the illustration, press the bushings from the control arm.

To install:

4. Position the busing in the control arm and using the tools shown, press the bushing in.

5. Using the flaring tool as shown in the illustration, flare the front bushing.

6. Install the rear bushing and install the control arm onto the vehicle.

7. Lower the vehicle and torque the control arm pivot shaft nuts to 92 ft. lbs. (125 Nm).

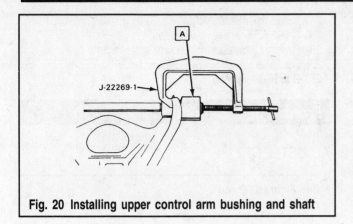

Fig. 20 Installing upper control arm bushing and shaft

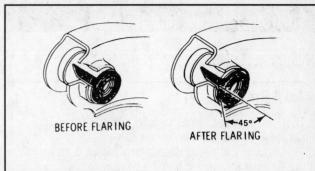

Fig. 24 Example of the lower control arm front bushing before and after flare

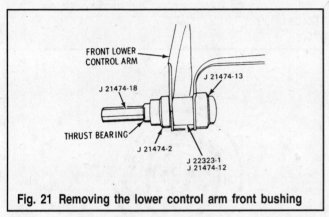

Fig. 21 Removing the lower control arm front bushing

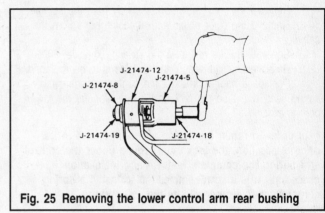

Fig. 25 Removing the lower control arm rear bushing

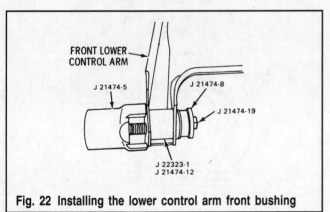

Fig. 22 Installing the lower control arm front bushing

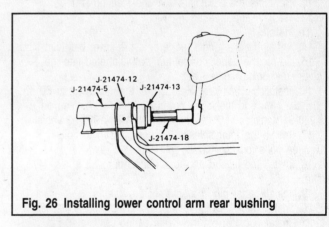

Fig. 26 Installing lower control arm rear bushing

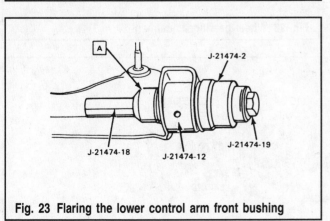

Fig. 23 Flaring the lower control arm front bushing

Rear Bushing
▶ **See Figures 25 and 26**

1. Remove the lower control arm assembly from the vehicle.

2. Using the tools as shown in the illustration, press the bushings from the control arm.

3. To install, position the busing in the control arm and using the tools shown, press in the bushing.

4. Install the front bushing, as required and install the control arm onto the vehicle.

5. Lower the vehicle and torque the control arm pivot shaft nuts to 92 ft. lbs. (125 Nm).

Steering Knuckle and Spindle

REMOVAL & INSTALLATION

▶ **See Figure 27**

1. Disconnect the battery negative cable.
2. Raise and support the vehicle safely.
3. Disconnect the ABS wheel speed sensor, if equipped.
4. Remove the tire and wheel assembly.
5. Remove the caliper assembly.
6. Remove the dust cap, cotter pin, nut and washer from the spindle.
7. Remove the hub and rotor assembly from the spindle.
8. Remove the rotor shield and attaching bolts from the spindle.
9. Separate the tie rod from the steering knuckle.
10. Remove knuckle seal, if the knuckle is to be replaced.
11. Position a floor jack under the control arm near the spring seat and raise the jack until it just supports the lower control arm.

➡**In order to retain the spring and control arm in its original position, the jack must remain under the control arm during the complete removal and installation procedure. It is also recommended to install a spring compressor to further secure the coil spring.**

12. Separate the ball joints from the steering knuckle.
13. Remove the steering knuckle.
    To install:
14. Install the steering knuckle onto the lower ball joint stud.
15. Lower the upper control arm ball joint stud into the steering knuckle tapered hole.
16. Install the ball joint nuts, torque the upper nut to 60 ft. lbs. (82 Nm) and the lower nut to 83 ft. lbs. (112 Nm) on 1990-91 vehicles or 79 ft. lbs. (107 Nm) for 1992-93 vehicles.
17. Install the rotor splash shield and attaching bolts. Tighten bolts to 124 inch lbs. (14 Nm).
18. Install the tie rod and torque the nut to 35 ft. lbs. (47 Nm).
19. Install cotter pin in all castellated nuts.
20. Install rotor, bearings, washer and nut and adjust.
21. Install a cotter pin in wheel bearing castellated nut.
22. Install dust cap.
23. Install caliper assembly.

24. Install wheel assembly.
25. Install ABS wheel speed sensor.
26. Remove jack assembly, lower the vehicle.
27. Reconnect the negative battery cable.
28. Road test vehicle.

Front Wheel Bearings

ADJUSTMENT

▶ **See Figures 28 and 29**

1. Raise the car and support it at the lower arm.
2. Remove the hub dust cover and spindle cotter pin. Loosen the nut.

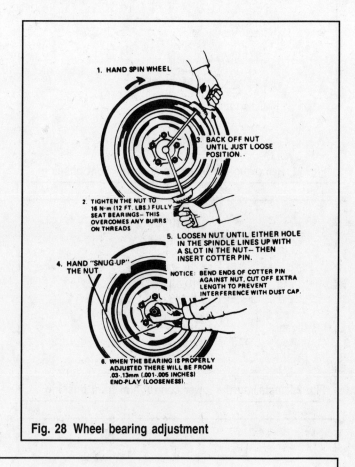

Fig. 28 Wheel bearing adjustment

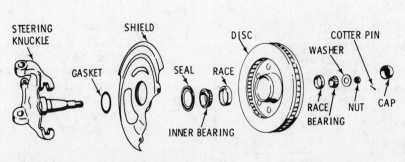

Fig. 27 Steering knuckle, rotor and wheel bearing assembly

Fig. 29 Wheel bearing dust cap removed to access wheel bearings for disassembly or adjustment

3. While spinning the wheel, snug the nut down to seat the bearings. Do not exert over 12 ft. lbs. of force on the nut.

4. Back the nut off ¼ turn or until it is just lose. Line up the cotter pin hole in the spindle with the hole in the nut.

5. Insert a new cotter pin. Endplay should be between 0.03-0.13mm. If play exceeds this tolerance, the wheel bearings should be replaced.

REMOVAL & INSTALLATION

1. Raise the car and support it at the lower arm. Remove the wheel. Remove the brake caliper and support it on a wire.

2. Remove the dust cap, cotter pin, castle nut, thrust washer and outside wheel bearing. Pull the disc/hub assembly from the steering knuckle.

3. Pry out the inner seal and remove the inner bearing. If necessary to remove the inner bearing races, use a hammer and a brass drift to drive the bearing races from the hub.

To install:

4. Clean all parts in kerosene or equivalent, DO NOT use gasoline. After cleaning, check parts for excessive wear and replace damaged parts.

5. Smear grease inside of hub. Install the bearing races into hub, using a hammer and a brass drift. Drive the races in until they seat against the shoulder of the hub.

6. Pack the bearings with grease and install the inner bearing in the hub. Install a new grease seal, be careful not to damage the seal.

7. Install the disc/hub assembly onto the steering knuckle. Install the outer bearing, thrust washer and castle nut. Tighten the nut until the wheel does not turn freely.

8. Back off the nut until the wheel turns freely and install the cotter pin. Install the dust cap, caliper and wheel. Lower the car.

PACKING

Clean the wheel bearings thoroughly with solvent and check their condition before installation.

✳✳CAUTION

Do not blow the bearing dry with compressed air as this would allow the bearing to turn without lubrication.

Apply a sizable amount of lubricant to the palm of one hand. Using your other hand, work the bearing into the lubricant so that the grease is pushed through the rollers and out the other side. Keep rotating the bearing while continuing to push the lubricant through it.

Front End Alignment

▶ **See Figures 30, 31 and 32**

CAMBER

Camber is the inward or outward tilting of the front wheels from the vertical. When the wheels tilt outward at the top, the camber is said to be positive (+). When the wheels tilt inward at the top, the camber is said to be negative (-). The amount of tilt is measured in degrees from the vertical and this measurement is called the camber angle.

CASTER

Caster is the tilting of the front steering axis either forward or backward from the vertical position. A backward tilt is said to be positive (+) and a forward tilt is said to be negative (-).

TOE-IN

Toe-in is the turning in of the front wheels. The actual amount of toe-in is normally only a fraction of a degree. The purpose of toe-in is to ensure parallel rolling of the front wheels. (Excessive toe-in or toe-out will cause tire wear.)

CASTER/CAMBER ADJUSTMENT

Caster and camber can be adjusted by moving the position of shims from the upper control arm shaft. Moving the shims from the forward/rearward position on the shaft adjusts caster. Adding or removing an equal amount of shims from the front and rear of the shaft adjusts camber.

TOE-IN ADJUSTMENT

Loosen the clamp bolts at each of the steering tie rod adjustable sleeves. With the steering wheel set straight ahead, turn the adjusting sleeves to obtain the proper adjustment.

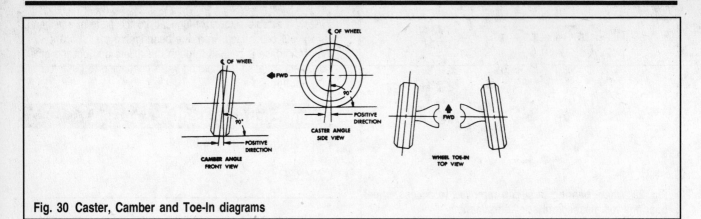

Fig. 30 Caster, Camber and Toe-In diagrams

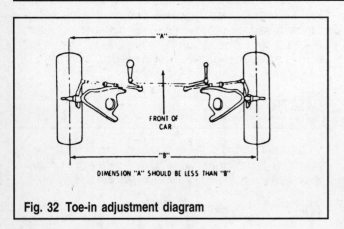

Fig. 32 Toe-in adjustment diagram

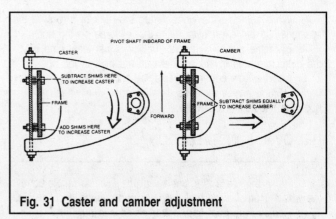

Fig. 31 Caster and camber adjustment

WHEEL ALIGNMENT

| Year | Model | Caster | | Camber | | Toe-in (in.) | Steering Axis Inclination (deg.) |
		Range (deg.)	Preferred Setting (deg.)	Range (deg.)	Preferred Setting (deg.)		
1990	Caprice	2P–4P	3P	0–1⅝P	¹³/₁₆P	¹/₃₂	0
1991	Caprice	2½P–4½P	3½P	0–1⅝P	¹³/₁₆P	¹/₃₂	0
1992	Caprice	2½P–4½P	3½P	0–1⅝P	¹³/₁₆P	¹/₃₂	0
1993	Caprice	2½P–4½P	3½P	1N–1P	0	¹/₃₂	0

N—Negative
P—Positive

REAR SUSPENSION

▶ **See Figures 33 and 34**

Coil Springs

REMOVAL & INSTALLATION

1. Raise and support the vehicle safely, place an adjustable support under the axle housing.

2. Disconnect the ABS rear speed sensor, if equipped. Remove the stabilizer shaft and control arm mounting bolt on the end of the rear axle affected.

3. If equipped, disconnect the height sensor link from the upper control arm by removing the attaching nut and sliding the sensor link stud out of the hole in the upper control arm.

4. Disconnect the brake line support bolt at the center of the axle housing. No brake lines need to be disconnected, therefore brake bleeding will not be necessary.

5. Remove the nut and washer from the shock absorber and disconnect the shock absorber from the bracket.

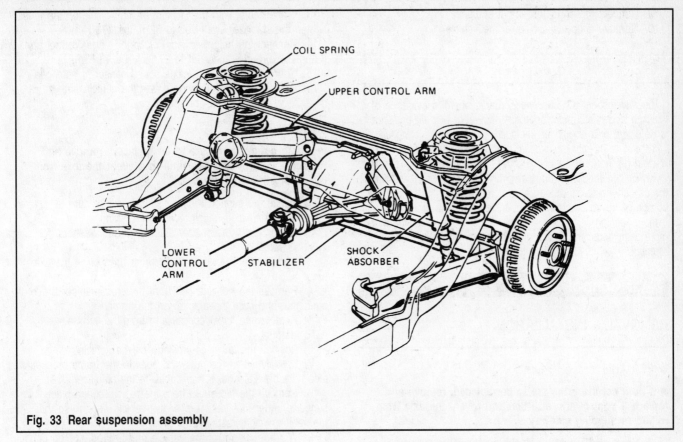

Fig. 33 Rear suspension assembly

Fig. 34 Rear suspension assembly

6. Carefully lower the axle housing enough to remove the spring. Be careful not to stretch the brake hose.

7. Remove the spring, upper and lower insulator, as equipped.

To install:

8. Install the upper insulator, lower insulator, as equipped, and the rear spring to the bracket on the frame seat. Point the coil leg toward the left side of the vehicle, at a right angle from the centerline of the vehicle.

9. Raise the rear axle back into place with the adjustable lifting device.

10. Install the rear shock absorber to the bracket, and tighten the nut to 48 ft. lbs. (65 Nm). Install the stabilizer shaft, control arm and mounting bolts at the rear axle.

11. Connect the rear brake line support bolt and tighten to 20 ft. lbs. (27 Nm).

12. Connect the height sensor link to the upper control arm, if applicable, and tighten nut to 27 inch lbs. (3 Nm).

13. Connect the ABS rear axle speed sensor, if equipped.

14. Lower vehicle and adjust the height sensor, if necessary.

Shock Absorbers

REMOVAL & INSTALLATION

1. Raise and safely support the vehicle. Be sure to support the rear axle housing.

2. Disconnect the air line, if equipped, from the shock. Turn the spring clip 90 degrees and pull gently on air line housing.

3. Remove the upper nuts and bolts from the shock absorber at the frame.

4. Using a wrench to hold the stud in place, remove the lower nut and washer from the shock at the rear axle housing. The stud must not be allowed to turn during this operation or damage may result in the bond between the bushing and stud.

5. Remove the shock.

To install:

6. Install the shock absorber and loosely connect the upper frame bolts and nuts.

7. Place the stud into the bracket on the axle housing and attach the nut and washer.

8. Holding the stud steady with a wrench, tighten to nut to 48 ft. lbs. (65 Nm). Either tighten the upper bolts at the frame to 20 ft. lbs. (27 Nm) or the nuts at the frame to 12 ft. lbs. (16 Nm), whichever is easier.

9. Connect the shock air line, if equipped.
10. Remove supports and lower the vehicle.

TESTING

Visually inspect the shock absorber. If there is evidence of leakage and the shock absorber is covered with oil, the shock is defective and should be replaced.

If there is no sign of excessive leakage (a small amount of weeping is normal) bounce the car at one corner by pressing down on the fender or bumper and releasing. When you have the car bouncing as much as you can, release the fender or bumper. The car should stop bouncing after the first rebound. If the bouncing continues past the center point of the bounce more than once, the shock absorbers are worn and should be replaced.

Rear Control Arms

REMOVAL & INSTALLATION

UPPER ARM

➡If both control arms are to be replaced, remove and replace 1 control arm at a time to prevent the axle from rolling or slipping sideways.

1. Raise and support the vehicle safely. Be sure to support the rear axle housing with a jackstand.
2. Disconnect the ABS rear axle speed sensor, if equipped.
3. If equipped, disconnect the height sensor link from the upper control arm by removing the attaching nut and sliding the sensor link stud out of the hole in the control arm.
4. Disconnect the stabilizer shaft bolts and washers from the upper control arm, for 1990 vehicles.
5. Remove the nut and bolt at the rear axle housing. Disconnect the upper control arm from the housing.
6. Remove the nut and bolt at the rear frame crossmember. Remove the upper control arm from the vehicle.
   To install:
7. Loosely attach the upper control arm to the rear frame crossmember using the nut and bolt.
8. Loosely attach the upper control arm to the rear axle housing using the nut and bolt.
9. For 1990 vehicles, loosely attach the stabilizer shaft and bolt.
10. Remove the jackstand from the rear axle and place supports under the tires. Lower the vehicle enough so the vehicle weight rests on the tires.
11. With the weight of the vehicle on the tires, tighten the bolt at the rear frame crossmember to 114 ft. lbs. (155 Nm) or the nut to 91 ft. lbs. (123 Nm). Either the nut or the bolt must be tightened, torque whichever is easiest to access.
12. With the weight of the vehicle on the tires, tighten the bolt at the rear axle housing to 80 ft. lbs. (108 Nm) or the nut to 70 ft. lbs. (95 Nm). Once again, torque whichever is easiest to access.

13. If applicable, with the weight of the vehicle on the tires, tighten the stabilizer shaft bolt to 52 ft. lbs. (70 Nm).
14. Connect the height sensor link to the upper control arm, if applicable, and tighten nut to 27 inch lbs. (3 Nm).
15. Connect the ABS rear axle speed sensor, if equipped.
16. Remove the tire supports, lower the vehicle and, if necessary, adjust the height sensor.

LOWER ARM

➡If both control arms are to be replaced, remove and replace 1 control arm at a time to prevent the axle from rolling or slipping sideways.

1. Raise and support the vehicle safely. Be sure to support the rear axle housing with a jackstand.
2. Disconnect the stabilizer shaft bolts and washers, for 1991-93 vehicles.
3. Remove the nut and bolt from the bracket on the axle tube.
4. Remove the nut and bolt from the crossmember brace, if equipped, and from the bracket on the frame.
5. Remove the lower control arm from the vehicle.
   To install:
6. Position the lower control arm on the vehicle.
7. Loosely install the nuts and bolts to the frame bracket, axle tube bracket and, if applicable, to the stabilizer shaft.
8. Remove the jackstand from the rear axle and place supports under the tires. Lower the vehicle enough so that the vehicle weight rests on the tires.
9. With the weight of the vehicle on the tires, tighten either the nut or the bolt, whichever is easiest to access. For 1990 vehicles tighten the lower control arm bolts to 122 ft. lbs. (165 Nm) or the nuts to 92 ft. lbs. (125 Nm). For 1991-93 vehicles tighten the lower control arm bolts to 74 ft. lbs. (100 Nm) or the nuts to 91 ft. lbs. (123 Nm).
10. If applicable, tighten the stabilizer bolts to 52 ft. lbs. (29 Nm).
11. Remove the tire supports and lower the vehicle.

Sway Bar

REMOVAL & INSTALLATION

1. Raise and safely support the vehicle. Be sure to support the rear axle housing.
2. Remove the bolts and screws securing the stabilizer shaft to the control arm.
3. Remove the stabilizer shaft from the bracket assembly. Remove the bracket assembly, if required.
4. Installation is the reverse of the removal procedure.

Automatic Level Control (ALC) System

▶ **See Figures 35, 36 and 37**

The ALC, formerly referred to as the Electronic Level Control (ELI) system, was used on 1988 and later vehicles and, keeps the rear of the vehicle level by automatically adjusting the rear trim height with varying vehicle loads. The system is activated when the ignition is on and excess weight is added to the

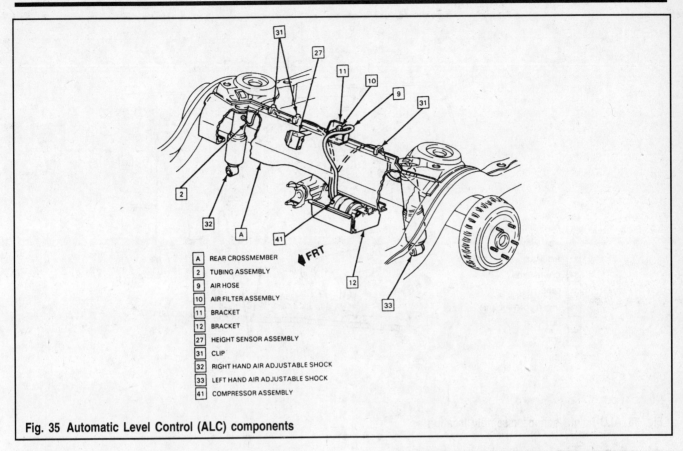

Fig. 35 Automatic Level Control (ALC) components

A	REAR CROSSMEMBER
2	TUBING ASSEMBLY
9	AIR HOSE
10	AIR FILTER ASSEMBLY
11	BRACKET
12	BRACKET
27	HEIGHT SENSOR ASSEMBLY
31	CLIP
32	RIGHT HAND AIR ADJUSTABLE SHOCK
33	LEFT HAND AIR ADJUSTABLE SHOCK
41	COMPRESSOR ASSEMBLY

vehicle. When the excess weight is removed from the vehicle, an exhaust solenoid connected to the battery positive, allows air to be released from the system even with the ignition off. This system is used in place of the standard rear shock absorbers.

Air Lines and Fittings

The air lines include spring clip connections with molded sealing shoulders in the retainer and on the end of the air line with double O-ring seals. Before making any air line disconnection, clean the connector and surrounding area. Turn the spring clip to release the connector. To reassemble, lubricate the O-rings with petroleum jelly and push the air line fully into the fitting.

Height Sensor Assembly

REMOVAL & INSTALLATION

1. Disconnect the battery ground cable.
2. Raise and safely support vehicle on jack stands.
3. Disconnect the electrical connector.
4. Remove the nut attaching link to upper control arm.
5. Remove the two bolts attaching height sensor assembly to rear crossmember.
6. Remove the height sensor from the vehicle.
7. Installation is the reverse of removal procedure.

ADJUSTMENT

➡The attaching link should be securely connected to the height sensor arm when any adjustments are made. For every 1 degree change in arm angle the trim height will change approximately ¼ inch. The arm angle may be changed a total of 5 degrees, resulting in a trim height change of approximately 1¼ inches.

1. Loosen the locknut securing the metal arm to the plastic arm.
2. To decrease the amount of suspension travel required to turn on compressor (To raise vehicle height), move the plastic arm to the top of the slot and tighten locknut.
3. To increase the amount of suspension travel required to turn on compressor (To lower vehicle height), move the plastic arm to the bottom of the slot and tighten locknut.

Compressor Assembly and Bracket

REMOVAL & INSTALLATION

1. Disconnect the battery ground cable.
2. Raise and safely support vehicle on jack stands.
3. Disconnect the air hoses and tubing assembly at the compressor assembly.
4. Remove the bolts retaining the mounting bracket with compressor assembly to rear crossmembers.
5. Remove the bolt attaching the ABS wheel speed sensor wire clip from the compressor mounting bracket, and remove the ABS wire clip from the mounting bracket.
6. Disconnect the compressor electrical connector.
7. Remove the mounting bracket with compressor assembly from the rear crossmember.
8. Remove the screws attaching the compressor assembly to mounting bracket, and remove the compressor assembly.
9. Installation is the reverse of removal procedure.

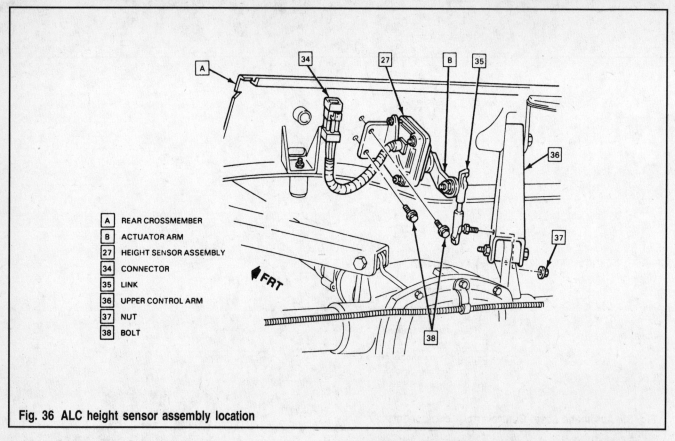

A	REAR CROSSMEMBER
B	ACTUATOR ARM
27	HEIGHT SENSOR ASSEMBLY
34	CONNECTOR
35	LINK
36	UPPER CONTROL ARM
37	NUT
38	BOLT

Fig. 36 ALC height sensor assembly location

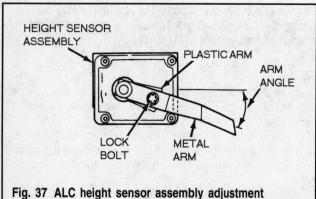

Fig. 37 ALC height sensor assembly adjustment

Air Shocks

With the exception of the air lines, the air shocks are removed in the same manner as the standard rear shocks. Refer to that procedure.

✳✳CAUTION

When replacement of an air shock is necessary, always replace it with an exact matching shock. Failure to do so could result in, an ill handling vehicle, physical damage and/or personal injury.

STEERING

✳✳WARNING

Before attempting any repairs involving the steering wheel or disassembly of it, ensure the Supplemental Inflatable Restraint (Air Bag) system is properly disarmed.

Air Bag

▶ See Figures 38 and 39

Disarming

1. Turn the steering wheel to align the wheels in the straight-ahead position.
2. Turn the ignition switch to the **LOCK** position.
3. Remove the SIR air bag fuse from the fuse block.

Fig. 38 SIR warning label located on radiator support advising driver that care must be used when working around steering column or sensors.

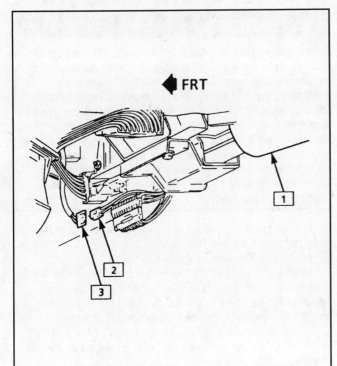

Fig. 39 SIR system disarming by disconnecting yellow 2-way connector at base of column. Follow proper arming and disarming procedures in text.

4. Remove the left side trim panel and disconnect the yellow 2-way SIR harness wire connector at the base of the steering column.

To enable system:

5. Turn the ignition switch to the **LOCK** position.
6. Reconnect the yellow 2-way connector at the base of the steering column.
7. Reinstall the SIR fuse and the left side trim panel.
8. Turn the ignition switch to the **RUN** position.
9. Verify the SIR indicator light flashes 7-9 times, if not as specified, inspect system for malfunction or contact the manufacturer.

SUPPLEMENTAL INFLATABLE RESTRAINT (SIR) COIL ASSEMBLY

✳✳CAUTION

After performing repairs on the internals of the steering column the coil assembly must be centered in order to avoid damaging the coil or accidental deployment of the air bag. There are 2 different styles of coils, 1 rotates clockwise and the other rotates counterclockwise.

Coil Centering Adjustment
▶ See Figure 40

1. With the system properly disarmed, hold the coil assembly with the clear bottom up to see the coil ribbon.
2. While holding the coil assembly, depress the lock spring and rotate the hub in the direction of the arrow until it stops. The coil should now be wound up snug against the center hub.
3. Rotate the coil assembly in the opposite direction approximately 2½ turns and release the lock spring between the locking tabs in front of the arrow.
4. Install the coil assembly onto the steering shaft.

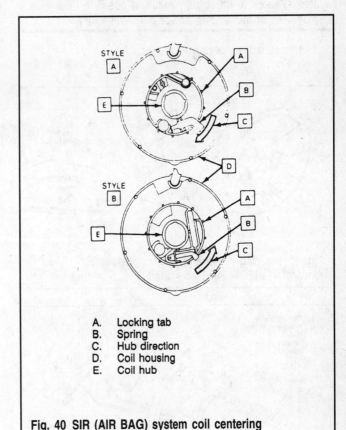

A. Locking tab
B. Spring
C. Hub direction
D. Coil housing
E. Coil hub

Fig. 40 SIR (AIR BAG) system coil centering

Steering Wheel

▶ See Figures 41 and 42

REMOVAL & INSTALLATION

➡ If the vehicle is equipped with S.I.R. (AIR BAG) system, ensure the prior disarming procedure is followed.

1990 CAPRICE

1. Disconnect the negative battery cable.
2. Remove the horn pad.
3. Disconnect the horn contact lead.
4. Remove the retainer and steering wheel nut.
5. Using a suitable steering wheel puller, remove the steering wheel.
6. Installation is the reverse of the removal procedure. Tighten the steering wheel nut to 31 ft. lbs. (42 Nm).

1992-93 CAPRICE

✳✳CAUTION

The vehicle is equipped with a Supplemental Inflatable Restraint (SIR) system, follow the recommended disarming procedures before performing any work on or around the system. Failure to do so may result in possible deployment of the air bag and/or personal injury.

1. Disconnect the negative battery cable.

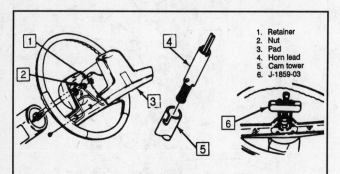

Fig. 41 Steering wheel and horn cap assembly removal — without Air Bag system

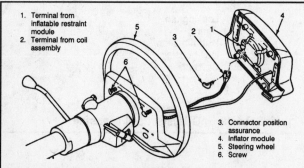

Fig. 42 Steering wheel and horn cap assembly removal — with Air Bag system

2. Disable the Supplemental Inflatable Restraint (SIR) system as follows:
   a. Turn the steering wheel so the vehicle's wheels are pointing straight-ahead.
   b. Remove the left sound insulator by removing the nut from the stud and gently prying the insulator from the knee bolster.
   c. Remove the SIR fuse from the fuse block.
   d. Disconnect the Connector Position Assurance (CPA) clip and yellow 2-way SIR harness connector at the base of the steering column.
3. Loosen the screws and locknuts from the back of the steering wheel using a suitable Torx® driver or equivalent, until the inflator module can be released from the steering wheel. Remove the inflator module from the steering wheel.

✳✳CAUTION

When carrying a live inflator module, ensure the bag and trim cover are pointed away from the body. In case of an accidental deployment, the bag will then deploy with minimal chance of injury. When placing a live inflator module on a bench or other surface, always place the bag and trim cover up, away from the surface. This is necessary so a free space is provided to allow the air bag to expand in the unlikely event of accidental deployment. Otherwise, personal injury may result. Also, never carry the inflator module by the wires or connector on the underside of the module.

4. Disconnect the coil assembly connector and CPA clip from the inflator module terminal.
5. Remove the steering wheel locking nut.
6. Using a suitable puller, remove the steering wheel and disconnect the horn contact. When attaching the steering wheel puller, use care to prevent threading the side screws into the coil assembly and damaging the coil assembly.
   To install:
7. Route the coil assembly connector through the steering wheel.
8. Connect the horn contact and install the steering wheel. When installing the steering wheel, align the block tooth on the steering wheel with the block tooth on the steering shaft within 1 female serration.
9. Install the steering wheel locking nut. Tighten the nut to 31 ft. lbs. (42 Nm).
10. Connect the coil assembly connector and CPA clip to the inflator module terminal.
11. Install the inflator module. Ensure the wiring is not exposed or trapped between the inflator module and the steering wheel. Tighten the inflator module screws to 25 inch lbs. (2.8 Nm).
12. Connect the negative battery cable.
13. Enable the SIR system as follows:
    a. Connect the yellow 2-way SIR harness connector to base of the steering column and CPA.
    b. Install the left sound insulator.
    c. Install the SIR fuse in the fuse block.
    d. Turn the ignition switch to the **RUN** position and verify that the inflatable restraint indicator flashes 7-9 times and then turns **OFF**. If the indicator does not respond as stated, a problem within the SIR system is indicated.

Turn Signal Switch

REMOVAL & INSTALLATION

▶ See Figures 43, 44, 45, 46 and 47

1990 Caprice

1. Turn the wheels of the vehicle to the straight-ahead position and set the ignition to **LOCK**. Disconnect the negative battery cable.

2. Remove the steering pad attaching screws. Lift pad up and remove the horn lead by pushing in on the insulator and turning counterclockwise.

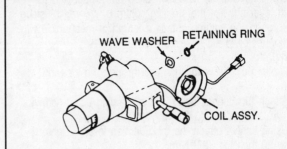

Fig. 46 Coil assembly removal — with Air Bag system

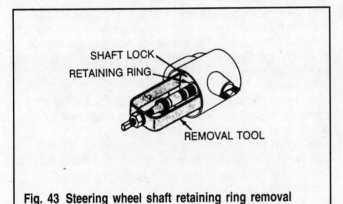

Fig. 43 Steering wheel shaft retaining ring removal

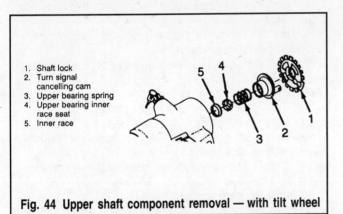

1. Shaft lock
2. Turn signal cancelling cam
3. Upper bearing spring
4. Upper bearing inner race seat
5. Inner race

Fig. 44 Upper shaft component removal — with tilt wheel

1. Multi-function lever
2. Screw
3. Hazard warning button
4. Spring
5. Hazard warning knob
6. Screw
7. Screw
8. Signal switch arm
9. Turn signal and hazard warning switch

Fig. 45 Turn signal and hazard switch removal

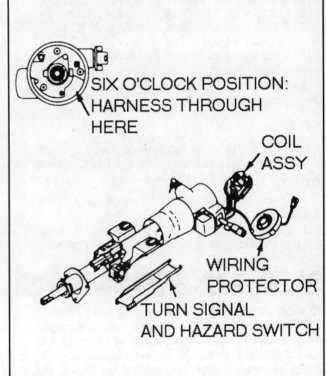

Fig. 47 Removing turn signal switch assembly

3. Remove the nut retainer and nut, and remove steering wheel with suitable puller. Remove the shaft lock cover.

4. Depress the shaft lock using tool J-23653 or equivalent. Remove the shaft lock retaining ring, the shaft lock and the shaft lock cover.

5. Remove the turn signal canceling cam and spring assembly. It may be necessary to turn the multifunction lever to the **RIGHT TURN** position. Remove the upper bearing spring, seat and inner race.

6. Rotate multifunction lever to the **RIGHT TURN** position and remove the screw and multifunction lever actuator arm.

7. Remove the wiring protector and hazard knob. Disconnect the switch wire connector at the lower end of the steering column.

8. Remove screws attaching the switch to the housing. Pull the switch out. If equipped with cruise control, the wiring

harness will have to be carefully pulled up through the gearshift lever bowl of the steering column. If wires must be pulled through the column, attach a length of mechanic's wire to the connector to aid in reassembly.

To install:

9. Gently pull the wiring harness through the steering column.

10. Attach turn signal switch to the housing using screws. Tighten to 30 inch lbs. (3.4 Nm).

11. Using screw, attach the multifunction lever. Tighten screw to 20 inch lbs. (2.3 Nm).

12. Install the inner race, upper bearing seat and upper bearing spring.

13. Install the turn signal canceling cam.

14. Using tool J-23653-B or equivalent, depress the shaft lock and install the shaft lock retaining ring.

15. Attach the shaft lock cover and steering wheel.

16. Tighten steering wheel retaining nut to 30 ft. lbs. (41 Nm) and attach nut retainer.

17. Attach the horn lead in cam tower by pushing inward and turning clockwise.

18. Attach steering pad with attaching screws and connect the negative battery cable.

1991-93

➡️If equipped with an air bag system, make certain to follow the recommended Disarming and Coil Centering procedure before and after repairs.

1. Disable the Supplemental Air Restraint (SIR) air bag system.

2. Remove the Torx® screws from the back of the steering wheel, disconnect the connector and remove the inflator module.

✳✳CAUTION

To avoid personal injury when carrying a live inflator module, make sure the bag and trim cover are pointed away. Always face the air bag assembly up, and never carry the inflator module by the wires or connector, otherwise personal injury may result if the module should deploy.

3. Disconnect the negative battery cable.

4. Remove the locking nut and use a suitable puller to remove the steering wheel.

5. Remove the coil assembly retaining ring and allow the coil assembly to hang.

6. Remove the wave washer.

7. Remove the shaft lock bolt guard:

  a. Turn the ignition switch to the **RUN** position.

  b. Rotate shaft so the blocking tooth is at 7 o'clock and bolt guard screws are accessible through large slots on lock shaft.

  c. Loosen screws on lock bolt guard and remove.

  d. Return ignition to the **LOCK** position.

8. Remove the shaft lock retaining ring using tool J-23653-C or equivalent.

✳✳CAUTION

Use a ½ inch wrench to hold the shaft of tool J-23653-C or equivalent, stationary when releasing the nut. Failure to do so may cause the tool to fly off and cause personal injury.

9. Remove the shaft lock, turn signal canceling cam, upper bearing spring, upper bearing inner race seat and inner race.

10. Turn the multifunction lever to the **RIGHT TURN** position and remove the multifunction lever and hazard knob assembly.

11. Remove the retaining screw and signal switch arm.

12. Remove the wiring protector from the steering column then disconnect the switch connector.

13. Remove the screws retaining the turn signal switch to the steering column, using care not to drop the screws in the column. Attach a length of mechanic's wire to the connector to aid in reinstallation and gently pull wire harness through the steering column.

To install:

14. Using the mechanic's wire, gently pull the turn switch connector through the steering column and attach switch connector to the vehicle wire harness.

15. Install the turn switch assembly and screws. Tighten turn switch mounting screws to 30 inch lbs. (3.4 Nm).

16. Install the signal switch arm and retaining screw. Tighten screw to 20 inch lbs. (2.3 Nm).

17. Install the hazard knob assembly and multifunction lever.

18. Install the inner race, upper bearing race seat and upper bearing spring.

19. Lubricate turn signal canceling cam with synthetic grease and install canceling cam assembly.

20. Install shaft lock and new shaft lock retaining ring using tool J-23653-C or equivalent.

21. Install shaft lock bolt guard as follows:

  a. Turn ignition switch to the **RUN** position.

  b. Rotate shaft until the block tooth is at the 7 o'clock position and bolt guard screw holes are accessible though large slots on lock shaft.

  c. Tighten screws on lock bolt guard until they bottom out, then torque to 20 inch lbs. (2.3 Nm).

22. Install the wave washer.

23. Install and center the coil assembly and retaining ring.

24. Connect wiring protector, if removed.

25. Install steering wheel, and tighten the locking nut.

26. Attach the inflator module.

27. Connect the negative battery cable and enable the SIR system.

Ignition Switch

▶ **See Figure 48**

➡️If equipped with an air bag system, make certain to follow the recommended disarming procedure before, and rearming procedure after, repairs.

1. Disconnect the negative battery cable and disable the air bag system, if equipped.

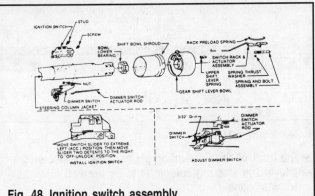

Fig. 48 Ignition switch assembly

2. Remove the column to instrument panel trim plates and attaching nuts.

3. Lower the steering column and disconnect the shift indicator cable.

4. Disconnect the ignition and dimmer switch wire connectors.

➡The steering column must be supported at all times to prevent damage.

5. Remove the switch attaching screws and remove the dimmer switch followed by the ignition switch.

To install:

6. Move the key lock to the **LOCK** position.

7. Move the actuator rod hole in the switch to the **LOCK** position.

8. Install the switch with the rod in the hole. Adjust the ignition switch as follows:

   a. 1990 — Place a 3/32 inch drill bit in the hole on the switch to lock the switch into position. Move the switch slider to the extreme left position then move the slider 1 detent to the right **OFF LOCK** position. Remove the drill bit.

   b. 1991-93 — Install the ignition switch in the **LOCK** position. Move the switch slider to the extreme right position and move the slider 1 detent to the left **LOCK** position. Depress switch mechanism slightly to insert a 3/32 inch drill bit into ignition switch.

9. Position and reassemble the steering column in reverse of the disassembly following the proper coil centering procedure. Enable the air bag system, if equipped, as follows:

   a. Connect the yellow 2-way SIR harness connector located at the base of the steering column.

   b. Install the SIR fuse to the fuse block.

c. Turn the ignition switch to **RUN** and verify the inflatable restraint indicator flashes 7-9 times and then turns off.

Ignition Lock Cylinder

REMOVAL & INSTALLATION

▶ See Figure 49

1990

1. Disconnect the negative battery cable.
2. Position the ignition lock cylinder in the **LOCK** position.
3. Remove the turn signal switch.
4. Remove key from lock cylinder. Remove the buzzer switch and clip.
5. Reinsert key into the lock cylinder and turn key to the **LOCK** position. Remove the lock cylinder retaining screw and the lock cylinder.

To install:

6. Match the key position upon removal of the lock cylinder. Be sure that the lock cylinder aligns the cylinder key with the keyway in the lock housing.
7. Push the lock all the way in and install the retaining screw. Tighten screw to 22 inch lbs. (2.5 Nm).
8. Install turn signal switch.
9. Connect the negative battery cable.

1991-93

➡This vehicle is equipped with an air bag system, make certain to follow the recommended disarming and coil centering procedure before and after repairs.

1. Disable the SIR system.
2. Disconnect the negative battery cable.
3. Remove the turn signal assembly.
4. Remove the SIR coil assembly from the column if necessary, as follows:

   a. Remove wiring protector.

   b. Attach a length of mechanics wire to the terminal connector to aid in reassembly.

   c. Carefully pull wire through the column.

5. Remove the key from the lock cylinder and remove the buzzer switch assembly.
6. Reinsert the key into the lock cylinder, be sure the key is in the **LOCK** position.

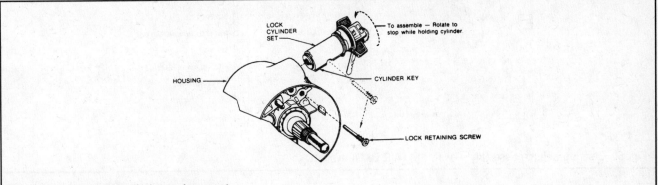

Fig. 49 Ignition lock cylinder replacement

7. Remove the lock cylinder retaining screw.

8. Remove the lock cylinder from the steering column.

To install:

9. Reinstall the lock cylinder set with key inserted. Attach with the retaining screw tighten at the steering column to 22 inch lbs. (2.5 Nm).

10. Insert the ignition key and turn it to the **RUN** position, and install the buzzer switch retaining clip, then return the key to the **LOCK** position.

11. Gently pull turn signal switch wiring connector through the steering column and allow assembly to hang freely.

12. Gently pull the coil assembly through the steering column and allow assembly to hang freely.

13. Install the turn signal switch assembly.

14. Be sure to follow proper SIR coil centering assembly.

15. Connect the negative battery cable and enable the SIR system.

Steering Column

REMOVAL & INSTALLATION

▶ **See Figure 50**

➡ **The front of dash mounting plates must be loosened whenever the steering column is to be lowered from the instrument panel.**

1. Disconnect the negative battery cable.

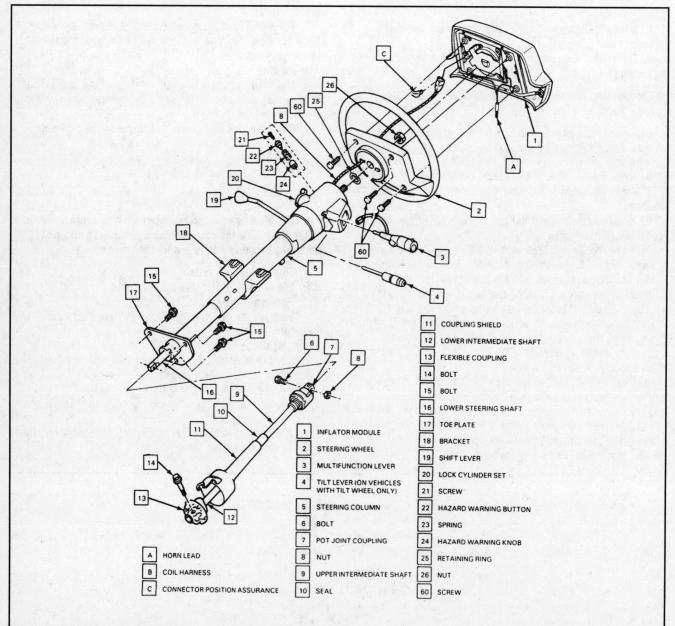

11	COUPLING SHIELD			
12	LOWER INTERMEDIATE SHAFT			
13	FLEXIBLE COUPLING			
14	BOLT			
15	BOLT			
16	LOWER STEERING SHAFT			
17	TOE PLATE			
18	BRACKET			
19	SHIFT LEVER			
20	LOCK CYLINDER SET			
21	SCREW			
1	INFLATOR MODULE		22	HAZARD WARNING BUTTON
2	STEERING WHEEL		23	SPRING
3	MULTIFUNCTION LEVER		24	HAZARD WARNING KNOB
4	TILT LEVER (ON VEHICLES WITH TILT WHEEL ONLY)		25	RETAINING RING
5	STEERING COLUMN		26	NUT
6	BOLT		60	SCREW
7	POT JOINT COUPLING			
8	NUT			
9	UPPER INTERMEDIATE SHAFT			
A	HORN LEAD	10	SEAL	
B	COIL HARNESS			
C	CONNECTOR POSITION ASSURANCE			

Fig. 50 Steering column assembly — with SIR (AIR BAG) system

2. On 1991-93 vehicles, disable the Supplemental Inflatable Restraint (SIR) system as follows:

a. Turn the steering wheel so the vehicle's wheels are pointing straight-ahead.

✳✳CAUTION

The wheels of the vehicle must be in the straight-ahead position and the steering column in the locked position before proceeding with steering column removal. Failure to follow this procedure will cause the SIR coil to become uncentered, resulting in damage to the coil assembly.

b. Remove the SIR fuse from the fuse block.

c. Remove the left sound insulator by removing the nut from the stud and gently prying the insulator from the knee bolster.

d. Disconnect the Connector Position Assurance (CPA) and yellow 2-way SIR harness connector at the base of the steering column.

3. Remove the nut and bolt from the upper intermediate shaft coupling. Separate the coupling from the lower end of the steering column.

4. Remove the steering wheel if the column is to be replaced or repaired on the bench.

5. Remove the knee bolster and bracket, if equipped.

6. Remove the bolts attaching the toe plate to the cowl.

7. Disconnect the electrical connectors.

8. Remove the capsule nuts attaching the steering column support bracket to the instrument panel.

9. Disconnect the shift indicator cable and gear selector rod from the column assembly.

10. Remove the steering column from the vehicle.

To install:

➡If a replacement steering column is being installed, do not remove the anti-rotation pin until after the steering column has been connected to the steering gear. Removing the anti-rotation pin before the steering column is connected to the steering gear may damage the SIR coil assembly.

11. Position the steering column in the vehicle.

12. Connect the shift indicator cable to the column.

13. Install the capsule nuts attaching the steering column support bracket to the instrument panel and tighten to 20 ft. lbs. (27 Nm).

14. Install the nut and bolt to the upper intermediate shaft coupling attaching the upper intermediate shaft to the steering column. Tighten the nut to 40 ft. lbs. (54 Nm).

15. Install the bolts attaching the toe plate to the cowl and tighten to 58 inch lbs. (6.5 Nm).

16. Connect the electrical connectors.

17. Remove the anti-rotation pin if a service replacement steering column is being installed.

18. Install the knee bolster and bracket, if equipped.

19. Install the sound insulator panel.

➡If SIR coil has become uncentered by turning of the steering wheel without the column connected to the steering gear, follow the proper adjustment procedure for SIR Coil Centering before proceeding.

20. Install the steering wheel.

21. Connect the negative battery cable.

22. Enable the SIR system as follows:

a. Connect the yellow 2-way SIR harness connector to the base of the steering column and CPA clip and install the SIR fuse.

b. Install the left sound insulator.

c. Turn the ignition switch to the **RUN** position and verify that the inflatable restraint indicator flashes 7-9 times and then turns **OFF**. If the indicator does not respond as stated, a problem within the SIR system is indicated.

Steering Linkage

REMOVAL & INSTALLATION

▶ **See Figure 51**

Pitman Arm

▶ **See Figure 52**

1. Raise and safely support the vehicle.

2. Remove the nut from the pitman arm ball stud.

3. Remove the relay rod from the pitman arm by using a tool such as J-24319-01 or equivalent. Pull down on the relay rod to remove it from the stud.

4. Remove the pitman arm nut from the pitman shaft and mark the relation of the arm position to the shaft.

5. Remove the pitman arm with tool J-5504 or tool J-6632 or equivalent. DO NOT HAMMER ON THE PULLER.

To install:

6. Position the pitman arm on the pitman shaft, lining up the marks made upon removal.

7. Position the relay rod on the pitman arm. Use J-29193 or J-29194 or equivalent to seat the tapers. A torque of 15 ft. lbs. (20 Nm) is required. With the tapers seated, remove the tool, then install a prevailing torque nut, and tighten to 35 ft. lbs. (48 Nm).

8. Set the relay rod height. Torque the idler arm-to-frame mounting bolts to 61 ft. lbs. (83 Nm).

9. Lower the vehicle.

Idler Arm

1. Raise the vehicle and support securely.

2. Remove the idler arm to frame nuts, washers, and bolts.

3. Remove the nut from the idler arm to relay rod ball stud.

4. Remove the relay rod from the idler arm by using J-24319-01 or equivalent.

5. Remove the idler arm.

To install:

6. Position the idler arm on the frame and LOOSELY install the mounting bolts, washers and nuts.

7. Install the relay rod to the idler arm, making certain seal is on the stud. Use J-29193 or J-29194 or equivalent to seat the tapers. A torque of 15 ft. lbs. (20 Nm) is required. With the tapers seated, remove the tool, then install a prevailing torque nut, and tighten to 35 ft. lbs. (48 Nm).

8. Set the relay rod height. Torque the idler arm-to-frame mounting bolts to 61 ft. lbs. (83 Nm).

9. Lower the vehicle.

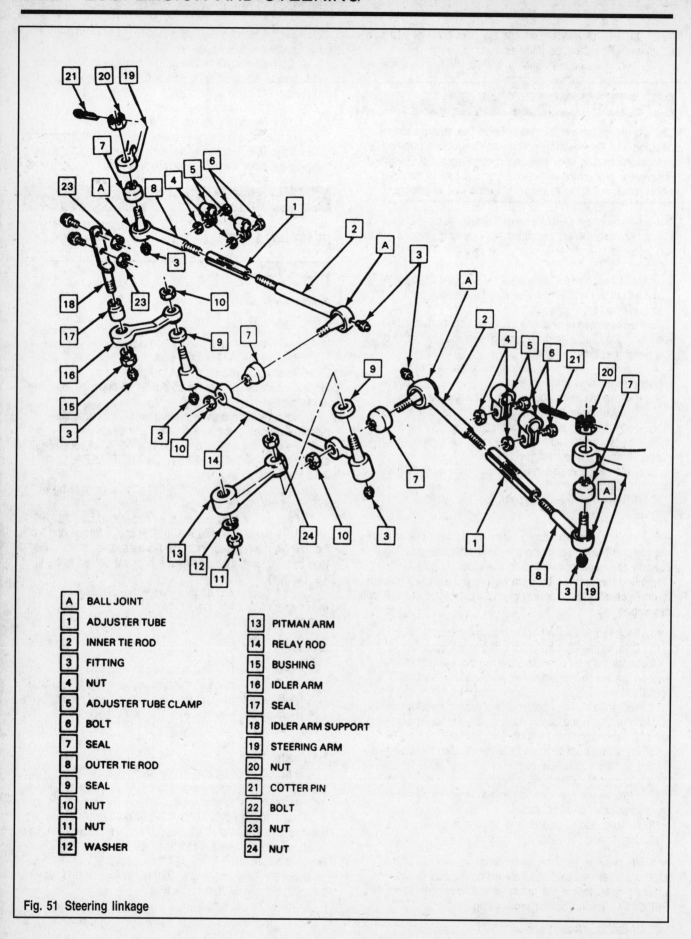

A	BALL JOINT		
1	ADJUSTER TUBE	**13**	PITMAN ARM
2	INNER TIE ROD	**14**	RELAY ROD
3	FITTING	**15**	BUSHING
4	NUT	**16**	IDLER ARM
5	ADJUSTER TUBE CLAMP	**17**	SEAL
6	BOLT	**18**	IDLER ARM SUPPORT
7	SEAL	**19**	STEERING ARM
8	OUTER TIE ROD	**20**	NUT
9	SEAL	**21**	COTTER PIN
10	NUT	**22**	BOLT
11	NUT	**23**	NUT
12	WASHER	**24**	NUT

Fig. 51 Steering linkage

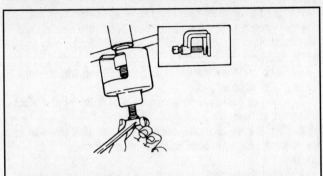

Fig. 52 Using pitman arm puller — tie rod tool pictured in upper right

Relay Rod

▶ See Figure 53

During production, the installed position of the relay rod is carefully controlled to assure that the rod is at the proper height. Both the left end and the right end of the relay rod must be held at the same height. The side-to-side height is controlled by adjusting the position of the idler arm.

Whenever disconnecting the relay rod assembly, it is important to first scribe the position of the idler arm-to-frame, and to reinstall the idler arm in the same position. Be sure to prevent the idler support from turning in the bushing, since that motion could result in improper relay rod height.

Whenever replacing the relay rod, or the idler arm, or the pitman arm, it is mandatory to establish the correct height.

1. Raise the vehicle and support on jackstands.

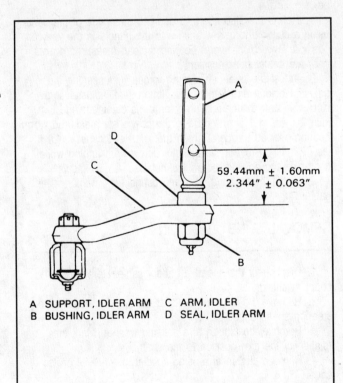

A SUPPORT, IDLER ARM   C ARM, IDLER
B BUSHING, IDLER ARM   D SEAL, IDLER ARM

59.44mm ± 1.60mm
2.344" ± 0.063"

Fig. 53 Ensure the relay rod height is correct. Adjust the relay rod height by turning the idler arm support into the bushing.

2. Remove the inner ends of the tie rods from the relay rod.

3. Remove the nut from the relay rod ball stud attachment at pitman arm.

4. Detach the relay rod from the pitman arm by using tool such as J-24319-01 or equivalent. Shift the steering linkage as required to free the pitman arm from the relay rod.

5. Remove the nut from the idler arm and remove the relay rod from the idler arm.

To install:

6. Install the relay rod to idler arm, making certain idler stud seal is in place. Use J-29193 or J-29194 or equivalent to seat the tapers. A torque of 15 ft. lbs. (20 Nm) is required. With the tapers seated, remove the tool, then install a prevailing torque nut, and tighten to 35 ft. lbs. (48 Nm).

7. Raise the end of the rod and install on the pitman arm. Use J-29193 or J-29194 or equivalent to seat the tapers. A torque of 15 ft. lbs. (20 Nm) is required. With the tapers seated, remove the tool, then install a prevailing torque nut, and tighten to 35 ft. lbs. (48 Nm).

8. Install the tie rod ends to the relay rod. Lubricate the tie rod ends.

9. Install the damper, if equipped.

10. Set the relay rod height. Torque the idler arm-to-frame mounting bolts to 61 ft. lbs. (83 Nm).

11. Lower the vehicle.

12. Check and, if necessary, adjust front end alignment.

Tie Rod Ends

▶ See Figures 54 and 55

1. Raise the vehicle and support securely.

2. Remove the cotter pins from the ball studs and remove the castellated nuts.

3. Remove the outer ball stud by using the ball stud puller. If necessary, pull downward on the tie rod to disconnect it from the steering arm.

4. Remove the inner ball stud from the relay rod using a similar procedure.

5. Remove the tie rod end or ends to be replaced by loosening the clamp bolt and unscrewing them.

To install:

6. Lubricate tie rod threads with chassis grease and install new tie rod(s). Make sure both ends are an equal distance from the tie rod and tighten clamp bolts.

7. Make sure ball studs, tapered surfaces, and all threaded surfaces are clean and smooth, and free of grease. Install

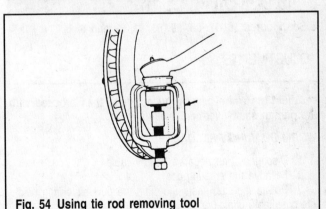

Fig. 54 Using tie rod removing tool

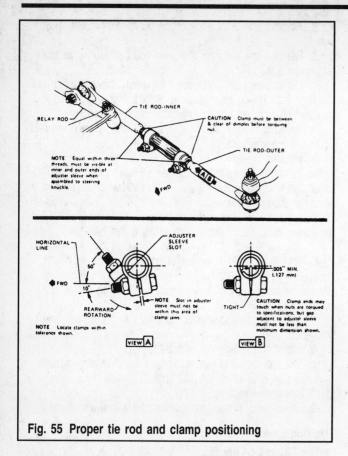

Fig. 55 Proper tie rod and clamp positioning

seals on ball studs. Install ball stud in steering arm and relay rod.

8. Rotate both inner and outer tie rod housings rearward to the limit of ball joint travel before tightening clamps. Make sure clamp slots and sleeve slots are aligned before tightening clamps. Make sure tightened bolts will be in horizontal position to 45 degrees upward (in the forward direction) when the tie rod is in its normal position. Make sure the tie rod end stays in position relative to the rod during the tightening operation. Tighten the clamps, and then return the assembly to the center of its travel.

9. Install ball stud nuts and torque to 35 ft. lbs. (47 Nm) Then tighten (do not loosen) further as required to align cotter pin holes in studs and nuts. Install new cotter pins.

10. Lubricate new tie rod ends and lower the vehicle.

Power Steering Gear

◗ **See Figures 56, 57, 58, 59, 60, 61, 62 and 63**

ADJUSTMENTS

➡**Adjust the worm bearing preload first, then proceed with the pitman shaft over-center adjustment.**

WORM BEARING PRELOAD

1. Disconnect the negative battery cable.
2. Remove the steering gear.
3. Rotate the stub shaft and drain the power steering fluid into a suitable container.
4. Remove the adjuster plug nut.

5. Turn the adjuster plug in (clockwise) using a suitable spanner wrench until the adjuster plug and thrust bearing are firmly bottomed in the housing. Tighten the adjuster plug to 20 ft. lbs. (27 Nm).

6. Place an index mark on the housing even with 1 of the holes in the adjuster plug.

7. Measure back counterclockwise ½ in. (13mm) and place a second mark on the housing.

8. Turn the adjuster plug counterclockwise until the hole in the adjuster plug is aligned with the second mark on the housing.

9. Install the adjuster plug nut and using a suitable punch in a notch, tighten securely. Hold the adjuster plug to maintain alignment of the marks.

10. Install the steering gear and connect the negative battery cable.

PITMAN SHAFT OVER-CENTER

1. Disconnect the negative battery cable.
2. Remove the steering gear.
3. Rotate the stub shaft and drain the power steering fluid into a suitable container.
4. Turn the pitman shaft adjuster screw counterclockwise until fully extended, then turn back 1 full turn.
5. Rotate the stub shaft from stop to stop and count the number of turns.
6. Starting at either stop, turn the stub shaft back half the total number of turns. This is the'Center" position of the gear. When the gear is centered, the flat on the stub shaft should face upward and be parallel with the side cover and the master spline on the pitman shaft should be in line with the adjuster screw.
7. Rotate the stub shaft 45 degrees each side of the center using a suitable torque wrench with the handle in the vertical position. Record the worm bearing preload measured on or near the center gear position.
8. Adjust the over-center drag torque by loosening the adjuster locknut and turning the pitman shaft adjuster screw clockwise until the correct drag torque is obtained: Add 6-10 inch lbs. (0.7-1.1 Nm) torque to the previously measured worm bearing preload torque. Tighten the adjuster locknut to 20 ft. lbs. (27 Nm). Prevent the adjuster screw from turning while tightening the adjuster screw locknut.
9. Install the steering gear and connect the negative battery cable.

REMOVAL & INSTALLATION

1. Disconnect the negative battery cable. Remove the coupling shield.
2. Remove the retaining bolts at the steering coupling to steering shaft flange.
3. Remove the pitman arm nut and washer. Mark the relation of the arm position to the shaft.
4. Remove pitman arm using special tool J-6632 or its equal.
5. Remove the fluid hoses and cap them to prevent foreign material from entering the system.
6. Remove the steering box to frame bolts. Remove steering box.

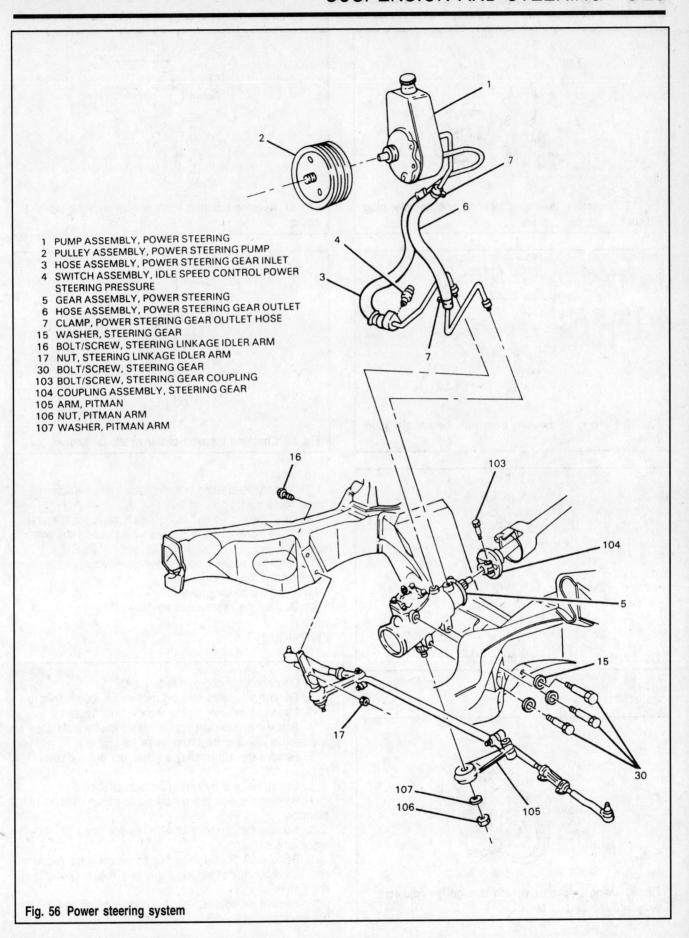

1 PUMP ASSEMBLY, POWER STEERING
2 PULLEY ASSEMBLY, POWER STEERING PUMP
3 HOSE ASSEMBLY, POWER STEERING GEAR INLET
4 SWITCH ASSEMBLY, IDLE SPEED CONTROL POWER
  STEERING PRESSURE
5 GEAR ASSEMBLY, POWER STEERING
6 HOSE ASSEMBLY, POWER STEERING GEAR OUTLET
7 CLAMP, POWER STEERING GEAR OUTLET HOSE
15 WASHER, STEERING GEAR
16 BOLT/SCREW, STEERING LINKAGE IDLER ARM
17 NUT, STEERING LINKAGE IDLER ARM
30 BOLT/SCREW, STEERING GEAR
103 BOLT/SCREW, STEERING GEAR COUPLING
104 COUPLING ASSEMBLY, STEERING GEAR
105 ARM, PITMAN
106 NUT, PITMAN ARM
107 WASHER, PITMAN ARM

Fig. 56 Power steering system

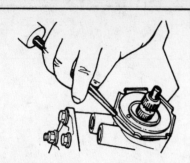

Fig. 57 Loosening the power steering gear adjuster plug locknut

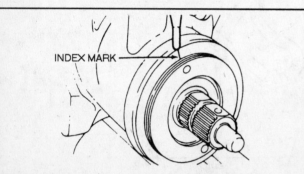

Fig. 58 Marking the housing even with the adjuster plug hole

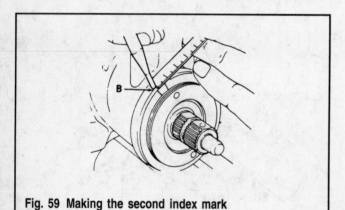

Fig. 59 Making the second index mark

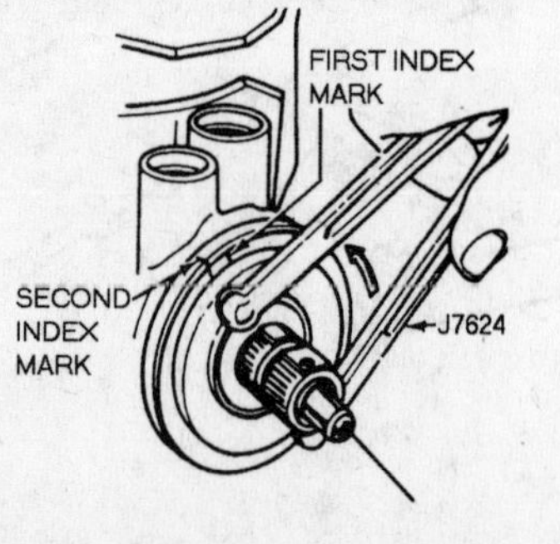

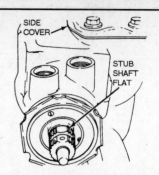

Fig. 61 Aligning the stub shaft parallel with the top cover

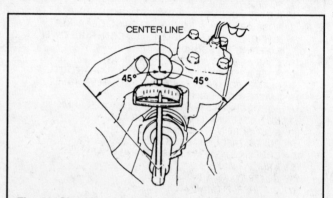

Fig. 62 Checking the over-center rotational torque

To install:

7. Position the steering box and secure with the steering box-to-frame bolts.

8. Install the pitman arm to the match marks made earlier.

9. Install the pitman arm nut and washer. Install the power steering hoses.

10. Install the retaining bolts at the steering coupling to steering shaft flange.

11. Install the coupling shield.

12. Connect the negative battery cable.

OVERHAUL

1. Disconnect the negative battery cable.

2. Remove the power steering gear as previously directed.

3. Clean any external grease and dirt from the unit.

4. Rotate the stub shaft back and forth over a drain pan and remove any fluid remaining inside the unit.

5. Remove the pitman shaft adjuster lock nut and cover bolts.

6. Center the gear by turning the stub shaft.

7. Remove the side cover, gasket and pitman shaft as an assembly.

8. Remove the pitman shaft from the side cover by unscrewing it.

9. Remove the housing end plug by removing the retaining ring. Use a punch inserted into the access hole to unseat the ring.

10. Remove the adjuster plug nut using a punch and hammer against the edge of the slots.

Fig. 60 Using a spanner wrench to align the adjuster plug with the second mark

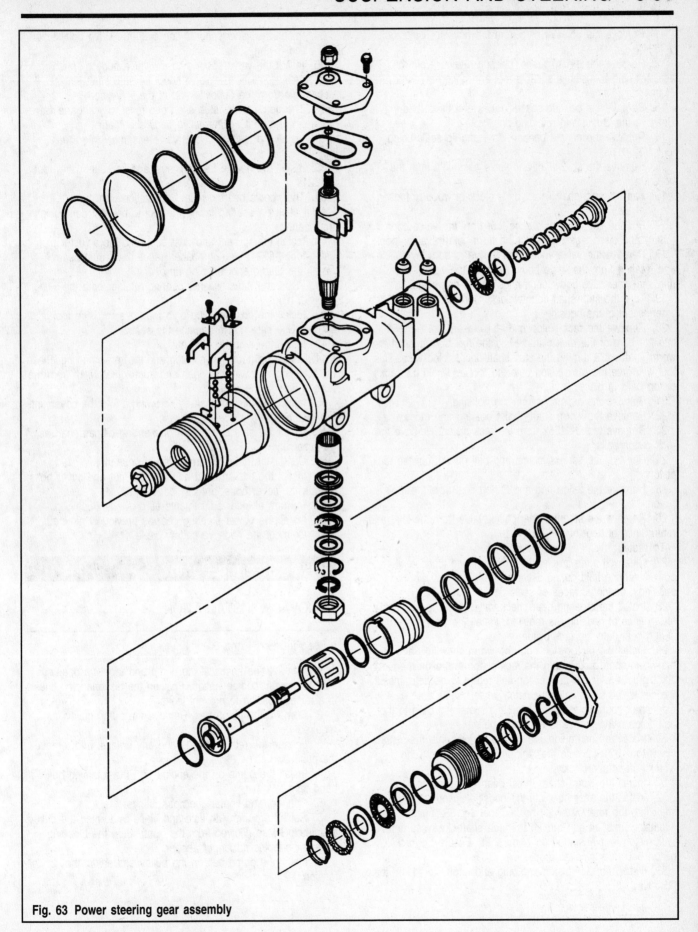

Fig. 63 Power steering gear assembly

11. Remove the adjuster plug from the housing using tool J-7624.

12. Remove the thrust washer bearing retainer from the adjuster plug by using a suitable tool and prying at raised area of bearing retainer.

13. Remove the bearing spacer, races and thrust bearing. Remove the O-ring and retaining ring.

14. Remove the needle bearing, dust and lip seals using tool J-6221.

15. Remove the stub shaft and valve assembly from the housing.

16. Tap the stub shaft lightly on a block of wood to loosen the shaft cap.

17. Pull the cap and valve spool out from the valve body 1/4″ (6mm) and disengage stub shaft pin from hole in valve spool.

18. Remove the valve spool from the valve body by pulling and rotating from the valve body. Remove the valve spool O-ring seal, the valve body teflon rings and O-ring seals.

19. Turn the stub shaft counterclockwise until the rack piston extends out of the housing.

20. Remove the rack piston end plug. Insert tool J-21552 into the bore of the rack piston. Hold the tool tight against the worm shaft while turning the stub shaft counterclockwise. This tool will force the rack piston onto the tool and hold the rack piston balls in place.

21. Remove the assembly from the housing.

22. Remove the worm shaft, thrust bearing and races.

23. Remove tool J-21552 from the rack piston. Remove the rack piston balls.

24. Remove the screws, clamp and ball guide from the rack piston.

25. Remove the teflon ring and O-ring seal from the rack piston.

26. Remove the steering gear check valve from the inlet and return lines of housing, as required.

To install:

27. Clean all parts in a suitable cleaner and lubricate with power steering fluid during assembly. Replace any worn bushings, bearings, races or seals.

28. Install the steering gear check valve from the inlet and return lines of housing, as required. Install the teflon ring and O-ring seal onto the rack piston.

29. Install the rack piston onto the worm shaft fully and align the worm shaft groove with the rack piston and align the worm shaft groove with the rack piston ball return guide hole. Install the black and silver balls alternately while turning the wormshaft counterclockwise. Install the remaining balls to the ball guide using grease to retain the balls.

30. Install the ball guide, clamp and screws onto the piston. Insert tool J-21552 onto the rack piston while turning the wormshaft counterclockwise.

31. Install the worm shaft, thrust bearing and races.

32. Install the assembly into the housing. Insert the worm shaft into the rack piston by holding tool J-21552 tightly against wormshaft and turning the stub shaft clockwise until rack piston is fully seated on worm shaft. Ensure the rack piston balls are installed properly.

33. Install the rack piston end plug and torque to 111 ft. lbs. (150 Nm).

34. Install the valve spool O-ring seal, the valve body teflon rings and O-ring seals.

35. Install the valve spool onto the valve body by pushing and rotating until hole in valve spool for stub shaft pin is accessible from the opposite end of the valve body.

36. The notch in the stub shaft cap must fully engage valve body pin and seat against valve body shoulder.

37. Install the stub shaft and valve assembly into the housing.

38. Install the needle bearing, dust and lip seals using tool J-6221.

39. The needle bearing must be installed with the identification on bearing facing the tool to prevent damaging the bearing.

40. Install the lip seal and dust seal onto the adjuster plug using tool J-6221. bearing spacer, races and thrust bearing. Install the O-ring and retaining ring.

41. Install the thrust washer bearing retainer onto the adjuster plug.

42. Install the adjuster plug onto the housing using tool J-7624. Use care not to damage the seals.

43. Install the adjuster plug nut.

44. Install the housing end plug and the retaining ring. Place the retaining ring with the open end approximately 1″ from the access hole in the housing.

45. Install the pitman shaft by screwing it into the cover until fully seated.

46. Install the side cover, new gasket and pitman shaft as an assembly.

47. Center the gear by turning the stub shaft.

48. Install the pitman shaft adjuster lock nut and cover bolts. Torque the cover bolts to 44 ft. lbs. (60 Nm).

49. Perform all gear adjustments as previously outlined.

50. Install the power steering gear as previously directed.

51. Connect the negative battery cable.

Power Steering Pump

REMOVAL & INSTALLATION

▶ **See Figures 64 and 65**

1. Remove the hoses at the pump and tape the openings shut to prevent contamination. Position the disconnected lines in a raised position to prevent leakage.

2. Remove the pump belt. Remove the pump pulley, as required

3. Loosen the retaining bolts and any braces, and remove the pump.

4. Install the pump on the engine with the retaining bolt hand tight.

5. Connect and tighten the hose fittings.

6. Refill the pump with fluid and bleed by turning the pulley counterclockwise (viewed from the front). Stop the bleeding when air bubbles no longer appear.

7. Install the pump belt on the pulley and adjust the tension.

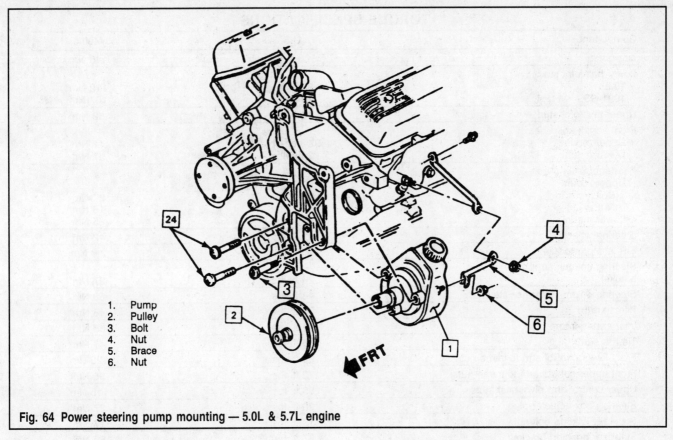

1. Pump
2. Pulley
3. Bolt
4. Nut
5. Brace
6. Nut

Fig. 64 Power steering pump mounting — 5.0L & 5.7L engine

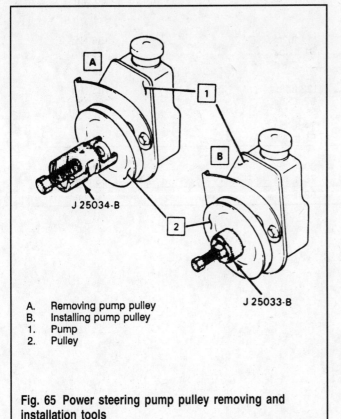

A. Removing pump pulley
B. Installing pump pulley
1. Pump
2. Pulley

J 25034-B

J 25033-B

Fig. 65 Power steering pump pulley removing and installation tools

SYSTEM BLEEDING

1. Fill the reservoir with power steering fluid.

➡**The use of automatic transmission fluid in the power steering system is NOT recommended.**

2. Allow the reservoir and fluid to sit undisturbed for a few minutes.

3. Start the engine, allow it to run for a moment, then turn it off.

4. Check the reservoir fluid level and add fluid if necessary.

5. Repeat the above steps until the fluid level stabilizes.

6. Raise the front of the vehicle so that the wheels are off of the ground.

7. Start the engine and increase the engine speed to about 1500 rpm.

8. Turn the front wheels right to left (and back) several times, lightly contacting the wheel stops at the ends of travel.

9. Check the reservoir fluid level. Add fluid as required.

10. Repeat step 8 until the fluid level in the reservoir stabilizes.

11. Lower the vehicle and repeat steps 8 and 9.

TORQUE SPECIFICATIONS

Component	U.S.	Metric
Lug nuts:	100 ft. lbs.	140 Nm
Lower ball joint stud		
1990:	83 ft. lbs.	112 Nm
1991–93:	79 ft. lbs.	107 Nm
Upper ball joint stud:	60 ft. lbs.	82 Nm
Front shock absorber		
Upper mount:	97 inch. lbs.	11 Nm
Lower mount:	20 ft. lbs.	27 Nm
Rear shock absorber		
Upper mount		
Bolt:	20 ft. lbs.	27 Nm
Nut:	12 ft. lbs.	16 Nm
Lower mount:	48 ft. lbs.	65 Nm
Steering wheel:	31 ft. lbs.	42 Nm
SIR inflator module:	25 inch lbs.	2.8 Nm
Steering column support bracket:	20 ft. lbs.	27 Nm
Steering column intermediate shaft:	44 ft. lbs.	60 Nm
Pitman arm:	35 ft. lbs.	48 Nm
Idler arm-to-frame:	61 ft. lbs.	83 Nm
Tie rod stud:	35 ft. lbs.	47 Nm
Front lower control arm to frame nuts:	92 ft. lbs.	125 Nm
Front upper control arm to frame nuts:	72 ft. lbs.	98 Nm
Upper control arm pivot shaft nuts:	85 ft. lbs.	115 Nm
Steering box adjuster plug:	20 ft. lbs.	27 Nm
Stabilizer linkage bolt/nut:	13 ft. lbs.	17 Nm
Stabilizer bushing bracket:	37 ft. lbs.	50 Nm
Rear control arm to frame crossmeber		
Upper		
Bolt:	114 ft. lbs.	155 Nm
Nut:	91 ft. lbs.	123 Nm
Lower		
1990		
Bolts:	122 ft. lbs.	165 Nm
Nuts:	92 ft. lbs.	125 Nm
1991–93		
Bolts:	74 ft. lbs.	100 Nm
Nuts:	91 ft. lbs.	123 Nm
Rear control arm to frame crossmeber		
Bolt:	80 ft. lbs.	108 Nm
Nut:	70 ft. lbs.	95 Nm
Rear stabilizer shaft:	52 ft. lbs.	70 Nm

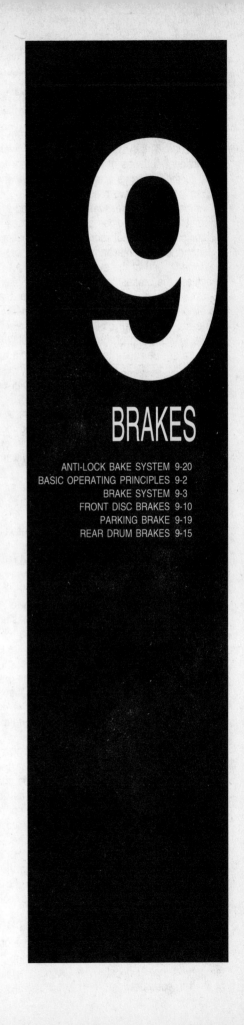

9

BRAKES

9

9

BASIC OPERATING PRINCIPLES

Hydraulic systems are used to actuate the brakes of all automobiles. The system transports the power required to force the frictional surfaces of the braking system together from the pedal to the individual brake units at each wheel. A hydraulic system is used for two reasons.

First, fluid under pressure can be carried to all parts of an automobile by small pipes and flexible hoses without taking up a significant amount of room or posing routing problems.

Second, a great mechanical advantage can be given to the brake pedal end of the system, and the foot pressure required to actuate the brakes can be reduced by making the surface area of the master cylinder pistons smaller than that of any of the pistons in the wheel cylinders or calipers.

The master cylinder consists of a fluid reservoir and a double cylinder and piston assembly. Double type master cylinders are designed to separate the front and rear braking systems hydraulically in case of a leak.

Steel lines carry the brake fluid to a point on the vehicle's frame near each of the vehicle's wheels. The fluid is then carried to the calipers and wheel cylinders by flexible tubes in order to allow for suspension and steering movements.

In drum brake systems, each wheel cylinder contains two pistons, one at either end, which push outward in opposite directions.

In disc brake systems, the cylinders are part of the calipers. One cylinder in each caliper is used to force the brake pads against the disc.

All pistons employ some type of seal, usually made of rubber, to minimize fluid leakage. A rubber dust boot seals the outer end of the cylinder against dust and dirt. The boot fits around the outer end of the piston on disc brake calipers, and around the brake actuating rod on wheel cylinders.

The hydraulic system operates as follows: When at rest, the entire system, from the piston(s) in the master cylinder to those in the wheel cylinders or calipers, is full of brake fluid. Upon application of the brake pedal, fluid trapped in front of the master cylinder piston(s) is forced through the lines to the wheel cylinders. Here, it forces the pistons outward, in the case of drum brakes, and inward toward the disc, in the case of disc brakes. The motion of the pistons is opposed by return springs mounted outside the cylinders in drum brakes, and by spring seals, in disc brakes.

Upon release of the brake pedal, a spring located inside the master cylinder immediately returns the master cylinder pistons to the normal position. The pistons contain check valves and the master cylinder has compensating ports drilled in it. These are uncovered as the pistons reach their normal position. The piston check valves allow fluid to flow toward the wheel cylinders or calipers as the pistons withdraw. Then, as the return springs force the brake pads or shoes into the released position, the excess fluid reservoir through the compensating ports. It is during the time the pedal is in the released position that any fluid that has leaked out of the system will be replaced through the compensating ports.

Dual circuit master cylinders employ two pistons, located one behind the other, in the same cylinder. The primary piston is actuated directly by mechanical linkage from the brake pedal through the power booster. The secondary piston is actuated by fluid trapped between the two pistons. If a leak develops in front of the secondary piston, it moves forward until it bottoms against the front of the master cylinder, and the fluid trapped between the pistons will operate the rear brakes. If the rear brakes develop a leak, the primary piston will move forward until direct contact with the secondary piston takes place, and it will force the secondary piston to actuate the front brakes. In either case, the brake pedal moves farther when the brakes are applied, and less braking power is available.

All dual circuit systems use a switch to warn the driver when only half of the brake system is operational. This switch is located in a valve body which is mounted on the firewall or the frame below the master cylinder. A hydraulic piston receives pressure from both circuits, each circuit's pressure being applied to one end of the piston. When the pressures are in balance, the piston remains stationary. When one circuit has a leak, however, the greater pressure in that circuit during application of the brakes will push the piston to one side, closing the switch and activating the brake warning light.

In disc brake systems, this valve body also contains a metering valve and, in some cases, a proportioning valve. The metering valve keeps pressure from traveling to the disc brakes on the front wheels until the brake shoes on the rear wheels have contacted the drums, ensuring that the front brakes will never be used alone. The proportioning valve controls the pressure to the rear brakes to lessen the chance of rear wheel lock-up during very hard braking.

Warning lights may be tested by depressing the brake pedal and holding it while opening one of the wheel cylinder bleeder screws. If this does not cause the light to go on, substitute a new lamp, make continuity checks, and, finally, replace the switch as necessary.

The hydraulic system may be checked for leaks by applying pressure to the pedal gradually and steadily. If the pedal sinks very slowly to the floor, the system has a leak. This is not to be confused with a springy or spongy feel due to the compression of air within the lines. If the system leaks, there will be a gradual change in the position of the pedal with a constant pressure.

Check for leaks along all lines and at wheel cylinders. If no external leaks are apparent, the problem is inside the master cylinder.

Disc Brakes

BASIC OPERATING PRINCIPLES

Instead of the traditional expanding brakes that press outward against a circular drum, disc brake systems utilize a disc (rotor) with brake pads positioned on either side of it. Braking effect is achieved in a manner similar to the way you would squeeze a spinning phonograph record between your fingers. The disc (rotor) is a casting with cooling fins between the two braking surfaces. This enables air to circulate between the braking surfaces making them less sensitive to heat buildup and more resistant to fade. Dirt and water do not affect braking action since contaminants are thrown off by the centrifugal action of the rotor or scraped off by the pads. Also, the equal clamping action of the two brake pads tends to ensure uniform, straight line stops. Disc brakes are inherently self-adjusting.

There are three general types of disc brake:
1. A fixed caliper.
2. A floating caliper.
3. A sliding caliper.

The fixed caliper design uses two pistons mounted on either side of the rotor (in each side of the caliper). The caliper is mounted rigidly and does not move.

The sliding and floating designs are quite similar. In fact, these two types are often lumped together. In both designs, the pad on the inside of the rotor is moved into contact with the rotor by hydraulic force. The caliper, which is not held in a fixed position, moves slightly, bringing the outside pad into contact with the rotor. There are various methods of attaching floating calipers. Some pivot at the bottom or top, and some slide on mounting bolts. In any event, the end result is the same.

All the cars covered in this book employ the sliding caliper design.

Drum Brakes

BASIC OPERATING PRINCIPLES

Drum brakes employ two brake shoes mounted on a stationary backing plate. These shoes are positioned inside a circular drum which rotates with the wheel assembly. The shoes are held in place by springs. This allows them to slide toward the drums (when they are applied) while keeping the linings and drums in alignment. The shoes are actuated by a wheel cylinder which is mounted at the top of the backing plate. When the brakes are applied, hydraulic pressure forces the wheel cylinder's actuating links outward. Since these links bear directly against the top of the brake shoes, the tops of the shoes are then forced against the inner side of the drum. This action forces the bottoms of the two shoes to contact the brake drum by rotating the entire assembly slightly (known as servo action). When pressure within the wheel cylinder is relaxed, return springs pull the shoes back away from the drum.

Most modern drum brakes are designed to self-adjust themselves during application when the vehicle is moving in reverse. This motion causes both shoes to rotate very slightly with the drum, rocking an adjusting lever, thereby causing rotation of the adjusting screw.

Power Boosters

Power brakes operate just as non-power brake systems except in the actuation of the master cylinder pistons. A vacuum diaphragm is located on the front of the master cylinder and assists the driver in applying the brakes, reducing both the effort and travel he must put into moving the brake pedal.

The vacuum diaphragm housing is connected to the intake manifold by a vacuum hose. A check valve is placed at the point where the hose enters the diaphragm housing, so that during periods of low manifold vacuum brake assist vacuum will not be lost.

Depressing the brake pedal closes off the vacuum source and allows atmospheric pressure to enter on one side of the diaphragm. This causes the master cylinder pistons to move and apply the brakes. When the brake pedal is released, vacuum is applied to both sides of the diaphragm, and return springs return the diaphragm and master cylinder pistons to the released position. If the vacuum fails, the brake pedal rod will butt against the end of the master cylinder actuating rod, and direct mechanical application will occur as the pedal is depressed.

The hydraulic and mechanical problems that apply to conventional brake systems also apply to power brakes, and should be checked for if the tests below do not reveal the problem. **Test for a system vacuum leak as described below:**
1. Operate the engine at idle without touching the brake pedal for at least one minute.
2. Turn off the engine, and wait one minute.
3. Test for the presence of assist vacuum by depressing the brake pedal and releasing it several times. Light application will produce less and less pedal travel, if vacuum was present. If there is no vacuum, air is leaking into the system somewhere.

Test for system operation as follows:
4. Pump the brake pedal (with engine off) until the supply vacuum is entirely gone.
5. Put a light, steady pressure on the pedal.
6. Start the engine, and operate it at idle. If the system is operating, the brake pedal should fall slightly toward the floor if constant pressure is maintained on the pedal.

Power brake systems may be tested for hydraulic leaks just as ordinary systems are tested.

BRAKE SYSTEM

All vehicles are equipped with independent front and rear brake systems. The systems consist of a power booster, a master cylinder, a combination valve, front disc assemblies and rear drum assemblies.

The master cylinder, mounted on the left firewall or power booster, consists of two fluid reservoirs, a primary (rear) cylinder, a secondary (front) cylinder and springs. The reservoirs, being independent of one another, are contained within the same housing; fluid cannot pass from one to the

other. The rear reservoir supplies fluid to the front brakes while the front reservoir supplies fluid to the rear brakes.

During operation, fluid drains from the reservoirs to the master cylinder. When the brake pedal is applied, fluid from the master cylinder is sent to the combination valve (mounted beneath the master cylinder), here fluid pressure is monitored and proportionally distributed to the front or rear brake systems. Should a loss of pressure occur in one system, the other system will provide enough braking pressure to stop the vehicle. Also, should a loss of pressure in one system occur, the differential warning switch (located on the combination valve) will turn ON the brake warning light (located on the dash board).

As the fluid enters each brake caliper or wheel cylinder, the pistons are forced outward. The outward movement of the pistons force the brake pads against a round flat disc or brake shoes against a round metal drum. The brake lining attached to the pads or shoes comes in contact with the revolving disc or drum causing friction, which brings the wheel to a stop.

In time, the brake linings wear down. If not replaced, their metal support plates (bonded type) or rivet heads (riveted type) will come in contact with the disc or drum; damage to the disc or drum will occur. Never use brake pads or shoes with a lining thickness less than 1/32" (bonded brakes) or 2/32" (riveted brakes).

Most manufacturers of disc pads provide a wear sensor, a piece of spring steel, attached to the rear edge of the inner brake pad. When the pad wears to the replacement thickness, the sensor will produce a high pitched squeal.

Adjustment

DISC BRAKES

Disc brakes are self-adjusting. No adjustment is possible or necessary. Check fluid level of reservoir, for as brake pads wear, the piston moves out and the piston void must be replaced with brake fluid.

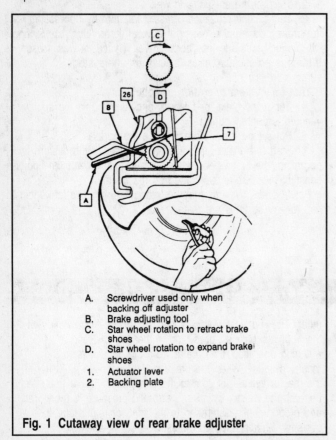

A. Screwdriver used only when backing off adjuster
B. Brake adjusting tool
C. Star wheel rotation to retract brake shoes
D. Star wheel rotation to expand brake shoes
1. Actuator lever
2. Backing plate

Fig. 1 Cutaway view of rear brake adjuster

DRUM BRAKES

▶ **See Figure 1**

The drum brakes are designed to self-adjust when applied with the car moving in reverse. However, they can also be adjusted manually. This manual adjustment should also be performed whenever the linings are replaced.

1. Use a punch to knock out the lanced area in the brake backing plate. If this is done with the drum installed on the car, the drum must then be removed to clean out all metal pieces. After adjustments are complete, obtain a hole cover to prevent entry of dirt and water into the brakes.

2. Use an adjusting tool especially made for the purpose to turn the brake adjusting screw star wheel. Use a small screwdriver to push the adjusting lever away from star wheel when adjusting brakes. Expand the shoes until the drum can just be turned by hand. The drag should be equal at all the wheel.

3. Back off the adjusting screw 12 notches. If the shoes still are dragging lightly, back off the adjusting screw one or two additional notches. If the brakes still drag, the parking brake adjustment is incorrect or the parking brake is applied. Fix and start over.

4. Install the hole cover into the drum.

5. Check the parking brake adjustment.

Brake Light Switch

REMOVAL & INSTALLATION

▶ **See Figure 2**

1. Disconnect the wiring harness from the brake light switch.

2. Remove the switch.

3. To install, depress the braked pedal, insert the switch into the tubular clip until the switch body seats on the clip. Clicks should be heard as the threaded portion of the switch are pushed through the clip toward the brake pedal.

4. Pull the brake pedal fully rearward (towards the driver) against the pedal stop, until the click sounds can no longer be heard. The switch will be moved in the tubular clip providing adjustment.

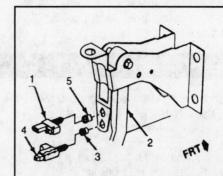

1. Release switch— cruise control
2. Brake pedal
3. Retainer
4. Stoplight switch
5. Retainer—cruise control switch

Fig. 2 Brake light and cruise control switch

5. Release the brake pedal, and then repeat Step 4, to assure that no click sound remains.

6. Connect the wiring harness to the brake light switch.

Master Cylinder

REMOVAL & INSTALLATION

▶ See Figure 3

➡ **Be sure to clean the area where the master cylinder is mounted, before beginning removal.**

1. Disconnect and cap or plug hydraulic lines to prevent fluid contamination or loss.

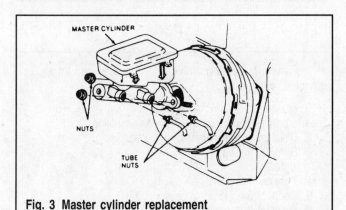

Fig. 3 Master cylinder replacement

2. Remove the attaching nuts.

3. If the combination valve bracket is mounted over the master cylinder on the power brake booster studs, pull the bracket from the studs and reposition it aside.

4. Remove the master cylinder.

To install:

5. Install the master cylinder on the power booster studs.

6. If applicable, install the combination valve bracket on the power booster studs.

7. Install the attaching nuts and tighten to 20 ft. lbs. (27 Nm) for all except 1991 vehicles or tighten to 15 ft. lbs. (21 Nm) for 1991 vehicles only.

8. Unplug hydraulic lines, attach to the master cylinder and tighten to 24 ft. lbs. (32 Nm).

9. Fill with approved brake fluid and bleed system.

OVERHAUL

▶ See Figures 4, 5 and 6

This is a tedious, time-consuming job. You can save yourself a lot of trouble by buying a rebuilt master cylinder from your dealer or parts supply house. The small difference in price between a rebuilding kit and a rebuilt part usually makes it more economical, in terms of time and work, to buy the rebuilt part.

1. Remove the reservoir cover and diaphragm. Discard any brake fluid in the reservoir.

2. Inspect the reservoir cover and diaphragm for cuts, cracks, or deformation. Replace any defective parts.

3. Depress the primary piston and remove the lock ring.

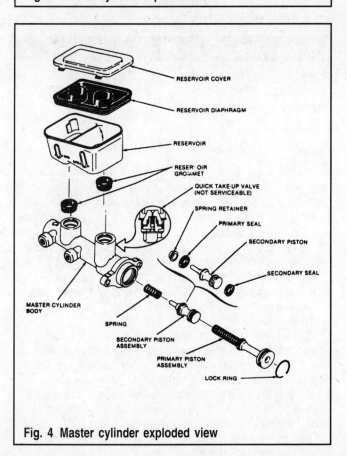

Fig. 4 Master cylinder exploded view

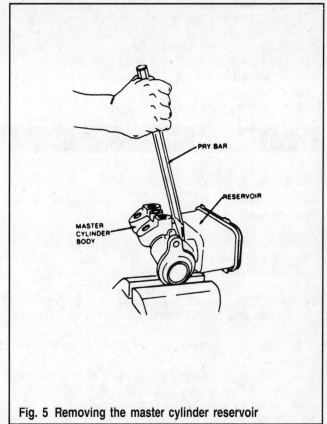

Fig. 5 Removing the master cylinder reservoir

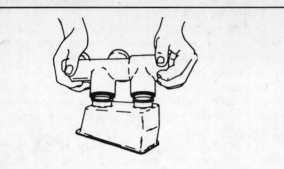

Fig. 6 Install the master cylinder-to reservoir with a rocking motion

4. Direct compressed air into the outlet at the blind end of the bore and plug the other outlet to remove primary and secondary piston.

5. Remove the spring retainer and seals from the secondary piston.

6. Clamp the master cylinder in a vise. Do not clamp it on the master cylinder body. Using a pry bar, remove the reservoir.

7. Do not attempt to remove the quick take-up valve from the body. This valve is not serviced separately.

8. Remove the reservoir grommets.

9. Inspect the master cylinder bore for corrosion. If corroded, replace the master cylinder. Do not use any abrasive on the bore.

10. Reassemble, using new seals and grommets. Lubricate all parts with brake fluid.

11. Install the reservoir grommets.

12. Install the reservoir.

13. Install the spring retainer and seals from the secondary piston.

14. Install primary and secondary piston.

15. Depress the primary piston and install the lock ring.

16. Fill with brake fluid. Install the reservoir cover and diaphragm.

17. Bleed brake system.

Power Brake Booster

REMOVAL & INSTALLATION

▶ **See Figure 7**

1. Disconnect the vacuum hose from the vacuum check valve and plug the hose.

2. Remove the 2 nuts holding the master cylinder, and combination valve bracket if applicable, to the power unit. Carefully position the aside, being careful not to kink any of the hydraulic lines. It is not necessary to disconnect the brake lines.

3. Loosen the 4 nuts that hold the power unit mounted on the firewall.

4. Disconnect the retainer, outer washer, air valve pushrod assembly and inner washer, as applicable, from the brake pedal. Do not force the pushrod to the side when disconnecting.

5. Remove the 4 mounting nuts and remove the power unit.

To install:

6. Place the power unit against the firewall and loosely attach nuts.

7. Connect the inner washer, air valve pushrod assembly, outer washer, and retainer to the brake pedal.

8. Tighten the power unit attaching nuts to 15 ft. lbs. (21 Nm).

9. Install the master cylinder and, if applicable, the combination valve bracket on the power booster mounting studs. Tighten bolts to specification.

10. Unplug and connect the vacuum hose to the vacuum check valve.

Combination Valve

REMOVAL & INSTALLATION

➡**This valve is not repairable and only serviced as a complete assembly.**

1. Disconnect the hydraulic lines from the valve. Plug the lines to prevent fluid loss and dirt contamination.

2. Disconnect the electrical connection.

3. Remove the valve.

To install:

4. Position the valve.

5. Connect the electrical connection.

6. Connect the hydraulic lines to the valve.

7. Bleed the brake system.

Brake Hoses

▶ **See Figures 8, 9 and 10**

REMOVAL & INSTALLATION

Front

1. Clean dirt and foreign material from both the hose and fittings.

2. Disconnect the brake pipe from the hose fitting using a backup wrench on the fitting. Be careful not to bend the frame bracket or the brake pipe.

3. Remove the U-clip from the female fitting at the bracket and remove the hose from the bracket.

4. Remove the bolt from the caliper end of the hose. Remove the hose from the caliper and discard the two copper gaskets on either side of the fitting block.

To install:

5. Use new copper gaskets on both sides of the fitting block. Lubricate the bolt threads with brake fluid. With the fitting flange engaged with the caliper orientation ledge, fasten the hose to the caliper and torque to 32 ft. lbs. (44 Nm).

6. With the weight of the car on the suspension, pass the female fitting through the frame bracket of crossmember. Fitting fits the bracket in only one position. With least amount of twist in the hose, install the fitting in this position. There should be no kinks in the hose.

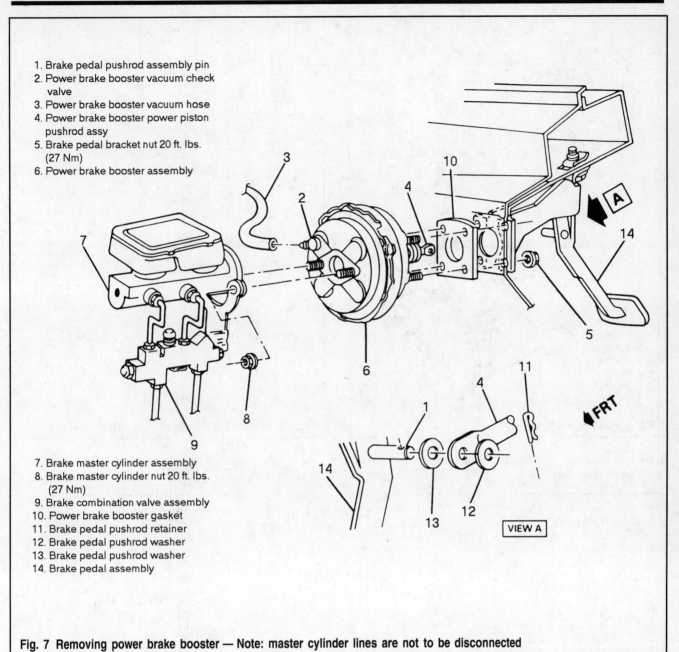

1. Brake pedal pushrod assembly pin
2. Power brake booster vacuum check valve
3. Power brake booster vacuum hose
4. Power brake booster power piston pushrod assy
5. Brake pedal bracket nut 20 ft. lbs. (27 Nm)
6. Power brake booster assembly

7. Brake master cylinder assembly
8. Brake master cylinder nut 20 ft. lbs. (27 Nm)
9. Brake combination valve assembly
10. Power brake booster gasket
11. Brake pedal pushrod retainer
12. Brake pedal pushrod washer
13. Brake pedal pushrod washer
14. Brake pedal assembly

Fig. 7 Removing power brake booster — Note: master cylinder lines are not to be disconnected

7. Install the U-clip to the female fitting at the frame bracket.

8. Attach the brake pipe to the hose fitting using a backup wrench on the fitting. Torque to 17 ft. lbs. (24 Nm).

9. Inspect to see that the hose doesn't make contact with any part of the suspension. Check in the extreme right hand and extreme left hand turn conditions. If the hose makes any contact, remove and correct.

10. Bleed the brake system.

Rear

1. Remove the two brake pipes from the junction block and with the use of a backup wrench, remove the hose at the female fitting. Be careful not to bend the bracket or pipes.

2. Remove the U-clip and take the female fitting out of the bracket.

3. Observe the position at which the junction block is mounted to the axle. When installing the new hose, be sure this junction block is in the same position.

4. Remove the bolt attaching junction block to axle.

To install:

5. Thread both the rear axle pipes into the junction block.

6. Bolt the junction block to the axle to 20 ft. lbs. (27 Nm). Torque the rear pipes to 17 ft. lbs. (24 Nm).

7. Pass the female end of the hose through the frame bracket. The female fitting will fit the bracket in only one position; without twisting the hose, position the female end in the bracket.

8. Install the U-clip.

9. Attach the pipe to the female fitting using a backup wrench on the fitting, torque to 17 ft. lbs. (24 Nm) again be careful not to bend the bracket or pipe. Check to see that the

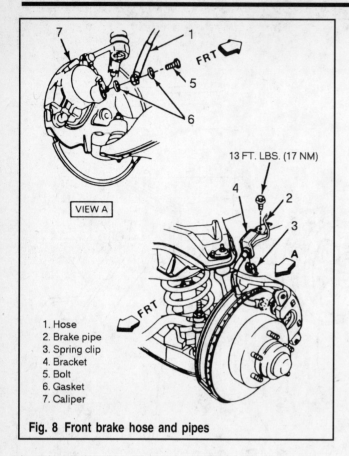

13 FT. LBS. (17 NM)

VIEW A

1. Hose
2. Brake pipe
3. Spring clip
4. Bracket
5. Bolt
6. Gasket
7. Caliper

Fig. 8 Front brake hose and pipes

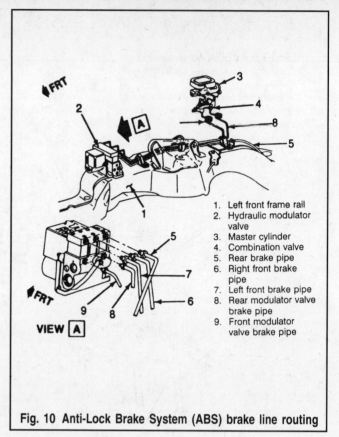

1. Left front frame rail
2. Hydraulic modulator valve
3. Master cylinder
4. Combination valve
5. Rear brake pipe
6. Right front brake pipe
7. Left front brake pipe
8. Rear modulator valve brake pipe
9. Front modulator valve brake pipe

VIEW A

Fig. 10 Anti-Lock Brake System (ABS) brake line routing

hose installation did not loosen the frame bracket. Re-torque the bracket, if necessary.

10. Fill and maintain the brake fluid level in the reservoirs. Bleed the system.

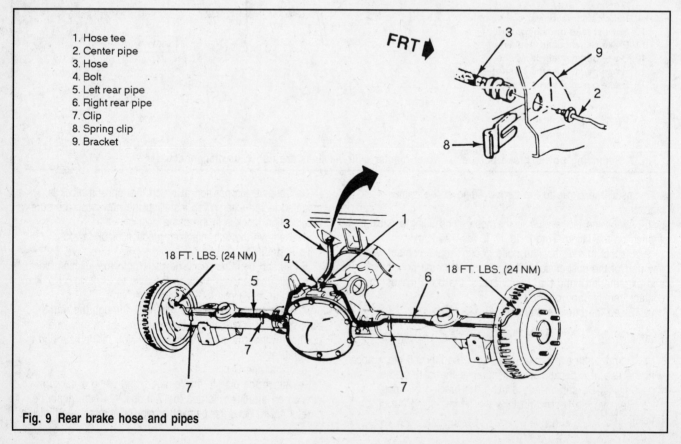

1. Hose tee
2. Center pipe
3. Hose
4. Bolt
5. Left rear pipe
6. Right rear pipe
7. Clip
8. Spring clip
9. Bracket

FRT

18 FT. LBS. (24 NM)

18 FT. LBS. (24 NM)

Fig. 9 Rear brake hose and pipes

Steel Pipes

▶ **See Figures 11 and 12**

When replacing the steel brake pipes, always use steel piping which is designed to withstand high pressure, resist corrosion and is of the same size.

✳✳CAUTION

Never use copper tubing, for it is subject to fatigue, cracking, and/or corrosion, which will result in brake line failure.

➡**The following procedure requires the use of the GM Tube Cutter tool NO. J-23533 or equivalent, and the GM Flaring tool No. J-29803, J-23530 or equivalent.**

1. Disconnect the steel brake pipe(s) from the flexible hose connections or the rear wheel cylinders, be sure to removal any retaining clips.
2. Remove the steel brake pipe from the vehicle.
3. Repair or replace the pipe as follows:
   a. Using new steel pipe (same size) and the GM Tube Cutter tool No. J-23533 or equivalent, cut the pipe to length; be sure to add 1/8 in. (3mm) for each flare.

➡**Be sure to install the correct pipe fittings onto the tube before forming any flares.**

   b. Using the Flaring tool NO. J-23530, J-29803 or equivalent, follow the instructions equipped with the tool to form double flares on the end of the pipes.

c. Using the small pipe bending tool, bend the pipe to match the contour of the pipe which was removed.
d. To install, reverse the removal procedures. Bleed the hydraulic system.

Bleeding

▶ **See Figures 13 and 14**

The purpose of bleeding the brakes is to expel air trapped in the hydraulic system. The system must be bled whenever the pedal feels spongy, indicating that compressible air has entered the system. It must also be bled whenever the system has been opened, repaired or the fluid appears dirty. You will need a helper for this job.

✳✳CAUTION

Never reuse brake fluid which has been bled from the brake system.

1. The sequence for bleeding is right rear, left rear, right front and left front. If the car has power brakes, remove the vacuum by applying the brakes several times. Do not run the engine while bleeding the brakes.
2. Clean all the bleeder screws. You may want to give each one a shot of penetrating solvent to loosen it; seizure is a common problem with bleeder screws, which then break off, sometimes requiring replacement of the part to which they are attached.

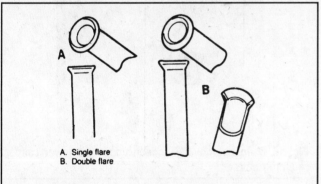

A. Single flare
B. Double flare

Fig. 11 Single flare (A) and Double flare (B) ends

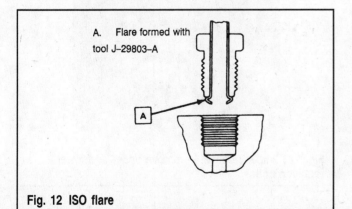

A. Flare formed with tool J–29803–A

Fig. 12 ISO flare

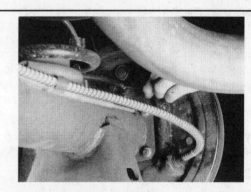

Fig. 13 Bleeding the rear brakes

Fig. 14 Bleeding the front brakes

3. Fill the master cylinder with good quality brake fluid.

➡Brake fluid absorbs moisture from the air. Don't leave the master cylinder or the fluid container uncovered any longer than necessary. Be careful handling the fluid; it eats paint. Check the level of the fluid often when bleeding and refill the reservoirs as necessary. Don't let them run dry or you will have to repeat the process.

4. Attach a length of clear vinyl tubing to the bleeder screw on the wheel cylinder. Insert the other end of the tube into a clear, clean jar half filled with brake fluid.

5. Have your assistant slowly depress the brake pedal. As this is done, open the bleeder screw ¾ of a turn and allow the fluid to run through the tube. Then close the bleeder screw before the pedal reaches the end of its travel. Have your assistant slowly release the pedal. Repeat this process until no air bubbles appear in the expelled fluid.

6. Repeat the procedure on the other three brakes, checking the level of fluid in the master cylinder reservoir often.

7. Upon completion, check the brake pedal for sponginess and the brake warning light for unbalanced pressure. If necessary, repeat the entire bleeding procedure.

FRONT DISC BRAKES

✳✳CAUTION

Brake pads contain asbestos, which has been determined to be a cancer causing agent. Never clean the brake surfaces with compressed air! Avoid inhaling any dust from any brake surface! When cleaning brake surfaces, use a commercially available brake cleaning fluid.

Brake Pads

INSPECTION

The pad thickness should be inspected every time that the tires are removed for rotation. The outer pad can be checked by looking in each end, which is the point at which the highest rate of wear occurs. The inner pad can be checked by looking down through the inspection hole in the top of the caliper. If the thickness of the pad is worn to within 0.030 inch (0.76mm) of the rivet at either end of the pad, all the pads should be replaced.

➡Always replace all pads on both front wheels at the same time. Failure to do so will result in uneven braking action and premature wear.

REMOVAL & INSTALLATION

▶ See Figures 15, 16, 17, 18, 19, 20, 21, 22 and 23

1. Siphon ⅔ of the brake fluid from the master cylinder reservoir. Loosen the wheel lug nuts and raise the car. Remove the wheel.

2. Position a C-clamp across the caliper and press on the pads. Tighten it until the caliper piston bottoms in its bore.

➡If you haven't removed some brake fluid from the master cylinder, it may overflow when the piston is retracted.

Fig. 16 Caliper removal — loosen upper and lower caliper retaining bolts

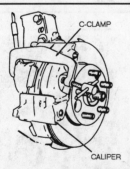

Fig. 15 Install a C-clamp and compress the piston into the caliper before removing the assembly

Fig. 17 Caliper removal — remove upper and lower retaining bolts

3. Remove the C-clamp.

➡The single piston design caliper uses either an Allen® head bolt or Torx® head bolt to secure the caliper to the mounting bracket. Do not use an Allen® socket in place of the Torx® socket, otherwise damage to the bolt may occur.

4. Remove the mounting bolts. Inspect the bolts for corrosion and replace as necessary.

5. Remove the caliper from the steering knuckle and suspend it from the body of the car with a length of wire. Do not allow the caliper to hang by its hose.

6. Remove the pad retaining springs and remove the pads from the caliper.

7. Remove the caliper bolt sleeves and the rubber bushings from the mounting bolt holes.

Fig. 18 Caliper removal — lift caliper assembly from mounting bracket

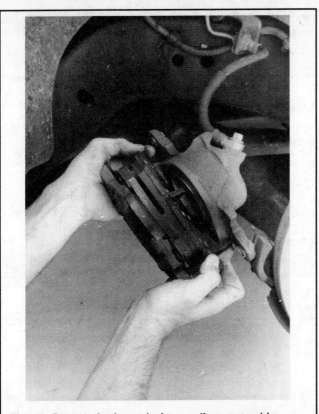

Fig. 19 Remove brake pads from caliper assembly

Fig. 20 Support caliper assembly out of the way using wire.

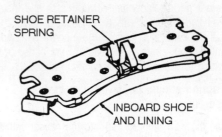

Fig. 22 Install the retaining spring on the inboard (piston side) pad

Fig. 21 Disc brake pads and caliper assembly retaining bolts

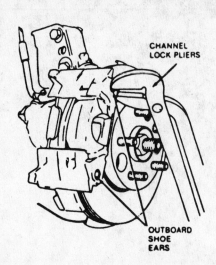

CHANNEL
LOCK PLIERS

OUTBOARD
SHOE
EARS

Fig. 23 Bend the outboard pad ears to ensure the pad does not vibrate in caliper mounting, causing noise during braking

To install:

8. Obtain a pad replacement kit. Lubricate and install the new sleeves and bushings with a light coat of silicone grease.

9. Install the retainer spring on the inboard pad. Apply a suitable anti-squeak paste to the back of the pads. Do not apply anything to the pad-to-rotor contact surface.

➡**A new spring should be included in the pad replacement kit.**

10. Install the new inboard pad into the caliper with the wear sensor at the leading of the shoe during forward wheel rotation.

11. Install the outboard pad into the caliper.

12. Use a large pair of slip joint pliers to bend the outer pad ears down over the caliper. The outer pad should not be loose when properly attached to the caliper.

13. Install the caliper onto the steering knuckle. Tighten the mounting bolts to 38 ft. lbs. (51 Nm). Install the wheel and lower the car. Fill the master cylinder to its proper level with a good quality brake fluid.

14. Pump the brake pedal slowly and firmly with the engine running before attempting to move the vehicle; bleed the brakes as required.

Brake Caliper

REMOVAL & INSTALLATION

◆ See Figure 24

> **✳✳CAUTION**
>
> Brake pads contain asbestos, which has been determined to be a cancer causing agent. Never clean the brake surfaces with compressed air! Avoid inhaling any dust from any brake surface! When cleaning brake surfaces, use a commercially available brake cleaning fluid.

1. Remove ⅔ of the brake fluid from the master cylinder. Raise the vehicle and remove the wheel.

2. Place a C-clamp across the caliper, positioned on the brake pads. Tighten it until the piston is forced into its bore.

3. Remove the C-clamp. Remove the bolt holding the brake hose to the caliper.

4. Remove the caliper mounting bolts. Inspect them for corrosion and replace them if necessary. Remove the caliper.

To install:

5. Position the caliper with the brake pad installed and install caliper mounting bolts. Mounting bolt torque is 38 ft. lbs. (51 Nm.) for the caliper.

6. Install the bolt holding the brake hose to the caliper and tighten to 18-30 ft. lbs. (24-40 Nm.).

7. Fill the master cylinder with brake fluid.

8. Install the wheels and lower the vehicle.

> **✳✳CAUTION**
>
> Before moving the vehicle, pump the brakes several times to seat the brake pad against the rotor.

OVERHAUL

◆ See Figures 25, 26 and 27

1. Remove the caliper.

2. Remove the pads.

3. Place some cloths or a slat of wood in front of the piston. Remove the piston by applying compressed air to the fluid inlet fitting. Use just enough air pressure to east the piston from the bore.

> **✳✳CAUTION**
>
> Do not try to catch the piston with your fingers, it can result in serious injury.

4. Remove the piston boot with a screwdriver, working carefully so that the piston bore is not scratched.

5. Remove the bleeder screw.

6. Inspect the piston for scoring, nicks, corrosion, wear, etc., and damaged or worn chrome plating. Replace the piston if any defects are found.

7. Remove the piston seal from the caliper bore groove using a piece of pointed wood or plastic. Do not use a

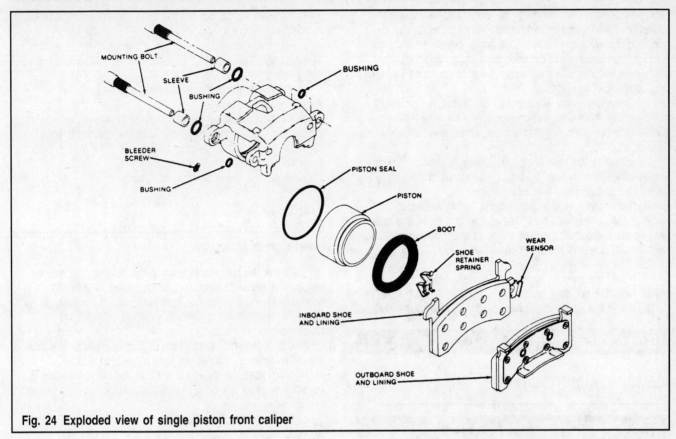

Fig. 24 Exploded view of single piston front caliper

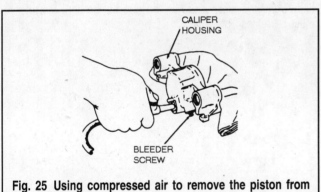

Fig. 25 Using compressed air to remove the piston from the caliper bore

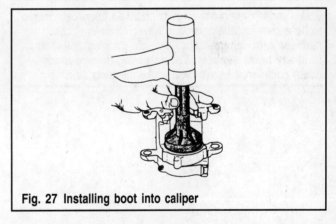

Fig. 27 Installing boot into caliper

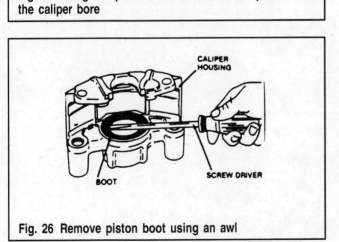

Fig. 26 Remove piston boot using an awl

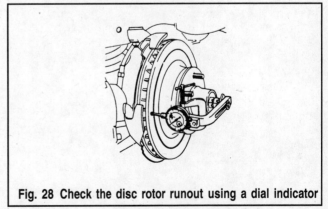

Fig. 28 Check the disc rotor runout using a dial indicator

screwdriver, which will damage the bore. Inspect the caliper bore for nicks, corrosion, and wear. Very light wear can be cleaned up with crocus cloth. Use finger pressure to rub the crocus cloth around the circumference of the bore — do not slide it in and out. More extensive wear or corrosion warrants replacement of the part.

8. Clean any parts which are to be reused in denatured alcohol. Dry them with compressed air or allow to air dry. Don't wipe the parts dry with a cloth, which will leave behind bits of lint.

9. Lubricate the new seal, provided in the repair kit, with clean brake fluid. Install the seal in its groove, making sure it is fully seated and not twisted.

10. Install the new dust boot on the piston. Lubricate the bore of the caliper with clean brake fluid and insert the piston into its bore. Position the boot in the caliper housing and seat with a seal driver of the appropriate size, or G.M. tool no. J-26267.

11. Install the bleeder screw, tightening to 80-140 inch lbs. (9-16 Nm). Do not over tighten.

12. Install the pads, install the caliper, and bleed the brakes.

Brake Disc (Rotor)

REMOVAL & INSTALLATION

✳✳CAUTION

Brake pads contain asbestos, which has been determined to be a cancer causing agent. Never clean the brake surfaces with compressed air! Avoid inhaling any dust from any brake surface! When cleaning brake surfaces, use a commercially available brake cleaning fluid.

1. Remove the caliper by following instructions of caliper removal procedure.

2. Remove dust cap, cotter pin, castle nut, thrust washer and outside wheel bearing. Pull the disc/hub assembly from the steering knuckle.

3. To install, position the disc/hub assembly to the spindle/steering knuckle.

4. Install the outside wheel bearing, thrust washer and castle nut. Tighten the castle nut until the bearing is snug. Back off the nut ¼ turn. Refer to Chapter 8 for Wheel Bearing Removal and Installation, and Adjustment.

5. Install the cotter pin and dust cap.

INSPECTION

▶ **See Figures 28 and 29**

1. Check the rotor surface for wear, scoring, grooves or rust pitting. Rotor damage can be corrected by refacing, consult your local garage or machine shop. If the damage exceeds the minimum thickness, which is stamped on the rotor, replace the rotor.

2. Check the rotor parallelism at four or more points around the circumference, it must not vary more than 0.0005" (0.013mm). Make all measurements at the same distance in from the edge of the rotor. Refinish the rotor if it fails to meet specification.

3. Measure the disc runout with a dial indicator. If runout exceeds 0.004 inch (0.10mm), and the wheel bearings are okay (runout is measured with the disc on the car), the rotor must be refaced or replaced.

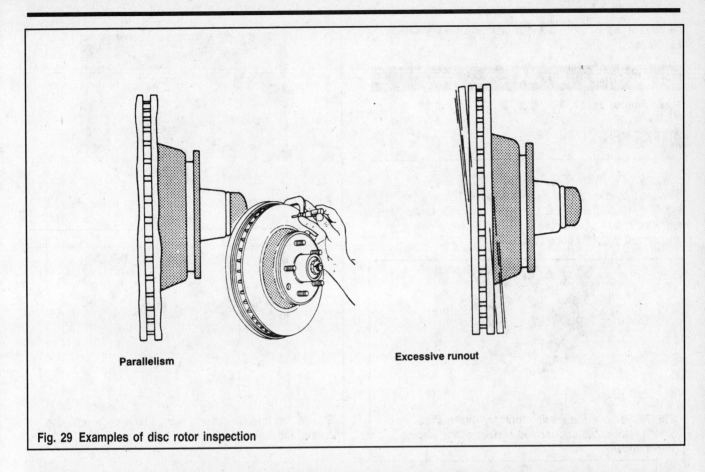

Parallelism   Excessive runout

Fig. 29 Examples of disc rotor inspection

REAR DRUM BRAKES

Brake Drums

REMOVAL & INSTALLATION

▶ See Figure 30

✳✳CAUTION

Brake shoes contain asbestos, which has been determined to be a cancer causing agent. Never clean the brake surfaces with compressed air! Avoid inhaling any dust from any brake surface! When cleaning brake surfaces, use a commercially available brake cleaning fluid.

1. Raise and support the car.
2. Remove the wheel or wheels.
3. Pull the brake drum off. Gently tap the rear edges of the drum to start it off the studs.

➡**It may be necessary to remove a retainer clip installed from the factory if this is the first time the drum has been removed.**

4. If extreme resistance to removal is encountered, it will be necessary to retract the adjusting screw. Knock out the access hole in the backing plate and turn the adjuster to retract the linings away from the drum.

Fig. 30 Drums which have never been removed come secured to the axle with retainer clips

5. Install a replacement hole cover before reinstalling drum.
6. Install the drums in the same position on the hub as removed.

DRUM INSPECTION

Check the drums for any cracks, scores, grooves, or an out-of-round condition. Replace if cracked. Slight scores can be removed with fine emery cloth while extensive scoring requires turning the drum on a lathe. Never have a drum turned more than 0.060 inch. The outside ring of the drum is generally stamped with the minimum and/or maximum inside diameter specification.

Brake Shoes

▶ See Figures 31, 32, 33, 34, 35, 36, 37, 38 and 39

ADJUSTMENT

Rotate the star wheel adjuster until a slight drag is felt between the shoes and drum, then back off 12 clicks on the adjusting wheel. Put the car in reverse and, while backing up, apply the brakes several times. This will allow the self-adjusters to complete the adjustment.

Fig. 33 Remove the trailing (secondary) brake shoe spring

Fig. 32 Remove the leading (primary) brake shoe spring — note the shorter pad surface of the leading brake shoe

Fig. 34 Remove the trailing (secondary) shoe retaining spring and adjusting lever

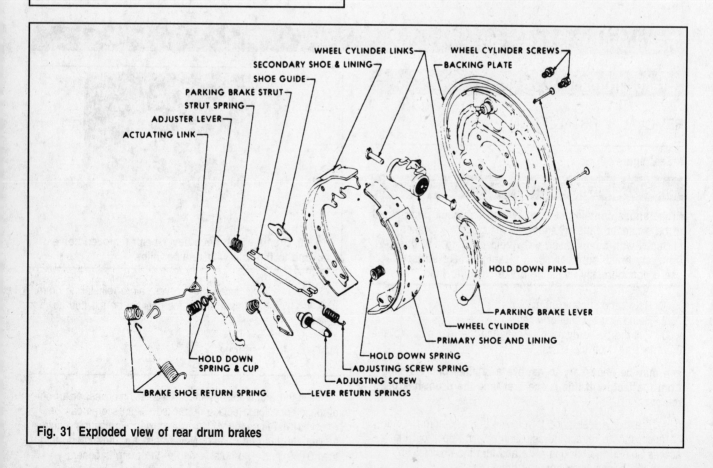

Fig. 31 Exploded view of rear drum brakes

Fig. 35 Remove the leading (primary) shoe retaining spring. Note the difference between the trailing brake shoe and retaining spring used with the self adjuster (left) and the leading brake shoe and retaining spring (right)

Fig. 36 Remove the parking brake strut and the brake shoe guide, then spread the shoes slightly apart and lift them over the axle flange

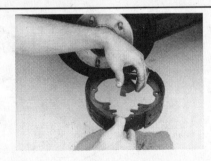

Fig. 37 Flip the shoes over and remove the emergency brake lever. Note: there is no need to disconnect the brake cable from the emergency brake lever.

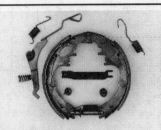

Fig. 38 Exploded view of the passenger side brake shoe assembly — the drivers side will be slightly opposite. Note the proper self adjuster and spring installation — Clean and lubricate the adjuster prior to installation

Fig. 39 Adjust the rear brakes prior to installing the drum. The drum should fit over the brake with a slight drag.

REMOVAL & INSTALLATION

✳✳CAUTION

Brake shoes contain asbestos, which has been determined to be a cancer causing agent. Never clean the brake surfaces with compressed air! Avoid inhaling any dust from any brake surface! When cleaning brake surfaces, use a commercially available brake cleaning fluid.

1. Raise and safely support the vehicle.
2. Remove the wheel and tire assemblies.
3. Remove the brake drum.
4. Remove the return springs.

5. Remove the hold-down springs and pins. Remove the lever pivot.

6. Remove the actuator link while lifting up on the actuator lever.

7. Remove the actuator lever and lever return spring.

8. Remove the shoe guide, parking brake strut and strut spring.

9. Remove the brake shoes and disconnect the parking brake lever from the shoe.

10. Remove the adjusting screw assembly and spring. Remove the retaining ring, pin from the secondary shoe.

To install:

➡**Any part or spring which may appear worn should be replace. The short shoe (primary) should be installed to the front of the vehicle and the long shoe (secondary) should be installed to the rear. After complete installation of the brake shoes a clicking sound should be heard when turning the adjusting screw or self-adjuster. Do not switch parts from the left or right brake assembly, the adjusters are designated Left and Right.**

11. Clean dirt from all parts and wire brush raised pads on backing plate. Lubricate backing plate pads and adjusting screw with brake grease.

12. Install the parking brake lever on the secondary shoe.

13. Install the adjusting screw and spring. Lubricate the adjusting screw with brake (white) grease. Ensure the spring does not come into contact with the adjuster.

14. Clean and lubricate the contact points of the backing plate. Install the brake shoe assemblies after installing the parking brake lever on the shoe.

15. Install the parking brake strut and strut spring by spreading the shoes apart.

16. Install the shoe guide, actuator lever and lever return spring.

17. Install the hold-down pins, lever pivot and springs. Install the actuator link on the anchor pin.

18. Install the actuator link into the actuator lever while holding up on the lever.

19. Install the shoe return springs. Install the brake drum. Install the wheel and tire assemblies.

20. Adjust the brake and lower the vehicle. Check emergency brake for proper adjustment.

Wheel Cylinders

▶ See Figures 40 and 41

REMOVAL & INSTALLATION

❊❊CAUTION

Brake shoes contain asbestos, which has been determined to be a cancer causing agent. Never clean the brake surfaces with compressed air! Avoid inhaling any dust from any brake surface! When cleaning brake surfaces, use a commercially available brake cleaning fluid.

1. Raise and support the car. Remove the wheel. Remove the brake shoes by following the Brake Shoe Replacement procedure.

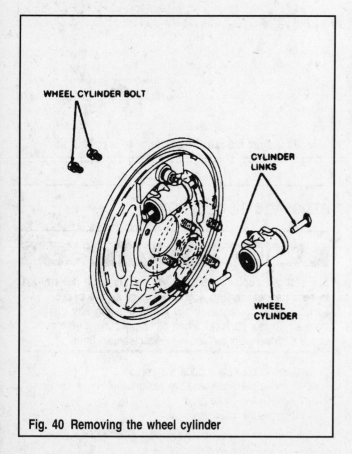

Fig. 40 Removing the wheel cylinder

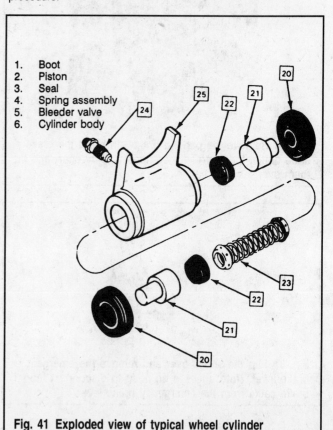

1. Boot
2. Piston
3. Seal
4. Spring assembly
5. Bleeder valve
6. Cylinder body

Fig. 41 Exploded view of typical wheel cylinder

2. Remove dirt from around the wheel cylinder inlet and pilot. Disconnect the inlet tube.

3. Remove the wheel cylinder retaining bolts. Remove the wheel cylinder.

4. To install, place wheel cylinder into position and install the retaining bolts. Torque the retaining bolts to 13 ft. lbs. (18 Nm).

5. Connect the inlet tube and torque 18 ft. lbs. (24 Nm). Complete installation by reversing the removal procedure. Bleed the brakes.

OVERHAUL

Overhaul kits for wheel cylinders are readily available. When rebuilding and installing wheel cylinders, avoid getting any contaminants into the system. Always install clean, new high quality brake fluid. If dirty or improper fluid has been used, it will be necessary to drain the entire system, flush the system with proper brake fluid, replace all rubber components, refill, and bleed the system.

1. Remove the wheel cylinder by referring to the Wheel Cylinder Removal procedure.

PARKING BRAKE

▶ **See Figure 42**

Cables

REMOVAL & INSTALLATION

Front

1. Raise the vehicle and support it safely.
2. Loosen equalizer enough to gain necessary cable slack.
3. Disconnect the front cable at the connector.
4. Disconnect the cable casing at frame by compressing retainer fingers and pulling outward.
5. Lower the vehicle.
6. Remove driver's side wheelhouse panel screws and panel bolts. Pull panel out to gain access to the front cable.
7. Disconnect the front cable and casing at the lever assembly, by compressing retainer fingers and pulling outward.
8. Remove the front cable and grommet from the vehicle.
To install:
9. Position front cable and grommet in vehicle.
10. Connect the front cable and casing at the lever assembly.
11. Install the wheelhouse panel bolts, tighten to 18 ft. lbs. (25 Nm), and screws, tighten to 89 inch lbs. (10 Nm).
12. Raise and safely support the vehicle.
13. Connect the cable casing at the frame and connect the cable to the connector.
14. Adjust the parking brake and lower the vehicle.

Rear

1. Raise the vehicle and support it safely.

2. Remove the rubber boots from the cylinder ends with pliers. Discard the boots. Remove and discard the pistons and cups.

3. Wash the cylinder and metal parts in denatured alcohol or clean brake fluid.

✳✳CAUTION

Never use a mineral based solvent such as gasoline, kerosene, or paint thinner for cleaning purposes. These solvents will swell rubber components and quickly deteriorate them.

4. Allow the parts to air dry or use compressed air. Do not use rags for cleaning since lint will remain in the cylinder bore.

5. Inspect the piston and replace it if it shows scratches.

6. Lubricate the cylinder bore and counterbore with clean brake fluid.

7. Install the seals (flat side out) and then the pistons (flat side in).

8. Insert new boots into the counterbores by hand. Do not lubricate the boots.

9. To install the wheel cylinder refer to the Wheel Cylinder Installation procedure.

2. Loosen the equalizer enough to gain cable slack, as necessary.

3. On the left side disconnect the cable from the connector and the equalizer. On the right side, disconnect the cable from the equalizer. Disconnect the cable and casing at the frame by compressing the retainer fingers and pulling outward. Disconnect the cable and casing from the axle housing clips.

4. Mark the relationship of the wheel to the axle flange and remove the tire and wheel assembly.

5. Remove the brake drum, the primary shoe return spring, secondary shoe hold-down spring and the parking brake strut, as necessary.

6. Compress the retainer fingers and loosen the cable and casing from the backing plate. Disconnect the cable from the parking brake lever and remove the cable.
To install:
7. Connect the cable and casing into the brake backing plate and attach to the parking brake lever.

8. Install the primary brake shoe return spring, secondary shoe hold down spring, parking brake strut and rotor.

9. Align the wheel and axle flange marks. Install the tire and wheel assembly.

10. On the left side connect the cable to the connector and the equalizer. On the right side, connect the cable and casing to the frame and to the axle housing clips. Then connect the cable to the equalizer.

11. Adjust the parking brake and lower the vehicle.

ADJUSTMENT

➡Before attempting to adjust the parking brake, verify the rear brakes are correctly adjusted. If rear brakes are adjusted properly, the parking brake original adjustment should not have to be changed.

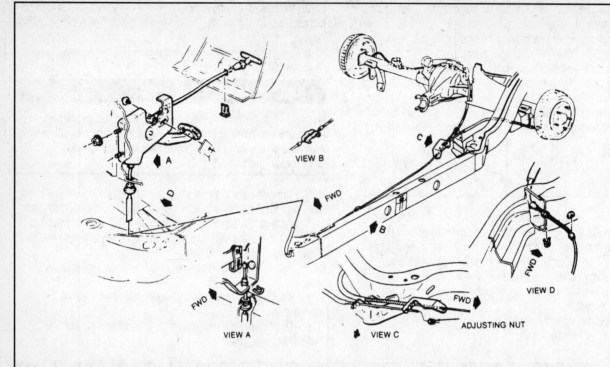

Fig. 42 Parking brake cables and lever assembly

1. Clean and lubricate the exposed threads of the adjuster rod, to either side of the nut.
2. Apply the parking brake 3 clicks for 1990 vehicles or 6 clicks for 1991-93 vehicles, then raise and support the vehicle safely.
3. Tighten the adjusting nut until the rear wheels can barely be turned backward, using 2 hands, but lock up when moved forward.
4. With the parking brake disengaged the rear wheel should turn freely in either direction with no brake drag.
5. Lower the vehicle.

Brake Lever

REMOVAL & INSTALLATION

1. Raise and safely support the vehicle.
2. Loosen the parking brake cable adjuster to relieve cable tension.
3. Lower the vehicle and remove the parking brake release handle from the lever assembly.

4. Remove the 2 nuts and 1 bolts securing the brake lever assembly to the vehicle.
5. Disconnect the parking brake warning light switch.
6. Remove the front parking brake cable from the brake lever assembly.
7. Remove the brake lever assembly from the vehicle.
To install:
8. Install the brake lever assembly into the vehicle. Install the 2 nuts and 1 bolts securing the brake lever assembly to the vehicle. Torque the bolt to 115 inch lbs. (13 Nm) and the 2 nuts to 13 ft. lbs. (17 Nm).
9. Install the front parking brake cable onto the brake lever assembly.
10. Connect the parking brake warning light switch wire connector.
11. Install the parking brake release handle onto the lever assembly.
12. Raise and safely support the vehicle.
13. Adjust the parking brake cable.
14. Lower the vehicle and check for proper parking brake operation.

ANTI-LOCK BAKE SYSTEM

Description and Operation

The purpose of the Anti-Lock Brake System (ABS) is to minimize wheel lockup during heavy braking on most road surfaces. The ABS performs this function by monitoring the speed of each wheel and controlling the brake fluid pressure to each front wheel and both rear wheels during a braking maneuver. This allows you (as the driver) to retain directional stability and steering capability.

ABS continuously monitors all of its components and uses several methods of determining a fault and notifying the driver of a system malfunction. When the vehicle is started, a functional check of the ABS electrical circuitry is performed. As the vehicle speed reaches 4 mph, a functional check of the hydraulic modulator takes place. During this check each valve is cycled and the pump motor is turned on briefly. You may hear or feel this check take place when the vehicle begins to move. This test will only occur with each ignition startup and is considered normal operation. If a malfunction should occur the Brake warning lamp or the Anti-Lock warning lamp will either stay on or begin to blink.

➡Only a qualified technician should perform diagnostics and repairs, due to the complexity of this system. However some system components will have to be removed in order to obtain access to other parts.

PRECAUTIONS

Failure to observe the following precautions may result in system damage.
• Before performing electric arc welding on the vehicle, disconnect the Electronic Brake Control Module (EBCM) and the hydraulic modulator connectors.
• When performing painting work on the vehicle, do not expose the Electronic Brake Control Module (EBCM) to temperatures in excess of 185°F (85°C) for longer than 2 hours. The system may be exposed to temperatures up to 200°F (95°C) for less than 15 minutes.
• Never disconnect or connect the Electronic Brake Control Module (EBCM) or hydraulic modulator connectors with the ignition switch ON.
• Never disassemble any component of the Anti-Lock Brake System (ABS) which is designated non-serviceable (for example: the modulator); the component must be replaced as an assembly.
• When filling the master cylinder, always use Delco Supreme 11 brake fluid or equivalent, which meets DOT-3 specifications; petroleum base fluid will destroy the rubber parts.

Modulator Valve

REMOVAL & INSTALLATION

▶ **See Figures 43, 44 and 45**

✳✳CAUTION

The modulator is not repairable and no screws on the modulator may be loosened. If the screws are loosened, it will not be possible to get the brake circuits leak-proof and personal injury may result.

1. Disconnect the negative battery cable.
2. Remove the air intake duct and resonator and move the upper coolant hose aside.
3. Disconnect the canister purge line at the canister and move aside.
4. Remove the retaining screw and remove the modulator valve cover.
5. Unlock the tab and disconnect the modulator valve electrical connector.
6. Remove the nut and disconnect the ground wire from the modulator.
7. Note the hydraulic brake pipe locations then disconnect and plug the lines from the modulator to prevent fluid contamination or loss.
8. Remove the 3 nuts retaining the modulator to the bracket.

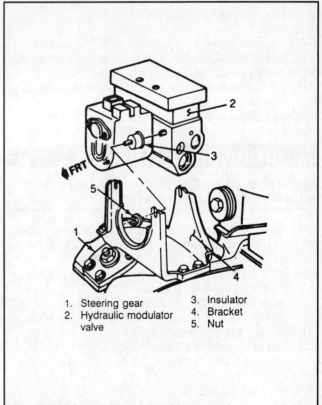

1. Steering gear
2. Hydraulic modulator valve
3. Insulator
4. Bracket
5. Nut

Fig. 44 ABS modulator assembly removal

Fig. 43 ABS modulator assembly located in the engine compartment near the alternator

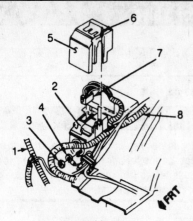

1. Forward lamp harness
2. Hydraulic modulator valve
3. Nut
4. Ground wire
5. Modulator valve cover
6. Screw
7. Modulator valve electrical connector
8. ABS wiring harness

Fig. 45 ABS modulator cover removed to access the solenoid and motor relays and electrical connector

9. Remove bracket taking care to protect the vehicle from any brake fluid spillage. If replacing the modulator assembly, remove the insulators from the modulator valve.

To install:

10. If applicable, install the insulators to the modulator valve.
11. Install the modulator valve to the bracket and tighten the 3 nuts to 89 inch lbs. (10 Nm).
12. If a new modulator is being used, remove shipping plugs from the valve openings.
13. Connect the hydraulic brake pipes to their original locations in the modulator and tighten to 11 ft. lbs. (15 Nm).

✳✳CAUTION

If brake pipes are switched (inlet vs. outlet) wheel lockup will occur and personal injury may result.

14. Install the ground wire and nut to the modulator, tighten nut to 25 inch lbs. (2.8 Nm).
15. Install the modulator valve electrical connector.
16. Install the modulator valve cover with the retaining screw and tighten to 13 inch lbs. (1.5 Nm).
17. Connect the canister purge line to the canister.
18. Install the air intake duct and resonator and move the upper coolant hose into position.
19. Connect the negative battery cable.
20. Use only DOT 3 hydraulic brake fluid, fill and bleed the brake system.
21. Road test the vehicle.

Electronic Brake Control Module (EBCM)

REMOVAL & INSTALLATION

▶ **See Figures 46 and 47**

For 1991 vehicles, the EBCM is located between the deck lid hinge pillar and the wheelhouse panel. For 1992-93 vehicles, it has been relocated under the left side instrument panel, above the brake pedal, on the DERM bracket.

To remove the EBCM simply verify the ignition switch is OFF and the negative battery cable is disconnected, remove the securing screws and disconnect the wire connector.

Front Wheel Speed Sensor

REMOVAL & INSTALLATION

▶ **See Figures 48, 49 and 50**

1. Disconnect the negative battery cable.
2. For the right side speed sensor, unclip the connectors from the clip and separate.
3. Raise and support the vehicle safely.
4. For the left side speed sensor, with the vehicle safely supported, unclip the connectors from the clip and separate.
5. Remove the sensor wiring harness mounting bolt and bracket from the frame rail.
6. Remove the sensor retaining bolt and remove the sensor from the knuckle assembly.

To install:

7. Coat the steering knuckle with anti corrosion compound 1052856 or equivalent, at the knuckle contact point.
8. Install the wheel speed senor to the steering knuckle and tighten the sensor retaining bolt to 71 inch lbs. (8 Nm).

➡**Proper installation of the wheel speed sensor cables is critical to proper operation of the ABS system. Make sure the cables are installed in the retainers. Failure to do this may result in contact with moving parts and the over extension of the cables, resulting in an open circuit.**

9. Connect the sensor wiring harness mounting bolt and bracket to the frame rail and tighten to 89 inch lbs. (10 Nm).
10. For the left side speed sensor, with the vehicle safely supported, attach the connectors and position them in the clip.
11. Lower the vehicle.
12. For the right side speed sensor, attach the connectors and position them in the clip.
13. Connect the negative battery cable and road test vehicle.

➡**The wheel speed sensor wires are labeled with either a white tag or white letter designating L (left) and R (right). It is of great importance that the speed sensors be installed in their proper sides.**

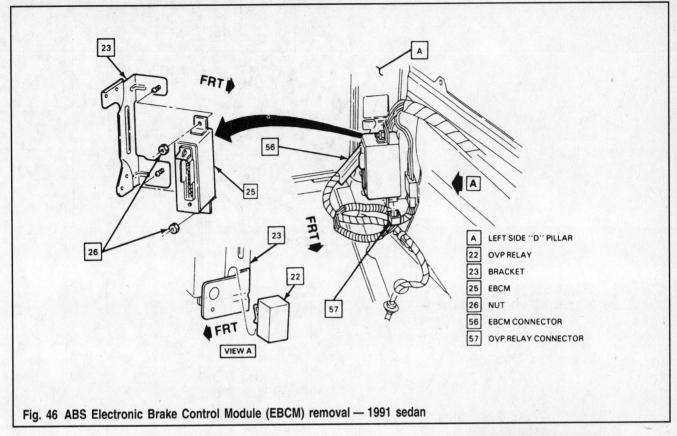

Fig. 46 ABS Electronic Brake Control Module (EBCM) removal — 1991 sedan

A	LEFT SIDE "D" PILLAR
22	OVP RELAY
23	BRACKET
25	EBCM
26	NUT
56	EBCM CONNECTOR
57	OVP RELAY CONNECTOR

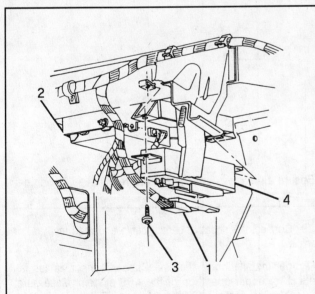

1. Electronic brake control module connector
2. Electronic brake control module bracket
3. Electronic brake control module bracket bolt/screw 53 in. lbs. (6 Nm)
4. Electronic brake control module assembly

Fig. 47 ABS Electronic Brake Control Module (EBCM) removal — 1992-93

Fig. 48 ABS front wheel speed sensor located on back of disc brake rotor shield

Rear Axle Speed Sensor

REMOVAL & INSTALLATION

▶ See Figure 51

1. Disconnect the negative battery cable. Raise and support the vehicle safely.
2. Disconnect the rear sensor assembly from the differential sensor connector.
3. Remove the sensor wiring harness from the retainer brackets.
4. Remove the sensor retaining bolt and remove the speed sensor from the rear axle housing.

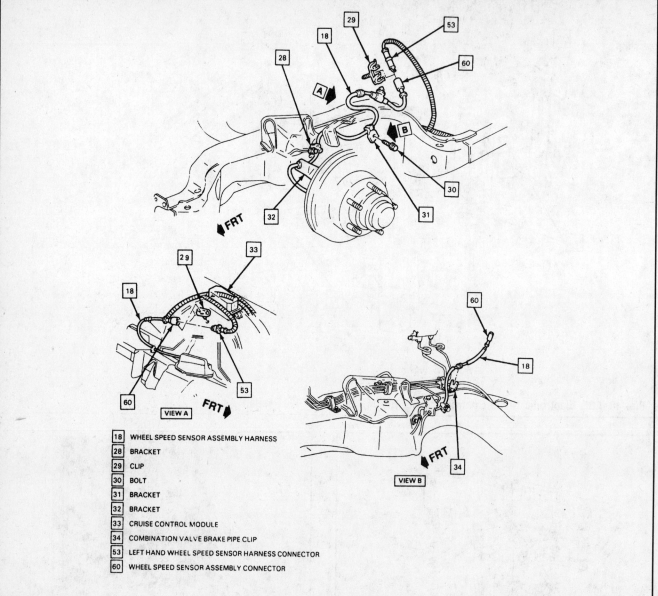

18	WHEEL SPEED SENSOR ASSEMBLY HARNESS
28	BRACKET
29	CLIP
30	BOLT
31	BRACKET
32	BRACKET
33	CRUISE CONTROL MODULE
34	COMBINATION VALVE BRAKE PIPE CLIP
53	LEFT HAND WHEEL SPEED SENSOR HARNESS CONNECTOR
60	WHEEL SPEED SENSOR ASSEMBLY CONNECTOR

Fig. 49 ABS left front wheel speed sensor wire harness routing. Ensure all harness connectors are re-installed in original location during speed sensor replacement

To install:

5. Install the sensor into the rear axle housing. The sensor is a tight fit but it must be pushed in by hand. Do not hammer the sensor into position.

6. Tighten the sensor retaining bolt to 71 inch lbs. (8 Nm).

7. Insert the sensor wiring harness into the retainer brackets.

8. Connect the rear sensor assembly to the differential sensor connector.

9. Lower the vehicle.

10. Connect the negative battery cable and road test the vehicle.

➡Proper installation of the wheel speed sensor cables is critical to proper operation of the ABS system. Make sure the cables are installed in the retainers. Failure to do this may result in contact with moving parts and the over extension of the cables, resulting in an open circuit.

Front Wheel Speed Sensor Ring

The front wheel speed sensor ring is an integral part of the brake rotor. The sensor ring is accessible for inspection by removing the brake rotor. If replacement of the wheel speed sensor ring is necessary, the brake rotor must be replaced.

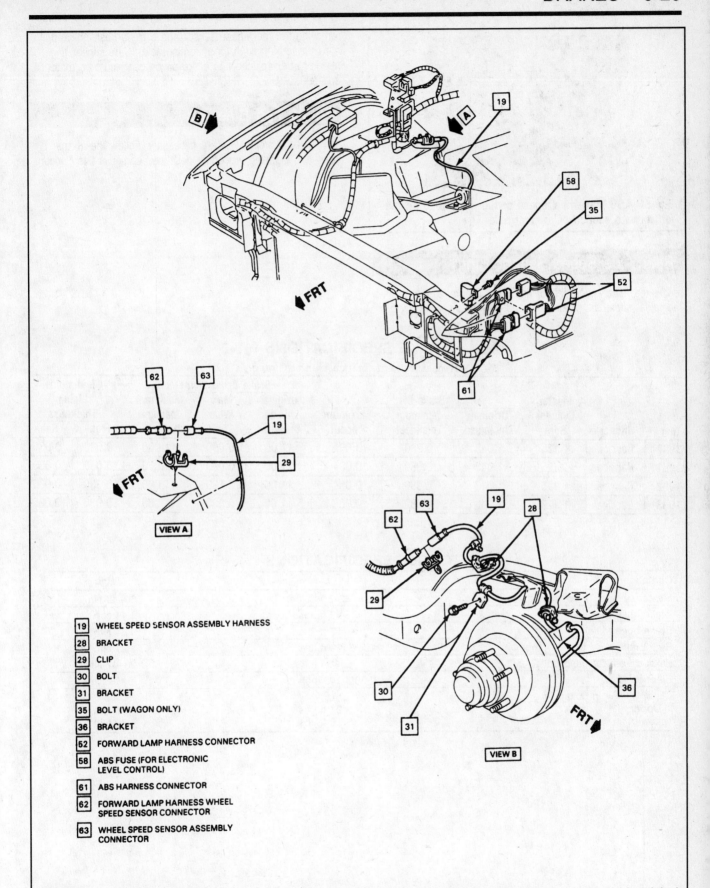

19 WHEEL SPEED SENSOR ASSEMBLY HARNESS
28 BRACKET
29 CLIP
30 BOLT
31 BRACKET
35 BOLT (WAGON ONLY)
36 BRACKET
52 FORWARD LAMP HARNESS CONNECTOR
58 ABS FUSE (FOR ELECTRONIC LEVEL CONTROL)
61 ABS HARNESS CONNECTOR
62 FORWARD LAMP HARNESS WHEEL SPEED SENSOR CONNECTOR
63 WHEEL SPEED SENSOR ASSEMBLY CONNECTOR

Fig. 50 ABS left front wheel speed sensor wire harness routing. Ensure all harness connectors are re-installed in original location during speed sensor replacement

Fig. 51 ABS rear wheel speed sensor is located on the left forward section of the rear axle.

Rear Axle Speed Sensor Ring

The rear axle speed sensor ring is an integral part of the rear axle differential pinion gear and may be inspected by removing the rear speed sensor and using a flashlight and mirror to look through the mounting hole. If the sensor ring needs to be replaced, the entire pinion gear must be removed and replaced.

Filling and Bleeding

No special procedures are necessary. Follow the normal filling and bleeding procedure described earlier in this Section.

BRAKE SPECIFICATIONS

All measurements in inches unless noted.

Year	Model	Master Cylinder Bore	Brake Disc			Brake Drum Diameter			Minimum Lining Thickness	
			Original Thickness	Minimum Thickness	Maximum Runout	Original Inside Diameter	Max. Wear Limit	Maximum Machine Diameter	Front	Rear
1990	Caprice	1.125	1.043	0.980	0.004	11.00	0.090	11.060	0.030	0.030
1991	Caprice	1.125	1.043	0.980	0.004	11.00	0.090	11.060	0.030	0.030
1992	Caprice	1.125	1.043	0.980	0.004	11.00	0.090	11.060	0.030	0.030
1993	Caprice	1.125	1.043	0.980	0.003	11.00	0.090	11.060	0.030	0.030

TORQUE SPECIFICATIONS

Component	U.S.	Metric
Master cylinder to booster	22–30 ft. lbs.	30–45 Nm
Brake hose to caliper	32 ft. lbs.	44 Nm
Brake hose to line	17 ft. lbs.	24 Nm
Rear brake hose to axle flange	20 ft. lbs.	27 Nm
Front caliper retaining bolts	21–35 ft. lbs.	28–47 Nm
Bleeder screw	80–140 inch lbs.	9–16 Nm
Cliper guide pin bolts Upper:	26 ft. lbs.	35 Nm
Lower:	16 ft. lbs.	22 Nm

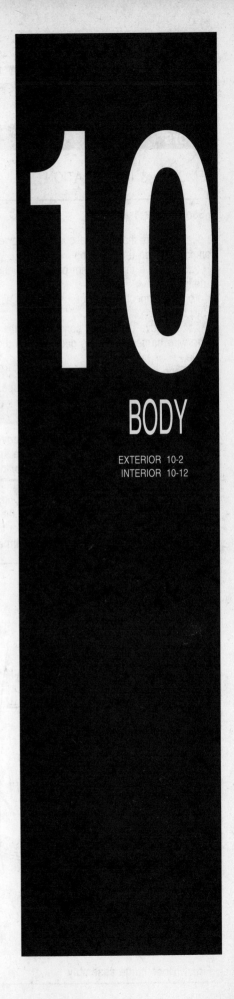

10

BODY

EXTERIOR 10-2
INTERIOR 10-12

EXTERIOR

Doors

REMOVAL & INSTALLATION

▶ **See Figures 1 and 2**

1. On doors that are equipped with power operated components, do the following:

   a. Remove the door trim panel and inner panel water deflector.

   b. Disconnect the wire harness from all components in the door.

   c. Remove the rubber conduit from the door, then remove the wire harness from the door through the conduit access hole.

2. Tape the area (on the door pillar and body pillar) above the lower hinge with cloth backed body tape.

✳✳CAUTION

Before performing the following step, cover the spring with a shop cloth or rag to prevent the spring from flying and possibly causing personal injury or damage.

3. Insert a long, flat-blade screwdriver under the pivot point of the hold-open link and over the top of the spring. The screwdriver should be positioned so as not to apply pressure to the hold-open link. Cover the spring with a shop cloth or

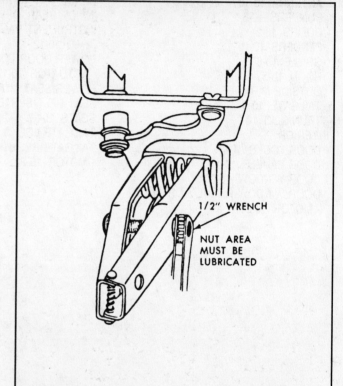

Fig. 2 Remove door hinge spring using tool J-36604 or flat bladed screwdriver

rag and lift the screwdriver to disengage the spring. The spring can also be removed by using tool J-36604 (or equivalent) door hinge spring compressor tool. The tool is stamped right side and left side. The tool stamped left side is used to service the right-hand hinge spring and vise-a-versa for the tool stamped right side.

4. With the aid of a helper to support the door, remove the lower hinge pin using a soft-headed hammer and locking type pliers. The helper can aid the hinge pin removal by raising and lowering the rear of the door. Loosen and support the front fender away from the body as necessary to gain access to the hinge bolts.

5. Insert a bolt into the hole of the lower hinge to maintain the door attachment during upper hinge removal.

6. Using a 13mm socket, remove the upper hinge bolts from the pillar. Remove the bolt from the lower hinge and remove the door from the body.

To install:

7. Replace the hinge pin clip.

8. With the aid of a helper, position the door and insert the bolt in the hole of the lower hinge.

9. Bolt the upper hinge to the body. The lower hinge pin is installed with the pointed end down.

10. Remove the screw from the lower hinge and install the lower hinge pin. The use of tool J-36604 or equivalent is recommended for installing the hinge spring.

➡**If the spring is installed before installing the lower hinge pin, damage to the hinge bushings may result.**

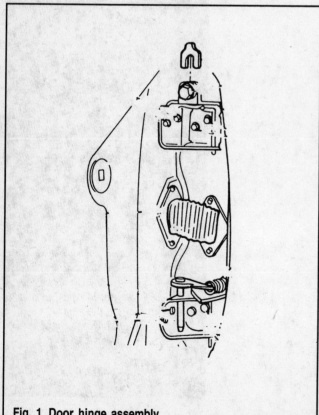

Fig. 1 Door hinge assembly

11. If the spring was removed using a screwdriver, install the spring as follows:

a. Place the spring in tool J-36604 or equivalent.

b. Place the tool and spring in a bench vise.

c. Compress the tool in the vise and install the bolt until the spring is fully compressed.

d. Remove the tool (with the compressed spring) from the vise and install in the proper position in the door lower hinge. A slot in one jaw fits over the hold-open link. The hole on the other jaw fits over the bubble.

e. Remove the bolt from the tool to install the spring.

f. Remove the tool from the door hinge (tool will fall out in three pieces). Cycle the door to check the spring operation.

12. Remove the tape from the door and the body pillars.

13. On doors with power operated components:

a. Install the wire harness to the door through the conduit access hole, then install the rubber conduit to the door.

b. Connect wire harness to all components in the door.

c. Install the inner panel water deflector and door trim panel.

Hood

REMOVAL & INSTALLATION

▶ See Figures 3 and 4

1. Open the hood and mark the position of the hood hinge assembly-to-hood by a scribe, caulk or paint. Remove the hood strut rod, on 1991 vehicles.

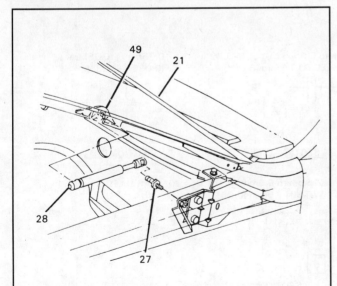

21 HOOD ASSEMBLY
27 STUD, HOOD STRUT BALL, 27 N•m (20 LB. FT.)
28 ROD ASSEMBLY, HOOD OPEN ASSIST
49 BRACKET ASSEMBLY, HOOD OPEN ASSIST ROD

Fig. 3 Hood gas strut rod removal — 1991-93

2. Remove the hood attaching bolts that are towards the front of the hood.

3. Slowly loosen the remaining hood attaching bolts.

4. With the aid of a helper, remove the bolts and remove the hood. Place the hood on a protected surface.

To install:

5. Position the hood over the hood hinge assembly with the aid of a helper and install the hood attaching bolts finger tight.

6. Align the hood to the match marks made earlier and tighten the hood attaching bolts.

7. Close the hood and check align.

ALIGNMENT

▶ See Figure 5

Slotted holes are provided at all hood hinge attaching points for proper adjustment - both vertically and fore-and-aft. Vertical adjustments at the front may be made by adjusting the rubber bumpers up and down.

To adjust the hood fore-and-aft move the hood forward or rearward until the hood clearances are equal and as specified in the illustration. If the hood is not properly coming into adjustment then the body panels may also need to be adjusted. To achieve the best results set the hood to any existing marks and make adjustments one at a time.

Trunk Lid

REMOVAL & INSTALLATION

▶ See Figure 6

1. Disconnect the negative battery cable. Open the trunk lid and place protective coverings over the rear fenders to protect the paint from damage.

2. Mark the location of the hinge-to-trunk lid bolts and disconnect the electrical connections and wiring from the lid, if equipped.

3. Using an assistant to support the lid, remove the hinge-to-lid bolts and the lid from the vehicle.

4. To install, reverse the removal procedures. Adjust the position of the trunk lid to the body.

ALIGNMENT

▶ See Figure 7

Rear compartment torque rods are adjustable to increase or decrease operating effort. To increase the amount of effort needed to raise the rear compartment lid or to decrease the amount of effort to close the lid, reposition the end of the rod to a lower torque rod adjusting notch. To decrease the amount of effort needed to raise the rear compartment lid or to increase the amount of effort to close the lid, reposition the end of the rod to a higher torque rod adjusting notch. Prop the trunk lid in full-open position to keep lid from falling when torque rods are disengaged from the torque rod bracket.

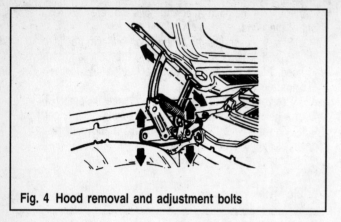

Fig. 4 Hood removal and adjustment bolts

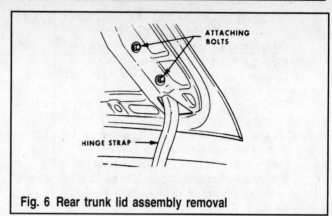

Fig. 6 Rear trunk lid assembly removal

ATTACHING BOLTS

HINGE STRAP

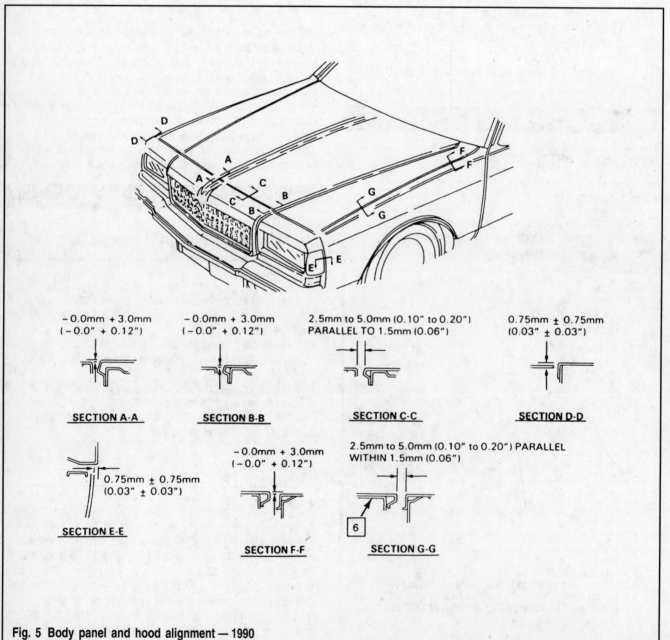

−0.0mm + 3.0mm
(−0.0" + 0.12")

SECTION A-A

−0.0mm + 3.0mm
(−0.0" + 0.12")

SECTION B-B

2.5mm to 5.0mm (0.10" to 0.20")
PARALLEL TO 1.5mm (0.06")

SECTION C-C

0.75mm ± 0.75mm
(0.03" ± 0.03")

SECTION D-D

0.75mm ± 0.75mm
(0.03" ± 0.03")

SECTION E-E

−0.0mm + 3.0mm
(−0.0" + 0.12")

SECTION F-F

2.5mm to 5.0mm (0.10" to 0.20") PARALLEL
WITHIN 1.5mm (0.06")

6

SECTION G-G

Fig. 5 Body panel and hood alignment — 1990

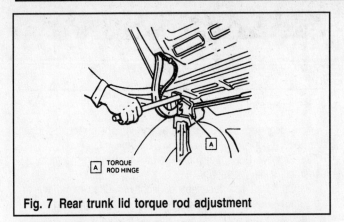

Fig. 7 Rear trunk lid torque rod adjustment

Tailgate

REMOVAL & INSTALLATION

▶ **See Figure 8**

1. Disconnect the negative battery cable.
2. Open the tailgate like a door until the tension is relieved from the torque rod. Remove the torque rod assist link retainer to body bolts.
3. Close the tailgate and open it as a gate.
4. Support the tailgate in the full open position. Remove the support cable to the left upper hinge striker assembly. Remove the left side quarter trim.

5. With the aid of an assistant, remove the left lower hinge to body retaining bolts.
6. Disconnect the electrical harness connector. Remove the screws retaining the electrical conduit to the tailgate assembly.

➡**With the tailgate open in the gate position and the right and left upper locks manually engaged, the tailgate is in a vulnerable position and could drop from the right lower lock if the locking rod and the outside handle are activated. Do not pull on the rod or activate the outside handle, as damage to the tailgate or personal injury could result.**

7. Manually latch the left upper lock. With the aid of an assistant support the tailgate, activate the right side door handle to unlock and free the right lower lock from the striker assembly.
8. Remove the tailgate assembly by lifting upward and than rearward.

To install:

9. Position the tailgate assembly in place on the vehicle.
10. Install the retaining bolts.
11. Install the electrical conduit to the tailgate assembly.
12. Connect the electrical harness connector.
13. Install the left quarter trim.
14. Install the left upper hinge striker assembly. Adjust the tailgate assembly, as required.
15. Connect the negative battery cable.

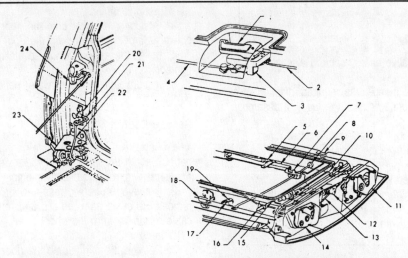

1. Handle—tailgate remote control
2. Rod—tailgate lock remote control
3. Control asm.—tailgate lock remote
4. Rod asm.—tailgate lock remote control to lock left side
5. Cam—tailgate glass regulator
6. Cam—tailgate inner panel
7. Plate—tailgate window guide right side
8. Bumper—tailgate window down stop
9. Retainer asm.—torque rod tailgate hinge
10. Rod—tailgate window blockout
11. Lock asm.—tailgate lower right side
12. Actuator asm.—electric lock
13. Rod asm.—tailgate upper to lower lock connection
14. Lock asm.—tailgate upper right side
15. Rod—tailgate inside locking to lock
16. Knob—door inside locking rod
17. Stop—tailgate window up
18. Retainer asm.—tailgate belt trim support
19. Stop—tailgate window up
20. Retainer—tailgate hinge torque rod link
21. Link—tailgate hinge torque rod
22. Rod—torque tailgate hinge
23. Hinge asm.—tailgate lower lt. side
24. Striker asm.—tailgate upper hinge lt. side

Fig. 8 Tailgate assembly

ALIGNMENT

The tailgate can be aligned slightly by loosening the hinge and/or the latch bolts. The bottom of the tailgate can be adjusted in or out by adding or removing shims between the hinge and body.

➡When adjusting the hinge/latch-to-body positions, be sure to use alignment marks as reference points.

BUMPERS

REMOVAL & INSTALLATION

Front
▶ **See Figures 9 and 10**

1. Disconnect the negative battery cable. Raise and support the vehicle safely.
2. Properly support the bumper. As required, disconnect all the necessary electrical connections at the turn signal assemblies and the cornering light housings.
3. On the vehicles without the energy absorber type bumper, remove the bolts from the frame and remove the bumper.
4. On vehicles equipped with the energy absorber type bumper, remove the bolts from the reinforcement to the energy absorber (each side) and remove the bumper assembly.
5. Installation is the reverse of the removal procedure.

Rear
▶ **See Figures 11 and 12**

1. Disconnect the negative battery cable. Raise and support the vehicle safely.
2. Properly support the bumper. As required, disconnect all the necessary electrical connections at the tail light assembly housings.
3. On the vehicles without the energy absorber type bumper, remove the bolts from the frame and remove the bumper.
4. On vehicles equipped with the energy absorber type bumper, remove the bolts from the reinforcement to the energy absorber (each side) and remove the bumper assembly.
5. Installation is the reverse of the removal procedure.

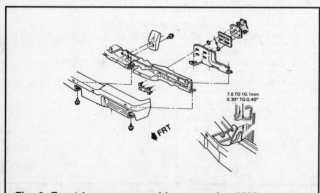

Fig. 9 Front bumper assembly removal — 1990

Grille

REMOVAL & INSTALLATION

▶ **See Figures 13 and 14**

1. Disconnect the negative battery cable. As required, open the hood.
2. Remove the sheet metal screws that retain the grille assembly to its mounting.
3. On some vehicles, the headlight trim rings may have to be removed before the grille assembly can be removed from the vehicle.
4. Remove the grille assembly from the vehicle.
5. Installation is the reverse of the removal procedure.

Outside Mirrors

REMOVAL & INSTALLATION

▶ **See Figures 15 and 16**

Standard Mirrors

1. Remove the door trim panel and detach inner panel water deflector enough to gain access to the mirror retainer nuts.
2. Remove the attaching nuts from the mirror base studs and remove the mirror assembly from the door.
   To install:
3. Position the mirror onto the door making sure the mirror gasket is properly aligned on the door outer panel.
4. Install the attaching nuts to the mirror base studs and tighten.
5. Install the inner panel water deflector and door trim panel.

Remote Control Mirrors

1. Remove the mirror remote control bezel and door trim panel. Detach the inner panel water deflector enough to expose the mirror and cable assembly from the door.
2. Remove the mirror base-to-door outer panel stud nuts, remove the cable from the clip and remove the mirror and cable assembly from the door.
   To install:
3. Position the mirror onto the door making sure the mirror gasket is properly aligned on the door outer panel.
4. Install the cable onto the clip and install the mirror base-to-door outer panel stud nuts. Torque to 72 inch lbs. (8 Nm).
5. Install the inner panel water deflector and door trim panel.
6. Install the mirror remote control bezel.

Power Operated Mirrors

1. Disconnect the negative battery terminal and, from the door trim panel side, remove the remote control mirror bezel, release and remove the door panel.
2. Disconnect wire harness connection from the remote mirror electrical switch.

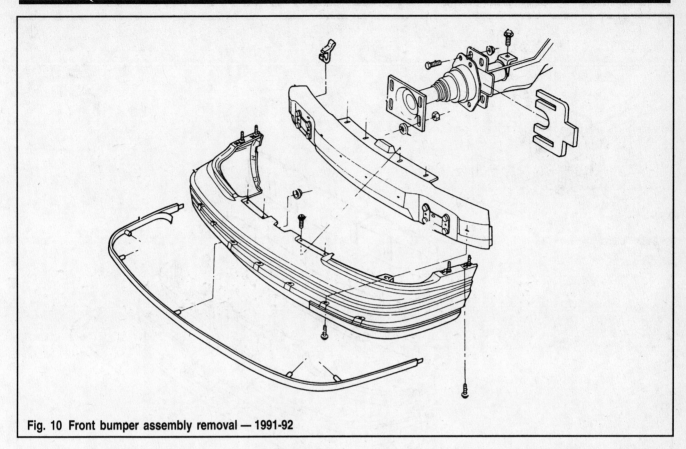

Fig. 10 Front bumper assembly removal — 1991-92

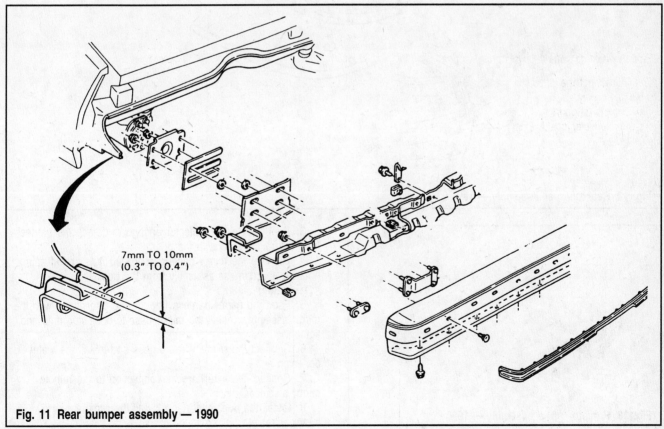

7mm TO 10mm
(0.3" TO 0.4")

Fig. 11 Rear bumper assembly — 1990

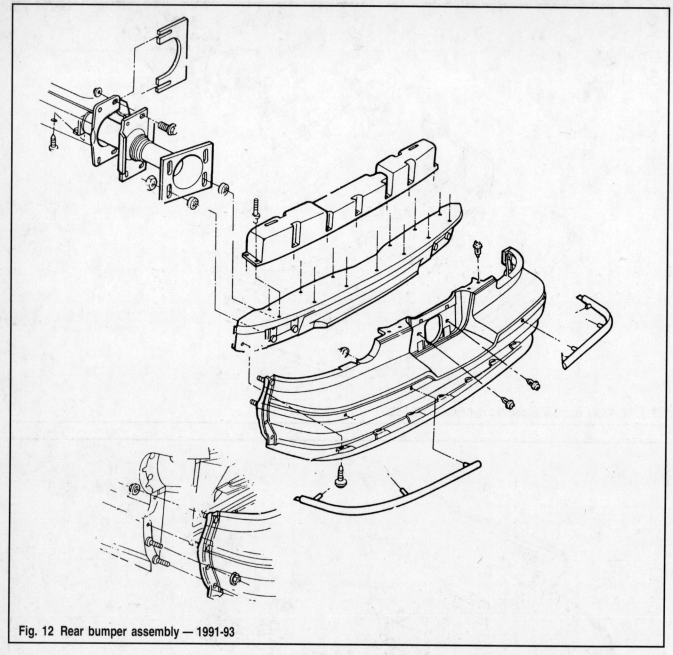

Fig. 12 Rear bumper assembly — 1991-93

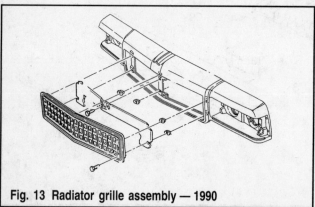

Fig. 13 Radiator grille assembly — 1990

3. Peel back water deflector enough to detach the harness from the retaining tabs in the door.

4. Remove the mirror base-to-door stud nuts and lift mirror housing and harness assembly from the door.

To install:

5. Feed the mirror harness through the door along with the mirror assembly. Install the mirror base-to-door stud nuts and tighten.

6. Connect the mirror wire harness and install the water deflector.

7. Connect the wire harness connection to the remote mirror electrical switch.

8. Install the door panel and install the remote control mirror bezel.

9. Connect the negative battery terminal.

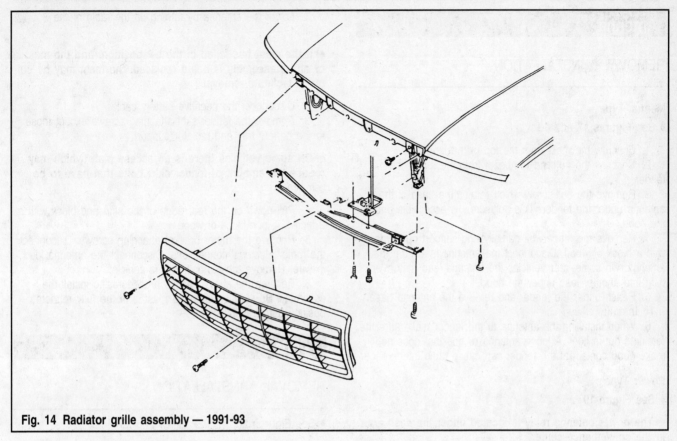

Fig. 14 Radiator grille assembly — 1991-93

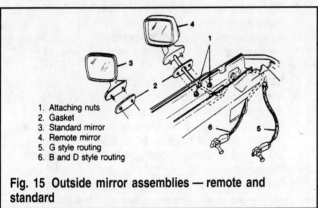

1. Attaching nuts
2. Gasket
3. Standard mirror
4. Remote mirror
5. G style routing
6. B and D style routing

Fig. 15 Outside mirror assemblies — remote and standard

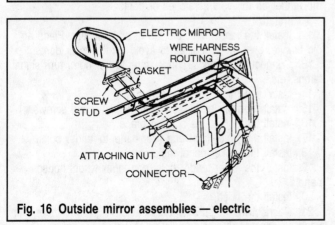

ELECTRIC MIRROR
WIRE HARNESS ROUTING
GASKET
SCREW STUD
ATTACHING NUT
CONNECTOR

Fig. 16 Outside mirror assemblies — electric

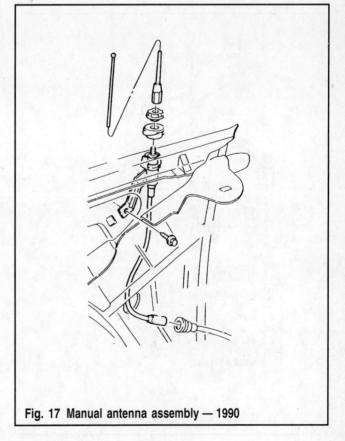

Fig. 17 Manual antenna assembly — 1990

Antenna

REMOVAL & INSTALLATION

Manual Type
▶ **See Figures 17 and 18**

1. Unscrew the mast from the top of the fender.
2. Unscrew the nut and the bezel from the top of the fender.
3. Remove the bolt/screw which retains the base of the antenna under the fender. This bolt/screw is accessible under the hood.
4. Remove the fenderwell partially and support outwards with a block of wood. Disconnect the antenna lead from the antenna. On some later vehicles the antenna lead may even plug into another lead under the hood.
5. Reach under the fender and remove the antenna base.
   To install:
6. When installing the antenna to the fender make sure the retaining nut is tight. A loose antenna or one that does not make good contact at the fender can cause radio interference.

Power Type
▶ **See Figure 19**

➡**The power antenna relay is located under the dash area in the convenience center.**

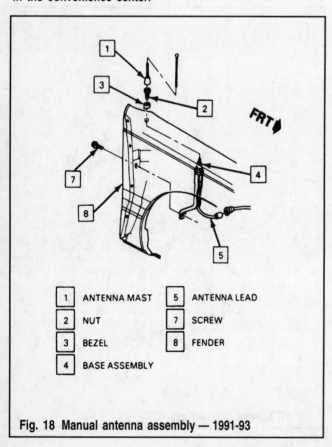

1	ANTENNA MAST	5	ANTENNA LEAD
2	NUT	7	SCREW
3	BEZEL	8	FENDER
4	BASE ASSEMBLY		

Fig. 18 Manual antenna assembly — 1991-93

1. Lower the antenna by turning off the radio or the ignition.

➡**If the mast has failed in the UP position, and the mast or entire assembly is being replaced, the mast may be cut off to facilitate removal.**

2. Disconnect the negative battery cable.
3. Remove the fender skirt attaching screws except those to the battery tray and radiator support.

➡**On some vehicles there is an access plate which may reduce the amount of fender skirt bolts that have to be removed.**

4. Pull down on the rear edge of the skirt and block with a 2 inch x 4 inch block of wood.
5. Remove the motor bracket attaching screws. Disconnect the motor electrical connections. Disconnect the antenna lead in wire. Remove the motor from the vehicle.
6. Reverse the above service procedures to install the assembly. Be sure the antenna mast is in the fully retracted position before installation.

Fenders

REMOVAL & INSTALLATION

▶ **See Figures 20, 21, 22, 23, 24 and 25**

1. Disconnect the negative battery cable.
2. Remove the hood.
3. Raise and safely support the vehicle.
4. Remove the lower fender bolts and inner wheel house panel.
5. Remove the rocker panel molding.
6. Remove the lower front filler panel-to-fender bolts.
7. Remove the bolt from the support brace.
8. Remove the front end fascia-to-fender nuts and screws.
9. Remove the hood hinge-to-fender bolts.
10. Disconnect all electrical connections from horn, turn signal lamps, etc.
11. Remove the fender by sliding rearward and outward, at rear, with the aid of an assistant. Place an old blanket over the fender as to avoid scratches or dents.
    To install:
12. Install the fender with the aid of an assistant. Place an old blanket over the fender as to avoid scratches or dents.
13. Connect all electrical connections to the horn, turn signal lamps, etc.
14. Install the hood hinge-to-fender bolts.
15. Install the front end fascia-to-fender nuts and screws.
16. Install the bolt at the support brace.
17. Install the lower front end filler panel-to-fender bolts.
18. Install the rocker panel molding.
19. Install the lower fender bolts and inner wheel house panel.
20. Install the hood.
21. Connect the negative battery cable. Align the fender and hood as necessary, placing existing shims in original positions.

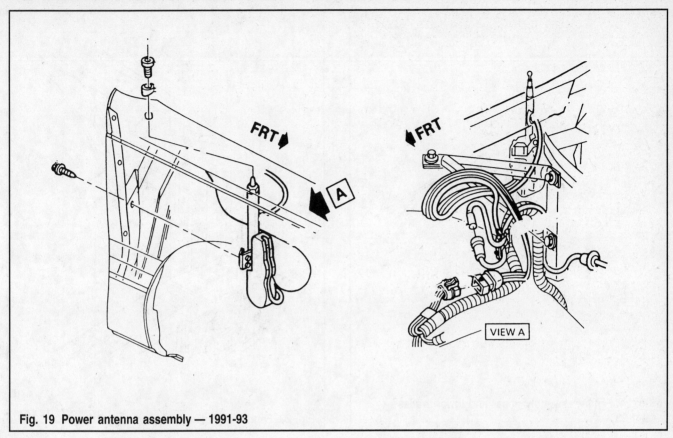

Fig. 19 Power antenna assembly — 1991-93

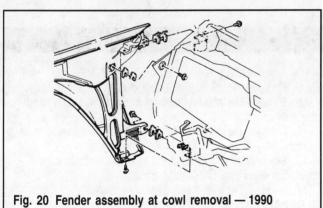

Fig. 20 Fender assembly at cowl removal — 1990

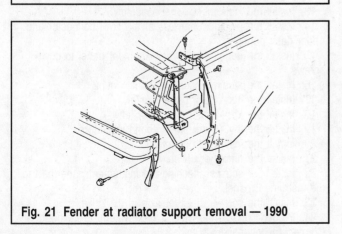

Fig. 21 Fender at radiator support removal — 1990

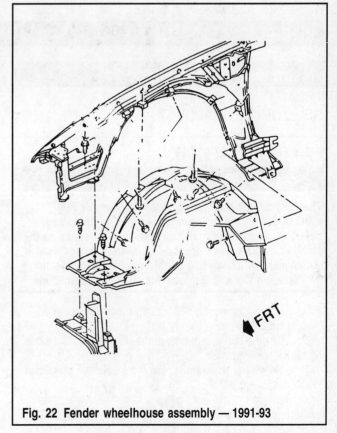

Fig. 22 Fender wheelhouse assembly — 1991-93

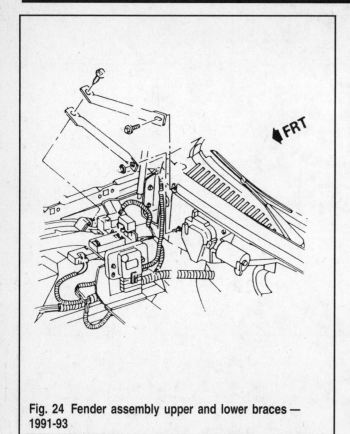

Fig. 24 Fender assembly upper and lower braces —
1991-93

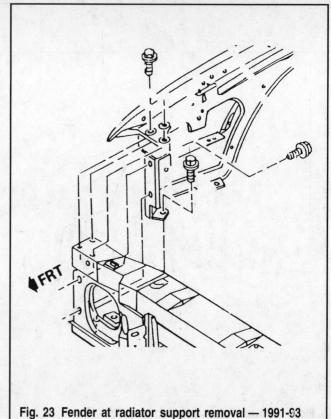

Fig. 23 Fender at radiator support removal — 1991-93

INTERIOR

Instrument Panel and Pad

REMOVAL & INSTALLATION

▶ See Figures 26, 27 and 28

✳✳CAUTION

The 1991-93 vehicles are equipped with an Air Bag system. Proper disarming of the system is necessary before proceeding with any disassembly or repairs to the steering column, dash or electrical system or possible deployment of the air bag might occur. Refer to Section 8 — Steering Column Removal for disarming procedure.

1. Properly disable the SIR air bag system, if equipped. Disconnect the negative battery cable.
2. Open the doors and remove the screws from the sides of the instrument panel.
3. Remove the screws attaching the instrument panel pad to the instrument panel.
4. Remove the defogger grilles and remove the screws located under the grilles and in the front of the panel pad.
5. Remove the instrument panel pad.
6. Remove the instrument panel sound insulators.

7. Remove the knee bolster and bracket.
8. Remove the instrument panel cluster.
9. Remove the steering column retaining nuts and lower the column.
10. Remove the upper and lower instrument panel to cowl screws.
11. Disconnect and remove the electrical harness at the cowl connector and under dash panel.
12. Remove the instrument panel assembly.
To install:
13. Install the instrument panel assembly.
14. Install the electrical harness at the cowl connector and under dash panel.
15. Install the upper and lower instrument panel to cowl screws.
16. Install the steering column retaining nuts.
17. Install the instrument panel cluster.
18. Install the knee bolster and bracket.
19. Install the instrument panel sound insulators.
20. Install the instrument panel pad.
21. Install the defogger grilles.
22. Install the screws attaching the instrument panel pad to the instrument panel.
23. Install the screws at either side of the grille.
24. Properly enable the SIR air bag system, if equipped. Connect the negative battery cable.

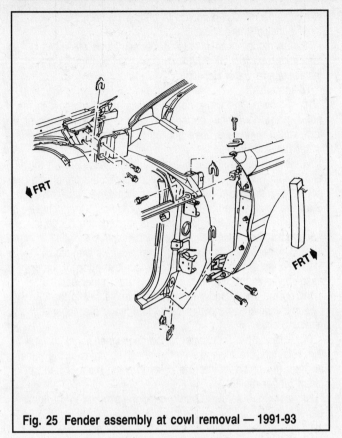

Fig. 25 Fender assembly at cowl removal — 1991-93

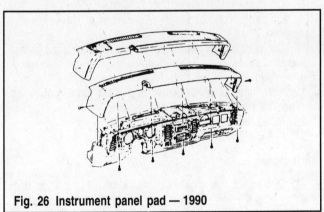

Fig. 26 Instrument panel pad — 1990

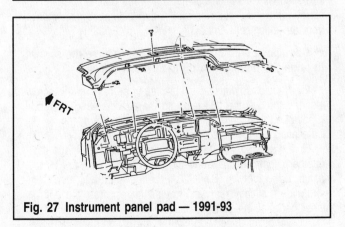

Fig. 27 Instrument panel pad — 1991-93

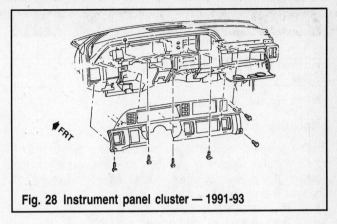

Fig. 28 Instrument panel cluster — 1991-93

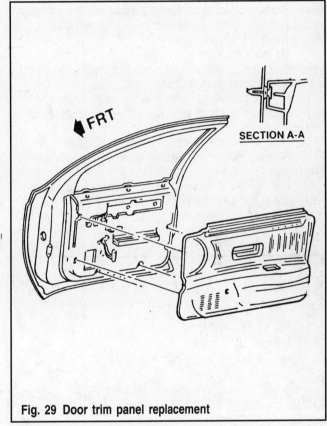

SECTION A-A

Fig. 29 Door trim panel replacement

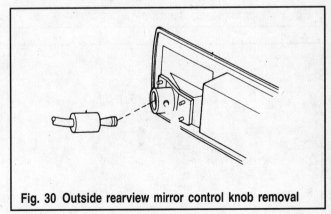

Fig. 30 Outside rearview mirror control knob removal

Door Panels

REMOVAL & INSTALLATION

▶ See Figures 29, 30, 31, 32, 33 and 34

Front Door

The one-piece trim hangs over the door inner panel across the top and is secured by clips down the sides and across the bottom. It is retained by screws located in the areas of the armrest and pull handle assembly.

1. Remove all the door inside handles.
2. Remove the door inside locking rod knob.
3. Remove the screws inserted through the door armrest and pull the handle assembly into the door inner panel or armrest hanger support bracket.
4. On models with remote control mirror assemblies, remove the control plate from the bezel on the trim pad and remove the control from the plate.
5. On models with power door lock controls located in the door trim panel, disconnect the wire harnesses at the switch assemblies.
6. Remove the remote control handle bezel screws.
7. Remove the screws used to hold the armrest to the inner panel.
8. Remove the screws and plastic retainers from the perimeter of the door trim panel using tool BT-7323A or equivalent and a screwdriver. To remove the trim panel, push

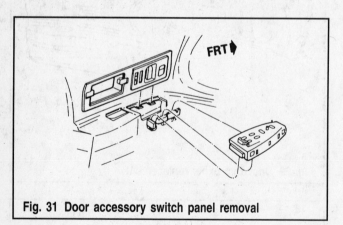

Fig. 31 Door accessory switch panel removal

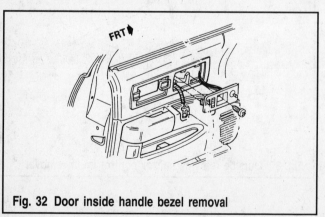

Fig. 32 Door inside handle bezel removal

the trim upward and outboard to disengage from the door inner panel at the beltline.

9. On models with a water deflector held in place by fasteners, use tool BT-7323A or equivalent to remove the fasteners and water deflector.

To install:

10. To install the water deflector, locate the fasteners in the holes in the door inner panel and press in place. Replace all tape which may have been applied to assist in holding the water deflector in place.
11. Before installing the door trim panel, make certain that all the trim retainers are installed securely to the panel and are not damaged. Where required, replace damaged retainers. Start the retainer flange into 1/4 inch (6mm) cutout attachment hole in the trim panel, rotate the retainer until the flange is engaged fully.
12. Connect all electrical components where present.
13. To install the door trim panel, locate the top of the assembly over the upper flange of the door inner panel, inserting the door handle through the handle slot in the panel and press down on the trim panel to engage the upper retaining clips.
14. Position the trim panel to the door inner panel so the trim retainers are aligned with the attaching holes in the panel and tap the retainers into the holes with the palm of hand or a clean rubber mallet.
15. Install the screws used to hold the armrest to the inner panel.
16. Install the remote control handle bezel screws.
17. On models with power door lock controls located in the door trim panel, connect the wire harnesses at the switch assemblies.
18. On models with remote control mirror assemblies, install the control to the plate. Install the control plate to the bezel on the trim pad.
19. Install the handle assembly and install the screws inserted through the door armrest.
20. Install the door inside locking rod knob.
21. Install all the door inside handles.

Rear Door

1. Disconnect the negative battery cable. Remove the door handles and the locking knob from the inside of the doors. If equipped with a switch cover plate in the door armrest, remove the cover plate screws, then disconnect the switch from the electrical harness.

➡**If equipped with door pull handles, remove the screws through the handle into the door inner panel.**

2. If equipped with an integral armrest, remove the screws inserted through the pull cup into the armrest hanger support. If equipped with an armrest applied after the door trim installation, remove the armrest-to-inner panel screws.
3. If equipped with two-piece trim panels, disengage the retainer clips from the front and the rear of the upper trim panel, using tool No. BT-7323A, then lift the upper door trim and slide it slightly rearward to disengage it from the door inner panel at the beltline.
4. Along the upper edge of the lower trim panel, remove the mounting screws. At the lower edge of the panel, insert tool No. BT-7323A between the inner panel and the trim panel,

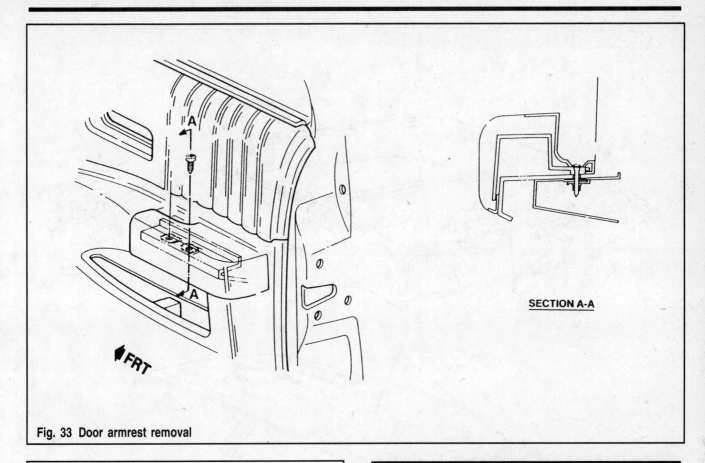

Fig. 33 Door armrest removal

SECTION A-A

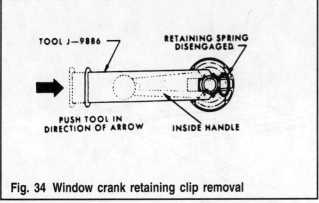

Fig. 34 Window crank retaining clip removal

the disengage the retaining clips from around the outer perimeter. To remove the lower panel, push the panel down and outward to disengage it from the door.

➡️**If equipped with courtesy lights, disconnect the wiring harness.**

5. If equipped with an insulator pad glued to the door inner panel, remove the pad (with a putty knife) by separating it from the inner panel.

6. To install, reverse the removal procedures.

Headliner

REMOVAL & INSTALLATION

▶ **See Figure 35**

1. Disconnect the negative battery cable.
2. Remove the dome lamp and sunshade.
3. Remove the coat hooks and seat belt escutcheons, by unsnapping from the headliner.
4. Remove the rear window opening molding.
5. Remove the rear quarter interior trim panels, body lock pillar panels and windshield side upper moldings.
6. Remove the headliner retaining clips and remove the headliner either through the rear passenger door or rear tailgate on wagon.
7. Installation is the reverse of the removal procedure.

Door Locks

REMOVAL & INSTALLATION

▶ **See Figures 36, 37 and 38**

1. Raise the door window. Remove the door trim panel and detach the inner panel water deflector enough to expose the access hole.

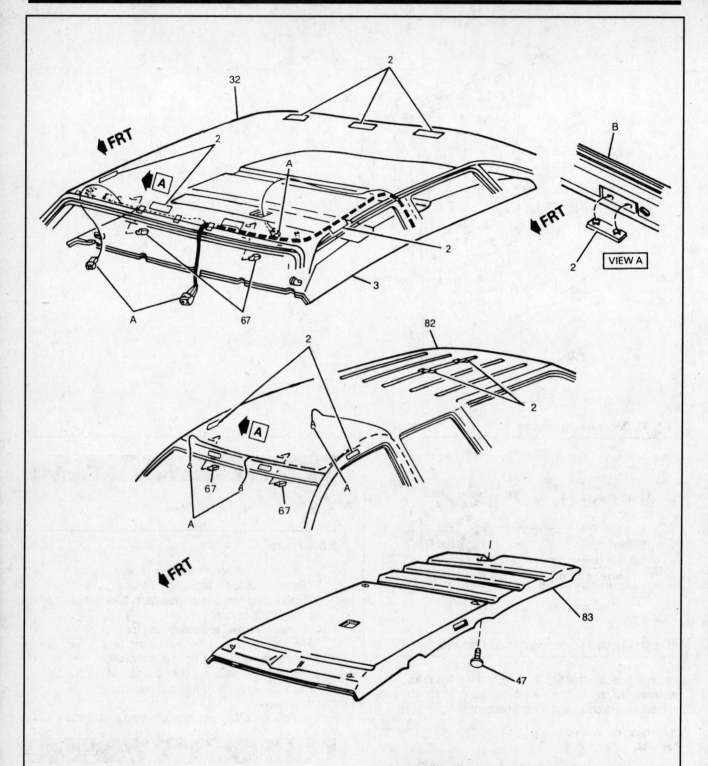

Fig. 35 Headliner assembly — 1991-93

A CONNECTOR, ELECTRICAL
B RAIL, ROOF
2 RETAINER, HEADLINING TRIM FINISH PANEL
  MOLDING
3 PANEL ASSEMBLY, HEADLINING TRIM FINISH

32 PANEL ASSEMBLY, ROOF (SEDAN)
47 RETAINER, HEADLINING TRIM FINISH PANEL
67 NUT, SUNSHADE ROD RETAINER
82 PANEL ASSEMBLY, ROOF (WAGON)
83 PANEL ASSEMBLY, HEADLINING TRIM FINISH

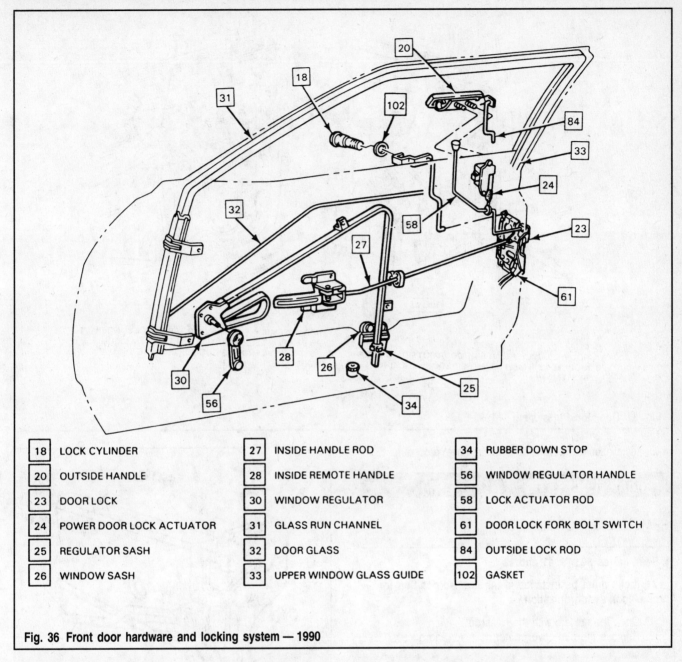

18	LOCK CYLINDER	27	INSIDE HANDLE ROD	34	RUBBER DOWN STOP
20	OUTSIDE HANDLE	28	INSIDE REMOTE HANDLE	56	WINDOW REGULATOR HANDLE
23	DOOR LOCK	30	WINDOW REGULATOR	58	LOCK ACTUATOR ROD
24	POWER DOOR LOCK ACTUATOR	31	GLASS RUN CHANNEL	61	DOOR LOCK FORK BOLT SWITCH
25	REGULATOR SASH	32	DOOR GLASS	84	OUTSIDE LOCK ROD
26	WINDOW SASH	33	UPPER WINDOW GLASS GUIDE	102	GASKET

Fig. 36 Front door hardware and locking system — 1990

2. Disengage the lock cylinder to the lock rod at the cylinder.

✳✿CAUTION

If removing the lock cylinder retainer by hand, wear gloves to prevent personal injury.

3. With a screwdriver or similar tool, slide the lock cylinder retainer forward until it disengages. Retainer can also be removed by hand by grasping anti-theft shield at the top of the retainer and rotating until disengaged. Remove the lock cylinder from the door.

4. To install, lubricate the cylinder with the proper lubricant.

5. Position the cylinder into place and rotate it until the cylinder engages. Install the cylinder retainer.

6. Engage the lock cylinder to lock rod at the cylinder.

7. Install the inner panel water deflector and door trim panel.

Power Door Lock Actuator

REMOVAL & INSTALLATION

1. Disconnect the negative battery cable. Remove the door panel.

2. Raise the window fully. Disconnect the electrical connector from the actuator.

3. Drive the rivet center pins out using an ⅛ in. punch and hammer, then using a ¼ inch drill bit, remove the rivet head.

4. Remove the actuator rod and remove the door lock actuator.

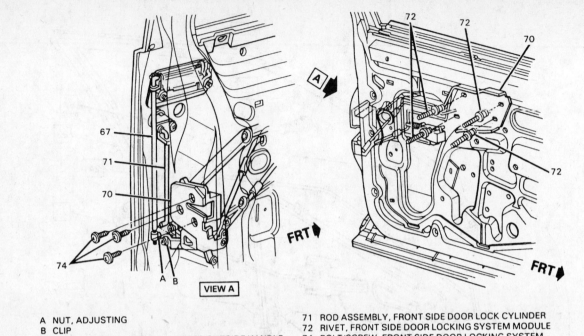

A   NUT, ADJUSTING
B   CLIP
67 ROD ASSEMBLY, FRONT SIDE DOOR OUTSIDE HANDLE
70 MODULE ASSEMBLY, FRONT SIDE DOOR LOCKING
     SYSTEM

71 ROD ASSEMBLY, FRONT SIDE DOOR LOCK CYLINDER
72 RIVET, FRONT SIDE DOOR LOCKING SYSTEM MODULE
74 BOLT/SCREW, FRONT SIDE DOOR LOCKING SYSTEM
     MODULE, 10 N·m (89 LB. IN.)

Fig. 37 Door locking system — 1991-93

5. Installation is the reverse of the removal procedure.

Tailgate Locks

REMOVAL & INSTALLATION

▶ See Figures 39, 40, 41 and 42

➡ All locks must be installed in the latched position for proper lock synchronization.

1. Open the tailgate with the glass up.
2. Remove the trim cover, water deflector and access panel.
3. Disconnect all necessary lock rods.
4. Disconnect all necessary wire connectors.
5. Remove the lock retaining screws and remove the lock assembly.
6. Installation is the reverse of the removal procedure. Use care when adjusting the right upper and lower locks while in the latched position, since the tailgate may drop from the left upper lock position.

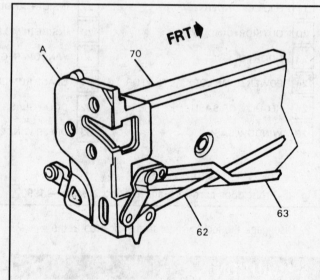

A   LATCH, DOOR
62 ROD, FRONT SIDE DOOR LOCKING
63 ROD, FRONT SIDE DOOR INSIDE HANDLE
70 MODULE ASSEMBLY, FRONT SIDE DOOR LOCKING
     SYSTEM

Fig. 38 Door lock latch — 1991-93

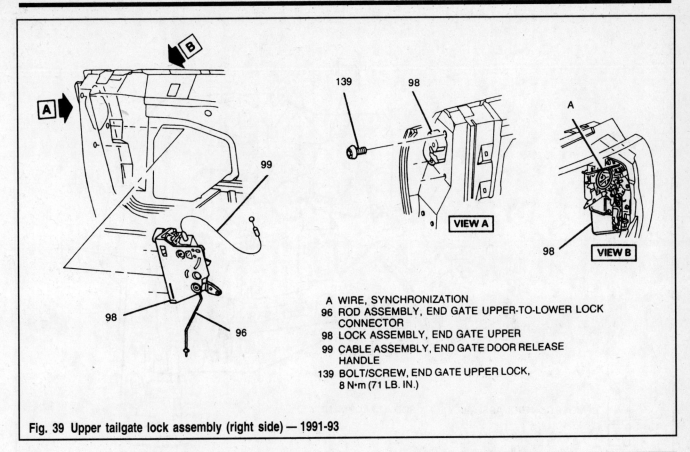

A WIRE, SYNCHRONIZATION
96 ROD ASSEMBLY, END GATE UPPER-TO-LOWER LOCK CONNECTOR
98 LOCK ASSEMBLY, END GATE UPPER
99 CABLE ASSEMBLY, END GATE DOOR RELEASE HANDLE
139 BOLT/SCREW, END GATE UPPER LOCK, 8 N•m (71 LB. IN.)

Fig. 39 Upper tailgate lock assembly (right side) — 1991-93

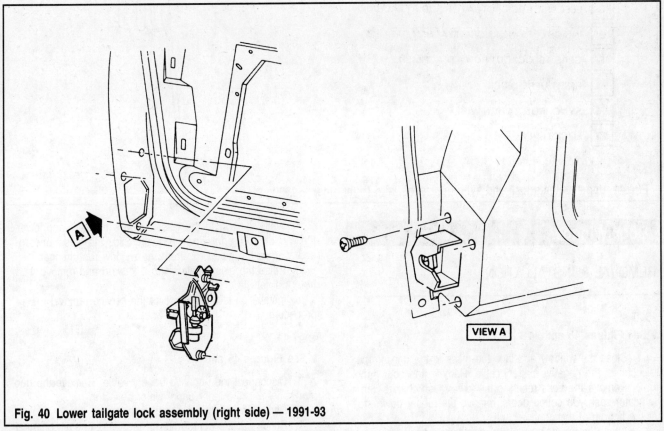

Fig. 40 Lower tailgate lock assembly (right side) — 1991-93

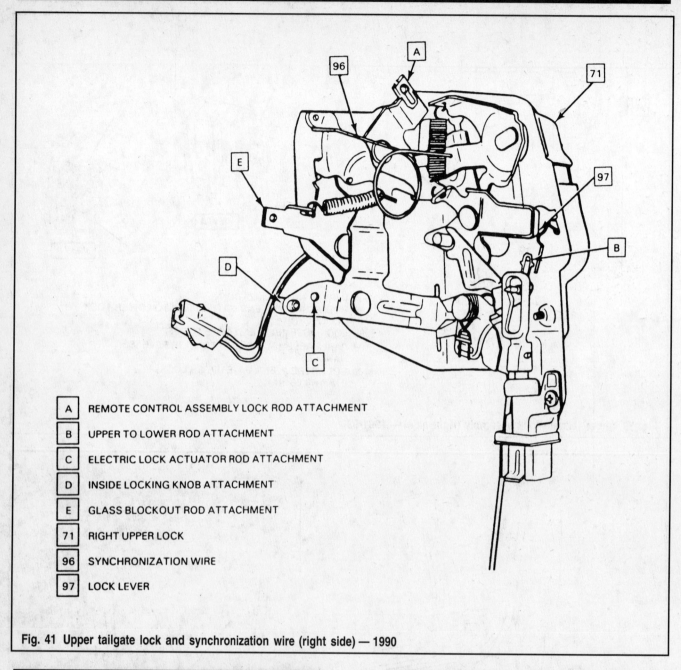

A	REMOTE CONTROL ASSEMBLY LOCK ROD ATTACHMENT
B	UPPER TO LOWER ROD ATTACHMENT
C	ELECTRIC LOCK ACTUATOR ROD ATTACHMENT
D	INSIDE LOCKING KNOB ATTACHMENT
E	GLASS BLOCKOUT ROD ATTACHMENT
71	RIGHT UPPER LOCK
96	SYNCHRONIZATION WIRE
97	LOCK LEVER

Fig. 41 Upper tailgate lock and synchronization wire (right side) — 1990

Door Window

REMOVAL & INSTALLATION

1990
▶ **See Figures 43 and 44**

1. Close the window and tape the glass to the door frame. Disconnect the negative battery cable. Remove the door panel.
2. Remove the bolts retaining the lower sash channel the regulator sash. On coupe doors, remove the rubber down stop at the bottom of the door.
3. Attach the window regulator and lower the window regulator to the full down position. Remove the regulator sash.

4. While supporting the glass, remove the tape and lower the window to the full down position. Slide the glass forward and remove the guide clip from the window run channel.
5. Raise the glass while tilting it forward and remove it from the vehicle.
6. Installation is the reverse of the service removal procedure.

1991-93
▶ **See Figures 45 and 46**

1. Disconnect the negative battery cable. Remove the door trim panel and the inner panel water deflector.
2. Raise the window to half-up position.
3. Punch out the center pins of the glass to sash channel attaching rivets.
4. Remove the front window channel and bolt.

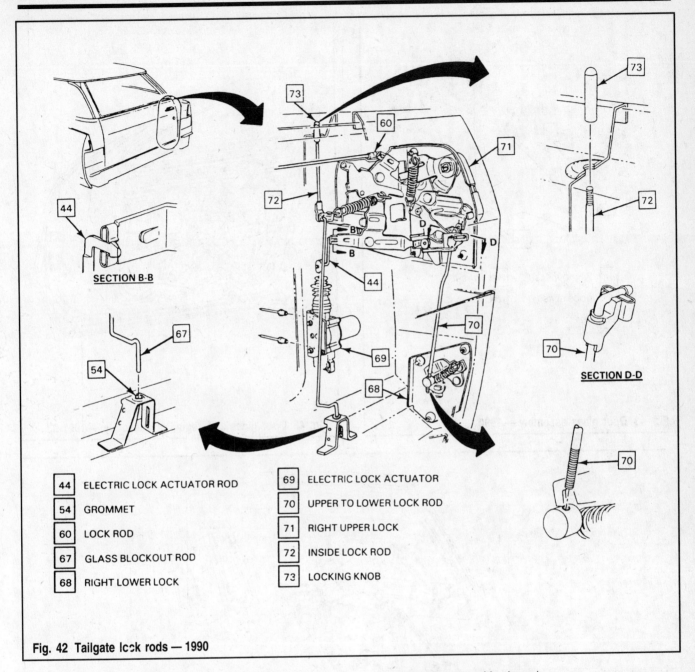

44	ELECTRIC LOCK ACTUATOR ROD
54	GROMMET
60	LOCK ROD
67	GLASS BLOCKOUT ROD
68	RIGHT LOWER LOCK

69	ELECTRIC LOCK ACTUATOR
70	UPPER TO LOWER LOCK ROD
71	RIGHT UPPER LOCK
72	INSIDE LOCK ROD
73	LOCKING KNOB

Fig. 42 Tailgate lock rods — 1990

5. Using a 1/16 inch drill bit, drill out the attaching rivets on sash channel.

6. Lower the glass to remove from the sash channel and remove the glass from the door.

7. To install, remove the drilled out rivets and shavings from the door.

8. Check the rivet bushings and retainers on the glass for damage. If necessary, remove the bushings using a flat-bladed tool covered with a cloth body tape. Install by snapping rivet retainer into the bushing.

9. Lower the glass into the door and position on the sash channel so the holes in the sash line up with the holes in the bushings and retainers.

10. Using rivet tool J-29022 or equivalent, install 1/4 inch peel type rivet (part No. 20184399 or equivalent) to retain the glass to sash channel.

11. Install the rear guide channel.

12. Before installing the trim parts, check the window adjustment for proper fit.

13. Install the inner panel water deflector and the door trim panel.

Door Window Regulator and Motor

REMOVAL & INSTALLATION

1990

1. Disconnect the negative battery cable. Remove the door trim panel and inner panel water deflector.

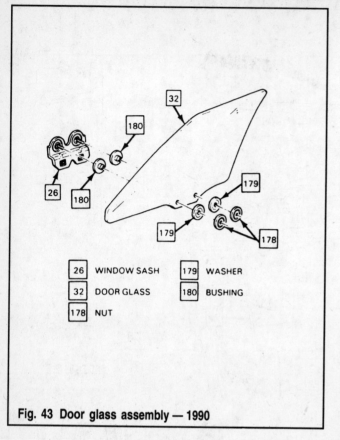

26 WINDOW SASH
32 DOOR GLASS
178 NUT
179 WASHER
180 BUSHING

Fig. 43 Door glass assembly — 1990

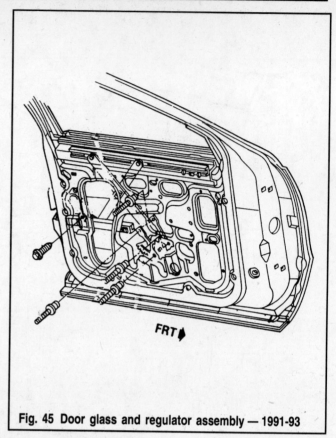

FRT

Fig. 45 Door glass and regulator assembly — 1991-93

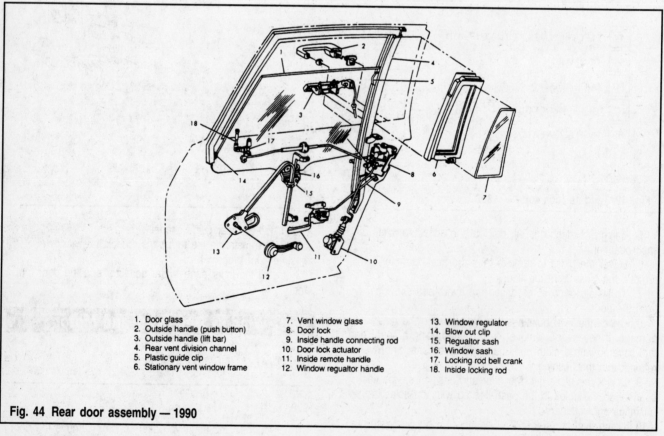

1. Door glass
2. Outside handle (push button)
3. Outside handle (lift bar)
4. Rear vent division channel
5. Plastic guide clip
6. Stationary vent window frame
7. Vent window glass
8. Door lock
9. Inside handle connecting rod
10. Door lock actuator
11. Inside remote handle
12. Window regualator handle
13. Window regulator
14. Blow out clip
15. Regualtor sash
16. Window sash
17. Locking rod bell crank
18. Inside locking rod

Fig. 44 Rear door assembly — 1990

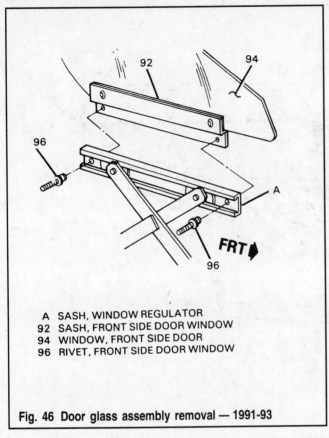

A   SASH, WINDOW REGULATOR
92 SASH, FRONT SIDE DOOR WINDOW
94 WINDOW, FRONT SIDE DOOR
96 RIVET, FRONT SIDE DOOR WINDOW

Fig. 46 Door glass assembly removal — 1991-93

2. Raise the window to full-up position and hold in place by inserting a rubber wedge door stops at the front and rear of the window between window and inner panel.

3. Remove the sash to regulator bolts.

4. Punch out the center pins of the regulator rivets; then drill out the rivets using a ⁵/₁₆ inch drill bit.

5. Move the regulator rearward and disconnect wire harness from the motor (if equipped).

6. Remove the regulator through the rear access hole.

To install:

7. Place the regulator through the rear access hole into the door inner panel. If electric regulator is being installed, connect the wire connector to motor prior to installing the regulator to the inner panel.

8. Locate the lift arm roller into the glass sash channel.

9. Using rivet tool J-29022 or equivalent, rivet regulator to the inner panel of the door using ¼ **x** ½ inch aluminum peel type rivets (part No. 9436175 or equivalent). If rivet tool is not available, use the following nut and bolt method:

   a. Install U-clips on the regulator at the attaching locations. Be sure to install the clips with clinch nuts on the outboard side of the regulator.

   b. Locate the regulator in the door inner panel. If the electric regulator is being installed, connect the wire connector to the regulator motor.

   c. Locate the lift arm roller in the glass sash channel.

   d. Align the regulator with clinch nuts to holes in the inner panel.

   e. Attach the regulator (and motor) to the door inner panel with M6.0 **x** 1 **x** 13 (¼-20 **x** ½ inch) screws (part No. 9419723 or equivalent) into ¼″ nuts with integral washers. Tighten the screw to 90-125 inch lbs. (10-14 Nm) torque.

10. Remove the rubber wedge door stops at the front and rear of the window between window and inner panel.

11. Install the inner panel water deflector and the door trim panel. Connect the negative battery cable.

1991-93

1. Disconnect the negative battery cable. Remove the door trim panel and inner panel water deflector.

2. Raise the window to full-up position and hold in place by inserting a rubber wedge door stops at the front and rear of the window between window and inner panel.

3. Remove the front door lock module assembly.

4. Punch out the center pins of the regulator sash to window rivets; then drill out the rivets using a ⁵/₁₆ inch drill bit.

5. Remove the bolt securing the regulator cam to the door panel. Disconnect wire harness from the motor (if equipped).

6. Punch out the center pins of the regulator rivets; then drill out the rivets using a ⁵/₁₆ inch drill bit.

7. Remove the regulator through the rear access hole.

8. Installation is the reverse of the removal procedure.

Tailgate Regulator and Motor

REMOVAL & INSTALLATION

▶ **See Figures 47 and 48**

1. Disconnect the negative battery cable. Remove the trim panel. Remove the window.

2. Disconnect the electrical connection from the electrical motor assembly.

3. Remove the regulator retaining bolts or rivets and remove the regulator and window motor as an assembly.

➡ **The regulator arm is under tension, due to the mounting of the electric window motor, and if the following operation is not performed, serious damage could result.**

4. Drill a ⅛ inch hole through the regulator backing plate and sector gear. Install a pan head 10-12 x ¾ inch screw through the hole, to lock the gear in place.

5. Separate the motor assembly from the window regulator.

6. Installation is the reverse of the removal procedure.

Front and Rear Glass

▶ **See Figures 49, 50 and 51**

➡ **Bonded windshields require special tools and special removal procedures to be performed to ensure the windshield will be removed without being broken. For this reason we recommend that you refer all removal and installation to a qualified technician.**

❊❊CAUTION

Always wear heavy gloves and safety glasses when handling glass to reduce the risk of injury.

When replacing a cracked windshield, it is important that the cause of the crack be determined and the condition corrected, before a new glass is installed. The cause of the crack may

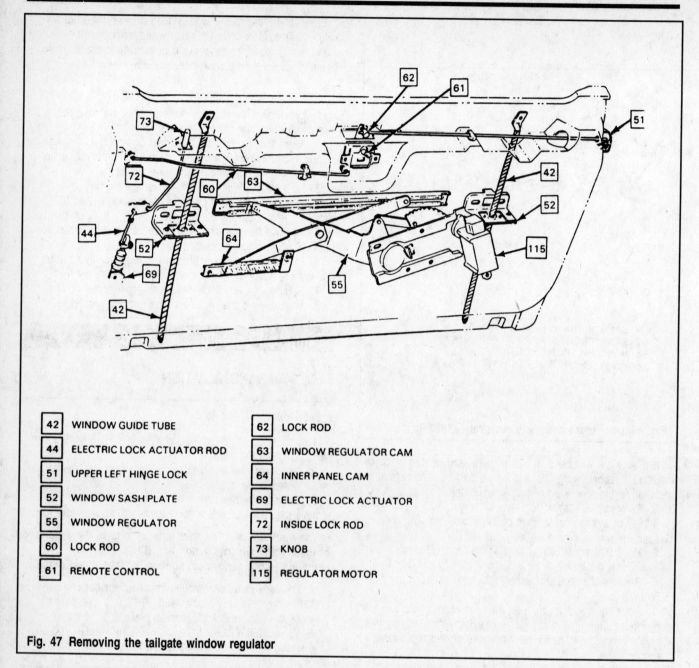

42	WINDOW GUIDE TUBE	62	LOCK ROD
44	ELECTRIC LOCK ACTUATOR ROD	63	WINDOW REGULATOR CAM
51	UPPER LEFT HINGE LOCK	64	INNER PANEL CAM
52	WINDOW SASH PLATE	69	ELECTRIC LOCK ACTUATOR
55	WINDOW REGULATOR	72	INSIDE LOCK ROD
60	LOCK ROD	73	KNOB
61	REMOTE CONTROL	115	REGULATOR MOTOR

Fig. 47 Removing the tailgate window regulator

be an obstruction or a high spot somewhere around the flange of the opening; cracking may not occur until pressure from the

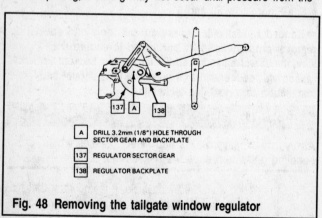

A	DRILL 3.2mm (1/8") HOLE THROUGH SECTOR GEAR AND BACKPLATE
137	REGULATOR SECTOR GEAR
138	REGULATOR BACKPLATE

Fig. 48 Removing the tailgate window regulator

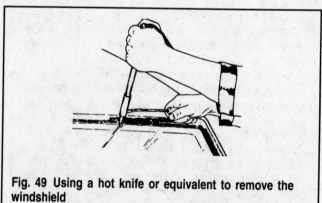

Fig. 49 Using a hot knife or equivalent to remove the windshield

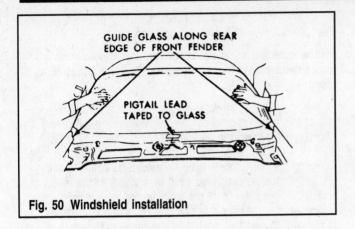

Fig. 50 Windshield installation

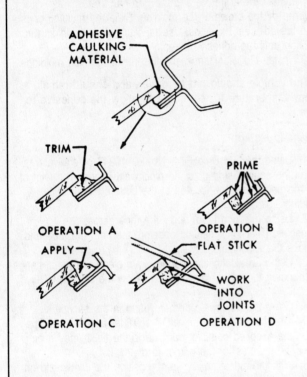

Fig. 51 Applying sealant to existing windshield to correct water leak

high spot or obstruction becomes particularly high due to winds, extremes of temperature or rough terrain.

When a windshield is broken, the glass may have already have fallen or been removed from the weatherstrip. Often, however, it is necessary to remove a cracked or otherwise imperfect windshield that is still intact. In this case, it is a good practice to crisscross the glass with strips of masking tape before removing it; this will help hold the glass together and minimize the risk of injury.

If a crack extends to the edge of the glass, mark the point where the crack meets the weather strip. (Use a piece of chalk to mark the point on the cab, next to the weatherstrip.) Later, examining the window flange for a cause of the crack which started at the point marked.

The higher the temperature of the work area, the more pliable the weather strip will be. The more pliable the weather strip, the more easily the windshield can be removed.

There are two methods of windshield removal, depending on the method of windshield replacement chosen. When using the short method of installation, it is important to cut the glass from the urethane adhesive as close to the glass as possible. This is due to the fact that the urethane adhesive will be used to provide a base for the replacement windshield.

When using the extended method of windshield replacement, all the urethane adhesive must be removed from the pinchweld flange so, the process of cutting the window from the adhesive is less critical.

REMOVAL & INSTALLATION

➡**The following procedure may be used for front and rear glass and requires the use of the Urethane Glass Sealant Remover (hot knife) tool No. J-24709-1 or equivalent, the Glass Sealant Remover Knife tool No. J-24402-A or equivalent.**

1. Place the protective covering around the area where the glass will be removed.
2. Remove the windshield wiper arms, the cowl vent grille, the windshield supports, the rear view mirror and the interior garnish moldings.

➡**If equipped with a radio antenna, embedded in the windshield, disconnect the cable connector from the windshield.**

3. Remove the exterior reveal molding and glass supports from the windshield.
4. Using the Urethane Glass Sealant Remover (hot knife) tool No. J-24709-1 or equivalent, and the Glass Sealant Remover Knife tool No. J-24402-A or equivalent, cut the windshield from the urethane adhesive. If the short method of glass replacement is to be used, keep the knife as close to the glass as possible in order to leave a base for the replacement glass.
5. With the help of an assistant, remove the glass.
6. If the original glass is to be reinstalled, place it on a protected bench or a holding or holding fixture. Remove any remaining adhesive with a razor blade or a sharp scraper. Any remaining traces of adhesive material can be removed with denatured alcohol or lacquer thinner.

➡**When cleaning the windshield glass, avoid contacting the edge of the plastic laminate material (on the edge of the glass) with a volatile cleaner. Contact may cause discoloration and deterioration of the plastic laminate. DO NOT use a petroleum based solvent such as gasoline or kerosene; the presence of oil will prevent the adhesion of new material.**

INSPECTION

Inspection of the windshield opening, the weather strip and the glass may reveal the cause of a broken windshield; this can help prevent future breakage. If there is no apparent cause of breakage, the weatherstrip should be removed from the flange and the flange inspected. Look for high weld or solder spots, hardened spot welds sealer, or any other obstruction or irregularity in the flange. Check the weatherstrip for irregularities or obstructions in it.

Check the windshield to be installed to make sure that it does not have chipped edges. Chipped edges can be ground off, restoring a smooth edge to the glass and minimizing concentrations of pressure that cause breakage. Remove no more than necessary, in an effort to maintain the original shape of the glass and the proper clearance between it and the flange of the opening.

INSTALLATION

To replace a urethane adhered windshield, a GM Adhesive Service Kit contains some of the materials needed and should be used to ensure the original integrity of the windshield design. Materials in this kit include:

1. One tube of adhesive material.
2. One dispensing nozzle.
3. Steel music wire.
4. Rubber cleaner.
5. Rubber Primer.
6. Pinchweld primer.
7. Blackout primer.
8. Filler strip (for use on windshield installations of vehicles equipped with an embedded windshield antenna).
9. Primer applicators.

Other materials required for windshield installation which are not included in the service kit, are:

10. GM rubber lubricant No. 1051717.
11. Alcohol for cleaning the edge of the glass.
12. Adhesive dispensing gun No. J-24811 or equivalent.
13. A commercial type razor knife.
14. Two rubber support spacers.

Short Method

1. Using masking tape, apply the tape across the windshield pillar-to-windshield opening, then cut the tape and remove the windshield.

2. Using an alcohol dampened cloth, clean the metal flange surrounding the windshield opening. Allow the alcohol to air dry.

3. Using the pinchweld primer, found in the service kit, apply it to the pinchweld area. DO NOT let any of the primer touch the exposed paint for damage to the finish may occur; allow five minutes for the primer to dry.

4. Cut the tip of the adhesive cartridge approximately ³/₁₅ inch (5mm) from the end of the tip.

5. Apply the adhesive first in and around the spacer blocks. Apply a smooth continuous bead of adhesive into the gap between the glass edge and the sheet metal. Use a flat bladed tool to paddle the material into position if necessary. Be sure that the adhesive contacts the entire edge of the glass and extends to fill the gap between the glass and the solidified urethane base.

6. With the aid of a helper, position the windshield on the filler strips against the two support spacers.

➡**The vehicle should not be driven and should remain at room temperature for six hours to allow the adhesive to cure.**

7. Spray a mist of water onto the urethane. Water will assist in the curing process. Dry the area where the reveal molding will contact the body and glass.

8. Install new reveal moldings. Remove the protective tape covering the butyl adhesive on the underside of the molding. Push the molding caps onto each end of one of the reveal moldings. Press the lip of the molding into the urethane adhesive while holding it against the edge of the windshield. Take care to seat the molding in the corners. The lip must fully contact the adhesive and the gap must be entirely covered by the crown of the molding. Slide the molding caps onto the adjacent moldings. Use tape to hold the molding in position until the adhesive cures.

9. Install the wiper arms and the interior garnish moldings.

➡**The vehicle should not be driven and should remain at room temperature for six hours to allow the adhesive to cure.**

Extended Method

1. Using the GM Strip Filler No. 20146247 or equivalent, install the sealing strip onto the pinchweld flange. The joint of the molding should be located at the bottom center of the molding.

2. Using masking tape, apply the tape across the windshield pillar-to-windshield opening, then cut the tape and remove the windshield.

3. Using an alcohol dampened cloth, clean the metal flange surrounding the windshield opening. Allow the alcohol to air dry.

4. Using the pinchweld primer, found in the service kit, apply it to the pinchweld area. DO NOT let any of the primer touch the exposed paint for damage to the finish may occur; allow five minutes for the primer to dry.

5. With the aid of an assistant, position the windshield on the filler strips against the two support spacers.

6. Cut the tip of the adhesive cartridge approximately ³/₈″ from the end of the tip.

7. Apply the adhesive first in and around the spacer blocks. Apply a smooth continuous bead of adhesive into the gap between the glass edge and the sheet metal. Use a flat bladed tool to paddle the material into position if necessary. Be sure that the adhesive contacts the entire edge of the glass and extends to fill the gap between the glass and the primed sheet metal.

➡**The vehicle should not be driven and should remain at room temperature for six hours to allow the adhesive to cure.**

8. Spray a mist of warm or hot water onto the urethane. Water will assist in the curing process. Dry the area where the reveal molding will contact the body and glass.

9. Install the reveal molding onto the windshield and remove the masking tape from the inner surface of the glass.

10. Press the lip of the molding into the urethane adhesive while holding it against the edge of the windshield. Take care

to seat the molding in the corners. The lip must fully contact the adhesive and the gap must be entirely covered by the crown of the molding. Use tape to hold the molding in position until the adhesive cures.

11. Install the wiper arms and the interior garnish moldings.

Inside Rear View Mirror

INSTALLATION

▶ **See Figure 52**

The rear view mirror is attached to a support which is secured to the windshield glass. This support is installed by the glass supplier using a plastic-polyvinyl butyl adhesive.

Service replacement windshield glass has the mirror support bonded to the glass assembly. To install a detached mirror support or install a new part, the following items are needed:
- Part No. 1052369, Loctite® Minute-Bond Adhesive 312 two component pack or equivalent
- Original mirror support (prepared per Steps 4 and 5 of the installation procedure) or replacement rear view mirror support
- Wax marking pencil or crayon
- Rubbing alcohol
- Clean paper towels
- Fine grit emery cloth or sandpaper (No. 320 or No. 360)
- Clean toothpick
- Six-lobed socket bit.

1. Determine the rear view mirror support position on the windshield. Support is to be located at the center of the glass

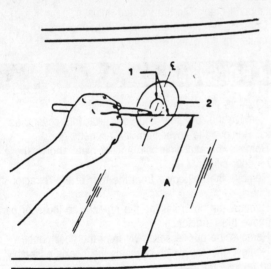

1. Locating circle and base of support line on outside glass surface
2. Circle on outside glass surface indicates area to be cleaned

Fig. 52 Locating and marking the bonded support on the windshield for the rear view mirror. Distance "A" should be 22″ for 1990 or 28-3/4″ for 1991-93 vehicles

27⅛ inch from the base of the glass to the base of the support.

2. Mark the location on the outside of the glass with wax pencil or crayon. also make a larger diameter circle around the mirror support circle on the outside of the glass surface.

3. On the inside of the glass surface, clean the large circle with a paper towel and domestic scouring cleanser, glass cleaning solution or polishing compound. Rub until the area is completely clean and dry. When dry, clean the area with an alcohol saturated paper towel to remove any traces of scouring powder of cleaning solution from this area.

4. With a piece of fine grit (No. 320 or No. 360) emery cloth or sandpaper, sand the bonding surface of the new rear view mirror support or factory installed support. If original rear view mirror support is to be reused, all traces of the factory installed adhesive must be removed prior to reinstallation.

5. Wipe the sanded mirror support with a clean paper towel saturated with alcohol and allow it to dry.

6. Follow the directions on the manufacturer's kit to prepare the rear view mirror support prior to installation on the glass.

7. Properly position the support to its premarked location, with rounded end pointed upward, press the support against the glass for 30-60 seconds, exerting steady pressure against the glass. After five minutes, any excess adhesive may be removed with an alcohol moistened paper towel or glass cleaning solution.

8. Install the mirror.

Seats

REMOVAL & INSTALLATION

▶ **See Figure 53**

Front

1. Operate the seat to the full-forward position. If six-way power seat is operable, operate seat to the full-forward and up positions. Where necessary to gain access to the adjuster-to-floor pan attaching nuts, remove the adjuster rear foot covers and/or carpet retainers.

2. Remove the track covers where necessary; then remove the adjuster-to-floor pan rear attaching nuts. Operate the seat to the full-rearward position. Remove the adjuster front foot covers; then remove the adjuster-to-floor pan front attaching nuts.

3. Disconnect the wire connectors and remove the seat belts. Remove the seat assembly from the car.

4. Prior to installing the seat assembly, check that both seat adjusters are parallel and in phase with each other.

5. Install the adjuster-to-floor pan attaching nuts by moving the seat forward and rearward and torque nuts to 15-21 ft. lbs. (20-28 Nm).

6. Check the operation of the seat assembly to full limits of travel.

REAR

The rear seat bottom may be removed by simply pushing rearward at the bottom of the seat, then tilt the assembly up and remove from the vehicle. The top (back portion) may be

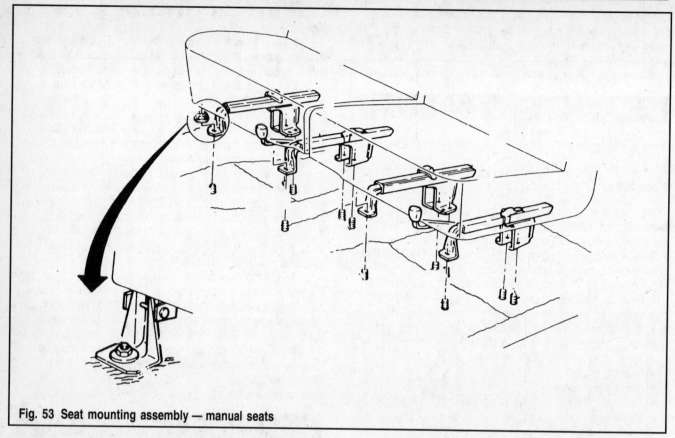

Fig. 53 Seat mounting assembly — manual seats

removed by removing the retaining bolts at the bottom of the seatback and lifting up on the assembly.

Power Seat Motor

REMOVAL & INSTALLATION

1. Remove the front seat assembly and place upside down on a clean protected surface.
2. Disconnect the motor feed wires from the motors.
3. Remove the nut securing the front of the motor support bracket to the inboard adjuster and withdraw the assembly from the adjuster and the gearnut drives.
4. Disconnect the drive cables from the motors and complete removal of the support bracket with the motor attached.
5. Grind off the peened over end(s) of the grommet assembly securing the motor to the support and separate the motor(s) as required from the support.
6. Before installation, drill out the top end of the grommet assembly using a 3/16 inch drill.
7. Install the grommet assembly to the motor support bracket and secure the motor to the grommet using 3/16 inch rivet.

8. Install the support bracket with the motor attached and connect the drive cables to the motors.
9. Install the support bracket nuts securing the front of the motor support bracket to the inboard adjuster.
10. Connect the motor feed wires to the motors.
11. Install the front seat assembly.

Seat Belt System

REMOVAL & INSTALLATION

1. Remove the rear seat and door pillar trim covers, as required. Remove the cover from the anchor plate.
2. Remove the attaching bolt, anchor plate and washer from the door pillar.
3. Remove the bolt cover from the rear of the retractor assembly.
4. Remove the bolt retaining the retractor to the floor panel and remove the retractor.
5. Remove the buckle assembly from the floor panel.
6. Remove the cap which conceals the buckle assembly bolt and remove the bolt.
7. Remove the seat belt warning wire from the drivers side buckle and remove the buckle assembly from the vehicle.
8. Installation is the reverse of removal. Tighten all bolts to 31-35 ft. lbs. (43-48 Nm).

TORQUE SPECIFICATIONS

Component	U.S.	Metric
Outside mirror	72 inch lbs.	8 Nm
Window regulator	90–125 inch lbs.	10–14 Nm
Seat-to-floor	15–21 ft. lbs.	20–28 Nm
Seat belt	31–35 ft. lbs.	43–48 Nm

GLOSSARY

AIR/FUEL RATIO: The ratio of air to gasoline by weight in the fuel mixture drawn into the engine.

AIR INJECTION: One method of reducing harmful exhaust emissions by injecting air into each of the exhaust ports of an engine. The fresh air entering the hot exhaust manifold causes any remaining fuel to be burned before it can exit the tailpipe.

ALTERNATOR: A device used for converting mechanical energy into electrical energy.

AMMETER: An instrument, calibrated in amperes, used to measure the flow of an electrical current in a circuit. Ammeters are always connected in series with the circuit being tested.

AMPERE: The rate of flow of electrical current present when one volt of electrical pressure is applied against one ohm of electrical resistance.

ANALOG COMPUTER: Any microprocessor that uses similar (analogous) electrical signals to make its calculations.

ARMATURE: A laminated, soft iron core wrapped by a wire that converts electrical energy to mechanical energy as in a motor or relay. When rotated in a magnetic field, it changes mechanical energy into electrical energy as in a generator.

ATMOSPHERIC PRESSURE: The pressure on the Earth's surface caused by the weight of the air in the atmosphere. At sea level, this pressure is 14.7 psi at 32{248}F (101 kPa at 0{248}C).

ATOMIZATION: The breaking down of a liquid into a fine mist that can be suspended in air.

AXIAL PLAY: Movement parallel to a shaft or bearing bore.

BACKFIRE: The sudden combustion of gases in the intake or exhaust system that results in a loud explosion.

BACKLASH: The clearance or play between two parts, such as meshed gears.

BACKPRESSURE: Restrictions in the exhaust system that slow the exit of exhaust gases from the combustion chamber.

BAKELITE: A heat resistant, plastic insulator material commonly used in printed circuit boards and transistorized components.

BALL BEARING: A bearing made up of hardened inner and outer races between which hardened steel balls roll.

BALLAST RESISTOR: A resistor in the primary ignition circuit that lowers voltage after the engine is started to reduce wear on ignition components.

BEARING: A friction reducing, supportive device usually located between a stationary part and a moving part.

BIMETAL TEMPERATURE SENSOR: Any sensor or switch made of two dissimilar types of metal that bend when heated or cooled due to the different expansion rates of the alloys. These types of sensors usually function as an on/off switch.

BLOWBY: Combustion gases, composed of water vapor and unburned fuel, that leak past the piston rings into the crankcase during normal engine operation. These gases are removed by the PCV system to prevent the buildup of harmful acids in the crankcase.

BRAKE PAD: A brake shoe and lining assembly used with disc brakes.

BRAKE SHOE: The backing for the brake lining. The term is, however, usually applied to the assembly of the brake backing and lining.

BUSHING: A liner, usually removable, for a bearing; an anti-friction liner used in place of a bearing.

CALIPER: A hydraulically activated device in a disc brake system, which is mounted straddling the brake rotor (disc). The caliper contains at least one piston and two brake pads. Hydraulic pressure on the piston(s) forces the pads against the rotor.

CAMSHAFT: A shaft in the engine on which are the lobes (cams) which operate the valves. The camshaft is driven by the crankshaft, via a belt, chain or gears, at one half the crankshaft speed.

CAPACITOR: A device which stores an electrical charge.

CARBON MONOXIDE (CO): A colorless, odorless gas given off as a normal byproduct of combustion. It is poisonous and extremely dangerous in confined areas, building up slowly to toxic levels without warning if adequate ventilation is not available.

CARBURETOR: A device, usually mounted on the intake manifold of an engine, which mixes the air and fuel in the proper proportion to allow even combustion.

CATALYTIC CONVERTER: A device installed in the exhaust system, like a muffler, that converts harmful byproducts of combustion into carbon dioxide and water vapor by means of a heat-producing chemical reaction.

CENTRIFUGAL ADVANCE: A mechanical method of advancing the spark timing by using flyweights in the distributor that react to centrifugal force generated by the distributor shaft rotation.

CHECK VALVE: Any one-way valve installed to permit the flow of air, fuel or vacuum in one direction only.

CHOKE: A device, usually a moveable valve, placed in the intake path of a carburetor to restrict the flow of air.

CIRCUIT: Any unbroken path through which an electrical current can flow. Also used to describe fuel flow in some instances.

CIRCUIT BREAKER: A switch which protects an electrical circuit from overload by opening the circuit when the current flow exceeds a predetermined level. Some circuit breakers must be reset manually, while most reset automatically

COIL (IGNITION): A transformer in the ignition circuit which steps up the voltage provided to the spark plugs.

COMBINATION MANIFOLD: An assembly which includes both the intake and exhaust manifolds in one casting.

COMBINATION VALVE: A device used in some fuel systems that routes fuel vapors to a charcoal storage canister instead of venting them into the atmosphere. The valve relieves fuel tank pressure and allows fresh air into the tank as the fuel level drops to prevent a vapor lock situation.

COMPRESSION RATIO: The comparison of the total volume of the cylinder and combustion chamber with the piston at BDC and the piston at TDC.

CONDENSER: 1. An electrical device which acts to store an electrical charge, preventing voltage surges.
2. A radiator-like device in the air conditioning system in which refrigerant gas condenses into a liquid, giving off heat.

CONDUCTOR: Any material through which an electrical current can be transmitted easily.

CONTINUITY: Continuous or complete circuit. Can be checked with an ohmmeter.

COUNTERSHAFT: An intermediate shaft which is rotated by a mainshaft and transmits, in turn, that rotation to a working part.

CRANKCASE: The lower part of an engine in which the crankshaft and related parts operate.

CRANKSHAFT: The main driving shaft of an engine which receives reciprocating motion from the pistons and converts it to rotary motion.

CYLINDER: In an engine, the round hole in the engine block in which the piston(s) ride.

CYLINDER BLOCK: The main structural member of an engine in which is found the cylinders, crankshaft and other principal parts.

CYLINDER HEAD: The detachable portion of the engine, fastened, usually, to the top of the cylinder block, containing all or most of the combustion chambers. On overhead valve engines, it contains the valves and their operating parts. On overhead cam engines, it contains the camshaft as well.

DEAD CENTER: The extreme top or bottom of the piston stroke.

DETONATION: An unwanted explosion of the air/fuel mixture in the combustion chamber caused by excess heat and compression, advanced timing, or an overly lean mixture. Also referred to as "ping".

DIAPHRAGM: A thin, flexible wall separating two cavities, such as in a vacuum advance unit.

DIESELING: A condition in which hot spots in the combustion chamber cause the engine to run on after the key is turned off.

DIFFERENTIAL: A geared assembly which allows the transmission of motion between drive axles, giving one axle the ability to turn faster than the other.

DIODE: An electrical device that will allow current to flow in one direction only.

DISC BRAKE: A hydraulic braking assembly consisting of a brake disc, or rotor, mounted on an axle, and a caliper assembly containing, usually two brake pads which are activated by hydraulic pressure. The pads are forced against the sides of the disc, creating friction which slows the vehicle.

DISTRIBUTOR: A mechanically driven device on an engine which is responsible for electrically firing the spark plug at a predetermined point of the piston stroke.

DOWEL PIN: A pin, inserted in mating holes in two different parts allowing those parts to maintain a fixed relationship.

DRUM BRAKE: A braking system which consists of two brake shoes and one or two wheel cylinders, mounted on a fixed backing plate, and a brake drum, mounted on an axle, which revolves around the assembly.

DWELL: The rate, measured in degrees of shaft rotation, at which an electrical circuit cycles on and off.

ELECTRONIC CONTROL UNIT (ECU): Ignition module, module, amplifier or igniter. See Module for definition.

ELECTRONIC IGNITION: A system in which the timing and firing of the spark plugs is controlled by an electronic control unit, usually called a module. These systems have no points or condenser.

ENDPLAY: The measured amount of axial movement in a shaft.

ENGINE: A device that converts heat into mechanical energy.

EXHAUST MANIFOLD: A set of cast passages or pipes which conduct exhaust gases from the engine.

FEELER GAUGE: A blade, usually metal, of precisely predetermined thickness, used to measure the clearance between two parts.

FIRING ORDER: The order in which combustion occurs in the cylinders of an engine. Also the order in which spark is distributed to the plugs by the distributor.

FLOODING: The presence of too much fuel in the intake manifold and combustion chamber which prevents the air/fuel mixture from firing, thereby causing a no-start situation.

FLYWHEEL: A disc shaped part bolted to the rear end of the crankshaft. Around the outer perimeter is affixed the ring gear. The starter drive engages the ring gear, turning the flywheel, which rotates the crankshaft, imparting the initial starting motion to the engine.

FOOT POUND (ft.lb. or sometimes, ft. lbs.): The amount of energy or work needed to raise an item weighing one pound, a distance of one foot.

FUSE: A protective device in a circuit which prevents circuit overload by breaking the circuit when a specific amperage is present. The device is constructed around a strip or wire of a lower amperage rating than the circuit it is designed to protect. When an amperage higher than that stamped on the fuse is present in the circuit, the strip or wire melts, opening the circuit.

GEAR RATIO: The ratio between the number of teeth on meshing gears.

GENERATOR: A device which converts mechanical energy into electrical energy.

HEAT RANGE: The measure of a spark plug's ability to dissipate heat from its firing end. The higher the heat range, the hotter the plug fires.

HUB: The center part of a wheel or gear.

HYDROCARBON (HC): Any chemical compound made up of hydrogen and carbon. A major pollutant formed by the engine as a byproduct of combustion.

HYDROMETER: An instrument used to measure the specific gravity of a solution.

INCH POUND (in.lb. or sometimes, in. lbs.): One twelfth of a foot pound.

INDUCTION: A means of transferring electrical energy in the form of a magnetic field. Principle used in the ignition coil to increase voltage.

INJECTOR: A device which receives metered fuel under relatively low pressure and is activated to inject the fuel into the engine under relatively high pressure at a predetermined time.

INPUT SHAFT: The shaft to which torque is applied, usually carrying the driving gear or gears.

INTAKE MANIFOLD: A casting of passages or pipes used to conduct air or a fuel/air mixture to the cylinders.

JOURNAL: The bearing surface within which a shaft operates.

KEY: A small block usually fitted in a notch between a shaft and a hub to prevent slippage of the two parts.

MANIFOLD: A casting of passages or set of pipes which connect the cylinders to an inlet or outlet source.

MANIFOLD VACUUM: Low pressure in an engine intake manifold formed just below the throttle plates. Manifold vacuum is highest at idle and drops under acceleration.

MASTER CYLINDER: The primary fluid pressurizing device in a hydraulic system. In automotive use, it is found in brake and hydraulic clutch systems and is pedal activated, either directly or, in a power brake system, through the power booster.

MODULE: Electronic control unit, amplifier or igniter of solid state or integrated design which controls the current flow in the ignition primary circuit based on input from the pick-up coil. When the module opens the primary circuit, the high secondary voltage is induced in the coil.

NEEDLE BEARING: A bearing which consists of a number (usually a large number) of long, thin rollers.

OHM:(Ω) The unit used to measure the resistance of conductor to electrical flow. One ohm is the amount of resistance that limits current flow to one ampere in a circuit with one volt of pressure.

OHMMETER: An instrument used for measuring the resistance, in ohms, in an electrical circuit.

OUTPUT SHAFT: The shaft which transmits torque from a device, such as a transmission.

OVERDRIVE: A gear assembly which produces more shaft revolutions than that transmitted to it.

OVERHEAD CAMSHAFT (OHC): An engine configuration in which the camshaft is mounted on top of the cylinder head and operates the valve either directly or by means of rocker arms.

OVERHEAD VALVE (OHV): An engine configuration in which all of the valves are located in the cylinder head and the camshaft is located in the cylinder block. The camshaft operates the valves via lifters and pushrods.

OXIDES OF NITROGEN (NOx): Chemical compounds of nitrogen produced as a byproduct of combustion. They combine with hydrocarbons to produce smog.

OXYGEN SENSOR: Used with the feedback system to sense the presence of oxygen in the exhaust gas and signal the computer which can reference the voltage signal to an air/fuel ratio.

PINION: The smaller of two meshing gears.

PISTON RING: An open ended ring which fits into a groove on the outer diameter of the piston. Its chief function is to form a seal between the piston and cylinder wall. Most automotive pistons have three rings: two for compression sealing; one for oil sealing.

PRELOAD: A predetermined load placed on a bearing during assembly or by adjustment.

PRIMARY CIRCUIT: Is the low voltage side of the ignition system which consists of the ignition switch, ballast resistor or resistance wire, bypass, coil, electronic control unit and pick-up coil as well as the connecting wires and harnesses.

PRESS FIT: The mating of two parts under pressure, due to the inner diameter of one being smaller than the outer diameter of the other, or vice versa; an interference fit.

RACE: The surface on the inner or outer ring of a bearing on which the balls, needles or rollers move.

REGULATOR: A device which maintains the amperage and/or voltage levels of a circuit at predetermined values.

RELAY: A switch which automatically opens and/or closes a circuit.

RESISTANCE: The opposition to the flow of current through a circuit or electrical device, and is measured in ohms. Resistance is equal to the voltage divided by the amperage.

RESISTOR: A device, usually made of wire, which offers a preset amount of resistance in an electrical circuit.

RING GEAR: The name given to a ring-shaped gear attached to a differential case, or affixed to a flywheel or as part a planetary gear set.

ROLLER BEARING: A bearing made up of hardened inner and outer races between which hardened steel rollers move.

ROTOR: 1. The disc-shaped part of a disc brake assembly, upon which the brake pads bear; also called, brake disc.
2. The device mounted atop the distributor shaft, which passes current to the distributor cap tower contacts.

SECONDARY CIRCUIT: The high voltage side of the ignition system, usually above 20,000 volts. The secondary includes the ignition coil, coil wire, distributor cap and rotor, spark plug wires and spark plugs.

SENDING UNIT: A mechanical, electrical, hydraulic or electromagnetic device which transmits information to a gauge.

SENSOR: Any device designed to measure engine operating conditions or ambient pressures and temperatures. Usually electronic in nature and designed to send a voltage signal to an on-board computer, some sensors may operate as a simple on/off switch or they may provide a variable voltage signal (like a potentiometer) as conditions or measured parameters change.

SHIM: Spacers of precise, predetermined thickness used between parts to establish a proper working relationship.

SLAVE CYLINDER: In automotive use, a device in the hydraulic clutch system which is activated by hydraulic force, disengaging the clutch.

SOLENOID: A coil used to produce a magnetic field, the effect of which is produce work.

SPARK PLUG: A device screwed into the combustion chamber of a spark ignition engine. The basic construction is a conductive core inside of a ceramic insulator, mounted in an outer conductive base. An electrical charge from the spark plug wire travels along the conductive core and jumps a preset air gap to a grounding point or points at the end of the conductive base. The resultant spark ignites the fuel/air mixture in the combustion chamber.

SPLINES: Ridges machined or cast onto the outer diameter of a shaft or inner diameter of a bore to enable parts to mate without rotation.

TACHOMETER: A device used to measure the rotary speed of an engine, shaft, gear, etc., usually in rotations per minute.

THERMOSTAT: A valve, located in the cooling system of an engine, which is closed when cold and opens gradually in response to engine heating, controlling the temperature of the coolant and rate of coolant flow.

TOP DEAD CENTER (TDC): The point at which the piston reaches the top of its travel on the compression stroke.

TORQUE: The twisting force applied to an object.

TORQUE CONVERTER: A turbine used to transmit power from a driving member to a driven member via hydraulic action, providing changes in drive ratio and torque. In automotive use, it links the driveplate at the rear of the engine to the automatic transmission.

TRANSDUCER: A device used to change a force into an electrical signal.

TRANSISTOR: A semi-conductor component which can be actuated by a small voltage to perform an electrical switching function.

TUNE-UP: A regular maintenance function, usually associated with the replacement and adjustment of parts and components in the electrical and fuel systems of a vehicle for the purpose of attaining optimum performance.

TURBOCHARGER: An exhaust driven pump which compresses intake air and forces it into the combustion chambers at higher than atmospheric pressures. The increased air pressure allows more fuel to be burned and results in increased horsepower being produced.

VACUUM ADVANCE: A device which advances the ignition timing in response to increased engine vacuum.

VACUUM GAUGE: An instrument used to measure the presence of vacuum in a chamber.

VALVE: A device which control the pressure, direction of flow or rate of flow of a liquid or gas.

VALVE CLEARANCE: The measured gap between the end of the valve stem and the rocker arm, cam lobe or follower that activates the valve.

VISCOSITY: The rating of a liquid's internal resistance to flow.

VOLTMETER: An instrument used for measuring electrical force in units called volts. Voltmeters are always connected parallel with the circuit being tested.

WHEEL CYLINDER: Found in the automotive drum brake assembly, it is a device, actuated by hydraulic pressure, which, through internal pistons, pushes the brake shoes outward against the drums.

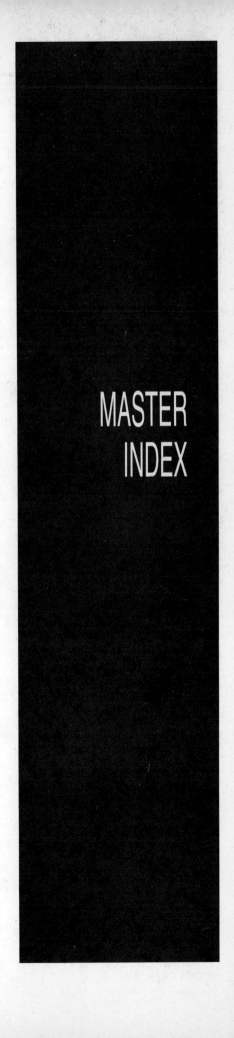

MASTER INDEX